Eyes of the Fleet

Also by David D. Bruhn

Ready to Answer All Bells

Wooden Ships and Iron Men: The U.S. Navy's Ocean Minesweepers, 1953–1994

Wooden Ships and Iron Men: The U.S. Navy's Coastal and Motor Minesweepers, 1941–1953

Wooden Ships and Iron Men: The U.S. Navy's Coastal and Inshore Minesweepers, and the Minecraft That Served in Vietnam, 1953–1976

MacArthur and Halsey's "Pacific Island Hoppers": The Forgotten Fleet of World War II

Battle Stars for the "Cactus Navy": America's Fishing Vessels and Yachts in World War II

We Are Sinking, Send Help!: The U.S. Navy's Tugs and Salvage Ships in the African, European, and Mediterranean Theaters in World War II

Eyes of the Fleet

The U.S. Navy's Seaplane Tenders
and Patrol Aircraft in World War II

Cdr. David D. Bruhn, USN (Retired)

HERITAGE BOOKS
2016

HERITAGE BOOKS
AN IMPRINT OF HERITAGE BOOKS, INC.

Books, CDs, and more—Worldwide

For our listing of thousands of titles see our website
at
www.HeritageBooks.com

Published 2016 by
HERITAGE BOOKS, INC.
Publishing Division
5810 Ruatan Street
Berwyn Heights, Md. 20740

Copyright © 2016 Cdr. David D. Bruhn, USN (Retired)

Heritage Books by the author:

Battle Stars for the "Cactus Navy": America's Fishing Vessels and Yachts in World War II

Eyes of the Fleet: The U.S. Navy's Seaplane Tenders and Patrol Aircraft in World War II

MacArthur and Halsey's "Pacific Island Hoppers:" The Forgotten Fleet of World War II

We Are Sinking, Send Help!: The U.S. Navy's Tugs and Salvage Ships in the African, European, and Mediterranean Theaters in World War II

Wooden Ships and Iron Men: The U.S. Navy's Ocean Minesweepers, 1953–1994

Wooden Ships and Iron Men: The U.S. Navy's Coastal and Motor Minesweepers, 1941–1953

Wooden Ships and Iron Men: The U.S. Navy's Coastal and Inshore Minesweepers, and the Minecraft that Served in Vietnam, 1953–1976

All rights reserved. No part of this book may be reproduced or transmitted in any form or by any means, electronic or mechanical, including photocopying, recording or by any information storage and retrieval system without written permission from the author, except for the inclusion of brief quotations in a review.

International Standard Book Numbers
Paperbound: 978-0-7884-5707-4
Clothbound: 978-0-7884-6416-4

To the United States Navy officers and men who served
aboard seaplane tenders, and the pilots and crews of
patrol planes that functioned as "eyes of the fleet"
in World War II

Contents

Foreword by Roland Nino Martinez	xiii
Acknowledgements	xv
Preface	xvii
1. Peril in the Java Sea	1
2. Seaplane Tenders	17
3. Patrol Wings/Fleet Air Wings	27
4. Attack on Pearl Harbor	29
5. Japanese Attack on the Philippines	55
6. Defense of the Netherlands East Indies	67
7. Australia's "Pearl Harbor"	91
8. Japanese Threat to Java Grows	99
9. Battle of the Java Sea and Duty in Australia	111
10. War in the Aleutians	123
11. Battle of Midway	145
12. War in the Americas	163
13. Guadalcanal Campaign	171
14. America Reinforces New Caledonia	193
15. A Swan in the South Pacific	203
16. French Morocco	215
17. European Theater	225
18. Central Pacific Campaign	235
19. Central Solomons Campaign	253
20. New Guinea and Bismarck Archipelago	277
21. Admiralty Islands Landings and Hollandia Operation	285
22. Western New Guinea Operations	297
23. Capture and Occupation of Saipan	311
24. South Palau Islands	323
25. Liberation of the Philippines	329
26. Assault and Occupation of Iwo Jima	353
27. Assault and Occupation of Okinawa	361
28. Third Fleet Operations against Japan	375
29. War's End	391
Postscript	397

Appendices
  A. Seaplane Tender and Patrol Squadron Battle Stars   405
  B. Presidential Unit Citations/Navy Unit Commendations   415
  C. Medal Citations for Officers and Men of USS *Heron*   417
  D. Patrol Wings/Fleet Air Wings   419
  E. Allied Vessels at Darwin, Australia during Attack   421
  F. Silver Star Citation for Lt. Comdr. Lester Wood   423
  G. Japanese Midway Invasion Force   425
  H. Crews of PBY Seaplanes that made a Night Torpedo   427
     Attack against Japanese Ships at Battle of Midway
  I. Restructuring of Pacific Fleet Aviation Forces   429
  J. Japanese Military Aircraft   431
  K. VPB-18 Navy Unit Commendation Citation   433
  L. Post-WWII Disposition of Seaplane Tenders   435
Bibliography   441
Notes   443
Index   483
About the Author   519

PHOTOS AND ILLUSTRATIONS

1-1: PBY-5A Catalina drops a torpedo in 1942-1943   2
1-2: *Evasion of Destruction* (painting by Richard DeRosset) depicts   11
     an attack by Japanese torpedo bombers on *Heron*
1-3: Capt. William L. Kabler, USN   13
2-1: *Avocet* carrying a SOC Seagull scout plane   18
2-2: *Osmond Ingram* under way   20
2-3: *Barnegat* under way in Boston Harbor   21
2-4: *Salisbury Sound* tending aircraft (painting by Richard DeRosset) 24
2-5: Navy carrier aircraft fly in formation over battleship *Missouri* 25
4-1: Gunners aboard *Avocet* search for Japanese planes   38
4-2: West side of Ford Island during Japanese attack   41
4-3: Burning PBY at Naval Air Station, Kaneohe Bay, Oahu   47
4-4: Sikorsky JRS-1 "flying boats" (amphibian aircraft)   52
5-1: *William B. Preston* before conversion to a seaplane tender   60
6-1: Capt. Frank D. Wagner, USN   69
7-1: *William B. Preston* during Japanese air raid on Darwin 93
8-1: *Langley* with a deck load of P2Y flying boats   102
8-2: Rear Adm. Thomas Alton Donovan, USN   107
10-1: *YP-72* serving as the flagship of the Alaskan Patrol 126

10-2: *Gillis* at sea	134
10-3: *Northwestern* burns after Japanese attack on Dutch Harbor	136
10-4: *YP-92* at sea following a snow storm	143
11-1: Midway Atoll	146
11-2: Pilots of PBY-5A seaplanes at the Battle of Midway	150
11-3: Cutter from the sunken Japanese aircraft carrier *Hiryu*	159
11-4: Japanese prisoners of war aboard *Ballard*	159
12-1: *Gannet* at sea	164
12-2: *Sumar* at sea	166
13-1: Destruction of *YP-346* by IJN *Sendai* off Guadalcanal (painting by Richard DeRosset)	180
13-2: World War II poster featuring Adm. William S. Halsey	186
14-1: Pontoon Pier at the Seaplane Base, Noumea	196
14-2: Rear Adm. Richard E. Byrd, USN	197
15-1: *Swan* serving as a seaplane tender in the early 1930s	204
15-2: Pago Pago Harbor, Tutuila, Samoan Islands	206
15-3: Vought OS2U Kingfisher observation floatplane	207
16-1: *Barnegat* under way off Boston Navy Yard	216
16-2: British Maj. Gen. John L. Hawksworth and Rear Adm. Richard L. Conolly, USN	223
17-1: PB4Y-1 Liberator on anti-submarine patrol	227
17-2: *Rockaway* tending a PBM Mariner seaplane	231
17-3: Tug towing a component of a Mulberry harbor	233
18-1: A Pollywog's Nightmare	238
18-2: Devastation on Kwajalein Island	246
18-3: Fifth Fleet ships anchored at Majuro Lagoon	248
18-4: PBM-3D patrol bomber at factory	249
19-1: *Chincoteague* off Mare Island Navy Yard	256
19-2: LCVP landing craft at Bougainville Island	265
19-3: Lt. Comdr. Richard M. Nixon, USNR	270
19-4: *Pocomoke* at sea	274
20-1: *Half Moon* at sea near Brisbane, Australia	278
21-1: *Tangier* liberty party on Los Negros Island	289
21-2: PB4Y-1 Liberator of Bombing Squadron VB-106	290
21-3: *Orca* off Houghton, Washington	293
22-1 Blast from explosives at Morotai Island	305
22-2: *Currituck* and *Tangier* at Morotai Island	306
23-1: PBM Mariner lifted aboard *Pocomoke*	317
23-2: Tenders and seaplanes at Saipan Island	318
25-1: *Cooper* underway in New York Harbor	336
25-2: Japanese "Zero" diving on the *Columbia*	345
25-3: *Mississippi* bombarding Luzon, Philippine Islands	348

26-1: Naval bombardment of Iwo Jima Island — 354
26-2: *Hamlin* at anchor in Tanapag Harbor, Saipan — 355
26-3: B29 bomber after crash-landing at Iwo Jima — 357
27-1: *Thornton* being towed into Kerama Retto harbor — 365
27-2: SP-5B Marlin patrol plane — 369
27-3: *Norton Sound* hoisting aboard a PBM Mariner — 372
28-1: PB4Y-2 Privateer patrol planes over Miami, Florida — 376
28-2: Seaplane anchorage at Buckner Bay, Okinawa — 377
28-3: PB2Y Coronado patrol bomber in flight — 384
28-4: Japanese "Shinyo" (suicide) explosive motorboat — 386
28-5: *Onslow* refueling a PBM Mariner seaplane — 388
29-1: Nimitz arrives at Tokyo Bay in a PB2Y seaplane — 394
29-2: Nimitz signs surrender document aboard *Missouri* — 394
29-3: Capt. Etheridge Grant, USN — 396
Postscript 1: *Norton Sound* launches a V-1 "loon" missile — 400
Postscript 2: *Dexter* entering San Francisco Harbor — 402

MAPS AND DIAGRAMS

1-1: Manila Bay area, Philippine Islands — 5
1-2: Philippine Islands: Luzon south to Mindanao — 6
1-3: Southern Philippines, Malaysia, Borneo, and Indonesia — 7
4-1: Navy Ships at Pearl Harbor on 7 December 1941 — 36
4-2: Bomb damage suffered by *Curtiss* at Pearl Harbor — 45
5-1: Philippine Islands — 56
5-2: Borneo and Celebes, Netherlands (Dutch) East Indies — 58
6-1: Netherlands (Dutch) East Indies; now Indonesia — 72
6-2: Allied Forces landings on Borneo — 82
6-3: Lesser Sunda Islands — 88
7-1: Darwin Harbor, Australia — 94
7-2: Continent of Australia — 97
8-1: Japanese movements south from the Philippines to Java — 100
10-1: PBY search for Japanese fleet approaching the Aleutians — 129
10-2: PBY and YP picket lines for approach of the enemy fleet — 131
10-3: Kiska Island — 139
11-1: Hawaiian Islands — 147
11-2: Portion of Japanese Midway Occupational Force — 149
12-1: Bermuda — 165
13-1: Guadalcanal and Tulagi, Solomon Islands — 173
13-2: Guadalcanal area — 175
13-3: Solomon Islands — 176

13-4: Santa Cruz Islands	177
14-1: New Caledonia Islands	194
14-2: Noumea, New Caledonia	195
15-1: Samoan Islands	205
15-2: Wallis Island	208
16-1: Mehedia, French Morocco	219
16-2: Port Lyautey, French Morocco	221
18-1: Principal Central Pacific route toward Japan	236
18-2: Funafuti Atoll, Ellice Islands	237
18-3: Tarawa Atoll, Gilbert Islands	243
18-4: Marshall Islands	245
19-1: MacArthur and Halsey's routes to New Britain	254
19-2: Central Solomon Islands	263
19-3: Southeast Papua New Guinea/New Britain area	264
19-4: Treasury Islands in the Solomon Islands	267
21-1: Advancement by MacArthur up New Guinea	286
21-2: Manus and Los Negros, Admiralty Islands	287
21-3: Hollandia area of New Guinea	292
21-4: Geelvink Bay/Vogelkop Peninsula area, New Guinea	294
22-1: PBY-5 glide attack on a small Japanese freighter	302
22-2: Morotai Island, New Guinea	304
23-1: Caroline and Mariana Islands	312
23-2: Landing beaches at Saipan Island	315
24-1: Palau Islands, Caroline Islands	324
27-1: Okinawa Islands	362
27-2: Search plan for Mariner aircraft at Okinawa	367
29-1: Fast aircraft carrier operations against Japan	392

Foreword

There are few people remaining today who have experienced flying in a thin-skinned seaplane and above all, noted the pulsing thin metal as it beats against the frame while the aircraft is in a slight dive to align itself with "rigging a ship" from the cardinal points. Some sixty years have passed since I decided to join up. As a nineteen year old young man from the southwest plains of Oklahoma, I had discovered that my love for photography was a part of the air branch of the Navy. After receiving my first orders to PATRON 46 at Naval Air Station, San Diego, a scant three miles from the Naval Training Center where I was attending boot camp, my company chief had to explain to me PATRON stood for Patrol Squadron. In less than three months after I reported for duty, the Squadron deployed to Naval Air Station, Sangley Point, Philippines.

I was fortunate to do two tours in the Far East, which entailed my spending much time in flight aboard Navy seaplanes, carrying out my duties as a squadron photographer. The relationship between the U.S. and China in the 1950s was volatile, particularly during the Taiwan/Formosa Straits conflict of 1958. The Chinese particularly did not like the Navy taking aerial photographs of the many atolls in the South China Sea. However, flying in "Gooney Birds" as the P5M Marlins were called at one time, was a thrill of a lifetime, as was being a part of aircraft flight crews that were totally devoted to their mission in the tradition of the Eyes of the Fleet. Although my naval experience was in a seaplane that was a successor to the PBY Catalinas and PBM Mariners, our pilots, navigators, and flight crews flew these birds with the same pride and devotion to our country as had the airmen in World War II.

I previously read CDR David Bruhn's *Wooden Ships and Iron Men* trilogy with great interest and pleasure. Devoted to the unsung and stalwart sailors that served aboard wooden minesweepers between 1941 and 1994, the literary treatment of this part of naval history is such that readers feel like they are witnessing events that very few knew about. When I learned that he was writing a new work on seaplanes and seaplane tenders during World War II, I felt sure that he would cover every aspect in glorious detail.

CDR Bruhn has now skillfully addressed a mostly neglected segment of the U.S. Navy, and given it the respectful historical attention it deserves. It was refreshing to find that Bruhn had chosen seaplanes and their seaplane tenders as his subject and described, in detail, their mission and important contributions. This almost totally ignored sector of our Navy's history has now come to light in the author's book *Eyes of the Fleet*. I look forward to this First Edition with anticipation and admiration of all Navy aviators.

PH-1 Roland Nino Martinez, USN (Retired)
Former Curator for Photography, VMMC San Diego
Vietnam Veteran's Association of America Life Member

Acknowledgements

I am grateful to Richard DeRosset for producing a dramatic and truly stunning painting for the cover art, titled "Evasion of Destruction." This magnificent work portrays a strafing run by three Japanese "Mavis" flying boats following their unsuccessful torpedo attack on the USS *Heron* (AVP-2) on 20 December 1942. *Heron* shot down one of the aircraft with her starboard 3-inch gun; her port gun had been disabled by earlier combat action. This final attack followed a series of earlier ones by twelve other enemy aircraft against the small seaplane tender as she sailed alone in the Java Sea.

Richard DeRosset holding one of the several cats with which he shares his art studio, while standing in front of a work in progress.

Richard has produced nearly 900 paintings and murals during his career as an artist, which followed much time spent at sea as a "white hat" in the U.S. Navy during the Vietnam War, crewmember of the fishing boat *Petrel* which caught fire and was lost at sea off the southern California coast, and master of the small merchant tanker MV *Pacific Trojan* that operated out of the Long Beach area.

But for his work, few depictions of small ships engaged in fiercely contested, but relatively obscure or unknown naval battles would find their way on to canvas. Only a few people admiring the cover art will recognize the 187-foot ship as a former *Lapwing*-class minesweeper, built during World War I. Fewer still will know that she was one of only nine of these type ships converted to seaplane tenders and employed as such before and during World War II. Since Richard is both an aviation and maritime artist, viewers can witness his prowess at both of these disciplines in a single painting.

Rob Hoole, a former Royal Navy mine clearance diving officer and commanding officer of HMS *Berkeley* (M40)—a *Hunt*-class countermeasure vessel—reviewed the chapter on the Normandy invasion. Hoole is a long-standing member of the Ton Class Association and a regular contributor to its publications. He is also founding Vice Chairman and Webmaster of the Royal Naval Minewarfare & Clearance Diving Officers' Association, and holds key positions in related organizations. Lastly, in addition to being an acknowledged expert on mine warfare, Hoole is a keen naval historian and author.

Roland Nino Martinez was kind enough to pen a foreword for the book. Nino was associated with seaplanes and seaplane tenders in the 1950s, well after the time period to which this work is devoted, but he shares the same passion for this area of naval aviation as did his predecessors. The "Eyes of the Fleet" were replaced decades ago by high-performance aircraft and intelligence-gathering satellites, but love of seaplanes endures among those who spent time in aircraft fitted with floats instead of wheels. Following duty with Patrol Squadron 46, Nino served aboard the new nuclear-powered guided missile cruiser *Long Beach* (CGN-9) and the elderly carrier *Bon Homme Richard* (CV-31). He completed his Navy career with Helicopter Anti-Submarine Squadron Two and Light Photographic Squadron Sixty-Three. Nino then worked for U.S. Customs for a while, and as a private investigator for fifteen years—occupations seemingly well-suited for someone who regularly made low passes over reefs of the South China Sea, including the Spratleys, to obtain photo reconnaissance.

I am particularly grateful to Lynn Marie Tosello for her work as the editor of this text. In addition to contributing both eloquence and substance to the work via her discerning eye and thorough work, I am grateful for her efforts in identifying nautical terms and Navy "fleet shorthands" requiring further explanation regarding their meaning.

Preface

This is the best goddam squadron in the world; and I'll lick anyone who says it ain't.

—Russel W. Woods, Aviation Machinist's Mate Third, flight engineer, Crew Two. These words, unoriginal as they were and spurred by the consumption of much beer at a last Harvey Point, North Carolina, squadron get-together before the deployment of VPB-216 to the Pacific Theater, reflected the attitude of all hands.[1]

Black Cat operations are a severe nervous and emotional strain on pilots and crews. In addition to the expected hazards of war – anti-aircraft fire, nightfighters, searchlights, etc. – there are the added tensions and strains caused by flight at night, frequently in poor weather, at altitudes well below surrounding terrain, for long and fatiguing periods of time, ending in dangerously low attacks made under instrument conditions. As a result, the incidence of "operational fatigue" amongst pilots and crews is disproportionately high. Some slight amelioration can be obtained by adhering to certain definite principles.

Most important of all, the plane commander must have the definite assurance that "out there" – on patrol – he is responsible, and his decisions are final and not subject to criticism by higher echelons of command upon his return from patrol. This does not mean, obviously, that military discipline should be relaxed and pilots permitted to disregard orders at will, nor does it mean that evidence of non-performance of duty should be disregarded; but it does mean that when a pilot reports that he could not get through the weather, or that enemy return fire was too intense and accurate to permit an attack, he will not be subjected to a fishy stare and a dissertation on what he should have done….

—Excerpt from Patrol Bombing Squadron VPB-34 War History describing the hazards routinely faced by PBY-5 patrol planes during night armed reconnaissance anti-shipping patrols. It reflects the seasoned perspective of combat veterans, versus the eager anticipation of war prior to arrival in the theater.

Because of the breadth of *Eyes of the Fleet*, I believe it is important to identify some limitations of the book, before progressing to an overview of it. Acts of valor and derring-do were abundant in naval aviation in World War II, including in patrol squadrons and patrol bombing squadrons. As such, an entire book could be devoted to a single parent Air Wing or, in some cases to a particular squadron—such books exist. It would also be possible to fill a book with nothing but descriptions of the air attacks made against seaplane tenders, and many books about significant battles and operations covered herein. Regarding the latter, a diversity of numerous such works already exists. In order to provide more space for the main themes of the book, I have thus tried to afford only as much background as that necessary to place in context the contributions of seaplane tenders and their patrol aircraft to the overall war effort.

Some readers will likely be disappointed that there is little material about the service of seaplane tenders in the American Theater, with the exception of one ship, and only limited coverage of those that served in the European Theater. A quick review of Appendix A, titled Seaplane Tender and Patrol Squadron Battle Stars, will reveal why the bulk of the book is devoted to the war in the Pacific. A majority of the Navy's seaplane tenders were sent there because the expansive ocean demanded large numbers of patrol aircraft to search for enemy forces. Moreover, unlike in Europe, there were relatively few airfields or airstrips available in the Pacific, until existing enemy facilities were captured or airfields built in concert with the movement of Allied forces toward Japan.

Although seaplane tenders did not earn any battle stars in the American Theater, some patrol squadrons and individual planes did, mostly in conjunction with convoy escort duties or anti-submarine operations. The Pacific Theater portion of the appendix includes all the numerous operations in which seaplane tenders, patrol squadrons, and patrol bombing squadrons earned battle stars. A few operations involved only land-based patrol planes, and in some cases, the aircraft of a squadron were split, with a detachment assigned to a tender, and the balance operating from a shore airbase.

The number of battle stars a unit (ship or patrol squadron) earned signified quantity of combat action. For extraordinary heroic action, a ship or squadron might also receive a unit award. The Presidential Unit Citation was the highest award for heroism a unit might receive and equivalent to the Navy Cross Medal for an individual. The Navy Unit Commendation was awarded to military units for heroism not sufficient to justify an award of the Presidential Unit Citation. The destroyer seaplane tender *McFarland* (AVD-10) earned the Presidential Unit Citation and the small seaplane tender *Heron* (AVP-2) a Navy Unit Commendation. Many patrol squadrons (VP) and patrol bombing squadrons (VPB) earned one or more of these laurels, a listing of which is provided in Appendix B.

U.S. ASIATIC FLEET ABANDONS THE PHILIPPINES

The book opens in Chapter 1 with the exploits of the seaplane tender *Heron* and her crew during the defense of the Netherlands East Indies, which followed retirement of the U.S. Asiatic Fleet south from Manila to the Java Sea. There was no expectation by the Navy that the very small fleet (with no ship larger than a cruiser) at Manila Bay could provide a credible defense of the Philippines. The existing war plan charged Adm. Thomas D. Hart to support the U.S. Army presence in the Philippines as long as the defense of the islands continued. However, due to its small size, all that could be reasonably expected, should Japanese forces invade the archipelago, would be for surviving units of the fleet to retire or fight a delaying action. Ultimately both actions occurred.

OVERVIEW OF THE SEAPLANE TENDERS, PATROL WINGS, AND FLEET AIR WINGS

Chapter 2 provides an overview of the seaplane tenders employed in World War II to maintain, refuel, and rearm the "eyes of the fleet"—initially scout planes and patrol planes, and later patrol bombers as well. Chapter 3 offers a very short summary of the organization and later the restructuring of Patrol Wings, which the Navy redesignated Fleet Air Wings on 1 November 1942. Wings were the parent organizations of Patrol Squadrons (VP), Patrol Bombing Squadrons (VPB), and Utility Squadrons (UT).

INITIAL ACTIONS IN THE PACIFIC THEATER

Chapters 4-11 progress through the early part of the war in the Pacific. The Japanese attacks on Pearl Harbor, the Philippines, and Darwin (Australia's "Pearl Harbor") are described as is the relatively short, but hard fought Allied defense of the Netherlands East Indies. The book then turns to action in the Aleutians and the Battle of Midway. Particularly during the Aleutian Islands portion of the Battle of Midway, PBYs played a key role as strike, as well as patrol aircraft.

WAR IN THE AMERICAS

The brief portion of the book devoted to the war in the American Theater, Chapter 12, focuses on the loss of the seaplane tender *Gannet* to the German submarine *U-653* off Bermuda.

GUADALCANAL, NEW CALEDONIA, AMERICAN SAMOA, AND OTHER SOUTH PACIFIC ISLANDS

Readers next travel in Chapters 13-15 to Guadalcanal in the Solomon Islands, New Caledonia (a French Territory strategically located on the northeast approach to Australia), and islands of the South Pacific at which seaplane tenders initially provided the only facilities available for seaplanes. The significance of American control of Guadalcanal, which the 1st Marine Division had captured from the Japanese on 7 August 1942, was not lost on the enemy—from it the Allies could expand their presence in the South Pacific while thwarting the Japanese thrust.

Amidst fears that Germany, with tacit support from large numbers of Vichy French (German sympathizers) on New Caledonia, might invite the Japanese to occupy the French Territory, a hastily gathered U.S. Army force embarked in merchant ships and sailed from New York City on 23 January 1942. Upon arrival, Task Force 6814 occupied New Caledonia supported by the seaplane tender *Tangier* which had arrived earlier.

For America, keeping open the 7,800-mile-long sea route from Panama to Sydney, Australia, was a strategic imperative. The northern route, west-southwest from Hawaii, was already controlled by the Japanese operating from island bastions. Only the southern route, via South Sea Islands, was available for use by ships carrying men and war materials to Australia. However, facilities in the South Pacific at which U.S. ground and air forces were based were primitive, prompting the Navy to dispatch Rear Adm. Richard E. Byrd, USN (Retired), to lead an inspection team in assessing the condition of the bases. Byrd was a pioneering American aviator, famous polar explorer, and Medal of Honor recipient who had been recalled to active duty. From 1942 to 1945 he headed missions to the Pacific, including surveys of remote islands for airfields.

AFRICAN AND EUROPEAN THEATERS

The action moves next in Chapters 16 and 17 to French Morocco and the Normandy coast. A single seaplane tender, the *Barnegat*, was involved in the invasion of French Morocco on 8 November 1942—a part of the larger Operation TORCH—which involved the participation of American ground troops in Europe/Africa for the first time.

The *Rockaway* was the single seaplane tender to support Operation OVERLORD, the invasion of Normandy, France. She performed patrol and convoy escort work in the English Channel, transported personnel and protected Allied beachheads against enemy air attacks, and served as flagship for Rear Adm. John E. Wilkes, USN.

Chapter 17 includes an account of the loss of Lt. Joseph P. Kennedy, Jr. (the older brother of future president JFK) in an aircraft loaded with high explosives on an attack mission against a German V-weapons site in France.

OPERATIONS FACILITATING/LEADING UP TO THE ALLIED LIBERATION OF THE PHILIPPINE ISLANDS

Following nominal coverage of the African and European Theaters, the remainder of the book is devoted to the war in the Pacific. Chapters 18-24 describe some of the operations supporting/leading up to the liberation of the Philippines. Adm. Raymond A. Spruance's Central Pacific Campaign, and Adm. William F. Halsey and Gen. Douglas MacArthur's advances up the Solomon Islands and New Guinea and through the Bismarck Archipelago overlay this action. Seaplane tenders and patrol planes were with the Fleet during the drive through the Central Pacific's Gilbert, Marshall, and Mariana Islands. They also supported the Admiralty Islands landings, Hollandia and other New Guinea operations, consolidation of the Northern Solomons, and the capture of the South Palau Islands.

Also described is the capture of the Green Islands. Among the naval personnel assigned to Green Island (the largest of the islands) was future American president Lt. Richard M. Nixon, USNR, who in the spring of 1944 ran the base air cargo office. He spent many free nights in the Pacific playing poker with other servicemen. Reportedly, his winnings were such that he was able to purchase a home after the war and also finance his first political campaign with them.

THE INVASION OF THE PHILIPPINES, IWO JIMA, OKINAWA, AND FINAL THIRD FLEET OPERATIONS AGAINST JAPAN

Chapters 25-28 cover the Allied landings at Leyte in November 1944, which launched the invasion of the Philippines, as well as the invasions of Iwo Jima and Okinawa, and Third Fleet Operations preceding Japan's surrender in August 1945. During this almost ten-month period, there was a dramatic increase in the number of battle stars earned by seaplane tenders and patrol squadrons. Part of this was due to the large Allied forces engaged in amphibious landings against very strong island defense forces, and associated combat at sea, in the air and ashore. Another factor was the dramatic increase by the Japanese in the numbers of kamikaze aircraft employed in attacks against naval and merchant ships and the frequency of their use.

While Navy ships (including seaplane tenders) and merchant vessels fought off suicide and conventional aircraft attacks, patrol planes carried out anti-shipping, anti-submarine patrol and search and reconnaissance flights as well as other duties. The increased tempo of the war in the Pacific theater required greater employment of seaplanes as bombers and for "Dumbo" operations. The term Dumbo referred to air-sea rescue operations, and their frequency was generally linked to the tempo of combat air operations, as increased missions resulted in a greater number of pilots and aircrews being shot down.

END OF WAR AND POST-WAR DEMOBILIZATION

The final chapter of the book covers the end of the war, which occurred following United States' detonation of atomic bombs over the cities of Hiroshima and Nagasaki. This action was deemed necessary by President Harry S. Truman, who wished to avoid massive American casualties expected to result from a planned invasion of the Japanese home islands. Despite the fact that by August 1945, Japan was for all practical purposes defeated, its leaders intended to fight on, even though fanatical resistance would likely result in hundreds of thousands of Japanese lives being lost.

The Postscript provides an overview of post-war occupational duty of seaplane tenders in the Pacific and Europe, the massive post-war demobilization of the U.S. military—which included the U.S. Navy—and the service of seaplane tenders retained by the Navy during the Korean and Vietnam Wars. Five tenders participated in the Korean War and three in the Vietnam War. The end of World War II marked the conclusion of large usage of seaplane tenders by the Navy. With no need to patrol expansive ocean areas in peacetime, the Service disposed of a majority of these type ships by sale or lease, or laid-up in "mothballs" in Reserve Fleets.

A SALUTE TO SEAPLANE TENDERS AND THE MEN WHO SERVED ABOARD THEM IN WORLD WAR II

There are hundreds of published works related to naval aviation and within this category several devoted to seaplanes, particularly the greatly beloved PBY "Catalinas." Information about seaplane tenders and the men aboard them who maintained, rearmed, and refueled planes is almost non-existent. There are several reasons for this. The war correspondents and historians with the Fleet generally did not ride tenders, except perhaps for the *Biscayne*, which was converted to an amphibious force flagship. They were aboard carriers, battleships, or large amphibious ships that served as admirals' flagships, and wrote stories about what they witnessed, the large battles, and about what they believed would be of most interest to Americans. Hollywood movie producers followed suit on the silver screen.

Many if not most Americans of a certain age have seen the 1976 war film *Midway*, and may recall that PBYs scouted for and located the Japanese fleet. Few are probably aware that the fabric-covered patrol planes were also dispatched during the Battle of Midway to conduct the first night torpedo attacks on enemy ships, or that during the Aleutian Islands part of the Battle of Midway, Adm. Chester Nimitz ordered Patrol Wing Four to "bomb the Japanese out of Kiska."

NAUTICAL TERMS AND USE OF THE BOOK'S INDEX

Some readers may find useful the definitions of some nautical terms sprinkled through the book:

- Abaft: Toward the stern, relative to some object ("abaft the deckhouse").
- Armada: A large fleet of warships, though the term may be used symbolically to signify any large moving group of vessels.
- Atoll: A ring-shaped coral reef or a string of closely spaced small coral islands, enclosing or nearly enclosing a shallow lagoon. The largest island of an atoll often has the same name as the atoll, just as the largest island of an island chain often has the same name as the chain.
- Bollard: A thick low post, usually of iron or steel, mounted on a pier or wharf, to which mooring lines from vessels are attached.
- Bowser: Portable fuel tank.
- Broach: To turn the ship broadside to heavy seas, or lose control of steering in following seas so that the ship is turned broadside to the waves. An extremely dangerous situation in steep seas since the ship may roll over and capsize.
- Bullnose: A closed chock (deck fitting through which mooring lines are fed) at the bow of a ship.
- Caliber: The bore-to-barrel-length ratio of a naval gun, obtained by dividing the length of the barrel (from breech to muzzle) by the barrel diameter to give a dimensionless quantity. For example, a 3-inch/50-caliber gun has a barrel length of 150 inches.

- Collier: Bulk cargo ship designed to carry coal especially many decades ago for naval use by coal-fired warships.
- D-Day: The unnamed day on which a particular operation commences or is to commence.
- Davit(s): A crane made of a swinging boom together with blocks and tackle, usually mounted in pairs, which may be swung over the side of a ship to lower and recover the launch or lifeboats.
- Dead in the water: Not moving (used only when a vessel is afloat and neither tied up nor anchored).
- Deckhouse: An enclosed structure built on the ship's upper or main deck, usually the navigating station though the term can refer to any simple superstructure on deck.
- Fathom: A unit of measurement equal to six feet, used to measure water depth.
- Freeboard: Vertical distance from a ship's weather deck to the surface of the water.
- General quarters: Battle Stations.
- Gun(s) opened: To begin firing a gun or guns.
- Jacobs ladder: A flexible hanging ladder consisting of vertical ropes or chains supporting wooden rungs that allow people to board a ship from a small boat.
- Land: To put ashore. Disembark.
- Lay to: To bring a ship to a stop in open water.
- Lighter: Flat-bottomed barge.
- Master: The commander of a non-military ship.
- Purse seiner: A type of fishing vessel that uses a net called a seine, which hangs vertically in the water and has along its bottom a number of rings. A line passes through all the rings, and when pulled, draws the net closed preventing the fish inside it from escaping.
- Rating: The rating of a sailor is a combination of rate (pay grade, as indicated by the number of chevrons he or she wears) and rating (occupational specialty, as indicated by the symbol just above the chevrons).
- Roadstead: A sheltered offshore anchorage area for ships.
- Seadrome: A floating airdrome serving as an intermediate or emergency landing place for aircraft flying over water.

Preface   xxv

- Stand (past tense stood): Of a ship or its captain, to steer, sail, or steam, usually used in conjunction with a specified direction or destination, e.g., "stand into port."
- Vessel: Any craft (from largest ship to smallest boat) that is capable of floating and moving on the water.

Former sailors picking up a book such as this one often want to ascertain whether or not it contains any references to a ship(s) in which they served. In acknowledgement of this fact, an extensive index is included. To reduce its size, multiple ships listed on the same page or pages in the text are combined into a single entry. Entries for American ships are located under their associated ship type headings. For example, the gunboats *Luzon* and *Oahu* are consolidated into a single entry under Ships and Craft, and the sub-categories: United States, Navy, combatants, and gunboats. A reader searching for a particular foreign ship should review all entries under the heading for that country.

Since a good portion of this book is devoted to U.S. Navy, Marine Corps, and Army Air Corps aviation, some readers will likely be most interested in searching for references to a particular Aviation Wing or Squadron or type of aircraft. This information may be found near the end of the index under the entry United States, and within the sub-categories Army, Navy, Marine Corps, or military aircraft.

1

Peril in the Java Sea

Any time more than one plane was sighted they were sure to be enemy.

—Lt. William L. Kabler citing an adage common in the Asiatic Fleet after its retirement south to the Netherlands East Indies following the Japanese invasion of the Philippines on 8 December 1941. This comment was in reference to there being no need to identify as the enemy two flights of planes approaching his ship, the USS *Heron*, on 31 December, which preceded a number of bombing, strafing and torpedo attacks on the seaplane tender.[1]

The morning of 31 December 1941, the *Heron* (AVP-2) was proceeding on a southerly course in the Molucca Sea—a part of the western Pacific within the Netherlands (Dutch) East Indies—when she came under the first of a series of withering attacks from Japanese aircraft that day. The small seaplane tender was assigned to Patrol Wing Ten, part of the small United States Asiatic Fleet, which had been forced to leave the Philippines following the Japanese invasion of the Archipelago. When war broke out on 7 December (the 8th in the Philippines), the Wing consisted of the twenty-eight PBY-4 Catalinas of Patrol Squadron VP-101, ten light seaplanes of its utility squadron, and the seaplane tenders *Langley*, *Childs*, *William B. Preston*, and *Heron*.[2]

Catalinas were the most-produced flying boat of World War II and at 66 feet in length with a wingspan of 104 feet, were fairly good sized. The utility squadron's supporting seaplanes, four J2Fs, five OS2Us, and one SOC, were smaller. The Grumman J2F Duck was a single-engine amphibious biplane used for utility and air-sea rescue duties. The Vought OS2U Kingfisher was an observation floatplane, whose normal armament was .30-caliber machine guns and two 100-pound bombs. It was the successor for the Curtiss SOC Seagull, a single-engine scout observation biplane, which would continue to serve much longer than expected during the war.

Chapter 1

Photo 1-1

PBY-5A Catalina drops an aircraft torpedo during tests in 1942-1943. Patrol Wing Ten utilized the earlier model PBY-4 aircraft during the Defense of the Java Sea.
U.S. Naval History and Heritage Command Photograph #NH 94118

Wing personnel were not surprised on 8 December, when they learned that the Japanese had attacked Pearl Harbor. The Catalina pilots had received orders in late November to begin carrying out patrols to the west of Manila, along the coast of Indo-China across the South China Sea. Up until 2 December, plane crews detected nothing alarming. On that day, however, a sighting was made of twenty Japanese merchant ships, including troop transports, present in Cam Ranh Bay, French Indochina (now Vietnam). The following day, there were fifty ships, including cruisers and destroyers. On 4 December, they had vanished. Forty-eight hours later, British patrols from Singapore spotted the Japanese armada moving westward across the Gulf of Thailand. On the 5th, 6th, and 7th of December, Wing Ten aircraft on patrol from Manila met Japanese planes patrolling in the vicinity of the Luzon coastline. Although not yet at war with one another, there was tension associated with these meetings. "Each outfit, of course, had their machine guns manned, kept a wary eye on each other and avoided each other like stiff-legged dogs."[3]

President Franklin D. Roosevelt was well aware that drumbeats warning of Japan's militaristic intentions were drawing nearer. He sent Admiral Thomas C. Hart, commander-in-chief Asiatic Fleet, a message on 1 December with the highest-secrecy classification directing him to undertake a classified operation. (A detailed account is provided in my book *Battle Stars for the "Cactus Navy": America's Yachts and Fishing Vessels in World War II*.) During hearings held in 1945, members of Congress stated their belief that this action—in which the patrol yacht *Isabel* was sent to reconnoiter Cam Ranh Bay with its heavy concentration of Japanese ships—had been intended to provoke a war with Japan.

JAPANESE INVASION OF THE PHILIPPINES

When Patrol Wing Ten received word that Pearl Harbor had been attacked, wartime watches were already in effect, planes were loaded with bombs with full crews and full allowances of ammunition aboard, and the Wing was ready in all respects for combat with the exception of final dispersal. Existing war plans directed seaplane tenders and aircraft to scatter to lakes, swamps, coves, bays or any other place with suitable cover and facilities. Prior to this action, the ships were situated as follows:

- *William B. Preston* (AVD-7) was at Davao Bay, Mindanao, in the southeastern Philippines, tending three Catalina seaplanes;
- *Heron* (AVP-2) was at the Balabac Straits—which connects the Sulu Sea in the southwestern Philippines with the South China Sea to the northwest—tending five OS2U Kingfishers;
- *Childs* (AVP-14) was on the east side of Manila Bay tending five Catalinas; and,
- *Langley* (AV-3), the flagship, was at Manila Bay as well, loading gas, oil, and stores.[4]

Nine of the remaining eighteen PBYs were operating from a lake called Laguna de Bay, located sixty miles southeast of Manila near the town of Los Banos. The others were at Olongapo in Subic Bay, sixty miles north of Manila. In ensuing days, the planes at Davao Bay conducted searches to the southeast of the Philippines scouting for enemy forces, those at Balabac Straits to the southwest of the archipelago toward Borneo, and those at Manila Bay and Subic Bay, to the west and northwest of Luzon.[5]

Japanese control of the skies quickly made it unfeasible for Patrol Wing Ten to remain in the Philippines. Enemy dive bombers and destroyers chased the *William B. Preston* out of Davao Bay and, on 12 December, Japanese "Zeros" attacked and destroyed seven PBYs refueling on the water in Subic Bay at Olongapo. By Sunday, 14 December, the Japanese were sending flights over Luzon daily and they had everything their own way over Manila Bay. This untenable position necessitated relocating the Wing's seaplanes and tenders southward. Such a move would also provide a reprieve for personnel fatigued by combat-related duties. *Childs* had been tending planes at night, which "meant that the crew was at [their] General Quarters stations a good bit of the day and they were at their fueling station for servicing the PBYs most of the night and it was becoming a 24-hour schedule and they were getting very little sleep."[6]

There was never any expectation that the Asiatic Fleet could remain in the Philippine Islands. The existing war plan charged it to support the U.S. Army presence in the Philippines as long as the defense of the islands continued. However, due to the fleet's small size, all that could be reasonably expected, should Japanese forces invade the archipelago, would be for it to retire or fight a delaying action. Ultimately both actions occurred. Following receipt of Navy Department orders on 20 November 1941 to fall back, Admiral Hart had begun to move his fleet southward.[7]

Patrol Wing Ten maintained its patrols until the fleet was safely down in southern Borneo and then brought up the rear. When the Wing withdrew from the Manila area, only seventeen Catalinas remained, of which eleven could fly. The six disabled PBYs had gasoline tanks, fuselages and wings full of holes from Japanese aircraft machine guns and shipboard anti-aircraft guns. The two remaining J2F Ducks also made their way south, crammed with five-gallon cans of gasoline to help extend their range. They landed where they could and gassed every so often until they reached Balikpapan, on the east coast of Borneo. They, and four OS2U Kingfishers that joined them, comprised the remaining planes of the utility squadron.[8]

Departing the Manila area on 14 December, *Childs* proceeded southwest to Cavite to load bombs, and then to Cebu in the southern Philippines to fuel before continuing southward to Balikpapan, Borneo. While she was moored at the Standard Oil dock at Cebu, an old Filipino man approached the ship. Lt. Comdr. John L. Pratt, the tender's commanding officer, described the man who apparently had previously served in the United States Navy:

> You could see that he had washed, and pressed, and polished his uniform, which showed signs of many years' wear. He came up to the dock, looked up at the bridge saluted and said, "Captain, I am ready for duty." Needless to say, we took him on board, and I believe he is still with Patrol Wing 10 and very proud of it, and we were very proud of him.[9]

Map 1-1

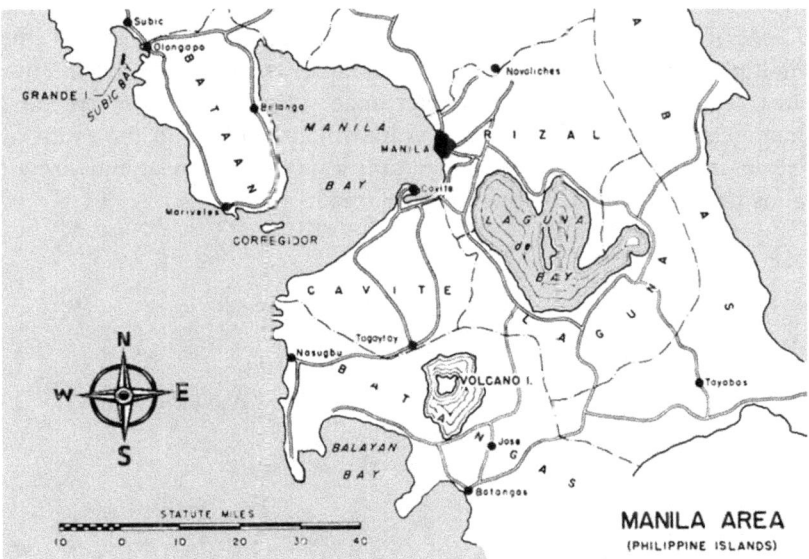

Manila Bay area of Luzon Island, Philippine Islands
Source: http://www.ibiblio.org/hyperwar/USN/Building_Bases/maps/bases2-p391.jpg

JOURNEY OF THE SEAPLANE TENDERS SOUTH

While *Childs* was in transit to Balikpapan, a Japanese submarine trailed her for almost a day. It would show up astern occasionally, but she was easily able to outdistance it each time, thereby avoiding attack. From Balikpapan, *Childs* and the other three seaplane tenders—the *Heron*, *William B. Preston*, and *Langley*—moved farther south into the Netherlands East Indies. Stretching 314 feet in length, the *Childs* and *William B. Preston* were sister ships; former destroyers commissioned in 1920. *Heron*, a 188-foot ex-World War I minesweeper, was smaller and two years older. At 542 feet in length the *Langley* was the largest of the three ships, and of even greater age, having been commissioned on 7 April 1913 as the collier *Jupiter*. Following conversion to the Navy's first aircraft carrier in 1920, she was renamed *Langley*. In 1937 the Navy converted her to a seaplane tender (AV-3). The *Langley* had been the first tender to leave the Philippines. She slipped out of Manila Bay under the cover of darkness the evening of 8 December and travelled south with the fleet oilers *Pecos* (AO-6) and *Trinity* (AO-13), escorted by the destroyers *Barker* (DD-213) and *Paul Jones* (DD-239). The Navy, judging the *Langley* to be particularly vulnerable to

6   Chapter 1

destruction by the enemy, sent her to Darwin, Australia, to serve as an aviation support ship. Because she had been designed to haul coal, the *Langley*'s designers had given her large cargo holds, and not the multiple compartments found in warships, which divide the interior area of a ship's hull into smaller spaces by the use of structural members. This made her more vulnerable to sinking in the event of battle damage. Moreover, she had only a modest outfit of anti-aircraft guns to protect herself from attack by enemy planes.[10]

Map 1-2

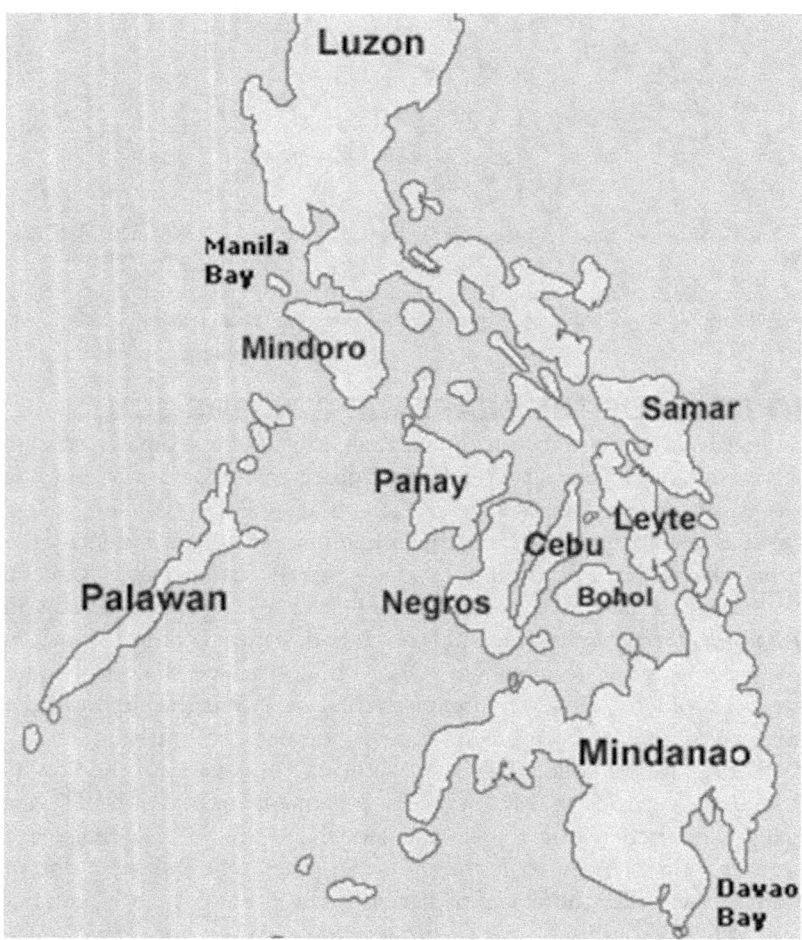

Philippine Islands: Luzon south to Mindanao

The tenders *Heron* and *William B. Preston* arrived at Balikpapan on 16 December, where aviation gasoline and fuel oil were available, and then proceeded to Soerabaja, a large port city in northeast Java. (This city is today Surabaya, Indonesia, and this name is used hereafter.) Aboard the *Heron*, crewmembers were very interested in Java and in enjoying some fine Dutch beer. There proved to be girls and good restaurants, as well as beer ashore, but leisure activities had to compete with the business at hand. All four tenders had reached Surabaya, but orders sent *Childs* and *Heron* to Ambon, a seaport and the main town on Ambon Island, a thousand miles to the northeast. The *Langley* was dispatched with the Wing's remaining three OS2Us to Darwin, the capital city of Australia's Northern Territory, situated on the Timor Sea. After a short period of supporting anti-submarine patrols from that port, she was ordered to Fremantle, 2,260 nautical miles southward along Australia's western coast. From Fremantle, her planes flew anti-submarine patrols and escorted Allied ships traversing nearby waters.[11]

Map 1-3

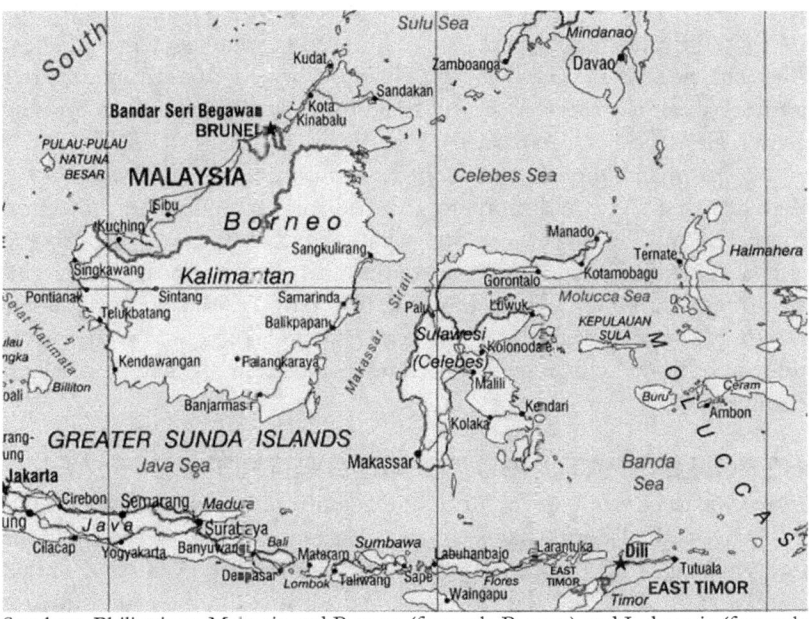

Southern Philippines, Malaysia and Borneo (formerly Borneo) and Indonesia (formerly the Netherlands East Indies)

The relocation of the *Langley* to Australia left the *William B. Preston* at Surabaya, and the *Childs* and *Heron* at Ambon, to tend planes that would serve as the U.S. Navy's "eyes of the fleet" for the defense of the Netherlands East Indies. A newly formed ABDA (American-British-Dutch-Australian) command, encompassing all Allied forces in South East Asia, had orders to hold the Japanese north of the Malay area for as long as possible. By this action, it was hoped the Allies could retain control of the Indian Ocean and the western sea approaches to Australia. The patrol wing was to conduct flights over the sea passages north of the Malay barrier in order to give adequate warning of any Japanese movements in force southward. The barrier was a notional line that ran down the Malayan Peninsula, through Singapore and the southernmost islands of the Dutch East Indies.[12]

Heron loaded the Wing's two Grumman J2F Ducks aboard and left Surabaya on Christmas Day, 1941. She reached Ambon four days later on 29 December. Ambon would prove to be a fairly good seaplane base; there was considerable gasoline available and it offered a good harbor with a ramp to haul out planes to work on and repair. *Childs* arrived with one OS2U, and the three planes immediately started to carry out patrols, searching to the north into the Halmahera Islands (the site of a Japanese naval base), the Molucca Passage, and adjacent Molucca Sea. Ten Catalina PBY-4s soon joined these aircraft, after damage they had received in the Philippines was "patched up" by the Dutch air station at Surabaya.[13]

Childs made herself at home at Ambon, finding a coral ridge along the shoreline she could moor to and endeavor to hide from detection by the enemy. Her crew cut down palm trees and lashed them to the ship's masts and stacks, and covered the remaining topside areas with palm fronds. This effort to look like part of the scenery, while assisting the shore facilities in rearming and refueling planes, was undertaken for self-preservation during Japanese air raids on island facilities.[14]

HERON DISPATCHED TO AID DESTROYER *PEARY*

Heron was sent from Ambon on 29 December to assist the *Peary* (DD-226), which had been attacked by two groups of aircraft the previous day while making the run south from Manila. By evading dropped bombs and torpedoes, the destroyer had escaped harm from a quartet of Japanese bombers with only minor strafing damage. However, an Australian PBY out on patrol had sighted the enemy aircraft, reported them, and misidentified the *Peary* as Japanese. As a result, three Australian Lockheed Hudson bombers, based at Ambon, appeared that evening and made two runs each on the destroyer. Shrapnel from near bomb misses killed one crewman and wounded two others, perforated the ship's hull plating in several places, including the steering compartment, and severed the steering cables.[15]

Steering by manual movement of the rudder, the *Peary* shaped a course across the Molucca Sea. In early morning on 29 December, she arrived at the tiny island of Maitara—located across a channel from Ternate, a much larger member of the Maluku group (also known as the Moluccas)—and moored to palm trees on its northeast side. *Heron* arrived at Ternate in early evening the following day. After four hours spent trying to convince local authorities that she and *Peary*, for whom she was searching, were American ships, she was informed that the destroyer had sailed earlier. Having failed to find her, *Heron* left to make the return transit to Ambon.[16]

HERON SURVIVES MULTIPLE AIRCRAFT ATTACKS

In mid-morning the following day, 31 December, *Heron* sighted a four-engine seaplane approaching at a low level. Because it resembled a Sikorsky VS-42 flying boat, a type flown by the Dutch, the ship's commanding officer, Lt. William L. Kabler, USN, ordered his gunners to hold fire until positive identification was made. As two "red meatballs" under the wings of the Japanese Kawanishi H6K "Mavis" became visible, all the ship's guns—two 3-inch mounts and four .50-cal. machine guns—opened. At 0930, the aircraft came in on a bombing run, but apparently machine gun fire discouraged it from dropping any ordnance on its first pass.[17]

The plane climbed to altitude and came back in on another attack. *Heron* maneuvered violently to avoid dropped 100-pound bombs, and they fell well clear of her. A third attack followed, but again caused no harm. About that time, a rainsquall developed to the southwest and the seaplane tender ran for the shelter it offered. Kabler believed that by these means he had evaded the enemy. However, at about 1100 when *Heron* came out of the squall, the plane was off her starboard beam, sitting on the water waiting patiently for the ship to reemerge. The aircraft continued to shadow the seaplane tender until mid-afternoon, when six more Mavis—two sections of three patrol planes each—arrived.[18]

About 1520, one of the sections broke off from the other and came in on a horizontal bombing attack. The first pass was apparently not to the planes' liking, and they swung around and came in up wind on a second attack. A third attack followed. Each time, the *Heron* maneuvered to avoid the dropped bombs. The second section then tried its luck. On the first run, 3-inch rounds hit one of the planes, which started smoking, dropped out of the formation, and retired northward. The two remaining aircraft made one more pass. As before, Kabler was able to dodge the free falling ordnance through rudder commands. Up to this point, three aircraft had dropped twenty-two 100-pound bombs, all of which the ship had managed to avoid. However, there would be no reprieve for *Heron* and her crew as still more enemy aircraft—five twin-engine land-based bombers, and three addition four-engine patrol planes—arrived overhead.[19]

The former were Mitsubishi G3M "Nell" bombers. Three weeks earlier, groups of this type and Mitsubishi G4M "Betty" bombers had attacked and sunk the battleship HMS *Prince of Wales* and the battlecruiser HMS *Repulse* off the eastern coast of Malaya. News of this tragedy stunned British Prime Minister Winston Churchill, who immediately recognized that British and American naval forces in the region now faced much graver damage:

> In all the war, I never received a more direct shock.... As I turned over and twisted in bed the full horror of the news sank in upon me. There were no British or American ships in the Indian Ocean or the Pacific except the American survivors of Pearl Harbor, who were hastening back to California. Over all this vast expanse of waters Japan was supreme, and we everywhere were weak and naked.[20]

The bombers made a pass over *Heron* but, apparently not liking the run, did not release any bombs. At 1600, after proceeding down wind and reversing course, they came in on a run dropping sticks of 100-pound bombs. The term "stick" denoted a group of several bombs, falling one above the other, straight down. The seaplane tender was unable to avoid them all. A shrapnel-loaded, high-explosive bomb hit a shackle near the top of her mainmast and detonated on contact, blasting holes of considerable depth in the steel mast, destroying one shroud shackle and block, slacking and damaging all shrouds, and dropping the boat boom on the motor launch in the starboard skids. The blast radiated in all directions from the point of impact. Shrapnel went through the 1 ¼-inch thick steel engine room hatch and ricocheted around the space. A bomb splinter penetrated the manhole cover (bronze ½-inch thick) to the rudder yoke compartment, located about seventy feet aft of the impact. Three other bombs hit the water and detonated off the ship's port bow at a distance of forty-five feet. Hot shrapnel penetrated her side (¼-inch plate) in about twenty-five places and started fires in the paint locker and commissary storeroom located on the upper level of the forward hold. Kabler described the bomb-blast damage to *Heron* and carnage among the crewmen topside:

> This attack damaged the ship considerably. Pieces of shrapnel from the bomb hit on the mainmast, cut all the stays to the boat booms, and injured most of the gun crew of the machine guns there. The near misses off the port bow set the paint locker in the forward store room on fire, damaged the port three inch gun and killed one of the lookouts and injured all of the gun crew on the port three inch gun and all the gun crews on the port machine guns.[21]

Photo 1-2

Evasion of Destruction by Richard DeRosset portrays a strafing run by three Japanese "Mavis" flying boats following their unsuccessful torpedo attack on the USS *Heron* (AVP-2) on 31 December 1942. *Heron* shot down one of the aircraft with her starboard 3-inch gun; her port gun had been disabled by earlier combat action. This final attack followed a series of earlier ones by twelve other enemy aircraft against the seaplane tender as she sailed alone in the Java Sea. Due to heroic actions by her captain and crew, *Heron* survived overwhelming odds during the long ordeal.

Fifteen minutes later, the three patrol planes (likely Mavis) which had been awaiting their turn, formed into a "torpedo anvil" at 1615 and came in on an attack. One approached on the ship's starboard bow, one on her port bow, and one on her port quarter. Fortunately, the aircraft did not synchronize their movements to arrive together, and Kabler was able to sequentially turn *Heron* "bow to" each of the planes as they released their torpedoes. This tactic is designed to minimize the cross-section a ship presents to a torpedo streaking toward it, and it worked. Each of the "fish" passed harmlessly down either the port or starboard side of the seaplane tender. Not deterred, the planes continued in and strafed *Heron*, causing additional personnel casualties aboard ship. The attack was not completely one-sided as *Heron*'s single operational 3-inch gun shot down one attacker.[22]

But for the near perfect actions of captain and crew over a period of several hours, the *Heron* would have been sent to the bottom by bombs or torpedoes from one or more of the fifteen Japanese aircraft. The demands made on the propulsion plant due to violent ship maneuvering by Kabler to avoid bombs and torpedoes, caused the engine room to become so hot and full of steam that watch standers donned gas masks. The twenty-four-year-old former minesweeper had not, in her recent past, been able to make more than about 10 knots. However, when the bridge demanded more speed, her engineers had gotten everything possible out of her old boilers and steam turbines, and had her up to about 14 knots at one time.[23]

Sadly, *Heron* suffered twenty-six casualties—almost half of her crew—due to bomb blasts and the strafing attack. Despite the harm done his ship by the enemy, Kabler tried to rescue the crew of the downed Mavis. Although aflame, it had succeeded in landing on the water nearby allowing its crew to abandon. After first sinking the plane with gunfire, Kabler twice maneuvered *Heron* through the surviving airmen, enabling rescue lines to be thrown them. The Japanese, however, refused to accept any assistance to save them. Concerned about the threat posed by any enemy submarines nearby, Kabler then departed the area. He explained:

> The crew escaped from the plane that was shot down while it was burning on the water, and seeing the crew in the water, we turned the ship back to try to pick them up. We stopped the ship and threw them life lines. They all refused the life lines and, since we were in submarine waters, it was not advisable to remain there for much time, so we proceeded on our course....[24]

That night, the crew extinguished the fires on board, pumped firefighting water out the forward hold—bringing the ship back on an even keel—and repaired her port three-inch gun. Badly battered, *Heron* arrived at Ambon the following morning. An officer ashore described the demeanor of the men aboard the seaplane tender thus: "Her crew was fighting mad, with fighting spirit and morale at the highest pitch. The ship obviously was not ready to fight immediately, but they were eager to return to get another shot at the Japs." After making port, *Heron*'s captain obtained medical care for her wounded and buried her dead. A military funeral for Chief Quartermaster Dennis Allmond, USN, and Coxswain Michael Borodenko, USN, was attended by the *Heron*'s officers and crewmembers as well as by a number of men from *Childs* and a large part of the native Dutch population.[25]

Photo 1-3

Formal photograph of Capt. William Laverett Kabler, USN, later in his career. Courtesy of NavSource
(http://www.navsource.org/archives/02/people/kabler_william_l.jpg)

Admiral Hart promoted Kabler to lieutenant commander and awarded him the Navy Cross Medal. (Kabler would retire from the Navy with the rank of rear admiral.) Two other individuals, Chief Boatswain William Harold Johnson, USN, and Machinist's Mate Second Class Robert Lee Brock, USN, also received the Navy Cross. Johnson and Brock were machine gunners who, despite being injured or wounded, continued to engage enemy aircraft from their exposed positions during prolonged combat. The *Heron*'s executive officer, Lt. Franklin Duerr Buckley, USN, received the Bronze Star for his direction of "accurate and effective anti-aircraft fire to destroy one and damage at least one more of the hostile bomber planes, thereby disrupting the Japanese attack." The associated medal citations are provided in Appendix C.[26]

SHORTLIVED DEFENSE OF THE JAVA SEA

Heron tended aircraft at Ambon while being patched up through the combined efforts of her own crew and that of *Childs* until 4 January 1942, when she was sent to Darwin, Australia, for additional repairs. This work was completed on the 19th, and she was ordered to Saumlaki, a port city and site of a Dutch garrison on the south end of Yamdena in the Tanimbar Islands. Saumlaki lay about 300 miles south of Ambon, which Allied forces would be forced to abandon on 26 January. *Heron* was only able to remain at Saumlaki for a short time until 5 February. By then Japanese forces had landed at Ambon and enemy patrols were coming too close to Saumlaki, resulting in the tender receiving orders to return to Darwin.[27]

Capt. John V. Peterson, USN, former commander Patrol Wing Ten, described in an interview in February 1944 the conditions that seaplane tenders and PBYs faced at Ambon prior to its abandonment:

> We could not operate there because we were almost always under continuous observation, bombardment or strafing. The Japanese had soon disposed of the few Dutch fighters and were continuously attacking the Australian Hudsons and our Catalinas on patrol. We then started a mobile operation from the following bases: Kendari in the Staring Bay area of the Celebes, the Tanimbar Islands group, Koepang in Timor, Soemba Islands, Flores Islands and Darwin, North Australia, as well as operating the patrols from Surabaya.[28]

When Wing Ten was forced to abandon Ambon, *Childs*, *Heron*, and *William B. Preston* continued to operate with two or three planes each at various islands. Usually they stayed in one area for a few days, fueling the planes at night. While the PBYs were out on patrol, the ships stood out to sea so that they would have maneuvering room in the event of an attack. This was the only means by which the tenders and their aircraft could survive and continue to carry out patrols as the Japanese moved south.[29]

During the latter part of January and early February, the Wing flew reconnaissance in the Makassar Straits, Balikpapan and Java Sea areas. The fabric-covered, lightly-armed seaplanes of Wing Ten were in truth entirely unsuited for the type of operations the Japanese forced them to undertake. That is, reconnaissance duties in the face of not only heavy anti-aircraft opposition, but also fighter opposition. Despite these shortcomings, their young pilots and flight crews persevered. Five Wing Ten personnel—three aviators and two enlisted plane crew members—would receive the Navy Cross Medal, and eleven aviators the Distinguished Flying Cross.[30]

Their sacrifices would, however, be for naught. During the Battle of the Java Sea and the ensuing Battle of Sunda Strait, 27 February-1 March, all of Dutch Rear Adm. Karel Doorman's Allied Striking Force, except four American destroyers, were destroyed by Japanese invasion forces. Following these devastating losses, the American-British-Dutch-Australia combined command effectively ceased to exist. Japanese amphibious forces invaded Java on 28 February and the remnants of the Allied navies fell back to Australia. Peterson described the final days of seaplane patrols:

> As soon as the Japanese had dispersed our surface forces in the battle of the Java Sea, they immediately started making landings north and west of Surabaya and at several other places along the north coast of Java. By this time the wing had about five or six effective patrol planes and they were rapidly deteriorating due to lack of spare parts such as generators, pumps of all kinds, and due to continuous operations. On the night of the 28th it was necessary to report to the High Command in abandoning that we could no longer carry out any patrols due to the poor conditions of our planes and especially our radio equipment. That is, we could send the planes out but we had no assurance that we would get any further reports.[31]

RETIREMENT TO AUSTRALIA
In the final days of the Allied defense of the Netherlands East Indies, all the combatant ships except for those engaged in the battle of the Java Sea had shifted around to Tjilatjap on the south coast of Java, which had a fairly good harbor. Wing Ten used this base for ten days

or so before the Allied command released the American forces from the Java area on 1 March. Remnants of the Wing found their way to Perth, a large city situated on the Swan River in Western Australia, by various means of transportation including aircraft, surface vessel, and submarine. *Heron* was sent to Broome, a coastal town about 1,400 nautical miles up the coast from Perth, where the Australian blood-red desert floor met the turquoise of the Indian Ocean against a palette of red earth, sandstone cliffs and white beaches. She transported excess Wing personnel, of which there were many because while many PBYs had been lost in combat the crews of most had been rescued. Following her arrival there, *Heron* made preparations to tend planes that were being dispatched to Broome as well.[32]

LAURELS FOR WING TEN PATROL SQUADRONS AND SEAPLANE TENDERS

In recognition of the collective heroic actions of the aviators of Patrol Wing Ten in the Philippines area and Netherlands East Indies, the Navy awarded Patrol Squadrons 22, 101, and 102 the Presidential Unit Citation, the highest award for heroism a unit might receive and equivalent to the Navy Cross Medal for an individual. The seaplane tender *Heron* received the Navy Unit Commendation for her actions during the defense of the Netherlands East Indies. The seaplane tenders *Childs*, *Heron*, and *William B. Preston*, and these three patrol squadrons earned battle stars for the period 8 December 1941 to 3 March 1942, during which they conducted offensive operations in the Philippines, covered the retirement of the Asiatic Fleet south to the Netherlands East Indies, and conducted reconnaissance and offensive operations in the unsuccessful Allied defense of the Java Sea.

Battle Stars for the Philippine Islands Operation

Ship or Squadron	Award Dates	Commanding Officer
Childs (AVD-1)	8 Dec 41-3 Mar 42	Comdr. John L. Pratt
William B. Preston (AVD-7)	8 Dec 41-3 Mar 42	Lt. Comdr. Etheridge Grant
Heron (AVP-2)	8 Dec 41-3 Mar 42	Lt. Comdr. William L. Kabler
VP-22	9 Jan-3 Mar 42	Lt. Comdr. Frank O'Beirne
VP-101	8 Dec 41-3 Mar 42	Lt. Comdr. John V. Peterson
VP-102	8 Dec 41-3 Mar 42	Lt. Comdr. Edgar T. Neale

2

Seaplane Tenders

> *The* Chincoteague *[AVP-24] long since has been repaired and has resumed her job. The account of her action is cited as one experience in the life of only one of the Navy's many seaplane tenders—those tough, darling little ships which hardly have been noticed by correspondents understandably more impressed by the majesty of the mighty aircraft carriers and the thrilling exploits of fighters, scout-bombers, and the hard-hitting torpedo planes.*
>
> —From an article published in *Flying Magazine* in October 1944, about damage the seaplane tender *Chincoteague* suffered on 17 July 1943 at Saboe Bay, Santa Cruz Islands, during attacks by Japanese bombers[1]

Navy seaplane tenders were employed during World War II to refuel, rearm, and repair the "eyes of the fleet," scout planes and patrol planes, and later in the war, patrol bombers. The ships could be positioned in any sizeable body of protected water where their tended aircraft could land and take off, and were particularly valuable in advance areas with no facilities for land-based reconnaissance aircraft. Large numbers of the Navy's tenders were devoted to the Pacific Theater during the war, due to the scarcity of existing airstrips or airfields across its vastness. As General MacArthur drove up through Papua-New Guinea, Admiral Halsey through the Solomon Islands, and Admiral Spruance through the Central Pacific toward the Japanese home islands, tenders supported the assault forces. Their patrol aircraft scouted for Japanese naval forces, and carried out attacks on enemy ships and shore targets as opportunities presented themselves. Once Naval construction battalion personnel ("Seabees") had built airstrips and supporting facilities in captured areas to host land-based fighter and attack aircraft, the seaplane tenders moved forward to new areas, repeating this cycle.

The Navy's use of seaplanes began in the 1920s, when several World War I-vintage *Lapwing*-class minesweepers were assigned a new mission, caring for seaplanes. These ships, often called "Bird-class" because they bore names of birds, received minimum modifications during their conversion to seaplane tenders. Changes were limited to removal of minesweeping gear, addition of storage tanks for aviation fuel, and provisions for berthing and messing aviation personnel. The converted ships retained their AM series hull numbers, denoting minesweeper, for many years until designated "minesweeper for duty with aircraft" on 30 April 1931. The Navy formally reclassified nine ships as small seaplane tenders on 22 January 1936, and assigned them new hull numbers ranging from AVP-1 through AVP-9.

Ex *Lapwing*-class Minesweepers, 187 feet, 1,350 tons

Lapwing AVP-1 (ex AM-1)	*Avocet* AVP-4 (ex AM-19)	*Swan* AVP-7 (ex AM-34)
Heron AVP-2 (ex AM-10)	*Teal* AVP-5 (ex AM-23)	*Gannet* AVP-8 (ex AM-41)
Thrush AVP-3 (ex AM-18)	*Pelican* AVP-6 (ex AM-27)	*Sandpiper* AVP-9 (ex AM-51)[2]

Photo 2-1

Small seaplane tender *Avocet* (AVP-4) carrying a Curtiss SOC Seagull scout observation biplane. The former *Lapwing*-class minesweeper still has her original unaltered stack in this photo, which was likely taken in the 1930s.
U.S. Navy Photograph 1 Hanson Place Brooklyn, New York
Courtesy of Tommy Trampp

DESTROYER SEAPLANE TENDERS

The Navy recognized that it would require much greater numbers of seaplane tenders in light of its Pacific Ocean strategy. In the event of hostilities, war plans called for the availability of widely-deployed seaplane detachments to scout for enemy naval forces—and its existing tender force offered only modest capabilities. The small, converted minesweepers could hoist small seaplanes, such as Curtiss SOC Seagull scout observation biplanes and Vought OS2U Kingfisher observation floatplanes, but could not hoist the newer, much larger Consolidated PBY Catalina flying boats. In 1938, the Sea Service began converting the first of fourteen ships drawn from different classes of World War I "flush-deck" destroyers for use as tenders, pending the availability of purposeful-built ships. The Navy considered the 314-foot "four pipers" pressed into these duties as too antiquated to serve as front-line combatants. However, being considerably larger than the former minesweepers, they could tend more aircraft, carry greater quantities of aviation fuel, and provide more services for planes and their crews than could the small seaplane tenders. The destroyers were also much faster, and more heavily armed ships.[3]

Each destroyer received substantial modifications to ready it for the new role. These included the removal of the two boilers in the forward fire room to facilitate installation of tanks, allowing for storage of 30,000 gallons of aviation fuel. The two forward stacks, now unnecessary, were removed as well. Other changes were made topside to support aviation personnel. These included the removal of the ship's torpedo tubes, waist guns, and 3-inch anti-aircraft gun, and the extension of the deckhouse aft in the area formerly occupied by the stacks. The latter alteration provided living and office space for an embarked squadron. A light crane was fitted amidships, and aircraft servicing boats were slung from davits in readiness for their new function.[4]

The first two destroyers chosen for conversion for use as mobile bases for PBY patrol planes were the *Childs* and *Williamson*. They began conversion following their reclassification on 1 July 1938. Their utilization in this new role was a success, leading to five more conversions authorized in 1939 and seven more in 1940. The first seven of these type fast tenders were originally designated AVP-14 through AVP-20. In August 1940, their designation, and those of the other seven ships of the class of fourteen ex-destroyers became seaplane tender (destroyer), and their hull numbers were changed to AVD-1 though AVD-14.[5]

Former "Flush Deck" Destroyers, 314 feet, 1,215 tons

Childs AVD-1 (ex DD-241, ex AVP-14)	*Goldsborough* AVD-5 (ex DD-188, ex AVP-18, later APD-32)	*Osmond Ingram* AVD-9 (ex DD-255, later APD-35)	*Greene* AVD-13 (ex DD-266, later APD-36)
Williamson AVD-2 (ex DD-244, ex AVP-15)	*Hulbert* AVD-6 (ex DD-342, ex AVP-19)	*Ballard* AVD-10 (ex DD-267)	*McFarland* AVD-14 (ex DD-237)
George E. Badger AVD-3 (ex DD-196, ex AVP-16, later APD-33)	*William B. Preston* AVD-7 (ex DD-344, ex AVP-20)	*Thornton* AVD-11 (ex DD-270)	
Clemson AVD-4 (ex DD-186, ex AVP-17, later APD-31)	*Belknap* AVD-8 (ex DD-251, later APD-34)	*Gillis* AVD-12 (ex DD-260)	

Photo 2-2

Destroyer seaplane tender *Osmond Ingram* (AVD-9) under way off Norfolk Naval Shipyard, Portsmouth, Virginia, on 10 July 1943.
U.S. Naval History and Heritage Command Photograph # NH 42922

Beginning in 1943, as new, purposeful-built *Barnegat*-class seaplane tenders began to replace them these ex-destroyers served in other roles including convoy escort, anti-submarine warfare, and local patrol, plane guard, and shakedown support for escort carriers. Most were reclassified as destroyers in 1943. Six of the AVDs—*George E. Badger, Clemson, Goldsborough, Belknap, Osmond Ingram* and *Greene*—were converted to high speed transports (APD-31 through 36) in March, April, and June 1944, for the support of amphibious operations.[6]

BARNEGAT-CLASS SMALL SEAPLANE TENDERS

In 1938, construction of seven newly-designed small seaplane tenders was authorized. The design of the lead ship incorporated desired capabilities identified during the service of the earlier tenders. These included:

- aircraft and weapons repair shops
- aircraft crew and support crew facilities
- weapons and fuel storage capacities
- operating range and ability to conduct operations independent of other fleet vessels, air defense and fire support capabilities
- ability to navigate and turn around in shallow or restricted waterways[7]

Drawing only thirteen feet of water, the 311-foot ships could navigate or anchor in shallow waters, and possessing twin screws (propellers), could maneuver easily in restricted waterways as well.[8]

Photo 2-3

Seaplane Tender *Barnegat* (AVP-10) under way in Boston Harbor, 1 January 1942, with an OS2U Kingfisher seaplane on her fantail.
Courtesy of Stephen P. Carlson: Boston Navy Yard Photograph 135-42, Boston National Historical Park Collection NPS Cat. No. BOSTS-10343

In addition to caring for seaplanes, the *Barnegat*s were intended to perform at-sea aircraft salvage, search and rescue and ship escort duties, in particular, escort of large seaplane tenders. Initial armament was two 5-inch/38-caliber gun mounts and four 20mm guns. Some ships received quad 40mm Bofors mounts in lieu of a 5-inch mount forward of the bridge and additional twin 40mm Bofors amidships, and 20mm guns aft, giving them enhanced anti-aircraft capabilities. Against low-flying enemy aircraft, a 40mm gun spanned the gap in performance between a small caliber 20mm AA gun and the much larger (but considerably slower to train and elevate) 5-inch gun. Many of the ships were also outfitted with sonar and depth charge racks to give them an anti-submarine capability.[9]

The keel of *Barnegat* (AVP-10) was laid in October 1939 and she was commissioned in July 1942. Thirty-five ships of the class were eventually built, but only twenty-nine served during the war as seaplane tenders. Four—*Mobjack, Oyster Bay, Wachapreague,* and *Willoughby*—were reclassified while still under construction as AGPs (motor torpedo boat tenders). The last two ships—*Timbalier* and *Valcour*—were not completed until after the war's end. *Barnegat*-class tenders were named after small bodies of water:

Barnegat-class Small Seaplane Tenders, 311 feet, 2,750 tons

Barnegat (AVP-10)	San Pablo (AVP-30)	Floyds Bay (AVP-40)
Biscayne (AVP-11)	Unimak (AVP-31)	Greenwich Bay (AVP-41)
Casco (AVP-12)	Yakutat (AVP-32)	Onslow (AVP-48)
Mackinac (AVP-13)	Barataria (AVP-33)	Orca (AVP-49)
Humboldt (AVP-21)	Bering Strait (AVP-34)	Rehoboth (AVP-50)
Matagorda (AVP-22)	Castle Rock (AVP-35)	San Carlos (AVP-51)
Absecon (AVP-23)	Cook Inlet (AVP-36)	Shelikof (AVP-52)
Chincoteague (AVP-24)	Corson (AVP-37)	Suisun (AVP-53)
Coos Bay (AVP-25)	Duxbury Bay (AVP-38)	Timbalier (AVP-54)
Half Moon (AVP-26)	Gardiners Bay (AVP-39)	Valcour (AVP-55)
Rockaway (AVP-29)		

LARGE SEAPLANE TENDERS

Fifteen large seaplane tenders served during World War II. Although designated seaplane tenders, they were often referred to as "large seaplane tenders" or "heavy seaplane tenders" due to their size. The first two of these tenders were a converted merchant ship and Navy collier, respectively. The *Wright* had been laid down in the builder's yard as a Hog Island type "B" cargo vessel, and was later fitted out as a lighter-than-air aircraft tender and commissioned *Wright* (AZ-1) on 16 December 1921. She was reclassified a heavier-than-air aircraft tender (AV-1) on 2 December 1926. The *Langley* was commissioned *Jupiter* (Collier #3) on 7 April 1913. She was later converted at Norfolk Navy Yard to the Navy's first aircraft carrier, and recommissioned *Langley* (CV-1) on 20 March 1922. Fifteen years later, she was modified again and reclassified a seaplane tender (AV-3) on 11 April 1937.

Large Seaplane Tenders

No Name Class

Wright (AV-1) 448-feet, 12,142 tons | *Langley* (AV-3) 542-feet, 19,360 tons

Curtiss-class, 527-feet, 13,880 tons

Curtiss (AV-4) | *Albemarle* (AV-5)

Currituck-class: 541-feet, 14,300 tons

| *Currituck* (AV-7) | Norton Sound (AV-11) | Pine Island (AV-12) | Salisbury Sound (AV-13) |

Tangier-class: 492-feet, 8,950 tons

Tangier (AV-8) | *Pocomoke* (AV-9) | *Chandeleur* (AV-10)

Kenneth Whiting-class: 492-feet, 8,000 tons

| Kenneth Whiting (AV-14) | Hamlin (AV-15) | St. George (AV-16) | Cumberland Sound (AV-17)[10] |

The two ships of the *Curtiss*-class—*Curtiss* and *Albemarle*—were the Navy's first purposeful-built large seaplane tenders, characterized by a large, high-freeboard hull with a relatively small superstructure. Crew accommodations and non-seaplane facilities were in the forward half of the ship, and a large seaplane working deck at the stern. Extensive maintenance shops were located in a large block structure forward of the working deck, which joined the main superstructure. Two large cranes—one at the rear of the superstructure and one farther aft at the stern—enabled the lifting of aircraft aboard. The ships also boasted heavy armament: two 5-inch guns forward and two atop the aft superstructure, with another two dual 40mm and twelve 20mm anti-aircraft guns added later.[11]

The four *Currituck*-class ships—*Currituck, Norton Sound, Pine Island*, and *Salisbury Sound*—were named for features on America's Alaskan and East Coasts. The major changes from the *Curtiss* design, upon which these ships were based, was one instead of two stacks, and related engine room and fire room modifications. A catapult was fitted aft to enable launching Marine Corps floatplane dive bombers in forward areas, but the tenders did not operate in this role. *Currituck* and *Norton Sound* served in the Pacific; the other two ships of the class were completed too late to see any combat service.[12]

The *Tangier, Pocomoke* and *Chandeleur* were Maritime Commission C3-Cargo Ships converted to seaplane tenders to fill an immediate need for additional tenders. The *Tangier* and *Pocomoke* had already been completed as the S.S. *Sea Arrow* and S.S. *Exchequer*, respectively, when acquired by the Navy. A third same-type ship was still unnamed and under construction when converted and commissioned *Chandeleur*. Modifications made to the merchant ships included fitting a seaplane working deck aft of the bridge superstructure, one level above the main deck, and a single large crane aft of the seaplane deck at the extreme stern. Provisions were made to carry seaplane servicing and utility boats on deck forward of the bridge, and cargo holds were converted for berthing, stores and spares storage, and repair shops. Initial armament was four single 5-inch/38 gun mounts; this configuration was later changed to one 5-inch and several 40mm guns. Conversion did not significantly alter the ex-cargo ships' appearance; they continued to look like freighters.[13]

Photo 2-4

Large seaplane tender *Salisbury Sound* (AV-13) tending P5M-2 Marlin anti-submarine patrol seaplanes at Tsugen Jima, Japan, in March 1957.
Painting by Richard DeRosset

The four ships of the *Kenneth Whiting*-class—*Kenneth Whiting*, *Hamlin*, *St. George*, and *Cumberland Sound*—were also constructed on C3-Special hulls. They were nearly identical to the *Tangier*–class ships. The crane was relocated to the forward end of the seaplane deck to provide room for a 5-inch gun mount aft.[14]

WAR DUTY AND SHIP LOSSES

U.S. Navy seaplane tenders operated in every theater during World War II. They supported the landings in North Africa; and at Sicily, Salerno, and Anzio as part of the Italian Campaign; the Normandy Invasion in northwest France; and the invasion of Southern France. Seaplane tending, patrol, and ship escort duties were performed in the Caribbean Sea, the Panama Canal Zone, and along the coasts of South America. In the Pacific, seaplane tenders earned their first battle stars at Pearl Harbor, and during unsuccessful defenses of the Philippine Islands and the Java Sea. As combat spread across the Pacific, stars were won in the Aleutian Islands and far to the south-southwest in the Solomons. Tenders also earned battle stars in the Santa Cruz, Gilbert, New Georgia, Bismarck, Western Caroline, and Marshall Islands. More stars were garnered in Western New Guinea, and at Saipan, at Leyte and Luzon in the Philippines and, as war drew nearer an end, at Iwo Jima and Okinawa. Five seaplane tenders—*Cumberland Sound*, *Gardiners Bay*, *Hamlin*, *Mackinac*, and *Suisun*—were among the ships present in Tokyo Bay on 2 September 1945 for the formal surrender of the Empire of Japan.[15]

Photo 2-5

Navy carrier aircraft fly in formation over the battleship USS *Missouri* (BB-63), during surrender ceremonies aboard the ship the morning of 2 September 1945. Army Signal Corps Photograph #SC 211863, now in the collections of the National Archives

The sixty-seven seaplane tenders that served during World War II collectively earned a total of 109 battle stars, all but six of them in the Asiatic-Pacific Theater. Three tenders were lost during the war—two to enemy action. The *Langley* was irreparably damaged by Japanese aircraft bombs south of Java in the Dutch East Indies, on 27 February 1942, and was sunk by the destroyer *Whipple* (DD-217). The *Gannet* was torpedoed and sunk by the German submarine *U-653* off Bermuda on 7 June 1942. Near war's end, the *Thornton* was involved in a collision with the fleet oilers *Ashtabula* (AO-51) and *Escalante* (AO-70) off Okinawa on 5 April 1945, and was later scraped.[16]

3

Patrol Wings/Fleet Air Wings

> *The organization of fleet aircraft as something seperate from a fixed air base makes for better organization and administration of the units concerned. The relationship to the fleet becomes at once clear-cut and definite and the place in the chain of command becomes freed from any dual status as partly a shore and partly a fleet unit.*
>
> —Observation regarding the establishment of Patrol Wings in October 1937[1]

Following post-World War I defense cuts, the U.S. Navy's remaining inventory of patrol aircraft was assigned to the naval air stations at Coco Solo, Panama; Norfolk, Virginia; San Diego, California; and Pearl Harbor, Hawaii. In ensuing years there were several reorganizations within the Navy. The most significant occurred on 1 January 1923 when the Navy merged the Pacific and Atlantic fleets to form a single United States Fleet, comprised of Battle Force (ex-Pacific Fleet), Scouting Force (ex-Atlantic Fleet), Control Force, and Base Force. During this reorganization, the Navy's small Asiatic Fleet remained a separate entity. There were also a series of lesser changes related to administrative and operational command of patrol aircraft. On 1 October 1937, patrol aviation was divided among five newly established Patrol Wings, whose administration was now separate from that of the fleet air base (formerly termed naval air station) to which they were assigned:

- Patrol Wing One at FAB San Diego, California
- Patrol Wing Two at Pearl Harbor, Hawaii
- Patrol Wing Three at Coco Solo, Panama
- Patrol Wing Four at Seattle, Washington
- Patrol Wing Five at Norfolk, Virginia[2]

REALIGNMENT OF THE FLEETS

In 1940, as part of America's response to Japanese expansionism and in an attempt to deter further aggression, the Navy realigned its forces in the Pacific, constrained by the reluctance of Congress to fund armaments for the defense of U.S. possessions and territories that might never be used, and a general aversion of the American people against war. It moved the "Battle Fleet" (formerly Battle Force) the Pacific component of the existing United States Fleet, from the west coast of the U.S. to Pearl Harbor in summer 1940 and that fall relocated the Asiatic Fleet from China to Manila Bay to strengthen the defense of the Philippines. These actions were followed on 1 February 1941 by a reorganization of the United States Fleet into three separate components: the U.S. Pacific Fleet, based at Pearl Harbor; the U.S. Atlantic Fleet (the former "Scouting Force" that comprised the Atlantic presence of the U.S. Navy), headquartered at Newport, Rhode Island; and the very small U.S. Asiatic Fleet, with no ship larger than a cruiser, at Manila Bay. The Asiatic Fleet retained its status as a force independent of the U.S. fleet, charged by the existing war plan to support the U.S. Army presence in the Philippines so long as the defense of the islands continued.[3]

EXPANSION OF NAVY PATROL/FLEET AIR WINGS

On 1 November 1942, the Navy redesignated the Patrol Wings—which had by then increased in number from five to twelve—Fleet Air Wings. Five additional Wings were later formed, totaling seventeen Fleet Air Wings. The Wings were numbered consecutively from one to eighteen, with the number thirteen omitted. Appendix D provides an overview of when and where the Patrol Wings were established, and based during the war.[4]

4

Attack on Pearl Harbor

FROM: SECNAV *[Secretary of the Navy]*
TO: ALNAV *[All Navy]*

WHILE YOU HAVE SUFFERED FROM A TREACHEROUS ATTACK YOUR COMMANDER IN CHIEF HAS INFORMED ME THAT YOUR COURAGE AND STAMINA REMAIN MAGNIFICANT. YOU KNOW YOU WILL HAVE YOUR REVENGE. RECRUITING STATIONS ARE JAMMED WITH MEN EAGER TO JOIN YOU.

THE SECRETARY OF THE NAVY

Waves of fighters and bombers launched from all six of Japan's first-rate aircraft carriers—the *Akagi*, *Hiryu*, *Kaga*, *Soryu*, *Shokaku* and *Zuikaku*—struck Pearl Harbor on 7 December 1941. With over 420 embarked aircraft, these ships constituted by far the most powerful carrier task force ever assembled. Their main targets were battleships and aircraft carriers; fortunately the Pacific Fleet's carriers were at sea. Secondary targets were airfields. Of first priority were Hickam Field, Wheeler Field, and Ford Island at Pearl Harbor, followed by elsewhere on Oahu, Kanoehe Naval Air Station, Bellows Field, and Ewa Marine Corps Station. The carriers were a part of Vice Adm. Chuichi Nagumo's Striking Force, positioned 275 miles north of Pearl Harbor. His goal was to wipe out the major part of the Pacific Fleet at Pearl Harbor and destroy all the military aircraft on Oahu. The Force had sortied from Tankan Bay in the Kurile Islands on 26 November, and set a course for Pearl Harbor across a part of the North Pacific generally avoided by merchant shipping. Nagumo's orders were to abandon the mission if detected, or should diplomacy work an unanticipated miracle. However, only one ship (a Japanese freighter) was encountered during the transit which was characterized by bad weather and rough seas.[1]

There was some concern among the Japanese about the PBY Catalina flying boats on Oahu, which had the range to find the enemy fleet and track it for hundreds of miles. The mission of the PBYs was scouting for submarines and enemy positions with an additional role of search and rescue. Unbeknownst to the Japanese, commander-in-chief Pacific Fleet, Adm. Husband E. Kimmel, USN, was reluctant to use the aircraft for extensive patrol, it being difficult to get parts for them. He calculated that if war with Japan broke out he would need those aircraft to patrol in advance of his fleet. As a result, very few PBYs were used for patrol, and search sectors were to the south of Oahu in the direction of the nearest Japanese possessions. None of the Catalinas were assigned to patrol northward, the direction from which the Japanese Fleet actually came. War Plan Orange (the U.S. strategy for dealing with a possible war with Japan) assigned patrolling to the Army. But on Oahu, there were only twelve B17 Flying Fortresses that were capable of long range patrols. Thus, neither the Navy nor the Army was maintaining patrols adequate to detect the approaching Striking Force.[2]

A patrolling Catalina did find a Japanese midget submarine just off the entrance to Pearl Harbor at 0700 on the morning of the attack. The PBY dropped its depth bombs and sent a coded message to its base at 0715, but by the time this message was decoded and passed on to Admiral Kimmel, enemy bombs had already begun falling.[3]

INITIAL ENEMY CONTACT

Contact with the submarine was first made at 0342 by the coastal minesweeper *Condor* (AMc-14), carrying out a routine sweep of a mile-wide area from the Pearl Harbor entrance out to the 100-fathom curve. As the officer of the deck and quartermaster of the watch peered through binoculars in an attempt to pierce the darkness ahead, they sighted the periscope of a submerged submarine off the entrance buoys of the harbor in a restricted defensive sea area where U.S. submarines were prohibited from operating submerged. A mere seventy-seven feet in length, *Condor*—the former fishing vessel *New Example*—was slightly shorter than the diminutive submarine (later identified as a Japanese Type-*A* midget), and was not ideally suited to deal with it. She was pulling sweep gear, which severely limited her maneuverability, had no depth charges, and was armed only with a single .50-caliber machine gun. *Condor* accordingly informed the *Ward* (DD-139), patrolling nearby, of this contact by visual signal. The destroyer instituted a search and at about 0637 sighted the periscope of a submarine apparently trailing the general stores issue ship *Antares* (AKS-3), as it approached the harbor entrance to Pearl Harbor.[4]

Ward witnessed a PBY (from squadron VP-14) circle and drop what appeared to be, two smoke pots near the object. At 0645, the destroyer commenced her attack, firing one salvo each from her No. 1 and 3 guns, followed by depth charges on the submarine. At 0651, the destroyer sent a radio message to the commandant, Fourteenth Naval District: "We have dropped depth charges upon sub operating in defensive sea area." The commanding officer, however, after reflecting that this message might not be interpreted as showing a surface submarine contact, two minutes later sent the supplementary message: "We have attacked fired upon and dropped depth charges upon submarine operating in defensive sea area." This message was received by the Bishop's Point radio station, relayed to the officer in charge, Net and Boom Defenses, Inshore Patrol, and delivered by the communications watch officer, Fourteenth Naval District, to the duty officer, who notified his chief of staff. However, because the message moved with excruciating slowness upward through the chain of command, the base commander didn't receive a report of the submarine until just shortly before Japanese carrier aircraft initiated an unprovoked attack on the U.S. Pacific Fleet inside the harbor.[5]

Sixty-one years later, on 28 August 2002, two deep diving submersibles operated by the Hawaii Undersea Research Laboratory found the midget submarine sunk by the *Ward*. The wreckage lies in 400 meters of water about five miles off the mouth of Pearl Harbor. Five of the midgets had been transported by *I* type "mother" submarines and launched near the entrance to Pearl Harbor the night before the attack. At least one of the 2-man submarines penetrated the harbor, where it was sunk by the destroyer *Monaghan* (DD-354). Another drifted around to the east coast of Oahu and was captured there the day after the attack. In 1960, the fourth was discovered on the sea floor off the harbor entrance. The final submarine remains unaccounted for to date.[6]

TASK FORCE 9

Rear Adm. Patrick N. L. Bellinger, USN, was the senior naval air commander present at Pearl Harbor. He was commander Task Force 9, comprised of Patrol Wings One and Two; had direct command of Patrol Wing Two; and was commander Naval Base Defense Force. The latter role involved coordinating the air activities for the protection of the Hawaiian Islands. Wing Two was well established in the area, having been created from the former Hawaiian Patrol Wing on 1 October 1937. Based on Ford Island at Pearl Harbor, it boasted four patrol squadrons—VP-21, 22, 23, and 24—but one, VP-21, was temporarily at Midway Atoll. PBYs were organized into patrol squadrons that nominally had a dozen aircraft. The V in VP denoted heavier-than-air, and P stood for patrol. Patrol Wing One at Naval Air Station, Kaneohe Bay, was new to the Hawaiian area, having arrived there from San Diego during the latter half of 1941. Its skipper, Comdr. Knefler McGinnis, USN, worked directly for Admiral Bellinger, and was responsible for squadrons VP-11, 12, and 14.[7]

Commander Task Force 9 and Patrol Wing Two: Rear Adm. Patrick N. L. Bellinger, USN

Seaplane Tender	Location on 7 Dec 1941	Patrol Squadron	Location on 7 Dec 1941
McFarland (AVD-14)	off Maui	VP-21 (12 planes; 7 in air, 1 under repair)	Midway Atoll
Swan (AVP-7)	Pearl Harbor	VP-22 (12 planes)	Pearl Harbor
Tangier (AV-8)	Pearl Harbor	VP-23 (12 planes; 1 under repair)	Pearl Harbor
Thornton (AVD-11)	Pearl Harbor	VP-24 (6 planes; 4 in air, 1 under repair)	Pearl Harbor

Commander Patrol Wing One: Comdr. Knefler McGinnis, USN

Seaplane Tender	Location 7 Dec 1941	Patrol Squadron	Location 7 Dec 1941
Avocet (AVP-4)	Pearl Harbor	VP-11 (12 planes)	Kaneohe Bay
Curtiss (AV-4)	Pearl Harbor	VP-12 (12 planes; 1 under repair)	Kaneohe Bay
Hulbert (AVD-6)	Pearl Harbor	VP-14 (12 planes; 3 in air, 2 under repair)	Kaneohe Bay
Wright (AV-1)	En route Pearl Harbor from Midway Atoll		

That Sunday morning, 7 December, the condition of readiness within the task force was "Baker 5" (50 percent of assigned aircraft on four hours' notice to be prepared for flight) with machine guns and ammunition in all planes not undergoing maintenance work. In addition, VP-21 at Midway, VP-23 at Pearl Harbor, and VP-11 at Kaneohe Bay were in condition "Afirm 5" (100 percent of aircraft on 4 hours' notice). The four hours was primarily set to permit personnel rest and in no way reflected the material readiness of the aircraft.[8]

Twenty-four operational PBYs were present at Pearl Harbor at the time of the attack, all on the ground. VP-14 at Kaneohe Bay had the duty at the time the first bomb fell; responsibility for all Hawaiian

Islands-based search patrols for the 24-hour period from 0800, 6 December to 0800, 7 December. Kaneohe Bay lay about nine miles northeast of Pearl Harbor on the Mokapu Peninsula in Honolulu. The below table duplicates parts of the one that precedes it, but provides additional information regarding numbers and status of patrol aircraft that morning:

Squadron/Location	Number of Seaplanes	Type
VP-11/Kaneohe Bay	12	PBY-5
VP-12/Kaneohe Bay	12 (1 under repair)	PBY-5
VP-14/Kaneohe Bay	12 (3 in air on dawn patrol, 2 under repair)	PBY-5
VP-21/Midway Atoll	12 (7 in air on search, 1 under repair)	PBY-3 & PBY-4
VP-22/Pearl Harbor	12	PBY-3
VP-23/Pearl Harbor	12 (1 under repair)	PBY-5
VP-24/Pearl Harbor	6 (4 in air off Maui, participating in exercises, 1 under repair)[9]	PBY-5

Six of the eight seaplane tenders assigned to Task Force 9 were among the Pacific Fleet ships present at Pearl Harbor. *Wright* was en route to Hawaii after having delivered cargo and passengers to Midway Atoll, and would reach Pearl Harbor the following day. The *McFarland* was relatively near, at sea off Maui taking part in anti-submarine exercises. Upon learning of the attack, she patrolled to the southwest before returning to Oahu on 9 December.[10]

COMMENCEMENT OF AIR ATTACK

Tora, Tora, Tora.

—Coded message sent by Capt. Mitsuo Fuchida, who led the first wave of attacks, to indicate the Americans had been caught by surprise.[11]

The time of the first attack on Pearl Harbor is easily remembered in that it occurred with the hoisting of the morning preparatory signal for eight o'clock colors. At that time, 0755, Japanese dive bombers appeared over Hickam Field which, located adjacent to Pearl Harbor, was the principal army airfield in Hawaii and the only one large enough to accommodate B17 bombers. Seconds later, torpedo planes and dive bombers came in from various compass directions to concentrate their attacks on the battleships moored at Pearl Harbor.

Admiral Bellinger broadcast at 0758 to all ships present the warning: "Air raid. Pearl Harbor, this is no drill."[12]

The entire attack would last one hour and fifteen minutes. The enemy aircraft strike force consisted of 353 planes, including 40 torpedo planes, 103 high-level bombers, 131 dive bombers, and 79 fighters. The remaining aircraft flew combat air patrol overhead the Japanese carriers to provide them protection. Aboard the enemy carriers, the first wave of over 180 aircraft—torpedo planes, high-level bombers, dive bombers and fighters—was launched in the darkness and flew off to the south. A second attack wave of similar size, but with more dive bombers and no torpedo planes, was then sent off into the emerging morning light. Near Oahu's southern shore, five midget submarines were trying to make their way into Pearl Harbor's narrow entrance channel.[13]

While an estimated eighteen planes engaged in the attack on Hickam Field, approximately nine dive bombers from out of the northeast bombed and strafed Naval Air Station, Kaneohe Bay, concentrating on seaplanes on the ground, in the water, and at the hangar. Of the PBYs on Oahu that morning, all but eleven would be destroyed or temporarily knocked out of action. Following the opening attack, air strikes continued. The primary objectives of the Japanese pilots were the heavy ships and aircraft at Pearl Harbor and Kaneohe Bay. Damage to light forces, hangars and other buildings were incidental to the destruction of large ships and aircraft ashore.[14]

ACTIONS BY SEAPLANE TENDERS' GUN CREWS

> *This vessel brought down one Japanese torpedo bomber by .50 cal. AA fire from berth S-3 at the Submarine Base, Pearl Harbor, in the engagement at about 0758, December 7, 1941, and shared in bringing down a bomber at about 0820.*
>
> *This vessel went to general quarters when the Japanese attack was first sighted by the watch aboard, and is believed to have been the first ship in the fleet to open fire. The torpedo bomber was headed west over East Loch preparatory to launching her torpedo against battleships off Ford Island. No other anti-aircraft [rounds] were being fired at this plane when brought down. The bomber appeared to be making a horizontal bombing run in the direction of drydock No. 1. In both cases almost certain hits were averted.*
>
> —Lt. Comdr. James Mills Lane, USN, commanding officer USS *Hulbert* (AVD-6), describing actions by the seaplane tender during the air attack on Pearl Harbor.[15]

Ford Island (located in the East Loch of the harbor) bore the brunt of the attack. Moored along its east side in "battleship row" were seven of the eight battleships at Pearl Harbor. The eighth, *Pennsylvania* (BB-28), was in dry dock at the Navy yard, situated adjacent to Pearl City, for overhaul. *Utah* (AG-16), a former battleship converted to a mobile target for fleet gunnery, was moored on the west side of Ford Island. A secondary, but important target was Naval Air Station, Pearl Harbor on Ford Island. In addition to the other aircraft at the station that morning, there were two dozen PBYs parked near the seaplane ramp. Nagumo knew these planes, if undamaged, were capable of locating his fleet: six carriers, a screen of nine destroyers and a light cruiser, a support force of two battleships and two heavy cruisers, three fleet submarines to patrol the flanks, and a supply train of seven or eight tankers. Thirty-three of the seventy aircraft on the ground on Ford Island would be destroyed during the prolonged Japanese air raid.[16]

The enemy attack began that morning when a "Val" dive bomber dropped a 550-pound bomb on ramp #4 at the south end of Ford Island; the location of Patrol Squadron 22's twelve aircraft. The explosion and ensuing fire completely destroyed six PBY-3s, damaged one PBY-3 beyond repair, and put the remaining five seaplanes out of commission for one to ten days. A second bomb struck the small arms magazine at the corner of the hangar and fire burned about two-fifths of the structure before the blaze was brought under control. A third bomb struck the underwater portion of ramp number four.[17]

Of the six seaplane tenders at Pearl Harbor, *Curtiss* would suffer the most damage and greatest number of personnel casualties. She lay at berth X-22 in the channel off the west side of Ford Island. A second tender, *Tangier*, was moored between her and the *Utah*. Across Ford Island on its southeast corner, *Avocet* was in berth F-1 near "battleship row." To the southeast, *Swan* rested on the Marine Railway dock in boiler upkeep, not far from the *Pennsylvania*. The final two seaplane tenders, *Thornton* and *Hulbert*, were moored at the submarine base, a little farther to the southeast, in berths S-1 and S-3.

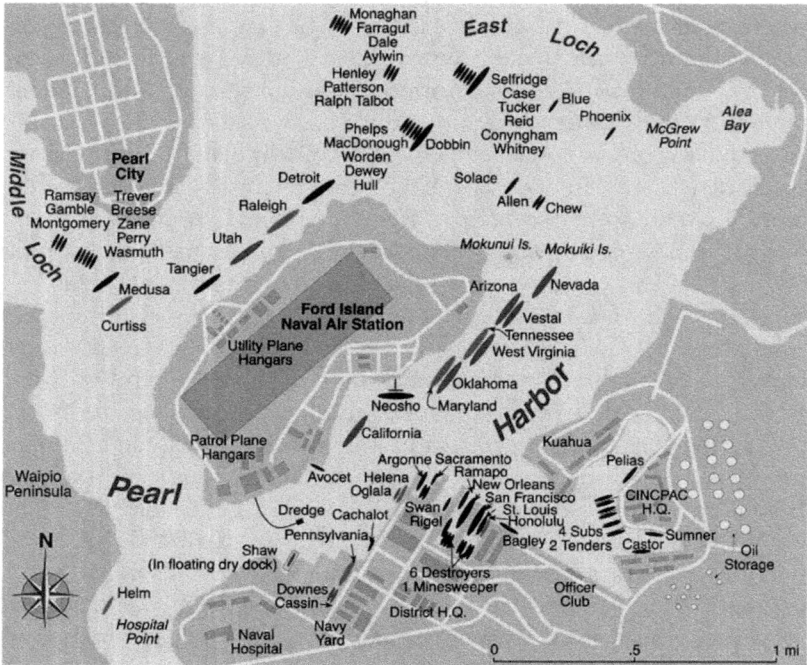

Units of the Pacific Fleet present at Pearl Harbor the morning of 7 December 1941.

ENEMY ACTION IN THE VICINITY OF THE SUB BASE

Aboard the *Thornton*, the general alarm called "all hands" to their air defense stations as the attacks commenced. The ship's 5-inch/50 gun mounts were too slow to engage fast moving enemy aircraft, and the 20mm and 40mm guns which would later serve as the Navy's principal anti-aircraft batteries aboard ships were not yet available in the fleet. Thus, only her machine guns and rifles offered the destroyer seaplane tender a means of self-defense:

- Four .50-caliber machine guns
- Three .30-caliber Lewis machine guns
- Three .30-caliber Browning automatic rifles
- Twelve .30-caliber Springfield rifles[18]

Thornton's .50-caliber machine gun battery opened fire at 0758 followed by that of other weapons. Combined fire from *Hulbert* and *Thornton* .50s immediately brought down a torpedo plane in mid-channel between the submarine base and the officer's club. It burst into flames and fell into the water, its torpedo unlaunched. *Hulbert* also shared in bringing down a bomber making a horizontal run at about 0820. A few minutes later, a hit was made on a dive bomber under fire from the miscellaneous auxiliary *Sumner* (AG-32), *Hulbert*, and *Thornton*, which proved non-lethal. The plane, with its tail on fire, escaped southward over Honolulu's Halawa district.[19]

Sumner, *Hulbert*, and *Thornton* later engaged several enemy aircraft making an attack on the *Neosho* (AO-23) as she shifted berths. The fleet oiler had gotten underway at 0842 after chopping her mooring lines to bollards as no assistance was available for casting them off. After backing away from the pier, *Neosho* barely cleared the battleship *Oklahoma* (BB-37), which had capsized to port. The planes turned away from the withering fire, after which the third one strafed personnel on the Fleet Landing at Merry Point. The aircraft in the vicinity of the *Thornton* were torpedo planes, except for the three that assailed *Neosho*, which appeared to be light bombers or fighters.[20]

Men aboard the *Thornton* witnessed about eighteen torpedo planes initiate attacks against "battleship row" from the Merry Point channel area. After passing over the Merry Point landing and leveling off at between 25 and 50 feet in altitude, the aircraft launched torpedoes along a front stretching from a point opposite the submarine base to one opposite Kuahua Island.[21]

A sighting was also made from the *Thornton* of fifteen horizontal bombers flying at high altitude, about 8,000 feet, which bombed Hickam Field and the battleships. The aircraft were formed in three groups of five planes each, flying in a V-formation. Dive bombers seen in the area near the *Pennsylvania* were plummeting down at angles of between 65 and 75 degrees. They came in from the northwest and southeast almost simultaneously. Despite their close proximity to the morning's action, the *Hulbert* and *Thornton* were unscathed by it.[22]

NAVY YARD AND THE EAST SIDE OF FORD ISLAND

Swan was in the Marine Railway at the Navy Yard undergoing boiler upkeep. She witnessed at 0755 the initial bomb dropped on the south seaplane ramp at the Ford Island naval air station. Her 3-inch anti-aircraft battery opened fire eight minutes later. Fuses were set for 2.1 seconds and local gun control was used because target bearings were changing so rapidly. As her gunners scored a direct hit on a plane, which crashed in flames beyond the dry dock area, members of the engineering department not handling ammunition began placing the ship's boilers in commission. *Swan*, like *Hulbert* and *Thornton*, suffered no material harm or men killed during the air attacks. One member of a gun crew, the port 3-inch gun pointer, was injured slightly by machine gun fire. Pointers were selected based on their ability to shoot straight, in conjunction with such qualities as good eyesight, nerve, and a cool, unexcitable disposition.[23]

Photo 4-1

Gunner pointers aboard *Avocet* search for enemy planes to take under fire. *Nevada* (BB-36) is at right, with her bow on fire. Beyond her is the destroyer *Shaw* (DD-373), also aflame. Smoke at left comes from the destroyers *Cassin* (DD-372) and *Downes* (DD-375), ablaze in Drydock Number One.
U.S. Navy Photograph #80-G-32445

Avocet was moored at the Naval Air Station dock, a short distance from the *California* (BB-44), the nearest battleship along "battleship row," which stretched to the northeast. Her general quarters alarm called all hands to battle stations after a bomb explosion was heard and Japanese planes were sighted attacking the aircraft hangars on Ford Island. *Avocet*'s two 3-inch/50 anti-aircraft guns opened, and the first shot from the starboard gun hit a torpedo plane turning away from the *California*, causing it to burst into flames and crash near the naval hospital. The seaplane tender also fired at dive bombers attacking the *Nevada* (BB-36), but scored no hits.[24]

In separate action, high-altitude bombers dropped four bombs near the *Avocet*. Fortunately, they struck the harbor floor without detonating; muddy water rising to the surface revealed their impact sites. During the morning's action, *Avocet* expended 144 rounds of 3-inch and about 1,750 rounds of .30-caliber. Her commanding officer, Lt. William G. Johnson Jr., praised the actions of the men behind the guns in a report, noting "the gun crews worked the guns deliberately and with apparent total disregard for their own safety." *Avocet*'s only casualty was a crewman wounded slightly in the forearm by a spent bullet.[25]

NORTHWEST SIDE OF FORD ISLAND

> *At 0843 – Enemy submarine sighted off the starboard bow, distance about 800 yards. Opened fire with #1 A.A. [anti-aircraft] gun (3"/50) fired six shots. USS CURTISS also firing five inch gun at submarine. 0844 ceased firing at submarine, due to fouling of target by [the destroyer] USS MONAGHAN [DD-354]. 0845 USS MONAGHAN ran over location where submarine was sighted, probably ramming it and dropped two depth charges. This was a fine piece of work and the Commanding Officer of MONAGHAN, in my opinion, should be commended for an excellent and rapid action.*
>
> —Comdr. Clifton A. F. Sprague, USN, commanding officer USS *Tangier* (AV-8), describing in a report the Japanese attack on Pearl Harbor.[26]

The *Curtiss* and *Tangier* suffered the most damage and casualties of the six seaplane tenders at Pearl Harbor, because enemy planes targeted them as well as other nearby large ships and aircraft and aviation facilities on Ford Island. The Japanese pilots focused their attacks on "high value units" and *Tangier* and *Curtiss*, at 492 and 527 feet in length, respectively, were more important targets than the smaller tenders. *Avocet* and *Swan*—converted 187-foot World War I vintage minesweepers able to support only a few aircraft—posed little threat to the Japanese Fleet. Similarly, *Hulbert* and *Thornton*, although larger at 314 feet and possessing greater capabilities, were antiquated former "flush deck" destroyers, having been commissioned in 1919-1920.

In addition to danger posed by aircraft, the *Curtiss* and *Tangier* also faced an enemy submarine threat. The first hint of such to ships at Pearl Harbor came at 0745 when the destroyer *Monaghan* (DD-354) received orders to get underway and rendezvous with the destroyer

Ward off the harbor entrance to assist her in finishing off a submarine. *Monaghan*, moored north of Ford Island in a nest with Destroyer Division 2 ships, left anchorage at 0815. Her commanding officer described carnage encountered as the ship passed west of Ford Island while proceeding outbound to sea, and of sighting and taking a submarine inside the harbor under attack:

> UTAH, seen to be hit before 0800, had capsized and sank, the RALEIGH was down by the bow, apparently hit forward by a torpedo. Heavy ships moored to Eastward of Ford Island were still under heavy torpedo and dive bombing attack, with several listing heavily. ARIZONA was seen to blow up but time was not observed.
>
> Shortly after getting underway, word was received that a submarine had been sighted in the channel off Beckoning Point. The Submarine was seen almost immediately from the Bridge and Control. The CURTISS had the submarine periscope under fire at the moment. MONAGHAN proceeded to attack, taking the periscope under fire also. While still about 100 yards away the submarine conning tower and bow of the submarine were suddenly exposed and a torpedo was fired down the side of the MONAGHAN which later exploded on the beach at the Northern end of the harbor. Submarine was attacked by ramming and depth charges, and sank immediately.[27]

Although not identified by the *Monaghan* as being a participant in the action, *Tangier* also took the submarine under fire. Earlier that morning, general quarters had been sounded aboard the seaplane tender at 0758, as the first of a group of Japanese planes passed along her port side at an altitude of about 400 feet, headed to Marine Corps Air Station Ewa, located seven miles west of Pearl Harbor on Oahu. The rising sun insignia on the wings of the planes left no uncertainty as to whether it was a real attack.[28]

Tangier opened fire two minutes later as crewmen arrived at their gun stations. Loud explosions were heard from Ford Island, where bombs dropped on a hangar full of PBYs gutted the structure. Comdr. Clifton A. F. Sprague, USN, *Tangier*'s commanding officer, estimated that the first wave of dive bombers and torpedo planes consisted of from forty to fifty aircraft. The planes came in generally from a heading of 50° true, flying down Ford Island on the port side of the seaplane tender. The only exception was three torpedo planes that launched torpedoes at about 0803 at the *Utah*; they came from the north. Reports by men positioned aft on *Tangier* differed as to whether all three torpedoes hit the *Utah*, or whether two hit her and one slid between her stern and *Tangier*'s stern. The former battleship took two hits, and immediately started to list to port. As her crew began to abandon, she rolled over onto her side and capsized.[29]

Photo 4-2

The west side of Ford Island during the Japanese attack on Pearl Harbor. Visible are (left to right): *Tangier*, the capsized *Utah* (AG-16), *Curtiss* in the distance directly behind *Utah*, the repair ship *Medusa* (AR-1), and the stern of *Raleigh* (CL-7), which is listing after a torpedo hit.
USAAF photograph, U.S. National Park Service Pearl Harbor gallery (courtesy of Robert Hurst and NavSource)

The light cruiser *Raleigh*, located on the opposite side of the *Utah* from *Tangier*, was hit amidships by a torpedo and took such a list to port it appeared she might capsize. Her commanding officer issued an order that all men not at the guns were to jettison topside weight, and to put the ship's two scout planes in the water first. The torpedoes aboard the ship, minus their warheads, were pushed overboard and beached at Ford Island. Torpedo tubes, catapults, steel cargo boom, stanchions, boat skids, life rafts and booms were also jettisoned, and both anchors let go. As crewmen topside worked furiously to decrease the list and thereby keep the cruiser afloat, her gun crews helped to destroy five enemy aircraft.[30]

Tangier's guns poured out full fire at Japanese planes flying down her port side at about 300 to 500 feet in altitude. A hit was made on the engine compartment of one of the planes, as evidenced by white smoke emitting from the aircraft as it passed over Waipio Peninsula, directly west of Ford Island, at low altitude. During a slight lull in the action, damage control parties used the time to verify proper closure of all watertight doors, hatches, and ports, and readiness of fire hoses for use. A few changes were also made to better optimize the use of personnel, as described by the executive officer:

> Damage control parties, ammunition supply, and belting parties were checked and redistribution of personnel made where necessary to eliminate bottle necks.... Practically no changes were made except to use the 5" – 51 caliber gun crew and ammunition supply party to supplement the 3" and .50 caliber machine gun ammunition and belting parties. The 5" – 51 caliber gun not being an A.A. gun was of no value to us and the personnel were required as indicated above. During this time our boats in the water were used for rescuing *UTAH* survivors.[31]

The *Tangier* received a report at 0833 of a Japanese submarine in the channel. Her #1 3-inch gun opened fire ten minutes later following a sighting of the sub about 800 yards distant off her starboard bow. *Curtiss* concurrently fired 5-inch rounds at it. Cease fire was ordered aboard *Tangier* at 0844, due to *Monaghan* fouling the firing bearing while making a run to ram and depth charge the target. In desperation, the *I-22* fired both her torpedoes toward the *Curtiss* and *Monaghan*. One of the "fish" grounded on Ford Island; the other hit a pier off Pearl City. *Monaghan* sank the sub at 0845. The wreck was recovered in ensuing days and later used as fill material during construction of a new pier at the Pearl Harbor submarine base.[32]

It was later learned that five midget submarines had been transported to Pearl Harbor on the decks of the same number of larger mother-submarines. The battery powered 78-foot Type-*A* midgets each carried two torpedoes. One of the subs, *I-18*, was depth-charged in Keehi lagoon outside Pearl Harbor between the harbor entrance and Honolulu. U.S. Navy divers located her wreckage on 13 June 1960 with both torpedoes still aboard. *I-24* lost her way due to a malfunctioning gyrocompass, and eventually grounded herself at Waimanalo Beach on Oahu's east shore. She was captured with both torpedoes unfired and her commanding officer became the first Japanese POW of the war. *I-20* was sunk by gunfire from the *Ward*. Sixty-one years later, on 28 August 2002, two deep diving submersibles operated by NOAA's Hawaii Undersea Research Laboratory located the wreckage about five miles off the entrance to Pearl Harbor with both torpedoes still aboard. *I-22* was sunk by the *Monaghan* as described. The fifth midget, *I-16*, sent a radio report the evening of 7 December claiming credit for sinking the *Arizona*. (Photographic analysis conducted later suggested that a submarine inside the harbor successfully fired torpedoes at the battleships *West Virginia* and *Oklahoma*.) *I-16* was not retrieved by any of the mother-submarines and her final resting place remains unknown.[33]

AIRCRAFT ATTACKS AGAINST *TANGIER* INCREASE

The preceding attacks against *Tangier* and other ships in the vicinity were only a prelude of what was to come in the next few minutes. A report by Comdr. Clifton A. F. Sprague, later described the devastation aircraft wrought on *Arizona* and *Nevada*, as well as separate attacks made on his ship, the *Tangier*.

> 0850 – NEVADA underway heading out the channel, struck in bow by torpedo or bomb. A larger explosion was heard and a pillar of smoke and flame rolled up for about two hundred feet from position occupied by NEVADA. The ARIZONA is now violently afire, appears that oil tanks are burning. ARIZONA's smoke obscures damage on other battleships, forward of her.
>
> A second wave of attackers started coming in. From now on the Japanese planes made deliberate bombing attacks on TANGIER. Shot off tail of one Japanese plane just as he had passed abeam to starboard. This plane crashed in Middle Loch in back of CURTISS and [the repair ship] MEDUSA. The plane was hit by .50 cal. Machine gun bullets and the tail was shot off by the 3"50 cal. forward [gun] battery.[34]

As a second wave of attackers came in, *Tangier*'s gunfire riddled a Japanese plane, which went out of control and crashed on the shoreline near Beckoning Point. A bomb dropped by another plane made a direct hit on the *Curtiss*. Sprague estimated that there were about twenty-seven aircraft in the second wave, and the same number in one that followed it:

> 0910 – Third wave of bombing attack came in again, about twenty seven planes. This might be delayed planes of second attack. Riddled another Japanese plane, flying up our port side, engine caught fire, then part of fuselage forward of the pilot burst into flame, pilot got his plane around 90° to right and...deliberately crashed his plane into CURTISS. Plane crashed into CURTISS near after stack, into boat crane and A.A. gun station and started a good size fire.[35]

Within only a few minutes between 0913 and 0920, the *Tangier* was the target of five bombs dropped by five separate planes. One fell on Ford Island; the pilot did not press home his attack, as the others did, and the ordnance fell short because he turned away early. The other four aircraft made their drops from about 300 feet away while in shallow dives. All four were very close misses, and the explosions muffled, apparently because the bombs buried themselves in silt on the harbor floor. *Tangier* was struck in forty-two places by fragments, but only two penetrated the side of the ship, and the only casualties suffered were three men on deck who received superficial wounds. No enemy planes approached *Tangier* after 0920. When the action ended, she had expended 217 rounds of 3-inch/50 (forward battery), 198 rounds of 3-inch/23 (aft battery), and 23,000 rounds of .50-caliber machine gun ammunition that morning.[36]

CURTISS DAMAGED WITH HIGH CASUALTIES

Almost immediately after the aircraft attacks commenced that morning, the *Curtiss* was strafed by fighter planes as men topside observed bomb hits on the VP-22 hangar at the Naval Air Station. Gun crews were ordered to "fire individually on any target making an offensive approach." The ship's .50-caliber machine guns opened fire at 0803, and two minutes later her 5-inch battery in local control. During ensuing air action, enemy bombers under heavy fire made an unsuccessful attack on the ship at 0825. This thwarted attempt was followed by visual detection aboard the *Curtiss* of an undersea threat.[37]

At 0836, a sighting was made of a periscope about 700 yards on the ship's starboard quarter. Following an order to the 5-inch battery to "fire on submarine," No. 3 gun fired one round over the periscope and two just short and directly at it, and No. 2 gun opened fire as well. The midget sub surfaced at 0840, with the conning tower and a section of bow visible, and fired a torpedo up the North Channel toward a destroyer. *Curtiss*'s No. 3 gun scored two hits on the conning tower, and the order was given "Cease firing on submarine."[38]

Air action soon resumed. At 0905, gunfire from the *Curtiss* hit one of three planes pulling out of a dive over Ford Island. Set afire, and out of control the aircraft crashed into the starboard side of the seaplane tender against No. 1 crane. The gas tank exploded creating an inferno amongst the plane wreckage on the boat deck, forcing temporary abandonment of No. 3 Gun. A different group of planes made a direct attack on the *Curtiss* a few minutes later. The aircraft releasing their bombs from about 300 feet while in a glide at about thirty degrees to the horizon. One bomb hit the seaplane tender's stern mooring buoy and two fell clear of the ship. The remaining bomb hit the starboard side of the boat deck, passed through the carpenter shop on the superstructure deck, and aviation radio repair shop on the upper decks, into and across the hangar, and finally detonated on the main deck.[39]

Diagram 4-2

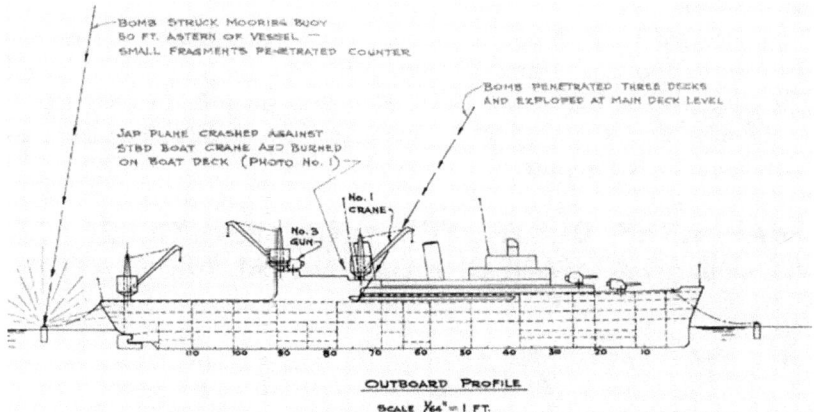

USS *Curtiss* Bomb Damage, December 7, 1941 Pearl Harbor, Bureau of Ships, Navy Department, April 20, 1942

The explosion blew a 20-foot diameter hole in the main deck, destroying bulkheads, decks, equipment and fixtures within a radius of thirty feet. Fires broke out in many places on six decks, which were not completely extinguished until 1430. Cork used extensively in the seaplane tender for insulation ignited and burned rapidly in the damaged areas. The direct hit was probably by a 550-pound, general purpose bomb containing 132 pounds of TNT. *Curtiss* suffered twenty men killed, one missing and presumed dead, and fifty-eight men injured due to the bomb blast or resultant fires. The seaplane tender had been designed under treaty restrictions that forbade the use of armor in auxiliary ships. In the *Currituck* (AV-7) and other newer large seaplane tenders, the ship's third deck was two inches thick over the middle sixty percent of its length, providing additional protection for magazines and propulsion machinery spaces. This feature aboard the *Curtiss* would probably have stopped the bomb splinters that entered her engine room. Thirty-three of the most grievously injured men aboard the tender were transferred to the hospital ship *Solace* (AH-5), and the others were retained on board.[40]

Chapter 4

USS *Curtiss* Crewmen Killed in Japanese Attack on Pearl Harbor

F1c Joseph I. Caro	S1c Edward S. Haven Jr.	AS Jesse K. Milbourne
S2c Lee H. Duke	MATT2c Anthony Hawkins Jr.	RM2c Dean B. Orwick
S1c Clifton E. Edmonds	AS Thomas Hembree	MATT2c William J. Powell
Cox John W. Frazier	AS Andrew King	S1c Wilson A. Rice
S2c Nickolas S. Ganas	S2c Robert S. Lowe	S2c Howard A. Rosenau
S2c George H. Guy	AS James E. Massey	RM2c Benjamin Schlect
F1c Kenneth J. Hartley	S1c Maurice Mastrototaro	SF1c Joseph Sperling

The deceased were all enlisted men. The long titles of their ratings used in the above table are: AS (Apprentice Seaman), Cox (Coxswain), F1c (Fireman 1st Class), MATT2c (Mess Attendant 2nd Class), RM2c (Radioman 2nd Class), S1c (Seaman 1st Class), S2c (Seaman 2nd Class), and SF1c (Shipfitter 1st Class).[41]

SEAPLANES DESTROYED AND MEN KILLED OR WOUNDED AT KANEOHE BAY NAVAL AIR STATION

> *His complete disregard for his own life, in staying with his machine gun, although many times wounded, is the kind of American fighting spirit necessary to victory.*
>
> —Adm. Chester W. Nimitz, commander-in-chief Pacific Fleet, remarking on the courage of Chief Aviation Ordnanceman John William Finn, USN, in the face of almost certain death, during the Japanese attack on Naval Air Station, Kaneohe Bay, on 7 December 1941.[42]

The first indication commander Patrol Wing One had that anything was amiss on the morning of 7 December was receipt of a message from patrol aircraft *14-P-1* out on dawn patrol reporting that it had dropped a depth bomb on and had sunk an enemy submarine a mile off the Pearl Harbor entrance. Comdr. Knefler McGinnis later learned that the destroyer *Ward* had carried out the attack on the sub, and the plane had added its bomb in assistance. When this report was received it seemed so implausible that the first reaction was that it must have been a case of mistaken identity as some U.S. Navy submarines were scheduled to enter Pearl Harbor that morning. While trying to verify that patrolling aircraft had the necessary information concerning these submarines, nine enemy fighters appeared over Naval Air Station,

Kaneohe Bay, and while circling at low altitude strafed the control tower on the hill, and the four patrol planes moored in the bay.[43]

This was followed by an attack on other aircraft on the seaplane ramp, the first being an OS2U-1 Kingfisher, which was thoroughly riddled. All the planes on the water were set on fire, and some of those on the beach. Squadron personnel got machine guns in action against the attacking planes, and punctured the fuel tanks of at least two aircraft.[44]

Photo 4-3

Sailors attempt to save a burning PBY at Naval Air Station, Kaneohe Bay, Oahu, during the Japanese air raid.
U.S. Navy Photograph #NH 97432 from the collections of the U.S. Naval History and Heritage Command

After the first wave there was a few-minutes lull before another attack by six to nine fighters. All attacks were directed at the seaplanes on the ground, in the water, and in the hangars, but there was some strafing of cars and quarters incident to the main attack. Squadron personnel attempted to save the planes not on fire and those not too far gone. Men thus engaged were strafed by machine gun fire, as were personnel in automobiles attempting to get to the hangar area. Following the first two attacks, squadron personnel directed all their efforts to getting aircraft that could possibly be saved clear of the area of burning planes.[45]

An attack wrought by a group of bombers, which followed earlier strafing attacks by fighter aircraft, caused the greatest number of personnel casualties. McGinnis described the devastation:

> About 0930 a formation of nine, 2 seater bombers, came in formation over the Bay, more or less following the coast line from Kahuku point, at an altitude of about 1000 to 1500 feet and dropped bombs on the hangar occupied by Patrol Squadrons ELEVEN AND TWELVE. This attack caused the loss of the greatest number of personnel as considerable men were in the hangar getting replenishment ammunition.... Immediately behind this wave of bombers were nine additional bombers and it is uncertain whether or not they dropped bombs—so much smoke was in the area and people stunned by the first wave that this point is uncertain...[46]

Following the bombing attack, there was a third strafing attack at 1000. During the series of attacks that morning, all of the planes at the base were put out of commission. These included thirty-three patrol planes, one OS2U-1, and the J2F-1 belonging to the Air Station. The only planes not destroyed were three that were on dawn patrol. One of these was attacked by a number of fighters and received considerable bullet holes, but remained operational. McGinnis later praised the bravery of his people throughout the prolonged air raid:

> The conduct of all personnel throughout the entire attack was magnificent, in fact, too much so. Had they not with no protection, deliberately set themselves up with machine guns right in line with the drop of the attacking and strafing planes and near the object of their attack, we would have lost less men. It was, due to this reckless resistance that two enemy planes were destroyed and six or more were sent away with heavy gas leaks.[47]

Seventeen personnel of Patrol Squadrons 11, 12, and 14 were killed in the air attack on Naval Air Station, Kaneohe Bay, and another eleven men were seriously injured. The four officers killed were naval reserve (USNR) ensigns, and the thirteen enlisted men all regular navy (USN). Titles of rates: AMM1c (Aviation Machinist's Mate 1st Class), AMM2c (Aviation Machinist's Mate 2nd Class), AMM3c (Aviation Machinist's Mate 3rd Class), AOM3c (Aviation Ordnanceman 3rd Class), Sea1c (Seaman 1st Class), and Sea2c (Seaman 2nd Class).

Patrol Wing One Casualties

Squadron Eleven	Squadron Twelve	Squadron Twelve
Ens. R. S. Foss	Ens. L. Fox Jr.	AMM2c W. S. Brown
Ens. J. G. Smartt	Ens. R. W. Uhlmann	AMM1c D. T. Griffin
AOM3c J. D. Buckley	Sea2c G. W. Ingram	AMM1c R. A. Watson
AMM1c C. M. Formoe	AMM2c C. Lawrence	
AMM3c M. A. Manning	Sea2c C. W. Otterstetter	**Squadron Fourteen**
Sea2c J. H. Robinson	AMM3c R. K. Porterfield	AMM3c L. G. Newman[48]
Sea1c L. D. Weaver		

But for Chief Petty Officer John W. Finn, USN, who would receive the Medal of Honor for his extraordinary heroism that day, the casualties would undoubtedly have been even greater. Finn was with his wife, Alice, at their apartment about a mile from the hangar when he heard gunfire that morning. Driving to the base, he was initially not sure that it was anything but a drill. Then he heard a plane come roaring in behind him, and upon glancing up he saw the rising sun on the underside of the wing, as the pilot made a wing-over. By the time Finn arrived at the hangar, most of the PBYs were on fire.[49]

Once on scene, he quickly took over a .50-caliber machine gun and mounted it on a moveable tripod platform used for training. This action exposed him, like other squadron personnel manning guns, to enemy strafing fire. Finn later commented about this shortcoming, "We could have done a better job if we had had those mounts. Every man was determined to find a machine gun to fight back and we did what we could to fight and turn them away." Finn continued to fire at enemy planes from his exposed position for two hours, during which he was shot in the left arm and foot, and received multiple shrapnel wounds on his scalp, chest and stomach, and right elbow and thumb. He said in an interview many years later that the planes had been so close he could see the pilots' faces.[50]

Chief Petty Officer Finn received the Congressional Medal of Honor on 15 September 1942, the first award of the nation's highest decoration for heroism, of the war. Of the fourteen other such medals awarded for the Pearl Harbor attack, his was the only one for combat. The other awardees received their medals for rescue attempts; ten posthumously. By then, Finn was no longer an enlisted man, having received a Limited Duty Officer's commission in 1942. A copy of his medal citation follows:

The President of the United States of America, in the name of Congress, takes pleasure in presenting the Medal of Honor to Lieutenant John William Finn, United States Navy, for extraordinary heroism, distinguished service, and devotion above and beyond the call of duty. During the first attack by Japanese airplanes on the Naval Air Station, Kaneohe Bay, on 7 December 1941, Lieutenant Finn promptly secured and manned a .50-caliber machinegun mounted on an instruction stand in a completely exposed section of the parking ramp, which was under heavy enemy machinegun strafing fire. Although painfully wounded many times, he continued to man this gun and to return the enemy's fire vigorously and with telling effect throughout the enemy strafing and bombing attacks and with complete disregard for his own personal safety. It was only by specific orders that he was persuaded to leave his post to seek medical attention. Following first aid treatment, although obviously suffering much pain and moving with great difficulty, he returned to the squadron area and actively supervised the rearming of returning planes. His extraordinary heroism and conduct in this action were in keeping with the highest traditions of the U.S. Naval Service.[51]

UTILITY SQUADRON PLANES SEARCH FOR ENEMY

Of the sixty-seven PBYs of Patrol Wings One and Two that were either present at, or operating from, Kaneohe Bay and Pearl Harbor at the time of the attack, all but a dozen were destroyed, damaged, or left unflyable. Only four of the PBYs on the ground at Pearl Harbor (of VP-23) escaped destruction or being knocked out of action during the first wave of attacks. They were immediately made ready for flight. Attired in pajamas, Capt. Francis M. Hughes, USN, was the first U.S. Navy pilot in the air after commencement of the air raid, airborne in a PBY before the attack was over. The remaining three flyable planes were in flight directly after the attack. (The planes, each loaded with four 1,000-pound bombs, were given a search sector of 225° to 270° true, out to five hundred miles from Pearl Harbor. This effort to find the enemy fleet was unsuccessful, as was that of the four VP-24 planes previously engaged in anti-submarine exercises off the coast of Hawaii. These aircraft were given search sectors by radio, but the results, like those of the other PBYs, were negative.[52]

One bright point for naval aviation that morning was the actions of Ens. John Edwards and other pilots, co-pilots, and air crew personnel of Utility Wing, Pacific Fleet. Following the initial attacks, of all the aircraft units present at Pearl Harbor, Utility Squadron One and Two were the most nearly intact. Thus, utility planes were used for the purpose of scouting and search. Between 0950 and 1638, the Wing had eight planes aloft.[53]

Ens. John P. Edwards, USNR, took off in a Sikorsky JRS-1 flying boat. These type planes were used primarily by Pan America Airways and were known as "Baby Clippers" in airline service. They could accommodate between 18 and 25 passengers and had a cruising speed of slightly over 100 mph. Those planes in naval service were armed only with hand-held rifles and later with "jury-rigged" single .30-caliber and single .50-caliber side guns and a single .30 cal. free gun in the nose.[54]

Three other pilots and two co-pilots followed Edwards up in three more JRS-1 flying boats, accompanied by ad hoc crews:

- Lt. (jg) James W. Robb, Jr., USNR
- Lt. Gordon E. Bolser, USNR, and Ens. Nils R. Larson, USNR
- Lt. (jg) Wesley H. Ruth, USNR, with Aviation Chief Machinist Mate Emery C. Geise (Naval Aviation Pilot) as his copilot[55]

Edwards, Robb, Bolser, Larson, and Ruth were awarded the Navy Cross for courageously piloting utility planes armed only with rifles. Edward's medal citation is representative of the others:

> The President of the United States of America takes pleasure in presenting the Navy Cross to Ensign John Perry Edwards, United States Naval Reserve, for extraordinary heroism in operations against the enemy while serving as Pilot of an airplane in Utility Squadron ONE (VJ-1), and for extraordinary courage and disregard of his own safety during the attack on the Fleet in Pearl Harbor, Territory of Hawaii, by Japanese forces on 7 December 1941. Although contact with the enemy meant almost certain destruction and despite the lack of any armament in this type plane, Ensign Edwards voluntarily piloted a JRS amphibian plane, equipped only with Springfield rifles, in search for and to obtain information of the enemy forces. Ensign Edwards' outstanding courage, daring airmanship and determined skill were at all times inspiring and in keeping with the highest traditions of the United States Naval Service.

While the brave men who accompanied them in their scratch crews also received appropriate commendations, only one, Sergeant Thomas E. Hailey, USMC, received the Navy Cross. Hailey had left the battleship *Oklahoma* after she had been ordered abandoned, helped rescue shipmates from the oily water, and then manned an anti-aircraft gun aboard the *Maryland*. After making the shore on Ford Island, he volunteered to go up in one of the Sikorskys armed only with a rifle and still wearing only the "skivvies" (underwear) in which he had swum away from the capsized *Oklahoma*.[56]

Photo 4-4

Utility Wing pilots flew Sikorsky JRS-1 planes like these while searching for the enemy fleet following the Japanese attack on Pearl Harbor—which were unarmed (except for Springfield rifles aboard them).
U.S Naval History and Heritage Command Photograph #2015.05.01

PEARL HARBOR GALVANIZES AMERICAN PEOPLE

The unprovoked Japanese attack on Pearl Harbor spurred the United States into war. Japan, by its strategic blunder, brought Americans together, from all walks of life, in grim determination to win victory in the Pacific, despite a majority of whom had been opposed to their country entering the war in Europe. Sunset at Pearl Harbor that day found the battleships *Arizona, California,* and *West Virginia* sunk, the *Oklahoma* capsized at her berth, and *Maryland, Nevada, Pennsylvania,* and *Tennessee* damaged. Also damaged were the cruisers *Helena, Honolulu,* and *Raleigh,* and the destroyers *Cassin, Downes,* and *Shaw.* Of the auxiliary ships present, the minelayer *Oglala* was sunk, and the seaplane tender *Curtiss,* repair ship *Vestal,* and the *Utah* damaged. (Other ships and Naval District craft received minor damage.) After being torpedoed, the ex-battleship *Utah* had rolled over and capsized at her berth, a few degrees short of being exactly upside down.[57]

The Japanese attack claimed the lives of more than 2,500 people, wounded 1,000 more and damaged or destroyed 18 American ships and nearly 300 airplanes. Almost half of the casualties occurred aboard the battleship *Arizona,* hit four times by Japanese bombers.[58]

The seaplane tenders and patrol squadrons present at Pearl Harbor received battle stars as did the *McFarland* at sea off Maui and VP-21 at Midway Atoll:

Ship	Award Date	Commanding Officer
Curtiss (AV-4)	7 Dec 1941	Capt. George Thomas Owen
Tangier (AV-8)	7 Dec 1941	Comdr. Clifton A. F. Sprague
Hulbert (AVD-6)	7 Dec 1941	Lt. Comdr. James Mills Lane
McFarland (AVD-14)	7 Dec 1941	Lt. Comdr. Joseph L. Kane
Thornton (AVD-11)	7 Dec 1941	Lt. Comdr. Wendell F. Kline
Avocet (AVP-4)	7 Dec 1941	Lt. William G. Johnson Jr.
Swan (AVP-7)	7 Dec 1941	Lt. Finley E. Hall
VP-11	7 Dec 1941	Lt. Comdr. Leon W. Johnson
VP-12	7 Dec 1941	Lt. Comdr. John P. Fitzsimmons
VP-14	7 Dec 1941	Lt. Comdr. William T. Rassieur
VP-21	7 Dec 1941	Lt. Comdr. George T. Mundorff Jr.
VP-22	7 Dec 1941	Lt. Comdr. Frank O'Beirne
VP-23	7 Dec 1941	Lt. Comdr. Francis M. Hughes
VP-24	7 Dec 1941	Lt. Comdr. T. U. Sisson

5

Japanese Attack on the Philippines

> *Pat Wing 10 whose headquarters was in Cavite on Sangley Point, was composed of two squadrons, Pat Squadron 101 and 102. VP-101 was based at Cavite on Sangley Point and Pat Squadron 102 was based at Olongapo on Subic Bay [about sixty miles north of Manila]. We did normal operations such as we would do in peace time, gunner and bombing, but every so often we would have a war scare out there and we would start patrols.*
>
> *The conditions of the aviation part of the armed forces in the Philippines to my mind was very inadequate. All that we had were some cruiser-based SOC's and the Catalinas and Patrol Wing 10.*
>
> —Lt. Comdr. Clarence A. Keller Jr., USN, describing the prewar activities and condition of the Asiatic Fleet's Patrol Wing Ten in the Philippine Islands.[1]

The morning of 8 December 1941 in the Philippines (the 7th at Pearl Harbor across the International dateline), Patrol Wing Ten planes were out on dawn patrols, but made no enemy sightings or contacts. Capt. Frank D. Wagner, USN, commander Aircraft, Asiatic Fleet and commander Patrol Wing Ten, was based ashore at Naval Air Station, Cavite. Upon learning of the attack on Pearl Harbor, he directed all planes to load with two 500-pound bombs each and to disperse to their pre-assigned war operating bases, all of which were within sixty miles of Manila. The distribution of aircraft was 1/4 at Olongapo, 1/4 operating from a lake called Laguna de Bay (located sixty miles southeast of Manila near the town of Los Banos), 1/4 in Manila Bay off Nichols Airfield basing on the seaplane tender *Childs*, and 1/4 at Cavite, south of Manila Bay. He ordered the patrols to the northwest and northeast to use one-half their planes daily, with the other half standing by as an attack group. Lt. Comdr. John V. Peterson, USN, at Los Banos, commanded the Attack Group.[2]

The seaplane tender *Langley*, a converted aircraft carrier, was at Manila Bay loading gas, oil and supplies. The remaining two tenders of Wing Ten were monitoring sea approaches to the Philippines. *William B. Preston* (AVD-7) with three PBY-4s was in Malalag Bay off Davao

Gulf on the southeastern coast of Mindanao. Her planes patrolled the eastern approaches to the Celebes Sea. *Heron* was at Port Ciego on the southeastern tip of Palawan Island, with four OS2Us covering the western approaches to the Celebes Sea.³

Map 5-1

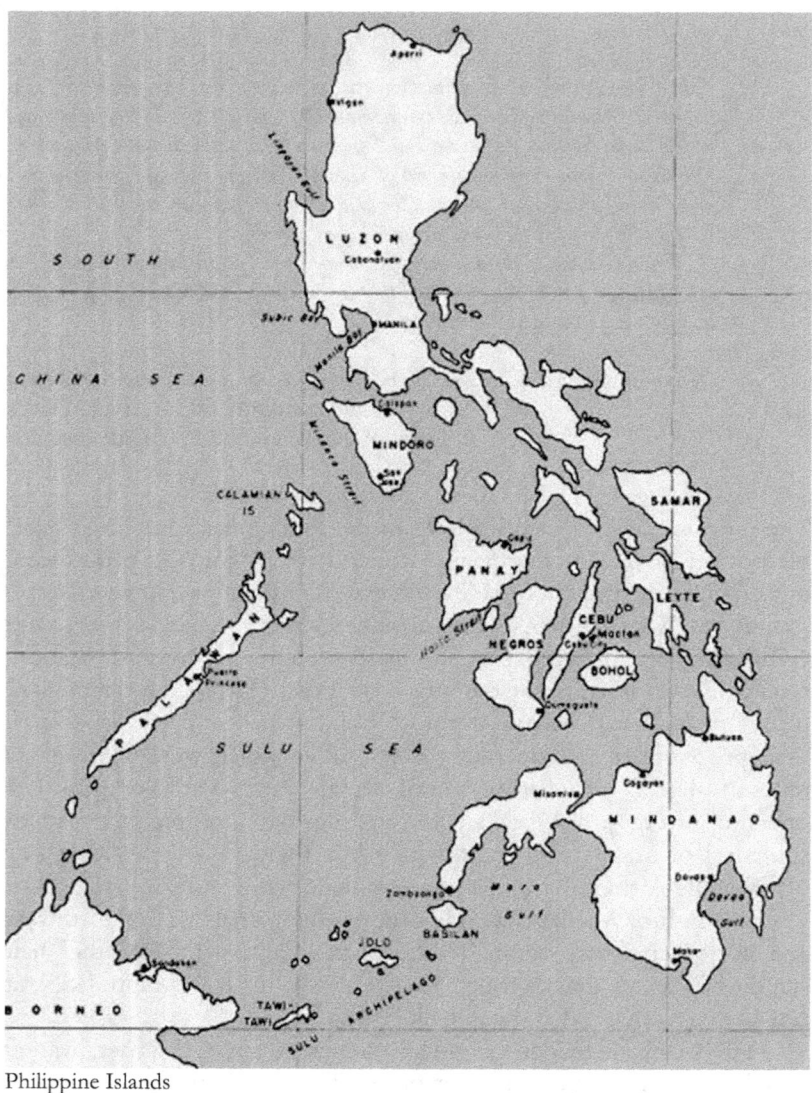

Philippine Islands

The units of Patrol Wing Ten at the onset of war are listed below, along with the identities of squadron commanders and commanding officers of seaplane tenders:

Commander Patrol Wing Ten: Capt. Frank D. Wagner, USN
(Twenty-eight PBY-4s and the planes of the Utility Unit)

Aviation Units/Tenders	Commander/Commanding Officer
Patrol Squadron 101: PBY-4s	Lt. Comdr. John V. Peterson, USN
Patrol Squadron 102: PBY-4s	Lt. Comdr. Edgar T. Neale, USN
Utility Unit: 5 OS2Us, 4 J2Fs, 1 SOC	Lt. Jack C. Renard, USN
Langley (AV-3)	Capt. Felix B. Stump, USN
Childs (AVD-1)	Lt. Comdr. John L. Pratt, USN
Heron (AVP-2)	Lt. William L. Kabler, USN
William B. Preston (AVD-7)	Lt. Comdr. Etheridge Grant, USN[4]

Admiral Thomas C. Hart, commander-in-chief Asiatic Fleet, had begun sending some of his ships to the Netherlands East Indies in the latter part of November, and various units of the fleet would follow at intervals all through December. The combatant ships gathering in the East Indies were formed into a strike force designated Task Force 5, under the command of Rear Adm. William A. Glassford Jr., USN. Glassford had commanded the Asiatic Fleet's Yangtze River Patrol in China prior to its withdrawal to the Philippines. He had left Shanghai on 29 November 1941 aboard the gunboat *Luzon* (PR-7) in company with the *Oahu* (PR-6) bound for Manila. The gunboats rendezvoused with the minesweeper *Finch* (AM-9), and submarine rescue ship *Pigeon* (ASR-6) the next day and sailed together, reaching the Philippines on 4 December. With Glassford then available for new duties, Hart assigned him as commander Task Force 5.[5]

Glassford left by plane in the late morning on 8 December for Iloilo, about 250 miles south-southeast of Manila, to embark in the heavy cruiser *Houston* (CA-30), which had been ordered there to await his arrival. That evening *Langley* and the fleet oilers *Pecos* (AO-6) and *Trinity* (AO-13), protected by the destroyers *Barker* (DD-213) and *Paul Jones* (DD-239), slipped out of Manila Bay under the cover of darkness. The group then proceeded south to join the *Houston* and light cruiser *Boise* (CL-47) off Panay, an island southeast of Mindoro.[6]

Upon rendezvousing, the ships formed a column, with *Houston* as the guide, followed by *Boise*, *Langley*, *Trinity*, and *Pecos*. *Barker* and *Paul Jones* took position in the van (off to the sides of the forward part of the formation) to screen for submarines. After entering the Celebes Sea, Glassford received orders to turn back with the cruisers to escort a submarine tender convoy following a day behind. *Langley* took over command of the oilers and destroyers, and the group continued southward to Borneo via Makassar Strait, which separates the islands of Borneo and Celebes.[7]

During passage of the strait on 13 December, *Pecos* with *Paul Jones* as an escort departed the convoy for Balikpapan, Borneo, and the light cruiser *Marblehead* (CL-12) joined and took over command. *Trinity* entered Balikpapan the next morning to go alongside the oil dock to load fuel, and *Langley* and *Marblehead* anchored in the harbor. Other Asiatic Fleet ships arrived at Balikpapan that day and the next to fuel. On 16 December, *Heron* and *William B. Preston* joined them. That afternoon a group of ships, including the *Langley* and *Preston*, formed up in Makassar Strait and sailed south for Java.[8]

Map 5-2

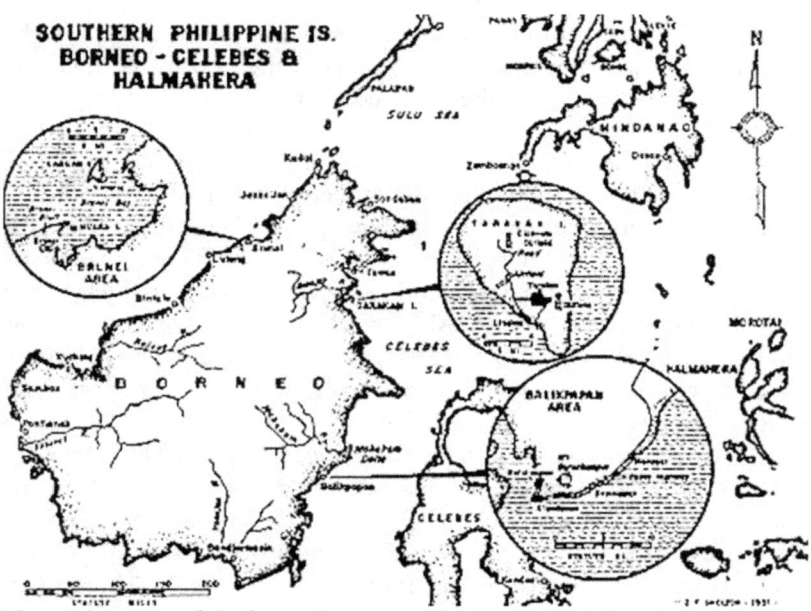

The northern part of the former Borneo is today Malaysia and Brunei, and Indonesia in the south, makes up the rest of the large island. Celebes is now Sulawesi, Indonesia. *The Army Air Forces in World War II: Vol. V, The Pacific: Matterhorn to Nagasaki June 1944 to August 1945*

ATTACK ON THE *WILLIAM B. PRESTON*

Having provided an overview of the Asiatic Fleet and the ships and aircraft of Patrol Wing Ten, we return to the early days of the defense of the Philippines. Shortly after 0300 on 8 December, the destroyer seaplane tender *William B. Preston* intercepted a radio message from commander-in-chief Asiatic Fleet: "Japan has commenced hostilities, govern yourselves accordingly." Lt. Comdr. Etheridge Grant, USN, not knowing exactly where the Japanese had commenced hostilities, put his ship on a war footing. One of the three PBY-4s tended by the "Williebee" took off at 0330 on a patrol of the eastern approaches of the Celebes Sea. Grant shifted his ship's anchorage away from the moorage of the other two Catalinas to lessen the chance that an enemy plane might damage both her and the PBYs with a single bomb. Meanwhile, sailors belted ammunition for the ship's four .50-caliber Browning machine guns, and took down awnings employed to shield crewmen from the tropical sun, to provide lookouts better visibility.[9]

William B. Preston had been commissioned a destroyer on 23 August 1920, at Norfolk, Virginia—too late to serve in the First World War. When the size of the U.S. Navy was reduced by the Washington Disarmament Conference, she was consigned with many other ships to "Red-Lead Row." There she remained, in obscurity, until selected for conversion to a seaplane tender on 18 November 1939. She entered the New York Navy Yard soon thereafter, where workmen removed her four 21-inch triple-torpedo tube mounts, half her 4-inch gun battery, her single 3-inch/23 anti-aircraft gun, and her depth-charge racks. Boilers one and two, the forward stacks and all associated engineering machinery and piping were also taken out. The elimination of most of her weapons and one-half of her propulsion plant provided the space necessary for the ship to function as a tender for a twelve-plane patrol squadron.[10]

Other modifications included the installation of a 30,000-gallon aviation-fuel tank, as well as living spaces for embarked aviation personnel. A newly constructed deckhouse extended from the bridge to the galley. Four .50-caliber machine guns replaced the two 4-inch guns atop the galley deckhouse, and the existing searchlight platform was strengthened to allow it to support a boat derrick and gear. Two 30-foot motor launches, each capable of carrying a 600-gallon fuel bowser, were added, carried in cradles aft of the searchlight platform, to augment two 26-foot motor whaleboats. Plane refueling booms were installed on each quarter to complete her new aircraft fueling system. Finally, freed-up space in her magazines held forty-eight 500-pound bombs in addition to 4-inch gun rounds.[11]

Unfortunately, the first rising sun seen that morning was the emblem on the wings of Japanese planes. At about 0800 as Grant went forward to check the progress of preparations to slip the anchor chain (eliminating time required to bring in the anchor should instant maneuverability be desired), a lookout shouted, "Aircraft!" Grant sprinted to the bridge as Japanese planes swept around the narrow neck of land that shielded Malalag Bay from the Gulf of Davao. A group of about eighteen "Kates" (Nakajima Type 97 B5N bombers) and nine "Claudes" (Mitsubishi A5M4 Type 96 fighters) from the carrier *Ryujo* roared in low over the water, their cowl guns winking fire. The Claudes quickly shot to pieces patrol planes *101-P-4* and *101-P-7* which tethered to their mooring buoys were "sitting ducks." The aircraft sank beneath the waters of the bay as survivors struck out for shore. Ens. Robert G. Tills, USN, was killed, and Radioman Third Albert E. Layton, USN, wounded in the attack.[12]

Photo 5-1

Undated photo of *William B. Preston*, well before her conversion to a seaplane tender. Photograph from the collection of the Vallejo Naval and Historical Museum (courtesy of Darryl Baker and NavSource)

The *William B. Preston* lowered a boat to pick up survivors as she prepared to make a dash for the open sea. After slipping her anchor chain, the seaplane tender zigzagged across the bay as Claudes and Kates attacked the fleeing ship. Four times the planes came over and each time, Grant was able to skillfully evade dropped bombs through the use of violent ship maneuvers. The tender emerged from the attack unscathed and returned to the bay to pick up her boat and the survivors from the Catalinas. The first wave of Japanese planes had strafed and sunk the two PBYs, but the enemy did not go unscathed.

The retiring aircraft left one of their own behind, a victim of the ship's .50-caliber battery, claimed by the sea. *William B. Preston*, the first unit of the Asiatic Fleet to come under attack, survived the battle.[13]

Thereafter four Japanese destroyers appeared, searching the gulf for the tender and any remaining planes. The alertness of lookouts paid dividends and *William B. Preston* was able to slip away unnoticed. Grant received orders to retire southward to Polloc Harbor, at the northeastern corner of Moro Gulf bordering Maguindanao. After she arrived there the next day, 9 December, three PBY-4s and two OS2U Kingfishers which had been attached to *Heron* at Balabac Strait, joined the ship. After being informed that Japanese troops had landed on Mindanao and were marching overland to Polloc Bay, Grant prepared to depart. The seaplane tender stood out on 10 December bound for Tutu Bay on the east coast of Jolo, one of the southernmost islands of the Sulu Archipelago. Planes *101-P-6* and *102-P-27*, and the OS2Us, took flight for the same destination; carburetor trouble forced *101-P-3* to remain behind.[14]

CATALINAS ATTACK JAPANESE SURFACE FORCE

On 8 December, patrol plane searches seaward of the Philippines had netted nothing; no sign of Japanese forces. Wing personnel witnessed the bombing of Iba, an Army airfield on the western coast of Luzon, and heard the bombing of Clark and Nichols Air Fields also located on Luzon. A very strong force of Japanese fighters, bombers, and dive bombers attacked all U.S. Army airfields in the vicinity of Manila the first day of hostilities. The Japanese did not hit the Subic Bay area for several days, perhaps due to weather conditions; visibility there was normally obstructed by clouds a good portion of the time.[15]

On the morning of 10 December, Lt. Clarence A. Keller Jr., USN, piloting PBY *102-P-7* sighted a Japanese surface force which he believed included two battleships. (They were actually the heavy cruisers *Ashigara* and *Maya*, part of Vice Adm. Ibo Takahashi's Northern Covering Force which also included the cruiser *Kuma*, and destroyers *Asakaze* and *Matsukaze*.) Keller described the incident:

> We took off at dawn and I was out about an hour on my leg when I noticed over on the starboard side a small-float plane, very low, heading in the opposite direction. We turned towards him but he turned away and I resumed my patrol. About twenty minutes later on the horizon I sighted a naval force. I headed towards them and identified them as two battleships, a cruiser, and two destroyers. At the time, the first thing that came to my mind was that it was a British force.[16]

Keller approached no closer, made a contact report to Patrol Wing Ten to the effect that he had sighted this force, and continued his patrol. About a half hour later, he received communications from the Wing asking if he still had contact. After replying in the negative and told to resume contact, Keller headed back in a southerly direction. Relocating the enemy he approached from almost directly astern and a bit on the starboard quarter of the formation of ships:

> I got down low on the water, about fifteen feet off the water, and cut across their stern at about seven thousand yards distant, maybe a bit closer. As I got directly astern of them the ships did a "ships left" [turn to port] and started firing at me with their ack-ack [anti-aircraft guns] and also their secondary batteries. The ack-ack was a bit astern of me. We could feel the burst in the plane, however, and the splashes from the secondary battery were long, I would say about five hundred yards over and ahead of us. I soon opened up the range so far that they ceased firing and they resumed their southerly course which at that time they were heading about 180. The cloud conditions that day were cumulus clouds, and I climbed...[17]

From 2,500 feet altitude, a position of relative safety above the clouds, Keller tracked the formation which was then about a hundred miles off the Philippine coast, headed north, and making greater speed. He continued to send position updates to Wing headquarters at Cavite until a flight of PBY-4s armed with bombs arrived:

> I saw the attack force come in...led by Commander J[ohn]. V. Peterson, who was commander of Patrol Squadron 101. They came in, made their drop, and just as they dropped, they were aiming at the rear battleship, he changed course to the starboard. As the salvo landed, his stern swung into the pattern and he continued going in a circle to the right and then he straightened out and zig-zagged off in a northerly direction and stopped and he was dead in the water and smoking when I left.[18]

After Peterson received word that Keller had sighted this force, he prepared to strike it with the five planes he had available at Los Banos. The planes took off at 0830, and after arriving in the Manila area began their search off the coast. Peterson found the Japanese ships at about 1130. The group was zigzagging at about 23 to 24 knots in a northwesterly direction, the sea was fairly rough and there were two layers of overcast, broken clouds over the sea. The five fabric-clad PBY-4 patrol planes posed to strike the warships below had neither armor nor self-sealing gas tanks to help ensure their survivability. These improvements were later made to provide aircrews greater protection when taking fire and reduce the possibility of seaplanes catching fire or exploding when hit. Peterson described the attack:

> I waited until the two layers [of cloud cover] which were broken overlapped, that is there was a clear area over the Task force and then made a bombing run on the largest battleship, which I believe to be the *KONGO*. The Japs set up a terrific anti-aircraft fire as soon as we started our bombing run. We were in close formation and were knocked about a good bit by the AA bursts. Sometimes there were as many as fifteen hundred burst[s] all round us. Some of them were as big as shade trees and others were smaller bursts. The fire was fairly accurate, but usually above and behind us although some burst ahead of us. It was difficult to make the bombing run, but we had an excellent bomber who stuck to his job and he made what I consider a very good run on the *KONGO*. We dropped and then immediately dispersed by previously arranged plan, each plane taking cover in the nearest cloud bank with instructions to rendezvous 50 miles on the reverse course to Manila as soon as the [flight] leader arrived there.[19]

Peterson was only able to remain for a short time to assess battle damage as he was now the single focus of the ships' anti-aircraft batteries. "We were being fired on and the burst[s] were getting close and knocking us about a bit." He had earlier observed bombs hit all around the stern of the battleship, and three or four direct hits which he believed had damaged her rudders and propellers. He witnessed the ship turn in a circle and slow, while steering a sort of wavering course, and eventually stop, after which the task force proceeded on its way, leaving her behind.[20]

PBY-4 PREVAILS AGAINST JAPANESE ZERO

Five PBYs out on patrol to the northeast of Luzon were recalled to load torpedoes and follow up Peterson's attack on the now crippled Japanese ship. One of these planes was shot down by enemy fighters just east of Manila. The other four returned and each was fueled and rearmed with one torpedo and two 500-pound bombs. They were in the process of taking off when twenty-seven bombers accompanied by fighters arrived overhead to make the first bombing attack on Cavite Navy Yard. The fighters engaged the four torpedo-laden patrol planes trying to get airborne, and shot up two badly, forcing them down.[21]

Ens. Robert McConnell landed *101-P-28* in Laguna de Bay east of Manila, while *101-P-2* flown by Lt. Harmon T. Utter, put down fifty miles off the coast. Before being forced to ditch, Utter bested a Japanese Zero in combat. Twisting and turning to evade the fast, maneuverable fighter, he steadied the PBY just long enough for the bow gunner, Chief Aviation Machinist's Mate Earl D. Payne, to hit the enemy with a burst of .30-caliber. Struck in the cockpit and engine compartment, and with its fuselage on fire, the plane plunged into Manila Bay. Utter received the Distinguished Flying Cross Medal, and was credited with being the first Navy pilot to bring down a Zero in the Pacific War:

> The President of the United States of America takes pleasure in presenting the Distinguished Flying Cross to Lieutenant Harmon Tischer Utter, United States Navy, for extraordinary heroism while participating in aerial flight, while serving as Pilot of an airplane in Patrol Squadron ONE HUNDRED ONE (VP-101), Patrol Wing 10 (Patwing-10), in action against enemy Japanese naval forces at Luzon, Philippine Islands, on 10 December 1941. Despite the fact that the plane was heavily laden with a torpedo and bombs, his skillful piloting made it possible for his crew to shoot down one enemy Japanese fighter. In addition to this action the subsequent skillful landing of his injured plane in a heavy sea without further injury to it or its personnel made possible to have the plane in service again on the following day.[22]

The DFC, America's oldest military aviation award, established by Congress on 2 July 1926, could be awarded to anyone in the Air Corps of the Army, Navy or Marine Corps for heroism or extraordinary achievement while participating in aerial flight.

The remaining two PBYs arrived at the approximate position of the crippled Japanese ship at dusk, but in evading the fighters they had consumed much of their gas and could only mount a brief search. They combed the area for as long as their fuel permitted. Not having located their target, they returned to Manila to find that the Japanese bombing attack on Cavite had almost completely wiped out the Navy Yard. The first and third salvos of bombs had blanketed the yard, and the whole place appeared to the pilots to be a mass of flames. The intervening salvo landed in the bay between Wing headquarters on the Cavite Air Station and the Navy Yard.[23]

WING TEN SUFFERS THE LOSS OF MANY PLANES

On 12 December, commander Patrol Wing Ten received a report that native lookouts at Lingayen Bay had sighted a considerable force of Japanese combatant ships moving along the coast toward Manila Bay. The seven PBYs at Olongapo (*101-P-10*, and *102-P-16, 17, 18, 19, 20, and 21*) were sent out to attack with bombs as many of the ships as possible. However, a seaward search from Mindoro to Lingayen Gulf found no vessels whatsoever. The Japanese by this time had occupied airfields in north and northwest Luzon. The enemy must have spotted the PBYs, because when the Catalinas returned to Olongapo five or six hours later to refuel at their mooring buoys, Japanese fighers came in behind them and destroyed all seven planes on the water. This was a severe blow to the Wing, and would be the greatest single loss sustained in one operation during the early days of the war. Mercifully, only two individuals, Ens. J. C. Watson, USNR, and ACMM George Sceek, were killed. The crews of moored PBYs and shore anti-aircraft batteries claimed two downed Zeros.[24]

The PBY crews and supporting personnel with plane and engine spare parts were moved by truck to Laguna de Bay. By this time the sky over Manila was continually occupied by the Japanese. Wing Ten continued to try to find targets for its aircraft in areas where fighter opposition might not be expected, but this was hard to do, and planes were being badly shot up. The base at Cavite was still intact, but communications equipment derangement forced commander Patrol Wing 10 to embark aboard *Childs* in Manila Bay, from which all operations were now being directed. Recognizing that operations could not long continue in the Manila area, Admiral Hart directed the Wing to move south.[25]

6

Defense of the Netherlands East Indies

> *We didn't know quite what to do but one thing I had in mind was not to speed up because that would look as though we were in a hurry to get away from them. We couldn't turn back because we would have been bottled up. We didn't have enough armament to engage any one of the ships and furthermore we had a valuable cargo of gasoline remaining and many spare parts and a considerable amount of stuff that belonged to Patrol Wing 10, which was needed by our airplanes which were operating from Java. Incidentally we had none of our own planes with us at this time.*
>
> —Capt. John L. Pratt, USN, former commanding officer of the seaplane tender *Childs* (AVD-1), describing discovering a force of six Japanese destroyers, one cruiser, and several transports strung out across the path his ship had intended to follow upon leaving Kendari, in early morning darkness on 24 January 1942. Later that day the Japanese Sasebo Special Naval Landing Force captured Kendari, Celebes, Dutch East Indies.[1]

The experiences and combat actions of *Childs*, from her movement south from the Philippines in December 1941 to the Dutch East Indies, operations there, and retirement to Australia in March 1942, are representative of other Wing Ten seaplane tenders as well. Operating in largely Japanese controlled areas, she was forced to move constantly between small islands, hiding during the day in rain squalls or next to the shore under canopy, and at night, under the cloak of darkness, stand out to sea to fuel and service patrol planes. By these means she was able to survive an encounter with a group of Japanese warships, and attacks by bombers and fighter aircraft.

DEPARTURE FROM THE PHILIPPINES

In darkness on Sunday night, 14 December, *Childs*—with the Wing commander and his staff and all the spare parts that could be gathered together on board, along with ammunition and so forth—sailed southward from Manila Bay. Finding the entrance to the channel through the defensive minefield leading out of the bay was difficult due to a lack of navigational aids. All the lights had been turned off. The seaplane tender's commanding officer, Comdr. John L. Pratt, knew the course through the channel, but it was fairly narrow. He was considering how he could traverse it in the dark when the person that was handling the searchlight on Corregidor (an island at the entrance to the bay) flashed the light just once on the entrance buoys and Pratt was able to steer a safe course. Passage through the channel required several turns; prior to each one, the searchlight flashed once on the buoys directly ahead. The timing of these actions was perfect, and the assistance provided could not have been better.[2]

In early afternoon on 15 December, *Childs* entered Cebu harbor at Cebu Island in the southern Philippines, and moored at the Standard Oil Docks. After being fueled she left there just after dark. (Details about this visit are covered in Chapter 1.) Like leaving Manila Bay, the channel going out was difficult to navigate without lights. Pratt was prepared to launch a boat to lead the ship through it when the beacon on the church in Cebu was turned on. Once clear of the harbor, the seaplane tender headed south through Surigao Strait and down past the Gulf of Davao. The Japanese were occupying this area of Mindanao for use as a base and their destroyers had been running in and out of there for days, but *Childs* had no difficulty in getting past in the dark. The *Heron*, *Langley*, and *William B. Preston* were at this time also headed south to Balikpapan.[3]

Back in the Manila Bay area, it had become apparent to the pilots and plane crews that with the Japanese aircraft controlling the skies, the enemy would eventually find and destroy the remaining units of Wing Ten. Accordingly, it was decided to consolidate as many patrol planes as possible at Lake Lanao (Malanao) on the island of Mindanao in the southern Philippines. The operational planes of VP-101 and 102 took flight on 15 December, leaving behind several pilots, and about a hundred seventy-five enlisted men and some enlisted pilots. The remnants of the Wing that reached the lake consisted of about twelve planes, augmented by two or three more the following day. This group remained at Mindanao for two days, awaiting orders from Capt. Frank D. Wagner, who was proceeding south aboard *Childs*.[4]

On 17 December, the planes were directed to proceed south and join up with the *Childs* at Manado on the northeast tip of the Celebes Islands group. During their stay at the lake, off-duty pilots and plane crews had enjoyed being housed at various local inns during some particularly severe weather. Those aboard planes on the water were hard pressed to prevent damage to the aircraft from wind and wave.

However, collectively Wing personnel found time for much needed rest and aircraft maintenance prior to their departure. While en route to Manado, new orders directed the group to proceed farther south to Balikpapan, which presented some challenges. The pilots lacked good charts of the area, requiring some guesswork on their part regarding proper flight headings. Moreover, they had no idea what recognition procedures would be required upon arrival, causing some concern they might be shot down. They also did not know what the port looked like from the air, or the condition of mooring facilities. Nevertheless, everything worked out all right.

Photo 6-1

Capt. Frank D. Wagner, USN (center) receiving the Distinguished Service Medal from the Secretary of the Navy, the Honorable Frank Knox, at left is Rear Adm. Randall Jacobs, USN, Chief of Bureau of Personnel. Wagner would be promoted to Rear Admiral after leaving command of Wing Ten, and subsequently serve as Deputy Chief of Naval Operations (Air) and Commander Air, Seventh Fleet, during the war. (Source: Bureau of Naval Personnel Information Bulletin, July 1942)

Lt. Comdr. John V. Peterson, commander Patrol Squadron 101, described in an interview in February 1944 the period spent at the lake and ensuing flight to Balikpapan:

> The group I was in command of at Lake Lanao had a very bad time during our stay there because of severe weather conditions

and a storm of almost hurricane force which nearly dashed all of our planes on the rocks. Our anchors would not hold and we only kept the planes out of danger by taxiing all night of the seventeen[th] and most of the next day.

Sometime prior to our arrival there, the Wing had placed considerable gasoline, oil and buoys in a shed at the Dansalan pier of Lake Lanao, so we were able to get a little rest here, repair some of our airplanes and generally make ready for the next jump.

We took off with 12 planes and two J2F's from Lake Lanao and headed for Manado early morning of the 18th of December. When we were about half way to Manado, I received a message from Commander Patrol Wing 10 stating that the *CHILDS* had been bombed by the Japanese in that area and that I was to proceed to Balikpapan and refuel from the *HERON* and *PRESTON* which should be there by this time.

We made good our landfall and landing and tied up to some buoys which the *HERON* had planted in that area. One of our planes had one bad engine and was forced to go to Manado with the two utility J2F's. This was not because they wanted to, but because the J2F's couldn't make the entire trip to Balikpapan [due to limited fuel capacity] and the bad engine on the one Catalina precluded him going any further than Manado. However, by the time these planes arrived at Manado the Japs had left and they were able to secure gasoline to make the jump to Balikpapan the next day where we rendezvoused.[5]

The planes remained in Balikpapan from 18-20 December. *Childs* rendezvoused with them there, and for the first time since the beginning of the war, Wing Ten had most of its force together, a total of sixteen aircraft: patrol planes *101-P-1*, *3*, *6*, *8*, *9*, and *11*; *102-P-23*, *25*, *26*, and *27*; four OS2Us and two J2Fs. Aviation mechanics changed the engine on PBY *102-P-23* and checked those of the other aircraft, ensuring readiness to proceed to Surabaya in force.[6]

CHILDS' BRIEF STOP AT MANADO BAY, CELEBES

The *Childs* had entered Manado Bay on Manado on 17 December to service Patrol Wing planes. As she stood into the bay, a sighting was made of several Dutch three-engine Dornier aircraft a short distance away. The first plane passed alongside, exchanged challenges, gave a big wave, and then flew off, followed by another plane and then another. They appeared to be very happy to see the seaplane tender. Another plane then showed up, a four-engine aircraft similar to a Sikorsky transatlantic plane that looked very much like a commercial aircraft. As the plane approached overhead on a parallel course, no markings could be seen. When abreast of *Childs*, the plane, which proved to be Japanese, turned and flew directly over the ship and bombs began falling around the tender. Pratt described the attack:

> Just as he got within about 300 yards and at an altitude of some 800 feet, very low, we saw Jap markings on him and at the same time he released his bombs.
>
> Our boys on the guns saw this at the same time and started shooting. They filled him full of lead and as he went over, you could see the details of the plane very closely. We saw the gun in the rear gunner's compartment fly up and evidentially they had killed the gunner. The plane was smoking somewhat and was badly hit but I believe that most of the shells that were fired from .50 calibers went in the plane a little too far aft to get the pilot, and he disappeared in the distance.
>
> The bombs [six or seven] fell about 300 yards, I guess 300 yards off our portside. It was a bad miss on his part, having come over at only 800 feet and having us cold turkey, but anyway they fell about 300 yards off to the side and off he went.[7]

RETIREMENT SOUTHWESTWARD TO SURABAYA

Following the enemy's discovery of *Childs* at Manado Bay, Wagner decided that it would be prudent for the ship to relocate some distance away from there, either to the south or the west. He elected to continue tender support at Balikpapan, about seven hundred miles to the west-southwest, and directed planes still en route to Manado Bay to proceed there instead. After servicing the PBY with the bad engine and two J2Fs, the seaplane tender left for Balikpapan in late afternoon. She was shadowed for the remainder of that day and the next morning by a Japanese submarine. Each time it showed up astern, the former destroyer increased speed sufficiently to remain clear of the threat.[8]

Childs arrived at Balikpapan Bay on 19 December, serviced patrol planes, and took on aviation gasoline and diesel from the fuel docks. She also gave supplies to *Heron*, similarly occupied with tending planes. *Langley* and *William B. Preston* had earlier departed Balikpapan bound for Makassar, a major seaport and trading center on the island of Celebes (now Sulawesi), in the Netherlands East Indies. Upon the completion of provisioning and providing services, *Childs* left en route to Surabaya, Java, at which the Asiatic Fleet was to base. Following arrival at the port city in late afternoon on the 21st, she moored alongside Holland Pier to fuel, load supplies, and provide crew liberty.[9]

Map 6-1

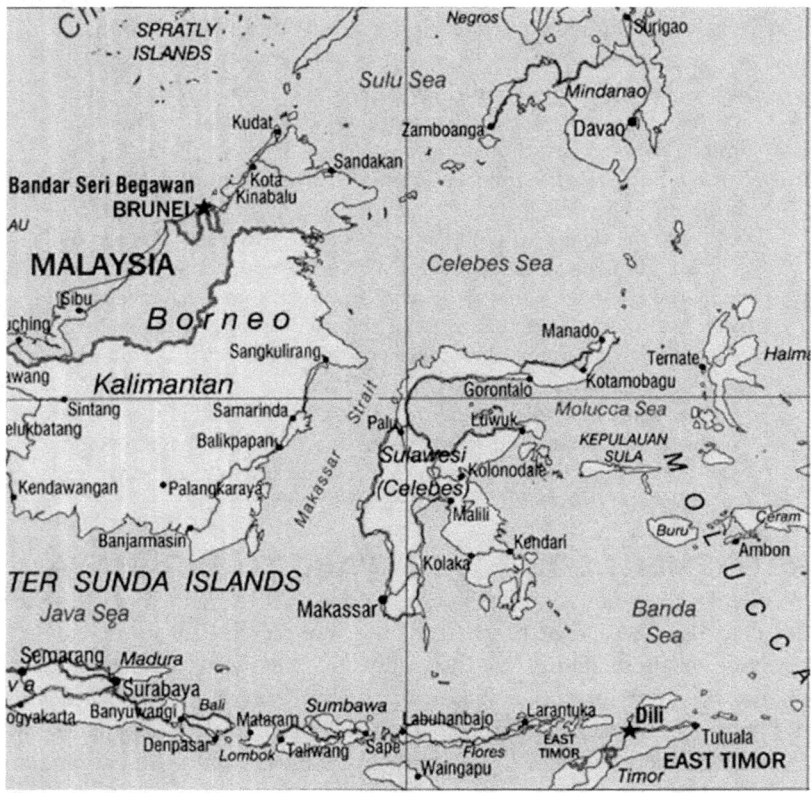

Netherlands (Dutch) East Indies; now Indonesia

In the coming days in late December, Rear Adm. William A. Glassford, commander Task Force 5 (the strike force of the Asiatic Fleet), set up a command post at Surabaya and held preliminary conferences with appropriate Dutch authorities. Thereafter, the task force would be organized into the ABDA striking force under Vice Adm. Conrad E. L. Helfrich of the Royal Netherlands Navy. The acronym ABDA reflected that the force was comprised of American, British, Dutch, and Australian elements. The ABDA Theater included the Dutch East Indies, Burma, the Philippines, the South China Sea, and the northeastern part of the Indian Ocean.[10]

Patrol Wing Ten set up headquarters at Air Base, Soerabaya (Surabaya) where it functioned for the remainder of the Java Sea Campaign. The ABDA deputy commander, Lt. Gen. George H. Brett, USAAF, chose Captain Wagner to command the American and Dutch seaplanes but eventually, due to pressure from the Dutch, put Kapitein ter Zee G. G. Bozuwa, head of the Dutch Naval air service, in charge. Wagner served as deputy of the Allied Air Reconnaissance Group, comprised of the Marineluchtvaartdienst/Royal Netherlands Naval Air Service, Patrol Wing Ten, and No. 205 Squadron, Royal Air Force.[11]

ABDA Command Structure

Supreme Commander	Field Marshall Sir Archibald Wavell, British Army
Deputy Commander	Lt. Gen. George H. Brett, U.S. Army Air Forces
Commander of land forces (ABDA Land)	Lt Gen. Hein ter Poorten, Netherlands East Indies Army
Commander of air forces (ABDA Air)	Air Chief Marshal Sir Richard E. C. Peirse, Royal Air Force
Commander of naval forces (ABDA Afloat) until 12 February 1942	Adm. Thomas C. Hart, United States Navy
ABDA Afloat after 12 February 1942	Adm. Conrad E. L. Helfrich, Royal Netherlands Navy

The main objective of the ABDA command was to maintain control of the "Malay Barrier" (or "East Indies Barrier"), a notional line running down the Malayan Peninsula, through Singapore and the southernmost islands of Netherlands (Dutch) East Indies. In short, to stop the advance of Japanese forces, which in late December were establishing themselves in the southern Philippines—at Davao on Mindanao, and to the southwest at Jolo, an island in the Sulu Archipelago within the Mindanao group—from which points they would later invade the Dutch East Indies. Davao and Jolo provided the Japanese airfields from which to launch attacks and set up parallel drives southward, one down through the Molucca Sea and another down the Makassar Strait.[12]

Adm. Thomas C. Hart, who would command the Allied naval forces, arrived at Surabaya from Manila Bay aboard the submarine *Shark* (SS-174) the evening of 1 January 1942. There, he found the command post of Task Force 5 established in the outskirts of the city in buildings which had been supplied by the Dutch Navy. The base facilities were considerable, but congested and quite vulnerable to attack from the air. In consideration of this, Glassford had sent the Asiatic Fleet's auxiliary ships, spares, munitions, and special supplies to Darwin, Australia, a very long distance to the southeast.[13]

PBY-4 CATALINAS ATTACK ENEMY SHIPS AT JOLO

Wing Ten's aircraft took flight from Balikpapan on 20 December for Surabaya, with the exception of *102-P-23*, which joined the others there the following day. In recognition of the Wing's aircraft losses in the Philippines, VP-101 and 102 were merged into one squadron under the command of Lt. Comdr. John V. Peterson. In a separate action, Lt. Jack C. Renard, who commanded the utility squadron, was detached from this duty to serve on Capt. Wagner's staff, and Lt. E. L. Phares, the executive officer, took over from him. For the first couple of days at Surabaya, Peterson and others were kept busy meeting with Dutch authorities, studying the geography of the country, and making provisions for the obtainment of replacement bombs, accessories and everything else they could get from the Dutch.[14]

After receiving orders to relocate to Ambon, a seaport on a same-named island a thousand miles northeast of Surabaya, the Catalinas began flight movements there on 23 December, in groups of three and four. By Christmas Day all usable PBYs had arrived at Ambon. The two J2Fs at Surabaya were hoisted aboard *Heron* and one of the four OS2Us taken aboard *Childs* for transport to Ambon. *Langley* took the remaining three OS2Us with her to Australia.[15]

In an effort to prevent enemy use of Jolo in the Philippines' Sulu Archipelago, six PBYs were sent on 26 December to make a daytime bombing attack on shipping while the Japanese were landing forces on and fortifying the island. The flight, led by Lt. Burden R. Hastings, USN, took off from Ambon in the late afternoon and arrived over the enemy naval force, consisting of a cruiser, destroyers and transports, off Jolo Harbor in early morning the following day. The pilots and plane crews had been briefed that there was a ship-to-shore landing taking place, but no fighter aircraft in the area. The latter information proved patently incorrect. Jolo was well protected by two dozen land-based Zero fighters, each more maneuverable and heavier armed than an ungainly, fabric-covered seaplane functioning as a patrol bomber.[16]

As the first section of three PBY-4s commenced a bombing run on a transport ship and a cruiser standing off the harbor, they were met by three Zeros. Hastings' plane (*P-1*) was shot down before reaching the drop point, and he and all but two of his crew were killed. (The Navy later awarded Hastings the Navy Cross - posthumously). The two survivors made it ashore on Jolo, and were found by Moros who turned them over to the Japanese. The men were subsequently publicly executed. As the remaining two planes (*P-6*, flown by Lt. (jg) Jack B. Dawley, USN, and *P-9* by Ens. Elwyn L. Christman, USNR) started their runs, they came under attack from Zeros, and were also subjected to ship and shore anti-aircraft battery and machine gun fire. Nevertheless, they pressed home their attacks and released their bombs over targets below. Reports later received by Patrol Wing Ten indicated that ships were hit and probably beached in that area due to damage incurred.[17]

Dawley piloted his Catalina (*P-6*) through heavy anti-aircraft fire and fighter opposition to deliver an attack on the cruiser. After enemy fire killed both the waist gunners aboard the flying boat, Aviation Machinist's Mate Second Evren C. McLawhorn manned the two guns alternately, refusing to abandon his post despite being wounded seven times. Following the ignition of ammunition cases aboard the plane by enemy gunfire, and despite the pain of his wounds, McLawhorn calmly jettisoned them. By this action, taken at the risk of his own life, he likely saved those of others.[18]

Dawley landed the damaged plane two hundred yards off Jolo's south shore. As soon as it hit the water, the surviving crewmembers jumped out and swam to the island. With his plane (*P-9*) aflame from damage inflicted on it by Japanese fighters, Christman had had to ditch in the Sulu Sea as well. However, he and the other surviving members of his plane crew were much worse off than those of *P-6*, because they came down well to the west of Jolo, necessitating a very long swim from the sinking plane. Both waist gunners had been killed and *P-9* lost another man who, wounded, drowned trying to make it to shore. In the days that followed, Dawley led his men and the survivors of *P-9* down through the Sulu Archipelago to Tarakan—a small marshy island off northeastern Borneo at which Dutch military forces were based.[19]

In preceding aero combat, waist gunner Aviation Machinist's Mate First Andrew K. Waterman had shot down one Zero and after being wounded had continued to fire at other Zeros until enemy bullets killed him. A second waist gunner, Aviation Machinist's Mate First Joseph Bangust, was also killed while firing at attacking fighter aircraft. Radioman First Robert L. Pettit, drowned during the thirty-hour swim made by the survivors to the nearest island. He also had been wounded in combat and, despite his wounds, had continued to carry out his duties after the aircraft was flooded with aviation gasoline from perforated tanks, which then caught fire. Chief Aviation Machinist's Mate Donald D. Lurvey saved the life of Ens. William V. Gough Jr., by returning to the burning plane to obtain a life ring for Gough, without which he would have perished. The chief then kept the pilot headed toward shore during the long swim, which Gough could not have done without assistance.[20]

76   Chapter 6

The group of nine survivors of the two PBYs was able to make a long, furtive boat voyage to Borneo through Japanese-controlled waters, by island hopping as much as possible. By this means the men were able to avoid open waters plied by enemy ships and aircraft. They first travelled in a vinta, then a lipa (indigenous craft paddled by natives), and finally in a diesel-powered, wooden launch, which had been condemned due to its leaky, rotten hull. Following many days of hardship and uncertainty about whether or not they would make it, the aviators sighted in late morning on 7 January the lightship marking the entrance to Tarakan Harbor. Sunbaked, attired in cast-off Moro clothing, and sporting heavy, 11-day beards, they identified themselves. Shortly thereafter the men were able to bath, shave, procure fresh clothing, and imbibe glasses of gin.[21]

The identities of the casualties and survivors of the bombing raid, along with a summary of the awards for valor received and the names of plane crew members, if known, are provided below. The acronym DFC refers to the Distinguished Flying Cross:

First Flight of PBY-4 Aircraft

Patrol Plane *P-1*

Lt. Burden R. Hastings, USN	Casualty	Navy Cross
Ens. R. F. Chambers, USNR	Casualty	
Ens. M. W. Miller Jr., USNR	Casualty	
ACMM Louie R. Erreca, USN	Casualty	
AMM1c Clyde H. Evans, USN	Casualty	
AMM3c Paul R. Moses, USN	Casualty	
CRM Clyde G. Parks, USN	Casualty	
RM1c Amon W. Gates, USN	Casualty	

Patrol Plane *P-6*

Lt. (jg) Jack Baldwin Dawley, USN	Survivor	Navy Cross
Ens. Ira W. Brown Jr., USNR	Survivor	DFC
AMM1c Dave W. Bounds, USN	Survivor	
AMM2c Evren C. McLawhorn, USN	Survivor	Navy Cross
AMM2c Earle B. Hall, USN	Casualty	
RM1c N. T. Whitford, USN	Survivor	
RM3c James M. Scribner, USN	Casualty	

Patrol Plane *P-9*

Lt. (jg) Elwyn L. Christman, USNR	Survivor	Navy Cross
Ens. William V. Gough Jr., USNR	Survivor	
ACMM Donald D. Lurvey, USN	Survivor	Navy Cross
AMM1c Andrew K. Waterman, USN	Casualty	Navy Cross
AMM1c Joseph Bangust, USN	Casualty	Navy Cross
RM3c Paul H. Landers, USN	Survivor	
RM1c Robert L. Pettit, USN	Casualty	Navy Cross

Second Flight of PBY-4 Aircraft

Patrol Plane *P-23*
Lt. John J. Hyland, USN
(No casualties among plane crew)

Patrol Plane *P-25*
Lt. (jg) Tomas E. L. McGabe, USN
(No casualties among plane crew)

Patrol Plane *P-11*
Lt. (jg) LeRoy C. Deede, USN	Survivor	DFC
Ens. Edgar Hazelton	Survivor	
AMM1c John Cumberland	Survivor	
RM2c Glen Dockery	Survivor	

(No casualties among plane crew; identities of other survivors unknown)[22]

The second section could not make bombing runs due to heavy fighter opposition. Lieutenant John J. Hyland, USN, led the section with Lieutenants (junior grade) Tomas E. L. McGabe, USN, and Leroy C. Deede, USN, piloting the other patrol planes. One of the planes was shot down and landed in the open sea south of Jolo. The other two jettisoned their bombs and returned to Ambon, the only PBYs of the bombing raid to survive the mission.[23]

Deede, his *P-11* crippled by anti-aircraft fire and opposed by Zeros, successfully evaded the enemy and landed at sea. For these actions and the downing of a Japanese fighter aircraft, he was awarded the Distinguished Flying Cross. So too was Lt. Duncan A. Campbell, USN, the plane commander of *P-3*, which rescued the crew of *P-11*.[24]

OPERATIONS AT AMBON, CORAM ISLANDS

Wing Ten operations during this period involved flights mainly over central and eastern Dutch East Indies waters. Patrol planes were widely dispersed, which made it difficult for the enemy to locate and destroy them on the water, and they made full use of the *Childs*, *Heron*, and *William B. Preston*. By virtue of the pilots' skill in using cloud cover to avoid contact with fighters, the planes were able to reconnoiter hostile waters and air space in the face of strong Japanese air forces.[25]

The *Childs* arrived at Ambon on 28 December and anchored in the bay, and Commander Pratt went ashore to report to Captain Wagner. Lt. Comdr. Clarence A. Keller Jr., USN, also arrived about this time with four planes. He reported to the senior naval officer, Captain Hecking, Royal Netherlands Navy, and also to Wing Commander Scott, Royal Australian Air Force. He received tasking to conduct patrols north-northwest of Ambon up the Molucca Passage toward the Celebes Sea. Thereafter, PBYs carried out searches of the passage, up to about latitude two degrees north and also patrolled northward into the Halmahera Sea. One Hudson light bomber accompanied each pair of Catalinas on patrols. The Royal Australian Air Force (RAAF) coastal reconnaissance aircraft had exceptional maneuverability for a twin-engine plane, and contributed much-desired combat capabilities, having more guns and a larger weapons load than the PBYs.[26]

All of the units of the Asiatic Fleet that travelled south from the Philippines reached the waters of the Dutch East Indies without much damage, except for the destroyer *Peary* and the seaplane tender *Heron*. *Peary* was attacked by three RAAF Hudson bombers after an Australian PBY on patrol misidentified her as Japanese. The *Heron* was sent from Ambon to provide assistance to *Peary*. After failing to locate her, the seaplane tender began the return transit to Ambon during which she came under a series of enemy aircraft attacks. *Heron* reached port on 1 January 1942, battered and with two men dead and half of her crew wounded. This action is described in Chapter 1.[27]

Shortly thereafter, Lt. Comdr. John V. Peterson, commander VP-101, assumed the additional duties of commander, Patrol Wing Ten from Captain Wagner. This made sense as Peterson was located with the Wing's aircraft at Ambon. Wagner continued to serve at Surabaya as commander Aircraft, Asiatic Fleet, and on 15 January 1942, he also assumed duties as deputy commander, Air Reconnaissance Group under ABDA Air.[28]

Patrol Squadron 101 planes carried out attacks in the Molucca Passage against Japanese transports and ships engaged in amphibious movement and landings in the area of Manado on Celebes Island. However, these efforts only slowed the establishment of an enemy air base within striking range of Ambon. Once it became operational, the squadron received almost a daily bombing and working over from Japanese land-based planes, which included the loss of VP-22 aircraft sent to Ambon from Hawaii to augment VP-101. Peterson explained:

> At first they attacked us with seaplanes. Later the attacks came most any time. This curtailed our operations somewhat. However, we continued to carry out our patrol in that area. On 9 and 10 January, we were reinforced by Squadron 22, which had flown out from Pearl Harbor. This group had PBY5 airplanes, but did not have self-sealing gas tanks or armor in their aircraft. Unfortunately, two of these planes upon their rendezvous with us at Ambon flew right into a Japanese attack on Ambon and were destroyed the first day.[29]

GRAVE RISKS TO SHIPS ALSO EXIST AT AMBON

Recurrent air attacks against Ambon obviously also presented much danger to any ships present at Ambon, and Commander Pratt believed that *Childs* was in danger of being sunk in the harbor. Particularly after he witnessed on 7 January 1942, what appeared to be a flare over the Ambon Bay seaplane base at Halong followed by a salvo of bombs dropped from a group of five to seven Japanese planes over Laha Airfield. Pratt also received a report that enemy aircraft had bombed the barracks at Ambon, apparently guided in by a native sergeant who was shot while he was setting a signal flare near the structures. There had been suspicions that such a thing had occurred during previous bombing raids, but this was the first time someone had been caught in the act.[30]

Pratt shifted the seaplane tender to a spot along the beach in the inner harbor where there was a steep bank and water deep enough to work her in against it. Once the ship was moored, related actions were undertaken to hide *Childs* from the view of enemy aircraft:

> By putting out a stern anchor we...hauled her in parallel to the bank and tied her up to the trees on the bank and after that we began to camouflage her. The crew went ashore and cut down small trees out of the jungle and hauled them aboard by lines and we completely covered the ship with trees and foliage and ferns and so forth.
>
> After this stuff had dried out, this camouflage had dried out, the ship smelled like a large spice pantry, because we hadn't realized we were in the Spice Islands and most of these trees and their foliage that was put on the ship were such things as nutmeg, and cinnamon, etc. A very delightful odor that permeated the ship at all times.[31]

The seaplane tender's crew was not overworked in ensuing days because a little air station set up on the opposite side of the inner harbor provided most of the patrol plane support. Aircraft directed to *Childs* for service would approach the little camouflaged island by taxiing along the shore until they could move under the leafy roof rigged over the ship. In this way, the planes were well concealed during the time in which they were being fueled or serviced. And, the hideout proved its worth. Japanese aircraft bombed Ambon, but did not attack the tender. She may not have been considered an important enough target, but in any case the officers and men aboard her were able to watch the bombings from their leafy bower with considerable confidence in their safety.[32]

On 9 January 1942, *William B. Preston* arrived at Ambon for an overnight stop before departing for Kendari in the Staring Bay area of the Celebes. *Childs* left Ambon the same day the *Preston* arrived, having been ordered to Surabaya. Ship movement in the open sea could be potentially very dangerous for her, because she possessed neither radar nor sound gear (sonar) and had to depend entirely on visual sighting to detect enemy ships or aircraft. She did usually carry one Kingfisher observation floatplane between her two after boats. The small aircraft could be hoisted aboard very nicely, and was of great value for reconnaissance. Following a report of smoke on the horizon, *Childs* dodged into an indentation of a nearby island. Sporting a coat of dark green paint, she blended well with the jungle backdrop. Pratt described finding, after creeping out of the island sanctuary, that the producer of the smoke was an innocuous merchantman, and not an enemy warship:

> I went up on the forecastle and sat with my legs astride the jackstay with a pair of binoculars and coached the Officer of the Deck in bringing the ship out of this little bay very slowly so that we could see around the point and we sat there with the bow just barely protruding beyond the point searching the area and watching for this ship that we had seen. Soon she showed up and we saw that she was a merchant steamer and then we went on our way.[33]

Elsewhere on 9 January, a Japanese invasion force commanded by Rear Adm. Hirose Sueto sortied from Davao on Mindanao bound for Tarakan, Borneo, a day's journey away. The force consisted of sixteen transports, four minesweepers, and two seaplane tenders carrying 2 Kure Special Naval Landing Force, 2 Base Force, and elements of 56 Independent Mixed Brigade. The transports were screened by a strong escort of four light cruisers and fifteen destroyers, and 21 Air Flotilla provided air cover. Tarakan Island, then part of the Dutch East Indies, fell to the enemy three days later on 12 January. Soon thereafter, elements of the Tainan Air Group arrived to provide air support for planned continual Japanese movements south. Samuel Eliot Morison artfully described the strategy that Japanese military forces would employ in their conquest of the Netherlands East Indies:

> The manner of the Japanese advance resembled the insidious yet irresistible clutching of multiple tentacles. Like some vast octopus it relied on strangling many small points rather than concentrating on a vital organ. No one arm attempted to meet the entire

strength of the Abda fleet. Each fastened on a small portion of the enemy and, by crippling him locally, finished by killing the entire animal...

The Japanese spread their tentacles cautiously, never extending beyond the range of land-based aircraft unless they had carrier support. The distance of each advance was determined by the radius of fighter planes from airfields under their control. This range was generally less than 400 miles, but the Japanese made these short hops in surprisingly rapid succession. Amphibious operations, preceeded by air strikes and covered by air power, developed with terrifying regularity. Before the Allies had consolidated a new position, they were confronted with a system of air bases from which enemy aircraft operated on their front, flanks and even rear.[34]

Having captured Tarakan, Balikpapan with its rich oilfields and strategically important airfields was the next target of the Japanese sweep southward. The 56th Mixed Infantry Group under Maj. Gen. Shizuo Sakaguchi had orders to take Balikpapan with as little damage as possible to its oilfields, oil installations and airfields. Units of the Asiatic Fleet tried to prevent this action. On 23 January, Destroyer Division 59—*John D. Ford* (DD-288), *Paul Jones* (DD-230), *Parrot* (DD-218), and *Pope* (DD-225)—entered Balikpapan Bay under the cover of darkness. Lying at anchor were sixteen Japanese transports and three torpedo boats.[35]

The destroyers fired several patterns of torpedoes, sinking four of the transports and one torpedo boat as Japanese destroyers assigned to cover the landing searched in the adjacent Makassar Strait for non-existent Allied submarines. These enemy ship losses did not prove an impediment as almost all the troops aboard the transports had already been transferred to landing craft. The Japanese assault unit landed without meeting resistance and by dawn had taken the airfield. From there it advanced southward and occupied Balikpapan City the night of the 25th. Dutch garrison troops had withdrawn and the Japanese entered the city without a fight.[36]

Map 6-2

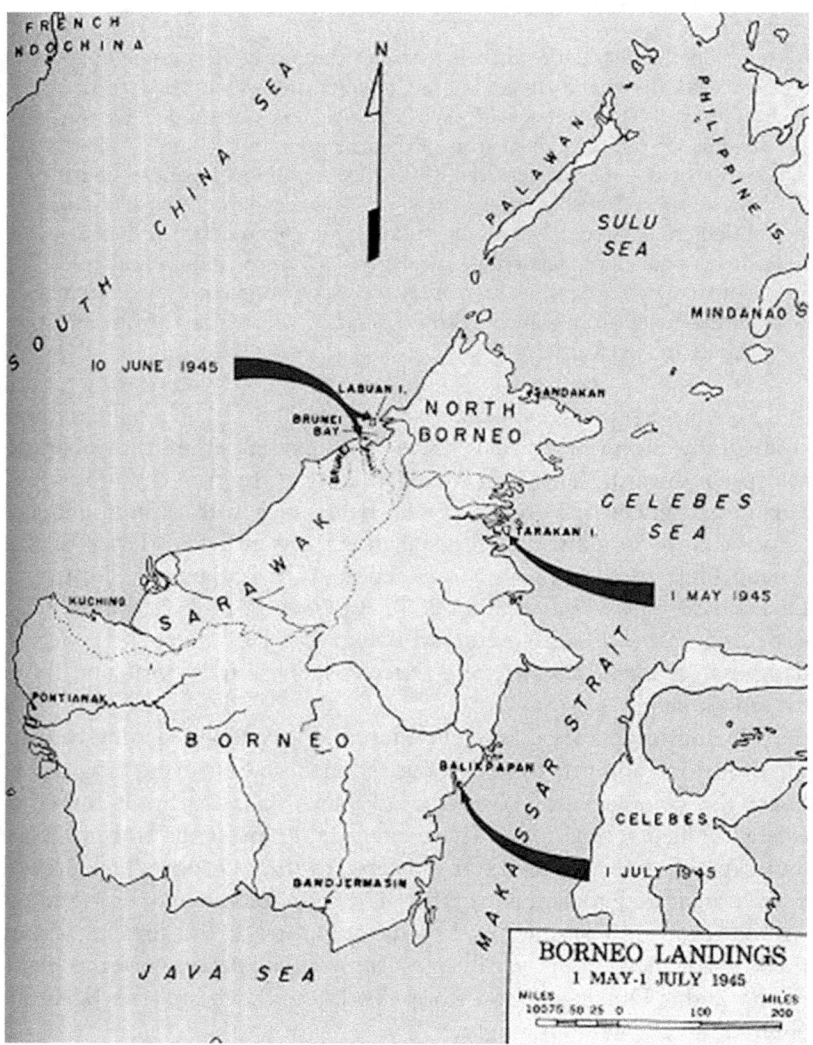

Oil rich and strategically important areas of Borneo (Tarakan Island, Brunei Bay, Labuan Island, and Balikpapan) captured by Japanese forces early in the war, which Allied forces retook between 1 May and 1 July 1945.
Source: http://www.lib.utexas.edu/maps/historical/engineers_v1_1947/borneo_landings_1945.jpg

FALL OF AMBON

Wing Ten continued to fly patrols from Ambon until mid-January 1942, when the area became untenable. Peterson had been ordered to Surabaya on 11 January, following his relief by Lt. Comdr. Edgar T. Neale as commander Ambon Group. A few days later, there was a heavy air raid on Ambon. Twenty-six Japanese bombers escorted by ten fighters arrived overhead in early afternoon on 15 January and dropped many bombs. Two Dutch Brewster F2A Buffaloes bravely attempted to intercept the flight. The largely obsolete fighter aircraft, being unstable and overweight, were shot down. Two PBY Catalinas (No. *7* and *8*) landed on the water and were immediately attacked. Both were damaged and beached, but suffered no personnel fatalities. A third patrol plane (No. *10*) was also damaged. The following day, Peterson ordered Patrol Squadron 101 to evacuate Ambon, following which Neale with four PBYs took flight for Surabaya.[37]

Peterson described the squadron's final days at Ambon, and patrol operations staged thereafter from a number of island areas:

> We could not operate there because we were almost always under continuous observation, bombardment or strafing. The Japanese had soon disposed of the Dutch fighters and were continuously attacking the Australian Hudsons and our Catalinas on patrol. We then started a mobile operation from the following bases: Kendari in the Staring Bay area in the Celebes, the Taninbar Islands group, Koepang in Timor, Soemba Islands, Flores Islands and Darwin, North Australia, as well as operating the patrols from Surabaya.
>
> Ambon was abandoned on 26 January, and those planes which were left in good condition were brought to Surabaya or Darwin. The tenders, the *CHILDS*, *HERON* and *PRESTON* continued to base two or three planes at a time at the various islands I have just mentioned. Usually they stayed in one area about two or three days, fueling the planes at night and while the planes were on patrol they stood out to sea so that they would have maneuvering room in case of an attack. This was about the only way we could exist and carry out patrols in this area as the Japs moved south.[38]

Three Japanese battalions landed at Ambon on 30 January 1942, and after four days of bitter fighting, forced the inadequately prepared and under-equipped Australian and Dutch forces on the island to surrender. The Australian "Gull Force" of about 1,100 men had arrived in Ambon on 17 December 1941, after a three-day trip from Darwin. It comprised the 2/21st Battalion, which was part of the 23rd Brigade, 8th Australian Division, together with anti-tank, engineer, medical and other detachments. Their orders were to join Netherlands East Indies troops—about 2,500 men, some of the best units of the NEI army—to help defend the Bay of Ambon and airfields at Laha and Liang. During combat with the Japanese, some small groups of soldiers escaped and made their way back to Australia. However, almost 800 surviving Australians and about 300 Dutch were captured and held as prisoners of war in their former barracks at Tan Tui, north of Ambon town. Nine months later, about 500 of these prisoners were transferred on 25 October to a camp at Bakli Bay on Hainan, an island off mainland China in the South China Sea.[39]

CHILDS' RETURN TO SURABAYA

After leaving Ambon on 9 January, and reaching Surabaya on 12 January, the *Childs* entered the Navy Yard to have some improvements made to render her a little less vulnerable to air attack. There were no proper materials at hand, but the Dutch were very cooperative. Shipyard workers shaped some boiler plate, the strongest material available, to serve as splinter shields around the .50-caliber guns and provide gunners at least some protection from bomb fragments. They also removed the obsolete gun director above the bridge for the purpose of weight compensation and stored it ashore. Following its removal, reinforcing steel was laid on the deck above the bridge and covered with poured cement to provide additional protection for the bridge team. Cement blocks about three inches thick, eighteen inches long and a foot wide were fabricated and packed in around the bridge to serve as a splinter shield. Lastly, the main mast was taken down and the foremast cut off to make the ship more stealthy. The masts had been quite high and could be seen at a considerable distance.[40]

DELIVERY OF AVIATION FUEL TO KENDARI

Childs left Surabaya on 20 January with 30,000 gallons of 100 octane gasoline in her tank as well as a deck load of gasoline drums bound for Kendari, about six hundred nautical miles east-northeast of Surabaya. The drums of highly flammable gasoline piled all over her upper decks made the crew uneasy. They knew they were headed north and that their ship was much more flammable than usual. Seaplane tenders were often referred to as firecrackers, and this one, with the extra load of gasoline, was now more or less a giant firecracker and headed into enemy territory. *Childs* was to get the drums to the airfield on Kendari for use by Army bombers, which after launching from Java airfields had to refuel prior to flying strikes against Davao on Mindanao. The bombing run from Java to Davao and back was just a little bit too long for the B17s. Pratt had been briefed that the mission could be "a bit ticklish" because the Japanese were very near Kendari and that he would have to use every means available to escape detection.[41]

The *William B. Preston* had visited Kendari earlier and reported to Wing Ten on 13 January that it was not a suitable base for planes without a tender, that one Japanese scout plane had been sighted there, and that two USN patrol planes from Surabaya and one from Ambon had arrived there. Leaving Kendari, the seaplane tender made her way to Kebola Bay, Alor Island, the largest of a same named island chain north of Koepang (now Kupang), Timor. Two PBYs of Patrol Squadron 22 took flight from Surabaya on 18 January to join her.[42]

Childs reached Kendari on 21 January via a narrow, winding passage and anchored in the bay. Arrangements were made to begin unloading immediately, and a lot of gasoline was discharged that night. At daylight the following morning, Pratt moved his ship alongside a bank in the channel through which she had entered the bay. After mooring, the crew covered her completely with trees, scrubs, palms and ferns as they had done in Ambon. The quality of their efforts was proven later that day when two Japanese reconnaissance planes came over at a very low altitude and apparently failed to sight the seaplane tender.[43]

Around dusk, *Childs* left her hiding place and moved back to the unloading site, where she continued discharging gasoline This work lasted throughout the night. The seaplane tender got underway shortly before dawn on the 24th, and proceed out the channel. Upon clearing it at 0530 she encountered a force of six Japanese destroyers, one cruiser, and several transports strung out across her intended path. After studying the enemy ships carefully Pratt turned to his executive officer, who was also viewing them with his binoculars, and asked him "Sam, do you see what I see?" Sam looked at him, grinned, and said nonchalantly, "Tsh! Tsh! Tsh!" At about this time one of the destroyers flashed a challenge to the tender with a searchlight. When queried by the signalman on watch regarding the proper response, Pratt directed him to answer it with the same signal they had received.[44]

While Pratt wondered whether or not this reply would placate the enemy, a heavy rain squall developed and slowly approached *Child*'s starboard bow from across the bay. Just as the Japanese started challenging again, the squall covered the ship. Recognizing that his ship had precious little time to escape almost certain destruction, Pratt took rapid actions:

We immediately speeded up to 25 knots and ran at this speed for three or four miles over to the southern shore of the bay. And when we ran out of rain we were under cover of the high bluff that formed the southern bank.

The ship was painted dark green and furthermore we had stretched a dark green tarpaulin, which is a large piece of canvas, over the stacks. It had been pulled up somewhat in the manner of a sail to disguise the silhouette of the ship. All of this blended in very well with the jungle and we felt reasonably safe when four more destroyers were reported on our port bow, heading directly toward us. These came on at a high rate of speed and the ship went into her regular General Quarters routine, namely the gunnery officer commenced calling down the ranges for use to open fire and the [fire] hoses were led out on deck and turned on, the magazines were opened up.

These destroyers kept on coming, the range dropping slowly until the range got down to 12,000 yards, at which point they turned, went into column and steered on [passed] by on our port hand. They hadn't seen us against the background of this green jungle.[45]

Having escaped detection, Pratt proceeded very slowly to the southern headland, eased the seaplane tender around the promontory and rang up full speed. After running for about fifteen minutes, three Zeros appeared and began staffing her. The ship's guns opened fire and repulsed the attack, and the planes pulled off. Pratt then set a course to the northeast to try to get around behind the Japanese. About twenty minutes later while headed for the open sea, three more Zeros attacked the ship. Anti-aircraft fire from the seaplane tender brought down the leader of the group and the other two planes retired. Following this second attack Pratt set a course for the Tukang Besi Islands across the Banda Sea.[46]

Upon reaching the islands, *Childs* coasted slowly through them trying to hide until darkness, because Pratt knew the cruiser previously encountered would have one of its scout planes out searching for his ship. Sure enough a scout plane showed up around 1415. The aircraft circled slowly overhead and then made a bombing run. Pratt ordered a hard turn just as the plane released its bombs and they missed badly. There was great interest in watching the plane depart because, if it began descending the cruiser was nearby and would soon be upon them. However, the plane kept its altitude as it headed northwest indicating the parent ship was still some distance away. *Childs* ran southeast at high speed until nightfall, and then changed course and headed for Java. After arriving at Surabaya, she remained through month's end. New orders on 30 January directed relocation of the tender eastward for the purpose of operating aircraft from dispersal bases at various islands.[47]

The first bombing attack of Surabaya occurred on 3 February. The Dutch fighters in the area were beaten in combat and mostly lost in the air and then, as was common, Japanese aircraft directed a majority of their efforts at air installations. The enemy also caught and destroyed a considerable number of aircraft on the ground, but no U.S. Navy planes were lost. PBY aircrews had fully learned about the dangers to themselves if they were found where enemy fighter aircraft expected them to be. The availability of support from the tenders permitted frequent changes in seaplane bases of operations, which was their salvation and allowed them to continue reconnaissance work in the face of strong enemy forces.[48]

As it turned out, *Childs* had cleared Kendari on 24 January just as a Japanese expeditionary force arrived to occupy the island. As the enemy continued to advance southward, Allied ships did considerable running in February to lay down gasoline along the "Malay Barrier." The fuel was for U.S. Army Air Force planes that were to be ferried by sea from Darwin to Java for its defense. The *Langley*—which would sail on 22 February from Fremantle, Australia, for Tjilitjap, Java, and would be sunk by Japanese bombers en route there—was one of the ships thus employed. Details about her loss and that of the fleet oiler *Pecos* are taken up in the following chapter.[49]

SERIES OF TEMPORARY SEAPLANE BASES

Childs arrived at Timor on 1 February, anchored, and fueled some Dutch planes and two of the Wing's. From Timor, she made her way to Soemba, one of the Lesser Sunda Islands. Pratt recalled challenges posed by a night arrival and expressed his admiration for the planes awaiting the tender which, despite having to taxi the reef-infested waters, were able to find her in the dark:

> We went in there at night and it was rather difficult to find an anchorage…. We put out a small motor launch, the Exec[utive Officer] got in the motor launch and he went slowly ahead, sounding [continuously monitoring the water depth with a lead line] until he got to a point where the bottom shoaled off and there we dropped our anchor. In the morning we found ourselves about a quarter of a mile from the beach.

Our planes were already there and they found us in the dark, how they did it, I don't know, because that part of the bay was filled with reefs and it was a nice bit of seamanship on the part of the planes to get out to us. But we managed to secure them, put out buoys for them, [and] give them gasoline.[50]

The following morning, *Childs* got underway and proceeded to Waworada Bay at Sumbawa, another of the Lesser Sunda Islands. After setting up an advance base in the slender bay facing the Indian Ocean and putting out mooring buoys, PBYs came in and were fueled. They then began conducting patrols, flying northward to discover and report on any enemy activities in that area.[51]

Map 6-3

Lesser Sunda Islands comprised of a string of volcanic islands stretching eastward from Java toward northwest Australia. The Greater Sunda Islands include Sumatra, Java, Borneo, and Celebes.

Japanese reconnaissance planes came over the bay daily and the only way the tender could avoid detection was to run about fifty miles out to sea each morning. If a dark cloud developed near her and produced a line squall, she would hide in it and drift with the rain as much as possible during the day. In early evening, *Childs* would head back to the bay to find the planes awaiting her. She would commence servicing them and changing pilots. Plane crews would also be fed, aircraft refueled, and minor engine work performed such as changing spark plugs and oil.[52]

The PBY pilots had mastered taking off from small harbors or island indentations at night, assisted by ship's force personnel. Signalmen aboard *Childs* trained searchlight beams down the side of the tender so that the pilots could see the ship clearly, and if they still had difficulty finding the designated takeoff point, a boat was sent out from the ship to serve as a guidepost.[53]

ALLIED SHIPS DAMAGED IN MAKASSAR STRAIT

Meanwhile, *Childs* received new orders sending her to Tjilatjap, a harbor on the southern side of Java. While en route there she passed the damaged cruiser *Marblehead* (CL-12) and *Houston* (CA-30). Seeing them out of commission caused consternation among her crew, as these were the two largest and most capable warships of the Asiatic Fleet.[54]

Dutch Rear Adm. Karel Doorman, aboard his flagship the Dutch light cruiser De Ruyter, had received a report of an aircraft sighting of three Japanese cruisers, several destroyers, and about twenty transports near the southern entrance to Makassar Strait. Wasting no time, he had led the ABDA Striking Force out of Bunda Roads, Madura Island (near Surabaya) at midnight on 4 February. The force was capable, comprised of three cruisers—*Houston* and *Marblehead*, and Dutch cruiser *Tromp*—and eight destroyers—*Barker* (DD-213), *Bulmer* (DD-222), *John D. Edwards* (DD-216), and *Stewart* (DD-224), and four Dutch destroyers including *Banckert*, *Piet Hein*, and *Van Ghent*. A glaring weakness was lack of supporting air cover to protect it from enemy aircraft. Four valiant Dutch flying boats came to provide their assistance, but would all be shot down by Japanese fighter aircraft in the ensuing battle.[55]

The Allied naval force was attacked later that morning by a group of twin-engine Nells. These aircraft were units of the Japanese Eleventh Air Fleet operating from newly captured Kendari. At 0949 a sighting was made of four groups of nine bombers each approaching from the east at about 17,000 feet. The Allied ships scattered to allow each to bring more weapons to bear on the threat, but the bombers focused their efforts on the cruisers. *Marblehead* was hit by three bombs, and would have sunk but for the extraordinarily courageous and effective actions of her crew. *Houston* lost her after gun turret and suffered heavy personnel casualties—sixty men killed. Dropped bombs straddled the *De Ruyter*, knocking out her fire control system.[56]

Childs arrived at Tjilatjap on Sunday, 8 February, camouflaged the ship and for the next two weeks took care of a group of British Catalinas and serviced planes of Wing Ten. Her duties as general aviation headquarters for the port came to an end on 21 February, when she was ordered to Cocos, because of fears that Tjilatjap would soon be bombed. Cocos, one of the Keeling Islands, lay southwest of Christmas Island about midway between Australia and Sri Lanka.[57]

That same day, Australian, British, Dutch, and American ships began searching for Japanese forces which might be attempting to make landings in the Java area, and to give what opposition they could to the enemy advance. The Allied naval forces were then operating under a new commander. Admiral Thomas C. Hart had turned over command of ABDA Afloat to Dutch Admiral Conrad E. L. Helfrich at Lembang, a town in west Java, on 14 February 1942.[58]

7

Australia's "Pearl Harbor"

> *The scenes in the harbour during the raid were horrific, with ships on fire, oil and debris everywhere, ships sinking, and ships run aground. The merchant ship* Neptuna *was berthed alongside the wharf. It received a direct hit and blew up. The tremendous explosion was ear-shattering and sent debris flying up to half a kilometre.* Neptuna *had been loaded with depth charges and ammunition.*
>
> —Stoker 2nd Class Charlie Unmack, an engineer aboard the minesweeper HMAS *Gunbar*, describing the carnage vested by a Japanese air raid on Darwin, Australia, on 19 February 1942.[1]

In late morning on 19 February 1942, as the 480-ton minesweeper HMAS *Gunbar* stood out of Darwin, a seaport in northern Australia on the Timor Sea, a group of her sailors were off duty and topside enjoying the scenery. Suddenly, they sighted a formation of planes approaching over East Head. As sunlight glinted off the aircraft, the men commented on the good formation they were keeping. Years later, Charlie Unmack recalled the approach of what would prove to be Japanese planes and the ensuing attack on the ships and shore facilities at Darwin:

> At first we thought these planes were ours, and then we noticed some silver-looking objects dropping from them. It was not long before we knew what they were as they exploded in smoke and dust on the town and waterfront. More Japanese planes came in from another direction. These were dive bombers, and they attacked the ships in the harbour. We saw a couple of planes crash into the sea. I thought they were ours.
> Then it was our turn for some attention. They began strafing us from almost mast height. As the only armament we had against aircraft was a Lewis machine gun, and this had been disabled by a Japanese bullet hitting the magazine pan, the skipper was firing at them with his .45 revolver. This strafing went on for approximately half an hour before my first taste of action ended. Our casualties were nine wounded out of a crew of thirty-six, and

one of these died on the hospital ship [HMAHS] *Manunda* on the following day. The skipper had both knees shattered by Japanese bullets.²

The attack on *Gunbar* was only a very small part of the action that day from 188 Japanese planes launched against Darwin. Throughout the first attack, horizontal bombers from land bases concentrated, in the main, on fixed targets as dive bombers from carriers in the Timor Sea attacked ships in the bay. The first attack and one that followed were led by Comdr. Mitsuo Fuchida. He was experienced in this role, having headed the first wave of aircraft in the attack on Pearl Harbor eleven weeks earlier. The air raid on Darwin was the largest Japanese attack since Pearl Harbor, and the first time since European settlement that mainland Australia had been attacked by a foreign enemy.³

Being the largest town in Northern Australia and situated on the Timor Sea, Darwin was a key defensive position against an expected invasion by Japan. To help guard against this possibility Australia had developed its military ports and airfields, built coastal batteries and anti-aircraft guns and steadily enlarged its garrison of troops. The Japanese viewed Darwin as a key port for the Allied ships, planes and forces defending the Dutch East Indies. Over the course of the war, Nipponese pilots would fly sixty-four raids on Darwin and thirty-three raids on other targets in Northern Australia.⁴

During the attacks against Darwin on 19 February, Japanese fighter aircraft strafed land targets and shipping as dive bombers attacked ships in the harbor, the military and civilian aerodromes and the hospital. The dive bombers were escorted by fighter planes to protect them from allied planes. The only air defenses the Allies had were ten fighter planes. Only one of these survived engagements with enemy fighters during the first attack, in which the Japanese suffered only one or two aircraft losses. The second air raid shortly after noon concentrated mainly on the Royal Australian Air Force base and its airstrip.⁵

WILLIAM B. PRESTON DAMAGED; *PEARY* SUNK

The *William B. Preston* was anchored in the east arm of Darwin Harbor that morning, with her crew following the normal shipboard routine. Earlier, patrol planes had been sent out on assigned missions, and the crew mustered at 0800. Following muster, a working party of nineteen men had left the ship. The commanding officer, Lt. Comdr. Etheridge Grant, also went ashore to arrange for a delivery of much needed fuel and gasoline to the seaplane tender.⁶

Photo 7-1

William B. Preston (AVD-7) under way during the Japanese air raid on Darwin.
U.S. Naval History and Heritage Command Photograph #NH 43658

Morning activities were altered at 0950 by the sudden appearance of Japanese aircraft. Twenty minutes later, the seaplane tender was attacked by dive bombers as she zigzagged toward open sea. Her executive officer, Lt. Comdr. Lester O. Wood, USN, had slipped the anchor chain and gotten under way in order to be able to dodge falling bombs. It was ship's policy to keep the main engines warmed up in advance areas, enabling almost immediate use of propulsion plant machinery. At 1010, while making over 20 knots and in a right turn, *William B. Preston* and the destroyer *Peary* were attacked by four dive bombers. The tender had available for self-defense, in addition to her four permanently mounted .50-caliber machine guns, another five .50s and four .30-caliber guns salvaged from destroyed airplanes, mounted throughout the ship. As the planes dove at an angle of about thirty degrees with their wheels down, .50-caliber fire caused two aircraft to turn away, but the remaining two persisted in their attack.[7]

Multiple bombs from one of the planes hit the *Peary* and flames immediately enveloped her. The first one exploded on her fantail; the second, an incendiary bomb, on her galley deckhouse; the third did not explode; the fourth hit forward and set off ammunition magazines; and the fifth, another incendiary, exploded in her after engine room. A .30-caliber machine gun on her after deckhouse and a .50-caliber gun on the galley deckhouse valiantly continued to fire throughout the attack, but provided little deterrence. Eighty men aboard the destroyer were killed in the attack, another thirteen were wounded, and in early afternoon, the *Peary* sank stern first.[8]

Map 7-1

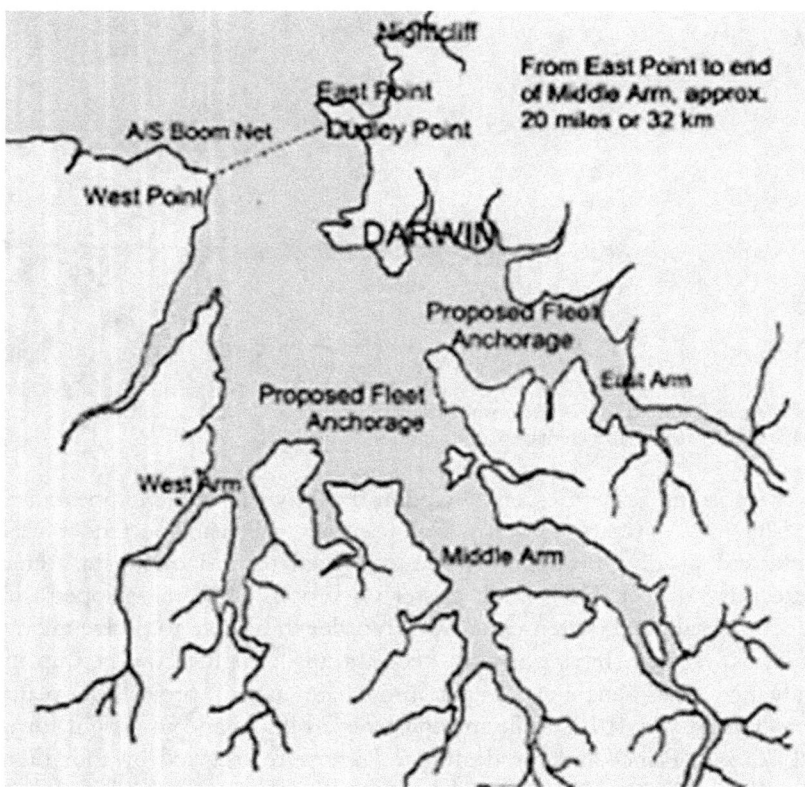

During Australia's "Pearl Harbor" on 19 February 1942, the *William B. Preston* cleared her anchorage in the east arm of Darwin Harbour and sped toward open water to gain sea room necessary to dodge aircraft bombs.
Chart is from the article "Fixed Naval Defences in Darwin Harbour 1939 – 1945" by Pat Forster, http://www.navy.gov.au/history/feature-histories/fixed-naval-defences-darwin-harbour-1939-1945

A bomb from the second plane hit the *William B. Preston*, portside, just forward of the after deckhouse and detonated; another was a near miss off her port quarter. The bomb that struck her demolished the auxiliary radio room and battery shop, knocked the after 4-inch gun out of action, blasted one large hole in the main deck and several small holes, and carried away the wheel ropes and steam lines to the steering engine. Shrapnel riddled the stacks, gasoline bowser, after searchlight, and deck locker. The blast had caused hull seams aft to open and this derangement and entry of water from a bomb-fragment hole in the ship's bottom, necessitated continuous pumping to keep her afloat.[9]

Of immediate concern was the spread of fire resulting from the bomb-blast. Lt. Eugene C. Rider, USN, was at his battle station on the galley deckhouse directing the actions of the anti-aircraft battery when his sighted flames in the vicinity of the after deckhouse. Recognizing that the executive officer, whose battle station would normally have been aft with the damage control party, was on the bridge, and all but one of the after repair party had been killed by the blast, he went aft to supervise fighting the fire. The blaze was in the immediate vicinity of 30,000 gallons of fuel oil and fifty 500-pound bombs. Additionally, ammunition (4-inch shells) inside the nearby ship's pyrotechnic locker had detonated and the locker was already on fire. Rider quickly organized the personnel in the vicinity, and directed their efforts toward isolating and extinguishing the blaze in the face of continued strafing attacks. He later received the Silver Star Medal for his heroic actions.[10]

Four of the twelve crewmembers who were killed (or who later died as a result of wounds sustained that day) were awarded Silver Star Medals posthumously. Within a few minutes after the general quarters alarm sounded that morning, ammunition party members Machinist's Mate Second Harvey E. Oswald and Fireman First Floyd D. Parks had, on their own initiative, manned a machine gun and opened fire on the enemy, helping force some of the attackers to keep their distance. Oswald and Parks lost their lives a short time later when the bomb struck the ship. Chief Machinist's Mate Eugene Blair and Metalsmith Second LeRay Wilson also lost their lives taking actions that potentially saved the ship. They went below deck to close all watertight doors and hatches to increase the survivability of the ship, and had just completed this action when the bomb blast killed them as well. A large bomb fragment penetrated the hatch of a compartment located above the port shaft alley, and continued downward through the bottom of the ship. Had Blair and Wilson not "dogged down" a number of doors and hatches (fastened them shut with toggle-type clamps), adjacent compartments would have flooded as well, and made keeping the ship afloat problematic.[11]

Steering only by engines orders (twisting the ship by going ahead on one engine and backing the other), Lieutenant Commander Wood, the executive officer, proceeded out of the bay at maximum speed leaving behind the commanding officer and the other men ashore. After the attack subsided, rudder control was restored to the bridge via commands to the steering gear compartment and manual movement of the rudder. When a Mavis attacked the ship in mid-afternoon, Wood was able to avoid the dropped bombs, which fell harmlessly into the sea. For his actions while in temporary command of the *William B. Preston*, he received the Silver Star Medal. The award citation can be found in Appendix F.[12]

That evening, burial services were conducted at sea for the eleven crewmen who lost their lives during the first attack. Two others were wounded, one of whom later died of his wounds. The deceased, all regular Navy (USN), included three metalsmiths (M1c and M2c), three seamen (S1c), two machinist's mates (CMM, MM2c), one fireman (F1c), one ship's cook (SC2c), one aviation ordnanceman (AOM2c) and one aviation machinist's mate (AMM1).[13]

Individual	Award	Individual	Award
CMM Eugene Blair	Silver Star	F1c Floyd D. Parks	Silver Star
AOM2c E. F. Gluba		S1c A. F. Pidinkowski	
M1c R. A. Johnson		SC2c J. H. Roberts	
M1c L. L Kerns		AMM1 F. J. Simpson	
S1c William Knight		S1c O. N. Vibert	
MM2c Harvey E. Oswald	Silver Star	M2c LeRay Wilson	Silver Star

The seaplane tender entered Derby, 800 nautical miles southwest of Darwin on Australia's northwest coast, following the second attack. Unhappily, the ship touched a shoal entering port, dinging her starboard propeller, which reduced effective speed to 8 knots. The commanding officer and the other men left behind on shore at Darwin rejoined the *William B. Preston* at Derby. All of the ship's boats had been blasted over the side or left behind when she cleared Darwin, and two of her four planes were seen burning as she had left there. A third had failed to return to the ship. The single remaining PBY had collected Lt. Comdr. Etheridge Grant and the others and brought them to Derby. Grant had been blown out of a motorboat while endeavoring to return to his ship during the attack.[14]

Leaving Derby, the *William B. Preston* proceeded to Broome, Australia, located about a hundred and twenty miles south-southwest as the crow flies further down the coast. On 24 February 1942 she was joined there by the *Childs* and *Heron* who assisted ship's force in making emergency repairs of the battle damage. The *Preston* obtained two replacement boats at Broome, and two additional aircraft sent there to join her. As Java fell, her three planes were used to assist in the evacuation of Surabaya and Tjilatjap.

Map 7-2

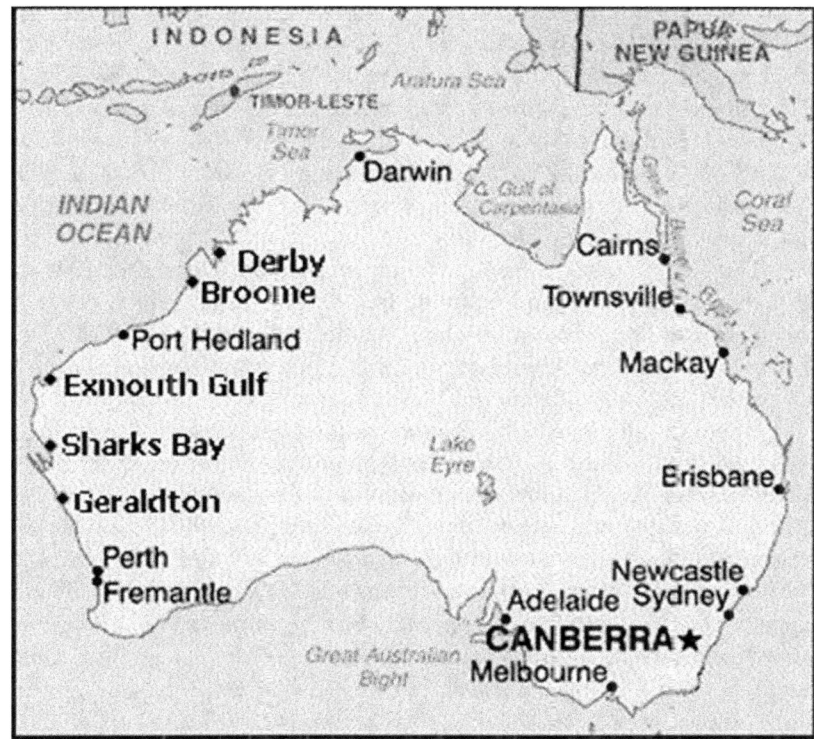

Continent of Australia

The tender was commended for her service by commander Patrol Wing Ten and, needing additional repairs, was sent to Fremantle, Australia. There not being sufficient facilities at Fremantle, she was then routed on to Sydney on the eastern coast of Australia. There she received a much needed overhaul and repair period. Her old 4-inch guns were replaced by 3-inch anti-aircraft guns, and 20mm Oerlikons were added to augment her anti-aircraft capability. Following the completion of all work, the *William B. Preston* proceeded to Fremantle and reported for duty to commander, Patrol Wing Ten, in June 1942.[15]

BATTLE STARS AND BATTLE HONOURS

Nine Allied ships were sunk as a result of the Japanese air raid on Darwin on 19 February 1942, and many others damaged by bombs or machinegun fire. The ships sunk were the destroyer USS *Peary* (DD-226), transports USAT *Mauna Loa*, and USAT *Meigs*, cargo ship M.V. *Neptuna*, coal hulk HMAS *Kelat*, lighter HMAS *Karalee*, patrol boat HMAS *Mavie*, tanker M.V. *British Motorist*, and troop ship S.S. *Zealandia*. A summary of the vessels present at or in the vicinity of Darwin that day is provided in Appendix E.[16]

The *Peary* received a battle star for the period 8 December 1941 to 19 February 1942 for the Philippine Islands Operation, which covered the air raid on 19 February in which the destroyer was lost. *William B. Preston* received a battle star for the same operation for the period 8 December 1941 to 3 March 1942.

Japanese air raids on Darwin and other areas of mainland Australia and offshore islands continued through mid-November 1943. Twenty-eight Royal Australian Navy channel patrol boats and Naval Auxiliary patrol craft actively involved in defense of Darwin during the Japanese air/submarine campaign of 19 February 1942–12 November 1943 received Battle Honours DARWIN 1942–43. These ships were the *Chinampa, Coongoola, Deloraine, Gunbar, Ibis, Kangaroo, Kara Kara, Karangi, Katoomba, Kiara, Koala, Kookaburra, Koompartoo, Kuru, Larrakia, Mavie, Moruya, Platypus, Red Bill, Southern Cross, Swan, Terka, Tolga, Townsville, Vigilant, Warrego, Warrnambool,* and *Wato*.[17]

8

Japanese Threat to Java Grows

During the latter part of January and early February 1942, Patrol Wing Ten flew reconnaissance operations in the Balikpapan and Java Sea area of the Makassar Strait. This was done by sending out three or four patrols in the strait as far north as Samarinda, Borneo, east to Celebes, down the island's west coast to Makassar (a historic port for spices and sailing ships and the capital city of Dutch Celebes), and back to the Java area. During an interview in 1944, Capt. John V. Peterson explained why PBY pilots referred to this area as Cold Turkey Lane." This term is a euphemism for being killed.

> There was no protection to speak of, we had no fighters, for protecting our bases and the Japs were in terrific numerical strength in this area. In fact they had airplanes based at Tarakan, Balikpapan, Samarinda [Borneo], Bandjermasin [a seaport on the south coast of Borneo] and later Bali [an island located only a little more than 100 miles by air from Surabaya, Java]. Almost daily our planes were attacked. However, they were usually able in the early part of their patrols to get back in some shape or other by taking cloud cover or by getting down on the water and using evasive action. They reported the movements daily of the Japanese Fleet down from Tarakan to Balikpapan to Makassar and later to Bali.
>
> The Java Sea action which took place later was the last large enemy movement which Patrol Wing 10 shadowed and did the reconnaissance work for during these patrols in the Makassar area, which is the Makassar-Balikpapan area. The wing worked with and under first Admiral Hart's command, and then Admiral Helfrich's command. During that time we supplied all the surface [ship] forces of all the allied commands with daily and almost hourly reports of the movement of the Japanese forces to the south. We also supplied this information to the Nineteenth Bombardment Group, U.S.A.A.F., which was based in Java. When we could find an isolated [enemy] ship we made bombing attacks on that ship and sometimes with success.[1]

Map 8-1

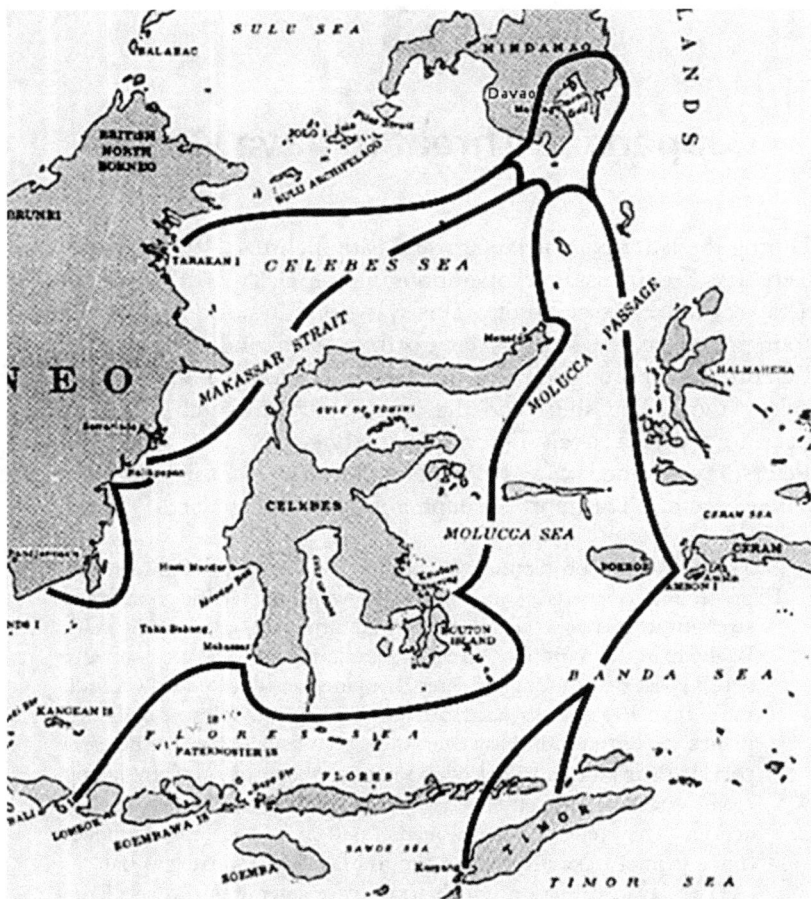

The movements of Japanese forces from Davao, Mindanao, southward to Java in the Netherlands East Indies resembled the tentacles of an octopus.

The Japanese were then preparing to capture Java in the largest amphibious operation yet attempted in the war. Vice Adm. Jisaburo Ozawa led the Western Attack group out of Camranh Bay on 18 February, bound for the Anambas Islands west of Borneo in the South China Sea. Upon arrival there, the three cruisers, six destroyers, minesweeper, and escorted fifty-six transport ships and cargo vessels awaited the approach of D-day. On the 19th, the Eastern Attack Force under Rear Adm. Shoji Nishimura in the light cruiser *Naka* left Jolo in the Sulu Archipelago. In addition to the flagship, six destroyers escorting forty-one transports comprised the force. Rear Adm. Takeo

Takagi's Eastern Covering Group—three cruisers and seven destroyers—formed in Makassar Strait off Borneo on 25 February. These combatant ships proceeded well ahead of the transports en route to Java, to meet whatever challenge the Allies might offer.[3]

LOSS OF THE *LANGLEY*

During the Allies buildup for the defense of Java, the *Langley* was lost to enemy action. Ironically, the aging seaplane tender had been sent to Darwin early in the Java Sea Campaign because she was considered too vulnerable for frontline work. She would be the only Patrol Wing Ten tender sunk due to damage inflicted by the Japanese. Launched in 1912 by the Mare Island Navy Yard as the collier *Jupiter* (AC-3), she had been converted in 1920 to the Navy's first aircraft carrier, *Langley* (CV-1). She was also the first surface ship equipped with a turbine-electric propulsion system: two huge electric motors powered by steam-turbine engines. In 1936, the *Langley* was designated a seaplane tender and entered Mare Island Navy Yard for the work necessary to configure her for her new role. Modifications included cutting off the forward portions of her flight deck which shortened it by about forty-one percent. The remaining deck was available for parking seaplanes, for transport, or to work on them. She was also fitted with eight fueling stations along her main deck, and the aircraft hangars and workshops (former coal bunkers) needed when she was a CV, became living quarters and repair parts storerooms.[4]

Following the *Langley*'s arrival at Darwin on 1 January 1942, she had supported Patrol Wing Ten and provided assistance to the Royal Australian Air Force in conducting anti-submarine patrols. On 11 February, she was ordered to Fremantle to collect a shipment of Army P40E Warhawk fighter aircraft to be ferried to Tjilatjap, Java. *Langley* stood out of Darwin on 17 February (two days before the big Japanese air raid there) and arrived the following day at Fremantle, a port city in Western Australia at the mouth of the Swan River.[5]

In early afternoon on 22 February, as an Australian Army band played "Farewell to Thee," *Langley* sailed from Fremantle in Convoy MS-5 with the U.S. Army transport *Willard A. Holbrook*, U.S. merchantman M.V. *Sea Witch*, and the Australian troop transports S.S. *Duntroon* and S.S. *Katoomba*, under escort of the light cruiser *Phoenix* (CL-46). *Katooma*, built in 1913, was a coal burner. To the displeasure of the convoy commander, she emitted black smoke continually and was a poor station keeper as well. The *Langley* was loaded to capacity. In addition to her usual stores and crew, she had aboard thirty-three Army Air Corps pilots and twelve enlisted crew chiefs from the 35th

Pursuit Group, and thirty-two P40E fighters. Twenty-seven aircraft were parked on her flight deck; the remaining five were crowded onto the main deck beneath it.[6]

That evening, Admiral Helfrich ordered the *Langley* to break away from the convoy and make a dash toward Tjilatjap. The shortage of aircraft was then so severe on Java that the Dutch were desperate for the ready-to-fly P40Es she had aboard. The seaplane tender departed the convoy at 2305 and set out alone. Four days later the destroyers *Edsall* (DD-219) and *Whipple* (DD-217), operating out of Tjilatjap, were ordered to rendezvous with the *Langley* to serve as escort ships for her. About 0720 the following morning, they took up screening stations on the seaplane tender. The weather was fair, with winds from the east-northeast and scattered alto-cumulus clouds.[7]

Photo 8-1

Langley (AV-3) with a deck load of P2Y flying boats and a utility seaplane. P2Y wings are stored on the after portion of her small flight deck. Date photo taken is unknown. U.S. Navy photograph from Norman Polmar's book *Aircraft Carriers*

In late morning that day, 27 February, *Edsall* made an emergency signal "aircraft sighted," upon which *Langley* immediately went to general quarters. Seven large twin-engine, silver colored land-based bombers were sighted approaching from the east at about 15,000 feet. Days earlier, Japanese troops had landed unopposed at Denpasar, on the southern end of Bali in the Netherlands East Indies, and captured the Dutch airfield located there. This gave the enemy an advance air base two miles off the eastern shore of Java. These planes, a squadron of Mitsubishi G4M "Betty" bombers led by Lt. Yoshinobu Tanabata, were from there. Two three-plane Vs were formed, with one behind the other. The remaining seventh plane was tucked in behind the second V. Each carried one 551-pound bomb on the rack beneath its fuselage.[8]

The *Langley*'s anti-aircraft armament consisted of four 3-inch guns on her flight deck, four .50-cals mounted on the corners of the signal bridge and a few men armed with Browning Automatic Rifles (BARS). The BARS, designed for use by infantry would be worthless in an anti-aircraft attack. So too would be the two large 5-inch guns on the bow, and two like them on the stern, intended for defense against other ships. The pedestal-mounted 3-inch guns appeared to offer the best chance to beat off an air attack. However, any such optimism would prove to be a false hope. Developed in World War I, these type guns could only reach targets up to about 12,000 feet in altitude.[9]

The seaplane tender was zigzagging, as a defense measure against any enemy submarines in the area, with *Langley*'s commanding officer, Comdr. Robert P. McConnell, USN, conning the ship from the open signal bridge. This station offered him unimpeded visibility of the surrounding area, but required that his orders be conveyed by voice tube to the officer of the deck on the navigating bridge directly below. The OOD had to then relay these rudder and engine commands to the helmsman and lee helmsman, resulting in some delay between ordered actions and accomplishment of them.[10]

The first in a series of air attacks against the tender commenced shortly before noon, at 1154, when a stick of bombs landed in the water well ahead of *Langley*. McConnell had wisely not waited until witnessing the release of bombs before taking measures to evade them. He ordered the rudder full right when the angle of the approaching planes was ten degrees short of being directly overhead. By this means, the ship received minimal damage which McConnell described in a report:

> The first salvo landed off the port bow on what would have been the ship's course projected prior to the turn. The closest bomb appeared to fall about one hundred feet from the ship. The ship shook violently but no damage was sustained other that the plating on the port side forward being riddled by bomb splinters, and superficial damage to the bridge.[11]

Destroyers *Whipple* and *Edsall* opened fire on the attacking aircraft with .50-caliber and 3-inch/23 guns, but the altitude of the planes prevented any effective results. The same was true of 3-inch fire from *Langley*'s guns. Following the initial attack, her gunners continued to fire at Betty bombers in range as they circled for a new approach, but scored no hits. No bombs were dropped on the second attack at 1203. Anti-aircraft fire and radical maneuvers by *Langley* during the final phase of the approach of the planes appeared to disrupt their setup for attack. The group made a third run at 1212. This time, the aircraft compensated for the evasive moves of the ship and dropped a tighter group of bombs—with deadly results:

> The *Langley* suffered five bomb hits on this salvo and sustained damage from two near misses on the port side, and one near miss on the starboard side.... #5 bomb hit on starboard side aft, penetrating flight deck, staff officers' quarters, and exploded against lower starboard structure on deck winch machinery. This last bomb set fierce fires. Fleet reserve pyrotechnics had been struck [moved] below to torpedo storage at "clear ship" [order to remove or relocate flammable materials] early in the voyage. Fires broke out on main deck in boats and in airplanes...and in the after part of the ship in the wooden deckhouses.... After the bomb salvo landed the ship was strafed by Japanese fighters only one of which (six) made a determined attack; some damage was sustained from aircraft cannon fire from this one plane.[12]

Following the bombing runs, several fighters appeared from the east at 1242 and started diving on and strafing *Langley*, already battered and aflame, with machine gun fire. The single-engine planes with belly tanks had come from Bali. No more than four planes, which made repeated attacks at about a 45-degree angle, were in sight at a time. No runs were made on the destroyers, and the attacks ceased about 1300.[13]

Prior to commencement of the strafing attacks, McConnell had put the ship on a course and speed necessary to obtain zero relative wind across the flight deck. This was done to avoid fanning the mass of flames resulting from bomb explosions, and damage control parties had gradually subdued the fires. *Langley* also had a 10-degree list to port because of the influx of seawater resulting from near bomb misses piercing her hull below the waterline. At 1225, in an effort to bring the ship back to an even keel, McConnell had ordered that five of the damaged planes on the port side be jettisoned (pushed) over the side. However, neither the removal of 104 tons of aircraft from the flight deck, nor the transfer of liquids between storage tanks corrected this impairment, due to seawater continuing to enter the ship.[14]

In addition to engine room flooding, the fire room bilges were awash, and there was water about four feet deep in the port turbo-electric motor pit. Following the strafing attack, McConnell set a course for Tjilatjapjap, hoping to make shallow coastal waters off Java, and gave the order for all hands to "prepare to abandon ship, make ready boats and life rafts for lowering." Although this directive was a precautionary measure, many crewmen misunderstood it and jumped overboard. The *Edsall*, trailing *Langley*, retrieved them from the sea.[15]

By early afternoon the ship's list had increased to 15 degrees. At 1332, McConnell gave the order to abandon ship, followed by at about 1345, the attendant "over the side." All remaining men and officers then abandoned and made their way to *Whipple*, about twenty-five yards off *Langley*'s starboard side. *Langley*'s No 4 motor launch, one motor whaleboat, and seven of eight life rafts constructed from empty gasoline drums and two of four balsa rafts had been lowered to the water's edge. *Edsall* cruised about picking up men in the water, as did the launch and whaleboat. Following a report by the executive officer that all men were clear, the commanding officer and executive officer left the *Langley*. McConnell went aboard the *Whipple*. The executive officer took the motor launch and located additional men who were put aboard *Whipple*. At 1358, *Whipple* fished the last survivor out of the water. *Edsall* had the men from the boats and rafts aboard her.[16]

Due to the rescue work of the destroyers, the seaplane tender's losses were limited to seven men killed and sixteen missing and presumed dead. Eleven men had been wounded including two pilots. Commander Destroyer Division 57 (Comdr. Edwin M. Crouch, USN), embarked aboard *Whipple*, reported the destroyer had recovered 308 officers and men of the *Langley*, and *Edsall* had the remaining 177 survivors. Following the *Langley*'s abandonment, Crouch ordered the seaplane tender sunk to prevent any possibility that the Japanese might salvage her.[17]

The *Whipple* fired nine 4-inch rounds into the ship's starboard side at 1428, with no apparent effect except to start more fires. Four minutes later the destroyer followed up with a torpedo. It penetrated the *Langley*'s starboard side and hit her gasoline storage tank, creating a high order detonation as intended, but the ship stubbornly remained afloat. A second torpedo fired into her port side appeared to finish off the dying ship. Engulfed by flames, with a 20-degree port list and down by the bow, she began to settle and when last seen was low in the water. Aware that additional aircraft might appear at any time, Crouch decided it would be unwise to tarry in the area to witness *Langley*'s final death throes. At his suggestion, Rear Adm. William A. Glassford sent the gunboat *Tulsa* (PG-22), minesweeper *Whippoorwill* (AM-35), and a plane from Tjilatjap to search for additional survivors and to confirm *Langley*'s sinking. The ships found nothing; a Dutch PBY later reported that the seaplane tender had indeed sunk.[18]

106   Chapter 8

The destroyers with the survivors cleared the area of *Langley*'s demise, seventy-four miles south of Tjilatjap, and headed west at 25 knots. That evening orders were received to transfer survivors to the fleet oiler *Pecos* (AO-6) in the lee of Christmas Island. The island in the Indian Ocean, 1,600 miles northwest of Perth, had been named by William Mynors, captain of the English East India Company vessel *Royal Mary*, when he sailed past the island on Christmas Day in 1643. The *Pecos* arrived in the vicinity of the British Phosphate Company dock on the north side of the island the morning of 28 February, and lay to off Flying Fish Cove waiting to embark the *Langley* personnel.[19]

A motor launch piloted by Mr. E. Craig, a British nationalist and employee of the company, approached the oiler. Aboard it was Lt. Comdr. Thomas A. Donovan, *Langley*'s First Lieutenant. Donovan had been sent to board the *Pecos* in order to explain the plan for transferring the survivors. However, as the launch made the ship's side a line trailing into the water fouled the boat's propeller. At about the same time an air alarm sounded and three Japanese twin-engine, land-based bombers appeared overhead from the direction of Sumatra. As the powerless boat began to drift away from the *Pecos*, Craig leaped from its bow onto the ship's Jacobs ladder. Donovan, who was seated amidships, was unable to disembark; when last seen the boat was drifting in the harbor, its propeller still fouled. Donovan was a very popular officer, and *Langley*'s crew later expressed much criticism regarding him being left behind, and no effort subsequently made to send one of the destroyers back to get him.[20]

Donovan was captured by the Japanese on 31 March 1942, and held as a prisoner of war at Makassar, Celebes, and Batavia, Java until after the end of hostilities. Following his return to U.S. Military control in September 1945, he was awarded the Legion of Merit. The medal citation reads in part:

> An inspiring and dignified leader throughout three and one-half years of incredible hardships, cruel mental strain and humiliating punishment, Commander Donovan justly earned and held the respect not only of fellow Americans and Allied nationals but also of the fanatical enemy, consistently maintaining an unbelievably high morale among the United States prisoners whom he fearlessly defended as a distinct and undaunted national group.[21]

Donovan also received the Bronze Star "for meritorious services from 13 to 28 September 1945 in the recovery and evacuation of American Prisoners of War and internees from Batavia, Java. Although suffering from the effects of imprisonment, he exerted every effort in behalf of others who had been held by the Japanese." Donovan would remain in the Navy after the war and retire as a rear admiral at the end of his career.

Photo 8-2

Rear Adm. Thomas Alton Donovan, USN
Courtesy of the United States Navy Memorial Navy Log

The Japanese bombers over Christmas Island dropped a stick of six bombs, which landed in the water just off the deck, and then lingered in the vicinity but did not drop any more bombs. The departing ships found shelter from scrutiny in a rain squall that came up from the east. When the squall passed, the group headed south at *Pecos*' best speed, about 12 knots. A single large twin-engine bomber was in sight for about an hour, but then disappeared northward.[22]

JAPANESE DIVE BOMBERS SINK THE *PECOS*

After seemingly having reached a relatively safe area of the ocean, the *Pecos* reduced her speed to bare steerageway in early morning darkness on 1 March, and put her motor launch over the side. Five trips to the *Whipple* and three to the *Edsall* brought 276 and 177 *Langley* survivors, respectively, to the oiler. Thirty-two of the *Langley* survivors aboard *Whipple*—Army Air Corps personnel—had been transferred to the *Edsall* at Christmas Island. They were to be taken to Java to fight as infantrymen. This seemingly incomprehensible decision was made at a time when American, British and Australian servicemen were leaving by whatever means available, after it had become obvious that no means existed to prevent the Japanese from taking the island. Once the survivors were aboard, the *Pecos* set a course for Fremantle. The destroyers went their separate ways; *Whipple* headed for Cocos Island, southwest of Christmas Island, and *Edsall* toward Tjilatjap, Java.[23]

Pecos's normal crew complement was about 125 officers and men, but she had departed Tjilatjap two days earlier with nearly twice that number aboard, 15 officers and 227 men. The additional personnel were survivors from the cruisers *Houston* and *Marblehead*, and destroyer *Stewart* (DD-224). These ships had been damaged in the Battle of Makassar Strait on 4 February. With the addition of the *Langley* survivors, there were now nearly seven hundred men cramped aboard the 475-foot oiler.[24]

Earlier, in recognition of the threat that the Japanese posed, Comdr. Paul E. Abernethy, USN, had directed that a large number of bamboo poles be brought aboard the *Pecos* and be lashed to her upper decks before she sailed from Tjilatjap. They were to be used for flotation by men for whom there were no boats or rafts and whom also did not have life jackets, should the oiler be sunk in combat.[25]

Shortly before noon on 1 March, three carrier-based Japanese dive bombers appeared out of the direction of the sun, and dropped three bombs, all which missed the *Pecos*. A second group of three planes then tried their luck; one of the bombs hit just aft of the fleet oiler's No. 1 three-inch gun, killing and wounding several of the gun crew. During these attacks, and those to come, Abernethy used maximum rudder angle to try to dodge each bomb.[26]

In the next few hours, three waves of bombers in groups of six, six, and nine arrived about one hour apart overhead *Pecos*. The planes were from the carriers *Akagi*, *Hiryu*, *Kaga*, and *Soryu*, part of an attack force eighty miles to the east that included the battleships *Hiei* and *Krishima* and the heavy cruisers *Chikuma* and *Tone*. After a patrol plane spotted the oiler and reported its location, four squadrons of Val dive bombers had been launched in sequence, one from each carrier. Each of the aircraft, painted brown, made two dives on *Pecos*, dropping one bomb on each approach. The dives were made at an angle of about 45 degrees and the attacks were from almost any direction. Of the fifty or so bombs that were dropped, five hit the oiler, and damage wrought by these bombs and six near misses proved fatal to her.[27]

Pecos sank in late afternoon at latitude 14°, 30' south, longitude 106°, 30' east. Toward the end of the action, several additional enemy planes appeared; the last one strafed men in the water astern of the sinking ship. Only two motor whaleboats and some balsa rafts were launched, leaving a majority of the survivors in the water scattered in groups over a wide area. *Whipple* arrived on the scene about 1930 and began picking up survivors, including those in one of the whaleboats. The destroyer was retrieving men from the water at 2141, when the ship's sonar operator reported the sound of screw beats (propeller noise) from a submarine. *Whipple* charged off and dropped several depth charges, then circled in an effort to gain echo contact with the sub. Unsuccessful, she resumed rescue operations. After picking up what appeared to be a good echo contact, she circled once again, endeavoring to make an attack. Four more depth charges were dropped and contact was lost.[28]

Following a subsequent report of the sighting of a submarine, commander Destroyer Division 57 had a tough decision to make. Should *Whipple* remain in the area and risk being torpedoed with the loss of the ship, crew and survivors from several ships aboard, or clear the area with the 220 survivors from *Pecos* retrieved thus far—8 officers and 63 men from *Pecos*, and 9 naval officers, two army officers, and 138 men from *Langley*. Comdr. Edwin M. Crouch decided to clear the area, an action supported by the commanding officers of *Whipple*, *Pecos*, and *Langley*. The destroyer's departure southward at 20 knots left the bulk of the men that had abandoned *Pecos* as she sank, to die in or on the sea. Some had perished prior to the arrival of *Whipple* due to their wounds, lack of adequate floatation—many men were dependent on hanging on to individual bamboo poles for their survival—or because they had simply given up, and sank into the abyss. Those still afloat and left behind likely perished within the next several hours, although men in the remaining whaleboat or rafts may have lasted for days. Crouch sent a message to commander, U.S. Naval Forces, Southwest Pacific, Vice Adm. William A. Glassford, at 0028 on 2 March 1942 reporting the ship loss and suggesting that any ships heading toward Australia search the area where *Pecos* sank.[29]

Whipple arrived at Fremantle about 2100 on 4 March, whereupon the wounded survivors were transferred to the hospital, and the others furnished clothing and quarters ashore. Of the nearly 700 officers and men that had been aboard *Pecos*, her commanding officer lost about seventy-one percent of his expanded crew—which included survivors from the *Houston*, *Marblehead*, and *Stewart*—and *Langley*'s captain (McConnell) lost at least sixty-seven percent of his officers and men. The following morning, nearly all the survivors boarded the troop transport *Mount Vernon* (AP-22) for passage to the United States, joining civilian and military escapees from the Philippines.[30]

In a written report on the loss of *Pecos*, dated 21 May 1942, Crouch included an account by Quartermaster Second J. D. Toone, USN, of having sighted a submarine:

> I was alongside a balsa raft which had burned and injured men in it. About 60 or 70 men in all, in or alongside that raft.... Just as it was getting real dark she [*Whipple*] was headed straight for our raft moving slowly when a submarine broached about five or six feet, about 600 or 800 feet off her starboard bow. He was about on a bow bearing. Two very shells [from a flare gun] were fired directly at it by the fellow in our raft so the WHIPPLE could see it. The submarine immediately submerged and I did not see it again. The ship turned to port at the time he submerged. The fellows in our raft through the WHIPPLE must have seen it. When I came on board I said something to one of the WHIPPLE crew about it and he said they heard the engines of the submarine.
>
> The submarine was very large. She had a peculiar tapering conning tower. It had an oval slant starting at deck and then went perpendicular. I have never seen a friendly submarine conning tower like it.[31]

9

Battle of the Java Sea and Duty in Australia

The fighting spirit and morale of the personnel of my force continued to be of the highest order. Our deficiencies in material strength, as compared to the force brought to bear by the enemy, were offset in a larger measure than is perhaps realized by the steadfast spirit and morale of our officers and men, who, in general, maintained the highest traditions of the United States Navy.

—Vice Adm. William A. Glassford Jr., USN, commander Naval Forces, Southwest Pacific, remarking on the manner in which the officers and men serving aboard the remnants of the Asiatic Fleet had stood up to the constant activity and strain over the course of the Java Sea Campaign and during its culminating battle, in which the Allied force was soundly defeated, sealing the fate of ABDA and presaging the fall of the entire Malay barrier to the Japanese.[1]

The relatively short, but hard fought Allied defense of the Netherlands East Indies came to a bitter end with the defeat of the ABDA Striking Force by Japanese naval forces in the Battle of the Java Sea fought on 27 February 1942 and the ensuing Battle of Sunda Strait. The latter series of skirmishes lasted through 1 March. Before describing these events, a comparison of the relative strengths of the Japanese naval forces marshaled for the invasion of Java and the ABDA force available to defend it is in order. The ships of the Japanese Southern Striking Force (Vice Adm. Nobutake Kondo), Eastern Attack Group and Western Attack Group, and supporting Eastern and Western Covering Groups are consolidated by ship type in the table to illustrate the disparity between the forces available to Kondo and those of Dutch Rear Adm. Karel Doorman, RNN, embarked in the light cruiser HNMS *De Ruyter*.

The principal battle on 27 February was characterized by a series of thrusts and parries, bursts of gunfire and firing of torpedoes, over a period of five or six hours. The battle began as a large Japanese invasion force approached the east end of Java, which Admiral Doorman believed was headed for Surabaya. Doorman had sailed with the heavy cruisers USS *Houston* and HMS *Exeter*, light cruisers HNMS *De Ruyter* and HNMS *Java* and ten destroyers from Surabaya Bay the previous day to engage the main convoy. In late afternoon, he sighted Rear Adm. Takeo Takagi's Eastern Covering Group—four cruisers and thirteen destroyers—thirty miles northwest of Surabaya.[2]

ABDA Combined Striking Force	Japanese Java Invasion Forces
	Aircraft Carriers (7)
	Akagi, Hiryu, Kaga, Ryujo, Shokaku, Soryu, Zuikaku
	Battleships (1)
	1 BB with the Carrier Group
Heavy Cruisers (2)	**Heavy Cruisers (13)**
USS *Houston* (sunk)	*Ashigara, Atago, Haguro, Kumano, Maya,*
HMS *Exeter* (damaged)	*Mikuma, Mogami, Myoko, Nachi, Suzuya, Takao*, plus 2 CA with the Carrier Group
Light Cruisers (3)	**Light Cruisers (6)**
HNMS *Java* (sunk),	*Jintsu* (damaged), *Naka, Natori, Sendai,*
HNMS *De Ruyter* (sunk)	*Yura*, plus 1 CL with the Carrier Group
HMAS *Perth* (sunk)	
U.S. Destroyers (5)	**Destroyers (57)**
USS *Alden*, USS *John D. Edwards*,	*Akebono, Arashi, Asagumo* (damaged),
USS *John D. Ford*, USS *Paul Jones*,	*Hagikaze, Harusame, Hatsukaze, Ikazuchi,*
USS *Pope* (sunk)	*Kawakaze, Maikaze, Minegumo, Murasame,*
British Destroyers (3)	*Nowaki, Samidare, Sazanami, Tokitsukaze,*
HMS *Electra* (sunk)	*Ushio, Yamakaze, Yudachi, Yukikaze*, plus
HMS *Encounter* (sunk)	25 DDs with the Western Attack Group,
HMS *Jupiter* (sunk)	9 DDs with the Carrier Group, and 4
Dutch Destroyers (3)	additional DDs of the Transport Group
HNMS *Evertsen* (destroyed), HNMS	**Patrol Craft (6)**
Kortenaer (sunk), HNMS *Witte de With*	PCs 4, 5, 6, 16, 17, 18
(hit by a bomb on 1 March while in	**Minewarfare Ships (3)**
drydock and scuttled the following day)	Minelayer *Wakataka*, Minesweepers 15, 16
	(1 minesweeper sunk)
	Seaplane Ships (2)
	1 Seaplane Carrier, 1 Seaplane Tender
	Transports and Freighters (97)
	(1 transport sunk and 3 forced aground)[3]

In the battle that followed, Doorman's American, British, Dutch, and Australian force fought valiantly, but suffered from old weapon systems; and lack of air cover, common tactical signals, and training time as a single unit. The Japanese ships used their 24-inch torpedoes to effect, sinking the destroyer HNMS *Kortenaer*, and their gunfire was accurate as well. An 8-inch round hit the flagship, HNMS *De Ruyter*, but failed to explode. The heavy cruiser HMS *Exeter* was not so lucky; an armor-piercing round struck her, continued its downward trajectory into the magazine beneath an anti-aircraft gun mount, and detonated. Crippled by damage from the resultant explosion of munitions, she slowed to one-half her normal speed, and the Allied force began to withdraw to cover her.[4]

In the failing light conditions of late afternoon and evening, and with the entire battle area wreathed or shrouded in smoke, Doorman tried, on several occasions, to double back and attack the Japanese transports screened by the covering force, but he was intercepted each time. The destroyer HMS *Electra* poured gun rounds into the light cruiser *Jintsu*, but in an unequal exchange with other enemy ships was herself sunk, and a second destroyer, HMS *Jupiter*, was lost to an uncharted minefield. Finally, in a devastating torpedo attack from the Japanese heavy cruisers *Haguro* and *Nachi*, both *De Ruyter* and *Java* were hit and sank in a matter of minutes, taking Doorman to his death. The two remaining Allied ships, cruisers USS *Houston* and HMAS *Perth*, then fled westward toward Tanjong Priok (a port on the northern coast of Java), where they signaled to Admiral Helfrich the tragic results of the Battle of the Java Sea. The ABDA force had been nearly annihilated while the Japanese lost not a single ship (one destroyer was badly damaged), and the transports of the enemy invasion force were untouched.[5]

The final grim fighting played out between 28 February and 1 March in the Battle of Sunda Strait. On the 28th, the cruisers USS *Houston* and HMAS *Perth* steamed boldly into Banten Bay, near the northwest tip of Java, hoping to damage the Japanese invasion fleet situated there. After evading nine torpedoes launched by the destroyer *Fubuki* as they approached the bay, the cruisers sank one transport and forced three others to beach, but then encountered overwhelming forces. A destroyer squadron blocked Sunda Strait—their only means of retreat following this action—and the heavy cruisers *Mikutma* and *Mogami* hastened to intercept. *Perth* came under fire at 2336 and sank five minutes into the new day on 1 March owing to 8-inch gunfire and four torpedo hits. *Houston*, fought on alone, scoring gunfire hits on three destroyers and sinking a minesweeper, but was hit by multiple torpedoes (four) and rolled over and sank thereafter.[6]

Separately, the damaged heavy cruiser HMS *Exeter* and destroyers HMS *Encounter* and USS *Pope* departed Surabaya on the 28th, hoping to make it safely to Ceylon (today Sri Lanka), nearly 1,800 nautical miles to the west-northwest. They were surrounded by several groups of patrolling Japanese cruisers and destroyers and summarily dispatched.

Exeter was hit numerous times by gunfire and finished off with a torpedo, and *Encounter* was fatally hit and abandoned. *Pope*, a World War I destroyer, was damaged by dive bomber attacks and sunk by cruiser gunfire in the early afternoon on 1 March.[7]

The remaining two Dutch ships were also lost. HNMS *Evertsen* departed Tandjong Priok an hour after the *Houston* and *Perth*, due to boiler limitations. She set a course for Sunda Strait, hoping to catch up, and later witnessed "star shells" light up the night sky and tracers flying from the two cruisers engaged in battle with the Japanese ships. *Evertsen* hoped to avoid the Japanese forces in the vicinity. However, the destroyers *Murakumo* and *Shirakumo*, which were on patrol to protect the southern flank of the Bantam Bay landing site, found her and opened fire. Hit, and with unextinguishable fires reaching a magazine aboard the Dutch destroyer that could not be flooded, her captain beached her on a coastal reef near Seboekoe Besar, an island in the Sunda Strait. Nine members of her crew were killed and the others captured and imprisoned for the duration of the war. *Evertsen*'s commanding officer died as a POW in April 1942. HNMS *Witte de With* was hit by an aircraft bomb on 1 March while resting in drydock, and was scuttled the following day.[8]

The only units of the ABDA Striking Force to escape destruction were the four old American destroyers of Destroyer Division 58—*Alden*, *John D. Edwards*, *John D. Ford*, and *Paul Jones*. Doorman had instructed the division commander, Comdr. Thomas H. Binford, USN, prior to the battle, to retire to Tanjong Priok once his ships had expended all their torpedoes. Binford, upon quitting the battle had decided to fuel at Surabaya. The division left Surabaya on 28 February and headed south through the Bali Strait. By hugging the shoreline and laying smoke at high speed after being sighted in the strait, the "tin cans" escaped encirclement by Japanese forces closing in on Java, and made it safely to Australia.[9]

Admiral Helfrich formally announced in late morning on 1 March, that the Governor General of the Netherlands East Indies had dissolved the ABDA naval command. Admiral Glassford had earlier ordered all American ships to Exmouth Gulf, Australia, and the British commander, Rear Adm. Arthur Palliser, ordered the Royal Navy units there as well. The previously mentioned four destroyers, along with *Parrott* (DD-218) and *Whipple* (DD-217)—which made good their escape from Tjilatjap—cruiser *Marblehead* (CL-12), patrol yacht *Isabel* (PY-10), and gunboat *Tulsa* (PG-22) were the only combatant ships of the Asiatic Fleet to survive the Java Campaign. The seaplane tenders *Childs*, *Heron*, and *William B. Preston*; destroyer tender *Black Hawk* (AD-

9); and minesweepers *Lark* (AM-21) and *Whippoorwill* (AM-35) also made it to Australia.[10]

JAPANESE AIR RAID ON BROOME, AUSTRALIA

Prior to the abandonment of Java, there had been fear that should the Japanese bomb the base at Tjilatjap, due to the nature of the harbor and the large number of vessels present, the first ships to sortie would clog its entrance and the remainder would not be able to get out. As a result, *Childs* had left Tjilatjap on 21 February bound for Cocos Island, little more than a sand spit way out in the Indian Ocean southwest of Christmas Island. She was about halfway there when a change in orders directed her to proceed to Broome, Australia. The *Heron* and *William B. Preston* were also headed for Western Australia, and PBYs had begun transporting excess plane crews from aircraft lost in combat from Surabaya to the Australian coastal towns of Derby and Broome.[11]

Broome, which lay about 1,200 nautical miles north of Perth, was being used as the Australian end of an air shuttle service from Java. Hundreds of evacuees had been ferried there in Dutch, American, and Australian military and civil aircraft, and the town was overflowing with military personnel and refugees. People slept wherever they could while waiting for flights to continue their journeys south. Since the loss of Darwin, Broome had become the most important staging and refueling point for evacuees from Java en route to Perth.[12]

William B. Preston and *Heron* were at Broome when *Childs* arrived there on 26 February, scheduled to leave together that day. The former destroyer was crippled, having damaged both screws and bent her port propeller shaft when she hit a shoal entering Derby. As a result, *Heron* had been ordered to escort *William B. Preston* to Perth. Commander Pratt was unsure what his ship's mission would be at Broome; it appeared she was to tend the flying boats using the port.[13]

After anchoring, Pratt went ashore and happened to find Rear Adm. William R. Purnell, USN, sitting in a cottage on the top of a hill in a little town that resembled an Arizona cow town in its offseason. He had been Admiral Hart's chief of staff prior to the latter officer's relief by Admiral Helfrich on 14 February. The admiral and Pratt chatted for a few minutes before Purnell asked why he was there. Pratt replied that he had come in under orders but did not like the looks of things, and that he would like to leave a boat equipped to service planes at Broome, and move the *Childs* a little further out of Japanese bombing range. Purnell, who needed to go to Perth, then said "Well, what are we waiting for?" The two men returned to *Childs* together and in early evening the tender, "with the authority of the senior Asiatic Fleet officer" present, stood out of Roebuck Bay and set a course southwest toward Exmouth Gulf.[14]

Her departure proved fortunate for ship and crew, as a few days later Japanese fighters attacked Broome without warning on 3 March 1942. Twenty-five Allied aircraft were destroyed and dozens of people killed or wounded in the air raid, which lasted not more than twenty minutes. Many of the casualties were Dutch women and children packed into flying boats in the harbor waiting to be ferried ashore or waiting to depart for southern destinations. Pratt described what had transpired:

> Shortly thereafter the Japs came into Broome and cleaned out everything in the harbor. This was a terrible thing because a large number of Dutch planes had just landed, bringing in their women and children and as it was at low tide, there is a high rise of tide in that harbor, they were unable to get ashore and they were still in the planes when the Japs came in.
>
> They sank every plane and the water was full of women and children, some of them very young. Some of them were shot up, the sharks got some and a large number were lost. Our boat which we had left there was able to rescue about 50 people.[15]

An exact accounting of all the people that died in the raid, and the identities of many, will never be known. The Dutch casualties were buried in the Broome War Cemetery, but later removed and reburied in a special area in the Karrakatta cemetery in Perth. Many of the dead were not identified and lie today in unmarked graves.[16]

EXMOUTH GULF BOUND

After *Childs* departed Broome, a sighting was made aboard ship of a four-engine enemy patrol plane, and Pratt and Parnell stood on the bridge, waiting for it to begin a bombing run. A crewman with binoculars watched its bomb rack. The aircraft came in at about 8,000 feet and when it got to the appropriate bombing angle, the seaplane tender sped up just a little. When the man with the glasses reported "Here they come," Pratt ordered the rudder put hard over and engines increased to full speed. By these tactics, the ship had always avoided bombs by a considerable margin and did so again.[17]

After reaching her destination, Exmouth Gulf, the seaplane tender moved to its lower end, where she would set up a base and become sort of an evacuation center as well. The breeze coming off the land was cool and dry and, after long months operating around steaming hot jungle areas, this change was very refreshing and the crew slept under blankets for the first time in more than a year. The tender anchored about a mile from the beach, after feeling her way down the gulf because she did not have a chart of that part of it. Two of her PBYs had flown ahead to spot reefs in the entry channel and she had proceeded without too much difficulty. *Childs* anchored in an area of the gulf called the Bay of Rest. It really was such for her crew, this being the first place they had felt any real security in three months.[18]

EVACUATION OF PATROL WING TEN FROM JAVA

Wing Ten staff, aircrews, and patrol planes at Surabaya hurriedly left there in early morning darkness on 1 March. They had received a report from PBY *P-5* that the Japanese Eastern Force was off the beaches at Kragan on Java's northern coast, about sixty miles away. Wagner ordered Peterson to evacuate his people from Surabaya to Exmouth Gulf. The pilots received word to leave Java about 0200, and by 0400 were on their way south to Australia. All personnel were evacuated by air. The normal crew of a PBY was seven men: a plane commander, who was an officer; a second pilot, also an officer; an aviation pilot, normally an enlisted man; two mechanics and two radiomen. In Lt. Comdr. Clarence A. Keller's plane alone, there were about thirty people. When the planes reached the gulf, *Childs* was waiting for them.[19]

That night, Pratt received a dispatch from Java asking if he could send two planes to Tjilatjap, to evacuate Captain Wagner and a good many other officers who were still there. The three PBYs Pratt had available were in very bad shape. They had not received maintenance for several hundred hours and were barely able to get off the water and fly. The three pilots, Lt. Duncan Campbell, Lt. John Hyland, and Ens. Robert LeFever, were being briefed that the mission required a five hundred mile flight over open water, and the Japanese had control of the air over Java. Their only comment was, "When do we start?"[20]

They took off that evening and flew all night, landing in Java the following morning. Upon departure later that day, Hyland's plane (*P-3*) was unable to take off due to engine problems, and he joined LeFever's plane, replacing him as senior pilot in the left-hand seat. PBYs *P-10* (LeFever) and *P-46* (Campbell) took aboard two full plane loads of personnel including Wagner and some members of his staff; *P-3* was destroyed to prevent its capture by the Japanese. Following Wagner's arrival at Exmouth Bay, it was decided that the location was too exposed to the elements and the Japanese to be a suitable advance base, and that everything would be moved south to Perth.[21]

SOUTH TO PERTH, AUSTRALIA

> *Recreational facilities, living conditions, and food were superior at PERTH.... It is to be noted that great strides towards international goodwill and cementing of relations between nations were taken during this period as respects the personal and social contacts made by and between the Australian people and our small slice of the American populace. Not the least, by far, was the excellence of the native Australian brew, which contributed to this mutual understanding.*
>
> —History of Patrol Squadron VP-33, lauding duty at Perth from 26 October 1943 to 5 February 1944.[22]

Childs remained in Exmouth Gulf for several more days before receiving orders to go to Perth. En route there, she stopped at Geraldton, where the town hosted a big dance. As Pratt looked over his crew he noted that they resembled a bunch of pirates, having not had access to a supply ship or small stores for three months. The men wore tropic clothing despite it being cool, and were dressed in every manner imaginable. The Seaman's Aid, a British organization, came aboard with sweaters and wool clothing to help alleviate this situation. Turned out in liberty attire, the crew went ashore and had a fine time. Many men became boisterous but nothing out of line occurred and everyone enjoyed the dance.[23]

From Geraldton, *Childs* proceeded down the coast to Perth. Following arrival there, Pratt managed to obtain two Orliken guns from the Army and have them installed on the seaplane tender just before he was relieved of command. The existing .50-caliber guns had proven useful in repelling Zeros or other low flying strafing aircraft. His crew had driven off two bunches of them without too much difficulty. However, enemy bombers just stayed above the range of the machine guns and bombed at will.[24]

DUTY IN AUSTRALIA

> *What was left of the Wing consisted of two airplanes, and they were ensconced on a sand spit which was located in the Swan River – a very ideal operating place and one that we later developed into a sizable air station. We [VP-21] combined with the remnants of all the Asiatic Fleet squadrons, VJ and ship units, and formed a single squadron which consisted then of fourteen Catalinas and several SOC's, Kingfishers and J2F's; we had seven types of airplanes in all*

and nine types of engines, and no spares of any kind. We set up Quonset huts for the men to house in. The officers were all barracked in various civilian homes around the city and Headquarters was set up in a life insurance building in town, very comfortably located.

We built a ramp, took over a boat house from the university and built an operations office and gasoline mooring sites and in general provided everything that you get on an air station.

—Comdr. George T. Mundorff, Jr., USN, commander Fleet Air Wing Ten, describing the arrival of VP-21 (which he had previously commanded) at Perth, Australia, on 7 April 1942 to reinforce Patrol Wing Ten.[25]

In recognition of the horrific losses of Patrol Wing Ten, Adm. Chester W. Nimitz, commander-in-chief Pacific Fleet, ordered Patrol Squadron VP-21 and its twelve PBY-5s from Pearl Harbor to Perth. When VP-21 arrived at Perth in April 1942, to join the remnants of the Wing, there were no adequate seaplane bases anywhere on Australia's west coast except at Perth on the Swan River. The Navy tried to remedy this situation as explained by Comdr. George T. Mundorff Jr., USN:

We established advanced bases at Geraldton, roughly 200 miles north of Perth; Shark Bay, Exmouth Gulf, and at a place we named Heron Haven after the USS *HERON* which is still out there on the job. It's close to Nichol Bay and it is merely a lee behind some islands and makes really a very nice operating base for patrol boats.

We had to survey the coast in order to find these places because we found that the charts of the area in most cases were not any newer than 1850-60. The coast line as indicated on the charts is in many cases as much as 10 or 12 miles out from the actual position, and in almost no instance does the coast line resemble that shown on the chart.[26]

The Navy did not have perfect understanding of Australia's western coast in April 1942, and none of these additional sites proved satisfactory. Shark Bay, a very large expanse of water about 430 nautical miles north of Perth on the westernmost point of the Australian continent, was very rough and subject to large swells. The same thing was true of Exmouth Gulf, two hundred miles or so further up the coast, where the Wing lost several planes. There was also nothing suitable from Exmouth eastward around northern Australia to Darwin. The north coast from Port Hedland to Darwin had a tidal range of 22-28 feet, and corresponding tidal currents, which ran 10-12 knots in some places.[27]

Patrol Squadron VP-34 was based at Geraldton in autumn 1943, which was still little more than a landing area, equipped to fuel planes and house crews. The harbor was inadequate for normal landings or take-offs, requiring operations to be conducted from unprotected waters outside it. Leased private residences in the heart of the town, served as quarters and offices. The food was good and recreation facilities were representative of those found in any small town.[28]

Childs and *William B. Preston* took turns providing services and accommodations for aircraft and flight crews at Exmouth Gulf and Heron Haven in northwest Australia. The operating areas in both places were large and unobstructed, but very poorly sheltered from seas apt to be quite rough. While based at these locations, VP-34 found that "recreation opportunities were limited to swimming and throwing rocks at Wallabies."[29]

The operations of the Wing in Australia included: escort, patrol, bombing, training and utility. Escort operations involved providing protection for ship convoys routed between 150 to 600 miles offshore. Inshore escort duties were performed by the Royal Australia Air Force whenever it had the means to do so. When it did not, the Wing tried to cover this responsibility. Its efforts, and those of the Australians, were not always adequate because of a chronic shortage of planes. Mundorff explained:

> We provided day and night coverage and from the point of view of Task Force 71, to which we were attached, I feel that we fell far short of what was desired because the demand for protection far exceeded our capacity and that of the combined efforts of ourselves and the RAAF because around the southwest corner of Australia there are better than 80 ships a week. Of those which pass there, only a very small percentage can be protected. Patrols were flown daily. They consisted of various sectors, the longest of which required 15 hours to fly. The others averaged about 10 hours. We never cancelled any, excepting at Exmouth, where the swells were frequently so high as to make it impossible to take off with a fully loaded plane. We conducted night operations at all these places and also night offensive scouting which took us up toward Java and Timor.[30]

During the latter part of Mundorff's tenure as commander Fleet Air Wing Ten (former Patrol Wing Ten), half of the Wing relocated to Australia's east coast and set up an advanced base at Palm Island, just north of Townsville. It was the main rearward base on Australia's east coast and corresponded to Perth on the west. Two advanced bases were established at Samarai and Jenkins Bay, in the southeast corner of New Guinea, equipped with a reasonable amount of gear, spare parts, barracks and the other things one might expect at such facilities.[31]

LAURELS FOR PATROL WING TEN AND TENDERS

In recognition of their heroic actions in the Philippines and Netherlands East Indies, the Navy awarded Patrol Squadrons 22, 101, and 102 the Presidential Unit Citation, the highest award for heroism a unit might receive and equivalent to the Navy Cross Medal for an individual. The *Heron* received the Navy Unit Commendation for the defense of the Netherlands East Indies. This ribbon is awarded by the Secretary of the Navy to military units for heroism in action against the enemy not sufficient to justify an award of the Presidential Unit Citation. These ships and squadrons also received a battle star for the period indicated in the table below:

Patrol Squadron	Presidential Unit Citation	Battle Star
Patrol Squadron 101	8 Dec 1941-3 Mar 1942	8 Dec 1941-3 Mar 1942
Patrol Squadron 102	8 Dec 1941-3 Mar 1942	8 Dec 1941-3 Mar 1942
Patrol Squadron 22 (sent from Hawaii to augment Wing Ten)	8 Dec 1941-3 Mar 1942	9 Jan-3 Mar 1942
Seaplane Tender	Navy Unit Commendation	Battle Star
Childs (AVD-1)		8 Dec 1941-3 Mar 1942
Heron (AVP-2)	17 Dec 1941-3 Mar 1942	8 Dec 1941-3 Mar 1942
William B. Preston (AVD-7)		8 Dec 1941-3 Mar 1942

In addition to these unit awards, the Navy conferred decorations or promotions to fifty-seven aviators of Wing Ten for their actions during three months of fierce action against numerically superior Japanese forces in the Southwest Pacific. The Wing began combat in the Philippines with forty-two aircraft and arrived in Australia with two. Fifteen officers and five enlisted men received the Navy Cross, the Distinguished Service Medal, or the Distinguished Flying Cross. Ten officers and men of the seaplane tenders *Heron* and *William B. Preston* received Navy Cross, Silver Star, or Bronze Star Medals:

Patrol Wing Ten

Distinguished Service Medal
Capt. Frank Dechant Wagner, USN

Navy Cross Medal
Lt. Burden Robert Hastings, USN	Posthumously
Lt. Jack Baldwin Dawley, USN	
Lt. (jg) Elwyn Lewis Christman, USNR	
RM1 Robert Lee Pettit, USN	Posthumously
ACMM Don Dexter Lurvey, USN	
AMM1c Joseph Bangust, USN	Posthumously
AMM1c Andrew Kenneth Waterman, USN	Posthumously
AMM1c Evren C. McLawhorn, USN	

Silver Star Medal (Army Award)
Lt. Comdr. Edgar T. Neale, USN

Distinguished Flying Cross Medal
Lt. (jg) Ira W. Brown Jr., USNR	
Lt. (jg) Richard Bull, USNR	Posthumously
Lt. Duncan A. Campbell, USN	
Ens. John F. Davis, USNR	
Lt. (jg) LeRoy C. Deede, USN	
Lt. Charles C. Hoffman, USN	
Lt. Clarence Armstrong Keller Jr., USN	
Comdr. John Valdemar Peterson, USN	
Lt. (jg) John Mott Robertson, USNR	Posthumously
Lt. (jg) William S. Robinson, USN	Posthumously
Lt. Comdr. Harmon Tischer Utter, USN[31]	

Heron (AVP-2)

Navy Cross Medal
Lt. William Leverette Kabler, USN	31 December 1941
Chief Boatswain William Harold Johnson, USN	31 December 1941
Machinist's Mate Second Robert Lee Brock, USN	31 December 1941

Bronze Star Medal
Lt. Franklin Duerr Buckley, USN	31 December 1941

William B. Preston (AVD-7)

Silver Star Medal
Lt. Comdr. Lester Orin Wood, USN	19 February 1942
Lt. Eugene Carter Rider, USN	19 February 1942

Silver Star Medal (Posthumously)
Chief Machinist's Mate Eugene Blair, USN	19 February 1942
Machinist's Mate Second Harvey E. Oswald, USN	19 February 1942
Fireman First Floyd D. Parks, USN	19 February 1942
Metalsmith Second LeRay Wilson, USN	19 February 1942

10

War in the Aleutians

[They] would sink if rammed by a barnacle.

—Comdr. Charles E. Anderson, USNR, Dutch Harbor captain-of-the-port, remarking on the state of a group of World War I-era destroyers and former fishing boats (YPs) that comprised the so-called "Alaskan Navy" in early 1942[1]

In spring 1942, the Allies were in desperate straits, and not just in the Pacific. German U-boats had sunk almost five hundred ships off America's East Coast, and Japanese submarines had sunk a few vessels and shelled refineries and installations on the West Coast. United States naval forces in the Pacific were driven back to Hawaii and the West Coast, and Japan knew that U.S. strategy was limited to holding a line of defense that began in New Guinea, extended northward through Samoa and Midway, and was anchored at Dutch Harbor in the Aleutians.[2]

One bright moment for America occurred on 18 April 1942 when a group of U.S. Army Air Force B25s, led by Lt. Col. James H. ("Jimmie") Doolittle, launched from the carrier *Hornet* (CV-8) in the Central Pacific and bombed Tokyo. While the damage inflicted by the sixteen bombers was small, the psychological effect of an air raid on Japan was huge. The Japanese high command disagreed about the site from which the raid had originated. Some argued that the bombers had been launched from carriers, while others believed their origin to be an airfield in Alaska. Flying such a distance through the pervasive inclement weather of the Aleutians, which included harsh winds and blizzards, however, would have been impossible. While Attu, the westernmost island in the Aleutians, lay 1,746 nautical miles from Tokyo, the nearest U.S. base was located on Umnak Island, 260 miles farther east, 2,006 long miles from Japan's capital city. In preparation for the Doolittle raid, engineers had taken desperate measures to increase the fuel storage aboard the bombers. Modifications included removing tail guns to create space for a rubber fuel tank in the tail section (and installing broomsticks painted like machine gun barrels to provide the impression of a defensive capability), and loading ten five-gallon gas cans aboard for manual addition to gas tanks while in flight. These actions increased the range of the planes to 2,000 miles under optimum flying conditions—no headwinds, storms, or navigation errors.[3]

Following the raid, Adm. Isoroku Yamamoto, who was already obsessed with destroying American sea power, expanded his plans to include offensive operations against U.S. military installations in the Aleutians. His first attempt to destroy the American fleet had taken place in early May in the Battle of the Coral Sea, during which Japanese torpedo and dive bombers sank the carrier *Lexington* (CV-2) and damaged the *Yorktown* (CV-5). His new strategy focused on both Midway Island and the Aleutians. Japanese carrier aircraft would strike Dutch Harbor, Unalaska Island; while farther west, occupational forces landed on Adak, Kiska, and Attu. Yamamoto envisioned that this first strike would draw the American fleet away from Pearl Harbor and north toward Alaskan waters, enabling his Combined Fleet to engage it near Midway after having captured the island for use by his own planes.[4]

CODEBREAKERS LEARN OF YAMAMOTO'S PLANS

The Japanese offensive planned for early June would not be a surprise. A team of Pacific Fleet cryptanalysts broke Japan's top secret naval code on 15 May and were able to piece together Yamamoto's plan to occupy Midway and the Aleutians. Informed of this intelligence, Admiral Nimitz established Task Force 8 under Rear Adm. Robert A. Theobald (who had been serving as his commander of Pacific Fleet destroyers) on 21 May. Nimitz had only two operational carriers available, the *Enterprise* and *Hornet* (repairs to *Yorktown* were not expected to be finished before August) and required the majority of his fleet to oppose the Japanese at Midway. He was thus only able to provide Theobald with a force of five cruisers—*Indianapolis* (CA-35), *Louisville* (CA-18), *Honolulu* (CL-48), *St. Louis* (CL-49), and *Nashville* (CL-43)—and units of Destroyer Division 11—*Gridley* (DD-380), *McCall* (DD-400), *Reid* (DD-369), and *Humphreys* (DD-236). Theobald would also have command of the sparse U.S. Navy, Army, and Canadian forces already based in Alaska. These forces consisted of the so-called "Alaskan Navy" commanded by Capt. Ralph C. Parker, USN; nearly two hundred planes (mostly Army bombers and fighters) under Maj. Gen. Simon B. Buckner Jr., USA; and the twenty Navy

Catalina PBY seaplanes of Patrol Wing Four. Having received his orders to prepare Alaska against a Japanese attack, Theobald left Pearl Harbor aboard the destroyer *Reid* bound for Kodiak, headquarters of the Alaskan Naval Sector.[5]

THE ALASKAN NAVY

Five years before the war, Alaska was virtually undefended. Its only naval facility was a seaplane base at Sitka, a seaport on Baranof Island in the Alaska Panhandle that faced the Gulf of Alaska. As a result of recommendations made by the Hepburn Board, which reviewed America's national defense structure, new construction followed, and by September 1941 bases at Sitka, Kodiak, and Dutch Harbor had been commissioned as naval air stations, with the latter two ready to receive submarines. In mid-1940 the Army sent Colonel Buckner to Alaska to prepare the territory for the possibility of war with Japan. The Navy quickly followed suit by creating an Alaskan Sector under the Thirteenth Naval District and appointing Parker to command it.[6]

The associated allocation of forces to Parker was, to be very generous, "modest"—a single ship, the *Charleston* (PG-51). Between 6 November 1940 and 27 November 1941, the 328-foot gunboat made five cruises, patrolling the long section of coastline from Seattle to Aleutian and Alaskan waters. During a cruise from 23 January to 15 March 1941, an embarked survey party put ashore in a series of small ports found a scarcity of existing infrastructure and little hint of the buildup in Army personnel. A crewman observed in his diary that there was nothing at Hunter Bay or Latouche, nothing at Sawmill Bay except for sawmills, and absolutely nothing at Cold Bay. He humorously described Petersburg as "just a little burg too," Juneau as "still just Juneau," Sitka as "still [a] mud-hole," and Yakutat as also "just a little burg." The flagship encountered few units of the Alaskan Navy during the expedition, except for Yard Patrol Craft (YPs) based at Dutch Harbor.[7]

Captain Parker had only the *Charleston* until he was able to procure three Seattle fishery boats—the *YP-72* (ex-cannery tender *Cavalcade*), the *YP-73* (ex-cannery tender *Corsair*), and the *YP-74* (ex-purse seiner *Endeavor*)—and outfit them for use as patrol craft. The "YP boats" operated from Dutch Harbor under local command of Comdr. Charles E. ("Squeaky") Anderson, USNR, a Swede and Alaskan, said to be the only sailor alive who really knew Aleutian waters. (His nickname was a pun on his loud, piercing voice.) By May 1942, Parker's navy had grown to include two old World War I four-stack destroyers, three Coast Guard cutters, and a few more YPs, none, except for the *Charleston*, fitted with sonar or guns larger than three-inch. The YPs were among a group of halibut and purse seiners converted in 1941 by Olson & Winge Marine Works of Seattle, Washington—the first yard in the Pacific Northwest to undertake a full program of Army-Navy repair and modification work—for Navy use as supply ships. These fifteen vessels, whose hulls were sheathed with ironbark, a tropical wood, would range up and down the Pacific Coast from the Canal Zone to the Aleutians and into the Bering Sea. Standard modifications included accommodations for additional crewmen, transformed stowage space for military uses, and mounted armament.[8]

Photo 10-1

Prior to World War II, *YP-72*, the former purse seiner *Cavalcade*, served as the flagship of the Alaskan Patrol. During the Aleutian Islands portion of the Battle of Midway, the 87-foot wooden vessel carried out picket ship, patrol and other duties that included towing a propellerless PBY-5A into Port Moller.
U.S. Navy Photograph #239470

ADDITIONAL YPS SENT NORTH

By May 1942 the number of YPs operating in the Alaskan Sector as units of the local defense force had increased significantly. A summary of the duties or status of these vessels as of the fifteenth of the month follows:

Ship Name or Designation (Former Type Vessel/Name and Name of Commanding Officer)	Length Feet	Year Built	Assigned Duty/ Status
Section Base, Cordova			
YP (*Northern Light*)			in repair at Cordova
Section Base, Dutch Harbor			
YP (*Washington*)			patrol section waters
YP (ex-motor vessel *Point Reyes*)			patrol section waters
YP-86 (ex-purse seiner *Pacific Fisher*)	73.6	1937	patrol section waters
YP-88 (ex-purse seiner *Adventure*)	74.6	1937	patrol section waters
YP-93 (ex-purse seiner *Margaret F.*)	69	1937	patrol section waters
YP-94 (ex-purse seiner *Western Chief*)	76.4	1936	patrol section waters
Section Base, Ketchikan			
YP (ex-fishing vessel *Hiram*)			patrol section waters
YP-197 (ex-FWS *Brown Bear*)	114.8	1934	in repair at Seattle
YP-250 (ex-gas fishing boat *Spencer*)	64	1913	in repair at Seattle
YP-251 (ex-halibut schooner *Foremost*, Jack L. Hull, Chief Boatswain's Mate, USCG)	79.7	1924	in repair at Seattle
YP-401 (ex-*Monterey*)	110	1917	en route to Seattle
Section Base, Kodiak			
YP-72 (ex-cannery tender *Cavalcade*)	87	1940	patrol section waters
YP-74 (ex-purse seiner *Endeavor*)	72.1	1937	in repair at Cordova
YP-95 (ex-purse seiner *Nordic Pride*)	74.8	1940	in repair at Seward
YP-148 (ex-purse seiner *Western Queen*)	85	1940	patrol section waters
YP-151 (ex-purse seiner *Sunrise*)	80.2	1931	patrol section waters
YP-152 (ex-purse seiner *Western Traveler*)	78.8	1937	patrol section waters
YP-155 (ex-purse seiner *Storm*)	74.7	1939	patrol section waters
Section Base, Sitka			
YP (ex-*Bendora*)			patrol section waters
YP-73 (ex-purse seiner *Corsair*)	84.5	1937	patrol section waters
YP-85 (ex-purse seiner *Nick C. II*)	72.1	1939	patrol section waters
YP-92 (ex-purse seiner *Helen B.*, Lt. Harold Wright)[9]	72.3	1938	patrol section waters

Captain Parker still had too few YP boats available for patrol of Alaskan and Aleutian waters. This shortfall was partially alleviated on 25 May when twenty-two YPs—*72-73, 83-84, 86, 88, 94-96, 148-149, 151-155, 197, 333, 338, 396-397,* and *401*—were reassigned to the Northwest Sea Frontier from local defense forces of the Thirteenth Naval District. Rear Adm. Charles S. Freeman, USN, commanded the Northwest Sea Frontier—comprised of both the Alaskan Sector and Northwestern Sector. He was also commandant of the subordinate Thirteenth Naval District and thus controlled both sea frontier and local defense forces. The reallocation of particularly seaworthy district craft to sea frontiers was prompted by a Navy directive limiting local defense force vessels to those craft that could not be used in the open sea under favorable conditions. A rigorous selection of craft was to be made for transfer from local defense forces to sea frontier forces on a temporary basis. The justification for the action was the Navy's desire to "keep on top of enemy subs." Commanders were to make every effort to keep the vessels at sea two-thirds of the time. On 28 May 1942, the YPs began operations as a part of Task Force 8.[10]

PRELUDE TO BATTLE

Rear Adm. Theobald arrived at Kodiak on 28 May and immediately called a conference of his commanders to explain his general plan of organization and operation, and to allow them to review his draft operation plan. In attendance were Maj. Gen. Simon B. Buckner Jr., USA (commanding general Alaskan Defense); Brig. Gen. William O. Butler, Air Corps, USA (commanding general Eleventh Air Force); Capt. Ralph C. Parker, USN (commander Alaskan Sector); and Capt. Leslie E. Gehres, USN (commander Patrol Wing Four). The overarching guidance of the OpPlan was brief and to the point:

> This force will, in coordination with the Army, oppose the advance of the enemy in the Aleutian-Alaska Area, taking advantage of every favorable opportunity to inflict strong attrition.[11]

Based on information gleaned by his codebreakers, Nimitz provided Theobald with the projected composition of the Japanese Northern Force expected to attempt to seize bases in the Aleutian Islands area. Theobald subsequently received intelligence that this force would arrive off Kiska on 31 May or 1 June 1942, that Unalaska Island was the objective, and that he should expect an air attack on Dutch Harbor between 31 May and 3 June, followed by a landing attack between 1 and 4 June.[12]

DEPLOYMENT OF SCOUTING FORCES

All shipping was ordered out of the Umnak area in anticipation of the Japanese attack, and on 30 May, Task Force 8 units—the submarines *S-34* and *S-35*, gunboat *Charleston*, minesweeper *Oriole* (AM-7), seaplane tenders *Casco* (AVP-12), *Williamson* (AVD-2), and *Gillis* (AVD-12) and Coast Guard cutters and YPs—were en route to their stations in Aleutian Peninsula waters. The two "S-boats" were units of Submarine Division 41, comprising the Submarine Group, and the tenders were support ships for the seaplanes and three scouting planes of Patrol Wing Four. These aircraft, along with one flight of Army

Bombardment Squadron 36, comprised the Air Search Group. The Surface Search group was made up of the *Charleston*, *Oriole*, cutters *Haida* (WPG-45), *Onondaga* (WPG-79), *Cyane* (WPC-105), *Aurora* (WPC-103), and *Bonham* (WPC-129); and fourteen YPs.[13]

Diagram 10-1

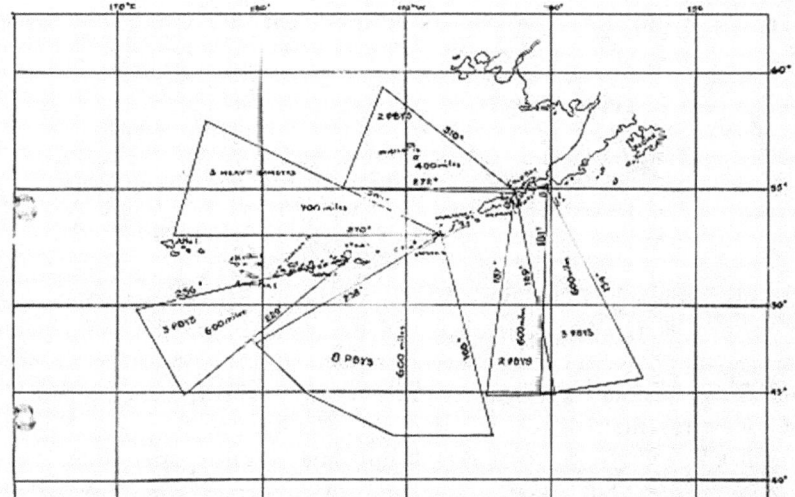

Patrol Wing Four began searching the fog-shrouded Aleutian Islands for the Japanese Northern Force on 29 May 1942.
Commander Task Group 8 1 Operational Plan No. 1-42

Theobald had initiated seaplane patrol flights on 29 May, a day before deployment of the patrol craft to picket stations on the Pacific and Bering Sea approaches to Dutch Harbor. The seaplane tenders were tasked to support Army aircraft as well as Navy planes. *Casco* was assigned to base at Cold Bay to provide services to the four PBYs of Task Group 8.1.2 under Lt. Comdr. James S. Russell, provide torpedoes and servicing to Army and Navy aircraft, and function as an interceptor radar station for Army pursuit planes. *Williamson* was to provide services for an equal number of PBYs (Lt. Comdr. Charles E. Perkins' Task Group 8.1.3) operating from Sand Point on Popof Island. Lastly, *Gillis* was to operate in the Akutan Pass area as a rescue and homing vessel for Task Group 8.1.1, the Dutch Harbor Unit under Lt. Comdr. Paul Foley Jr. Comprising this unit were twelve PBYs and one B17. A fourth tender, *Hulbert*, would later arrive at Kodiak from Pearl Harbor, in mid-afternoon on 6 June, due to an urgent requirement for additional such ships. From Kodiak, *Hulbert* proceeded to Dutch Harbor via a stop at Cold Bay on 8 June, where she transferred passengers, mail and freight to *Casco*. Arriving at Dutch Harbor late the following morning, she moored alongside the Army transport USAT *President Fillmore* to take fuel and then stood out again, bound for Sand Point, per new orders. Upon her arrival there on 10 June, she tended four planes of Squadron 43.[14]

Tender	Initial Assignment	Planes Tended	Officer in Charge
Casco	Cold Bay	TG 8.1.2 (VP-42)	Lt. Comdr. James S. Russell, USN
Williamson	Sand Point, Popof Island	TG 8.1.3 (VP-43)	Lt. Comdr. Charles E. Perkins, USN
Gillis	Dutch Harbor	TG 8.1.1 (VP-41)	Lt. Comdr. Paul Foley Jr., USN
Hulbert	Sand Point, Popof Island	TG 8.1.3 (VP-43)	Lt. Comdr. Perkins, USN

Information about the YP boats assigned to the Surface Search Group is sketchy, as is information about conditions and any enemy forces they encountered. However, the experiences of the flagship *Charleston* were likely typical. A meeting of ships' commanding officers with representatives of commander, Alaskan Sector, on 29 May finalized arrangements for establishing the surface patrol lines. The *Charleston* left Dutch Harbor the following morning for Akutan Pass, which separates Unalaska from Umnak Island. Arriving on her station in the early morning on 31 May, she found the weather misty, with visibility decreasing at times to 200 yards, rough seas, and strong winds. The weather in the Aleutian Islands, especially toward the western part, is among the worst in the world. When sudden blasts of cold dense wind, called "williwaws," sweep down from snow and ice fields of coastal mountains, winds may increase to gale proportions; speeds of 100 knots are not uncommon. When these conditions occur, heavy seas and strong currents running through passes and channels near jagged island shorelines and shoals make navigation extremely hazardous. Rain is common even on good days and when it is not raining, there is normally fog. Moreover, it is a peculiarity of the area that fog and wind may persist together for many days at a time.[15]

The first day of June found *Charleston* patrolling in misty fog, which allowed occasional stretches of visibility up to ten miles, and a cloud ceiling that varied in height from zero to 1,500 feet. In early evening, winds increased to gale force and the seas became rough. The following day, there were gale force winds with a 2,000 foot ceiling and 10 mile-maximum visibility; both decreased over the course of the day during which the patrol ship saw and heard nothing. On 3

June the seas were fairly smooth, with an overcast sky blocking any sunlight; visibility was between one-half and three miles. That night the sky was dark, and there was no indication of enemy forces in the vicinity. The following morning, crewmen felt a heavy thud against the ship's hull, believed due to a submarine-fired torpedo that failed to explode. There was, however, no sighting of an enemy submarine, aircraft, or ship. The weather worsened during the forenoon, with winds reaching gale force, creating long swells.[16]

Map 10-2

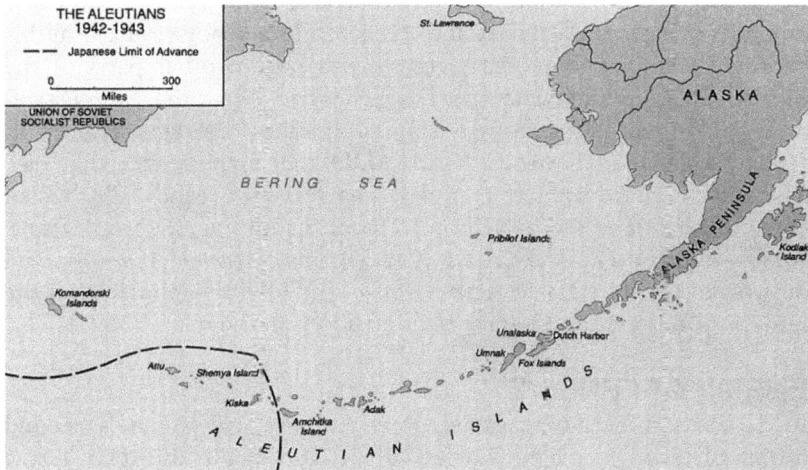

PBY Catalina seaplanes and YPs patrolled fog-shrouded Aleutian waters in search of the Japanese Fleet during the Battle of Midway.

DISPOSITION OF TASK FORCE 8

Theobald, embarked in the cruiser *Nashville* (CL-43), departing Kodiak in company with the oiler *Sabine* (AO-25) on the afternoon of 1 June to rendezvous at sea with other units of the main body. Having dispatched his submarines, patrol planes, and surface picket vessels to scout for the Japanese force, and having positioned the Destroyer Striking Group—*Case* (DD-370), *Brooks* (DD-232), *Sards* (DD-243), *Kane* (DD-235), *Dent* (DD-116), and *Humphreys* (DD-236)—at Makushin Bay, Theobald intended to use Army land-based aircraft and, as opportunity allowed, his own cruisers to engage the enemy. The *Case*, a new destroyer, and five older World War I "four stackers" were to remain in Makushin Bay to serve as "weapons of opportunity." While almost certain destruction awaited the ships if caught out by the Japanese, the large inlet southwest of Dutch Harbor offered a backdrop of land to help screen them from enemy air and radar detection. The defensive air patrol that the Army maintained over its airfield on Umnak Island, seventy-five miles southwest, would also afford a measure of protection. Meanwhile, should the Japanese advance sufficiently close, the destroyers might have an opportunity to dash out under the cloak of darkness to launch a torpedo attack on enemy cruisers and transports.[17]

Theobald, who believed that the Japanese would try to seize Dutch Harbor by landing troops ashore somewhere between Umnak in the eastern Aleutians and Cold Bay on the tip of the Alaska Peninsula, positioned his small force south of Kodiak in order to defend the eastern Aleutians and Alaska. He did not yet have all his allocated ships, as some were still en route from other parts of the Pacific. By 2 June the destroyer *Humphreys* had joined the *Nashville* and *Sabine* to screen them from enemy submarines; the light cruiser *St. Louis* (CL-49) and destroyer *Gilmer* (DD-233) arrived later that day. The only contact sighted that day was the submarine *S-27*, which crossed in front of the formation. The next morning, a group of four ships—the cruisers *Indianapolis* (CA-35) and *Honolulu* (CL-48), and destroyers *Gridley* (DD-380) and *McCall* (DD-400)—appeared on the horizon and proceeded to take their positions in the main body.[18]

ENEMY OFFENSIVE

In darkness a few hours earlier, Rear Adm. Kakaji Kakuta's Second Mobile Force—the light carriers *Ryujo* and *Junyo* and two heavy cruisers, screened by destroyers—had made a run in toward Dutch Harbor in preparation to launch an attack. His primary object was to strike Dutch Harbor, and thereby deflect Nimitz's forces from Midway. However, he also had orders to destroy installations that might facilitate an air invasion of Japan, and to cover and support the Kiska and Adak-Attu occupation forces. The carriers reached their launch position, 165 miles south of Dutch Harbor, undetected around 0250, having eluded both the search planes and the picket line of Coast Guard cutters and YPs. The same fog that shielded the enemy hindered aircraft in navigating over water. The *Junyo* attack group turned back half-way to the target, while the *Ryujo*'s planes found clear skies over parts of Dutch Harbor, allowing them to strike targets ashore. Many of the planes, though, were unable to find their way back to their ships and, once their fuel was expended, fell into the sea.[19]

FIRST ATTACK ON DUTCH HARBOR

At 0645 Theobald received a dispatch from Naval Air Station, Dutch Harbor stating that it had been attacked by a group of torpedo bombers and fighter aircraft. The planes appeared without warning, but the air base had been at dawn battle stations daily and heavy anti-aircraft fire opened immediately. Enemy fighters strafed a Catalina seaplane taking off for Kodiak, resulting in two crewmen killed and another injured, and damaged another four PBYs nearby. Bombers hit fuel tanks, a radio station, warehouses, and barracks at Fort Mears, setting fire to some structures and increasing casualties to eighteen soldiers, three sailors, one Marine, and one civilian.[20]

During and immediately after the strike on Dutch Harbor, there were numerous contacts between Catalinas and enemy aircraft, mostly as PBYs were returning to base to refuel before resuming their patrols. Slow and ungainly by comparison, the flying boats wisely tried to avoid exposure to enemy fighters. The pilot of one Catalina did encounter two adversaries more to his liking—a pair of unarmed single-engine observation planes. He shot one down, and later apologized for letting the other escape.[21]

Following the first attack, Theobald's orders to the main body—the destroyers at Makushin Bay and six submarines under his command—remained, "Exploit favorable opportunity to deliver attrition attacks upon enemy forces...." A greater number of enemy bombers with their fighter escort were sent against Dutch Harbor the following day. Although Catalinas made occasional contact with Japanese ships, U.S. Army bombers, flying from Cold Bay and Umnak to the west of Dutch Harbor, had been unable, due to the conditions, to make effective attacks on the enemy carrier force.[22]

ARRIVAL OF ADDITIONAL PATROL CRAFT

Prior to the first attack, five additional patrol vessels—the cutter *Onondaga* (WPG-79) and YPs *72*, *74*, *151*, and *155*—had arrived at Dutch Harbor on the morning of 3 June and then had stood out to sea: *YP-74* in company with the destroyer *Talbot* (DD-114) to proceed to her station; seaplane tender *Gillis* with YPs *72*, *151*, and *155* for a special mission; and *Onondaga* to clear the harbor until it was safe to return. Dispatched to rescue two aircraft forced down east of Akutan Island, the *Gillis* searched that area and in the vicinity of Tigalda Island with negative results. She then proceeded through Unimak Pass to examine the north side of Akun Island, again without success. *Gillis* next received orders to locate and recover a plane shot down fifteen miles southeast of Scotch Cap lighthouse on Unimak. She searched those waters and the coastlines of all the islands in the area to no avail. The cutter *Nemaha* had retrieved the plane, but had not reported its recovery in order to maintain radio silence. *Gillis* returned to Dutch Harbor during the afternoon of 4 June and moored at the oil dock to receive much-needed fuel. There were few ships in port; available destroyers had been absorbed by Task Force 8, and YPs and other small craft were engaged in patrol and mercy activities.[23]

SECOND ATTACK ON DUTCH HARBOR

At 1635 the air station alert sounded. *Gillis* set general quarters and, after clearing the fuel dock, was directed to provide protection for the S.S. *President Fillmore* and the S.S. *Morlen*, which were just getting underway. At 1751, as she was leaving port with the two ships in trail, the seaplane tender sighted a formation of approximately twenty-six Japanese aircraft approaching through Akutan Pass to attack Fort Mears and Dutch Harbor.[24]

Photo 10-2

Seaplane tender *Gillis* (AVD-12) at sea on 14 February 1941.
U.S. Navy Photograph #80-G-13141, now in the collections of the National Archives

Gillis opened fire with her forward 3-inch mount, diverting the aircraft from the *Fillmore* and *Morlen*. The formation then split into smaller groups of high altitude bombers, dive bombers, and fighters. Dive bombers made a run at the fuel tanks at the dock where the seaplane tender had been only a few minutes earlier, setting them aflame, but did not emerge unscathed, as one plane was hit streaming smoke as it pulled out of its dive. Two aircraft mounted a strafing attack on the *Fillmore*, which proved to be anything but an easy target. In addition to her normal ship armament, the Army troop transport had a deck-loaded battery of 37mm guns consigned for delivery to Cold Bay, giving her twenty-two anti-aircraft guns. Once in action their combined muzzle flashes made it appear to an observer off the ship that she was on fire. Having found the transport a "tough slog," the planes broke off and attacked the *Gillis*. Her 20mm and .50-caliber gunfire forced them to retire, with one trailing smoke as it rounded Priest Rock on its way out of Akutan Pass. The tender's 3-inch guns had kept horizontal bombers at a high altitude, and sent into the sea one of three planes attempting to approach undetected by flying low along the shoreline. Thereafter, all Japanese aircraft withdrew.[25]

Lt. Comdr. Norman F. Garton, *Gillis*' commanding officer, later received the Silver Star for the actions of his ship that day, as detailed in the medal citation:

> The President of the United States of America takes pleasure in presenting the Silver Star to Lieutenant Commander Norman Farquhar Garton, United States Navy, for conspicuous gallantry while serving as Commanding Officer of the Seaplane Tender U.S.S. *GILLIS* (DD-260), in action against enemy Japanese forces during the Aleutian Islands Campaign, Territory of Alaska, in June and July 1942. As a result of the training he gave his crew, his brilliant combat leadership and his indefatigable devotion to duty, the *GILLIS* shot down four and probably five enemy aircraft and made possible the first intensive continuous bombing of enemy concentrations on Kiska Harbor, thereby contributing greatly to the successful operations of Patrol Wing Four. His conduct throughout was in keeping with the highest traditions of the United States Naval Service.[26]

While the damage inflicted by the enemy was not sufficient to knock out Dutch Harbor as an operating base, aircraft destroyed four fuel tanks, demolished a wing of the hospital, damaged an uncompleted hangar, and partially destroyed the old steamship S.S. *Northwestern*. The dilapidated vessel (constructed in 1889 in Chester, Pennsylvania, as the *Orizaba*) was beached for use as a barracks ship. Fort Mears suffered the destruction of four bombers, three fighters, and two seaplanes; casualties increased the death list to forty-three. A group of enemy fighters made a strafing run on Fort Glenn, sixty-five miles west on Umnak Island. Army pursuit planes from Otter Point airfield shot down two of the aircraft and the remaining seven withdrew without inflicting any damage.²⁶

Photo 10-3

S.S. *Northwestern* burns after the attack by Japanese carrier planes on 4 June 1942. U.S. National Archives Photograph #80-G-215398

As soon as the raid developed, Army and Navy planes had initiated a search for the enemy carriers and made contact with Japanese ships several times. However, on almost every occasion, the enemy was able to vanish into fog banks before large air forces could be concentrated against them. Theobald had envisioned that Catalina scout planes would locate and maintain contact with the enemy until heavy bombers, if available, could mass an attack. The practice of the PBYs was to send contact updates until forced to withdraw to refuel, and to launch an attack before their departure, with enemy carriers being the most important target.²⁷

TASK FORCE COMMANDER VISITS KODIAK

On learning of the second attack on Dutch Harbor, Theobald ordered the commanding officer of the *Indianapolis* to take command of the main body, and the admiral set out in the *Nashville* for Kodiak, accompanied by the *Gridley*. En route he received a succinct update just prior to midnight:

> 11 bombers and 7 fighters attacked Dutch Harbor at 1808 W [local time]. SS *Northwestern* and warehouses lost. Details will follow.[28]

Following his arrival at Kodiak on the morning of 5 June, Theobald went ashore to confer with the commanders of the Air Search Group, Air Striking Group, and Alaskan Sector. During the meeting he emphasized the absolute necessity to concentrate planes of the Air Striking Group for immediate attack following location of the enemy, and to keep the task force commander informed of operations. Theobald had ordered the units of the main body to maintain radio silence in order to prevent the enemy from pinpointing their location through use of high-frequency direction-finding equipment. However, this policy prevented him from transmitting timely instructions, which instead had to be delivered to the recipient by a ship detached from the main body. Following the conference, Theobald returned aboard the *Nashville* and left Women's Bay at 1605.[29]

SEAPLANE AND CREW CASUALTIES MOUNTING

After leaving the meeting, commander, Air Search Group sent a dispatch to Theobald informing him of the steady degradation of the Catalinas, their nearly expended stamina of pilots and crews, and an existing, desperate need for additional planes:

> Originator declares not more than 14 doubtfully effective Catalinas remaining now. Operational and combat losses in maintaining contact are mounting and Army air has not yet struck effective blow. Pilots and crews at limit of endurance after 48 hours continuous flying and fighting despite usual Aleutian weather. This night will just about end them. Must have replacements or these Japs will give us the slip.[30]

Nashville and *Gridley* rejoined Task Group 8.6 south of Kodiak on 6 June, and Theobald resumed command of the main body. In the late afternoon of the following day, he received a dispatch from Naval Air Station, Kodiak summarizing air attacks on enemy forces, and offering the good news that all but one crew of downed aircraft had been recovered. The message conveyed in part:

Latest count of attacks 4 June one torpedo by Catalina ineffective due engine failure. Bombing of CV [aircraft carrier] by Catalina repulsed by AA [anti-aircraft] hits. Dive bombing on CV with torpedo by B26 ineffective [.] Torpedoes on CA [heavy cruiser] by 2 B26 2 hits claimed. Torpedo on CV by B26 repulsed by AA. Bombs on CV by B17 results undetermined.

14 Catalinas now effective including 2 replacements received 5 June.... All lost Catalina crews except 1 definitely recovered by [seaplane] tenders or fish boats [YPs]. Exception last seen 4 June with fish boat nearby.[31]

No enemy contacts were made the following day due to heavy fog, and all plane crews were experiencing extreme fatigue due to constant alerts, lack of proper facilities at dispersal points, and endless flying.[32]

ENEMY OCCUPATION OF ATTU AND KISKA

Meanwhile, on 6 June, under cover of fog, Japanese forces had begun the occupation of Attu and Kiska whose only military installations were meteorological outposts. Reports from these stations ceased the next day, and while it was not unusual for either station to miss broadcasting one or more weather updates, it was curious for both stations to miss all of them. On 10 June, after the fog had abated somewhat, a PBY reported substantial Japanese forces on both islands: four ships in Kiska harbor, one probably a cruiser and one a destroyer; and at Attu, a tent camp and numerous small boats and landing barges.[33]

That evening, having learned that Japanese forces had occupied Kiska and Attu, Captain Gehres sent a dispatch to the *Gillis* directing that all seaplanes out on night patrol return to base by way of Kiska and, fuel state permitting, drop their bombs on the enemy. The seaplane tender was then at Atka, 350 miles west of Dutch Harbor, having relocated there earlier that day to tend PBY Catalinas scheduled to operate from the small island.[34]

NIMITZ ORDERS CATALINAS TO BOMB JAPANESE OUT OF KISKA

On the evening of 11 June, Nimitz ordered commander, Patrol Wing Four to bomb the Japanese out of Kiska, superseding Theobald's employment of the PBYs as primarily a search group, with Army bombers as the strike force. On receipt of these orders, Captain Gehres directed every unit operating with the Wing to attack the enemy in Kiska continuously with bombs and torpedoes. The "Atka-

Kiska-*Gillis* bombing shuttle" had actually begun earlier that day when, at 0345, Gehres (embarked in *Gillis*) started sending planes with 500-pound bombs to Kiska as quickly as they could be loaded. Aircraft from Patrol Squadrons VP-41, 42, and 43 arrived at Atka from Cold Bay, Dutch Harbor, and Otter Point (on Amnak Island) in execution of the operation, described thus by Gehres:

> For the next forty-eight hours there occurred what I believe to be one of the most remarkable exhibitions of pure tenacity of purpose that has ever occurred in any military or naval force. Every plane available to PatWing 4 shuttled almost continuously from Dutch Harbor to Kiska, back to Atka for refueling and rearming thence back to Kiska. This was kept up day and night until *Gillis* has issued all her supply of bombs and every pumpable gallon of aviation gasoline. She was then relieved by *Hulbert*.[35]

Map 10-3

Kiska, Aleutian Islands
ONI Combat Narratives: The Aleutians Campaign (Washington DC: 1945)

On 11 June, following the departure of the four VP-43 planes she was tending to attack Kiska, *Hulbert* had proceeded from Sand Point to Nazan Bay, Atka, to top off fuel and gasoline and to augment the facilities of *Gillis*. There were no other tenders available for such duty. *Casco* was furnishing services at Cold Bay, and *Williamson* at Kodiak. Following her arrival at Nazan Bay at 2052 on 12 June, *Hulbert* anchored in company with *Gillis*.[36]

By 12 June, enemy forces and anti-aircraft installations at Kiska had increased sufficiently that it was extremely hazardous for seaplanes to attempt to enter the harbor either under the overcast or from above through breaks in the cloud cover. Gehres summarized the damage that the planes had sustained and described the tactic adopted by pilots to minimize losses. Their strategy entailed plummeting downward through solid cloud cover, finding a target visually upon breaking through, and immediately dropping their bombs and pulling up to minimize the possibility of taking fire or crashing:

> [Three] planes...returned from bombing raids so riddled with machine gun fire and anti-aircraft shell fragments that they would not float. Two sank on landing. One was beached, but it was necessary to burn and abandon it. Despite this heavy anti-aircraft damage only one crew member was killed and two wounded.
>
> The attacks were invariably made diving through the overcast at the speed, unheard of for PBY's, of 250 knots and dropping the bombs by "seaman's eye" method, then making a four-hand pullout back into the overcast. During this two day period of continuous bombing, there were contacts, bomb hits, and combats too numerous to list in detail...[37]

Having been recalled from picket ship duties, the units of the Surface Search Group were conducting normal patrol and escort duty from section bases under the direction of commander, Alaskan Sector. Some YPs were also searching for crews of downed Catalinas and performing general salvage work amid challenging conditions. One "fishboat," in urgent need of fuel, water, and provisions, approached *Charleston* which was patrolling nearby. However, rough seas and force-six winds prevented her from coming alongside for replenishment. The gunboat ordered the YP to proceed to Dutch Harbor via Unalga or Akutan Pass for supplies and then return to station.[38]

On the afternoon of 23 June, *Gillis* reported that her gasoline would be expended that night, and she was ordered to evacuate the Aleuts living on Atka and "scorch" the earth before her departure from the island. However, with 24 seaplanes moored in Nazan Bay at one time, and 68 officers and over 170 men on board resting while their aircraft were refueled and rearmed, a Japanese scout plane suddenly appeared over the harbor and then departed hastily westward to avoid pursuit. With both her location and that of her charges now disclosed to the enemy, the tender received orders to evacuate immediately. Gehres described the subsequent actions:

Planes still unfueled and armed were apportioned the *Gillis*'s remaining gas and bombs as rapidly as possible. Those refueled with sufficient gas to make the trip immediately took off for Dutch Harbor via Kiska. Others had barely enough gas to reach Umnak and had to go direct. Five planes were left at the buoys with no gas for them until the *Hulbert* could arrive at 2000. Leaving these planes at the moorings, the *Gillis* proceeded to another anchorage, sent ashore [a] party of men who obtained gasoline from a cache which was useless for planes, spread it on the village of Atka and burned the village.[39]

The *Gillis* removed the school teacher and his wife, Mr. and Mrs. McKee, but could not evacuate the village natives as they had scattered to the hills when the Japanese aircraft appeared. Meanwhile, the *Hulbert* had arrived and refueled the remaining planes as *Gillis* loaded them with bombs, and the PBYs set off for Dutch Harbor via Kiska. Late that night, at 2340, the *Gillis* departed bound for Kodiak, arriving at the air station in the early evening on 15 June.[40]

The first army bombers had arrived over Kiska on 12 June and were quickly initiated by the Japanese. During the initial attack, the flight leader of a group of five B24s made the mistake of attempting a long, straight-away bombing run at 1,700 feet in the face of heavily concentrated anti-aircraft fire. Struck by gunfire in the bomb bay, the lead plane exploded and disintegrated in the air. Eight drops were made by the other planes near a cruiser with no apparent damage. The four B24s then dropped six bombs from a safer 18,000 feet, and observed resultant fires on a cruiser. Three heavy cruisers, two light cruisers, and twelve seaplanes were present in the harbor with two light cruisers or destroyers entering port, and a carrier ten miles to the north.[41]

The Aleutian portion of the Battle of Midway ended in mid-June 1942 with enemy forces occupying two islands of little value. Theobald's expectation of a fleet action had not materialized and the Aleutians battle became a contest of air power, as had Midway. Reconnaissance flights during the latter part of the month revealed that while a majority of the Japanese ships had apparently withdrawn, the remaining strong landing forces on Kiska and Attu were digging in and establishing advance bases on the barren islands. Amid the stalemate in the Territory of Alaska, the Navy dispatched two additional flag officers to the theater. On 22 June Rear Adm. W. W. Smith, who had been Nimitz's chief of staff, reported to commander, Task Force 8, embarked aboard the *Indianapolis*, and assumed command of the main body. Theobald and his staff then relocated to

Naval Air Station, Kodiak. Four days later, Rear Adm. John W. Reeves, Jr., formerly commander, Northwest Sea Frontier, relieved Capt. Ralph C. Parker as commander, Alaskan Sector.[42]

AFTERMATH

In spite of some American concerns that the enemy occupation of Attu and Kiska signaled a Japanese intention to push eastward, there was no plan to invade the Alaskan mainland, Canada, or the United States. Although the Aleutian offensive was conceived by Yamamoto as a diversion to draw American naval forces away from Pearl Harbor, it was also defensive. Control of the western Aleutians by Japan would deny the United States the capability to launch air strikes against the empire from the islands as a prelude to an invasion. However, the brutal weather conditions and challenging terrain of the region that made sea, air, and land operations so formidable also made an Aleutians-Alaska invasion route unattractive to both American and Japanese strategists. Major General Buckner succinctly characterized the implausibility of such means to reach the United States:

> They might make it, but it would be their grandchildren who finally got there; and by then they would all be American citizens anyway![43]

There was, of course, great public sentiment against relinquishing a part of the Alaska Territory to the enemy, no matter how worthless. However, no immediate major countermove was possible due to the commitment of a large part of the Pacific Fleet to the impending campaign in the Solomon Islands.[44]

During the Aleutians campaign, additional YPs had arrived in Alaskan waters to augment existing patrol forces. On 15 June 1942, twenty-five YPs were operating from six section bases, while two from Ketchikan were undergoing repairs at Seattle. Called "YP boats" or "fish boats," these YPs would continue to carry out unheralded and sometimes heroic tasks for the duration of the war. The patrol craft, largely former seiners 75 to 104 feet in length, were commanded by young reserve officers, often on their first tour of sea duty. Operations around Kodiak and Dutch Harbor, and the uncharted reefs and rocky beaches of the bleak Aleutians, tested the mettle of these little ships, particularly when they were iced down and wallowing in masthead-high seas.[45]

Photo 10-4

Crewmen of the 72-foot *YP-92*, former purse seiner *Helen B.*, on deck after a snow storm.
Courtesy of Earl W. Mundy Jr., NavSource:
www.navsource.org/archives/14/143109203.jpg

LAURELS FOR PATROL SQUADRONS

> *Anyone who has operated patrol planes knows the long hours before and after each flight which must be devoted to preparations for the next flight during a protracted flight operation of this kind. Anyone who has taken part in tender based operations also knows the endless hours spent in fueling, arming, taxiing, boating, and the confusion of other preparations for flight operations. It can fairly be said that the pilots and crews of this squadron enjoyed no rest during the operating period outlined above. In contrast to this it can also be fairly said that most of their operations were conducted in a region renowned as among the worse in the world for flying, and incidentally, a region with which most of the pilots were not acquainted. Their operations involved night flights, landings, and take offs from open roadsteads and tiny Aleutian Harbors without benefit of any aids to night flying or navigation. All flights after June 10 were made in search of or to attack the enemy with no protection other than their own guns. All flights were successfully completed. During the period commencing June 11, the squadron shifted its base several times and based on three different tenders. If greater difficulties and dangers have been safely overcome by airmen the author has not heard of them.*
>
> *No praise is too great for these officers and men.*

—Lt. Comdr. Frederick N. Kivette, USN, commanding officer of
USS *Williamson* (AVD-2), in a report on the operations of
Patrol Squadron Forty-three dated 14 June 1942[46]

Commander Patrol Wing Four, in his endorsement of Kivette's report, praised Squadrons 43 and 51. He noted that the two units of VP-43—one from San Diego led by Lt. Comdr. Carroll B. Jones, and one from Tongue Point, Astoria, Oregon, led by Lt. Comdr. H. L. Ray—and a VP-51 Alameda, California unit under Lt. Comdr. D. T. Day Jr., deserved to be listed with the great accomplishments of naval aviation. Almost without exception, the pilots of these units had no experience in Alaskan operations, and their parent squadrons had no periods of preparation. In Captain Gehres' words:

> They came with only what they could carry in the planes. Yet in less than four full days out of California, these squadrons were dropping bombs on the enemy in Kiska in the face of increasingly heavy opposition, and kept it up for nearly forty-eight continuous hours.[47]

Lt. Comdr. Norman F. Garton, commanding officer of the *Gillis*, received the Silver Star Medal for heroism. Patrol squadrons VP-42 and VP-43 received the Navy Unit Commendation (abbreviated NUC in the below table), and VP-51 a battle star. The table also lists the other patrol squadrons and tenders that took part in, or supported operations against Japanese forces in Aleutian waters from late-May through mid-June 1942. The squadron and ship commanding officers were all Regular Navy (USN).

Unit	Award Dates	Commanding Officer
VP-41		Lt. Comdr. Paul Foley Jr.
VP-42	NUC (1 Jun-1 Aug 1942)	Lt. Comdr. James S. Russell
VP-43	NUC (8 Jun-1 Aug 1942)	Lt. Comdr. Carroll B. Jones, and Lt. Comdr. H. L. Ray
VP-51	Battle Star (3-6 Jun 42)	Lt. Comdr. D. T. Day Jr.
Casco (AVP-12)		Comdr. Thomas S. Combs
Gillis (AVD-12)		Lt. Comdr. Norman F. Garton
Hulbert (AVD-6)		Lt. Comdr. James Mills Lane
Williamson (AVD-2)		Lt. Comdr. Frederick N. Kivette

11

Battle of Midway

Our citizens can now rejoice that a momentous victory is in the making. Perhaps we will be forgiven if we claim we are about midway to our objective.

—Adm. Chester W. Nimitz, June 1942

Commonly referred to as an island, Midway, located 1,141 nautical miles west-northwest of Honolulu, is actually a coral atoll, six miles in diameter, comprised of three islands: Sand, Eastern and Spit. The atoll's name is said to come from its location midway between San Francisco and Tokyo. It was first discovered in 1859, and the United States, recognizing its strategic importance, claimed it eight years later, in 1867, when Capt. William Reynolds, commanding the screw sloop-of-war *Lackawanna*, raised the American flag over the atoll. Under Navy direction, the construction of facilities for Catalina seaplanes began in March 1940, and Naval Air Station, Midway was commissioned on 18 August 1941. Despite its small size, the station hosted an airstrip on Eastern Island, as well as a hangar for seaplanes and other facilities on larger Sand Island.[1]

STRATEGIC IMPORTANCE OF THE ROCKY ATOLL

Two Japanese destroyers shelled the island on the night of 7 December 1941, withdrawing at 2200 after killing four men and wounding ten, damaging some buildings, and destroying one patrol plane. The token attack signaled that Midway held little interest to the enemy. However, two weeks later, the fall of Wake Island—a U.S. territory hosting a naval base two thousand nautical miles west of Honolulu—dramatically increased the strategic importance of Midway to the United States, and thereby to Japan as well. Located 1,027 nautical miles northeast of Wake and nearer Pearl Harbor, the atoll then became the western-most American outpost in the Central Pacific. From Midway shore-based seaplanes could fly patrols toward the Japanese-held Marshall Islands and Wake, checking on enemy activities and guarding against further attacks on Hawaii. The Japanese coveted Midway for use as a base from which empire forces could launch attacks on Pearl Harbor. However, because Midway lay beyond the range of Wake Island-based search planes, the enemy could not monitor U.S. naval activity on or near the atoll.[2]

Photo 11-1

Midway Atoll, 24 November 1941. Eastern Island, then the site of Midway's airfield, is in the foreground. Sand Island, location of most other base facilities, is across the entrance channel.
U.S. Navy photograph #80-G-451086, now in the collections of the National Archives

BUILDUP OF STATION DEFENSES

Nimitz visited Midway in early May 1942 to inspect its defenses and confer with the local commanders. As the Japanese threat became more eminent, he dispatched more ground and air forces to the atoll, crowding Eastern Island with Marine Corps, Navy, and Army Air Force planes. Fifteen PBY-5As (six from VP-24, seven from VP-44, and three from VP-51), equipped with retractable tricycle landing gear to enable amphibious operation, were based ashore on Eastern Island, and fourteen older PBY-5s from VP-23 at the seaplane facility on Sand Island. In addition, VP-91 was sent to Barking Sands airfield, on Kauai, in order to cover the ocean between Hawaii and Midway.[3]

Map 11-1

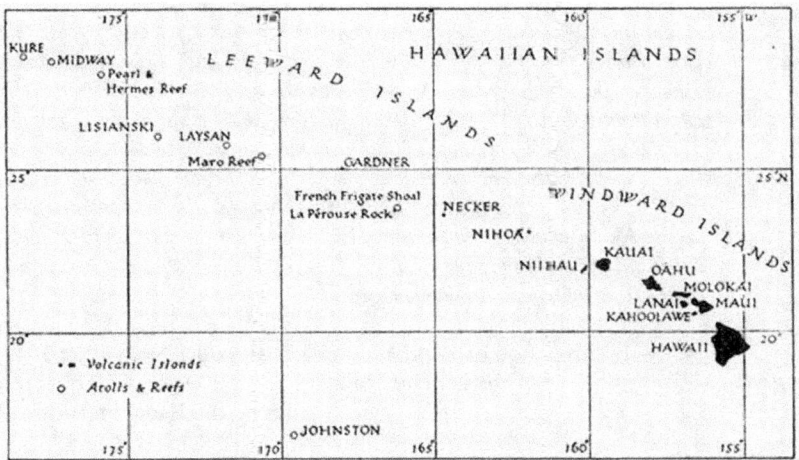

Hawaiian Islands
Source: http://www.lib.utexas.edu/maps/historical/pacific_islands_1943_1945/hawaiian_islands.jpg

On 29 May, the seaplane tender *Ballard* (AVD-10) and PT boats of Motor Torpedo Boat Squadron 1 arrived at Midway to bolster seaward defenses, and four ex-San Diego tuna clippers arrived to augment local defense forces. In anticipation of an impending air battle, the YPs were positioned near some small islands southeast of the station to refuel aircraft and rescue downed aviators. The *YP-284* (ex-*Endeavor*) was allocated to Lisianski, *YP-290* (ex-*Picaroto*) to Laysan, *YP-345* (ex-*Yankee*) to Gardner Pinnacles, and *YP-350* (ex-*Victoria*) to Necker. Other local defense force units were stationed near Midway or at other nearby lesser islands, reefs or shoals:

Midway Island	*PT-20*, *PT-21*, *PT-22*, *PT-24*, *PT-25*, *PT-26*, *PT-27*, and *PT-28*
Kure Island	*PT-29*, *PT-30*, and four small patrol craft
French Frigate Shoals	*Ballard* (AVD-10), *Thornton* (AVD-11), *Clark* (DD-361), and *Kaloli* (AOG-13)
Pearl and Hermes Reef	*Crystal* (PY-25) and *Vireo* (ATO-144)

By 4 June, the military forces stationed on or around Midway were as ready as possible to face the oncoming Japanese.[4]

PBY NIGHT TORPEDO ATTACK ON JAPANESE INVASION FORCE

> *About 0915, 3 June (+12), we saw one PBY [44-P-4 piloted by Ens. Jack Reid] circling formation about 600 miles west of MIDWAY, but no attack. About 1700 the same day, we were attacked by 9 B-17's. They were at different altitudes.... They surprised us, and [we] did not have time to open fire. The nearest bombs landed about 200 meters from a ship. No damage. We saw PBY's later but they did not attack. About midnight that same night we were attacked by two or three more PBY's. One dropped a torpedo which hit the tanker* Akebono Maru *in the bow. Eleven men were killed and 13 wounded but it did not sink, only slowed down. The PBY's also strafed the column of ships killing a few men but did no damage.*
>
> —Interrogation of Capt. Yasumi Toyama on 1 November 1945, former chief of staff, Second Destroyer Squadron during the Battle of Midway.[5]

> *This is a historical incident, being the first night torpedo attacks by our patrol planes on surface ships.*
>
> *The initial contact, and subsequent success of the attack, were in large measure made possible by the radar installation. Night torpedo attack, employing radar, represents one of the few profitable offensive uses of our patrol seaplanes.*
>
> —Rear Adm. Raymond A. Spruance, USN, chief of staff U.S. Pacific Fleet[6]

The morning of 3 June, PBY *44-P-4* reported at 0925 "Main body bearing 261°, distance 700 miles, six large ships in column." The same plane reported at 1100 that this force consisted of eleven ships on course 090, speed 19 knots. (These ships were actually a portion of the Japanese occupational force, identified in Appendix G, and not the main body.) Following receipt of the second report, a force of nine B17s armed with four 600-pound bombs each was ordered to attack this "main body." Taking off about 1230, the bombers found the enemy in late afternoon about 570 miles from Midway. The naval force consisted of the cruiser *Jintsu* (the flagship), and transports and cargo vessels screened by destroyers. The battleships and heavy cruisers the American bombers expected to find were several miles away. The B17s split into three flights of three planes each, and made their bomb drops from 8,000, 10,000, and 12,000 feet respectively. Heavy anti-aircraft fire precluded the planes from remaining in the area to observe the results of the attack. Reports from the aircraft commanders indicated that a heavy cruiser and a transport had been hit and a second cruiser was believed hit at the stern."[7]

Diagram 11-2

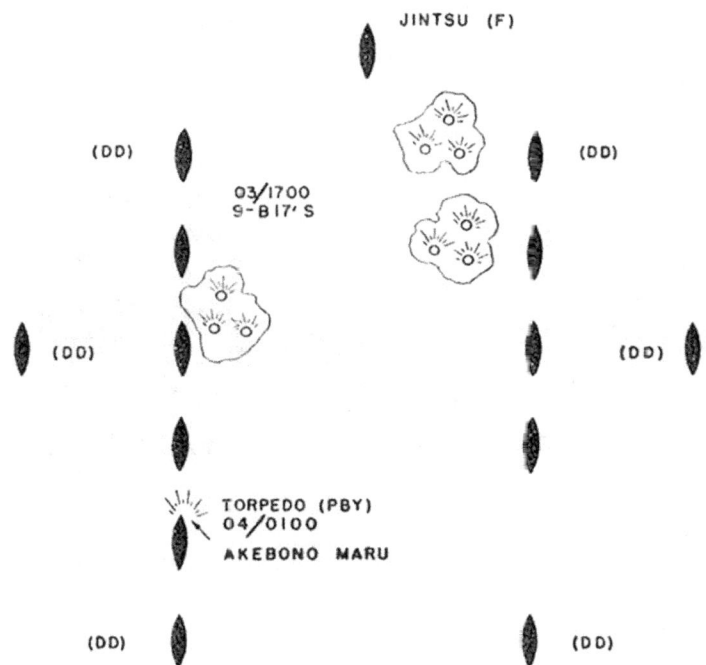

Diagram of the attacks made on 3-4 June on a portion of the Japanese occupational force approaching Midway, first by B17 bombers and then four PBY-5A seaplanes. United States Strategic Bombing Survey [Pacific], Annex A., of Capt. Yasumi Toyama's, IJN, 1 Nov 1945 interrogation (Courtesy of Ibilio Hyperwar Project)

Before the bombers had returned to Midway, and with the results of their mission unknown, a flight of four PBY-5A Catalinas, took off on a historical mission, the first night torpedo attack by patrol planes on surface ships. The planes were each armed with a single Mk. 13 torpedo. Lt. William L. Richards, USN, the executive officer of Patrol Squadron 44 and flight leader, received orders at about 2000 to "locate this force, deliver a torpedo attack, and return to base." The priority for attack was aircraft carriers, followed by battleships, and transports.[8]

When the flight left Midway that night at 2115, the weather was clear with some broken cumulus clouds at 1,000 feet. The lead plane turned on its formation lights and tail light, so that the other three PBYs could follow it in the darkness. They had their lights extinguished to reduce the possibility of detection by the enemy.

Lead plane:	*24-P-12*	Lt. William L. Richards, USN
Second plane:	*24-P-7*	Lt. (jg) Douglas C. Davis, USNR
Third plane:	*24-P-11*	Ens. Gaylord D. Propst, USNR
Fourth plane:	*51-P-5*	Ens. Allan Rothenberg, USNR[9]

Photo 11-2

Pilots of the four PBY-5A Catalina patrol bombers that flew the torpedo attack mission against the Japanese Fleet's Midway Occupation Force during the night of 3-4 June 1942. From left to right: Lt. (jg) Douglas C. Davis, Ens. Allan Rothenberg, Lt. William L. Richards, and Ens. Gaylord D. Propst.
U.S. Navy Photograph #80-G-64819, now in the collections of the National Archives

At about midnight, Rothenberg lost contact with the formation while climbing through a cloud area. An hour later, Propst became separated while going through a bank of clouds. The flight leader was unaware that two of his aircraft were no longer with him because they were showing no lights. Fifteen minutes after the second plane became detached radar contact was made by the flight leader at 0115 on "about ten ships" ten-to-twelve miles on the port beam of his aircraft. Richards came left to the bearing of the formation of ships. At 0120 the enemy force was visually sighted in the moonlight about seven miles dead ahead. The two remaining planes of the flight were at 3,000 feet, the moon was bright, and there were scattered cumulus between 1,000 and 2,000 feet. The silhouettes of the larger Japanese ships were clearly visible in the moonlight, although the heads of the two columns were obscured by cloud coverage.[10]

Richards circled once, to ensure that the planes following him had seen the enemy. After this maneuver, he was slightly abaft the port beam of the enemy formation. Richards gave the attack signal and began a glide downwards with engines throttled back and all lights extinguished. He selected the last large ship in the first column as his target. It presented the biggest silhouette and had been reported as possibly being a carrier, but as the range closed could be identified as a large transport or cargo ship of about 7,000 tons. As the flight leader continued his run in "up moon" for the attack, the plane continued to descend until it was about 100 feet off the water at 800 yards from the target ship. Immediately after launching his torpedo, Richards made a sharp right circling turn over the stern of the ship and then proceeded to a prearranged rendezvous point. Two crewmen serving as lookouts in the waist station of the plane reported a huge explosion and heavy smoke below as it passed over the ship, which would prove to be the tanker *Akeboro Maru*.[11]

Davis started his attack run in immediately after the leading plane, but unsatisfied with his position, withdrew to the north behind a cloud as he climbed to about 2,000 feet. As he began his approach about six minutes later, he controlled the plane's rudder and torpedo director, as Ens. R. J. Ney, his co-pilot, operated the elevators and ailerons. Just as Richards had done, he attacked "up moon" in a glide with throttles cut back. As he closed his target, the formation made a rapid turn to starboard, and the destroyers screening the group of transports began breaking formation. Davis described the ensuing torpedo attack:

> Began approach in at 1500 feet on enemy's port beam...maneuvering and descending with cut [silent] guns. Leveled off at 50-75 feet; airspeed 115 [knots] indicated. Dropped [torpedo] at 0150, range 200 yards. Target at drop had turned 90° to stbd; consequently drop was made from astern. Only then did transport open fire. Port waist gunner strafed decks on pull up. Retirement made to stbd. Several ships opened fire. Returned to

assess damage and identify further. Encountered more Destroyers and Anti Aircraft and machine gun fire.[12]

Davis reported that the enemy tracer fire was either red or pink in color, and that anti-aircraft explosives were white. A post-combat inspection revealed machine gun holes in the plane's wings, tail, and bow, evidence of damage from explosive bullets, and damage to the aircraft's bomb sight.[13]

After losing contact with the formation Ens. Gaylord D. Propst, piloting the third plane, had maintained course and speed and was able to pick up the target visually. He made his attack coming out of a wide spiral, with the final approach being made from the quarter into a "moon path." He launched his torpedo on what he believed to be the largest ship, the second from the end of the column. Immediately after he dropped the torpedo fifty feet off the water, 800-900 feet from the target, anti-air and machine gun fire opened on his plane. Propst made a feint to the right, and then a tight left turn. As he withdrew, he was attacked by a lone Japanese plane, believed to be a ship-based fighter, but was able to escape through judicious use of the scattered clouds available for cover.[14]

Ens. Allan Rothenberg, the pilot of the fourth plane and the first to lose contact with the PBY flight, had also continued to search. He contacted an advance screen of Japanese ships at 0030 and was fired at ineffectively by anti-aircraft guns. An unidentified, but believed enemy plane also made several approaches on him, but did not engage, and no shots were fired. At 0123, distance 520 miles from Midway, Rothenberg again encountered AA fire, ineffective as before. Unable to locate the enemy and with only one-half his fuel supply remaining, he turned back toward Midway, jettisoning his torpedo before landing at Laysan Island.[15]

Lt. (jg) James Clair Nolan, USNR, Rothenberg's co-pilot, described, in a personal diary entry, being sent out to find and attack the Japanese naval force, and encountering an enemy plane:

> Just about ready to turn in when we got the word that the four of us PBYs (the "reserve striking force") were going out immediately on a night torpedo attack. The B-17s reported the Japs bearing 261, distance 572 miles at about three o'clock that afternoon. We were to go out and get as many as possible—with PBYs!
>
> Climbed in our planes and took off at 8:30 p.m. . . . About 400 miles out we thought we saw anti-aircraft fire on our right, but due

to the rotten weather we couldn't see anything on the water. Soon the moon started to show through the clouds once in a while. When we reached the 520-mile mark about 1:30 Thursday morning and started to turn around, the waist hatch gunners spotted a plane tailing us. It blinked a red identification light at us a few times, so we knew it was a Jap, as our planes don't carry red identification lights. Just as we were about to fire on him he disappeared.

Can't understand why he didn't fire at us. A few seconds later anti-aircraft fire started going off around us. We circled looking for some ships, but could see nothing—pitch black. Thought we'd go back to where we saw the first anti-aircraft fire as the Japs should have been closer to Midway in 10 hours than 520 miles. . . . Started back, hoping to run into the Japs at about the 400-mile mark—but there was nothing we could see. The Eastern sky started to get light. . . . About 5:30 it turned light and about 6 the sun came up. About 6:30 our radio started to hum—the morning patrols out of Midway were spotting Japs North, West and South.[16]

Having failed to locate any enemy warships and low on fuel, the PBY headed back to Midway. Nolan worried that his plane would be shot down by a carrier-launched Japanese bomber or fighter or, alternatively, that it would run out of fuel and end up in the sea:

A report came through of a large body of Jap planes headed for Midway—we figured out they were only about 50 miles behind us. Would we beat them to Midway, or would they catch us and shoot us down? And, incidentally, where was the goddammed atoll called Kure Island, which we were supposed to pass over before approaching Midway? Our gas was getting low, the air and sea were swarming with Japs, and we weren't positive of our position, due to the impossibility of taking drift sights at night. [We] were beginning to feel desperate when I spotted Kure Island off to our right on the horizon. No one else could see it, even after flying toward it for 10 minutes.

As we got to Kure (with sighs of relief from all hands) and turned toward Midway (about 30 miles away over the horizon) I got a jolt—there, rising from the island which was just below the horizon, were the initial columns of dirt and smoke indicating exploding bombs. Our base was being bombed! And now the smoke was rising in dense billows while new plumes of dust and sand continued to shoot skyward. We couldn't see the Jap planes however. How we had missed contacting each other I shall never know—my luck was with me.[17]

Having avoided contact with one or more heavily armed, and maneuverable Japanese aircraft, which would have likely resulted in certain death, Nolan's priority was to liaison with the *YP-284* at Lisianski to refuel. She and the other three YPs each had about 3,000 gallons deck-loaded in drums for just that purpose:

> Headed for Lisianski Island, where a YP boat was supposed to be available for fueling...but could see nothing due to the heavy rain squalls. [We] circled around helplessly with an awful feeling in our hearts. Suddenly, below us, through the rain, I spotted the light blue water that indicates a submerged coral head. I knew then that we were right on top of the island. A few more circles and through a break we spotted the island—about 100-by-50 yards of coral covered by sand, with millions of birds flying about and a few seals sleeping on the sand. Circled looking for the YP boat and after 15 minutes of futile searching, decided to take our last chance and try for Laysan Island—120 miles away and we had only about 110 gallons of gas left—it would be close.
>
> An hour's flying brought us to Laysan and, thank God, there was a YP boat [the *YP-290*] with a pair of planes already fueling from her. We had six gallons left. Landed in the fairly rough water with a few nasty jolts, but luckily popped no rivets from the hull. Settled down to wait for our turn to fuel. I climbed up onto the top wing in the sun and, peeling off my shirt, went blissfully to sleep. After many hours of waiting we finally started fueling late in the afternoon. It continued 'til after dark. Decided to stay tied to [the] YP tender overnight.
>
> Climbed up onto top wing about 9 p.m. and turned in.[18]

The four seaplanes proceeded individually back toward their base upon completion of the attack. Upon arrival in the vicinity of Midway, they received by radio broadcast at 0641 "Air Raid Midway. Midway is now undergoing air raid." All planes set a course for Lisianski Island, over which they found a weather front of moderate intensity and about 80-100 miles wide. Propst in PBY *24-P-11* was forced to land at sea in the vicinity of Lisianski out of gas. (The crew would be rescued in early evening on 6 June. The plane itself was beyond salvage and was sunk by gunfire.) The other three planes diverted to Laysan.

Davis in PBY *24-P-7* landed at Laysan at 1000, with ten to twenty gallons of fuel remaining and several bullet holes in his aircraft. The flight leader, Richards in *24-P-12*, arrived there forty-five minutes later with less than fifty gallons remaining. Rothenberg, piloting *51-P-5*, arrived at 1105 to find, as described by Nolan, the other two planes receiving fuel from *YP-290*, the ex-tuna boat *Picaroto* from San Diego. Short of tenders, the Navy had dispatched her and three other former tuna boats (from a group of fourteen that had arrived at Pearl Harbor from San Diego) to Midway to function as such for the "eyes of the fleet."[19]

The three PBYs at Laysan returned to Pearl Harbor the following day. Nolan described arriving there to a celebration of the Navy's decisive victory in the second of five naval battles in the Pacific in which aircraft would play the predominant role:

> Awoke in the morning. Took on another 100 gallons, giving us nine hundred in all. Radioed Midway for instructions. They ordered us to return to Pearl Harbor. . . . Got a greasy egg sandwich from the tender [*YP-290*]. . . . Took off with a few mighty crashes on wave tops. Headed home and arrived at dusk. The newspapers are all howling over "our great victory at Midway." Seems as though the Japs got a good pasting. That's the first fight I've been in with them that my side won.[20]

Lieutenant Commander Richards noted in his report on the night torpedo attack that with the exception of himself, all pilots and crews involved in the mission had flown into Midway from Pearl Harbor on the afternoon of 3 June. "With a ten-hour flight already completed that day, and with no rest, all hands were more than willing to embark on an all-night combat mission." In the thirty-one hour period ending at 1100 on 4 June, each of the crews had been in the air a total of about twenty-three and a half hours. For three of the crews, this was followed by a flight back to Pearl Harbor the following day. The fourth crew was down at sea for about fifty-three hours before being rescued.[21]

BATTLE SUMMARY

The air battle of 4 to 7 June, conducted by Task Forces 16 and 17 formed around the carriers *Yorktown* (CV-5), *Enterprise* (CV-6), and *Hornet* (CV-8), brought about the resounding defeat of the Combined Fleet. Admiral Yamamoto suffered the loss of four carriers, *Akagi*, *Kaga*, *Soryu*, and *Hiryu*, with all their aircraft and many crew members (estimated at 275 planes, 2,400 men). Two, and probably three, battleships were also damaged, two heavy cruisers sunk, three or more heavy cruisers and one light cruiser damaged, three destroyers sunk, and four transport and cargo vessels hit, with an estimated total loss of 4,800 personnel. The U.S. Navy lost only the *Yorktown* and the destroyer *Hammann* (DD-412) with 92 officers and 215 men killed, and about 150 planes lost or damaged beyond repair.[22]

The Catalina seaplanes assigned to Naval Air Station, Midway played a key role in the battle. A flight of the scout planes made contact with the Japanese support force 700 miles west of Midway on 3 June and, in darkness early the following morning, made a high-level bombing attack against it. Three hours later, at 0430, both sides launched scout planes to search for one another's carriers. American PBYs spotted the Japanese carriers at 0520. However, pursued by Zero fighters and immersed in a deadly game of "cat and mouse" in the clouds above the Japanese Fleet, the scouts were unable to make a contact report until 0545. Twenty minutes later, a second and more detailed report followed. In the interim, Midway radar detected an incoming air raid and scrambled all planes still on the island. Battle was soon joined, the most significant part of which culminated at 1020 when dive bombers from the *Yorktown* and *Enterprise* arrived over the Japanese carriers, whose fighter protection had been spent destroying previous waves of attackers. This circumstance left the flattops, crammed with fully armed and fueled strike aircraft that had yet to launch, defenseless against the American raiders. In a span of five minutes, the strike fleet and Japan's dreams of victory and empire were engulfed in flame and destruction.[23]

EFFECT OF THE BATTLE OF THE CORAL SEA AND BATTLE OF MIDWAY ON THE JAPANESE FLEET

> *The loss of five carriers in May and June with several others damaged made it necessary to reorganize our striking forces. We wanted to capture MIDWAY to prevent another air attack upon JAPAN similar to the attack on 18 April [The Doolittle Raid]. We also wanted to use it for search as we did MARCUS and WAKE [islands]. We did not think the American forces were so strong as they were at MIDWAY. The loss of the carriers was later felt in our operations. We were unable to use seaplanes for long-range reconnaissance because we had to convert seaplane tenders like the* Chitose *to aircraft carriers. We also had to convert the [battleships]* Ise *and* Hyuga *(BB's, to carriers so they were lost to us for a long time. After MIDWAY we were defensive trying to hold what we had instead of expanding.*

—Response by Capt. Yasumi Toyama to the question, "Did the Battle of MIDWAY have any effect upon your planning?" during an interrogation of the former chief of staff Second Destroyer Squadron on 1 November 1945.[24]

CONTRIBUTIONS OF THE SEAPLANE TENDERS

The seaplane tenders *Ballard* (AVD-10) and *Thornton* (AVD-11) carried out routine duties in support of preparations for and during the Battle of Midway. The sister ships were former four-stack destroyers, commissioned in June, and July 1919, respectively. After World War I, *Ballard* was placed "out of commission in reserve" on 15 June 1922 and "laid up" in a reserve fleet in the San Diego area. She was placed in "commission in ordinary" on 25 June 1940. *Thornton* towed her to Union Yard of Bethlehem Steel Corp., San Francisco, for conversion to seaplane tender. She was placed in full commission on 2 January 1941 and reported to commander Aircraft, Scouting Force, Pacific Fleet for duty. Following the Japanese attack on Pearl Harbor on 7 December 1941, *Ballard* entered Navy Yard, San Francisco, for the replacement of her old 4-inch surface guns with two dual-purpose 3-inch guns. The new guns were installed on her fo'c'sle and after deckhouse. Ordered to join the fleet at Pearl Harbor, *Ballard* arrived there on 28 January 1942.[25]

In support of the buildup of Midway, *Ballard* left Pearl Harbor on 25 May for French Frigate Shoals, escorting several PT boats and carrying as a passenger the movie director John Ford. Ford, already a naval reserve officer, had gone on active duty after the Japanese attack on Pearl Harbor, and headed a documentary film unit. He would win back-to-back Academy Awards for *The Battle of Midway* (1942) in 1943 and for *December 7th* (1943) in 1944. After stopping at French Frigate Shoals on 26 May to refuel PT boats there, *Ballard* continued on to Midway with her own group of PT boats. It was necessary to refuel the motor torpedo boats while underway from the ship's aviation gasoline tank. *Ballard* arrived at Midway on 29 May, bade farewell to Ford and his assistant as they left the ship on their assignment, and took her departure for Pearl Harbor a few hours later.[26]

Two days after arriving back at Pearl Harbor, *Ballard* left again on 3 June for French Frigate Shoals. She refueled a squadron of PBYs there on 4 June, and then continued on to Midway with a much needed cargo of aviation gasoline and bombs. The seaplane tender reached Midway on 6 June, unloaded her cargo and then went in search of a downed PBY. She found the plane on 7 June, took it in tow, and delivered it to Midway the following day. That same day, *Ballard* received orders to investigate a rubber life raft sighted by a plane and to look for other survivors. On 12 June, she picked up a life raft with an unidentified body in it, as well as two balsa rafts and a rubber raft that were empty. *Ballard* returned to Midway on the 14th, offloaded the rafts, refueled, and then immediately departed for the western search area[27]

While combing her assigned area, she sighted a life boat containing thirty-five Japanese. As the *Ballard* approached the boat, articles were seen going over the side. By the time she got alongside, the boat was completely divested of anything that might be of military value to the U.S. Navy.[28]

The Japanese were taken aboard, stripped of all their clothing, searched, and put in a "bull pen" (enclosed area) on the quarterdeck. One of the prisoners died during the night from internal injuries and was buried at sea the next day, 20 June. The men were engineers from the aircraft carrier *Hiryu*. After an attack on their ship by a group of twenty-four SBD Dauntless dive bombers launched from the aircraft carrier *Enterprise* (which included ten refugees from the *Yorktown*, lost during the Battle of Midway) one of the men went topside, and discovered that the ship had been abandoned. He went below to the engine room and spread the word. The remaining engineers immediately lowered a life boat, and rigged a blanket as a sail. They had been in the boat for about two weeks. Upon her return to Midway the following day, *Ballard* turned the prisoners over to the Marine Corps commander.[29]

Battle of Midway 159

Photo 11-3

Cutter from the sunken Japanese aircraft carrier *Hiryu*, suspended from the starboard boat davits of USS *Ballard*, at Midway circa late June 1942.
U.S. Navy Photograph #80-G-79981-21, now in the collections of the National Archives

Photo 11-4

Japanese prisoners of war on board USS *Ballard* after being rescued from a lifeboat.
U.S. Navy Photograph #80-G-79974-1, now in the collections of the National Archives

Thornton was on station from 27 May to 3 June in the vicinity of French Frigate Shoals. Following her arrival there from Pearl Harbor she delivered supplies and radio equipment to the Marine Group on East Island, and then took up patrol duties nearby. The purpose of military forces on and around the shoals was to prevent enemy submarines from using the area as a refueling point for flying boat raids on Oahu, which had previously occurred. On 4 March 1942, two Kawanishi H8K "Emily" flying boats had made an ineffective bombing attack on Pearl Harbor due to cloud cover. The planes had launched from a field in the Marshall Islands and been refueled by submarines in sheltered waters off French Frigate Shoals. Included in Adm. Isoroku Yamamoto's plans for the Midway operation was an aerial reconnaissance mission above Pearl Harbor (code named OPERATION K) to determine whether there were any American carriers there. Naval patrols off the shoals had been increased, and a Japanese submarine sighting of two American warships at anchor there resulted in cancellation of the plan[30]

Thornton was under way during the day and lay to, or anchored near East Island at night to conserve fuel and prolong her time on station. During this period, she made no enemy contacts and sighted no vessels. She was relieved of these duties by *Ballard* on 4 June, and departed for Port Allen, Kauai. *Thornton* returned to French Frigate Shoals on 8 June and took up standby duty; anchored but "ready to slip cable and get underway in 30 seconds." She departed for Pearl Harbor the following day.[31]

LAURELS FOR SEAPLANE PILOTS AND CREWMEN

Pilots and crewmen of PBY Catalina seaplanes received medals of valor for their actions during the Battle of Midway. The pilots of the four PBY-5As—which made the first-ever night torpedo attack against enemy combatant ships at the Battle of Midway—received the Silver Star. The associated citation for Lt. Comdr. William L. Richards, USN, is representative of those of the other individuals:

> The President of the United States of America takes pleasure in presenting the Silver Star to Lieutenant Commander William Leroy Richards, United States Navy, for extraordinary heroism in the line of his profession as Pilot of a PBY Patrol airplane in Patrol Squadron FORTY-FOUR (VP-44), Patrol Wing TWO, and Commander of a flight of four PBY planes during operations of the U.S. Naval and Marine forces on Midway Islands against the invading Japanese Fleet on 4 and 5 June 1942. On the night of 3

and 4 June his flight successfully located the enemy at a distance of 560 miles from the base and attacked with torpedoes from close range. This successful surprise attack contributed greatly to the ultimate success of our forces in the Battle of Midway. His courage and devotion to duty were in keeping with the highest traditions of the United States Naval Service.

Appendix H identifies the plane crew members of the four PBYs.

BATTLE STARS FOR PATROL SQUADRONS

The below listed squadrons earned Battle Stars, as also did a two-plane detachment from VP-13 (PB2Y-2 aircraft *13-P1* and *13-P4*):

Squadron	Award Date	Squadron Commander
VP-13 Det.	3-5 Jun 42	Lt. William M. Nation
VP-23	3-5 Jun 42	Lt. Comdr. Francis M. Hughes
VP-24	3-6 Jun 42	Lt. Comdr. John P. Fitzsimmons
VP-44	3-6 Jun 42	Lt. Comdr. Robert C. Brixner
VP-51	3-6 Jun 42	Lt. Comdr. D. T. Day Jr.

12

War in the Americas

It is submitted that should enemy submarines operate off this coast, this command has no forces available to take adequate action against them, either offensive or defense.

—Commander, North Atlantic Naval Coastal Frontier,
22 December 1941[1]

One hundred five United States ships earned a battle star in the American Theater during the war; none of them seaplane tenders. Seventy-eight of the ships were Navy, twenty-two were merchantmen, and the remaining five, Coast Guard. Merchant ships with Navy Armed Guard units aboard to man gun mounts installed to provide a measure of self-protection could receive battle stars if eligible. The 105 battle stars awarded to ships in the American Theater was many fewer than the 3,820 and 13,653 in the European and Pacific Theaters, respectively. One reason for this great disparity was that naval forces in the latter theaters operated in much closer proximity to greater numbers of enemy forces.[2]

German U-boats (and to a much lesser degree Japanese submarines) constituted almost the entire threat to shipping in the Americas. The undersea boats were hard to find and destroy as they went about their business of sending hundreds of merchant ships to the bottom. This was particularly true early in the war before there were sufficient Allied naval vessels available to escort merchant convoys and form anti-submarine hunter-killer groups. (The mission of these groups, each comprised of a group of destroyers formed around a small aircraft carrier, was to seek out and kill U-boats.) In other theaters, enemy aircraft, ships and patrol craft, shore battery fire, and mines all posed a threat to ships, in addition to submarines.

The scope of this book does not permit adequate coverage of the war in the Americas, and only a single example of the horrific shipping losses to submarines is provided. Japanese submarines sank three merchant vessels off the west coast of the United States, and German

U-boats sank hundreds of merchantmen off America's east and gulf coasts, and in the Gulf of Mexico and the Caribbean.

Photo 12-1

Small seaplane tender *Gannet* (AVP-8) at sea on 4 May 1937.
U.S. Naval History and Heritage Command Photograph #NH 53818

GANNET SUNK BY GERMAN SUBMARINE *U-653*

In the early evening on 2 June 1942, the small seaplane tender *Gannet* (AVP-8) received orders from commandant U.S. Naval Operating Base, Bermuda, to rendezvous with HMS *Sumar* off the entrance channel to Bermuda. The two ships were to proceed in company to the rescue of the survivors of the S.S. *Westmoreland*, torpedoed by *U-566* the preceding day. A plane had sighted life boats from the British steamship 220 miles north of Bermuda. *Gannet* was then operating to the southwest of Bermuda. The British territory—located about six hundred miles off Cape Hatteras, North Carolina—occupied a strategically important position, commanding the approaches to the middle of the Atlantic seaboard, and its historic importance was longstanding. HM (His/Her) Majesty's Dockyard, Bermuda, located on Ireland Island at Grassy Bay, had been the Royal Navy's principal base in the Western Atlantic since American independence.[3]

The U.S. Navy had established a combined Naval Air Station/Naval Operating Base on Hamilton Island on 1 July 1941. This action followed a Destroyers for Bases Agreement in which fifty elderly destroyers were transferred from the United States to the UK in return for the right of the U.S. Navy and Air Forces to set up bases in British territories, including Bermuda. Darrell's Island, about a mile and a half to the east in Bermuda's Great Sound, was developed as an auxiliary seaplane base. *Gannet* was serving as tender to Wing Five's Patrol Squadron 74, which provided coverage in the approaches to Bermuda. She also was the communication center for all aircraft operations in the area.[4]

Map 12-1

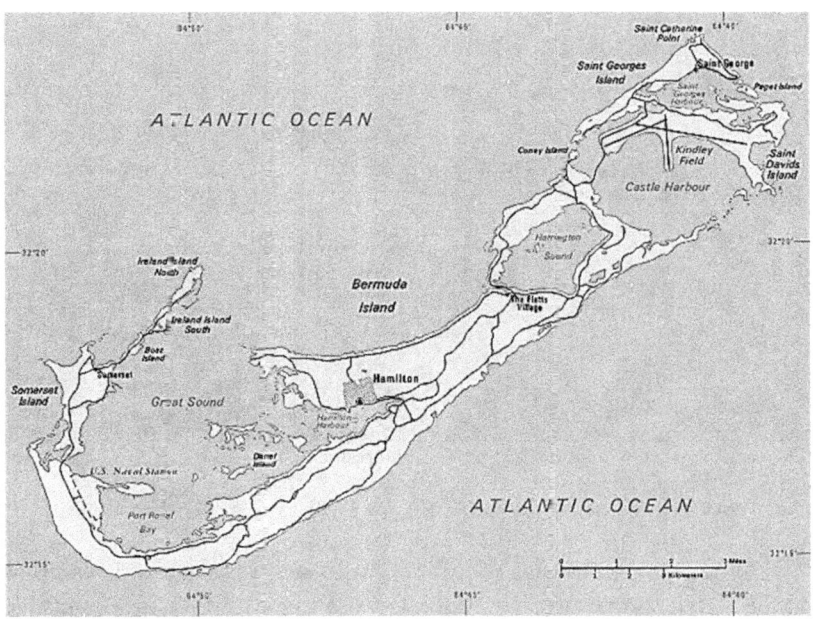

Bermuda hosted United States as well as Royal Navy and Royal Air Force military installations during World War II, as result of a 99-year lease granted by the United Kingdom to the United States in 1939.

The *Gannet* made contact with HMS *Sumar* in darkness on 3 June, five miles east of Mount Hill Light. Following verification of her identity by blinker, *Sumar* took up her patrol sector one thousand yards ahead of the seaplane tender. A few hours later, when there was sufficient light for the seaplane tender's commanding officer, Lt. Francis E. Nuessle, USN, to view his escort, he was dismayed to find that she was a converted yacht with a maximum speed of about 10 knots, and no radio. He had expected a corvette at least. The *Sumar* had been built in the United States in 1926 for an American owner, and later sold in 1941 to the British government and commissioned into the Royal Navy. She was fitted with ASDIC (sonar) and hydrophone equipment along with depth charges, giving her anti-submarine capability.[5]

Photo 12-2

The yacht *Sumar* was built in 1926 by Todd Shipyards Corp., Brooklyn, New York, for David C. Whitney and named after his wife Susan Marshall.
Courtesy of Grosse Point Historical Society, www.gphistorical.org/whitney.html

During the afternoon of 3 June, the *Sumar* reported to *Gannet* that her ASDIC was completely inoperative, and that she would continue to monitor her hydrophone equipment for any sounds of underwater contacts. *Gannet* was operating in Readiness Condition II (modified for submarine attack) and in Material Condition Baker. In addition to her normal steaming watch, a complete crew was on deck for one 3-inch/50-caliber gun as well as five designated lookouts. Three of the lookouts were stationed on the forward machine gun platform, and the other two on the after machine gun platform. All watertight doors in the ship were closed except for one door between the forward seamen's and petty officers' living quarters, which was permitted to remain open for access and purposes of ventilation.[6]

As the two ships transited toward the area in which they were to search for *Westmoreland*'s life boats, *Gannet* received dispatches from time to time giving the positions of enemy submarines, with orders to attack them if encountered. Such submarine location information was obtained by RDF (radio direction finding) equipment. Unbeknownst to authorities in Bermuda, the Canadian steamship S.S. *Cathcart* and the American Mallory Lines passenger ship S.S. *Henry R. Mallory* had picked up the *Westmoreland*'s master and other survivors—fifty-nine crewmen and five members of the Navy Armed guard—shortly after the sinking. (Two crewmen and one gunner were killed during the attack. The survivors were landed ashore at Halifax and New York.)[7]

On 5 June, a dispatch was received identifying an area in which patrol planes sent out from Bermuda would be searching. The two ships joined them, but later that day winds of up to 40 knots raised a heavy sea, which *Sumer* could ride out only on a most favorable course. Accordingly, the formation proceeded on various courses and speeds suitable to the patrol yacht. The two ships received orders the following day to return to Bermuda. That night the sky was partially overcast, the sea was smooth with a slight fog rising from the water, the western horizon was black, and there was slight illumination in the eastern sky.[8]

In early morning darkness on 7 June, *Gannet* was hit at about 0300 by a torpedo, below the waterline on her starboard side. The detonation caused both boilers to explode, blasted some crewmen topside overboard, and the seaplane tender immediately took a 15° list to starboard. A lookout later reported that he had seen a greenish flash close aboard to starboard immediately before the explosion. No warning of enemy contact had been made by *Sumar*.[9]

All hands above deck and some below were momentarily stunned by the concussion. Once recovered, gun captain Boatswain's Mate John M. Bohannon aroused his crew and loaded the starboard gun, but in the darkness no enemy was visible. The torpedo detonation had ruptured both forward and after fireroom bulkheads and through a large hole in the ship's side, the boiler rooms, the engine room and the forward compartments were filling rapidly. All machinery stopped at once due to the influx of seawater, and electrical power was lost.[10]

The commanding officer ordered preparations made to abandon ship, and seamen topside cast the life rafts adrift and unfastened the ship's three boats in the skids. Lack of time and electrical power prevented them from being lowered. Signalman First Loren W. McLaughlin fired five stars from a Very pistol as a distress signal. The list increased to well over 45° and Nuessle ordered all hands into the water on the port side. Filling rapidly, *Gannet* rolled steadily over onto her beam, down slightly by the bow, and sank four minutes after being hit. None of the ship's boats floated clear. Apparently they were trapped and carried under by the mast and boat boom as the seaplane tender twisted and slipped into the abyss.[11]

Seven officers and fifty-five men reached the three life rafts. The remaining fifteen members of ship's complement went missing. It was believed that a majority of these men, who were in the fire rooms or forward living spaces, had died instantly from the explosion. The survivors joined the rafts together, put their injured shipmates into them, and made them as comfortable as possibly. The remaining men, some in rafts and the others swimming alongside, steeled themselves to their situation and awaited rescue.[12]

Lt. W. L. Pettingill, piloting a Martin Mariner PBM-1 patrol bomber (*74-P-2*), found the survivors that afternoon and landed in rough seas to give assistance. After identifying the occupants of the rafts as the survivors of the *Gannet*, he reported this information to Naval Operating Base, Bermuda. He then took aboard ten badly injured men and returned to base; one of the men died en route. Lt. Comdr. J. W. Gannon, piloting *74-P-7*, found the rafts that evening. He landed and took eleven men aboard and after taking off, was able by circling overhead to attract the attention of *Hamilton* (DMS-18). The destroyer minesweeper then picked up the remaining forty-one survivors. Lt. Francis E. Nuessle considered the rescue of his men providential, noting in a report:

> The *HAMILTON* prior to the rescue happened to be passing in the vicinity and fortunately sighted the airplane circling above the rafts. The survivors swimming and clinging to the rafts up to their shoulders in the sea, could not have endured the storm which commenced in that area early the following morning.[13]

However, he erred in his assumption. Rear Adm. Jules James, USN, commandant Naval Operating Base, Bermuda, had directed *Hamilton* to proceed to the scene and rescue survivors. He had also ordered the destroyer *Trippe* (DD-403) to put to sea and patrol to the north, and the ocean tug *Owl* (AT-137) to search on her return trip from Norfolk, Virginia. *Hamilton* finding the survivors could be considered preordained, good planning, chance, or some combination of these factors depending on one's beliefs. Small margins often determined whether or not the survivors of ships sunk in frigid North Atlantic waters died, or were spared.[14]

U.S. NAVY DISPLEASED ABOUT *SUMAR*'S ACTIONS

> *At the time of the attack the SUMAR, equipped with listening gear but no radio was 500 to 700 yards ahead of the GANNET. She arrived [in port at Bermuda at noon on 7 June] in part in ignorance of the character of the action.*
>
> — Vice Adm. Adolphus Andrews, USN, Commander Eastern Sea Frontier, war diary entry, June 1942

Rear Adm. Jules James was unhappy, to say the least, that *Sumar* had left the *Gannet* to her fate and returned to Bermuda, after the seaplane tender was torpedoed. In a meeting with Lieutenant Nuessle regarding the *Gannet* sinking, he discussed the statement of the commanding officer of the *Sumar*, indicating that distress signals fired by Very pistol were mistaken for change-of-course signals. Nuessle informed him that besides the distress signals fired from the rafts, five were fired from aboard the *Gannet* before she sank, and that he personally witnessed three of them in the air at the same time. Nuessle also told the admiral that during the four days the two ships had been together, *Gannet* had made a great many changes of course, all communicated by blinker signal.[15]

Vice Adm. Adolphus Andrews' observation in the quoted material that such action by *Sumar*'s commanding officer was due in part to ignorance, was understated to say the least. One of the conditions of the U.S. Navy regarding the *Sumar* incident was that her captain, a lieutenant of the Royal Canadian Naval Voluntary Reserve, no longer command any Allied ships. There were heated exchanges of letters between Rear Adm. Jules James and his Royal Navy counterpart, Adm. Sir Charles R. Kennedy-Purvis, commander-in-chief, American and West Indies Command. The gist of the correspondence between them was that the Americans didn't want to be given substandard ships and inferior commanders who passed up an opportunity for bravery and glory in counter-attacking a U-boat and rescuing their allies. The British retorted that if the *Gannet* was so lacking, why was it sent on a mission for which it was grossly ill-suited?[16]

The lieutenant in question was put ashore. He went on to command by September 1943, Naval Reserve Division HMCS Cataraqui (also spelt Cararagin) in Kingston, Ontario. By June 1945 he was in command of HMCS Chippawa, a naval reserve division in Winnipeg, Manitoba where 28,000 Canadian naval personnel had to be processed for civilian life after the war. It was the Canadian Navy's rough equivalent of being sent to Siberia.[17]

INADEQUATE NAVY SHIPS TO COMBAT U-BOATS

> *The YP-389 reveals the difficulties involved in converting small vessels for war purposes.... She assumed this duty only because no ships adequate to the task were available in the Frontier.*
>
> —Vice Adm. Adolphus Andrews, USN, Commander Eastern Sea Frontier, war diary entry, June 1942

The above observation by Vice Admiral Andrews concerned the loss of the 110-foot yard patrol craft *YP-389* built as the former fishing trawler *Cohasset* for R. O'Brien and Co. of 34 Boston Fish Pier. Hastily acquired and converted for war duty, she had been sent to patrol a defensive minefield off Cape Hatteras, North Carolina, despite her single bow-mounted 3-inch deck gun being inoperable. There the *U-701* found and sank her. During the first six months of a German submarine offensive, which had begun with *U-123* sinking the British freighter S.S. *Cyclops* in Canadian waters on 11 January 1942, some 397 ships, totaling over two million tons, had been sunk.[18]

Andrews, whose Eastern Sea Frontier extended from Maine to South Carolina, had few resources initially to combat the threat: seven cutters, four converted yachts, three 1919-vintage patrol boats, two gunboats dating from 1905, and four wooden-hulled submarine chasers. In an effort to obtain vessels quickly with which to patrol East Coast waters, the Navy sought out regional fishing vessels and yachts, and pressed old 75-foot Coast Guard cutters into service. These were the conditions under which the *Gannet* was lost.[19]

13

Guadalcanal Campaign

In the South Pacific, Fleet Air Wing One planes helped track the enemy's naval forces as they moved southward for the engagement now known as the battle of the Coral Sea. During long day and night vigils they watched "The Slot" for movements of the "Tokyo Express," and reconnoitered the entire Solomons area prior to and during the bitter struggle for Guadalcanal and adjacent islands.

—Rear Adm. John Perry, USN, commander Patrol Wing One in Hawaii, which on 1 November 1942 was redesignated Fleet Air Wing One. Detachments from the Wing operated from bases in the South Pacific. Their aircraft, along with those of Wing Two, supported the Guadalcanal Campaign.[1]

THE BATTLE OF THE CORAL SEA

Following the Battle of Midway, the Pacific Fleet's primary focus in the second half of 1942 was supporting operations in the Solomon Islands, and specifically the island of Guadalcanal. The Guadalcanal Campaign was spurred by the Japanese occupation of Tulagi, a small island nestled in a bay at Florida Island opposite Guadalcanal, on 3 May 1942. The enemy's advances in the region had provided the impetus for the Battle of the Coral Sea, which preceded the Battle of Midway. Fought during 4–8 May between the Imperial Japanese Navy and naval and air forces from the United States and Australia, it would be the first great naval action between aircraft carriers and the first naval battle in which no ship on either side sighted the other.[2]

The Pacific Fleet's intelligence staff had learned that the Japanese were planning a three-pronged offensive in the Southwest Pacific. The plan, termed Operation MO, called for the invasion forces of Rear Adm. Kiyohide Shima to occupy Tulagi in the lower Solomons and establish a seaplane base from which Noumea could be neutralized. Rear Adm. Sadamichi Kajioka's invasion group would capture and occupy Port Moresby in Papua, and Vice Adm. Takeo Takagi's carrier striking force would enter the Coral Sea from the east and destroy any Allied forces that might interfere with this plan.³

Admiral Nimitz did not have even half the forces available to the Japanese, but he assigned all he had to Rear Adm. Frank J. Fletcher, whom was in command of the Allied naval forces in the South Pacific. Task Force 17 was centered-around the aircraft carriers *Lexington* and *Yorktown*. Most of the ships of Gen. Douglas MacArthur's navy in Australia, which would later be named the Seventh Fleet, also joined as well as three cruisers—HMAS *Australia, Hobart,* and USS *Chicago*—and a few destroyers under Rear Adm. John G. Crace, Royal Navy.⁴

Although a tactical victory for the Japanese in terms of tonnage sunk, the battle proved to be a strategic victory for the Allies. Japanese carrier-based Kates (Nakajima B5N torpedo bombers) and Vals (Aichi D3A Navy Type 99 bombers) sank the carrier *Lexington* (CV-2) and a bomb from a Val damaged the *Yorktown* (CV-5). The Japanese, in turn, lost the light carrier *Shoho* and suffered damage to the fleet carrier *Shokaku*. A second fleet carrier, *Zuikaku*, took over a month to replace her depleted aircraft complement. Neither of the latter two ships took part in the Battle of Midway the following month, while the *Yorktown* was repaired and did. The loss of the Japanese carriers ensured a rough parity in aircraft between the two adversaries and contributed significantly to the U.S. victory in that battle.⁵

STRATEGIC IMPORTANCE OF GUADALCANAL

Japan wanted an air field in the Solomons from which its land-based bombers could provide air cover for the advance of Imperial land forces to Port Moresby, the capital city of Papua and the site of an Allied base (the territories of Papua and New Guinea were combined after World War II into a single territory that today is known as Papua-New Guinea). The thousands of troops based there were the Allies' last line of defense before Australia. Having found Tulagi fit only for a seaplane base, on 5 July Japanese forces landed on Guadalcanal, twenty miles across the New Georgia Sound (which Allied servicemen referred to as "The Slot") from Tulagi, and began the rapid construction of Lunga Point Airfield (later, Henderson Field following its capture by U.S. Marines) from which the empire's planes could menace the shipping lanes to Australia.⁶

Map 13-1

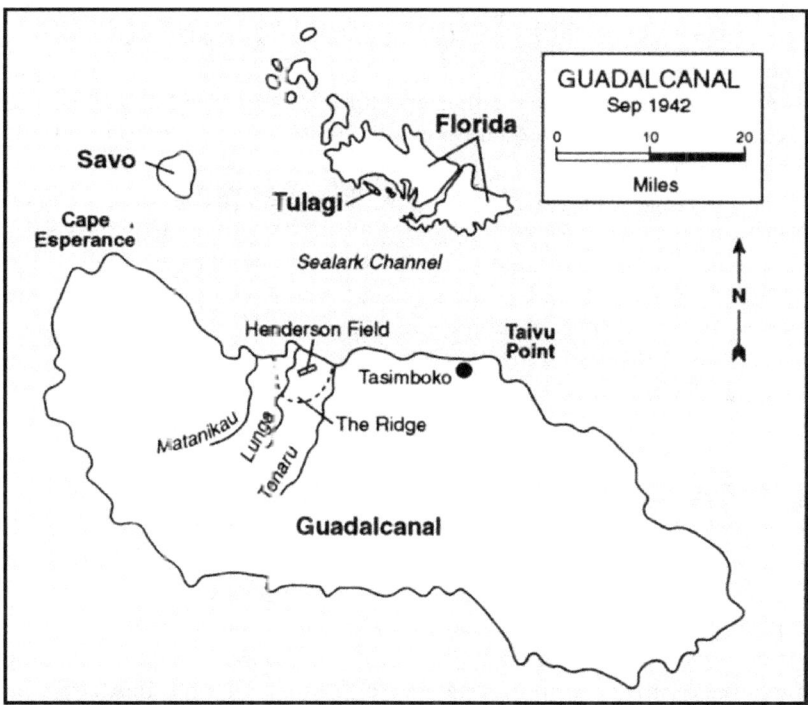

Tulagi, a small island nestled inside the bay of Florida Island, lay twenty miles across the New Georgia Sound (of which the Sealark Channel was a part) from Guadalcanal. (Source: www.nps.gov/history/history/online_books/npswapa/extContent/ usmc/pcn-190-003130-00/sec6.htm)

ALLIED AIRSTRIKES AGAINST TULAGI

In late June, PBYs flew strikes against the Japanese positions at Tulagi. They were tended by the large seaplane tender *Curtiss* (AV-4)— flagship of Rear Adm. John S. McCain, USN, commander Aircraft, South Pacific. The *Curtiss*, accompanied by the destroyer seaplane tender *McFarland* (AVD-14), had arrived at Noumea, New Caledonia, from Hawaii on 16 June. En route the two ships had made stops at Pago Pago, Samoa, and Tongatabu in the Tonga Islands.[7]

The *Curtiss* relieved the *Tangier* (AV-8) of her air operations duties on 20 June, and all personnel of VP-14 and VP-71 transferred to her. *Tangier* departed Noumea the following day bound for San Francisco and an overhaul. *Curtiss* would serve as both a seaplane tender and headquarters for commander Aircraft, South Pacific, during the Solomon Islands Campaign, and also as a repair and supply ship for destroyers and other small ships engaged in the forthcoming battle for Guadalcanal. On 25 June, two PBY-5s of VP-71 took off to make a bombing attack on Tulagi and Gavutu Harbor with McCain present in one of the flying boats to observe. The night mission was unsuccessful due to the weather conditions. Bad weather also forced the cancellation of subsequent missions on 10 and 13 July to bomb the Tulagi-Gavutu area.[8]

In July, land-based planes from "Bomber One"—an airfield on Espiritu Santo in the New Hebrides, located approximately 650 miles southeast of Guadalcanal—struck the Lunga Point airstrip on Guadalcanal as well as Japanese ground troops, supply functions and surface bastions. This bombing would prepare the way for landings by the 1st Marine Division in the Guadalcanal-Tulagi area on 7-9 August 1942, under the protection of planes from Espiritu Santo and aircraft carriers.[9]

GUADALCANAL-TULAGI LANDINGS

In an effort to prevent the Japanese from using Guadalcanal to launch air attacks on Allied shipping in the South Pacific, 11,000 members of the 1st Marine Division landed at Guadalcanal on 7 August and captured the airstrip at Lunga Point, as well as the Japanese encampment at Kukum on the west side of Lunga Point the following day. That same afternoon, after fierce fighting, Marines discharged at Tulagi took the Japanese-held island, as well as the smaller islands of Gavutu and Tanambogo. The airstrip on Guadalcanal was renamed Henderson Field, and its occupation and use by Allied forces temporarily halted Japanese expansion in the South Pacific.[10]

In support of the landings, the seaplane tender *Mackinac* (AVP-13) had entered Maramasike Estuary at the south end of Malaita Island in the early afternoon on 7 August. One of the eight PBYs maintained aboard her flew ahead as she entered the passage between Malaita Island and Maramasike Island, dropping float lights upon coral heads to assist the ship in navigating the shoal water. From 7 to 9 August her planes scouted waters to the northwest in the direction of the Japanese base at Rabaul, 564 nautical miles from Guadalcanal on the northern tip of the island of New Britain, for enemy forces.[11]

The *Mackinac* and the destroyer minesweeper *Tracy* (DM-19) received orders on 10 August, to retire to Espiritu Santo due to the threat that Japanese operating in the area posed to them. McCain had earlier relocated the *Curtiss* from Noumea to Espiritu Santo to be nearer the action.[12]

Map 13-2

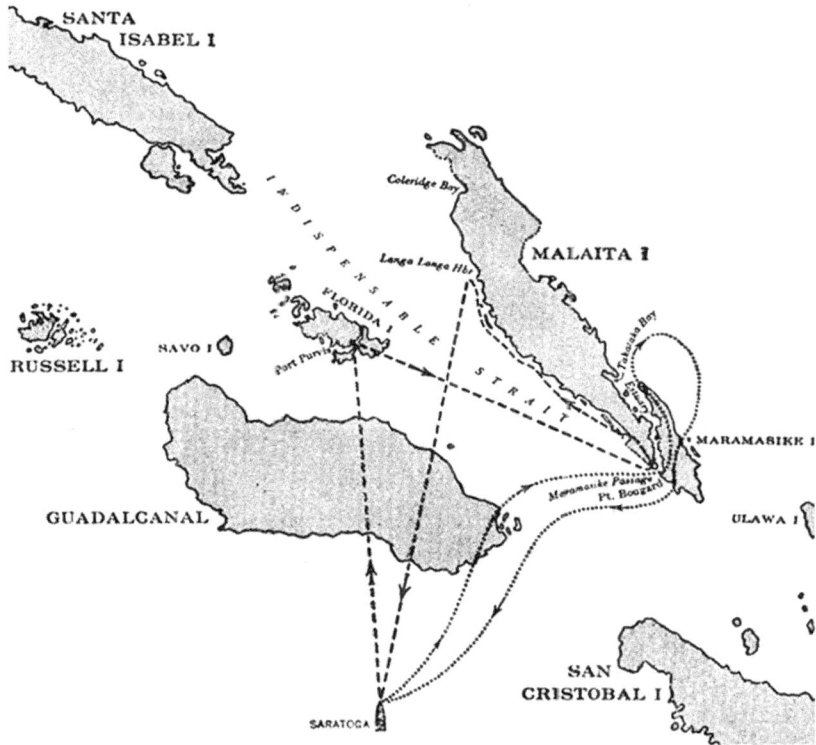

Air searches made by aircraft aboard the carrier *Saratoga* (CV-3), during the period in which the *Mackinac* was based in an estuary separating Malaita and Maramasike Islands to enable her patrol aircraft to search ocean waters to the northwest for enemy forces.
ONI Combat Narratives: Solomon Islands Campaign: I. The Landing in the Solomons, 7-8 August 1942 (Washington DC: 1943)

Throughout the prolonged, bloody Battle of Guadalcanal from 7 August 1942 to 9 February 1943, Espiritu Santo would serve as a Naval Air Base, staging area and supply point. From Bomber One, Army, Navy and Marine heavy and medium bombers made around-the-clock runs on enemy troops, installations and fleets in the greater Solomons area. Units of the patrol squadrons in the area reconnoitered the enemy's movements. From her anchorage in Segond Channel, the *Curtiss* tended planes of VP-11 and VP-23 conducting surveillance and anti-submarine patrols during the landings. In ensuing weeks, Patrol Squadrons VP-24, 71, and 91 would also fly missions from the Segond Channel seaplane base in support of the American forces on Guadalcanal.[13]

Map 13-3

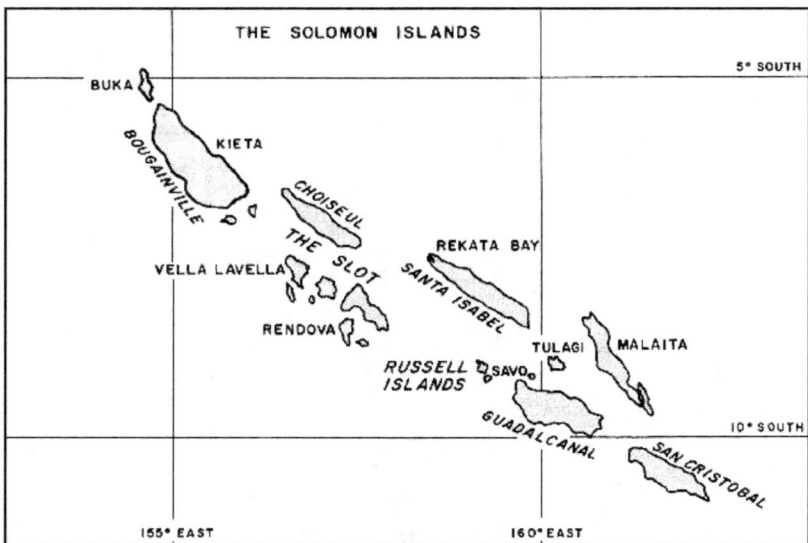

Guadalcanal in the Solomon Islands was a bitterly contested piece of real estate. Its capture by U.S. ground troops, supported by air and naval forces, after months of combat with Japanese on the island, preceded continued Allied movement northwestward up through the enemy-held Solomons.
(Source: http://www.ibiblio.org/hyperwar/USN/ACTC/img/actc-35.jpg)

The significance of American control of the island—from which the Allies could expand their presence in the South Pacific while thwarting the Japanese thrust—was not lost on the enemy. Guadalcanal became a pivotal piece of island real estate, one that both sides wanted to control and to which they were willing to commit large numbers of forces. By day, aircraft from Henderson Field controlled the skies, allowing U.S. Navy transports and small vessels to operate in the area with some degree of safety. At night, however, command of these waters shifted as IJN (Imperial Japanese Navy) warships, then cloaked by darkness from air attack, raced down the slot between the northern and southern Solomons with supplies and troops to resupply Japanese land forces—and to assault Allied ships caught outside the protected harbor of the fortified island of Tulagai.[14]

BALLARD AND *MACKINAC* SHELLED BY ENEMY SUBMARINES

> *The searches were really "hot" from then on. Almost daily sightings and attacks on enemy subs were made by our search planes as well as their being attacked by enemy planes. On 12 September, two subs surfaced at the entrance to GRACIOSA BAY and shelled the MACK, BALLARD, and our planes. We returned fire—the results not determined.... Permanent retirement was ordered to ESPIRITU the next day, and from there operations were conducted. The general situation quieted down somewhat although we continued to have our scares at ESPIRITU.*
>
> —Comdr. Horace B. Butterfield, USN, commanding officer USS *Mackinac*, describing conditions at Nendo Island.[15]

In September 1942 the destroyer seaplane tender *Ballard* (AVD-10) and the small seaplane tender *Mackinac* (AVP-13) were based at Nendo in the Santa Cruz Islands, which lay 335 nautical miles east-southeast of Guadalcanal. Higher command recognized that the two ships were exposed to enemy attack in this forward position, but considered the risk justified. From Nendo, PBY-5s were able to search waters well to the north for enemy forces and thus help to protect the right flank of the Allied line of communications to Guadalcanal. An enemy attack against the seaplane tenders came in the early morning darkness on 12 September, but not from Japanese aircraft as anticipated.[16]

Map 13-4

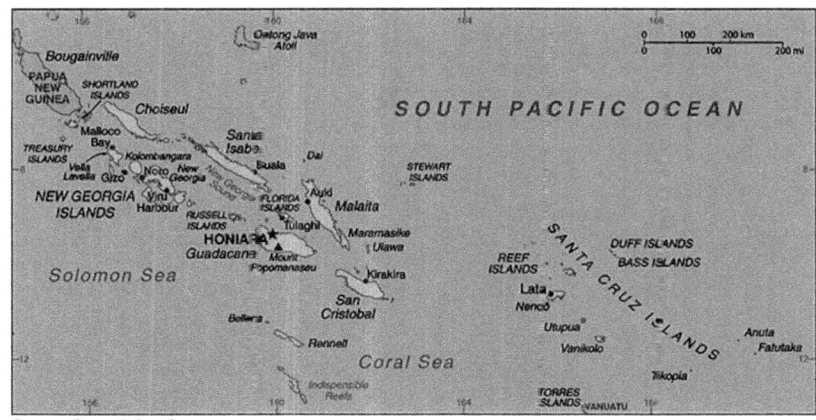

Santa Cruz Islands

Chapter 13

The *Ballard*, commanded by Lt. Comdr. D. R. Brokenshire, USN, came under fire at 0200 from an enemy vessel unsighted in the gloom, but believed to be a surfaced submarine. Two minutes later the *Ballard*'s guns commenced firing star shells in an effort to illuminate the threat. Enemy fire ceased at 0204, presumably as the sub prepared to dive and slip away after having fired an estimated six rounds. Once star shell illumination began to erode the darkness cloaking the submarine, it would have been prudent for her to submerge. *Ballard* ceased fire at 0207, having expended eleven rounds of star shell and one round of anti-aircraft common. The latter type round was used against aircraft or lightly armored ships; a direct hit on the sub would have likely sunk her. Ordered by commander Aircraft South Pacific to clear Nendo immediately, the ships withdrew southward to Espiritu Santo.[17]

In addition to the *Ballard* and *Mackinac*, two other Patrol Wing Two tenders, the *Curtiss* and *McFarland*, were then in the South Pacific tending PBY-5 Catalinas of Patrol Squadrons VP-11, 14, 23, 51, and 72. The number of patrol planes and tenders in the Pacific in mid-1942 was insufficient, and this shortfall was made worse when a tender was unavailable while undergoing maintenance or repair of combat damage. To optimize the use of tenders, one or more might be temporarily assigned to another Wing. Such was the case with *Avocet* and *Thornton*, then operating with Wing Four in Alaskan waters.

Location of Patrol Wing Two Tenders on 1 September 1942

Tender	Location	Tender	Location
Avocet (AVP-4)	Operating in Alaskan waters with Patrol Wing Four	*Swan* (AVP-7)	Navy Yard, Pearl Harbor
Ballard (AVD-10)	South Pacific	*Tangier* (AV-8)	Navy Yard, Mare Island
Curtiss (AV-4)	South Pacific	*Thornton* (AVD-11)	Operating in Alaskan waters with Patrol Wing Four
Mackinac (AVP-13)	South Pacific	*Wright* (AV-1)	At sea[18]
McFarland (AVD-14)	South Pacific		

MCFARLAND BOMBED BY JAPANESE AIRCRAFT WITH MANY CREWMEN KILLED OR WOUNDED

> *For some weeks after the bombing all hands spent a considerable period every day at gun stations watching enemy planes overhead. At times the tactical situation became such that it seemed that the whole Solomons area would fall to the enemy. At no time did anyone aboard lose their nerve.*
>
> —Lt. Comdr. John C. Alderman's, USN, commanding officer of the seaplane tender *McFarland* (AVD-14), assessment of the situation at Guadalcanal after his ship came under attack by Japanese bombers on 16 October 1942, resulting in many personnel casualties[19]

In early October 1942, the destroyer seaplane tender *McFarland* underwent a partial overhaul alongside the *Curtiss* at Espiritu Santo. As previously noted, in addition to her flagship and seaplane tender duties, the *Curtiss* also served as a supply and repair ship. Following all repairs, the *McFarland* loaded a deck cargo of aviation gasoline and lubricants the morning of 14 October from the Liberty ship S.S. *Irvin McDowell*. She departed for Guadalcanal that afternoon, under orders to deliver twelve torpedoes and two hundred drums of AvGas to Lunga Point. She was then to proceed to Vanikoro Island in the Santa Cruz island group to relieve sister ship *Ballard* (AVD-10), anchored in Peou Bay tending patrol planes.[20]

As the *McFarland* approached Lunga Point in the early afternoon on 16 October, she observed the yard patrol craft *YP-239* aground and under fire from an enemy gun in the vicinity of Kokumbona, a village on Guadalcanal's north coast. The 113-foot YP—the ex-San Diego tuna boat *Challenger*—was flying the signal flags "Emerg Hypo" requesting assistance. However, Lt. Comdr. John C. Alderman, USN, considered his ship's cargo too valuable to risk rendering assistance to the YP. Thus, the *McFarland* proceeded onward along her navigational track, out of range of the Japanese gun, toward Lunga lagoon.[21]

YP-239 would soon be the only surviving member of three ex-tuna boats at Guadalcanal, which were a part of a larger group of boats acquired by the Navy from San Diego's Portuguese fishing community for naval service. Fitted with machine guns and depth charges, and sporting new coats of grey paint covering their traditional white hulls, the three wooden vessels had been sent to Guadalcanal to serve as supply ships in support of U.S. forces on Guadalcanal and Tulagi, principally the First Marines. Tragically, *YP-346* (ex-*Prospect*) had been destroyed a week earlier, on 9 September, by gunfire from the Japanese light cruiser *Sendai*. Nine days hence, gunfire from three Japanese destroyers would send *YP-284* (ex-*Endeavor*) and the fleet tug *Seminole* (AT-65) to the bottom on the morning of 25 October during the second battle for Henderson Field. These losses would leave only *YP-239* of the YP component of the small numbers of vessels that comprised the so-called "Cactus Navy." Cactus was the military code word for Guadalcanal.22

Photo 13-1

Night Action off Tulagi by Richard DeRosset depicts the destruction of USS *YP-346* by the Japanese light cruiser IJN *Sendai* off Guadalcanal on 8 September 1942

A chapter of my book *Battle Stars for the "Cactus Navy": America's Fishing Vessels and Yachts in World War II* is devoted to the heroic actions of the crews of these small ships. YPs served as tugs, dispatch boats, rescue craft, troop and supply ferries, and transports for minor amphibious operations while plying the dangerous waters between Guadalcanal and Tulagi during the latter part of 1942.

YP-239 was refloated several hours later, having suffered only superficial damage, and returned to Tulagi. The ex-tuna boat had been required to shoulder more work following the loss of the ex-*Prospect*, and her tasking would be even greater after the loss of the ex-*Endeavor*. In recognition of his ship's herculean efforts, Chief Warrant Officer Howard H. Branyon, USN, would receive the Navy Cross Medal for "extraordinary heroism and devotion to duty in action against the enemy while serving [as the] Commander of Patrol Ship *YP-239*, in the waters between Tulagi and Guadalcanal, Solomon Islands, during the period from 1 September 1942 to 2 November 1942."[23]

In the early afternoon that day, 16 September, *McFarland* anchored about 500 yards east of Lunga Point on the northern coast of Guadalcanal, and began discharging her cargo to boats ferrying it ashore. The cargo included 37mm ammunition, aircraft flares, twelve torpedoes, 188 drums of aviation gas, and twenty drums of aviation lubricant. Boats returning to the seaplane tender brought ambulatory patients, totaling sixty servicemen, for evacuation to Espiritu Santo, and one hundred passengers. The deck cargo was soon unloaded, and discharge of additional gasoline from the ship's tank continued. At 1700, friendly fighter aircraft were sighted patrolling overhead. Lt. Comdr. Leroy C. Simpler, USN—a passenger and commander of VF5 (a squadron of F4F Wildcats)—commented that such activity normally meant that enemy planes were expected.[24]

At 1710, Alderman received a report from shore that a submarine periscope had been sighted rounding Lunga Point from the west. The special sea detail was set, anchor weighed, and the seaplane tender got under way on an easterly course with a large pontoon barge made up along her starboard side and a tank lighter on her port side. Aboard the barge was a deck load of 400 drums of fuel. Alderman believed that by maintaining a 1/3 ahead bell (5 knots), he could evade the sub and concurrently discharge the remainder of the tender's bulk gasoline to the lighter. However, a new threat soon developed.[25]

As the *McFarland* was proceeding eastward, she was attacked at 1750 by nine Vals (Japanese Aichi type 99 dive bombers) approaching from her starboard side. The planes each carried two bombs on racks outboard of their fixed landing gear. As the aircraft dove steeply downward at a sixty-degree angle in preparation for releasing their bombs, all hands manned their battle stations and ship's speed was increased to "full ahead." The *McFarland*'s starboard 20mm guns opened fire and maintained a "barrage of steel" directed at her assailants throughout the entire attack. One plane was downed, and another one, damaged and wobbling after being hit, jettisoned its bombs after passing over the ship without releasing them. Two .50-caliber machine guns located on the ship's after deckhouse kept up their fire until a bomb hit knocked them out of action. The starboard 3-inch gun, which required more time to train and elevate, expended only a single round during the fast-paced action.[26]

Alderman "conned" the ship (gave all engine and rudder orders himself) throughout the attack. Quickly recognizing that the barge and lighter alongside were hindering maneuverability, he ordered them cast off. There were several near bomb misses off the port side of the *McFarland*. The explosion from one blew a signalman off the port bridge bulwarks, and propelled an officer and an enlisted man on the bridge wing into the pilot house. Fortunately, many of the bombs fell astern of the ship because of a dramatic increase in speed ordered by the commanding officer.[27]

As planes overhead released their bombs, men below observed the rear seat occupant throwing out small black objects, believed to be incendiary devices and possibly hand-grenades. One of these may have hit the barge which, cast off, was then off the ship's starboard quarter. Her gasoline ignited and the flames were at least a hundred feet high. Those aboard the *McFarland* viewing the inferno presumed that no one could have survived; that the barge crew (twelve Navy men and Marines) had been consumed by fire.[28]

Fortunately, this was not the case. Boatswain's Mate Second Robert Lee Rheindt, the coxswain of one of the landing boats that had been ferrying cargo ashore, quickly laid his craft alongside the aflame barge and by this action saved the lives of six of the men aboard it, for which he received the Navy Cross. The associated medal citation incorrectly identifies the *McFarland*'s hull number as DD-237 (instead of AVD-14), which was her designation as a destroyer before and after her service as a seaplane tender:

> The President of the United States takes pleasure in presenting the Navy Cross to Robert Lee Rheindt, Boatswain's Mate Second Class, U.S. Navy, for extraordinary heroism and devotion to duty while serving on board the Destroyer U.S.S. *McFARLAND* (DD-237), in action against the enemy when his vessel was attacked by nine enemy dive bombers while unloading cargo and embarking wounded personnel in Lunga Roads, Guadalcanal, on 16 October 1942. When enemy bombers dove at our vessels loaded with gasoline and explosives, Boatswain's Mate Second Class Rheindt, standing by in a landing boat, saw a bomb hit a barge carrying aviation gasoline, which immediately burst into flames. Observing men covered with blazing oil, he unhesitatingly maneuvered his boat through smoke and flames near the furiously burning barge and rescued six men before the intense heat and spread of the flames drove him off.[29]

The most deadly bomb drop—one that would kill or wound 55 of the 296 ship's company and passengers aboard the *McFarland*—was yet to come. The last plane to attack the ship scored a direct hit in the vicinity of her depth charge rack on the port side of the fantail, setting off at least one depth charge. The resultant explosion, much larger than those from the preceding bomb blasts, blew the entire stern of the seaplane tender off and threw men off their feet. The steering was also damaged, mandating the use of engines only to coax the injured seaplane tender in the general direction of Tulagi.[30]

As the *McFarland* began to settle rapidly by the stern with a port list, orders were given to flood her forward peak tanks (used for boiler feed water storage), pump oil from a group of tanks aft to the forecastle group forward, and to shift all personnel to the starboard side of the ship. These rapid actions brought her back to an even keel, and it appeared that she would likely remain afloat. However, the life boat was lowered to the rail, the gripes were cast off on her other boat and all life rafts were made ready to drop in case the ship should sink. As these actions were carried out, the pharmacist's mate administered morphine to the seriously wounded, and stretcher bearers carried them forward to sick bay for treatment by the medical officer.[31]

The *McFarland* established communications with the signal station on Gavutu Island at 1925 and requested the services of a YP boat and "Higgins boats" (LCVP landing craft) for towing services and transfer of the wounded. In lieu of these type vessels, motor torpedo (PT) boats and tank lighters arrived from Tulagi a short time later. An attempt by a PT boat to take the ship in tow was unsuccessful. While awaiting the arrival of a larger and much more powerful YP, the passengers and wounded were transferred to the tank lighters. *YP-239*—which earlier that afternoon had been aground and under enemy fire—appeared at 2055 and took the *McFarland* in tow for Tulagi Harbor. The damaged seaplane tender anchored at 2340 just off "D" Medical Company Hospital, and the ship's crew began the process of identifying and transferring the dead for burial.[32]

McFarland's commanding officer, Lt. Comdr. John C. Alderman, later received the Navy Cross for his actions during extended service in the Guadalcanal area, and in particular for saving his ship, as described in the following citation:

> The President of the United States of America takes pleasure in presenting the Navy Cross to Lieutenant Commander John Clement Alderman, United States Navy, for extraordinary heroism and distinguished service in the line of his profession as Commanding Officer of the Destroyer U.S.S. *McFARLAND* (DD-237), while on special missions in the Solomon islands area during the period 8 August 1942 to 18 October 1942. On repeated occasions, Lieutenant Commander Alderman

courageously entered the Solomon waters to assist in the task of protecting the valuable supply lanes to Guadalcanal, in support of our land and sea defenses of that island. With utter disregard for his own safety, he exposed himself to the ever-present danger of hostile air attacks. On one occasion, his ship was so damaged by enemy fire that it was almost lost. By his perseverance, determination and technical ability, he made the necessary repairs to his ship, under the most adverse conditions, so that she was able to continue in the service of her country. His heroic conduct was in keeping with the highest traditions of the Naval Service.[33]

The personnel casualties aboard the *McFarland* would undoubtedly have been much greater but for the actions of Lt. Col. Harold W. Bauer, USMC, commander Marine Fighting Squadron VMF-212. As vividly described in the citation for the Medal of Honor he received for this and other combat actions during the same period, he single-handedly shot down four of the Japanese aircraft that had attacked the seaplane tender. The citation reads in part:

After successfully leading 26 planes on an over-water ferry flight of more than 600 miles on 16 October, Lieutenant Colonel Bauer, while circling to land, sighted a squadron of enemy planes attacking the U.S.S. *McFarland*. Undaunted by the formidable opposition and with valor above and beyond the call of duty, he engaged the entire squadron and, although alone and his fuel supply nearly exhausted, fought his plane so brilliantly that four of the Japanese planes were destroyed before he was forced down by lack of fuel.

Bauer, possibly the finest fighter pilot in the Marine Corps, had picked up the moniker "Indian Joe" at the U.S. Naval Academy because of his height, high cheekbones, and dark features. He was shot down two months later, on 14 November 1942, during aerial combat with two Japanese Zeros north of the Russell Islands in the Solomons. No trace of his remains were ever found.[34]

While incapacitated and undergoing repairs, *McFarland* took refuge up the Tulagi River, concealed from the view of enemy planes above by shrubbery along its bank. Efforts to make the damaged ship marginally seaworthy proved lengthy. Just before the Thanksgiving holiday, the *Ballard* delivered food and fuel to her at Tulagi. Following the completion of makeshift hull repairs, the *McFarland* proceeded to Espiritu Santo for additional work. She left there on 17 December bound for Pearl Harbor, arriving on the 29th. On 17 April 1943, the *McFarland* sailed from Hawaii for America's west coast. She was redesignated DD-237 on 1 December 1943 and homeported at San Diego. For the remainder of the war, destroyer *McFarland* performed plane guard duties for carriers engaged in training exercises and pilot qualification landings (involving being in position to rescue downed aviators forced to eject from aircraft).[35]

BATTLE OF THE SANTA CRUZ ISLANDS

> *It now appears that we are unable to control the sea in the Guadalcanal area. Thus our supply of the positions will only be done at great expense to us. The situation is not hopeless, but it is certainly critical.*
>
> —Assessment by Adm. Chester W. Nimitz, commander-in-chief U.S. Pacific Fleet, on 15 October 1942 of the bleak situation American naval forces then faced in the Guadalcanal area. That same day, Nimitz chose Vice Adm. William F. Halsey (a man known throughout the Pacific for his fighting spirit) to replace Vice Adm. Robert L. Ghormley as commander South Pacific Force.[36]
>
> *Attack – Repeat – Attack!*
>
> —Order sent by Vice Adm. William F. Halsey to Rear Admirals Thomas C. Kinkaid and George D. Murray, Commander Task Force 16 and 17, respectively, on 26 October 1942.[37]

During September and October 1942, there was an escalation in the fighting between Japanese and American forces on and around Guadalcanal, with reinforcements pouring in on both sides. United States military planners were determined to keep the supply lines with Australia open while the Japanese were just as determined to cut them. In October, the Japanese decided to launch a major offensive to gain control of Henderson airfield on Guadalcanal, eliminate the 10,000 American troops on the island, and destroy all allied warships in the Solomons area. A massive naval force left Truk in the Caroline Islands, home base of the Japanese Combined Fleet, on 11 October to provide cover for the invasion forces with four aircraft carriers, four battleships, ten cruisers, and 30 destroyers. Truk lay 795 miles north-northwest of Guadalcanal.[38]

Two American carriers, *Enterprise* (CV-6) and *Hornet* (CV-8), the battleship *South Dakota* (BB-57), six cruisers, and fourteen destroyers were available to oppose this formidable armada. Vice Adm. William

F. Halsey, who had just taken command of the U.S. South Pacific Force, ordered his force to move north of the Santa Cruz Islands to intercept the Japanese Fleet and keep them from supporting the invasion force. The ensuing battle of the Santa Cruz Islands took place on 26 October without contact between surface ships of the opposing forces; all of the action was between aircraft. The *Enterprise*'s planes bombed the carrier *Zuiho*, knocking her out of action as far as the battle was concerned, and planes from the *Hornet* severely damaged the carrier *Shokaku* and the heavy cruiser *Chikuma*. The *Shokaku* would be out of the war for nine months.[39]

Photo 13-2

World War II poster featuring Adm. William F. Halsey, USN.
U.S. Naval History and Heritage Command

The *Hornet* was attacked by Aichi D3A Val dive bombers and a flight of Nakajima B5N Kate torpedo planes. Significant damage to the carrier necessitated that she be taken in tow by the heavy cruiser *Northampton* (CA-26). While under tow, another flight of torpedo planes struck. One put a torpedo into her starboard side, and seawater flowing in through her hull created a significant list. Following orders by Halsey for American forces to sink the carrier, her commanding officer Capt. Charles P. Mason, USN, ordered all hands to abandon ship. After survivors were picked up, the destroyers *Anderson* (DD-411) and *Mustin* (DD-413) attempted to scuttle the *Hornet* with torpedoes and gunfire, but she stubbornly remained afloat. Two Japanese destroyers—the *Akigumo* and *Makigumo*—later finished her off with four long lance torpedoes.[40]

The Battle of the Santa Cruz Islands was the fourth carrier battle of the Pacific campaign and the fourth major naval engagement fought between United States and Japanese naval forces during the lengthy and strategically important Guadalcanal campaign. Vice Adm. Chuichi Nagumo, commander of the Japanese forces, characterized the results of the naval battle in his report to the Combined Fleet Headquarters:

> This battle was a tactical win, but a shattering strategic loss for Japan. Considering the great superiority of our enemy's industrial capacity, we must win every battle overwhelmingly in order to win this war. This last one, although a victory, unfortunately, was not an overwhelming victory.[41]

SEAPLANES ATTACK JAPANESE CAPITAL SHIPS

> *B17s and PBYs operating out of Espiritu Santo were of great service in search. They also conducted a number of offensive strikes.... Soon after midnight on the 26th [of October] one of these [PBYs] launched a torpedo from 500 yards at a large carrier; at this close distance the torpedo probably did not have sufficient run to arm. About the same time a second PBY attacked another enemy force and from a low altitude made two 500-lb bomb hits on a heavy cruiser.*
>
> —From a report by Adm. Chester W. Nimitz, commander-in-chief, U.S. Pacific Fleet, to Adm. Ernest J. King, commander-in-chief, U.S. Fleet, on the battle of the Santa Cruz Islands[42]

Prior to and during the battle of the Santa Cruz Islands, the *Curtiss* tended planes from VP-11, 23, 24, 51, and 91 from her anchorage in Segond Channel, Espiritu Santo. In addition to routine, ongoing antisubmarine patrol, ten PBYs and six B17s searched the northern semicircle from Espiritu Santo out some 650 to 800 miles each day. Augmenting these efforts were searches by PBYs tended by the *Ballard* at Vanikoro in the Santa Cruz Islands. At 1250 on 25 October, a search plane from Espiritu Santo found two Japanese carriers and their escort ships northeast of Guadalcanal and 360 miles west-northwest of Task Force 61, and made a contact report. Twelve hours later a search plane reported the enemy's current position. Task Force 61 was then about 300 miles to the southeast closing at 20 knots. At 0410 on 26 October, a PBY reported a large carrier and six other vessels about two hundred miles from Task Force 61's position.[43]

The "eyes of the fleet" had done their job, locating enemy carriers and other units of the Japanese Fleet for attack by more survivable fighters and bombers. Yet, having carried out their primary duty, Catalina seaplanes flew attacks on capital ships. In late evening on 26 October, three PBYs left Espiritu Santo to hunt carriers. By this time, the Japanese were withdrawing the remnants of their fleet farther west. At around midnight, Lt. (jg) Donald Jackson, the pilot of *51-P-6*, found the carrier *Junyo* but failed to damage it with a torpedo attack. In an effort to strike a deadly blow, he drew too near the ship before launching his torpedo—providing insufficient time for it to arm before reaching the target.[44]

The pilot of a second PBY, Lt. Melvin K. Atwell, attacked what he believed in the gloom to be a heavy cruiser, but which proved to be a destroyer screening the carrier *Zuikaku*. Atwell pressed home a dive bombing attack on the ship in the face of heavy anti-aircraft fire and shrapnel damage to his plane, and made two bomb hits abaft the destroyer's forward stack. The following description of the action is from the citation for the Navy Cross Atwell received for extraordinary heroism in action against the enemy on 27 October 1942:

> At about 0030, PBY airplane *91-P-4*, piloted by Lt. Melvin K. Atwell, USN, contacted a suspicious object on radar about thirty miles distance. He closed to a point where the dark outline of a large ship could be seen moving in an easterly direction at a high speed. Shortly after contact the ship moved under a 1,500 foot overcast and stopped. Lieutenant Atwell circled over the ship twice at low altitude in an unsuccessful attempt to identify it. He then climbed back to 1,500 feet and at 0150 when about two miles from the ship the plane was fired upon by two bursts of 20-mm.

followed by a 5" AA projectile which burst under its starboard wing. Lieutenant Atwell decided upon a dive bombing attack and attacked immediately from about 1,400 feet as the ship opened up with heavy anti-aircraft fire and commenced to gain headway. The Co-Pilot, Lieutenant Mather, dropped the two starboard 500-pound contact bombs at about 650 feet altitude. These bombs landed about 75 feet on the target's starboard quarter. The Pilot released the two port bombs of the same type at about 600 feet altitude while still in a dive. Both bombs were seen to explode abaft the first stack of the target which was illuminated by the explosion and identified as a Japanese heavy cruiser of the *AOBA* class. All anti-aircraft fire ceased after the last two bombs hit. The plane suffered numerous but not serious hits from shrapnel and the concussion from the bombs exploding blew out radio tubes and lights. Recovery from the dive was affected at about 20 feet above the sea. No personnel were injured. The pilot suspected gasoline leaks and immediately headed for his base. About 20 minutes later a large orange flash was seen in the vicinity of his former target. About ten minutes later a larger and more prolonged orange flash was seen in the same position.

The two patrol planes that had flown attacks on the enemy ships (one from VP-51 and the other from VP-91) and their crews returned safely to Espiritu Santo from their mission.[45]

AMERICAN FORCES PREVAIL ON GUADALCANAL

Japanese forces made several attempts to retake Henderson Field between August and November 1942. The naval and land battles, and the smaller skirmishes and raids of the Guadalcanal Campaign culminated in the naval battle of Guadalcanal fought between 12 and 15 November. The battle was the last Japanese attempt to land enough troops to retake Henderson, but it was unsuccessful. The inability of the Japanese to capture the airfield doomed their effort on Guadalcanal, and they evacuated their remaining forces by 7 February 1943, conceding the island to the Allies. The importance of the Guadalcanal Campaign was summarized by Adm. William F. Halsey Jr., USN, commander, South Pacific Force and South Pacific Area:

> Before Guadalcanal the enemy advanced at his pleasure—after Guadalcanal he retreated at ours.[46]

LAURELS FOR SEAPLANE TENDERS/SQUADRONS

The *McFarland* received the Presidential Unit Citation for the period 20 June to 16 October 1942, in which she operated in waters around Guadalcanal. She would be the only seaplane tender thus honored during the war. The associated text for the award follows:

> For outstanding performance during action with enemy Japanese forces in the Southwest Pacific Area, June 20 to October 16, 1942. Serving in turn as a seaplane tender, escort vessel, patrol boat, and cargo and troop carrier, the *McFARLAND*, under constant threat of hostile attack, delivered urgently needed supplies to American troops on Guadalcanal until eventually disabled by Japanese dive bombers and towed to port for repair. Her restoration to combatant status, at a time when she might easily have been given up for lost, is a distinctive tribute to the courageous tenacity of her officers and men.

The *McFarland* also earned a battle star for her actions on 16 October during the attack on her by a flight of Japanese bombers. Although severely damaged, she survived and returned to service. The *Curtiss*, *Mackinac*, and *Thornton* received one or more battle stars for the landings on Guadalcanal and Tulagi, the capture and defense of Guadalcanal, or the battle of the Santa Cruz Islands, as did Patrol Squadrons VP-11, 12, 14, 23, 24, 51, 72, 91.[47]

Battle Stars for Guadalcanal and the Santa Cruz Islands

Guadalcanal-Tulagi Landings

Ship	Award Period	Commanding Officer
Curtiss (AV-4)	7-9 Aug 1942	Capt. Wilson P. Cogswell, USN
Mackinac (AVP-13)	7-9 Aug 1942	Comdr. Norman R. Hitchcock, USN
VP-11	7-9 Aug 1942	Lt. Comdr. Clayton C. Marcy
VP-23	7-9 Aug 1942	Lt. Comdr. Francis M. Hughes

Capture and Defense of Guadalcanal

Ship	Award Period	Commanding Officer
Curtiss (AV-4)	10 Aug 42-8 Feb 43	Capt. Wilson P. Cogswell, USN
McFarland (AVD-14)	16 Oct 1942	Lt. Comdr. John C. Alderman, USN
Thornton (AVD-11)	20 Nov 42-8 Feb 43	Lt. Comdr. James P. Walker, USN
VP-11	10 Aug 42-8 Feb 43	Lt. W. P. Schroeder
		Lt. Comdr. Clayton C. Marcy
VP-12	15 Dec 42-8 Feb 43	Comdr. Clarence O. Taff
VP-14	10 Aug 42-8 Feb 43	Lt. Comdr. Clifford M. Campbell
VP-23	10 Aug 42-8 Feb 43	Lt. Comdr. Francis M. Hughes
		Lt. Comdr. James R. Ogden
VP-72	10 Aug 42-8 Feb 43	Comdr. Sidney J. Lawrence
VP-91 FE	10 Aug 42-8 Feb 43	Lt. Comdr. Joe B. Paschal
		Lt. Comdr. James O. Cobb

Battle of Santa Cruz Islands

Ship	Award Period	Commanding Officer
Curtiss (AV-4)	26 Oct 1942	Capt. Wilson P. Cogswell, USN
VP-11	26 Oct 1942	Lt. Comdr. Clayton C. Marcy
VP-23	26 Oct 1942	Lt. Comdr. James R. Ogden
VP-24	26 Oct 1942	Lt. Comdr. William L. Richards
VP-51	26 Oct 1942	Lt. Comdr. William A. Moffett Jr.
VP-91 FE	26 Oct 1942	Lt. Comdr. Joe B. Paschal

14

America Reinforces New Caledonia

> *Noumea is a French city whose citizens acted unfriendly in the extreme. I might go so far to say that they glared at we Yanks. The reason, we were to learn, was that they were Vichy French and Nazi sympathizers. It is a strange feeling to be hated, seemingly for no reason at all. One trip ashore was enough for all of us.*[3]
>
> —Bos'n Kenneth G. Adams, USNR, commanding officer of YP-347 (ex-San Diego tuna boat *Star of the Sea*), describing hostility encountered during a visit to Noumea in November 1942.[1]

In the aftermath of the attack on Pearl Harbor, the U.S. government decided in January 1942 to send troops to New Caledonia to fortify and defend it against a feared Japanese attack. An Australian garrison based there was insufficient to defend the 250-mile long, 31-mile wide island, and would later be withdrawn except for a small detachment, following the arrival of American forces. New Caledonia was a French Territory and former penal colony, strategically located on the northeast approach to Australia. From New Caledonia westward to Australia there was only the open Coral Sea. This made the island vulnerable to enemy forces wishing to sever the route by which ships were transporting men, materials, and munitions from America's west coast and the Panama Canal to reinforce Australia.[2]

Compounding the island's susceptibility to attack were fears that Germany with tacit support might invite the Japanese to occupy New Caledonia. The French high commissioner had committed the French population's loyalties to the Free French organization in September 1940, shortly after France had fallen to German forces. However of the 25,000 French (there was an estimated 55,000-60,000 people in New Caledonia, including the Loyalty Islands), some still supported the Vichy French government. The French State was the formal title of France's puppet Vichy administration installed by the Nazis after they conquered France in 1940, but "Vichy France," "Vichy Regime," "Vichy government," or "Vichy" were commonly used to describe the government which, officially neutral, collaborated with the Axis powers from July 1940 to August 1944.³

Map 14-1

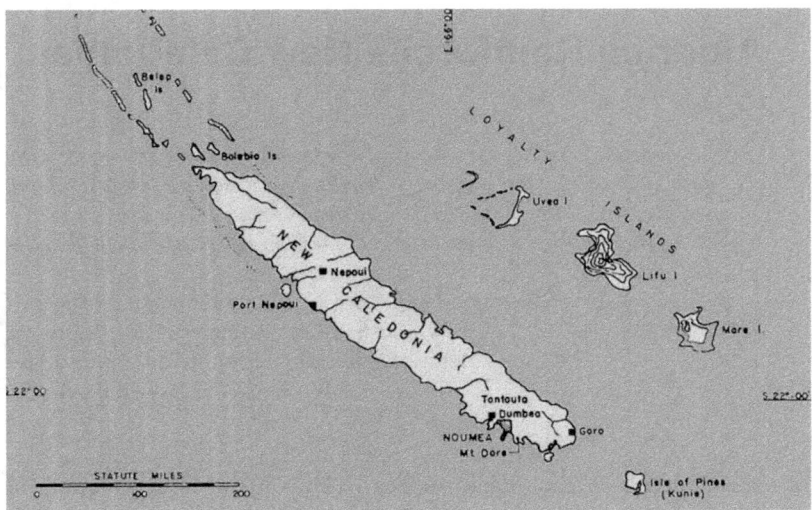

The French Colony of New Caledonia, comprising dozens of islands, lay northeast of Brisbane, Australia, across the Coral Sea.
Building the Navy's Bases in World War II History of the Bureau of Yards and Docks and the Civil Engineer Corps 1940-1946 Volume II

U.S. ARMY TASK FORCE 6814/AMERICAL DIVISION

At Brooklyn, New York, a hastily gathered Army force scraped together with units from all across America embarked aboard eight merchant ships—S.S. *Argentina*, S.S. *Barry*, S.S. *Cristobal*, S.S. *Erickson*, S.S. *McAndrew*, S.S. *Santa Elena*, S.S. *Santa Rosa* and the S.S. *Island Mail*—and sailed in convoy on 23 January. Comprising the elements of Task Force 6814 were the headquarters and detachment, two National Guard infantry regiments, two battalions of medium artillery, two engineer regiments plus a battalion, two ordnance companies and parts of two others, a signal company and MP Platoon, an evacuation and two station hospitals, plus a medical regiment, post office, finance and chemical units.⁴

The Task Force stopped at Melbourne to load guns (Australia British 18-pounders and 25-pounders) and embark two Australian officers and a crew of expert NCOs to instruct the Americans in the operation and nomenclature of the new weapons. Upon arrival at Noumea on 12 March 1942, Maj. Gen. Alexander M. Patch, USA, assumed active command. Because intelligence reports indicated an air attack might be expected, the troops went over the side in landing nets and dispersed to the hills. No attack developed, and the task force began fortifying island defenses and conducting field training.[5]

The constitution and organization of the Americal Division was authorized on 27 May 1942, the only Army division formed outside of United States territory during the war. (A distinction it would repeat two decades later when reformed during the Vietnam War.) The name Americal had been proposed by Pfc David Fonseca of the 26th Signal Company; the contraction was meant to suggest both America and Caledonia, the division's birthplace. The Americal Division would be the first Army unit sent to Guadalcanal. As it arrived piecemeal that summer and early autumn, its soldiers were fed into combat beside the battle-hardened First Marines. On 9 December 1942, the Americal Division relieved the 1st Marine Division on Guadalcanal.[6]

Map 14-2

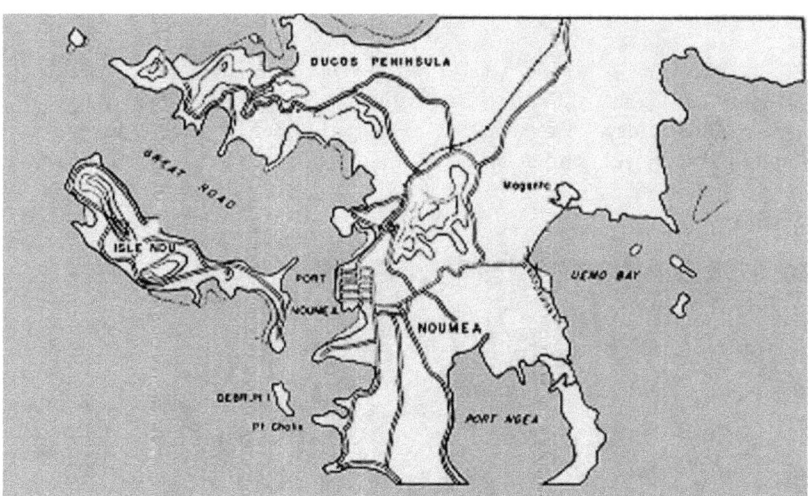

Noumea, at the southern end of the island of New Caledonia, was developed as the main Fleet Base in the South Pacific. Great Road was also known as Noumea Harbor.
Building the Navy's Bases in World War II History of the Bureau of Yards and Docks and the Civil Engineer Corps 1940-1946 Volume II

INITIAL SEAPLANE OPERATIONS

Functioning since 4 March 1942 as seaplane tender for a half squadron (six planes) of PBY-5s, the *Tangier* (AV-8) arrived at Noumea from Hawaii prior to Task Force 6814. Anchored in Great Road, she also furnished all services necessary to patrol aircraft passing through the area, and miscellaneous services to U.S. Army field forces in New Caledonia. The naval establishment at Noumea was, like Task Force 6814, ad hoc. On 10 June, Capt. T. J. Peyton, USN, arrived to take over the post of Captain of the Port, bringing with him eight officers and 143 men to install underwater defenses and an administrative unit. As might be expected, there were growing pains. In mid-June, a group of officers representing the Navy Department visited Noumea to inspect progress made. Their report identified deficiencies, including some related to the Navy men ashore:

> The naval personnel present were hastily organized in the U.S. with resulting confusion. Many have no pay accounts, service records, health records, inoculations, allotments or proper clothing. Some were merchant marine reserves reporting for first naval duty and had no uniforms. The transport [ship in which they travelled] could not outfit them. Some dungarees were obtained in Samoa. The small stores for this base have not yet arrived. The Army at Noumea is providing clothes for these men....
>
> Morale of the few naval forces present is satisfactory. Movies are available through the Army. The mail situation is unsatisfactory. Time has not permitted athletics. There are no local entertainment facilities.[7]

Photo 14-1

Pontoon Pier at the Seaplane Base, Noumea.
Building the Navy's Bases in World War II History of the Bureau of Yards and Docks and the Civil Engineer Corps 1940-1946 Volume II

Rear Adm. Richard E. Byrd, USN (Retired) noted in his report that fifteen PBY-5s, one PBY-5A, and five OS2U-3s were based with the *Tangier* in Noumea Harbor, and all land-based aviation was under the cognizance of the U.S. Army. Byrd was a pioneering American aviator, famous polar explorer, and Medal of Honor recipient who had been recalled to active duty. His World War II service was mostly as the confidential advisor to commander U.S. Fleet and chief of Naval Operations, Adm. Ernest J. King. From 1942 to 1945, Byrd headed missions to the Pacific, including surveys of remote islands for airfields.[8]

Photo 14-2

Rear Adm. Richard E. Byrd, USN
Naval History and Heritage Command Photograph NH 105371

Rear Adm. John S. McCain, USN, embarked aboard the *Tangier*, was taking over the base facilities on Ile Nou at Noumea, where the Royal Australian Air Force maintained a small seaplane base detachment without aircraft. McCain had recently become the first commander of a new aviation organization, "Aircraft South Pacific." The plan was to construct a temporary aircraft base camp to handle eighteen patrol bombers (VPB), and to quarter 75 officers and 250 men. The weather conditions for flying at Noumea were generally favorable. And, although the island was mountainous with few flat places where emergency landings could be made, there were numerous sheltered coves where, in a difficulty, seaplanes could land or takeoff.⁹

SUPPORT FOR THE BATTLE OF THE CORAL SEA

A few weeks earlier, prior to Admiral McCain assuming his new role, the *Tangier* and her tended patrol planes had played a supporting role in the Battle of the Coral Sea. On 29 April 1942, Comdr. George H. DeBaun learned that he had been designated commander Search Group (Task Group 17.9), a component of Rear Adm. Frank J. Fletcher's Task Force 17. DeBaun, the commanding officer of *Tangier*, was in charge of his ship, the planes assigned to him, and also was concurrently the senior officer present afloat (SOPA) at Noumea. He had been titled commander Task Unit 9.6.2, working for commander Patrol Wing Two (Task Force 9) in Hawaii.¹⁰

For the first four days in May, *Tangier*'s patrol planes conducted their standard search; three aircraft flying a parallel search on course 340° true from Noumea out a distance of 700 miles, with the PBYs spaced fifty miles apart. In the early afternoon of 4 May, six VP-71 aircraft arrived to supplement those of VP-72 then operating, bringing the complement to twelve. The following day, DeBaun implemented commander Task Force 17's directives:

> Six planes make daily search, covering sector from Noumea between bearings 305 and 360 as far to the northwest as the boundary of the Southwest Pacific Area and as far north as latitude 11-30 S. plus a triangle within the points, latitude 15-00 S. longitude 168-40 E., latitude 16-30 S. longitude 171-40 E., latitude 18-15 S. longitude 168-45 E.

Operational Order 2-42 further bade him to: "Modify these searches if later developments indicate a need therefor and keep the Task Force Commander advised," and also to "Trail any enemy surface units encountered, reporting contact promptly."¹¹

The search results that day, like those of previous ones, were negative regarding the detection of enemy forces. On 6 May, four more PBY-5s of VP-71 arrived to augment the existing patrol, and the next day theee more, as reliefs for the balance of VP-72. At 0721 the following morning, the *Tangier* received a report of a ship having been sunk by a Japanese sub and survivors in the water west of Bulari Pass, off Noumea. (This would prove to be the Greek cargo ship S.S. *Chloe*.) In response to the submarine threat in the area, DeBaun sent a dispatch to commander Patrol Wing Two, "Request authority to retain three planes VP-72 for anti-submarine air patrol up to limit of extended engine time. Also request six more planes be assigned *Tangier* at once for anti-submarine patrol."[12]

On 8 May, the air patrol reported at 1045 a sighting of a boat of the S.S. *John Adams* with twelve people in it. Named after the second President of the United States, the *Adams* was the first Liberty ship sunk by enemy action in World War II. She had left Noumea bound for Brisbane, Australia, carrying 2,000 tons of aviation gasoline in barrels. About 140 miles into her 900-mile voyage, she was hit by a torpedo fired by the *I-21*. The ship was blacked out and running at 12 knots with four lookouts posted, but none saw the torpedo approaching. The detonation of the warhead ripped a hole in her port side causing the after part of the ship to erupt into flames. As the fire spread, the master, Conrad Peterson, ordered the ship abandoned. Three lifeboats were launched, but eight Navy Armed Guard members aft were prevented from reaching the boats by the fire; they jumped off the stern into the sea. Sadly, five perished, the only casualties of the fifty men onboard.[13]

DeBaun directed the patrol plane to inform the boat to expect help the following day, to note its position on a chart, and to return to base. That afternoon, two destroyers, the *Helm* (DD-388) and *Henley* (DD-391), stood into Noumea Harbor and reported for anti-submarine patrol duty. In late afternoon, the air patrol reported sighting a second boat of *John Adams* seventy miles to the southeast of Amedee Light—a lighthouse sited on a small island thirteen miles off Noumea. The boat was under power and headed for New Caledonia (and would land on its own).[14]

The following day, 9 May, DeBaun instructed the plane in Sector A to search for survivors of the destroyer *Sims* (DD-409) and the oiler *Neosho* (AO-23). The former had sunk and the latter was sinking due to enemy action at the battle of the Coral Sea. The *Henley* was to proceed to the probable area of the *Neosho* and *Sims* survivors; en route, she was to search for the *John Adams* boat off Amedee Light. *Helm* was to pick up the other *John Adams* boat. The air patrol was to continue to search for survivors, to check on the probably landing of the No. 1 boat off Amedee Light and to locate the other boat for the *Helm*. A PBY sighted the boat *Helm* was searching for at 1425, and directed her to the area. The destroyer picked up thirteen survivors at 1727. The first boat would make land by itself; the status of the third boat was unknown.[15]

After putting down the *John Adams*, the *I-21* had found the S.S. *Chloe* on 7 May, and had sunk her as well. Comdr. Kanji Matsumura fired two Type 95 torpedoes at the Greek cargo ship, both exploded prematurely. He then surfaced, ordered the crew off the ship and sank the unarmed vessel with his deck gun. The *Chloe*, then about thirty-five nautical miles off Noumea, had been in passage from Newcastle, Australia, to Noumea. A PBY located *Chloe*'s lifeboats that afternoon and signaled HMAS *Wilcannia* (FYP-2), which was nearby. The small Australian patrol vessel picked up all thirty-five members of ship's company; there were no casualties.[16]

LOSS OF *NEOSHO* AND *SIMS* TO ENEMY AIRCRAFT

During the forenoon of 7 May, the destroyer *Sims* had been serving as anti-submarine escort for and patrolling ahead of the oiler *Neosho*. At 0930, fifteen Japanese high-altitude horizontal bombers attacked the two ships but did no damage. Ten more aircraft attached the *Sims* at 1038. By skillful maneuvering, she evaded the nine bombs that were dropped. A third attack made against the two ships by thirty-six dive bombers shortly before noon was devastating. *Neosho* was soon a blazing wreck, but still afloat, as the result of seven direct hits and a plane that dove into her. *Sims* was attacked from all directions. The destroyer defended herself as best she could, but was hit by three 500-pound bombs; two of which exploded in the engine room.[17]

The *Sims* commanding officer, Lt. Comdr. Wilford M. Hyman, ordered Chief Signalman R. J. Dicken to take charge of the starboard motor whaleboat and go aft in it and put out the fire in the after deckhouse and flood the after magazines. The port boat had been previously launched, and sank immediately. The starboard boat was holed, but kept afloat by stuffing life jackets in the opening and by continuous bailing. In addition to Dicken, six other sailors comprised the boat crew. As the boat proceeded around the bow to the lee side of the ship aft, the destroyer buckled amidships and began to sink, stern first. As she slipped into the deep, there was a tremendous explosion from her torpedoes or depth charges, which lifted the ship ten to fifteen feet out of the water.[18]

Chief Dicken, in the whaleboat, retrieved from the water all the men he could find, and whom appeared to still be alive. He succeeded in saving a total of fifteen men, including himself, and began looking for life rafts with other survivors. His search was fruitless, so he headed toward the *Neosho*, which had about a 25-degree list and was burning. The men in the whaleboat remained with the oiler, still afloat despite severe damage, until they were rescued by the *Henley* on 11 May. At 1245 that day, a patrol plane sighted the *Neosho* and survivors, and directed the destroyer (located fifty miles southwest of the oiler) to the *Neosho*. The *Henley* took aboard 123 survivors of the *Sims* and *Neosho* and delivered them to Brisbane. Prior to her departure, on orders from commander Destroyer Division 7, the destroyer sank the *Neosho* with a torpedo and 5-inch/38 gunfire. In ensuing days, patrol planes continued to search for additional crewmen adrift in rafts, but without success. *Helm*, which had continued the search after the *Henley*'s departure, arrived at Brisbane on 18 May She had found four survivors on the 16th, one of whom died shortly after being taken aboard. They had been part of a group of about sixty-eight men in four life rafts lashed together. The others had succumbed from a lack of water and from exhaustion.[19]

COMMANDER AIRCRAFT, SOUTH PACIFIC

A few days later, Rear Admiral McCain assumed command of Aircraft, South Pacific on 20 May 1942. This action took place aboard his flagship, *Tangier*, anchored at Great Road, Noumea. McCain was responsible for direct operational control of all shore and tender-based aircraft in the South Pacific, and for the training and indoctrination of all naval aircraft in the area. He was permitted to delegate certain aspects of his command to air organizations on the various islands under his command. A listing of the admirals that headed Aircraft, South Pacific and other Pacific Fleet aviation commands during the war is provided in Appendix I.[20]

In the coming months, Noumea would be developed as the main Fleet base in the South Pacific, assuming the extensive functions planned originally for Auckland, New Zealand. It would also serve as a staging area for the development of other advance bases, such as Guadalcanal; and on 8 November 1942, became headquarters for the Allied Commander of the South Pacific.[21]

PATROL WING ONE SENT FORWARD

Patrol Wing One, forerunner of Fleet Air Wing One, was based at Kaneohe Bay...on 7 December 1941. All except three of its planes were destroyed on the ground or water by the surprise Japanese attack. As soon as the Wing refitted, it continued to patrol from Kaneohe and began intensive training for future operations. A number of its search squadrons were moved forward to the New Hebrides and New Caledonia during the first half of 1942, but the greater part of the Wing remained in Hawaii until September. Early in that month it constructed its first forward base at Ile Nou, in Noumea's Harbor. Its forward

> *squadrons were subsequently first stationed at Ile Nou, at Espiritu Santo, and at Vanikoro in the Ellice Island Group.*
>
> —Rear Adm. John Perry, USN, Commander Fleet Air Wing One[22]

The role of the U.S. Navy and its aviation forces would expand rapidly during the war, which witnessed the increasing importance of carrier aviation as an element of striking power. The importance aircraft played in the Battle at Midway, and a growing demand for naval aviation forces, spurred Admiral Nimitz to recommend consolidation of administrative functions across aviation commands in the Pacific to create an efficient and effective command structure. Adm. Ernest J. King approved that recommendation and ordered the establishment of U.S. Naval Air Forces, Pacific Fleet. Its first commander, Rear Adm. Aubrey W. Fitch, USN, assumed his duties on 1 September 1942, the date on which the aviation commands' Carriers, Pacific Fleet, and Patrol Wings, Pacific Fleet, were abolished.[23]

One of Fitch's first actions was to relocate the headquarters of Patrol Wing One from Hawaii to Noumea. Previously, patrol plane units operating in the South Pacific Area consisted of detachments from many squadrons of Wings One and Two in Hawaii. Commander Wing One selected Patrol Squadrons VP-11, 72, and 91 to accompany him to the South Pacific and allocated to Patrol Wing Two all the remaining squadrons in the Hawaii area.[24]

Fitch directed commander Patrol Wing Two to transfer sufficient flight personnel to Wing One to provide the three squadrons, eighteen combat crews per squadron (44 officers and 124 men each). Eighteen reserve officers were to be provided for the headquarters squadron. The remaining squadrons of Patrol Wing One and those of Wing Two (VP-12, 14, 23, 24, 44, 51, and 71) were reorganized and Wing Two headquarters established at Naval Air Station Kaneohe.[25]

Forty-two operating PBY-5 aircraft were to be maintained in the South Pacific area via the transfer of aircraft from the Hawaiian area to meet attrition. To do so, Wing Two was to replace, in advance, those aircraft that had to be returned to the Hawaiian area for maintenance beyond the capacity of forces in the South Pacific area. Finally, rotation of flight crews between the two areas was to continue, as in the past, to provide for the replacement of combat weary flight crews with fresh ones from the Hawaiian area.[26]

15

A Swan in the South Pacific

There were those choice people who flew from [Pearl Harbor] Oahu to Puunene [Naval Air Station, Maui] and then those who went aboard the U.S.S. SWAN, a cross between a rowboat and a submarine. That trip proved most of our "salty" sailors had eaten the past few days and many graciously gave their digested food to the poor fishes. Our personal and squadron war stowed aboard and traveled mostly underwater. The loss of government and personal gear was extremely high, including all the bombsights, tools, spare equipment, oxygen masks and all squadron files. When the SWAN finally arrived at Kahului a group of thankful, weary lads departed vowing never to leave Maui unless the transportation was by air.

—Anecdote from the World War II history of Torpedo Squadron 3.[1]

Within days of the attack on Pearl Harbor, Japan swallowed up Guam, Indochina and Thailand, and by Christmas had taken Wake Island and Hong Kong. Within two months, her forces had occupied Manila, Singapore, and British Malaya (now called Malaysia). In March 1942 the Allies lost Java and Burma, and Japanese armies were in the Owen Stanley Mountains of New Guinea, with the coast of Australia almost in sight. In May, Corregidor surrendered, the Philippines fell, and Japan invaded the Solomon Islands. There was no let-up in the progress of the Japanese; it appeared they would win the war if they could continue their march to Australia and New Zealand and overrun them.[2]

Thus, keeping open the 7,800-mile-long sea route from Panama to Sydney was a strategic imperative. The northern route, west-southwest from Hawaii, was already controlled by the Japanese operating from island bastions. Only the southern route, via South Sea Islands, was available for use. From Bora Bora, the midway point, shipping destined for Australia had to sail through or close to a number of the island groups. First came the Cook Islands, then the Samoa, Tonga, and Fiji groups, and finally, a thousand miles or so from the Australian coast, the New Hebrides group and New Caledonia, forming the eastern rim of the Coral Sea. The utilization of these islands were critical to safeguarding the shipping route.³

One of the steps undertaken by the Navy to support the South Pacific supply line was the strengthening of American Samoa. The plan called for increasing facilities at the existing naval station at Tutuila and establishing two new advance bases to support land, sea, and air forces: on Upolu, an island under New Zealand mandate; and on Wallis, a French possession three hundred miles to the west. On both Upolu and Wallis, combined landplane and seaplane bases were to be built for the use of Navy and Marine Corps air units.⁴

SEAPLANE TENDER *SWAN*

The seaplane tender *Swan* (AVP-7) was sent to American Samoa to support Scouting Squadron VS-1D-14 and its handful of OS2U-3 Kingfishers until permanent facilities could be established ashore. The missions of the observation floatplanes were scouting for Japanese forces and providing anti-submarine coverage for friendly shipping in the area. The 187-foot *Swan*, like *Heron*, was a former minesweeper. Built by Alabama Dry Dock & Shipbuilding Co., Mobile, Alabama, she had been commissioned on 31 January 1919.⁵

Photo 15-1

USS *Swan* (AM-34) in the early 1930s, while serving as, but not yet designated, a seaplane tender.
U.S. Naval History and Heritage Command Photograph #NH 79072

Her first commanding officer, Lt. (jg) Fredman J. Walcott, United States Navy (Reserve Force), received the Navy Cross Medal "for exceptionally meritorious and distinguished service while in Command of the U.S.S. *Swan*, engaged in the important and hazardous work of clearing the North Sea of mines during World War I." Most of the 70,117 mines that comprised the North Sea Barrage had been laid by the Yankee Mining Squadron in 1918. The purpose of the barrier—which, at 230 miles in length and from 15 to 35 miles wide, stretched between Scotland and Norway—had been to bottle up German U-boats in their own waters, to prevent attacks against Allied shipping in the North Atlantic. In early 1919, *Heron, Swan,* and other *Lapwing*-class ships of Mine Division 2, had sailed from the United States for Kirkwall in the Orkney Islands, off the coast of northern mainland Scotland, to take part in the dangerous mine clearance operation.[6]

Following her return to America, *Swan* was decommissioned. Later recommissioned, she was assigned first to the Washington Navy Yard and then the Fifteenth Naval District, headquartered at Coco Solo in the Canal Zone. While based in Panama, she was designated "minesweeper for duty with aircraft" on 30 April 1931. In early 1934, *Swan* was reassigned to the Fleet Air Base at Pearl Harbor and, on 22 January 1936, she became officially a small seaplane tender with hull number AVP-7. *Swan* was assigned as a tender for Patrol Wing Two operating out of Pearl Harbor.[8]

PAGO PAGO, TUTUILA

Map 15-1

Samoan Islands (the correct spelling for the largest island is Savaii or Savai'i)

Swan left Pearl Harbor on 8 January 1942, bound for American Samoa, 2,276 nautical miles south-southwest of Honolulu in the central South Pacific. It, and Western Samoa (today, Samoa, an independent nation) comprised the Samoan Islands. American Samoa, located in the eastern half of the archipelago, consisted of a crescent-shaped group of seven islands and a few islets. Savaii, at the western end, was the largest and tallest island. The second largest, Upolu, lay southeast of Savaii, and Tutuila, the third largest, southeast of Upolu. Located east of Tutuila were three small islands (Ofu, Olosega, and Tau) whose combined land area was about eighteen square miles. Eastward of Tau Island, uninhabited Rose Atoll marked the eastern boundary. The ship arrived at Pago Pago Harbor ten days after leaving Hawaii, to tend the aircraft of VS-1D-14. Formed from a volcano crater, this harbor on the south coast of Tutuila was the best port in the South Seas.[9]

Photo 15-2

Pago Pago Harbor, Tutuila, Samoan Islands, 1899.
U.S. Naval History and Heritage Command Photograph #NH 1457

Fourteen days after the Japanese attack on Pearl Harbor, the Navy had ordered that VS-1D-14 be formed from two existing scouting squadrons, VS-1D-11 and VS-1D-13. The new squadron was commissioned at Naval Air Station Reeves Field, San Pedro, California, and sent to the Samoan Islands. Its OS2U-3 Kingfisher floatplanes were fitted with two .30-caliber guns, and were configured to carry two 325-pound depth charges. They also had been given self-sealing fuel tanks and armor protection. However, the weight of the intended ordnance proved a little too much for the monoplanes to lift, and thus they carried two 100-pound bombs when on patrol. Realistically, the scout planes had little chance of survival in an encounter with anti-aircraft batteries and, especially, with aircraft. Their job was to search for Japanese naval forces, report their position, and use clouds to hide from fighters until they could return to their base or tending ship.[10]

Photo 15-3

A Vought OS2U-3 Kingfisher being recovered by the cruiser USS *Baltimore* (CA-68) in 1944. These type aircraft were also carried by cruisers and battleships to spot gunfire, and search for enemy forces.
U.S. Navy Photograph #80-G-218123, now in the collections of the National Archives

The American Samoan Islands and Wallis Island (which lay within the Samoan area) were of strategic importance to the Allies, because of their location along the sea lanes from the U.S. West Coast and Panama, to Australia. The Navy was in the process of establishing an advance airbase and naval area in these islands to afford security to naval forces and shipping in the region, and to provide support to other island positions between the United States and Australia. To that end, a convoy had left San Diego on 6 January 1942. It included the ammunition ship *Lassen* (AE-3), oiler *Kaskaskia* (AO-27), transports S S. *Lurline*, S.S. *Matsonia*, and S.S. *Monterey*—carrying 4,800 men of the 2nd Marine Brigade—and the cargo ship *Jupiter* (AK-43).

Chapter 15

Despite concerns about the possibility of attack by Japanese forces, the group arrived safely at Pago Pago on 20 January.[11]

Map 15-2

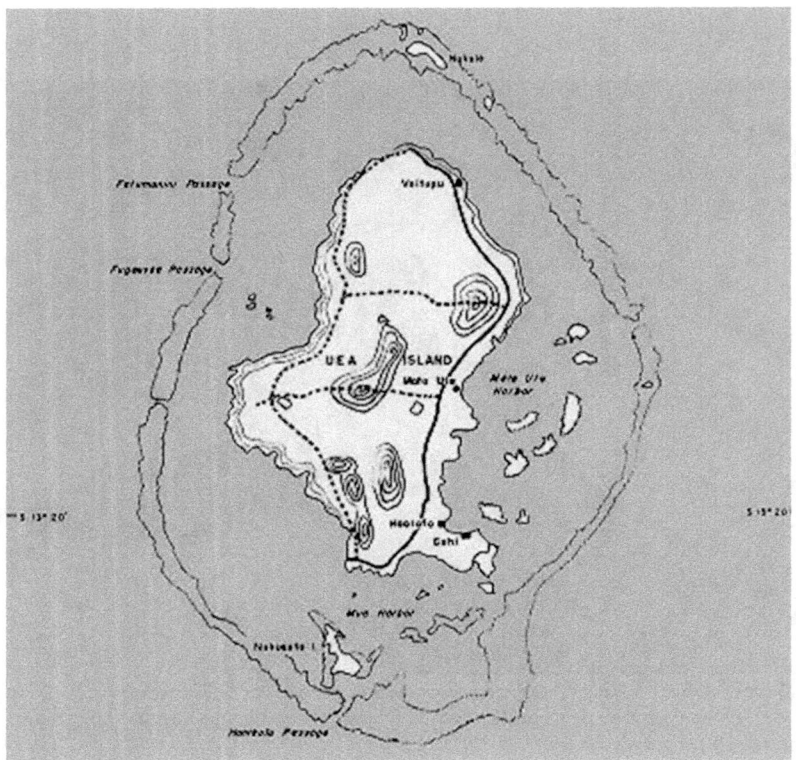

Wallis (Ile Uvea in French or Uea) Island
Building the Navy's Bases in World War II History of the Bureau of Yards and Docks and the Civil Engineer Corps 1940-1946 Volume II

Soon after that, construction of an airstrip at Tafune on the east coast of Tutuila Island, a little south of Pago Pago, was completed on 17 March 1942. Newly activated Marine Air Group 13 was then brought in from San Diego, for the air defense of American Samoa, and the 7th Marine Defense Battalion for island defense. By 1 June, there were 512 Navy and 7,483 Marine Corps personnel at Tutuila. These figures do not include one hundred men comprising the Fita Fita Guard, but do include 365 natives enlisted in the defense forces. The Fita Fita (soldier) Guard was a security organization comprised of Samoans recruited to help maintain law and order, and enlisted in the

Naval Reserve. The Marine Force, as then constituted, would likely have been capable of only repelling minor attacks or raids. Due to the island's rugged terrain, long coastline, and poor roads, it would have been difficult for the Marines to meet an enemy invasion force in sufficient numbers at a landing beach, or to get reinforcements quickly to an area to eject or contain the Japanese.[12]

The island's air striking force—made up of a small number of landplanes and amphibious aircraft—was also relatively weak. By June 1942, seaplanes were no longer operating from Pago Pago, resulting in the below listed aircraft being used for reconnaissance and off-shore air patrol in addition to serving as a standby attack force:

Quantity	Type Aircraft	Squadron
18	Grumman F4F-3 Wildcat fighters	VMF-111
2	North American SNJ-3 Texan trainers	VMF-111
17	Curtiss SBC-4 Helldiver scout bombers	VMO-151
5	Grumman J2F-5 Duck utility and air-sea rescue	Headquarters and Service Squadron

Despite Pago Pago being the safest and best ship harbor in the South Pacific, it had proved undesirable for the operation of seaplanes. This was due to the short takeoff run mandated by the geography of its harbor, and steep hills surrounding the harbor, which permitted take-offs only toward the entrance. Moreover, Tutuila received about 190 inches of rain a year, and squalls were frequent.[13]

RESCUE OF DOWNED FLIERS

Earlier, *Swan* had voyaged in mid-March to Pukapuka, 750 miles to the southeast in the remote Cook Islands, to retrieve three downed fliers from the aircraft carrier *Enterprise* (CV-6). Chief Petty Officer Harold Dixon, the pilot of a Douglas TBD Devastator torpedo bomber, had discovered while on an anti-submarine patrol that he was nearly out of fuel. Unable to return to the carrier, he ditched the plane in the ocean. Thus began a month-long ordeal for himself and his plane crew, bombardier Tony Pastula and radioman Gene Aldrich. During thirty-four days afloat on a tiny rubber raft, the men endured blazing sun, rough seas and hungry sharks, and would have perished but for rainwater caught in lifejackets and a paltry amount of scavenged food.

The men were able to spear a fish and a 4-foot shark with a knife, shoot a seabird with a .45-pistol, grab another one that alighted on the raft, and retrieve two water-soaked coconuts from the sea. Propelled by wind and wave, the raft drifted a thousand miles before finally washing up on Pukapuka, a coral atoll in the Cook Islands. Locals brought the men to the resident commissioner, who notified the Navy. Thereafter, *Swan* arrived at "Danger Island" (so called because of a treacherous, submerged reef, which precluded ships from anchoring in its beautiful lagoon) and whisked the men away and back to the fleet.[14]

UPOLU, AMERICAN SAMOA

Following her return to Pago Pago, *Swan* moored at Governors Dock, Naval Station Tutuila. She was one of only three ships attached to the naval station. The others, the tugs *Turkey* (AT-143) and *Kingfisher* (AT-135), were like *Swan* ex *Lapwing*-class minesweepers. Unlike her, the others retained minesweeping gear for use against moored mines. *Swan* remained at Pago Pago through 25 May, except for visits in April and May to Apia, on the north coast of Upolu. Apia had a poor harbor, and landings ashore had to be made in small boats. The climate on the island was more equable than that of Tutuila, having less average annual rainfall (about 110 inches) and average temperature a pleasant 77 degrees. But like at Tutuila, Marine Corps defense forces were assigned to Upolu, and there was also a naval air detachment and a naval construction battalion.[15]

The aviation facilities available to support seaplanes on Upolu consisted of a 20-foot ramp and quarters erected by VS-1D-14. The aircraft on hand on 3 June, were two J2F-5 and nine OS2U-3 seaplanes (two of which were in crates at Pago Pago). Existing mandates were that one J2F-5 and two OS2U-3 tender-based planes be temporarily maintained at Wallis Island for patrol purposes. The armament and performance of the Kingfishers was inadequate for any type of combat. Even when carrying two 100-pound bombs, the OS2U-3's fuel load had to be restricted to about ninety-nine gallons of gasoline, dramatically restricting its range of operation. VS-1D-14 had thirteen officer pilots, one enlisted pilot, one radio electrician, and sixty-eight other ratings. Temporary wooden huts served as quarters for the officers and men.[16]

Admiral Byrd's South Pacific Advanced Base Inspection Board team visited Apia in June 1942. His report highlighted deficiencies in the qualifications of assigned personnel, and the fact that some were fleet reprobates. These men would have been discharged from the naval service in peacetime. The report also noted that only meager amenities were available to the scouting squadron:

> The Naval Personnel was not well suited for this duty. The yeoman and storekeepers have no naval experience. No Chief Boatswain's Mate was provided, and one was transferred from the

Construction Battalion. This man had little Naval experience.... A high proportion of men, once sentenced to bad conduct discharges and who are on qualified probation, are among the Naval Personnel.

The Naval Unit has no athletic equipment but so far has had little time to use it. The unit has no movie machine, but can attend nearby Marine movies. No ship's [laundry] service has been established. The Post Exchange sends a truck around to all units weekly; often the supply of Post Exchange items are exhausted before the truck reaches the last of the outlying activities.

Beer is sold by the Post Exchange.

Very little mail has been received so far. That received was 5 or 6 weeks old.[17]

Logistic support for the scouting squadron was also limited; VS-1D-14 had six spare engines, and a few assemblies and spare parts. Due to the time required to obtain other needed items from the Navy's Bureau of Aeronautics (BuAero), the squadron deemed it best to initially get along with what help it could get from the Marine Corps garrison. Items required from BuAero included a liberal allowance of spare aircraft electrical, radio and other equipment that was adversely affected by moisture. Due to the heat and high humidity, all delicate mechanisms—instruments and radio equipment—deteriorated rapidly. The existing supply of aviation ordnance was marginal. There was a small quantity of 100-pound bombs for use by the OS2U-3 aircraft, but a shortage of belting links for .30-caliber ammunition.[18]

WALLIS ISLAND

Swan tended aircraft at Wallis Island from late May to early July 1942. Free French forces had occupied the island, which was pro-Vichy, on 26 May. United States forces arrived there the following day, and interviews with key officials followed. The French bishop at Wallis felt that all French people should give their allegiance to the Vichy government, and it seemed to disturb him greatly that Americans had occupied the island without permission from this government. It was felt, however, that over time he might change his perspective. There was also an influential German priest on the island who was violently pro-Axis, and whose continued presence on the island was considered undesirable. A king residing at Mata-Utu, the capital city on the eastern side of the island, ruled over the 5,000 natives on Wallis. In his capacity as the civilian administrator of the island, he received advice from the Resident Commissioner, a Free Frenchman, who was also the only civilian doctor on the island.[19]

Like at Upolu, a Marine force, naval unit, and construction battalion had been detailed to the island. The latter were independent organizations but under the commanding officer of the Marines. The air striking force was small, and the re-servicing facilities meager. On the positive side, a fringing coral reef surrounded the island, providing a natural barrier while still allowing ships to enter the lagoon at Gahi on the southeast coast. No facilities ashore then existed for land or seaplanes. The crews of two OS2U-3s and one J2F-5 were based aboard *Swan* moored at Mata-Utu. These seaplanes operated from the lagoon, which offered complete protection from the sea, but little from the wind.[20]

Following visits by the South Pacific Advanced Base Inspection Board to Tutuila, Upolu, and Wallis, which culminated in early June, Rear Admiral Byrd highlighted systemic deficiencies in the islands. His report concluded that due to prevailing weaknesses in self-defense, the island area required the protection of the fleet:

> The most dangerous deficiency noted was the inadequacy of the air forces and facilities in this area. The air striking force is small and the reservicing facilities meager. While landing fields are planned for all the islands, only one (that on Tutuila) existed at the time of the visit. The AA [anti-aircraft] protection was meager and particularly deficient in automatic cannon. It is not believed that these islands, at the time of the visit, could mutually support one another, as the means with which to do so are lacking. Had an attack been made at that time on any of the islands and particularly on Wallis, it would have quickly fallen and could have been used as a base by the enemy from which to launch attacks on the other islands. Until adequate air facilities and air forces exist on these islands, the reliance for protection of them must be placed on our sea forces. The [island] group is too far from other adjacent bases to allow adequate air support from any of them.[21]

Swan departed Wallis Island on 11 July for Pago Pago, to undergo two weeks of upkeep. Having fulfilled her responsibilities of tending the seaplanes and personnel of the scouting squadron until Navy "Seabees" could build facilities ashore, she stood out of the lagoon on 25 July bound for Pearl Harbor. *Swan* stopped briefly at Canton on the 28th, an atoll (one of the Phoenix Islands) located roughly halfway between Hawaii and Fiji. After entering Pearl Harbor on 4 August, she moored at the Navy Yard to commence a much needed overhaul. *Swan* left the yard on 28 October 1942, and proceeded to Kaneohe Naval Air Station on Oahu, to load ammunition and supplies.[22]

SOUTH SEAS "SUPPLY SHIP" DUTIES

When necessary, *Swan*, like other small Navy ships, served as a "maid of all duties." Through year's end and into 1943, she was employed principally as a cargo ship, hauling critically needed supplies and materials to island outposts. The tender proceeded out of Kaneohe Bay on the 30th and set a course for Canton, 1,660 nautical miles to the south-southwest. Under joint control of the United States and Britain, it was the site of an airstrip and was used as a stopover for the U.S. Navy Air Transport Service flights to Australia and New Zealand. A year later, in autumn 1943, Canton would also serve as a staging point for attacks on the Japanese-held Gilbert Islands.[23]

A patrol squadron that spent time on Canton in summer 1943 described it as being shaped like a limp quoit (ring) encompassing a large central lagoon well suited for seaplane operations. The base had exceptional repair and maintenance facilities, and a seaplane ramp to drag aircraft out of the water. Lodging and subsistence were less impressive. Quarters for officers and enlisted men consisted of Quonset Huts, as did the head, mess halls and all other types of establishments. The food was poor and the water brackish, but the Navy Seabees were good hosts, making available quarters and facilities to VP-34 personnel and providing a small ration of beer and movies. Swimming, softball, and volleyball were also available for recreation.[24]

Swan lay to off Canton for half a day on 7 November 1942, unloading men and materials, before departing for Suva, the principal port at Viti Levu in the Fijian Islands, a British Crown Colony. Fiji lay a thousand miles farther to the south-southwest and nearer Australia, and was another very important support point on the long South Pacific shipping route. *Swan* arrived at Suva on 13 November and moored at King's Wharf to load stores and supplies for delivery along her track back to Pearl Harbor. Stops included Funafuti, Ellice Islands, and Canton, Sydney, Hull, and Gardner in the Phoenix Islands.[25]

From Suva, it was a three-and-a-half day trek north to Funafuti which, located midway between Hawaii and Australia, was part of the British-owned Ellice island group. Some seven miles long and 50 to 150 yards wide, it had been developed that autumn to provide an air base and scouting and ferry point for aircraft en route to the South Pacific area. Its facilities would be most important later in connection with the U.S. thrust northwestward into the Gilbert and Marshall islands, but the base remained in a rudimentary condition for some time as later noted by VP-34 in August 1943:

This base was the most primitive of all, with crude quarters, poor food, inadequate sanitary facilities, and virtually non-existent repair and maintenance. Nearly all work, from maintenance to digging fox-holes and constructing heads, was performed by squadron personnel.²⁶

Following unloading of stores for the Resident Commissioner, *Swan* left Funafuti on 20 November, bound for Gardner Island in the Phoenix group. She arrived at Gardner (today named Nikumaroro) the morning of the 23rd and lay to while unloading stores for the British High Commissioner, Western Pacific. At completion, she set a course for Canton. Reaching there the following day, she unloaded stores and embarked administrative officers. She delivered them to Sydney Island along with stores, delivered stores to Hull Island, and later retrieved the officers and returned them to Canton. Leaving the Phoenix Islands, she proceeded northeast to Palmyra. The island, located 960 nautical miles south-southwest of Pearl Harbor, was the site of a naval air station. The "cargo and passenger ship," arrived at Navy Yard, Pearl Harbor on 14 December for the holidays. She left there at year's end on 30 December 1942, to make another run to Canton.²⁷

16

French Morocco

At 0740, Barnegat opened fire with No. 2 – 5" gun, and on one of the larger shore batteries, probably one of about 6" caliber. Opening range was 10,000 yards, the Control Officer's estimate, and the first burst was well over. A spot of down 1000 placed the second shot very close to the target. A total of eleven rounds were fired and it is believed the battery was silenced. At least the battery was not observed to fire again, and it had been, up until that time, quite active.

—Report by Comdr. Josephus A. Briggs, USN, commanding officer of the seaplane tender *Barnegat* (AVP-10), regarding his ship silencing an enemy gun after French batteries at Mehedia opened fire on transport ships of the Northern Attack Group during the Allied invasion of French Morocco[1]

In autumn 1942, the seaplane tender *Barnegat* (AVP-10) was stationed in Iceland. Attached to Patrol Wing Seven, but operating under commander, U.S. Naval Forces, European Waters, she was responsible for supporting British and Norwegian as well as American patrol planes. This duty necessitated the use of one of her crewmen, a Norwegian by birth, as an interpreter. Wing Seven air forces in Iceland operated in concert with the Royal Air Force Coastal Command and exiled Norwegian air forces based there. The mission of all the patrol planes was generally the same: protection of Allied shipping and anti-U-boat and anti-raider operations. The amorphous command arrangement based upon mutual agreement seemed to work well, because of the good judgment of the officers involved and perhaps due in part to the conditions that everyone faced. The severe weather—comparable to that in the Aleutians—imposed great hardships on aircraft and ships alike. Navigation in Icelandic waters was extremely hazardous, and even something as routine as anchoring offered the very real possibility of being driven aground by wind and wave. *Barnegat*'s duty in Iceland came to an end on 25 October when she departed Skerjafjordr bound for Londonderry Port, Lisahally,

Ireland. Embarked aboard the seaplane tender were personnel of VP-73, as well as torpedoes, bombs, and aviation equipment.[2]

Photo 16-1

Barnegat off Boston Navy Yard, Charlestown, Massachusetts on 1 January 1942. U.S. National Archives Photograph # 19-N-26612

Barnegat entered Lough Foyle Inlet on the north coast of Ireland, mid-afternoon on 27 October, and arrived at Lisahally in early evening. She left the United Kingdom's most westerly port the morning of 29 October and rendezvoused with Convoy WS-24 at a point six miles from Oversay Light, a lighthouse on a same-named island just off Rhynns Point, Scotland. Upon joining at 0830, *Barnegat* took her station as last ship in the center column. She steamed in company with the convoy until early afternoon on 2 November, when she departed to proceed independently to join Task Force 34. *Barnegat* made contact in early morning on 7 November with a destroyer of the task force, exchanged recognition signals, and reported for duty to Rear Adm. Monroe Kelly, USN, embarked in the battleship *Texas* (BB-35). Kelly was commander Battleships, Atlantic Fleet, and also for Operation TORCH (code word for the invasion of North Africa), commander Northern Attack Group (CTG 34.8).[3]

Kelly's naval force was to land its embarked troops and their equipment on assault beaches near the port city of Mehedia (also commonly spelled Mehdia), situated at the mouth of the Sebou River on French Morocco's Atlantic coast, and to provide fire support for the Army units ashore. His naval force was also to screen the transport area off the assault beaches, and to maintain anti-surface,

submarine and air patrols to deter enemy attacks The approximately 9,000 Army troops under Brig. Gen. Lucian King Truscott Jr., aboard transport ships of the Northern Attack Group, consisted of the following units:
- Sixtieth Infantry, Ninth Division, reinforced
- Ranger Detachment, United States Army
- One light armored battalion combat team, Second Armored Division

The mission of the 526 officers, 8,573 enlisted men, and 65 light tanks was to capture Mehedia, and Port Lyautey and its adjacent airfield, located about nine miles up the shallow and winding Sebou River. Seventy-six Army P40 Warhawk fighter aircraft staged aboard the auxiliary carrier *Chenango* (ACV-28)—a converted oiler—were to use the airfield for a subsequent attack on Casablanca, sixty-five miles to the south.[4]

The operations against the port town of Mehedia, and Port Lyautey upriver, were to be one component of the Allied three-pronged invasion of French Morocco. The main landing by the Central Attack Group was to be at Fedala, which lay a short distance north of Casablanca. The second landing by the Northern Attack Group was to be at Mehedia, to the north of Fedala. The third, by the Southern Attack Group was to be at Safi, 150 miles south of Casablanca. The small port and its docks would facilitate disembarkation of an armored detachment. At this time in the war, the Navy did not yet have tank landing ships to land tanks over beaches. Task Force 34 split up in the early morning on 7 November, to allow the attack groups to proceed to their various destinations. There was some fear that prevailing conditions might inhibit the landings; at that time of the year "heavy rollers" (waves) broke on the Moroccan coast with a very heavy surf.[5]

ASSAULT ON MEHEDIA/PORT LYAUTEY

The transport ships of the Northern Attack Group arrived in the transport area, located about seven miles off the mouth of the Sebou River, at 2321 on 7 November. Early the following morning the destroyers took their fire support stations at 0411. *Kearny* was positioned to the north of the river mouth, *Roe* to the south of it, and *Ericson* was held in reserve. The assault troops had begun boarding landing boats shortly after midnight that ranged from small rubber boats with outboard motors to craft capable of carrying 1,200 men.

The waves of assault craft formed around the three easterly transports, the *George Clymer*, *Henry T. Allen,* and *Susan B. Anthony.* The destroyer *Eberle*, and minesweepers *Osprey* and *Raven*, were responsible for escorting the waves to their lines of departure off the assault beaches. Two 63-foot boats carried aboard the oiler *Kennebec* were equipped with rocket projectors to permit lobbing explosives on enemy positions ashore prior to the arrival of the assault troops. The first boat was launched at 0242 and the second at 0412 in preparation for the amphibious assault.[6]

Northern Attack Group (Task Group 34.8)

Naval Gunfire Control Ships	Transport Ships	Transport Ships
Texas (BB-35)	*Algorab* (AK-25)	*Henry T. Allen* (AP-30)
Savannah (CL-42)	*Ann Arundel* (AP-76)	*Susan B. Anthony* (AP-72)
Ericson (DD-440)	*Electra* (AK-21)	*John Penn* (AP-51)
Kearny (DD-432)	*Florence Nightingale* (AP-70)	
Roe (DD-418)	*George Clymer* (AP-57)	

Anti-submarine and minesweepers	Other Ships
Livermoore (DD-429)	Seaplane tender *Barnegat* (AVP-10)
Eberle (DD-430)	Destroyer *Dallas* (DD-199)
Parker (DD-604)	Fleet oiler *Kennebec* (AO-36)
Raven (AM-55)	Merchant ship S.S. *Contessa*[7]
Osprey (AM-29)	

The first wave of assault craft landed at 0515, and seven waves (of eighteen or so craft each) made the beach before fire from enemy shore batteries compelled the transports to move farther offshore out of range of the guns. *Barnegat* was then positioned inshore of the line of transports and about three-and-one-half miles off the beach at Mehedia. Comdr. Josephus A. Briggs noted about the operation up to that point:

> At 0600, our light forces opened fire on shore establishments to cover the landing of our troops and at 0610 the shore batteries opened fire on the line of landing barges. At 0735, the shore batteries opened fire on the line of transports.[8]

A new threat also soon developed as Vichy fighters and two-engine bombers from the airfield at Rabat-Sale began to strafe and bomb landing craft. Moreover, assault troops making the beach were met ashore with bullets, bayonets, and 75mm fire from the 1st and 7th

Regiments Moroccan Tirailleurs (French Army designation for infantry recruited in colonial territories), the Foreign Legion, and naval ground units.[9]

Map 16-1

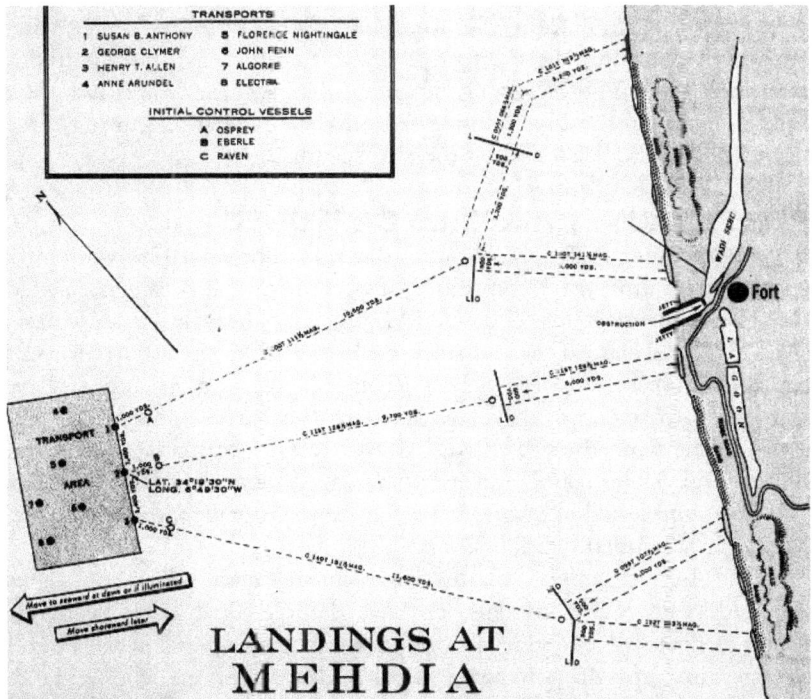

Barnegat was positioned shoreward of the transport area during the initial landings at Mehedia.

It had been unknown whether or not the Vichy French in North Africa would fight, and Admiral Kelly had instructions to not precipitate a conflict with the French if it could be avoided. Thus, there had been no shore bombardment preceding the amphibious assault to "soften up" the enemy defenses. At approximately 0630, the *Texas* broadcast first in French and then in English a message from Gen. Dwight D. Eisenhower, USA, the commander in chief of the forces landing in North Africa. French resistance continued with shore battery fire and aircraft attacks against ships offshore. At 0710 Kelly issued orders to the Northern Attack Group for a general offense. Thirty minutes later, *Barnegat* silenced one of the shore battery guns with 5-inch gunfire.[10]

By 0950 assault troops had established a beachhead south of the river mouth, but progress from then on was arduous. The garrison at the Kasbah—a walled fort on the heights above the Sebou River—which consisted largely of the French Foreign Legion, contested every inch of ground. Throughout D-day (8 November), *Savannah* bombarded fixed defenses and mobile batteries. In mid-afternoon *Texas* took ammunition dumps near Port Lyautey under fire, apparently with only slight effect. By late afternoon the shore batteries were silenced. The following morning, 9 November, *Savannah* took French tanks on the road coming from Rabat under fire, putting three out of action and causing the others to scatter.[1]

PORT LYAUTEY AIRFIELD CAPTURED

In early morning darkness, shortly after midnight on 10 November, a special demolition team comprised of two officers and fifteen enlisted men from the fleet tug *Cherokee* (AT-66), and the salvage ship *Brant* (ARS-32) breached a heavy steel cable boom designed to prevent passage by vessels up the Sebou River. Machine guns and artillery were sited to sweep the river adjacent to the barrier, and on a mesa south of the river, the walled Kasbah (fortress) in particular dominated the channel. The team returned to *George Clymer*, aboard which they had been embarked about 0430, seven hours after departing her side, with eight wounded members.[12]

The heroic actions of these seventeen men, all whom later received Navy Cross Medals, enabled the old flush-deck destroyer *Dallas* to make a harrowing passage in the face of adverse weather and enemy fire up the shallow, shoal-ridden river to the airfield. Embarked aboard her was a 75-man Raider Detachment, 3rd Battalion, U.S. Army. Upon reaching the riverbank the raiders encountered machine gun fire, but were able to occupy the airport immediately, and by the late morning the Army P40s from the *Chenango* were using the airport. *Dallas* remained at anchor until the mid-afternoon on 12 November when she stood downriver, passed through the jetties, and anchored off Mehedia Beach. The destroyer's commanding officer and two of her other officers, as well as a Free French pilot who personally steered the ship up the river, also received the Navy Cross. (The first chapter of my book *We are Sinking, Send Help: The U.S. Navy's Tugs and Salvage Ships in the African, European, and Mediterranean Theaters in World War II* describes this operation in detail.)[13]

Map 16-2

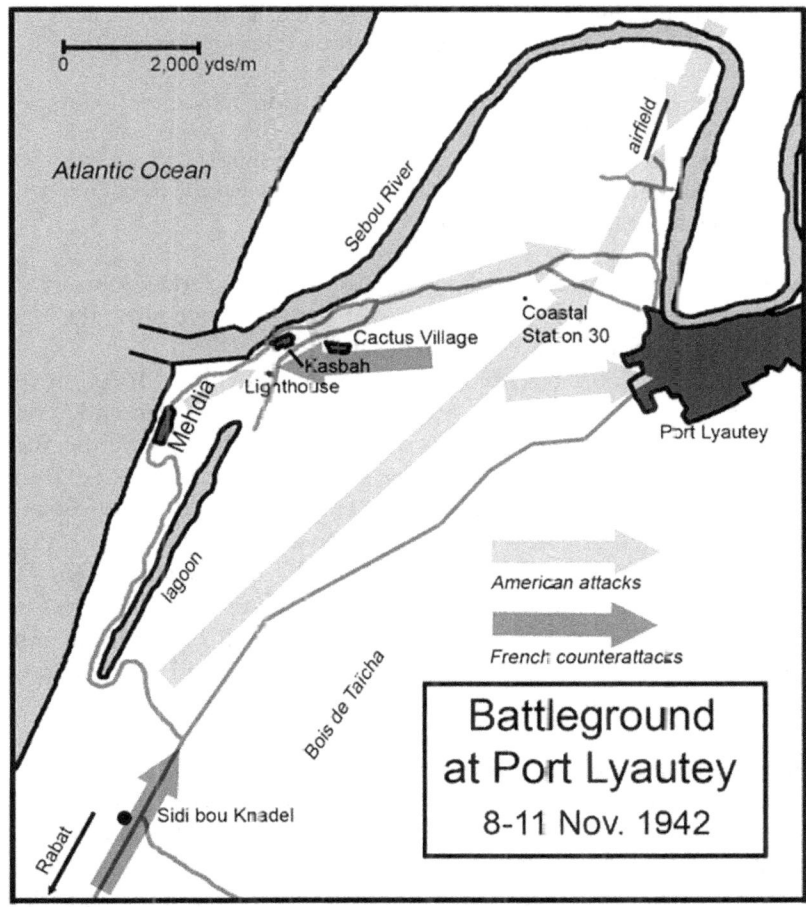

The breaching of a formidable steel cable boom guarding the mouth of the Sebou River was necessary for the destroyer *Dallas* to make a perilous passage up the river and land Army raiders to take the Port Lyautey airfield.

Following capture of the airfield the *Texas* broadcast the following message from Rear Admiral Kelly to the people of Port Lyautey:

> We have had to capture the fort at Mehdia. We have had to take your airfield at Port Lyautey. We have been forced to bombard the roads east of your city. We have had to bomb your trucks marching to reinforce you.

> These measures have been taken for only one reason: because your officials continue to oppose our purpose which is to assist in restoring France to Frenchmen and to Frenchmen alone. Such was the promise of the President of the United States. This promise will be kept.
>
> Why continue this unfortunate and useless resistance? You know that the United States because of its great power will not cease until it has broken the resistance of your chiefs.
>
> Join with us. Stop this useless waste of lives and use them later in the fight against your real enemy—Germany.

When no response to the message was forthcoming, Allied operations continued, and in the late morning that day, 10 November, the first U.S. planes landed at the Port Lyautey airfield.[14]

The S.S. *Contessa* started up the Sebou River at 1620 on 10 November. She was a rusty, dilapidated former Standard Fruit Company ship which, until taken over earlier in the year by the War Shipping Administration, had been used to haul bananas from Caribbean ports to the United States. How she found herself bound for Port Lyautey with 738 tons of gasoline and munitions to support the Army P40s is the subject of a book, titled *Twelve Desperate Miles: The Epic World War II Voyage of the SS Contessa* by Tim Brady. The *Contessa* ran aground shortly after passing the Kasbah and had to wait until high tide early the next morning to refloat her and allow her to complete the passage.[15]

Barnegat made the trip up the river on 11 November with the supply and maintenance requirements of VP-73. After receiving a French pilot on board at 1500, she proceeded up river and at 1745 moored in the river in the vicinity of the airport. The eleven PBY Catalina seaplanes of the squadron began arriving from Lyneham, England, two days later, and immediately began anti-submarine patrols. During the interim period, *Barnegat* landed her cargo of depth bombs, aviation gasoline, supplies and equipment necessary to support the planes. She continued tending the reconnaissance aircraft until Naval Air Station, Port Lyautey was well established and her services were no longer needed. *Barnegat* left Casablanca on 12 December to make the Atlantic crossing to America in convoy. She arrived at Boston, Massachusetts on 24 December 1942 for a much needed overhaul in drydock.[16]

Barnegat received a battle star for the period 8-11 November 1942 for the North African occupation, the only seaplane tender to be awarded one in that theater during the war. There was little need for the U.S. Navy to employ seaplane tenders in African, European and

Mediterranean waters, as established airfields were readily available ashore. A sister ship, *Biscayne* (AVP-11), arrived at Casablanca on 18 November 1942 and remained there until 25 April 1943 supporting patrol squadrons. She entered Mers-el-Kebir, Algeria, on 26 April and was fitted out in May as an amphibious force command ship. Over the next year-and-a-half, *Biscayne* received battle stars for the Sicilian occupation, Salerno landings, Anzio-Nettuno landings, and the invasion of southern France, all in the Mediterranean Theater. *Biscayne* was not formally reclassified as an amphibious force command ship (AGC-18) until 10 October 1944. (Thus designated, she would earn battle stars for Iwo Jima and Okinawa, a total of six during the war.)

Photo 16-2

British Maj. Gen. John L. Hawksworth and Rear Adm. Richard L. Conolly, USN, aboard the USS *Biscayne* on 6 September 1943, three days before the Salerno invasion. U.S. Navy Photograph #: 80-G-82331, now in the collections of the National Archives.

BATTLE STARS FOR TENDERS/VP SQUADRONS

In addition to the *Barnegat*, Patrol Squdron VP-73 received a battle star for the Algeria-Morocco Landings, as did one aircraft of Squadron 92.

North African Occupation: Algeria-Morocco Landings

Ship	Award Period	Commanding Officer
Barnegat (AVP-10)	8-11 Nov 42	Comdr. Josephus A. Briggs, USN
VP-73	8-11 Nov 42	Lt. Comdr. Alexander S. Heyward Jr.
VP-92 plane *P-6*	8-11 Nov 42	Lt. Comdr. J. A. Moreno

Sicilian Occupation

Ship	Award Period	Commanding Officer
Biscayne (AVP-11)	9-15 Jul 43	Comdr. Robert C. Young

Salerno Landings

Ship	Award Period	Commanding Officer
Biscayne (AVP-11)	9-21 Sep 43	Comdr. Robert C. Young

West Coast of Italy Operations: Anzio-Nettuno Advanced Landings

Ship	Award Period	Commanding Officer
Biscayne (AVP-11)	22 Jan-1 Mar 44	Comdr. Edward H. Eckelmeyer

Invasion of Southern France

Ship	Award Period	Commanding Officer
Biscayne (AVP-11)	15 Aug-25 Sep 44	Comdr. Edward H. Eckelmeyer, USN Lt. Comdr. R. H. Bates, USNR

17

European Theater

In order to forestall an invasion of Africa by Germany and Italy, which, if successful, would constitute a direct threat to America across the comparatively narrow sea from western Africa, a powerful American force equipped with adequate weapons of modern warfare and under American command is today landing on the Mediterranean and Atlantic coasts of the French colonies in Africa.

The landing of this American army is being assisted by the British Navy and Air Force, and it will in the immediate future be reinforced by a considerable number of divisions of the British Army.

This combined Allied force, under American command, in conjunction with the British campaign in Egypt, is designed to prevent an occupation by the Axis armies of any part of northern or western Africa and to deny to the aggressor nations a starting point from which to launch an attack against the Atlantic coast of the Americas.

In addition, it provides an effective second front assistance to our heroic allies in Russia.

—With these words,
President Franklin D. Roosevelt announced the
landing of American troops on African soil on
Sunday, 8 November 1942[1]

America's involvement in the African, European, and Mediterranean Theaters began on 7 November 1942 when American forces landed at Mehdia, Fedala, and Safi on the Atlantic coast of French Morocco, as joint British/American forces struck at the French Algerian cities of Oran and Algiers on the Mediterranean. The Vichy French government—which had been installed by the Nazis after they conquered France in 1940—was in control of French Morocco, Algeria, and Tunisia. The Allies were hopeful that the Vichy French forces would not fight, but they did with support from the German Air Force.

Following the successful conclusion if this operation, termed TORCH, Allied forces in early July 1943 crossed by water from North Africa to Sicily in the central Mediterranean. The invasion of Sicily launched the Italian Campaign. From there the Allies traversed the Strait of Messina to reach mainland Italy and invade Salerno, then pushed further up the west coast to Naples and Anzio against increasingly stiffer and more costly German resistance. At Anzio in January 1944, the drive toward Rome stalled. Allied forces came ashore behind enemy lines hoping to reach Italy's capital city more quickly. Instead, German forces pinned them on the beachhead and they suffered huge losses. The anticipated and actual results of the operation were characterized by British Prime Minister Winston Churchill in two different statements. The first held great promise: "Whoever holds Rome holds the title deeds of Italy." The second expressed his displeasure: "I had hoped we were hurling a wildcat into the shore, but all we got was a stranded whale."

Through sheer bravery and heroism the Allies held on and finally, with long-awaited reinforcements, broke out in late May and marched victoriously into Rome in June 1944. In recognition of the courage and sacrifice of the soldiers, sailors, and airmen at Anzio, twenty-two Americans were awarded the Congressional Medal of Honor, the most of any single battle of World War II. Two British soldiers received the Victoria Cross (the British equivalent of the Medal of Honor) for valour "in the face of the enemy." Following the disastrous Anzio operation, termed SHINGLE, a triumph elsewhere was desperately needed; it materialized at Normandy.[2]

NORMANDY INVASION – OPERATION OVERLORD

> *I remember the beach and the shellacking those poor guys took, and they never complained. We were shot at. We were hit once. I saw bodies floating around in the water and all that. The guys who didn't make it, that's what gets to me.*
>
> —Former Lt. (jg) Anthony Lucca recalling his service off Omaha Beach. He was an engineering officer aboard the seaplane tender *Rockaway*, whose duties included shuttling troops and VIPs by boat to the beach.[3]

The Allied invasion of Normandy, on the north coast of France across the English Channel from Britain, commenced on 6 June 1944 with simultaneous landings on five adjacent beaches. In total the Allies landed around 156,000 troops on D-day, which launched OVERLORD, code word for the operation to defeat Germany and free France. Both Allied and German forces suffered massive casualties during the battle of Normandy, which lasted until the end of August. Most occurred on the first day of assault landings, in which there were 2,499 American fatalities and 1,914 from the other Allied nations, a total of 4,413 dead. The total German casualties on D-day are unknown, but are estimated as being between 4,000 and 9,000 men.[4]

Allied ship losses for June 1944 included twenty-four warships and thirty-five merchantmen or auxiliaries sunk and an additional one hundred twenty vessels damaged. Scores of books have been written about the invasion of northern France. This short chapter is devoted to the contributions made by the seaplane tender *Rockaway* (AVP-29). There is also an account of the loss of Lt. Joseph P. Kennedy, Jr. (the older brother of future president JFK).[5]

Photo 17-1

PB4Y-1 Liberator patrol bomber flies out from the British coast for a Bay of Biscay anti-submarine patrol in November 1943.
U.S. National Archives Photograph #80-G-407692

ORDERS TO EUROPE

The *Rockaway* was a relatively new ship, having been commissioned on 6 January 1943 at her builder's yard, Associated Ship Building, Inc., Seattle, Washington. Following shakedown training, she became a unit of the Atlantic Fleet and was based in April 1943 at Norfolk, Virginia. Over the next several months, the seaplane tender delivered essential supplies and personnel to outlying bases in the North Atlantic; transferred a squadron from Newfoundland to England; carried cargo from Norfolk to the aircraft carrier *Ranger* (CV-4) at Scapa Flow in the Orkney Islands, Scotland; and delivered secret radar equipment to England for use in the Normandy invasion.[6]

On 1 May 1944, the *Rockaway* received orders from commander Air Force, Atlantic Fleet, Vice Adm. Patrick N. L. Bellinger, to load cargo, equipment and supplies, and embark personnel for transfer to Fleet Air Wing Seven in England. The Wing had been based at U.S. Naval Air Facility, Dunkeswell in Devon since 24 September 1943. One of its patrol bombing squadrons, VPB-103, was the first USN unit to train with the Royal Air Force, followed by VPB-105 and VPB-110. The Wing's PB4Y-1 Liberators (the Navy's designation for the B24 Liberator) and later PB4Y-2 Privateers flew anti-submarine patrols in the Bay of Biscay. Today, in the village church in Dunkeswell is a large commemorative brass plaque. Below the inscription "In Memory of These Officers and Men of the United States Navy Who Died for Their Country September 1943 to July 1945" are the names of the 182 members of Wing Seven who lost their lives during the war.[7]

OPERATION APHRODITE

> *Attempted first Aphrodite attack. Twelve August with robot taking off from Fersfield at One Eight Zero Five hours. Robot exploded in the air at approximately two thousand feet eight miles southeast of Halesworth at One Eight Two Zero Hours. Wilford J. Willy, Sr. Grade Lieutenant and Joseph P. Kennedy, Sr. Grade Lieutenant, both USNR, were killed. Commander Smith, in command of this unit, is making full report to U.S. Naval Operations. A more detailed report will be forwarded to you when interrogation is completed.*
>
> —Dispatch (formerly classified Top Secret) reporting the loss of Lieutenants Joseph P. Kennedy Jr. and Wilford J. Willy.[8]

Wing Seven operations included searchlight missions intended to force German submarines, operating on the surface at night and cloaked by darkness, to dive. If forced to emerge from the water's depths by day, they were easier prey for Allied forces. Prior to invention of the snorkel, a device which allowed submarines to remain below the surface while taking in air to operate their diesel engines, U-boats had to run on battery power when submerged. When the electrical charge on its batteries was low, the sub had to surface and operate diesel generators, putting it at much greater risk of detection and perhaps destruction.[9]

However, the odds associated with engaging enemy submarines in battle were not totally in favor of the Allies. As the war progressed, U-boats became more heavily armed with anti-aircraft defenses. In aircraft versus submarine actions, at least fifty-seven American planes were shot down by German submarine deck guns compared to only twelve U-boats lost to bombs, depth charges, or torpedoes [10]

Two of the Wing's casualties came by way of a secret program, code named APHRODITE. Two lieutenants, Joseph P. Kennedy, Jr. and Wilford J. Willy, assigned to VPB-110 at Dunkeswell, volunteered to serve in Special Attack Unit One. The two men were to pilot a PB4Y-1 Liberator loaded with high explosives in an attack against a German V-weapons site in France. Kennedy had in 1943 and 1944 flown numerous missions in a PB4Y-1, and was eligible for stateside duty. The use of this type plane was a variation in APHRODITE. The idea was to take old B17 Flying Fortresses that were no longer fit for regular duty, strip them of armor, armament and all non-essential equipment, and load them with several tons of a new British explosive called Torpex.[11]

It was hoped that these massive flying bombs could destroy or knock out of action German submarine pens and rocket launch sites against which traditional strategic bombing runs were proving ineffective. A significant drawback to this plan was critical limitations of the rudimentary navigation system employed to guide the drone aircraft, which could not handle take-offs. A pilot and a navigator were needed to get the plane off the ground and up to cruising altitude. After transferring control to a following aircraft with a radio control set, the flight crew would then bail out and parachute to safety. The unmanned plane was then to be guided by radio control downward to its target, detonating on impact.[12]

On the day of the mission, two Lockheed Ventura aircraft, with radio control sets, launched from RAF Fersfield, sixteen miles southwest of Norwich. Kennedy then took off in the explosive-packed PB4Y-1 and began a long and slow climb out toward the sea. Nearby, two P38 Lightning fighters served as escorts for the mission. As Kennedy and his flight engineer (Willy) proceeded eastward toward the coast, a sixth aircraft followed closely behind. The de Havilland Mosquito, a British multi-role combat aircraft, was fitted with a camera to film the operation. Aboard the plane—in a strange historical coincidence—was the second child of President Franklin D. Roosevelt, Col. Elliott Roosevelt, USAAF.[13]

After piloting the drone aircraft over England's Blyth Estuary, Kennedy and Willy transferred control of it to the Venturas. The men then prepared to bail out, after first arming the Torpex so that it would detonate if the PB4Y-1 hit its target. All went as planned until accompanying aircraft witnessed a thin trail of smoke coming from the plane's bomb bay, followed immediately by two explosions which totally obliterated the aircraft PB4Y-1 in midair. Both men were killed instantly and no traces of their bodies were ever found. They were each awarded the Navy Cross Medal posthumously.[14]

Aphrodite would prove to be a complete disaster. During more than a dozen missions, only one drone plane caused damage to the intended target. The first such was flown on 4 August 1944 utilizing four radio-controlled B17s. None of the targets were hit. Kennedy and Willy flew their mission on 12 August in a Navy PB4Y-1, carrying almost twice the explosive payload—21,170 pounds of Torpex—as had been aboard each Army bomber. The target was a German underground military complex in northern France near the hamlet of Mimoyecques. The Allies believed the facility was a possible launching base for V-2 ballistic missiles aimed at London. (Today, the former missile base, now named The Fortress of Mimoyecques, serves as a museum.)[15]

ATLANTIC CROSSING TO ENGLAND

Within days of receiving deployment orders to Europe, *Rockaway* left Norfolk in mid-afternoon on 6 May 1944, bound for Bristol, England. The ocean crossing was uneventful. Two days before voyage end, her gun crews expended 240 rounds of 20mm ammunition for training. Practice firing of 20mm and 40mm guns resumed the following morning. At 1637 that day, Trevose Head Light came into view seventeen miles distant in Constantine Bay off north Cornwall in southwest England. *Rockaway* passed Scarweather Light Ship abeam to port at 2200, continued inbound and anchored in Barry Roads in the Bristol Channel. She weighed anchor the following afternoon and proceeded into nearby Bristol. After marking time in Cumberland

Basin (the main entrance to the docks of Bristol) awaiting a favorable tide, she arrived at her destination that evening.[16]

Photo 17-2

Seaplane tender *Rockaway* (AVP-29) tending a PBM Mariner seaplane off Bahia, Brazil, probably during the spring of 1945.
U.S. Naval History and Heritage Command Photograph #NH 97495

The next day, Comdr. James H. Mills Jr., *Rockaway*'s commanding officer, discharged his passengers and cargo for Fleet Air Wing Seven, and then reported to Adm. Harold R. Stark, USN, for temporary duty. Stark was "double hatted." He commanded the Twelfth Fleet which had been established on 15 March 1943 from the U.S. naval forces assigned to him, and retained the title, commander Naval Forces, Europe (ComNavEur). With no pressing duties, the tender remained moored at Narrow Quay, Bristol, through month's end.[17]

Rockaway departed Bristol on 31 May for Barry Roads and upon arrival that evening, anchored. After "swinging at the hook" (remaining anchored) for a few days, she got underway around noon on 5 June, on the eve of the Normandy invasion, bound for the small seaside town of Lee-on-the-Solent, five miles west of Portsmouth on the south coast of England. Proceeding via the convoy route, she arrived there the following evening. News was received that day, 6 June, of the invasion of the French coast by Allied units.[18]

SUNDRY DUTIES

Because of the abundance of airfields in England from which fighters, bombers and other aircraft could operate, no requirement existed for the *Rockaway* to tend aircraft. She was therefore available for other tasks. Her duties during the invasion of France included: patrol and convoy work in the English Channel; transportation of Army and Navy personnel; protection of Allied beachheads against enemy air attacks; and flagship duty for Rear Adm. John E. Wilkes, USN. Wilkes, headquartered at Devonport, the naval base at Plymouth, had been responsible for the training and readiness of all USN landing and beaching craft in preparation for the invasion.[19]

Commander Mills received orders on 7 June to contact Capt. Edmond J. Moran at tug control at Lee-on-the-Solent and make arrangements to take him to sea on an inspection trip of tugs and their tows. He was an executive of Moran Towing in New York, who had been overseeing the Navy Rescue Tug Service along America's Eastern Seaboard and was a captain in the Naval Reserve. He was brought to England to organize and manage the towing forces in the Normandy invasion, and did so from Lee-on-the-Solent. In addition to the requirement for large tugs for cross-channel towing operations, there was a need for smaller tugs to tow Mulberry components to assembly areas off the English coast, and to position the components on the "Far Shore" during installation of Mulberry A and Mulberry B.[20]

The Allied forces were well aware of the strong German defenses around the ports of Western Europe. Because of this, the Allies did not consider it feasible to seize an existing port in the early stages of an invasion; they had to find another means of facilitating the unloading of supply ships at Normandy. The British solution to this problem was portable ports, code named "Mulberries."[21]

The *Rockaway* got underway on 8 June, with Moran aboard. Following his inspection, she returned to Lee-on-the-Solent and began embarking passengers for transport to the assault area. Among them was Commodore Howard A. "Pat" Flanigan, USN, commander Naval Forces, Europe's deputy chief of staff. The tender crossed the English Channel with the Transport Group the following day, and anchored off Omaha Beach in the Western Task Force area. At 2213, a report of an air raid sent ship's company to battle stations. *Rockaway*'s guns fired 120 rounds of 20mm and 32 rounds of 40mm at enemy planes, but none were seen to fall. It was later learned the aircraft had been dropping parachute mines. Flanigan and his party went ashore that day, 9 June (D+3), to contact U.S. authorities on the beach.[22]

Photo 17-3

Tug towing across the stormy English Channel one of the 150 concrete caissons which formed the main breakwaters of the Mulberry artificial harbors.
Official British photograph

In addition to ferrying ComNavEur staff and other passenger officers of the U.S. Army and Navy, the *Rockaway* also transported, in coming days, troops between England and the Normandy beachhead. This tasking included shepherding tug and tows crossing the channel, during which a brief encounter with E-boats occurred. This Allied term referred to a fast attack craft of the German navy. The German name for the craft was Schnellboot, meaning "fast boat," or S-Boot. There were different variants of the E-boat. All were more heavily armed, better in rough seas, and had much longer ranges than the American PT boat and the British Motor Torpedo Boat. E-boats were active in the channel that night (13 June) and other nights, attacking convoys of Allied ships en route to Normandy.[23]

A summary of the *Rockaway*'s duties during the invasion follows.

Date	Significant Activities
10 June	Underway from anchorage off Omaha Beach to visit various command ships and beachheads. Observed the heavy cruiser USS *Quincy* (CA-71) and battleship HMS *Warspite* (06) firing at German positions on the beach in the Utah area
11 June	Anchored off Lee-on-the-Solent

12 June	Off Selsey, England, to locate tugs and their tows scattered by enemy action the previous night, and to order them to return to Selsey
13 June	While patrolling the English Channel, fired two star shells at 0211 at a fast moving radar contact believed to be German E-boats reportedly operating in the area. Nothing seen, and the contact retired rapidly
14 June	Embarked U.S. Army generals Hughes, Crawford, Ross, and Lord, and other Army and Navy officers at Lee-on-the-Solent for transport to Omaha Beach
15-18 June	Transported military passengers between Lee-on-the-Solent and American beachheads at Normandy via some stops at Selsey
19 June	Escorted tugs and tows from Selsey to Omaha Beach
20 June	Broke (hoisted) the flag of Admiral Wilkes in *Rockaway* at Lee-on-the-Solent and embarked members of his staff
21-26 June	Anchored off Omaha beachhead in heavy seas; great storm damage inflicted to beach installations. Remained at anchor through 26 June.
26 June	Received orders from ComNavEur to proceed to Plymouth, England
27 June	Moored to the dock landing ship HMS *Oceanway* (F143) at Plymouth.

On the 20th, Admiral Wilkes, accompanied by a skeleton staff, shifted his flag from commander Landing Craft, Eleventh Amphibious Force headquarters at Plymouth to the *Rockaway*, and sailed for the assault area. Following his arrival there, Wilkes relieved rear admirals Don P. Moon and John L. Hall Jr. of their duties as commander Assault Force "Utah" and "Omaha," respectively. He would later, on 4 July, assume the duties of "Flag Officer, West," and subsequently those of a new command, U.S. Naval Bases, France.[24]

Rockaway arrived at Plymouth from the Omaha beachhead on 27 June. The following day, she loaded cargo and passengers as directed by commander Fleet Air Wing Seven for delivery to the United States. At 1330 on 29 June, the seaplane tender got underway to make the return Atlantic crossing to Norfolk, Virginia. The *Rockaway* earned a battle star for the Normandy invasion.[25]

Invasion of Normandy

Ship	Award Period	Commanding Officer
Rockaway (AVP-29)	6-25 Jun 1944	Comdr. James H. Mills Jr., USN

18

Central Pacific Campaign

The capture of Tarawa knocked down the front door to the Japanese defenses in the Central Pacific.

—Observation by Adm. Chester Nimitz regarding the acquisition of the Gilbert Islands, which came at a high cost in terms of lives lost.

The seaplane tenders *Curtiss* (AV-4) and *Mackinac* (AVP-13) departed Pearl Harbor at 0645 on the morning of 31 October 1943 bound for Funafuti, Ellice Islands to support the planned U.S. invasion of Tarawa. The *Curtiss* was the flagship of Task Force 57. Embarked aboard her was Rear Adm. John H. Hoover, commander Air Central Pacific. During forthcoming operations, Hoover's headquarters would be aboard *Curtiss*, anchored in Funafuti lagoon, with anti-submarine net protection and communication cables to shore. Hoover's tasking from Vice Adm. Raymond A. Spruance, commander Central Pacific Force, was to:

- Support the Central Pacific Campaign by Air Operations
- Defend and develop positions captured
- Construct and activate airfields on Makin, Tarawa, and Apamama[1]

The Central Pacific Force (Task Force 10) was a new command, established by Admiral Nimitz on 5 August 1943 with Spruance in charge. Its title would be short-lived. After overseeing the battle of Tarawa in November 1943, Spruance would guide his force as it advanced through the Gilbert Islands, and assaulted Kwajalein and Majuro Atolls in the Marshall Islands. For these successes, Spruance was promoted to admiral in February 1944. On 26 April 1944, the Central Pacific Force became the U.S. Fifth Fleet, which Spruance would command through war's end.[2]

THE GILBERT ISLANDS

The Gilbert Islands, which included Tarawa, Apamama, and Makin, were a group of coral atolls orientated in a roughly north-south line across the equator. The Japanese had invaded the British-held islands on the same day as the attack on Pearl Harbor and occupied them by 10 December 1941. The location of the islands immediately south and east of other important Japanese bases in the Carolines and Marshalls added to their strategic importance to the enemy. For the Allies, the Gilberts offered sites for airfields necessary for progress along the road through the Central Pacific toward Japan. The planned assault and capture of Tarawa and Makin in November 1943 was a part of the overall American strategy of conducting an offensive through Micronesia—the Gilbert, Marshall, and Caroline Islands—at the same time as MacArthur's New Guinea-Mindanao approach to Japan.[3]

Map 18-1

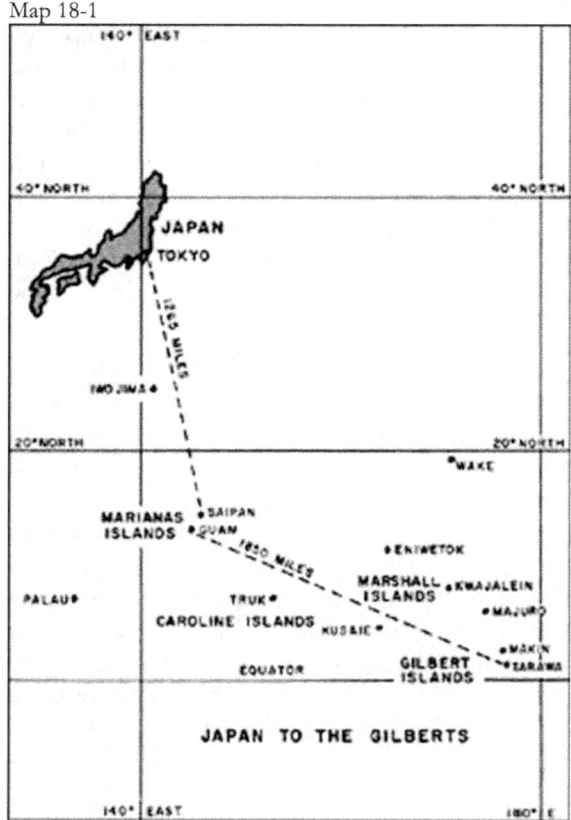

Principal route of the Central Pacific forces toward Japan
http://www.ibiblio.org/hyperwar/USN/ACTC/maps/actc-p735.jpg

In order to gain airbases capable of supporting operations across the Central Pacific to the Philippines and on to Japan, the U.S. needed to take the heavily defended Mariana Islands. However, use of land-based aircraft, to weaken enemy defenses and provide some measure of protection for the invasion forces, necessitated capturing the Marshall Islands, northeast of Guadalcanal. An enemy garrison and air base on Betio, one of the islands of Tarawa Atoll in the Gilberts, guarded against invasion forces arriving from Hawaii. Thus, the starting point for the planned invasion of the Marianas lay far to the east, at Tarawa.[4]

TRANSIT TO FUNAFUTI, ELLICE ISLANDS

A few days prior to departing Pearl Harbor, the *Mackinac* had put to sea to hone her gunnery. After clearing the harbor and arriving on the range, she fired her 5-inch/38 guns at a towed surface target, and then, at various courses and speeds, tracked and fired at an aerial target sleeve towed behind a plane. Drills that afternoon were devoted to practicing simulated depth charge attacks on a friendly submarine.[5]

Map 18-2

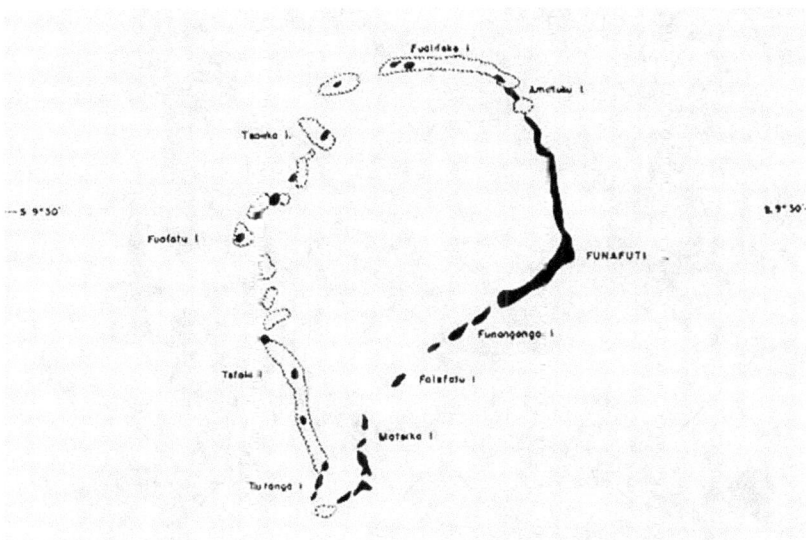

Funafuti Atoll, Ellice Islands

After leaving Pearl Harbor with the *Curtiss* on 31 October, *Mackinac* took station about 3,500 yards ahead of the large seaplane tender; acting as anti-submarine screen with the flagship serving as the

238   Chapter 18

formation guide. During the week-long transit southwest to the Ellice Islands, the two ships maneuvered in accordance with zigzag plans and exercised at general quarters. On 3 November, His Majesty, Neptunus Rex boarded the *Curtiss* with his Royal Court for a Crossing the Line ceremony. This traditional ritual associated with traversing the equator transformed the "Slimy Pollywogs" aboard ship into sons of Neptune, termed "Trusty Shellbacks."[6]

Illustration 18-1

Illustration titled A Pollywog's Nightmare, depicting some of the rituals in the ceremony from "The Royal Works - U.S.S. *Lexington*," a souvenir of the Neptune party held 20 May 1936 aboard the aircraft carrier *Lexington* (CV-2).

The *Mackinac* took leave of the flagship at 0700 on 7 November to proceed independently to render tender service at Nukufetau; another member of the Ellice Islands located fifty-seven nautical miles northwest of Funafuti Atoll. The *Curtiss* entered Te Ava Fuagea Channel at 0857, passed into Funafuti lagoon, and moored to a harbor buoy a short time later. To provide her protection from submarines, the yard net tender *Catalpa* (YN-5) rigged an anti-torpedo net around *Curtiss*. *Catalpa* was a unit of Service Squadron 4 based at the atoll and under the command of Capt. Herbert M. Scull, USN. The squadron consisted of the destroyer tender *Cascade* (AD-16) and twenty-three other ships and craft ranging from the repair ships *Phaon* (ARB-3) and *Vestal* (AR-4) through tugs and patrol craft to fuel-oil barges and 500-ton lighters.[7]

In the next few days, Admiral Hoover organized his forces for the support of Operation GALVANIC. Following preliminary carrier aircraft strikes on Tarawa and Makin, there would be, each day from 13-20 November, bombing runs by Army and Navy bombers on these atolls. In addition to seaplane tenders *Curtiss* and *Mackinac*, Hoover's Task Force 57 included the following Army and Naval air forces:

Striking Group (Task Group 57.2)	
Force	Aircraft
U.S. Army Heavy bombardment Groups 11 and 30, in Hawaiian area	90 VB(H)
Search and Reconnaissance Group (Task Group 57.3)	
Patrol Squadron VP-53, in Hawaiian area	12 PBY-5A
Patrol Squadron VP-72, in Hawaiian area	12 PBY-5
Heavy Bomber Squadron VB-108, at Canton	12 PB4Y-1
Medium Bomber Squadron VB-137, at Wallis	12 VB(M)
Medium Bomber Squadron VB-143, in Hawaiian area	12 VB(M)
Photographic Squadron VD-3, at Canton	6 PB4-Y
Ellice Defense and Utility Group (4th Marine Base Air Defense Wing)	
Fighter squadrons in Ellice Islands and at Wallis	90 VMF
Dive bombing squadrons at Wallis and Samoa	72 VMSB
Inshore patrol squadrons at Wallis and Samoa	24 VSO and VJ
Air transport squadron VMJ-353 at Samoa	12 VR
Army transports as assigned[8]	

ENEMY BOMBING ATTACKS ON ELLICE ISLANDS

On the eve of the commencement of B24 bomber strikes on the atolls, Hoover spoke to his military commanders on 12 November about the importance of focusing all efforts on one objective—that of killing Japanese and destroying their installations. The admiral explained the search problem, and emphasized that patrol planes must cover their assigned sectors accurately. He also suggested that island commanders obtain all the fire extinguishing apparatus possible, and as best they could set up anti-aircraft and fighter direction control.[9]

At a little past midnight, 0003 on 13 November, the radar operator aboard the *Curtiss* reported several "Bogies" (unidentified planes). This report was confirmed by radar ashore, which also indicated two groups of planes bearing 330 degrees true. Condition Blue was set and general quarters sounded on all ships and on Funafuti. This alert status meant "Air attack probable, unidentified aircraft in vicinity. All ships set Condition II." All hands were at battle stations when the planes were definitely identified as enemy and upgraded condition Red was established. Aircraft batteries on shore opened at 0045. Three minutes later, the planes made their first run and dropped bombs. The second run occurred at 0055 when the last bombs fell. As the flight of aircraft had approached Funafuti, it separated into two groups. One group of three planes made its run from the north. The other group of three went wide around the island to the east, then came in from the south. After the planes had disappeared from radar, condition White (All Clear) was reestablished. None of the ships had opened fire on the high-flying bombers, which were beyond the range of their anti-aircraft guns.[10]

Japanese aircraft—nine single planes and a three-plane formation—returned four days later and again attacked the base at Funafuti. The aircraft, believed to be twin-engine medium bombers, made individual runs from every direction dropping seventy to eighty large, medium and small bombs from 7,000 feet. The first of the aircraft, approaching singly from the northwest, was picked up on radar at 0337. The air raid warning sounded at 0400, enabling all hands to take cover before the first of ten bombing runs began at 0416. The island's Marine Corps anti-aircraft batteries—two 90mm batteries, three 40mm guns, and one .50-caliber machine gun—opened fire at 0420. Some ships in the lagoon were able to deliver 3-inch and 40mm fire as well. The *Curtiss* fired twelve rounds of 40mm after a shore search light illuminated one of the planes, which appeared to be a "Sally," Type 97. Dropped ordnance killed two Navy men, destroyed a B24 bomber and a C47 cargo plane, and damaged ten additional aircraft.[11]

PATROL SQUADRON 72

> *Evidence indicates that this Task Group was bracketed between two Japanese submarines operating to the westward of Tarawa. These submarines, instead of attacking themselves, used radio from a periscope antenna to home a large group of two-engine bombers carrying torpedoes in a successful attack below the level of satisfactory radar detection.*
>
> —Capt. Rudolph L. Johnson, USN, commanding officer
> USS *Independence* (CVL-22), describing a Japanese
> torpedo plane attack on the aircraft carrier
> off Tarawa on 20 November 1943.[12]

While serving as flagship and operations center for commander Air Central Pacific, the *Curtiss* also tended planes of Patrol Squadron 72. In addition to maintaining regular 600-mile, 10-degree sector patrols (three patrols per day average), the squadron also supplied a "Dumbo" plane for standby duty at Nanomea, an atoll at the extreme northwest end of the Ellice Islands group. Dumbo was the nickname for air-sea rescue aircraft, including flying boats, which could land on the water and perform rescues directly. The squadron also conducted Dumbo rescue operations at Tarawa and Makin prior to and during the seizure of the Gilbert Islands. Other functions included special searches, passenger flights, and photographic coverage.[13]

One of the most unusual tasking came on 21 November, when Lt. (jg) William H. Spradley in patrol plane *72-17* conducted a special flight to provide air coverage for the small aircraft carrier *Independence* (CVL-22). The carrier had been performing pre-landing strikes on Tarawa when, during a Japanese counter-attack, she was assaulted by a group of fifteen to eighteen twin-engine planes low on the water. The planes launched at least five torpedoes, one of which scored a hit on the carrier's starboard quarter. Between the sighting aboard ship of the torpedo's wake and its strike, six Bettys were shot down by *Independence* gun crews. Three of the downed aircraft had closed to within one hundred yards or less from the ship when hit. Seriously damaged, the *Independence* made her way to Funafuti arriving the morning of 23 November for repairs.[14]

CAPTURE OF TARAWA AND MAKIN

Two regiments from the U.S. 27th Infantry Division landed at Butaritari Island, Makin Atoll, on 20 November and following light Army losses—64 killed and 150 wounded—signaled "Makin taken," three days later. The assault on Tarawa that same day was bitterly contested. Heavily fortified, and garrisoned by several thousand Japanese troops on Betio, the principal island of the atoll, Tarawa had been attacked repeatedly from the air for weeks preceding the assault, and the previous day by naval shore bombardment. Although these efforts silenced the island's heavy guns and killed approximately half the Japanese troops, the enemy was able to concentrate the remaining forces beside the only beach where a landing was possible and inflicted heavy casualties. The 2nd Marine Division suffered 871 killed, an additional 124 men who would succumb to their wounds, and 2,306 wounded or missing in action. The fighting lasted nearly four days, at the end of which time Betio Island was considered secure, although subjected to air raids and isolated sniper action.[15]

THE *MACKINAC*'S ISLAND SHUTTLE SERVICE

After departing the *Curtiss* on 7 November, the *Mackinac* had entered harbor at Nukufetau in the Ellice Island Group, anchored and commenced delivering aviation gasoline to the beach. She arrived at Funafuti the following evening to go alongside the yard oiler *YOG-53* and replenish her stock of aviation fuel. Topped off, *Mackinac* stood out of the lagoon the morning of 10 November, bound for Wallis Island. Arriving there the next day, she anchored off Matalaa Point to embark the first ground echelon of Marine Scout Bomber Squadron VMSB-331 and load equipment for movement to Nukufetau. The squadron, which flew SBD Dauntless dive bombers, was to operate from Nukufetau during the invasion of the Gilbert Islands. The *Mackinac* arrived at Nukufetau on the 14th, disembarked the aviation unit and its gear, and pumped aviation gasoline to the beach. After completing this tasking, she returned to Funafuti on 19 November.[16]

MOVEMENT FORWARD TO TARAWA

Mackinac shuttled between Funafuti and Nukufetau a few more times before leaving Nukufetau for good on 29 November, bound for Tarawa. After anchoring in the lagoon at Tarawa in mid-afternoon on 1 December, she discharged a J2F plane and crew from Nukufetau and received aboard three crews of Squadron VP-72. Two seaplane moorings were then laid for tending one patrol and one Dumbo plane. In coming days the number of planes that *Mackinac* tended at Tarawa varied. Her charges on 10 December numbered five PBY Catalinas and six Lockheed PV-1 Ventura land-based patrol bombers.[17]

The balance of the month was characterized by periodic air raids. The first had occurred on 3 December, when a force of nine Japanese twin-engine bombers made individual runs on Betio Island (now under American control) on the south end of Tarawa Atoll, dropping ordnance on and in the vicinity of the airfield. Some fires were started and two planes were destroyed and others damaged. Enemy planes were engaged by shore batteries only. Japanese bombers came over once a day on 5, 6, 20, 23, and 27 December, and twice on the 12th and 24th, releasing ordnance over Tarawa from high altitude. As before, fires were started and planes were destroyed or damaged, but the ships and Catalinas present emerged from these attacks unscathed. On the last day of 1943, the *Curtiss* arrived at Tarawa from Funafuti, joining the *Mackinac*.[18]

Map 18-3

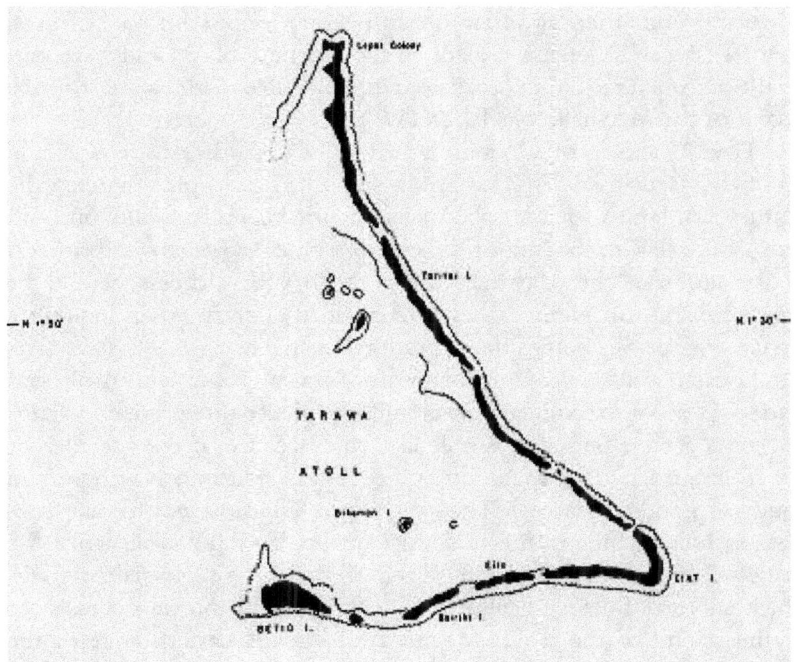

The 2nd Marine Division encountered heavy opposition after coming ashore on the lagoon side of Betio Island at Tarawa Atoll.
Source: http://www.ibiblio.org/hyperwar/USN/Building_Bases/maps/bases2-p315.jpg

INTO THE MARSHALLS (OPERATION FLINTLOCK)

> *Primary purpose of the search is information of the enemy, particularly ship movements. This information must be IMMEDIATE, ACCURATE, COMPLETE.... All search planes will carry some depth charges. Use any opportunity to attack enemy submarines, or small vessels.*
>
> —Commander Air Central Pacific's Operation Plan 1-44

The attack against the Gilbert Islands was a prelude to American forces gaining control of the Marshalls, the first step of Nimitz's planned drive through the Central Pacific on the road to Tokyo. The Marshall Island group was a former German colony. It had been given to Japan after World War I by the League of Nations in accordance with the South Pacific Mandate, which allowed Japan to take over all former German colonies in the Pacific north of the Equator. Since then, the islands had been an important part of both the offensive and defensive plans of the Japanese Navy, and were part of the perimeter of the Japanese empire. The code word for the assault of the Marshalls was FLINTLOCK.[19]

The objectives of Operation FLINTLOCK were to assault and occupy Kwajalein and Majuro Atolls. Nimitz's bold plan directed the capture of Majuro for the sake of its anchorage, and assaults on both ends of Kwajalein, the hub of the enemy's defense system. All the rest of the atolls in the Marshalls, even those with airfields, would be skipped; based on Nimitz's belief that Allied aircraft would neutralize Japanese air power before the operation began.[20]

Located 540 miles northwest of Tarawa, Kwajalein Atoll was made up of a triangular grouping of ninety-three small islands enclosing a huge 655 square mile lagoon. Because of the vast size of the atoll, Spruance's Expeditionary Force was split into Northern and Southern Landing Forces. The 4th Marine Division was to take Roi-Namur, twin islands in the northeast quadrant of the atoll, while the Army's 7th Infantry Division seized the island of Kwajalein itself, which lay forty-four nautical miles south of Roi-Namur in the extreme southeast end of the atoll. Majuro Atoll on the eastern edge of the Marshalls, would be seized in order to provide a fleet base and airfield for subsequent operations.[21]

AMERICAN TROOPS ASSAULT KWAJALEIN ATOLL

The entire island looked as if it had been picked up 20,000 feet and then dropped.

—Observation of a soldier quoted in U.S. Army history of the battle.

The 2nd Battalion, 23rd Marines landed on Roi on 1 February, a small island occupied mostly by an airfield and with little cover and few fortifications. Although it appeared completely deserted, some opposition was encountered, and naval ships took enemy installations on the north coast under fire. Organized resistance was quickly overcome, and mopping up operations completed the following morning. Marine losses were three killed and eleven wounded during the single day it took to secure the island.[22]

Map 18-4

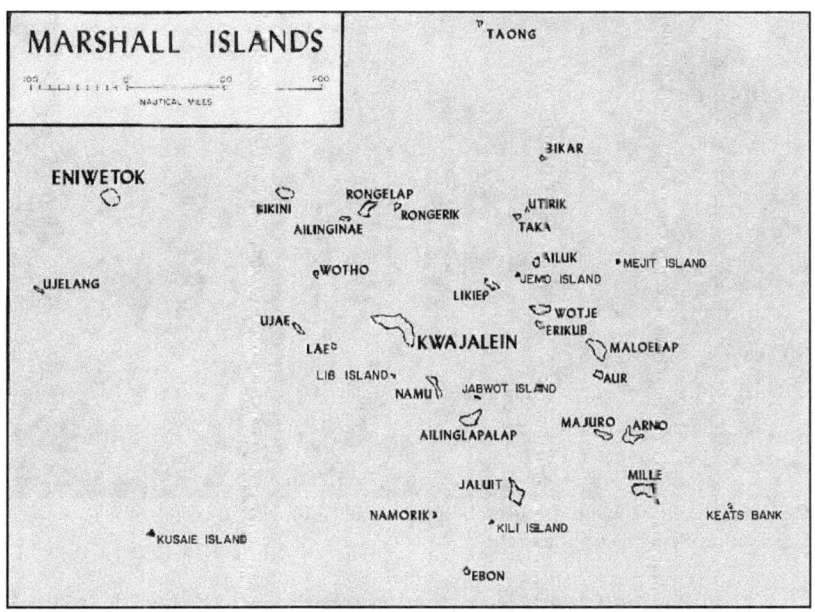

American forces landed on Kwajalein and Majuro during Operation FLINTLOCK, bypassing the other Japanese-held atolls in the Marshall Islands.
http://www.ibiblio.org/hyperwar/USMC/III/maps/USMC-III-7.jpg

The 24th Marines came ashore on Namur with little trouble, but the topography favored its defenders. There were numerous buildings and bunkers, and much of the island was covered by thick brush, which permitted an intricate network of defenses. Strong enemy opposition developed as soon as the Japanese force recovered from the preliminary naval gunfire, air bombardment, rocket firing, and machine gunning incident to the amphibious landing. Enemy harassment continued throughout the night, but each assault was beaten back. Approximately one hundred Japanese launched one serious attack; most of them were killed in hand-to-hand fighting. Fighting resumed in the morning with a company of medium and a company of light tanks supporting the Marine Regiment. Organized resistance ended at a little past noon.[23]

Photo 18-2

Devastation caused by pre-invasion bombardment of Kwajalein Island.
U.S. National Archives photograph

The 32nd and 184th regimental combat teams of the 7th Infantry Division began landing on Kwajalein at 0930 on 1 February. As the Army troops moved inland, armored amphibian tractors with 37mm guns and flamethrowers provided support. By nightfall six infantry battalions supported by four medium tank companies were ashore, having met little effective resistance. That evening Japanese defenders executed scattered counterattacks, but American artillery kept any large formations from gathering momentum. Infiltration by small enemy units resulted in some intermittent combat for most of the night, but by midnight it was estimated there were no more than 1,500 of the island's defenders remaining alive.[24]

The next morning, reserve battalions of the 32nd and 184th Regimental Combat Teams passed through the units landed on D-day, and tank-infantry teams attacked the remaining Japanese pockets of resistance. That night scattered groups of the enemy—comprised now of much smaller numbers—harassed rear areas, forcing units to defend themselves in all directions. By the morning of the third day there were few Japanese still alive and organized resistance ended shortly thereafter. The 7th Infantry suffered 177 killed and 1,000 wounded on Kwajalein. Few Japanese survived. An estimated fifty to seventy-five percent of the island defense force was killed in the preparatory bombardments, and more died in ensuing combat. Only 125 Korean laborers and 49 Japanese remained at the end.[25]

Following mopping-up operations by the 4th Marines on small islands near Roi-Namur, Kwajalein Atoll was declared secure. The 4th Marine Division suffered 737 casualties, including 190 killed. Estimated enemy losses totaled 3,472 dead, with 40 Korean laborers and 51 Japanese the only survivors.[26]

SMALL U.S. ARMY FORCE SEIZES MAJURO ATOLL

The second objective of Operation FLINTLOCK, Majuro Atoll, lay 220 nautical miles southeast of Kwajalein. Comprising Army Lt. Col. Sheldon's landing force was the Second Battalion, 106th Infantry, the Marine Corps Fifth Amphibious Corps Reconnaissance Company, and a headquarters garrison force. The Navy particularly desired the early seizure and development of Majuro for use as an advanced base in the Marshalls. Accordingly, detail plans had been made to (following occupation of the atoll), start immediately to clear lagoon waters of any mines, mark channels and anchorage areas, and install permanent buoys at the lagoon entrance.[27]

Assault plans were based on intelligence that there were 3-400 Japanese on islands in the atoll, probably concentrated on Darrit Island. On D+1, a detachment of scouts landed on entrance islands and were told by natives that there were about 300 Japanese on Darrit. Captain Jones, USMC, and the balance of the recon group came ashore on the seaward side of Dalap Island. He and his men canvased it and Uliga Island to the north prior to daybreak, and found no enemy on either one. Jones learned from an English speaking native that there were no Japanese on Darrit and only four in the entire atoll. This information proved to be true, and Majuro was occupied by late morning without a fight.[28]

The following day, 2 February, units of the fleet started to arrive, including the seaplane tender *Casco*. After anchoring in the lagoon at the east end of the atoll, her crew laid seaplane moorings and made general preparations for tending patrol planes of VP-202. Early that afternoon, PBM-3D Mariner patrol bombers began landing and found the operating conditions to be excellent.[29]

Photo 18-3

Ships of the U.S. Fifth Fleet anchored at Majuro on 25 April 1944, shortly before leaving to attack Truk Island in the Carolines, the main base for the Japanese Combined Fleet.
U.S. National Archives Photograph #80-G-225251

The *Casco* had arrived at Tarawa from Pearl Harbor on 31 January, and reported to Rear Admiral Hoover for duty. He dispatched her to Majuro Atoll the following day to tend PBM aircraft of Patrol Squadron 202. Prior to leaving Hawaii, all depth charges and depth charge racks were removed from *Casco*'s fantail and soundmen (sonar operators) transferred off the ship. This eliminated all her anti-submarine capabilities, but freed up additional deck space, allowing more efficient operations as a seaplane tender.[30]

On 6 February 1944, the *Casco* began retrieving her mooring buoys in preparation for shifting operations to Kwajalein Atoll. She stood out of Majuro lagoon that evening. After arriving at Kwajalein the following morning, she anchored off Ebeye Island and made preparations to tend the planes of VP-202, which thereafter began arriving from Majuro. Six days later, five PB2Y seaplanes of Squadron VP-102 arrived, to be based on the *Casco* while running searches out of Kwajalein along with VP-202.[31]

Photo 18-4

Portable covered work platforms protect mechanics from cold weather as they work on the engines of a PBM-3D patrol bomber at the Glenn L. Martin Aircraft Factory, Baltimore, Maryland, in February 1943.
U.S. National Archives Photograph #80-G-412754

CAPTURE OF ENIWETOK (CATCHPOLE)

> *Finally we killed them all. There was not much jubilation. We just sat and stared at the sand, and most of us thought of those who were gone—those whom I shall remember as always young, smiling and graceful, and I shall try to forget how they looked at the end, beyond all recognition*
>
> —Lt. Cord Meyer, USMC, describing the fighting on Parry Island during the assault of Eniwetok. The atoll was taken at a cost of 339 Americas killed and missing, and 2,277 Japanese.[32]

With Kwajalein taken, the next objective was to capture Eniwetok Atoll in the Marshall Islands. Located 326 miles west-northwest of Roi—and only 1,000 miles from the Mariana Islands—even the name of this western outpost of the Marshalls, which meant "land between the east and west," suggested the strategic importance of Eniwetok. Military commanders intended to use the atoll as an important staging point for U.S. Army, Navy, and Marine Corps forces in their progress from east to west toward Japan. The plan to capture Eniwetok and some lesser Marshall Islands was code named CATCHPOLE.[33]

On 17 February 1944, the 22nd Marine Regiment landed at Engebi Island on the north end of Eniwetok Atoll. The thousand or more Japanese defenders offered little resistance following prelanding shore bombardment, and Engebi was taken by late afternoon the next day, at the cost of eighty-five Marines killed.[34]

In southern operations against Eniwetok and Parry islands the opposing forces were much larger and enemy use on Parry of "hideyhole" concealment made the combat more difficult. Having learned via captured documents that these islands were defended by 2,155 troops of Maj. Gen. Yoshimi Nishida's 1st Amphibious Brigade, both battalions of the 106th Army Infantry Regiment and a Marine Reserve battalion assaulted Eniwetok Island. Fierce fighting ensued and after much effort, the island was secured in late afternoon on 21 February. The cost in American lives was 37 Marines killed and another 94 wounded. The Japanese garrison of about 800 men, except for 23 soldiers taken prisoner, was annihilated.[35]

Naval gunfire support ships offshore had a lot of time to pound Parry Island before Marines began coming ashore at 0900 on 22 February. Assault troops pushed forward behind tanks, with demolition and flame-thrower parties directly behind to destroy each enemy nest. By that afternoon, the Marines advanced to the island's southern end where the remaining Japanese were in the open. Eniwetok Atoll was taken at a cost of 339 Americans killed and missing, and 2,277 Japanese.[36]

There remained in the Marshall Islands, many atolls still occupied by Japanese forces, but only four hosted airbases. The Fifth Fleet had bypassed Jaluit, Mili, Maloelap, and Wotje, which could be isolated until war's end through the use of Allied air power. As a part of this effort, patrol aircraft continued to search swaths of ocean locating and reporting on enemy activity.[37]

EYES OF THE FLEET CONTINUE THEIR VIGILANCE

In mid-afternoon on 24 February, the *Chincoteague* stood out of Kwajalein en route to Eniwetok to tend planes there. Shortly before noon the following day, she passed Japtan Island abeam to starboard and proceeded to anchorage off Parry Island. That afternoon, planes of VP-72 (one PBY-5), 102 (one PB2Y-3) and 202 (eight PBM-3Ds) began arriving, and tending operations commenced. The aircraft at Kwajalein requiring repairs remained at Ebeye Island to be serviced by the *Casco*. The *Chincoteague* had arrived at Kwajalein from Hawaii only a few days earlier and had received VP-102 and VP-72 detachments aboard before proceeding to Eniwetok.[38]

Patrol planes conducted daily searches of a 180 to 300 degrees true sector from Eniwetok out to a distance of four hundred miles. At least one of the four VP-13 aircraft based at Tarawa (PB2Y-3s converted for transport-ambulance duty) was also tended by the *Chincoteague*.[39]

SEAPLANE TENDER/SQUADRON BATTLE STARS

The *Curtiss* and *Mackinac* received a battle star for the Gilbert Islands operation, and the *Casco* and *Chincoteague* one each for operations in the Marshall Islands. VP-72, a VP-13 detachment, and one plane of VP-53 earned battle stars for the Gilbert Islands, and the detachment one for Eniwetok Atoll as well.

Gilbert Islands Operation

Ship	Award Period	Commanding Officer
Curtiss (AV-4)	13 Nov-8 Dec 1943	Capt. Scott E. Peck, USN
Mackinac (AVP-13)	2-8 Dec 1943	Comdr. Paul D. Stroop, USN
VP-13 Det.	13 Nov-8 Dec 1943	Lt. Comdr. T. F. Connolly
VP-53 *P-1*	13 Nov-8 Dec 1943	Lt. Comdr. David Perry
VP-72	13 Nov-8 Dec 1943	Comdr. Sidney J. Lawrence

Marshall Islands Operation: Kwajalein and Majuro Atolls

Casco (AVP-12)	4 Feb 1944	Comdr. Earl R. DeLong, USN

Marshall Islands Operation: Occupation of Eniwetok Atoll

Chincoteague (AVP-24)	25 Feb 1944	Comdr. Robert A. Rosasco
VP-13 Det.	17 Feb-2 Mar 1944	Lt. Comdr. T. F. Connolly

19

Central Solomons Campaign

Following the successful Guadalcanal campaign (7 August 1942 to 21 February 1943), Admiral Halsey began a series of offensive operations against Japanese-held islands in the Central Solomons northwest of Guadalcanal. The strategy of Halsey's South Pacific forces and Gen. Douglas MacArthur's Southwest Pacific forces was to move northwest up through the Solomon Islands and up the New Guinea coast, respectively, then converge, and break through the Japanese-held Bismarck Archipelago. Allied control of the Vitiaz and Dampier Straits—sea passages between the southwest side of New Britain Island, and New Guinea—was a necessary step along MacArthur's planned New Guinea-to-the-Philippines invasion route.[1]

A huge impediment to both Halsey and MacArthur's plans was the powerful Japanese naval and air base at Rabaul on New Britain Island, from which attacks from the air and sea were being launched on Allied forces in the South and Southwest Pacific. By early 1943, some Allied leaders, and most notably MacArthur, wanted to focus on capturing Rabaul, but Japanese strength there and a lack of amphibious landing craft meant that such an operation was not practical in that year. Instead, on the initiative of the Joint Chiefs of Staff, Operation CARTWHEEL was developed to envelop and cut off Rabaul without capturing it, by simultaneous offensives in New Guinea and northward through the Solomon Islands The New Georgia Campaign, a series of battles that took place in the same named island group, in the central Solomon Islands from 20 June-25 August 1943, was also a part of CARTWHEEL, the Allied grand strategy in the South Pacific.[2]

The invasion of New Georgia, termed Operation TOENAILS, signaled both the beginning of the Central Solomons campaign and a new phase of the war, involving for the first time a sustained American strategic offensive. The ships involved directly or in support of the occupation of New Georgia included the *Chincoteague* (AVP-24), a seaplane tender based at Vanikoro in the Santa Cruz Islands, east-southeast of the Solomons.

Map 19-1

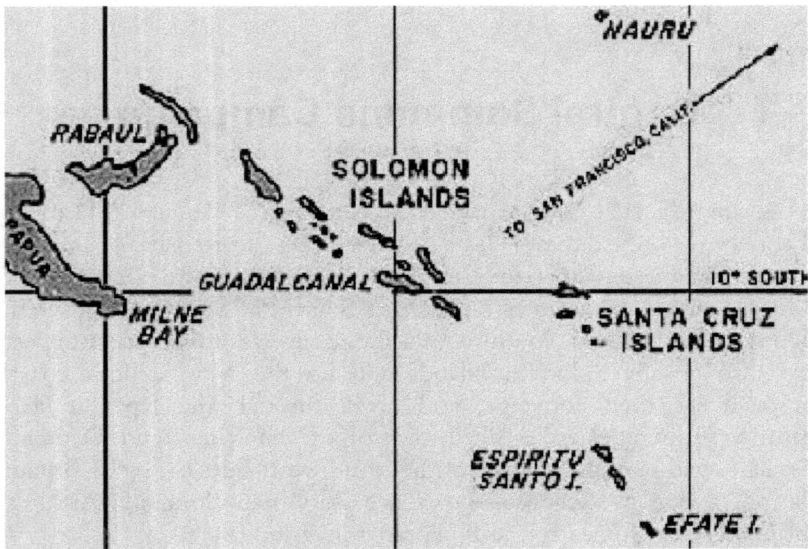

As MacArthur moved up the New Guinea coast, Halsey advanced northwest from Guadalcanal through the Solomons. The plan was for their forces to converge, and break through the Japanese-held Bismarck Archipelago. Allied control of the sea passages between New Britain Island (site of the powerful Japanese base at Rabaul) and New Guinea was a necessary step along MacArthur's planned New Guinea-to-the-Philippines invasion route.

ENEMY BOMBERS NEARLY SINK *CHINCOTEAGUE*

> *In spite of extensive damage and flooding,* CHINCOTEAGUE's *personnel succeeded in saving their ship. This achievement is all the more remarkable in view of the comparative inexperience of the crew. Only about a month had elapsed from the time the ship left San Diego upon completion of post shakedown repairs, until this action occurred.*
>
> —USS *Chincoteague* AVP24 War Damage Report No. 47

The *Chincoteague* (AVP-24) had relieved sister ship *Mackinac* (AVP-13) of her duties at Saboe Bay, Vanikoro on 6 July 1943. The Santa Cruz Islands, a part of the British Solomons Protectorate, included the big islands of Santa Cruz, Utupua, and Vanikoro; the Swallow or Reef island group; and the Duff group. The Swallow Islands were all quite small, the largest being not more than four miles in length. In 1766 an English vessel, the HMS *Swallow* commanded by Capt. Philip Carteret visited the islands, which he named after his ship. Resembling reefs, they were also called the Reef Islands.[3]

The *Mackinac* had established an advanced seaplane base at Vanikoro, 230 miles north of Espiritu Santo, on 12 November 1942. Positioning a tender there extended the ranges of PBYs based aboard the *Curtiss* (AV-4) anchored in Segond Channel at Espiritu Santo, New Hebrides. Using the advanced base, patrol planes from Espiritu Santo were able to fly 800-mile searches to the north scouting for enemy forces with stops at Vanikoro for fuel and crew rest. The *Chandeleur* (AV-10) relieved the *Curtiss* of her multiple duties as seaplane tender, flagship for commander Aircraft South Pacific Force, and repair and supply ship for destroyers and small craft engaged in the Solomons operation shortly thereafter on 9 July 1943.[4]

During the *Mackinac*'s tenure at Vanikoro, she tended an average of six planes that came from any or all of the various PBY squadrons at Espiritu Santo. A small PATSU (Patrol Aircraft Technical Service Unit) was based aboard the tender to perform aircraft service and minor maintenance work. As required, the *Mackinac* would make short trips to "Santo" for fuel and provisions. On such occasions, the *Thornton* (AVD-11) assumed her duties. Over the three month period immediately prior to her relief by the *Chincoteague*, the *Mackinac* had enjoyed a tranquil period of plane-tending. No enemy aircraft, surface craft, or submarines bothered her or appeared in the vicinity. This made it possible, weather permitting, to show nightly movies topside.[5]

After the *Chincoteague* dropped anchor in Saboe Bay, operations with PBY-5 Catalinas of VP-23 and 71 proceeded without incident for a week or so. The bright and shiny, new 2,800-ton *Barnegat*-class small seaplane tender was a mere two months old. A product of Lake Washington Shipyard in Houghton, Washington, she had been commissioned on 12 April 1943 and following shakedown training, had sailed from San Diego in June for Saboe Bay. *Chincoteague*'s first encounter with enemy aircraft came around noon on 14 July, when a plane believed to be on a photographic mission was sighted at about 15,000 feet overhead. The ship got underway, passed through the reef at the entrance to the bay and stood out to sea. She remained outside for about an hour before returning upon the departure of the aircraft. Her 5-inch/38 battery had opened fire at the high flying "snooper" with undetermined results.[6]

Operations returned to normal through the remainder of that day, and all of the next until early evening when, at 1847, a Japanese twin-engine bomber was picked up on radar. The plane was believed to be a Sally (Mitsubishi Ki-21 Type 97 heavy bomber). It circled for some minutes and then dropped two brilliant white flares about two thousand yards off the ship's port quarter, near the entrance to the bay. Taking full advantage of the darkness, the *Chincoteague* withheld anti-aircraft fire in order to not disclose her position.[7]

Photo 19-1

Seaplane tender *Chincoteague* off the Mare Island Navy Yard on 27 December 1943. U.S. Navy Photograph #NH 97710, from the collections of the Naval History and Heritage Command

Enemy aircraft attacks against the *Chincoteague* began in earnest the morning of 16 July, and continued through the afternoon of the 17th. The personnel casualties and material damage inflicted on her over this period would result in the Navy abandoning Vanikoro. Comdr. Ira E. Hobbs, *Chincoteague*'s commanding officer, described in a post action report the opening action. The other quoted material in the next few pages is from the same report.

> On the morning of the sixteenth at 0717, five Jap twin engined bombers were picked up by radar circling the bay and then sighted overhead. They released their bombs from an altitude of approximately eight thousand feet. The sticks fell about fifteen hundred yards from the ship, bursting in the jungle east of Saboe

Bay Head. Only the one run was made, the planes continuing on out of contact. A few hours later, at 1110, another formation was sighted overhead making a dummy run on the ship. Again these were thought to be the Sally type and this time there were nine of them flying in a close V of V's. On this run they passed on the starboard side heading out to sea. After circling about they came in from the sea, passing this time on the portside.[8]

Hobbs ordered the starboard anchor chain unshackled in order to get underway quickly, and as the tender set a course to exit the bay her gun crews opened fire. No ordnance was dropped and the planes disappeared eastward. Five minutes later they came in again, this time on a bombing run. They dropped sticks of three bombs each in a pattern. Maneuvering by the ship placed two sticks on her port quarter and one directly astern. The closest bomb fell about fifty feet away resulting in some minor splinter damage about her stern and to the sight of the number four 5-inch/38 gun. *Chincoteague* continued out to sea and later, after contact with the enemy was lost, returned to the bay at 1300 in order to receive VP-71. Its planes were to land for rest and fueling before proceeding on an overnight bombing mission.[9]

ATTACKS CONTINUE AND DAMAGE MOUNTS

During the preceding and all subsequent actions, the *Chincoteague*'s guns were fired by local control. She had no gun director and without one, anti-aircraft fire against distant targets was not of great value. The next morning, 17 July, the flight of six PBY-5s of VP-71 returned to Vanikoro from their mission. These planes, led by the squadron commander Lt. Comdr. C. K. Harper, USN, had struck Nauru Island, 675 miles north of Vanikoro, dropping six tons of bombs and scoring hits on the airstrip, dispersal areas, barracks, and the phosphate plant. The Japanese had invaded and occupied Nauru, in part because they intended to take over the island's important fertilizer industry.[10]

The small island hosted a Japanese airfield, and was home to the 67 Naval Guard Force, the Nauru Expeditionary Force of the 3rd Special Naval Base Force, and the Nauru Special Construction Unit of the Fourth Fleet. The PBYs had encountered intense but inaccurate anti-aircraft fire, and suffered no resulting damage. The last plane had just landed in Saboe Bay, when at 0725 the first stick of bombs from five twin-engine bombers bracketed the fo'c'sle of the *Chincoteague*. The enemy had come in at about eight thousand feet from the northwest, apparently having followed the patrol aircraft in.[11]

The seaplane tender got underway a minute later and headed for the entrance to the bay, as the bombers came in from the southeast on a second run. A stick of bombs fell about fifty yards astern of the *Chincoteague*, and the planes circled off in preparation for yet another attack. At 0738, just as she was emerging from the bay, bombs fell close aboard the ship. The one nearest, detonated about fifty feet off her starboard side. It ruptured gasoline lines, igniting fuel spraying from those lines along with nearby pyrotechnics. Fire parties were able to extinguish the flames by the use of fog nozzles. Numerous splinter holes were also made in the ship's hull.[12]

Chincoteague was making flank speed at the time of the attack, and maintained "maximum turns" clearing the passage through the reefs as, prior to reaching the open sea, no evasive action was practical other than going as fast as possible. At 0807 a new attack developed, as four planes came in from the ship's starboard quarter. Hobbs took evasive action using full rudder and flank speed, and all the dropped bombs fell clear. When contact with the enemy was lost, and due to VP-71 requiring fueling prior to its departure for Espiritu Santo, the tender returned to the bay at 0853.[13]

Upon receiving orders for the *Chincoteague* to depart there as well, Hobbs dispatched all patrol planes with the exception of three still needing fueling. The seaplane tender weighed anchor at 1020, leaving Bowser boats to refuel the remaining planes. By 1120 the ship had cleared the reefs and was standing out to sea. However, open water did not mean safety. An aircraft attack twenty-five minutes later killed ship's personnel and caused significant damage to the tender:

> Five Sallys overhead released sticks which bracketed the ship. We were maneuvering to the extreme degree again which helped to prevent any direct hits although some splinter damage was sustained. A few minutes later, having circled about into the sun they came in again. The stick of bombs again bracketed the ship. This time we received a direct hit from what is believed to be a 100 k.g. delayed action bomb which pierced three decks, the super, and main and second, before exploding in the after engine room. All after engineering personnel including the Chief Engineer were killed, as well as a fireman in the forward messing compartment. Number four gun went out of commission at the same time due to water damage.[14]

Damage to machinery in the after engine room reduced the speed the tender was able to make since the forward engines drove only the starboard propeller shaft. Additionally, loss of power to the steering gear mandated the use of hand steering during subsequent actions. At 1420, three bombers came in on a run at eight thousand feet releasing a series of green flares while heading into the sun. After circling about, they started their attack and the ship opened fire Dropped bombs bracketed the *Chincoteague*, resulting in personnel injuries and damage to the ship which stopped the tender dead in the water:

> At least one five hundred pound bomb falling along the port side stopped the forward engine room. The splinters and concussion produced by this stick resulted in considerable damage to personnel, the ship, and boats, one of which caught on fire. The remaining guns in commission from then on had to be manually operated.
> Number three five inch [gun] reported one Jap plane broke formation during this attack and veered off trailing smoke. This was the only observed result of our firing.[15]

A final attack occurred in mid-afternoon. A single plane bombed the immobile *Chincoteague*, but the ordnance fell two hundred yards abeam of the crippled ship.[16]

HERCULEAN EFFORTS BY CREW SAVE THEIR SHIP

But for her crew, the seaplane tender would have sunk. With the after engine room flooded and some after compartments partially flooded, and water coming in through splinter holes in the hull, the ship developed a heavy list to starboard. All available men including crews from the guns immediately joined together in a fight to save the ship. Bucket brigades went into action at 1500 working without cease in an effort to bail the ship out and handy billy pumps were pressed into service as well. These type gasoline-powered emergency pumps were used aboard Navy ships when electrical power was lost and normal pumping ability was not available.[17]

That night the struggle appeared to be hopeless until power could be obtained to operate electrical submersible pumps able to remove much higher volumes of water. Despite all efforts water levels continued to gain. However, all was not lost because flooding in the forward engine room could be controlled at a depth of a few feet. Once this became apparent, engineers started the 100kw diesel generator and then the 200kw generator. With electricity available, they then tried to start the Fairbanks-Morse main propulsion diesel engines. The first attempt to start one of them was unsuccessful. But on the second try, the diesel rumbled to life and the *Chincoteague* was able to get underway at 2350.[18]

An hour later, the destroyer seaplane tender *Thornton* (AVD-11) appeared on the scene and sent over via boat additional handy billys. These pumps were immediately put into service. With the *Thornton* as escort, the *Chincoteague* proceeded toward Espiritu Santo for nearly two hours, during which electrical fires twice started in the forward engine room and were extinguished with carbon dioxide. At 0245, a large fire broke out in this space, and an additional problem developed with a "runaway" engine:

> On the inboard engine the scavenging belt was seen to be filling with lubricating oil as well as diesel. It was immediately decided to secure the engine. However with the excess amount of oil present on the belt the engine continued to run. There was no means of control left; in a few seconds the engine began to overspeed, and in a few minutes to destroy itself. It was necessary to remove the crew, while the room was secured in an effort to smother the fire. At the same time foam generators were set up, the THORNTON came alongside, hoses were connected to her fire mains, and foam poured into the compartment.[19]

Fire parties fought the fire with fog nozzles and foam until about 0545 on the morning of 18 July when the last of the foam was expended. The fire appeared to be contained, but was still smoldering. After the engine room entry was battened down and air intakes to the space were covered with blankets and mattresses to prevent oxygen from restarting the fire, the *Thornton* cleared *Chincoteague*'s side and took her under tow. She broke the tow at 0740 due to a submarine contact, maneuvered to drop two depth charges, and resumed the tow after contact was lost.[20]

At 1217, the *Thornton* cast off the crippled seaplane tender because her charge was listing badly to starboard and in danger of sinking. The bucket brigades continued work, but the incessant flooding could not be checked and *Chincoteague*'s stern was settling with less than two feet of freeboard remaining. As the list varied between 12 and 18 degrees, Hobbs gave the order to lighten ship. Torpedoes, heavy machinery, winches and other weighty gear were jettisoned over the starboard side. This action, plus the use of additional pumps flown in by a PBY, and efforts by the bucket brigades enabled the crew to hold the flooding at bay and eventually to right the ship.[21]

At 1304, the *Thornton* once again came along the *Chincoteague*'s starboard side to furnish power for submersible pumps. She remained made up to her until the following morning—refusing to cast off that evening when an aircraft attack developed at 1743 just as the destroyer

Jenkins (DD-447) hove in sight. Three Japanese bombers made one pass at the *Jenkins*, than jettisoned their remaining bombs while trying, to no avail, to escape fighter aircraft. Three F4U Corsairs of Marine Fighting Squadron VMF-214, piloted by Maj. Bill Pace, and 1st Lieutenants Jack Petit and Dick Sigel, shot down all three Nells (Mitsubishi G3M medium bombers) in flames. A description of the air combat can be found in Bruce Gamble's book *The Black Sheep*:

> The Nells turned to the right and dived, but they were no match for the Corsairs' speed as they plunged into the rising darkness. The Nell on the outside of the turn fell behind, and from fifteen thousand feet Pace selected it as his target for an overhead run. It was just like gunnery practice. He came down on the bomber with a full deflection shot, with just the very tip of its tail in the outside ring of his gunsight, and triggered his guns. Incendiaries found the Nell's fuel tanks and the bomber promptly blew, a spectacular sight in the fading dusk.

Petit and Sigel finished off the other two bombers, and the actions of the Marines provided a great boost to morale aboard the *Chincoteague*.[22]

That night, 18 July, as the ship lay dead in the water, *Jenkins* and the destroyer minesweeper *Trever* (DMS-16), which had arrived at 1820 after the air attack, served as an anti-submarine screen. Meanwhile, pumping and bucket brigade efforts continued without stop.[23]

The following morning, heavy seas pounded the two seaplane tenders together, which created leaks in the *Thornton*'s fire room and forced her to cast off at 1021. Flooding aboard *Chincoteague* was now under control and the fire in her forward fire room was out. In late morning, the fleet tug *Sonoma* (AT-12) made the seaplane tender's side with more pumping equipment. She also had a *Chincoteague* motor launch with sixteen sailors aboard in tow, which she had come across earlier that morning. These were crewmen who had fueled the planes at Vanikoro, and then headed for Espiritu Santo in the open launch.[24]

The *Sonoma* took the *Chincoteague* in tow at 1220 and set a course for Espiritu Santo. From then until arrival in port the morning of 21 July, nothing of consequence occurred. Following the completion of temporary repairs at Espiritu Santo, the seaplane tender proceeded under tow for San Francisco; arriving on 4 September 1943.[25]

COMMANDING OFFICERS AND CREWMEN LAUDED

One officer and eight men were killed aboard the *Chincoteague* during the series of attacks by Japanese bombers. The Navy awarded the commanding officer of the *Chincoteague* and six of her crew either Silver

Star or Navy & Marine Corps Medals for personal valor, and the commanding officer of the *Thornton* the Silver Star Medal.

USS *Chincoteague* (AVP-24)

Individual	Medal
Comdr. Ira E. Hobbs, USN	Silver Star
Chief Carpenter's Mate Dale D. Huffman, USN	Silver Star
Chief Electrician's Mate Roy W. Nevills, USN	Silver Star
Chief Boatswain's Mate William B. Sedor, USN	Silver Star
Chief Motor Machinist's Mate Emra F. Castle Jr., USN	Navy & Marine Corps
Motor Machinist's Mate First Roy H. Knudsen, USN	Navy & Marine Corps
Aviation Chief Machinist's Mate Alagran H. Nordgram, USN	Navy & Marine Corps

USS *Thornton* (AVD-11)

Lt. Comdr. Frank E. Sellers Jr. USN	Silver Star[27]

But for the actions of Lt. Comdr. Frank E. Sellers Jr., the herculean efforts of the captain and crew of the *Chincoteague* to save their ship would have been for naught. His citation reads in part:

> Promptly going to the aid of the badly damaged U.S.S. *CHINCOTEAGUE*, Lieutenant Commander Sellers daringly and skillfully placed his ship alongside the burning seaplane tender and offered timely assistance in fighting rapidly spreading fire and pumping water from flooded spaces. Despite imminent threat of bombardment by attacking Japanese planes and serious damage inflicted upon his own ship from pounding against the stricken vessel, he voluntarily remained alongside the helpless craft until his services were no longer required.

TREASURY-BOUGAINVILLE ISLAND LANDINGS

> *Enthusiasm for the plan was far from unanimous, even in the South Pacific, but, the decision having been made, all hands were told to 'get going.'*
>
> *Worse than anything ever encountered before in the South Pacific.*
>
> —Comments by Adm. William F. Halsey regarding scheduled amphibious landings on Bougainville Island, and the beach conditions and terrain encountered. Most areas of the landing beaches were so narrow that two bulldozers could not pass abreast between jungle and sea.[28]

By July 1943, the South Pacific Command had decided that as part of the final phase of the Solomon Islands Campaign an assault should be made on Bougainville Island. In enemy hands the island constituted the next major obstacle to Halsey's forces driving northwest through the New Georgia Islands group. In the Allies hands it would provide a base for future operations against powerful Rabaul to the northwest. Japanese-held Bougainville hosted numerous airfields; two at the north end, two on the southern, a field and a seaplane base on the east coast, and a field on Shortland Island to the south. Enemy ground forces were concentrated in and around southern Bougainville, and garrisons were set up on the east coast and northern part of the island.[29]

Map 19-2

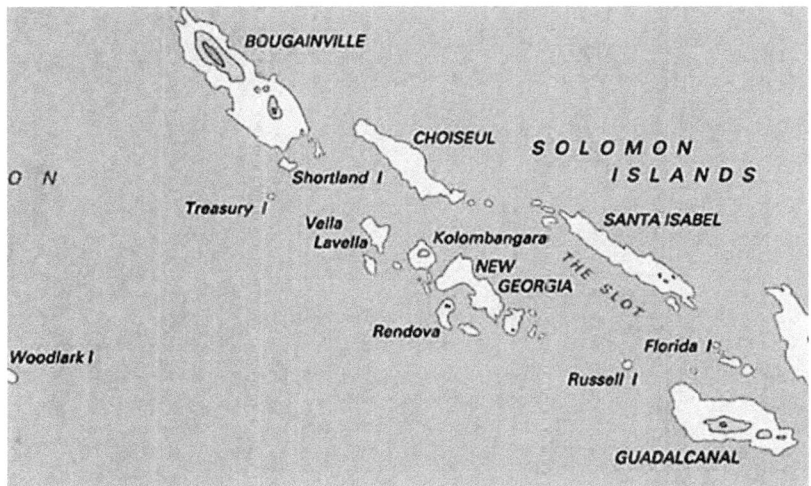

Central Solomon Islands

South Pacific forces had virtually completed occupation of the New Georgias with the capture of the Japanese airfield at Munda Point on New Georgia (the largest island in the group) on 5 August and landings on Vella Lavella ten days later. Occupation of Vella Lavella, also one of the New Georgia islands, was completed less than two months later. In October, the famed Black Sheep Squadron, VMF-214, led by fighter Ace Major Gregory "Pappy" Boyington moved forward from the Russell Islands to Munda. From there, F4U Corsair fighter aircraft could strike the next big objective, Japanese bases on Bougainville. (Boyington's VMF-214 was not the same squadron that had provided air cover for the *Chincoteague* in July. The Swashbucklers had been broken up in September and replaced by the Black Sheep, an entirely different unit that inherited its number.)[30]

In the Southwest Pacific, MacArthur's Allied forces took Salamaua and Lae in September. On 2 October, they captured Finschhafen, further up the eastern New Guinea coast, thus moving nearer to the Japanese base at Rabaul. Allied control of Finschhafen was considered necessary for the capture of the western cape of the Vitiaz Strait. It was also required for the development of the area by construction of airfields and naval facilities, creating a staging point for future operations against New Britain and the Bismarck Archipelago.[31]

Map 19-3

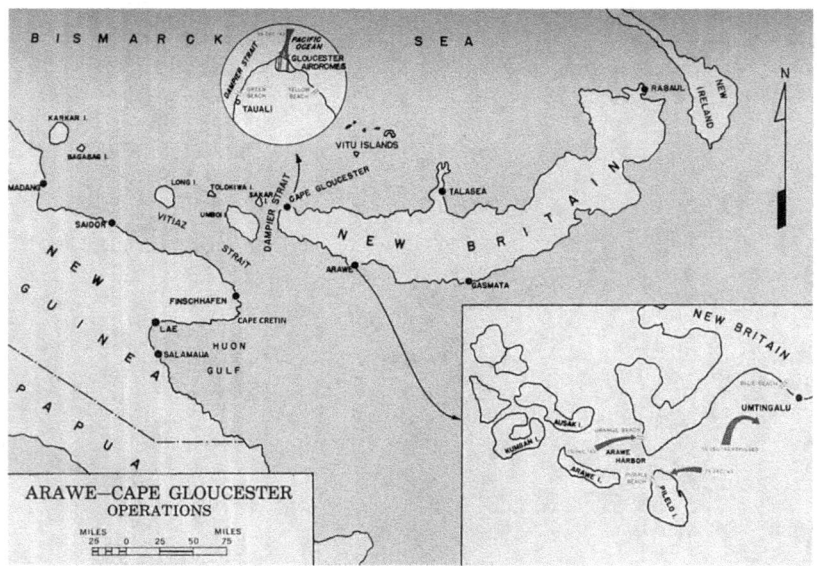

Southeast Papua New Guinea/New Britain area

TREASURY ISLANDS (OPERATION GOODTIME)

Later that month to the southeast in the Solomons, the invasion of the Treasury Islands on 27 October was a prelude to the much larger Bougainville expedition. The 8th Brigade Group of the 3rd New Zealand Division landed on the Treasury Islands, with 1,900 U.S. Marine support troops making up the balance of the amphibious force. It was a one-sided operation, with nearly 7,000 troops in total facing fewer than 250 Japanese. The Japanese chose to fight to the death and only eight were taken prisoner. Allied casualties were forty New Zealanders and twelve Marines killed, with additional wounded.[32]

BOUGAINVILLE (OPERATION CHERRY BLOSSOM)

In the much larger Bougainville assault, the 3rd Marine Division came ashore at Cape Torokina, on Empress Augusta Bay, on 1 November 1943. The purpose of the invasion of the largest and northernmost of the Solomon Islands was to gain and hold a strategic area around the beachhead only, since Lt. Gen. Harukichi Hyakutake, the island commander, had some 40,000 soldiers and 20,000 sailors under him. Construction of airstrips in this area of the long southwest coast of Bougainville would enable U.S. planes to strike Rabaul. Many miles of dense tropical rain forest separated the Empress Augusta Bay area from Japanese garrisons on Bougainville. The plan was for U.S. troops to build the airstrips before large numbers of enemy forces on the island could mount a sustained counterattack from land.[33]

Photo 19-2

Landing craft circle while awaiting the invasion of Bougainville on 1 November 1943 U.S. Marine Corps photograph taken from aboard the attack transport *American Legion* (APA-17).

This operation (code named CHERRY BLOSSOM) was a success and by February 1944, Japanese air strength at Rabaul had been eliminated. However, fighting on Bougainville would be protracted and last though the war's end. In November 1944, twelve Australian Army brigades replaced six U.S. Army divisions that were performing defensive roles in Bougainville, New Britain and the Aitape–Wewak area in New Guinea in order to free up the American units for operations in the Philippines. While the American units had largely conducted a static defense of their positions, Australian commanders mounted offensive operations designed to destroy the remaining Japanese forces in these areas. The value of these campaigns was controversial at the time and remains so today. Critics believe that they were unnecessary and wasteful of the lives of Australian soldiers involved, as the Japanese forces were already isolated and ineffective.[34]

SEAPLANE TENDER SUPPORT OF OPERATIONS

Five seaplane tenders—the *Chandeleur* (AV-10), *Chincoteague* (AVP-24), *Coos Bay* (AVP-25), *Pocomoke* (AV-9), and *Wright* (AV-1)—supported air operations during the Allied occupation of the Treasury and the Bougainville Islands. The *Coos Bay*, a product of Lake Washington Shipyards, Houghton, Washington, was a new ship, having been commissioned on 15 May 1943. Leaving Pearl Harbor on 30 July, she and the destroyer *Landsdowne* (DD-486) escorted the *Wright* (AV-1) to Pallikulo Bay at Espiritu Santo. Upon arrival on 11 August, *Coos Bay* reported for duty to commander Fleet Air Wing One.[35]

She was sent to Peou Bay on the southwest coast of Vanikoro Island to retrieve boats and other gear left behind by the *Chincoteague* in Saboe Bay, and which had been moved. On the night of 18 August, signal lights were observed across the reef, an area in which no ships were known to be. The next morning, as *Coos Bay* cleared the reef leaving Peou Bay, "sonar contract" was reported. With no room to maneuver to either attack or evade an enemy sub, Comdr. William Miller ordered flank speed and quit the area.[36]

Coos Bay joined the list of ships participating in the Solomons Campaign when she left anchorage in Segund Channel at Espiritu Santo on 11 October bound for Florida Island. Proceeding into Halavo Bay, the smoke and flames of the last Japanese air raid of the war on Guadalcanal could be seen twenty miles away across the Slot. As soon as the ship was anchored, the Air Officer and his men aboard her began establishing the *Coos Bay*'s first seadrome (A floating landing field). Patrol Squadron 71 then moved aboard and began carrying out PBY-5 search patrols.[37]

The living and working conditions aboard the tender with both ship's force and squadron personnel was crowded. Leisure was found and morale was maintained by converting Gamoni Island, popularly known as "Palm Island," to a recreation area. Good swimming and diving conditions were enjoyed by all, and an abundance of marine life produced some very good spear-fishermen.[38]

On 23 November, the *Coos Bay* moved to Tulagi Harbor, Rendova Island, in New Georgia. She took over the existing seadrome and tending of six to nine PBY-5s of Patrol Squadrons 14, 23, and 27. The seaplanes were engaged in air-sea rescue (Dumbo) missions, night snooper flights, anti-submarine missions and general utility flights. Ship support included housing and feeding the crews of the planes, seadrome maintenance, fueling and rearming aircraft, performing minor repairs of hull, engines and electronics gear, and maintaining a communications guard (monitoring radio circuits).[39]

Being able to land at sea and take off again, PBYs were ideally suited to carry out Dumbo missions. Dumbo planes in the Solomons were seaplanes stripped of all heavy gear to shed weight. Guns were manned for self-defense, but no bombs carried. These modified seaplanes engaged in rescuing pilots whose planes were shot down or failed for any reason. PBY-5s operating alone or escorted by fighters would be sent to pick up survivors. In many cases the planes had to land within easy range of shore-based artillery in order to rescue downed pilots. Fighter aircraft by diversion would try to keep the enemy as busy as possible during such operations.[40]

Map 19-4

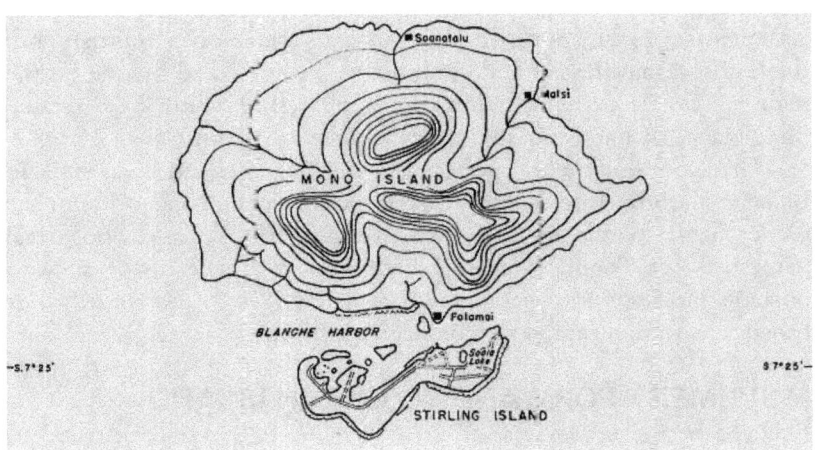

Treasury Islands in the Solomon Islands

Following her relief by the *Wright*, *Coos Bay* moved forward to Blanche Harbor, Treasury Islands on 28 December. This small island group, comprised of Mono and Stirling Islands, was commonly referred to as "Treasury." The occupation of these islands was intended to facilitate the construction of a radar station on Mono and use of Stirling as a staging area for an assault on Bougainville. From Blanche Harbor, the *Coos Bay* operated a six plane Dumbo unit, but there were usually six to nine seaplanes in the seadrome at any given time. Patrol Squadrons 14, 71, and 91 and the Royal New Zealand Air Force Maritime Squadron RNZAF No. 6FB operated from the tender at various periods during her four-and-one-half months at Treasury.[41]

Extensive air-sea rescue activity steadily increased the numbers of survivors brought aboard the *Coos Bay*. She made one rescue with her boats in the harbor at Treasury, after a fighter plane plunged into the water due to engine failure during takeoff from Stirling Field. Plane crash parties and fire and rescue parties were called away, and the pilot was retrieved from the water and taken back to the seaplane tender.[42]

RED ALERTS AND AIR RAIDS

Coos Bay was then the most forward-based surface ship in the Solomons Campaign. As such she was frequently subjected to enemy attacks. Red Alerts and air raids were so common that .30- and .50-caliber aircraft machine guns were employed to supplement her regular armament. During an enemy air raid on 13 January 1944, she was straddled by bombs but not damaged. The island command credited her with one Japanese plane shot down. Three weeks later, two enemy aircraft carried out a surprise early morning attack on 3 February, but the bombs again missed her. This attack was followed by one on the night of the 5th, in which ship's radar proved its worth by detecting three planes that shore-based radar had failed to identify.[43]

"Tokyo Rose" later asserted that the *Coos Bay* had been sunk in Blanche Harbor. Interestingly, this pronouncement came just after the tender had departed the Treasury Islands. Tokyo Rose, whose real name was Iva Toguri, was an American-born Japanese woman who hosted a Japanese propaganda radio program titled "Zero Hour." Her broadcasts were meant to demoralize U.S. troops.[44]

MOVEMENT FORWARD TO GREEN ISLAND

Relieved by the *Chincoteague* at Treasury, *Coos Bay* stepped forward to Green Island lagoon, arriving on 11 May to service PBYs and provide quarters for the crews while the main base was being constructed. The Green Islands lay thirty-seven miles north of Bougainville and one hundred seventeen directly east of Rabaul, New Britain. Green Island, the largest of the chain, had fallen to the 3rd New Zealand Division (less the 8th Brigade which had been used in the Treasuries operation) on 14 February 1944. Once under Allied control, Green Island became a forward base for the U.S. South Pacific Combat Air Transport Command (SCAT), which supplied material and mail to combat soldiers and evacuated the wounded. Among the naval personnel assigned to this base was future American president Lt. Richard M. Nixon, USNR. His war service is covered in the next section.[45]

The first three PBYs arrived at Green Island in April 1944. They belonged to VP-91, then land based at the Halavo Seaplane Base on Tulagi Island across the New Georgia Sound from Guadalcanal. The squadron also had seaplanes operating from two other advance bases, five at Treasury and two at Emirau Island in the Bismarcks. The seaplanes at the advanced bases were primarily for rescue (Dumbo) and general utility work, under the local control of commander Aircraft Solomons. This changed at Green Island on 27 May, when new tasking required VP-91 to fly five search sectors daily, maintain two anti-submarine planes in standby, and also carry out rescue duties. To meet these requirements, the planes at Treasury relocated to Green Island. In mid-June, VP-44 took over VP-91's duties, concurrent with the relief of *Coos Bay* by the *Chincoteague*.[46]

ALLIED NOOSE TIGHTENS AROUND REBAUL

The capture of the Green Islands and earlier of Emirau Island was part of an Allied plan to isolate Rabaul on New Britain, versus trying to take it from the Japanese. The U.S. 4th Marine Division, some four thousand men strong, had landed on Emirau on 20 March, after which the island was developed into an airbase, forming the final link in a chain of Allied bases surrounding Rabaul. One impediment to this plan was the enemy stronghold of Kavieng on New Ireland, which lay seventy-five miles southeast of Emirau and between the Green Islands and New Britain. Kavieng was considered as a target to be invaded by the 3rd Marines, but "top brass" decided the cost would be too high. Better to let Kavieng, like Rabaul, die on the vine. Particularly since aircraft and ships operating from Emirau would effectively cut off the Solomon Islands and the Bismarck Archipelago from the Japanese.[47]

NAVAL SERVICE OF RICHARD MILHOUS NIXON

Lieutenant Richard M. Nixon was a graduate of Duke University. He had been employed as an attorney for the Office of Emergency Management in Washington, D.C. when he accepted an appointment as lieutenant (junior grade) in the United States Naval Reserve on 15

June 1942. Following completion of aviation indoctrination training at Naval Air Station Quonset Point in Rhode Island, Nixon served until May 1943 as Aide to the executive officer at the Naval Reserve Aviation Base in Ottumwa, Iowa.[48]

Photo 19-3

Formal portrait of Lt. Comdr. Richard M. Nixon, USNR.

Seeking more excitement, he volunteered for sea duty and after reporting to commander Air Force, U.S. Pacific Fleet, he was assigned duties as officer-in-charge of the South Pacific Combat Air Transport Command at Guadalcanal and later at Green Island. His unit prepared manifests and flight plans for C47 cargo plane operations and supervised the loading and unloading of the aircraft.[49]

Nixon was transported to the South Pacific with hundreds of other servicemen aboard the S.S. *Monroe*, one of the "President" liners pressed into service as a troopship. At age seventy in an interview with Frank Gannon, he described the ocean crossing, which included him suffering chronic seasickness:

> It was a luxury liner fitted out for two hundred and fifty luxury passengers, and we had three thousand on it. We lived -- the officers were in bunks, three high on the walls and so forth and so on. [It] took seventeen days to get to Noumea, New Caledonia. And I remember the most unpleasant experience on that was not the fact that we had to wear life belts at times and so forth and so on, but was the fact that I was, of course, allergic to seasickness. And they used to bet -- we only had two meals a day. And my friends who were sitting at our table used to take bets among each other as to how long I'd stay at the table. I seldom got through a full meal.[50]

When asked by Gannon if he saw any action up the line during his duty in the Pacific, Nixon described enemy air attacks at Bougainville in January 1944:

> I think the most lively place I was in was Bougainville. There were about thirteen or fourteen days when we had air raids every night. One night it was pretty close. The Japanese plane used to come over. The way you could tell it was a Japanese plane is the motors were not synchronized. They go, "Dee-dee-dee-dee." Even without the air raid, you knew it was a Japanese plane coming over. And they were really harassing us because our Air Force had knocked down most of their power. One night...we heard this plane. It had come in very low. And we heard the bombs dropping as they came down the runway. "Rrrrrrrr." They were dropping. And we dived out of our cabin into the foxhole. As soon as we got out, we saw that our whole tent had been sprayed with bullets. It was a close one.[51]

In the spring of 1944, Nixon (now a full lieutenant having been promoted on 1 October 1943) ran the base air cargo office on Green Island. Formally named Nissan Island, Green Island was the largest of a group of eight islands on the north end of the Solomon Islands chain, just four degrees south of the Equator. It was also the site of the U.S. Navy/Marine Corps, New Zealand and Australian bases in the island chain. Nixon developed much respect for the "Seabees" (Naval Construction Battalion personnel) on the island, and it soon became apparent to him that they had the best chow. Seabees unloaded the infrequent refrigerated ships that stopped at the island, they manned the cold storage warehouse, and they delivered daily provisions to the many camp kitchens. Nixon related to Gannon:

> Well, the Seabees -- people wonder why I was so much for the hard hats. I talk about remarkable men, and they were remarkable. I remember one time on Green Island we were -- they were making an airstrip there, and it -- there was an air raid signal. But some of them were false. And these big Seabee guys, they'd be in the big bulldozers, they'd ignore the signals, and they'd keep working there, even in the middle of the night with their lights on in order to get the airstrip finished.
> Boy, they were something else. Most of them were from the east. This was the Twenty-Second Seabee Battalion. And I got to know them very well, and I ate with them because I was the head of a small detachment -- Army, Navy, Air Force were all members of it. I, being a naval officer, was the officer in charge, being a lieutenant and the ranking officer. And so I was able to select which mess we would use. Well, I turned down the Marine mess because the Marines can fight, but they couldn't cook. They were terrible cooks. I turned down the Army mess because they were almost as bad cooks...as the Marines. The only other mess was the Seabee mess, and it was the best.
> It wasn't because their cook was so good, but the Seabees, you know, they had access to a lot of things. They could put in a -- they could put in some flooring in your tent. They -- they could make various utensils and so forth. And so they would trade for meat and other vittles for their mess. And what they didn't trade, they stole. And they were very good.[52]

Upon finishing his tour of duty at Green Island, Nixon returned to the United States. From August through December of 1944, he was assigned to Fleet Air Wing Eight. He served through March 1945 at the Bureau of Aeronautics, Navy Department, Washington, D.C., before transfer to the Bureau of Aeronautics General Representative, Eastern District, headquartered in New York City. Nixon was released from active duty on 10 March 1946. He had become a lieutenant commander on 3 October 1945, and would gain another stripe when promoted to commander in the Naval Reserve on 1 June 1953.

Commander Richard M. Nixon, USNR, transferred to the Retired Reserve on 1 June 1966, two years before becoming the thirty-seventh president of the United States.[53]

While on active duty, he earned the American Campaign Medal, the Asiatic-Pacific Campaign Medal, and the World War II Victory Medal. Nixon was entitled to two engagement stars on his Asiatic-Pacific Campaign Medal for supporting air action in the Treasury-Bougainville operations and consolidation of the northern Solomons.[54]

CHINCOTEAGUE'S RETURN TO DUTY

The seaplane tender *Chincoteague* arrived at Green Island during the latter part of Nixon's tour there. Following repair of her battle damage at Mare Island Navy Yard in late December 1943, she had left the San Francisco Bay area and proceeded down the California coast to San Diego for crew training. Upon completion of all exercises, the ship and her new captain, Comdr. Robert A. Rosasco, USN, set a course for Pearl Harbor, arriving on 2 February 1944.[55]

Chincoteague stood out of Pearl Harbor ten days later and did not return to Hawaiian waters for seven months. During this period, she was continually on the move among the Solomon, Marshall, Gilbert, Mariana, New Hebrides and Phoenix Islands. As necessary, the ship carried freight, mail and passengers from place to place, but primarily engaged in tending aircraft. In concert with the western movement of the Pacific Fleet, she tended seaplanes at Kwajalein Atoll, Eniwetok Atoll, Treasury Island, and Green Island. *Chincoteague* joined sister ship *Coos Bay* at the latter island on 28 May. Many of the seaplanes she tended there, like those of the *Coos Bay*, were engaged in air-sea rescue (Dumbo) operations.[56]

Prior to her return to Hawaii, *Chincoteague* journeyed to Auckland, New Zealand, and transported aircraft engines back to Guadalcanal. She also escorted a group of PT boats from Funafuti, Ellice Islands, to Guadalcanal.[57]

LARGE SEAPLANE TENDER SUPPORT

From October 1943 to April 1944, the *Pocomoke* (AV-9) functioned as a transport ship for aviation personnel and gear. Such assignments made sense because the large seaplane tender was a former freighter, the *Exchequer*. At the completion of her construction at Pascagoula, Mississippi for the American Export Lines, she had then been the largest all-welded merchant ship ever built. She was launched on 8 June 1940. Relatively soon thereafter, the Navy acquired her from the

Maritime Commission on 16 October for outfitting for a new role and the seaplane tender *Pocomoke* was commissioned on 18 July 1941.[58]

Among her ports of call while supporting the Central Solomons Campaign were Canton Island, San Diego, Pearl Harbor, Palmyra Island, Pago Pago, Samoa, Espiritu Santo, San Francisco, Funafuti Atoll, Tarawa Atoll, Guadalcanal and Florida Island. One of the *Pocomoke*'s tasks was to transport Marine fighter squadrons. This job entailed carrying squadron personnel and their gear and all the planes as well.[59]

Photo 19-4

Large seaplane tender *Pocomoke* (AV-9) at sea.
U.S. Naval History and Heritage Command Photograph #NH 43513

One of the most memorable groups of passengers was famed Maj. Joe Foss and his Marine Night Fighter Squadron (VMF-532). The ship carried them and their F4U Corsair fighters from San Diego to Espiritu Santo in January 1944. As a Marine captain, Joseph Jacob Foss had received the Congressional Medal of Honor for service in the Guadalcanal Campaign from 9 October 1942-23 January 1943. While serving as executive officer and a pilot of Marine Fighting Squadron VMF-121 he flew the F4F-4 Wildcat. His medal citation reads in part:

> Engaging in almost daily combat with the enemy from 9 October to 19 November 1942, Captain Foss personally shot down 23 Japanese planes and damaged others so severely that their destruction was extremely probable. In addition, during this period, he successfully led a large number of escort missions,

skillfully covering reconnaissance, bombing, and photographic planes as well as surface craft. On 15 January 1943, he added three more enemy planes to his already brilliant successes for a record of aerial combat achievement unsurpassed in this war. Boldly searching out an approaching enemy force on 25 January 1943, Captain Foss led his eight F4F Marine planes and four Army P38's into action and, undaunted by tremendously superior numbers, intercepted and struck with such force that four Japanese fighters were shot down and the bombers were turned back without releasing a single bomb. His remarkable flying skill, inspiring leadership, and indomitable fighting spirit were distinctive factors in the defense of strategic American positions on Guadalcanal.[60]

WRIGHT AND *CHANDELEUR*'S SERVICE

The large seaplane tender *Wright* (AV-1), which had been named in honor of aviation pioneer Orville Wright, also transported Marine squadrons. She arrived at Espiritu Santo from Pearl Harbor in late July 1943 with the 31 officers and 238 men of Marine Fighting Squadron VMF-222. After landing them ashore, she remained at Espiritu Santo to tend planes of VP-14 and VP-24 during the first three months of the Central Solomons Campaign. *Wright* proceeded in late December to Rendova Island, New Georgia, and tended VP-14 until 17 January 1944, before shifting to Hawthorn Sound, New Georgia, where she tended VP-14 and 71 until mid-April. After leaving New Georgia, the seaplane tender entered Gavutu harbor, Florida Island, on 20 April, to load aviation stores and then continued on to Espiritu Santo for repairs that lasted through the end of May.[63]

The *Chandeleur*'s (AV-10) service during the Central Solomons Campaign was similar to that of *Pocomoke* and *Wright*. After tending VP-71 at Espiritu Santo from 1 July to 13 October 1943, she was ordered to cargo duty in support of the Treasury-Bougainville operations. Until 2 March 1944, she sailed between the New Hebrides and Guadalcanal, carrying men and aviation equipment. She then underwent a much-needed overhaul on the U.S. west coast, after which the seaplane tender made a round trip voyage to Pearl Harbor. The *Chandeleur* left Oakland, California on 18 May for Kwajalein and Eniwetok in the Marshall Islands, arriving 21 June 1944.[64]

SEAPLANE TENDER/SQUADRON BATTLE STARS

Six seaplane tenders—the *Chandeleur, Chincoteague, Coos Bay, Curtiss, Pocomoke*, and *Wright*—earned battle stars for one or more of the below listed operations. *Chincoteague*, gravely damaged by Japanese aircraft off

Vanikoro with men killed and injured, earned three battle stars; the last one following her return to duty after repair of battle damage. Patrol Squadrons VP-12, 24, 44, and 91 earned a battle star for consolidation of the southern Solomons, and components of VP-23, 54, 71, 81, and 91 for supporting air actions during Treasury-Bougainville operations.

Consolidation of Southern Solomons

Ship	Award Period	Commanding Officer
Curtiss (AV-4)	8 Feb-9 Jun 1943	Capt. Wilson P. Cogswell, USN
VP-12	9 Feb-23 May 43	Comdr. Clarence O. Taff
VP-24	8 Feb-9 Jun 43	Lt. Comdr. William L. Richards
VP-44	8 Feb-9 Jun 43	Lt. Comdr. Robert A. Rosasco
VP-91 FE	8 Feb-9 Jun 43	Lt. Comdr. James O. Cobb
		Lt. Comdr. E. L. Farrington

New Georgia-Rendova-Vangunu Occupation

Chincoteague (AVP-24)	17 Jul 1943	Comdr. Ira E. Hobbs, USN

Special operations: Action off Vanikoro

Chincoteague (AVP-24)	17-21 Jul 1943	Comdr. Ira E. Hobbs, USN

Treasury-Bougainville operation: Supporting Air Actions

Chandeleur (AV-10)	27 Oct 43-1 May 44	Capt. Albert K. Morehouse, USN
		Capt. Walter V. R. Vieweg, USN
Pocomoke (AV-9)	27 Oct 43-1 May 44	Capt. Curtis S. Smiley, USN
		Capt. Edward L. B. Weimer, USN
Wright (AV-1)	27 Oct 43-1 May 44	Capt. Frank C. Sutton, USN
		Capt. James E. Baker, USN
Chincoteague (AVP-24)	27 Oct 43-1 May 44	Comdr. Robert A. Rosasco, USN
Coos Bay (AVP-25)	27 Oct 43-1 May 44	Comdr. William Miller, USN
		Comdr. Delbert L. Conley, USN
VP-23 FE	27 Oct-15 Dec 43	Lt. Comdr. Frank A. Brandley
VP-54 FE	27 Oct-15 Dec 43	Lt. Comdr. Carl W. Schoenweiss
VP-71 FE	27 Oct-15 Dec 43	Lt. Comdr. C. K. Harper
VP-81 plane *P-7*	10 Dec 43-1 May 44	Lt. Comdr. E. P. Rankin
VP-91 FE	9 Nov-15 Dec 43	Comdr. E. L. Farrington

20

New Guinea and Bismarck Archipelago

Those planes don't look friendly to me.

—A radio transmission heard by the destroyer *Conyngham* (DD-371) from the *Lamson* (DD-367) to the *Mugford* (DD-389) and *Drayton* (DD-366), on 4 September 1943, regarding a flight of Japanese planes from Rabaul, approaching off New Guinea.[1]

Up to this point in the book, there has been no discussion of seaplane tenders supporting operations along the New Guinea coast. As new *Barnegat*-class tenders left their builder's yards in the United States, many were ordered to duty in the South or Southwest Pacific. The *San Pablo* (AVP-30), constructed by Associated Ship Building Inc., Seattle, Washington, was one of these ships. Following commissioning on 10 March 1943 and the completion of requisite training, she journeyed to New Guinea to join "MacArthur's navy," reaching Namoai Bay on 3 August. The small bay on the eastern side of Sariba Island lay inside larger, sheltered Milne Bay on the southeastern tip of Papua. Crossing the Pacific, the *San Pablo* made stops at Pearl Harbor, Espiritu Santo, Noumea, New Caledonia, and Brisbane, Australia.[2]

From her anchorage in Namoai Bay, the "newly minted" ship supported VP-101 in carrying out "Black Cat" activities against enemy shipping along the coast of New Guinea, New Ireland, New Britain, and in the waters of the Bismarck Sea. The term Black Cat referred to PBY Catalina seaplanes painted all black, which conducted night strikes against inter-island barge traffic as well as heavy shipping, harassed the enemy with bombing and strafing missions, and conducted photo intelligence. The squadron's PBY-5 aircraft also provided at-sea search and rescue support for downed Army fliers and sailors of sunken vessels, and transported high ranking officers, friendly coast watchers, and native guerrilla units.[3]

On 17 September, Patrol Squadron VP-11 relieved VP-101. The *Half Moon* (AVP-26) took over tending duties on 9 October, upon which *San Pablo* proceeded to Brisbane for repair, replenishment, and shore leave. The balance of the month was devoted to obtaining spare parts and replenishing stores, overhauling auxiliary machinery, and dry docking the ship for painting. A nearby Navy rest camp at Radcliffe was made available to the men who wished to spend their five-day leave there. Several officers took this opportunity to visit Sydney.[4]

Photo 20-1

Seaplane tender *Half Moon* (AVP-26) conducting turning trials on 10 February 1944, probably near Brisbane, Australia.
U.S. National Archives Photograph #80-G-223139

Upon completion of her overhaul and recreation period, the *San Pablo* was dispatched to Palm Island, thirty-five miles northeast of Townsville, Australia. After anchoring his ship in Challenger Bay on 4 November, Comdr. Stanton B. Dunlap, USN, reported for duty to deputy commander Fleet Air Wing Seventeen, Capt. Edwin R. Peck, USN. The *San Pablo* was charged with tending aircraft and other services at the island, mostly consisting of fueling and arming PBY-5 aircraft and fueling aircraft crash (rescue) boats. Palm Island was an excellent rear-area base, equipped to perform routine maintenance and all except major repairs to aircraft. The operating area was large, well-protected, and free of obstructions. Barracks and officer quarters for squadrons were wood frame buildings, which were clean and adequate, and the food was good. Swimming, beer, and movies provided ship's company and squadron personnel recreation.[5]

Occasionally other ships visited the island. The *YP-236* stood in on 16 November and anchored two hundred yards off the seaplane tender's starboard quarter. The 109-foot former tuna boat *Europa* was a long way from home. She was one of the many San Diego tuna boats the Navy had acquired early in the war and designated as yard patrol craft. Sporting a fresh coat of grey paint over their former glistening white hulls and armed with machine guns and depth charges, the wooden vessels were hurriedly dispatched to the Panama Canal Zone, Hawaiian Sea Frontier, or to the South or Southwest Pacific.[6]

San Pablo's rather mundane duties were broken on 19 November when she got under way for a day to compensate (adjust) magnetic compasses and conduct gunnery practice. Another day was spent at sea on the 24th, devoted to loss of steering, ship handling, and man overboard drills. The *San Pablo* continued her tending duties at Palm Island through mid-December, when she left to return to Namoai Bay. After arriving there the following day, she relieved the *Half Moon* and took up supporting VP-52's "Black Cat" operations. The squadron's flight personnel slept ashore at "Honey Hollow" and came aboard the ship mainly only for meals.[7]

The *San Pablo* and *Half Moon* were assigned along with the *Heron* to Task Unit 71.1.2, a part of Commodore Tomas S. Combs' Fleet Air Wing Seventeen. Combs was also commander Aircraft Seventh Fleet (Task Force 73), responsible for the aircraft and surface ships assigned to the Southwest Pacific Force. A summary of the Wing's seaplane tenders and patrol squadrons in December 1943 follows:

Task Group 73.1: Capt. Edwin R. Peck, USN
Task Unit 73.1.1

Squadron or Ship	Aircraft	Commanding Officer
Patrol Squadron VP-11	15 PBY-5s	Lt. Comdr. Clifford M. Campbell, USN
Patrol Squadron VP-34	PBY-5s	Lt. Comdr. J. G. Craig Jr, USN
Patrol Squadron VP-52	14 PBY-5s	Lt. Comdr. Harold A. Sommer, USN
Patrol Squadron VP-101	PBY-5s	Lt. Lauren E. Johnson, USN

Task Unit 73.1.2

San Pablo (AVP-30)		Comdr. Stanton B. Dunlap, USN
Half Moon (AVP-26)		Comdr. William O. Gallery Jr., USN
Heron (AVP-2)		Lt. John M. Norcott, USNR

PATROL SQUADRON 52

> *Today Patrol Squadron FIFTY TWO completes its tour of offensive night patrols against the enemy. Your splendid record of enemy shipping sunk and damaged adds a bright page to the history of Naval Aviation and will serve as*

> *inspiration and incentive to squadrons which follow. To all hands a hearty well done.*
>
> —Commander Aircraft Seventh Fleet commending VP-52 for its conduct of "Black Cat" operations in the Bismarck Sea during the latter part of 1943 and early 1944

From aboard the *Half Moon* at Namoai Bay, VP-52 had begun on 22 November 1943, a series of night anti-shipping missions through Dampier Straits and St. George's Channel into the Bismarck Sea. These missions (first flown by VP-101 in August) had originally been largely for reconnaissance. Subsequently, VP-11—operating under Comdr. William O. Gallery Jr., the commanding officer of the *Half Moon*—had made numerous attacks on Japanese vessels, including warships. Several different types of attack were tried, including medium-altitude glide or dive bombing runs in which ordnance release was made at 1,000 feet or higher, medium-altitude level runs, and torpedo attacks.[8]

The primary objective of the night searches when VP-52 began to conduct them was attacking enemy shipping. Experimentation with different types of attacks continued, much of it conducted by Gallery. Eventually the technique found to be the most successful was to approach an enemy ship at about 1,000 feet, glide or dive to practically mast-level and release bombs in train (sequentially). The usual aircraft ordnance load was two 500- and two 1,000-pound bombs, fused for a four and one-half second delay. During these attacks, the pilot did the targeting using seaman's eye and released bombs from the cockpit. It was not then known under what conditions night attacks by a plane as big and slow as a PBY were feasible. As such, Gallery left it almost entirely up to pilots to decide, on the spot, what type of attack to make, or whether to attack at all. Some of the factors considered were visibility, and whether or not the target was under the protection of escort vessels, aircraft, or shore batteries.[9]

Examples of the willingness of VP-52 pilots to press home their attacks in the face of adversity can be found in squadron history. On the night of 24 November 1943, William J. Lahodney, USN, carried out an attack on a cruiser escorted by three destroyers, operating seventy miles north of Rabaul:

> The force had already been alerted by a previous attack. In the face of intense anti-aircraft fire from all the ships, Lieutenant Lahodney glided to 150 feet before releasing his bombs, at least two of which hit the cruiser. His plane was badly damaged by the

anti-aircraft fire, but he was able to bring it safely back to his base.¹⁰

On another occasion, the night of 13 December, Lt. (jg) Rudolph Lloyd, USN, upon sighting a cruiser at anchor in the outer reaches of Kavieng Harbor, carried out an equally dangerous attack:

> There was a full moon, and the night was clear. Nevertheless, Lieutenant (jg) Lloyd pressed his attack to an extremely low altitude, scoring hits on the target. His plane was under intense anti-aircraft fire from the ship and numerous shore installations throughout his approach and retirement, but not badly damaged.¹¹

By the time VP-52's tour was completed on 31 December 1943, its PBY-5s had damaged two cruisers, two submarines (assessed by the squadron as sunk), and three destroyers. In addition, patrol aircraft had inflicted heavy losses on merchant shipping; 34,000 tons sunk, 10,000 tons probably sunk, and 32,000 tons damaged. Most of the squadron's one hundred thirty-seven missions had been devoted to anti-shipping. However, patrol coverage was provided for Seventh Fleet cruisers and destroyers bombarding Gasmate, New Britain, on the night of 29 November and to the Arawe invasion force on the night of 14 December 1943. Arawe was a very small harbor on the south coast of New Britain, which lay across the Dampier and Vitiaz Straits from New Guinea.¹²

Patrol Squadron 52 began on 1 January 1944 operating from Samarai Island off the southeastern tip of New Guinea, versus at Namoai Bay. This action was taken to free up the *San Pablo* for possible duty at an advanced position. Such an eventuality came to fruition. After continuing, for a while, to tend PBYs stopping at Namoai Bay, *San Pablo* left on 20 January for Langemak Bay, located 300 miles up the New Guinea coast, west-southwest of Rabaul. Arriving there the following day, she took up her new duties. The operating area was poor, permitting take-offs only toward the open sea and downwind. Operated from there the following month, VP-34 had to contend with an added hazard provided by floating debris of all kinds, most of it flotsam from moored freighters.¹³

The PBYs operating out of Samarai Island were now flying great distances on their "Black Cat" patrols, as part of an all-out attempt to wrest the waters of the Bismarck Sea from enemy control to prevent resupply of its beleaguered garrisons at Rabaul and Kavieng. These bases were receiving a daily pounding from Fifth Army Air Force planes operating from New Guinea and from Army and Marine Corps aircraft based in the Solomons. The "Black Cats" needed an advance base where they could "stage in" to receive services on the return flight to Samarai. The *San Pablo* met this requirement.[14]

In addition to fueling VP-52's patrol planes, the seaplane tender supported air-sea rescue work by those of VP-34 operating from Port Moresby. These planes were covering strikes by the Fifth AAF on Wewak, Hollandia, Madang, Rabaul, and Kavieng in New Guinea, and the Admiralty Islands. As such, it was considered advisable to keep at least two planes at Langemak Bay to cover emergency flights. VP-34 was assisted in this work by VP-52. Both squadrons were flying offensive patrols out of Samarai in addition to air-sea rescue work from Port Moresby and Langemak Bay. On 15 February, Lt. (jg) Nathan Gordon of VP-34 took off from Langemak Bay to cover a strike at Kavieng. Over a period of some two hours, he landed four times in the harbor at Kavieng to rescue fifteen officers and men of the Fifth AAF, during which he came under fire from enemy shore batteries, planes, and small craft. Details of the operation are cited in his Congressional Medal of Honor citation, which reads in part:

> For extraordinary heroism above and beyond the call of duty as commander of a Catalina patrol plane serving with Patrol Squadron Thirty-Four (VPB-34), in rescuing personnel of the U.S. Army Fifth Air Force shot down in combat over Kavieng Harbor in the Bismarck Sea, 15 February 1944. On air alert in the vicinity of Vitu Islands, Lieutenant Gordon unhesitatingly responded to a report of the crash and flew boldly into the harbor, defying close-range fire from enemy shore guns to make three separate landings in full view of the Japanese and pick up nine men, several of them injured. With his cumbersome flying boat dangerously overloaded, he made a brilliant takeoff despite heavy swells and almost total absence of wind and set a course for base, only to receive the report of another group stranded in a rubber life raft 600 yards from the enemy shore. Promptly turning back, he again risked his life to set his plane down under direct fire of the heaviest defenses of Kavieng and take aboard six more survivors, coolly making his fourth dexterous takeoff with 15 rescued officers and men. By his exceptional daring, personal valor, and incomparable airmanship under most perilous conditions, Lieutenant Gordon prevented certain death or capture of our airmen by the Japanese.[15]

DUTY AT LANGEMAK BAY, NEW GUINEA

> *USS* SAN PABLO – *This tender's operations consisted of supplying fuel for patrol planes returning from strikes deep inside Japanese held territory. Twenty red alerts were caused by Japanese planes in the vicinity of Langemak Bay, two of which resulted in bombs being dropped. No damage or casualties resulted to the USS* SAN PABLO *but other activities in the vicinity received both casualties and material damage.*
>
> *USS* SAN PABLO *was the advanced tender based at Langemak Bay from 1 February to 24 February.... Fifty-four red alerts were caused by Japanese planes in the vicinity of Langemak Bay and 19 bombs were dropped, doing no damage to the tender but scoring on other activities nearby. The USS* SAN PABLO *shot down one enemy aircraft.*
>
> —Commander Task Group 73.1 war diary entries for January and February 1944. The *San Pablo* carried out these duties from 21 January through 24 February 1944.

The fighter strip at Finschhafen was then under frequent surveillance by Japanese planes. Allied forces had captured Finschhafen in early October for use as a concentration point and staging area for future operations against New Britain and the Bismarcks. Located on the blunt eastern extremity of the Huon Peninsula, Finschhafen offered three ports. Ships arriving at Finsch Harbor entered from the north as a narrow, hook-shaped peninsula enclosed the port on the other three sides. Passage into the long, narrow inlet to Langemak Bay, southward of Finsch Harbor, was from the east. Dreger Harbor, located still farther south, was protected from the open sea by islands.[16]

During her five weeks at Langemak Bay, *San Pablo* witnessed over one hundred "alerts" and twelve bombings by enemy planes. The attacks were carried out by single planes during the day or by as many as six at night. The seaplane tender had the only heavy anti-aircraft guns in the vicinity and opened fire on several occasions. Her naval gunfire was directed by use of ship's radar ranges and bearings, and at altitudes received via radio communications from the Army command ashore. By employing these means to engage inbound Japanese planes still some distance away, *San Pablo* discouraged them from making close-in attacks.[17]

On the night of 23 January 1944, as she lay at anchor in the bay, a "Red Alert" warning from the Port Director was received aboard the

San Pablo at 2050, indicating an air raid was expected. Although the moon had not yet risen, visibility was excellent due to clear weather and bright starlight. Activation of the tender's general quarters alarm sent her crew scrambling to their battle stations. One minute later, all departments reported manned and ready.[18]

At 2055, the tender's 5-inch/38 gun battery commenced firing at two planes 15,000 yards distant that would close her to only 7,500 yards. Concurrently, shore batteries put up considerable anti-aircraft fire and the cargo ship *Ganymede* (AK-104) fired scattered 20mm bursts. The *San Pablo* ceased firing at 2106 having expended twenty-two rounds of ammunition. The attack was apparently made from seaward by three planes dropping bombs from Finschhafen to Langemak Bay. None of the twenty-one bombs fell in Langemak Bay proper, and the seaplane tender suffered no damage. Six dropped in the Dreger Wharf area, wounding three crewmen aboard the S.S. *John Muir* and causing superficial damage to the Liberty ship.[19]

SAN PABLO SHOOTS DOWN JAPANESE AIRCRAFT

San Pablo was credited with shooting down one enemy plane while at Langemak Bay. Following receipt of a "Red Alert" at 2251 the night of 6 February, her guns commenced firing at two enemy aircraft with running lights extinguished. Four planes participated in the attack, in which three Sallys dropped twelve 500-pound bombs in the Dreger area. The fighter airstrip was the target, and eye witnesses observed bursts of heavy 5-inch anti-aircraft fire within the formation of enemy planes over the target. One of the planes fell out of formation and headed out to sea, losing altitude as it retired. Since *San Pablo* had the only 5-inch guns in the entire Finschhafen area, she was credited by both the Army and Navy with a probable kill.[20]

PATROL SQUADRONS AWARDED PRESIDENTIAL UNIT CITATION FOR HEROISM IN BISMARCK SEA

	Presidential Unit Citation	
Unit	Award Period	Commanding Officer
VP-11	15 Sep 43–1 Feb 44	Lt. Comdr. Clifford M. Campbell, USN
VP-34	15 Sep 43–1 Feb 44	Lt. Comdr. J. G. Craig Jr., USN
VP-52	15 Sep 43–1 Feb 44	Lt. Comdr. Harold A. Sommer, USN

Battle Star
Eastern New Guinea Operation: Finschhafen Occupation

San Pablo (AVP-30)	21 Jan–17 Feb 44	Comdr. Stanton B. Dunlap, USN

21

Admiralty Islands Landings and Hollandia Operation

Within a week after the initial landing the First Cavalry Division had buried a Jap[anese] for each cavalryman landed on D-day, with estimated total garrison of between 4000 and 5000 troops.

—Commander Attack Group reporting on the Admiralty Islands operation, which was launched with a "reconnaissance in force" at Los Negros Island after an ineffective air reconnaissance had revealed no evidence of human activity. This misconception was discounted two days before the assault when Army scouts, who had gone ashore after being dropped off by a Catalina seaplane, reported that the area was "lousy with Japs."[1]

The capture and utilization of the powerful Japanese base at Rabaul, located on the northeast coast of New Britain, had been the main objective of Operation WATCHTOWER (which had opened with the landings at Guadalcanal in August 1942). However, after Allied movement up the New Guinea coast and finally into New Britain, the enemy stronghold still had close to 100,000 defenders. The garrison also had enough munitions, weapons, provisions, and supplies to withstand a long siege while inflicting large numbers of casualties on Allied invasion forces. Thus, the decision was made to bypass Rabaul and to instead, leap into the Admiralty Islands, which were ideally situated to develop facilities necessary to assist in isolating Rabaul and to support the approach to the Philippines. Manus, the largest island in the Admiralties—which spanned approximately 49 miles from east to west and 16 miles from north to south—offered ample space for military installations. Seeadler Harbor, on its northeast coast, could accommodate a task force. Los Negros Island, which located adjacent to Manus formed the eastern half of the harbor, had sufficient flat land to construct an airfield that would enable the Allies to deny the Japanese access to the Bismarck Archipelago and to dominate a 1,000-mile square of neighboring ocean whose corners were Bougainville,

Solomon Islands; Truk in the Caroline Islands; the Palau Islands; and Biak Island off northwestern New Guinea.[2]

Map 21-1

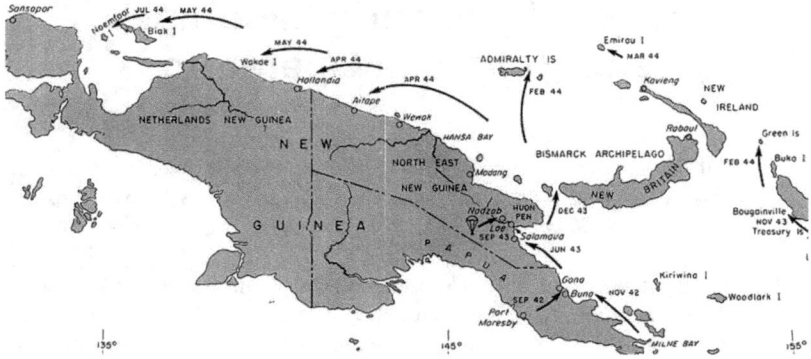

After defending Port Moresby, Papua, from a Japanese invasion, and establishing a base at Milne Bay, MacArthur's Australian and American forces advanced northwestward up the east coast of Papua and New Guinea along his road back to the Philippines.
(http://www.history.army.mil/books/AMH/Map23-43.jpg)

On the morning of 29 February 1944, the U.S. 1st Army Cavalry Division and detachments totaling 1,026 troops stormed ashore at Hyane Harbor, on the eastern shore of Los Negros Island. Planners had chosen the small, nearly landlocked Hyane, instead of the much larger and more accommodating Seeadler Harbor (some 15 miles long by 4 wide) or good beaches on the southeast coast of Los Negros, because the site was not an obvious choice and thus would likely not be as heavily defended. The landing force encountered little enemy opposition during daylight on D-day, but was heavily attacked that night and on the succeeding one. With the aid of Seventh Fleet gun batteries, abundant air power, and additional ground troops, the Americans advanced from Los Negros into Manus. By 3 April they were in control of Seeadler Harbor. A far better base than Rabaul (and nearer Japan), the Admiralties became one of the most important staging points in the last fifteen months of the Pacific War.[3]

SEAPLANE TENDERS ARRIVE AT ADMIRALITIES

During April [1944] Commander Seventh Fleet continued to endeavor to obtain additional squadrons of heavy patrol bombers for Commander Aircraft, Seventh Fleet, for use in patrolling the extensive area of open sea existing to the north of New Guinea. By the month's end, it had been decided to assign to Commander Aircraft, Seventh Fleet, Bombing Squadron One Hundred Forty-Six, consisting of PV-1 type aircraft.

—Commodore Thomas S. Combs, commander Aircraft, Seventh Fleet, citing in a war diary entry for April 1944 the expanding role of patrol planes within his command, including the addition of Lockheed PV-1 Ventura patrol bombers.

Map 21-2

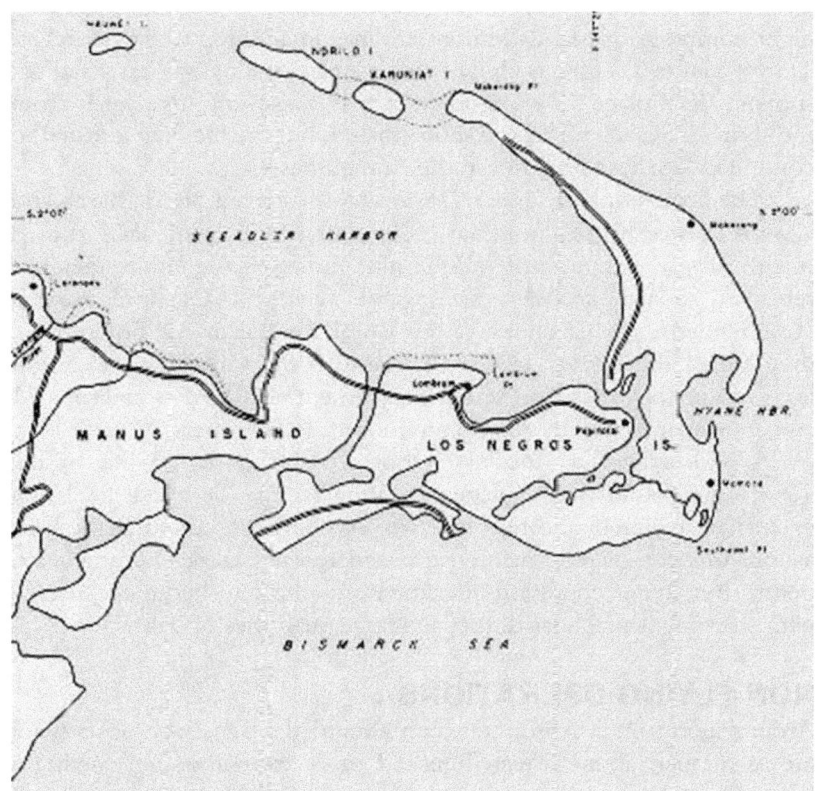

Manus and Los Negros, Admiralty Islands
(http://www.ibiblio.org/hyperwar/USN/Building_Bases/maps/bases2-p297.jpg)

San Pablo was the first seaplane tender to arrive in the Admiralties, entering Seeadler Harbor on 24 March 1944. While coming to anchor off Bear Point, a promontory of Los Negros Island in the southeast area of the harbor, men topside witnessed the bombardment of Pityilu, a small island off the northern coast of Manus, by three destroyers. Informed that there were Japanese ashore in the area bounding her intended anchorage, the tender moved to the eastern side of the harbor and laid buoys in preparation for the arrival of VP-33. The U.S. Army shelled the southern portions of Los Negros Island intermittently throughout the day and night for the first two days *San Pablo* was at anchorage.[4]

Commodore Thomas S. Combs, USN, boarded the *San Pablo* on 25 March and assumed duties as SOPA (Senior Officer Present Afloat), Seeadler Harbor. Search operations in the sea approaches to the Admiralties began that day with four planes flying five hundred miles northward on different sectors. By 28 March, seven planes of VP-33 and another seven of VP-52 were based at Seeadler, enabling night bombings of islands in the Carolines in addition to day searches. Thirty minutes before midnight on 1 April, enemy snipers fired six shots at PBY plane *52-48*, moored to a buoy seventy-five yards from the shore at Seeadler. All the shots missed, but the incident attested to continued Japanese presence in the Admiralties.[5]

The large seaplane tender *Tangier* (AV-8) arrived on 31 March and Combs hoisted his flag in her at 1300. Patrol Squadron VP-33 shifted to the *Tangier* with part of VP-52; nine crews of the latter squadron remained aboard *San Pablo*. During the week of 14-21 April, the *San Pablo* tended eight Catalinas of the Royal Australian Air Force while they mined the harbor at Woleai Island in the Carolines. The unit involved in this operation was a detachment of RAAF squadrons 11 and 20, accompanied by Air Commodore J. H. Summers.[6]

VP-34 arrived in Seeadler Harbor on 18 May for tending by the *Tangier* and found the seaplane operating area to be excellent, being extensive, sheltered, and relatively free of debris. Later, after the base ashore was completed, maintenance and repair facilities became even better, but living conditions declined and the bay became cluttered with shipping, small boat traffic, and large quantities of debris.[7]

NON-FLYING OPERATIONS

Around noon on 2 April, crewmen aboard the *San Pablo* observed a group of men about fifteen hundred yards from the ship waving a white flag. An armed party of eighteen men under the command of the executive officer left the tender in three boats to investigate. As the boats neared the beach, an order was given to the group of men ashore to remove their clothing and swim to the boats, where they were brought aboard and searched for weapons. The detainees proved to be Chinese whom had been captured by the Japanese in Hong Kong, and brought to the Admiralties as labor troops. They were turned over to the U.S. Army. [8]

Eight days later, a diving party overseen by *San Pablo*'s first lieutenant recovered approximately a hundred charts of waters adjacent to the Japanese Empire from a 200-ton Japanese ship that had been sunk in Lombrum Bay inside Seeadler Harbor. These charts were considered to be of such importance they were flown to Australia, safeguarded by a special courier, for reproduction.[9]

Photo 21-1

A *Tangier* (AV-8) liberty party on Los Negros Island on 14 June 1944, with their ship anchored in the right distance. Beer drinkers are in the foreground, swimmers beyond and a motor launch delivering more men to the pier, where they are collecting two bottles of beer apiece as they come ashore.
US National Archives Photograph #80-G-237133

HERON ARRIVED AT SEEADLER HARBOR

On the same day that the *San Pablo* had discovered the Chinese men at Seeadler Harbor, the *Heron* (AVP-2) left Samarai Island and proceeded through the China Strait en route to Namoai Bay, New Guinea. She arrived there in late afternoon. Although a seaplane tender, much of her work by this point in the war was non-aviation related. Being a former minesweeper able to pull heavy sweep gear at relatively slow speeds, she could also when necessary function as a fleet tug. In fact, many of her World War I sister ships still in service were serving as tugs. Following a single night in port, *Heron* stood out to sea on 3 April with two barges in tow, bound for Seeadler Harbor. That afternoon, she test fired her 3-inch main battery and smaller 20mm and .50-caliber anti-aircraft guns. She arrived at her destination shortly after midnight on 8 April with only a single barge in tow. The other had flooded, broke up and been sunk with gunfire during the transit.[10]

Heron was sent out from Seeadler Harbor the evening of 17 April to assist the *Wharton* (AP-7) after the transport grounded near the entrance to the harbor. Following several unsuccessful attempts to free the reef-gripped ship via tow line, *Heron* went alongside her and made up to her port quarter. At twenty-five minutes past midnight, she pulled *Wharton* free, and then returned to anchorage in the harbor. Three days later, *Heron* pulled an Army barge off "Red Beach."[11]

Photo 21-2

PB4Y-1 of VB-106 on patrol in the southwestern Pacific area in 1943-44.
Naval History and Heritage Command Photograph #75355

AIRCRAFT OPERATIONS AT THE ADMIRALTIES

In April, PBY-5 aircraft of Patrol Squadrons 33, 34, and 52, and PB4Y-1 aircraft of Bombing Squadron 106, conducted eight or more searches over water daily. The longest, in connection with landings at Hollandia, Tanahmerah Bay, and Aitapi, New Guinea, extended out as far as 1,000 miles from Seeadler Harbor; the shortest ones stretched 500 miles from that harbor. VB-106 operated from Nadzab in the Markham Valley of New Guinea through 11 April, and then from Momote Airfield in the Admiralties. Catalina and Liberator aircraft operating from the Admiralty Islands shot down eight enemy patrol planes, damaged or destroyed a number of small enemy ships and barges, and carried out the first Allied night strike on Wakde Island, off the northern coast of New Guinea. Seaplanes also conducted anti-submarine flights and air-sea missions in connection with strikes by U.S. Army Liberators on Japanese bases in the Carolines and the Geelvink Bay area at the northwestern end of New Guinea. VP-34 operating from aboard the *Half Moon* at Langemak Bay was tasked with carrying out air-sea rescue operations.[12]

HOLLANDIA, NEW GUINEA OPERATION

After taking the Admiralty Islands, MacArthur's next objective was to leapfrog the Japanese garrison at Wewak, New Guinea, into Hollandia, and to establish a new headquarters there. On 22 April 1944, the Allies launched the largest amphibious operation yet carried out in the Southwest Pacific involving over two hundred ships. It was intended to initiate the final stages of the isolation of Rabaul and involved concurrent landings at three locations on the northwest coast of New Guinea. The western landing took place at Tanahmerah Bay, the site of an enemy army and air force base. The central landing was thirty miles to the east-southeast in Humboldt Bay, and the eastern landing about ninety miles farther eastward at Aitape. Hollandia, the name by which the entire area would become known to American forces, was a tiny settlement nestled at the head of Challenger Cove, an arm of Humboldt Bay and formerly the eastern-most Dutch outpost in the Netherlands East Indies.[13]

The objective of the operation was to seize and occupy the Tanahmerah Bay-Humboldt Bay-Aitape areas, and to establish at Aitape minor air and naval facilities, and in the Humboldt Bay-Tanahmerah Bay areas a major airbase, minor naval facilities, and an intermediate supply base for the purpose of supporting further operations to the westward. Rear Adm. Daniel E. Barbey commanded the overall attack force and the attack group at Tanahmerah Bay, Rear Admiral William M. Fechteler the attack group at Humboldt Bay, and Capt. Albert G. Nobel, USN, that at Aitape. All the landings were a complete surprise which—following the intense pre-assault air and naval bombardment that broke the back of any resistance—eliminated Japanese opposition, resulting in practically no casualties during the landings. The enemy at Humboldt Bay retired into the hills and a party at Aitape left their defenses prior to the assault. Both Aitape airfields were captured by 22 April, and fighter operations commenced two days later. The airfields at Hollandia were taken thereafter, on 26 April 1944, and one strip was ready for use at month's end.[14]

Map 21-3

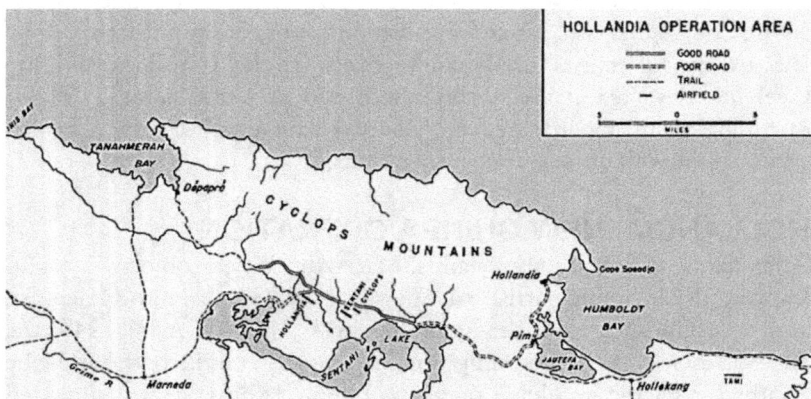

Following the Allies capture of Hollandia on the northeast coast of New Guinea, MacArthur's general headquarters relocated there from Brisbane, Australia. The naval, air, and troop supply base would support the landings on Leyte, and, thereafter, virtually everybody and everything en route to the Philippines campaign would pass through Hollandia.
(http://www.ibiblio.org/hyperwar/USA/USA-P-Approach/maps/USA-P-Approach-2.jpg)

PATROL PLANE OPERATIONS AT HOLLANDIA

San Pablo arrived at Humboldt Bay on 13 May and with the arrival of seven PBY-5 aircraft of Patrol Squadron VP-52 three days later began operations as Task Unit 73.1.2. The anchorage for the patrol planes was in shallow Jautefa Bay, located over three and one-half miles from the tender. Night searches were flown from Hollandia to the west and northwest up the New Guinea coast, to patrol the approaches to Wakde Island before an Allied invasion of the Wakde-Sarmi area planned for 17 May. Once the Tornado Task Force (163rd Regimental Combat Team of the 41st Division) commanded by Brig. Gen. Jens A. Doe, USA, was ashore, patrols were continued to prevent the Japanese from relieving or supplying their besieged troops. Other landings further to the west were covered by patrol planes at later dates. As a result of four operations—Wakde, Biak, Noemfoor, and Sansapor—MacArthur's forces would advance to Vogelkop on the northwest point of New Guinea, 550 miles west of Hollandia, in a little more than three months.[15]

VP-52 operating from the *San Pablo* also carried out some air-sea rescue work, but most of this work was done by VP-34 aboard the *Half Moon* in the southern part of Humboldt Bay. Patrol Squadron 34 considered its operating area to be good, extensive and well protected. However, its flight crews, like those of VP-52 aboard the *San Pablo*, were required to endure excessively long boat trips from their tender to seaplane moorings.[16]

San Pedro witnessed twenty-five "Red Alerts" during her stint at Hollandia, but the air strips ashore were the targets of all attacks. In addition to tending aircraft, she also fueled motor torpedo (PT) boats operating from the *Oyster Bay* (AGP-6) in Humboldt Bay. The *Oyster Bay* was a former *Barnegat*-class seaplane tender, which the Navy had reclassified as a motor torpedo boat tender during her construction at Lake Washington Shipyard, Houghton, Washington. With so many new seaplane tenders coming off the ways, it was no surprise that old warriors like *Heron*—whose service had been so critical early in the war—had been relegated to fleet tug work and sundry other duties. *Orca* (AVP-49), another one of the new *Barnegat*-class ships, relieved *San Pablo* of her duties on 26 May, whereupon the latter tender left for Sydney, Australia.[17]

Photo 21-3

Seaplane tender *Orca* (AVP-49) off Houghton, Washington, on 6 February 1944.
U.S. National Archives Photograph #19-N-61647

Built along the lines of a destroyer, though slightly larger in size, *Orca* had an anti-aircraft battery and anti-submarine armament to enable her to operate in isolated forward anchorages in support of Catalina or Mariner seaplanes. In addition to serving as a floating naval air station for an embarked squadron, she could also function as a forward radio communications station, weather station, and rescue agency for the planes based aboard her.[18]

As soon as VP-52 and headquarters personnel arrived aboard her, *Orca* began servicing patrol planes. That evening, 26 May, two planes departed on night searches. One flew reconnaissance and anti-submarine sweeps northwest of Biak Island for the protection of a cruiser task force, the other a reconnaissance and shipping search to the west of the Schouten Islands. These "Black Cat" operations involved night bombing attacks primarily against Japanese merchant ships and convoys. The squadron remained based on the *Orca* until 15 July, when the tender moved forward to Woendi lagoon, Biak Island. In the interim, its planes conducted anti-shipping operations over Geelvink Bay and along the coast of the Vogelkop Peninsula to the immediate northwest with mostly negative results. A PBY Catalina did, however, manage to put two bombs into a Japanese destroyer.[19]

Map 21-4

Geelvink Bay/Vogelkop Peninsula area of Dutch New Guinea
(http://www.ibiblio.org/hyperwar/USN/Building_Bases/maps/bases2-p278.jpg)

Two PBYs took off in the early evening on 3 June 1944 to search the Noemfoor-Manokwari-Sorong area. The island of Noemfoor lay off Geelvink Bay. At 2230, Lt. (jg) Walter A. Quinlan, USNR, in plane *52-47* sighted a large enemy destroyer twenty-three miles northwest of Manokwari. The unescorted warship was headed east, making 25-30 knots. The seaplane carried out a glide bombing attack from eight hundred feet, dropping four 500-pound bombs in train. Two of the bombs hit the ship; the other two were near misses, landing fifteen feet on either side of the bow. The destroyer lost all headway and lay dead in the water, after which the plane tried to approach it to observe the damage but was fired upon by heavy anti-aircraft fire. Quinlan returned to base at 0635 on 4 June. He later received the Distinguished Flying Cross for "extraordinary achievement while participating in aerial flight as Pilot of a Patrol Plane in New Guinea area on 3 June 1944."[21]

SEAPLANE TENDERS AWARDED BATTLE STARS

Ship	Admiralty Island landings Award Period	Commanding Officer
Heron (AVP-2)	8-17 Apr 44	Lt. John M. Norcott, USNR
San Pablo (AVP-30)	24 Mar-17 Apr 44	Comdr. Stanton B. Dunlap, USN
Tangier (AV-8)	31 Mar-17 Apr 44	Comdr. Richard M. Oliver, USN

Hollandia Operation: Aitape-Humboldt Bay-Tanahmerah Bay

Orca (AVP-49)	23 May-1 Jun 44	Comdr. Morton K. Fleming Jr., USN

22

Western New Guinea Operations

On the 14th of June, 1944 Lieutenant General Walter Krueger, Commanding General of the Sixth Army and of the Alamo Task Force, called General [Robert L.] Eichelberger for a conference at 1800K [local time]. The latter was at once informed that he would proceed without delay to Biak [Island, New Guinea] with the entire Headquarters I Corps and assume command of the Hurricane Task Force [principal combat component of which was the 41st Infantry Division, less the 163rd Regimental Combat Team]. It was explained that after continuous heavy fighting coupled with extremely unfriendly terrain, intense heat and scarcity of water, the infantry units within the task force were beginning to tire to a critical degree. It was further explained that the rather confused picture of the fighting at Biak indicated that the success of future operations was threatened.... General Eichelberger was also informed that the 34th Infantry was under orders to proceed to Biak to reinforce the Hurricane Task Force.

—Excerpt from an U. S. Army 41st Infantry Division report of 1944, "History of the Biak Operation 15-27 June 1944."

As MacArthur was concluding his New Guinea campaign and Spruance continuing his advance through the Central Pacific, Task Force 73 (Aircraft, Seventh Fleet) supported their combat operations. Three to four PB4Y patrols were flown daily in June 1944 from Wakde Island, New Guinea, to the northwest, covering the approaches to Allied held territory in northern New Guinea. Similarly, four daily PB4Y patrols from Los Negros in the Admiralty Islands covered the southerly approaches to the Palau Islands and Yap Island, and five PBY patrols from Seeadler Harbor covered ocean waters to the south of the western Caroline Islands. On 17 June, when it was believed that a large Japanese task force was approaching the Mariana Islands to engage the Fifth Fleet, PB4Y patrols from Los Negros were increased in range to 1,100 or more miles, and in number to five daily. A PB4Y sighted part of the enemy task force on the 19th, which included two front-line carriers. While reporting the sighting, the aircraft fended off an attack by two enemy fighter aircraft.[1]

Other Task Force 73 activities included conducting approximately four air-sea missions daily from Hollandia and Seeadler Harbor, and engaging in "Tom Cat" (night gunfire spotting) and "Black Cat" missions in the Geelvink Bay area and to the west, averaging two flights per night. In early June, a PBY on a night reconnaissance mission made two direct bomb hits on a destroyer attempting to reinforce the Japanese on Biak Island. In other action, PB4Ys operating from Wadke Island made direct hits on two medium-sized cargo vessels. Encounters with the enemy in June were not limited to Japanese shipping; Task Force 73 planes collectively shot down sixteen enemy aircraft and damaged three others over the course of the month.[2]

The large seaplane tender *Wright* (AV-1) contributed to these efforts after arriving at Hollandia, New Guinea on 23 June 1944 from duty with the South Pacific Force. She relieved the *Orca* of her duties as commander Task Group 73.2 the following day, at which time a detachment of VP-33 planes employed for air-sea rescue missions transferred aboard her from the *Orca*. Patrol Squadron 33 operated from the *Wright* in Humboldt Bay through 16 July, when the squadron relocated to Manus, Admiralty Islands. These flights provided cover for Army Air Force strikes on Wewak, Wakde, Biak, Noemfoor, Manokwari, Babo, Jefman Island, and Sagan, New Guinea, and for Allied landings at Wakde, Biak, and Noemfoor. In order to provide its personnel a reprieve from high-tempo operations, the squadron had earlier begun use of a rotation system to provide all hands a ten-day sojourn at a Navy Rest Camp in Southport, Australia.[3]

TASK FORCE 73/FLEET AIR WING 17 ACTIVITIES

Commodore Thomas S. Combs was relieved as commander Aircraft, Seventh Fleet (CTF 73) by Rear Adm. Frank D. Wagner on 9 July 1944. In a related action, Combs had turned over command of Fleet Air Wing Seventeen to Capt. Carroll B. Jones six days earlier. Wing administration was headquartered at Naval Air Facility Samarai, New Guinea, which also served as a base for the maintenance, service, and repair of PBY-5 aircraft. Samarai (the former capital of British, New Guinea) was a lovely tropical island with rich jungle verdure and frequent rains. More importantly to the Wing, Samarai offered a seaplane operating area that was extensive and fairly well sheltered from the prevailing winds, as well as excellent maintenance facilities including a seaplane ramp and a nose hangar. The latter term referred to a rectangular structure with solid walls on three sides. A sheet of canvas covered the remaining side, allowing the noses of planes to protrude through round openings in the canvas into the structure. By this means, mechanics could work inside engine compartments while sheltered from the environment. Living quarters for squadrons based on the island consisted of ancient government and private buildings; squadron offices were located in a former chapel. The food was good, as was the water obtained from large storage tanks in which rainwater was collected.[4]

Naval Air Facilities at Manus in the Admiralties and Biak Island off northwestern New Guinea were then under construction. Two regiments of the U.S. Army 41st Infantry Division had landed on Biak. This island was garrisoned by 11,000 men under Col. Naoyuki Kuzume, on 27 May. The invasion of Biak proved to be one of the most costly battles on the north coast. Initial efforts by the 41st Infantry Division went badly and the airfields MacArthur had promised would be available to support the invasion of Saipan on 15 July remained in Japanese hands. Japan viewed Saipan in the Mariana Islands as part of its homeland, as well as a link in its inner defense perimeter. Saipan was strategically important to the Allies, because from it the new B29 Superfortress long-range bombers could strike the Japanese home islands. In an effort to bolster the situation on Biak, Lt. Gen. Robert L. Eichelberger and the 34th Infantry were dispatched there. The Americas captured Mokmer Field on 22 June, but warfare continued until the end of July.[5]

Fleet Air Wing Seventeen's seaplane tenders were engaged in July in supporting patrol squadron operations, or transporting aviation stores, fuel, and supplies. *Tangier*, the flagship of commander Aircraft, Seventh Fleet, was based at Seeadler Harbor in the Admiralty Islands. *Wright* and *Orca* tended PBY-5 aircraft at Humboldt Bay and Woendi, one of the Schouten Islands north of Geelvink Bay. The other tenders were engaged primarily in support duties. *San Pablo* spent time in Sydney for repairs and crew recreation, and transported units of the Wing. *Half Moon* hauled aviation stores between Australia and New Guinea ports and the Admiralty Islands. *Heron* carried supplies and towed fuel barges between activities, and also tended "casual PBYs" at Humboldt Bay.

Ship	Squadron	Location	Dates
Half Moon (AVP-26)		Australian, New Guinea, and Admiralty Islands ports	
Heron (AVP-2)		Humboldt Bay, New Guinea Woendi Island, New Guinea	
Orca (AVP-49)	VP-34	Woendi Island, New Guinea	18-31 July
	VP-52	Humboldt Bay, New Guinea	3-16 July
San Pablo (AVP-30)		Sydney, Australia	
Tangier (AV-8)	VP-33	Seeadler Harbor, Admiralties	19-20 July
	VP-34	Seeadler Harbor, Admiralties	3-17 July
	VP-101	Seeadler Harbor, Admiralties	
Wright (AV-1)	VP-33	Humboldt Bay, New Guinea	3-16 July
	VP-52	Woendi Island, New Guinea	17-31 July[6]

SEAPLANE SUPPORT FOR U.S. FIFTH AIR FORCE

The *Wright*'s duty at Humboldt Bay supporting VP-33 air operations, involved furnishing air-sea rescue planes upon the request and order of commander Advanced Echelon, Fifth Air Force. The Echelon (a U.S. Army Air Wing) was originally based at Moresby, Papua, under Brig. Gen. Ennis C. Whitehead, USAAF, but had advanced up New Guinea behind MacArthur's forces. The Echelon had first moved forward to Finschhafen to support the landings on Los Negros Island by the 1st Cavalry Division with fighter cover, air resupply and limited air strikes. Its next move had been to Wakde, after the 163rd Infantry Regiment, 41st Infantry Division captured the island for use as a base from which to extend the range of Allied airpower in New Guinea.[7]

The Echelon then proceeded to Biak Island to utilize its airfields in support of the planned Morotai offensive, which would take place on 15 September 1944. The Allies wanted Morotai Island as a stepping stone for the invasion of the Philippines, and as a base from which the nearby large island of Halmahera—which hosted a Japanese garrison and eight airfields—could be neutralized. After strong enemy resistance on Biak delayed the capture of its airfields beyond the date they were expected to be operational, the Echelon moved its base of operations to nearby Owi Island.[8]

On 16 July, VP-33 planes left the *Wright* and she got underway from Humboldt Bay bound for Woendi Island. She arrived at Woendi Anchorage, Schouten Islands, the following day, and began tending squadron VP-52. Her duties there remained the same, furnishing air-sea rescue planes for commander Advanced Echelon, Fifth Air Force.[9]

CAPE SANSAPOR OPERATION

In early July 1944, following a landing at Noemfoor, with the intensity of fighting at Aitape building up, and with "mopping up" operations still under way at Biak and on the New Guinea mainland opposite Wakde, Rear Adm. Daniel E. Barbey, commander 7th Amphibious Force, had received orders to prepare for a landing on 30 July near Cape Sansapor on the Vogelkop peninsula. Capture of this headland at the northwestern end of New Guinea would signal (except for mopping up pockets of enemy resistance) the end of the New Guinea part of MacArthur's campaign. With the Vogelkop in Allied hands, MacArthur would be able to proceed directly into the Philippines, via a couple of island stepping stones en route.[10]

The landing at Sansapor took place as planned at 0700 on 30 July, with no enemy opposition encountered. A few hours later, assault troops captured two adjacent small islands against token resistance, during which one man in the landing force was wounded. The next day a battalion of U.S. troops moved in small boats along the twelve miles of coast to the village of Sansapor. On sighting the approaching American forces, the small garrison of Japanese troops based there fled to the hills. For Barbey's 7th Amphibious Force, the Sansapor operation marked the end of a trek of some 1,500 miles in one year from one end of New Guinea to the other. During that time "7th Phib" transported and landed every few weeks, groups of approximately 30,000 troops in little-known jungle areas to find, engage in combat, and destroy the stubborn enemy.[11]

Two weeks after the Sansapor invasion, engineers completed construction of an airstrip on nearby Middleburg Island, then the closest Allied base to the Philippines from which fighter aircraft could operate. "Black Cat" operations from Middleburg began on 22 August, when *Orca* arrived with VP-34 embarked. After she anchored at 0753, two crews of VP-11 reported aboard for temporary duty. In early evening, two planes took off on "Black Cat" missions to Ambon and Celebes Islands in the Dutch East Indies. Both of these missions achieved negative results. Five days later, a mission north of Davao on Mindanao marked the start of armed reconnaissance anti-shipping operations in the southern Philippines.[12]

The *Half Moon* arrived at Middleburg from Woendi Island on 25 August. VP-11 moved from *Orca* to her the next day, and she began tending the squadron's PBY-5 "Black Cats." The evening of 27 August, *Half Moon*'s guns opened on a Japanese plane making a bombing run on the island's airstrip. The plane paid little attention to the anti-aircraft fire and continued its run. The following evening brought a repetition of the same action. Realizing the enemy was concentrating on the airstrip and taking into consideration the inaccuracy of the planes' aim, which could result in the *Half Moon* being bombed, Comdr. Jack I. Bandy moved his ship about three miles away from the island each night as a precaution against being hit. The raids ceased after a few days, and *Half Moon*'s routine returned to normal.[13]

"BLACK CAT" ATTACKS ON JAPANESE SHIPPING

"Black Cat" missions to locate and attack shipping in Netherlands East Indies and Southern Philippine waters by the PBY-5s aboard *Orca* and *Half Moon* were ongoing. During one such mission, a "Black Cat" entered Manado Bay at Manado, one of the Celebes Islands, at 0425 on 27 August searching for shipping reported earlier that night by another Catalina. As the plane passed along the north shore, a total of five small vessels were sighted. Selecting a small freighter-transport anchored about a quarter-mile from the beach, the pilot made a bombing run from its port quarter to its starboard bow, as described in the associated VP-34 Aircraft Action Report:

> The bombardier released two 100 pound and two 500 pound bombs at 100 feet, as the plane was in a steep right turn made to correct heading. The first 100 was short; the first 500 was a direct hit amidships; the second 500 and 100 overshot. Two parafrags fell short. Two more similar runs were made to finish the ship off, but each time the bombs hung up and dropped off the wing long after the bomb release was pressed. However, on the second of these attacks a parafrag exploded on the superstructure.[14]

Diagram 22-1

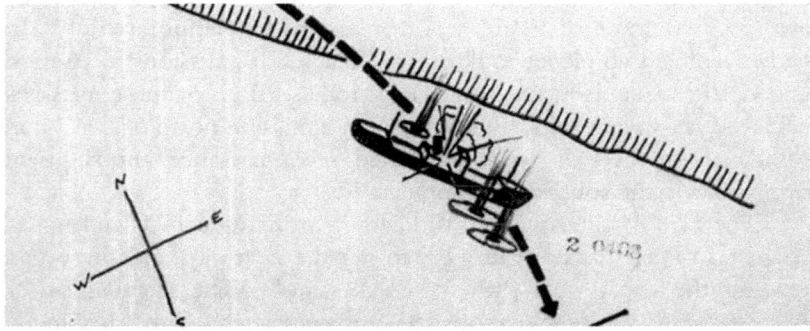

Sketch in an Aircraft Action Report depicting a "Black Cat" attack on a Japanese freighter.

The plane was lucky in that it encountered no anti-aircraft fire from either enemy ship or shore guns during three sequential runs at the target. Parafrag referred to a fragmentation bomb that utilized a parachute to slow its descent in order to allow the aircraft dropping it to escape the harmful effects while at the same time being able to fly in low and achieve maximum accuracy.¹⁵

On 1 September, VP-33 relieved 34 aboard *Orca* at Middleburg. Eleven days later *San Carlos* (AVP-51) replaced the *Orca* as tender for Squadron VP-33, upon which the latter ship proceeded to Sydney for a short dry-docking at Cockatoo Island. VP-33 flew night search and attack missions against enemy shipping in the Netherlands East Indies and Southern Philippines until 18 September, when the squadron moved forward to Morotai Island. From Morotai, VP-33 planes would continue between 19 September and 4 October to cover these areas, and would send the first Allied aircraft to Makassar Strait, Northern Borneo, Sulu Sea and Central Philippines since early 1942.¹⁶

MOROTAI ISLAND LANDINGS

> *The Fighter, Support Air and Air-Sea Rescue controls in the HQ [headquarters] staff had opportunity on D plus 1 of thoroughly testing their organization, communications and coordination during a gallant day-long battle to rescue a pilot in the water under the close fire of Japanese coast defenses at LOLOMATA which lies inside the narrows leading to KAOE BAY (HALMAHERA). The pilot was shot down by AA [anti-aircraft fire] during the early incoming CVE [aircraft carrier] fighter sweeps over HALMAHERA airfields. He landed in the water two miles off shore and drifted on his raft to shelter beside a fishing hulk within 300 yards of the beach where his position was constantly under fire from all calibers. He had been wounded in the hand and was therefore unable to paddle. Several efforts at rescue were made by a Catalina during his progress shoreward but in spite of fighters strafing the beach, [enemy] fire was too heavy and the flying boat was driven off at each attempt.*
>
> —Rear Adm. Daniel E. Barbey, USN, commander Task Force 77, describing actions taken to rescue a downed pilot, Ens. Harold A. Thompson. Eventually PT boats covered by smoke, bombing, and strafing, picked him up while under heavy fire.¹⁷

On 15 September 1944, the U.S. Army 31st Infantry Division and the 126th Infantry Regiment (32nd Division) stormed ashore on Morotai Island, unopposed. Lying three hundred miles northwest of Sansapor, Morotai was a member of the Molucca Islands. The assault troops were carried to the landing beaches by Barbey's 7th Amphibious Force. The occupation of Morotai was intended to isolate a Japanese garrison of about two divisions on nearby Halmahera Island, and provide a forward airbase and motor torpedo (PT) boat base for future operations. The immediate objective was to secure and hold the southern portion of Morotai, in order to establish air warning, aircraft, and light naval facilities. Radar was also to be sited on the N. Loloda Islands immediately northwest of the northern tip of Halmahera.[18]

Map 22-2

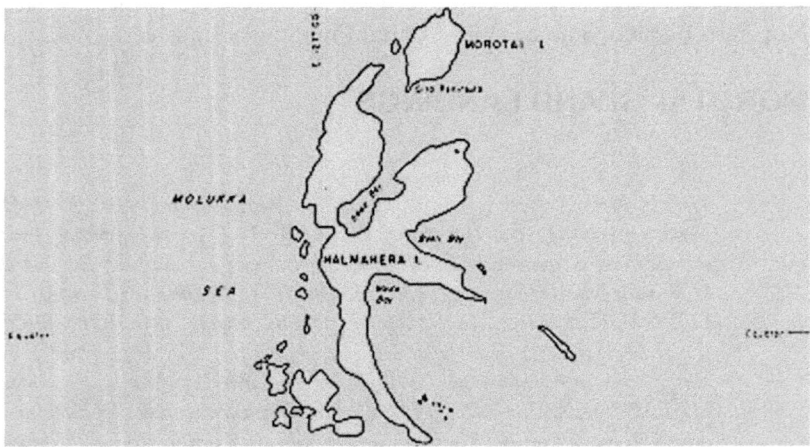

Morotai Island lay only ten miles east of the northern tip of Halmahera, on which the Japanese had a strong garrison. The Molucca (Molukka) Islands, of which they were both a part, lay 300 miles northwest of Sansapor, New Guinea.
http://www.ibiblio.org/hyperwar/USN/Building_Bases/maps/bases2-p309.jpg

Although the amphibious landing involved no enemy resistance, it was difficult due to the terrain. Coral heads and pinnacles extended seaward from the shoreline, and there was no observable approach channel, requiring the use of explosives to create one. Once ashore, vehicles bogged down in thick mud on the southern beaches of the island. The same type soil at the planned airfield site required Army engineers to find another location to construct the field. Once the airstrips were ready, B24 bombers of the U.S. Army's Thirteenth Air Force were flown in to Morotai.[19]

The seaplane tenders *Half Moon* and *San Carlos* arrived in company at Morotai on 18 September 1944. After anchoring between Soemoe Soemoe and Morotai Islands, the *Half Moon* began making preparations to tend planes of VP-11, while the *San Carlos* anchored off the southwest coast of Morotai Island. In mid-afternoon planes of VP-33 landed and moored to seaplane buoys she had laid. A third tender, the *Tangier*, arrived at Morotai three days later on 21 September. She anchored off Great Loleba Island and began tending VP-11 and 101 aircraft.[20]

Photo 22-1

Blast from explosives set by a Navy combat demolition unit to clear coral heads and open a channel at Morotai Island on 15 September 1944.
U.S. National Archives Photograph #80-G-258013

Red Alerts were common in September, occurring on almost a daily basis and sometimes more than once per day. During many of the air raids, Japanese planes were taken under fire by shore batteries only, being outside the range of the seaplane tenders. The first occasion for the *San Carlos* to fire her guns in anger occurred the night of 19 September. The tender went to general quarters at 1926 on receiving a Red Alert from the Senior Officer Present Afloat. Eight minutes later her radar detected a "bogie" approaching from abaft the ship's starboard beam, distance twenty miles. The aircraft closed rapidly, and ship's guns—#41 (twin mount 40mm), #43 (quad mount 40mm), and #21, #23, #25, and #27 (starboard 20mm battery)—opened fire as the target was illuminated by shore search lights. The single-engine, low-winged fighter, was flying at approximately 5,000 feet in altitude.[21]

Photo 22-2

Seaplane tenders *Currituck* (upper) and *Tangier* (lower) moored together at Morotai in October 1944, while supporting seaplane operations. Aircraft rescue (crash) boats are tied up alongside the *Tangier*, and OS2U floatplanes are on both ships' seaplane decks. U.S. Navy Photograph #80-G-1022364, now in the collections of the National Archives.

The plane altered course a little, continuing on a nearly parallel but slightly converging approach down the starboard side of the *San Carlos*. Her guns expended 235 rounds of 20mm and 80 rounds of 40mm, but to no avail due to evasive action by the target. At 2010, ship's radar detected a target nine miles distant. Seven minutes later, shore search lights illuminated what was believed to be the same plane flying at about 7,000 feet. The *San Carlos* took it under fire, and again failed to score any hits. A Red Alert at 2200 sent ship's company back to their battle stations, but no aircraft were detected. The tender secured from general quarters at 2310, and set readiness condition III.[22]

During an enemy air raid on 27 September, the *Tangier* opened fire at 1826 on a plane that dropped two bombs off her starboard quarter, at 2006 on one that crossed from her port bow to starboard bow, at 2009 at one passing overhead, and at 2052 at one approaching from her port bow. The fourth aircraft dropped four bombs, which fell about 750 yards off her stern. In each of these engagements, no observable hits were made on attacking planes. The *Half Moon* had a similar experience in early evening on 30 September. She expended 139 rounds of 20mm ammunition at an enemy plane, scored no hits and suffered no personnel casualties or damage to the ship.[23]

CATALINA SEAPLANE SINKS JAPANESE CRUISER

> *From the newest aviation mechanic and the squadron yeoman to the Captain [title of the squadron commander, a lieutenant commander] credit goes equally and unreservedly. Much credit must also go to the maintenance units who served our planes from the tenders, they were the ones who "sweated out" our safe returns and immediately swarmed over the planes before the props had really stopped turning over.*
>
> —War history of VP-33 describing duty of the squadron in September and October 1944, while embarked aboard the seaplane tender *San Carlos* at Morotai Island.[24]

While tenders at Morotai fended off enemy aircraft, PBY-5s operating from them continued to carry out "Black Cat" operations and conduct air-sea rescue missions. In thirty-three nights, Patrol Squadron VP-33 sank 103,500 tons of enemy shipping and damaged 53,500 tons. Of the five or six patrol plane commanders and their crews that compiled rather staggering records, Lt. (jg) William B. (Wild Bill) Sumpter, USN, and his crew stood out from all the rest, with 23,400 tons sunk and 2,800 more tons damaged. This was accomplished in part by sinking a heavy seaplane tender and two destroyer escorts in one bombing run. These ships were moored alongside each other, thus creating the opportunity, but the plane did not have to knock more than once. Of the four bombs expended, all scored direct hits, one each on the two destroyer escorts and two on the tender.[25]

On the night of 3-4 October 1944, while conducting "Black Cat" operations in the Northern Celebes area, Sumpter spotted two enemy light cruisers, one destroyer and one destroyer escort at anchor in Toli Toli Bay on the northwest coast of Celebes Island. The sighting was made possible by a full moon directly overhead. Because he believed the enemy had been alerted to his presence, Sumpter left the area, flying approximately fifty miles out to sea hoping to convince the Japanese they had not been detected. Wild Bill returned to the bay two hours later. Approaching from behind a hill at about 1,000 feet, he commenced a bombing run one-and-a-half miles away from his target, one of the light cruisers. When about a quarter mile distant from her, all four warships opened with intense light and medium anti-aircraft fire.[26]

Continuing the diving attack, during which his crew and plane were miraculously unharmed by enemy fire, Sumpter released his entire bomb load (four 500- and four 100-pound bombs) at 150 feet altitude. The run was made directly down the centerline of the cruiser, resulting in four of the bombs hitting and exploding slightly abaft amidships on her port side, and the same number hitting and exploding forward on the starboard side. Squadron war history cites the resultant battle damage:

> With a terrific detonation the entire ship burst into flame, and all hostile fire ceased for a sufficient length of time to allow the plane to pass two miles beyond the ship. Orbiting at that position, the pilot saw the cruiser burning furiously from bow to stern with intermittent internal explosions wracking the stricken vessel. Twenty minutes after the attack the flames suddenly appeared to be extinguished. Approaching to within one mile of the anchorage, and subjecting the area to a thorough search with binoculars, one cruiser, and two smaller ships could be seen. The spot where the target vessel had been moored was littered with debris and a mass of other undistinguishable flotsam. The ship was nowhere to be seen. The target vessel...was definitely sunk.[27]

For his heroic actions in attacking and sinking a Japanese cruiser, while taking fire from her and three other warships, Lt. (jg) William Benjamin Sumpter received the Navy Cross. The medal citation reads in part:

While patrolling the Toli Toli Bay, Northern Celebes, during hazardous conditions of bright moonlight and under constant and intense anti-aircraft fire, Lieutenant, Junior Grade, Sumpter made a gallant and courageous glide bombing attack on a 6,000-ton *KATORI* Class light cruiser, scoring eight bomb hits, the resulting explosion causing the warship to burn furiously for twenty minutes and then sink. His actions on this occasion showed an extraordinarily high degree of outstanding aggressiveness and heroic coolness under fire, and were in keeping with the highest traditions of the United States Naval Service.[28]

BATTLE STARS FOR SEAPLANE TENDERS

Five seaplane tenders—the *Half Moon, Orca, San Carlos, San Pablo,* and *Tangier*—received battle stars for Western New Guinea operations. The prerequisite for receiving an engagement star was participation in actual combat with the enemy, or for duty that was considered equally hazardous. The catch was, a unit could only receive one star for a single operation, no matter how many engagements. Since the *San Pablo* earned a star for Western New Guinea operations during the period 13-26 May 1944, she was not eligible for another for the below listed operations in which she otherwise met the criteria. The same was true for the *Half Moon, San Pablo,* and *Tangier*.

Western New Guinea Operations

Ship	Award Period	Commanding Officer
San Pablo (AVP-30)	13-26 May 44	Comdr. Stanton B. Dunlap

Western New Guinea Operations: Toem-Wakde-Sarmi Area Operation

Wright (AV-1)	22 Jun-16 Jul 44	Capt. James E. Baker
VP-115	1-21 Jun 44	Comdr. J. R. Compton

Western New Guinea Operations: Seventh Fleet Supporting Operations

Tangier (AV-8)	1 Aug-17 Sep 44	Capt. Richard M. Oliver
San Pablo (AVP-30)	12 Oct-7 Nov 44	Comdr. Chauncey S. Willard
	No BS	
VPB-11	7 Aug-6 Nov 44	Lt. Comdr. Thomas S. White
VP-52	26 Mar-19 Sep 44	Lt. Comdr. Harold A. Sommer
VPB-101	2 Jun-31 Aug 44	Lt. Comdr. Lauren E. Johnson
VP-115	26 May-31 Aug 44	Comdr. J. R. Compton

Western New Guinea Operations: Cape Sansapor Operation

Half Moon (AVP-26)	26-31 Aug 44	Comdr. Jack I. Bandy
Orca (AVP-49)	22-31 Aug 44	Comdr. Morton K. Fleming Jr.

Western New Guinea Operations: Morotai Landings

Tangier (AV-8)	15 Sep 44 No BS	Capt. Richard M. Oliver
Half Moon (AVP-26)	15 Sep 44 No BS	Comdr. Jack I. Bandy
San Carlos (AVP-51)	15 Sep 44	Lt. Comdr. De Long Mills
San Pablo (AVP-30)	15 Sep 44 No BS	Comdr. Chauncey S. Willard
VPB-71	15 Sep 44	Comdr. Norman C. Gillette Jr.
VPB-101	15 Sep 44	Lt. Comdr. Marvin T. Smith
VPB-104	15 Sep 44	Lt. Comdr. Whitney Wright
VPB-137	15 Sep 44	Lt. Comdr. John A. Porter
VPB-146	15 Sep 44	Lt. Comdr. Jesse P. Robinson Jr.

23

Capture and Occupation of Saipan

This force will capture, occupy and defend SAIPAN, TINIAN, and GUAM, will develop airfields in these islands and will gain control of the remaining MARIANAS, in order to operate long range aircraft against JAPAN, secure control of the Central Pacific and isolate and neutralize the central CAROLINES.

When directed by the commander Central Pacific Task Forces, [commander Forward Area, Central Pacific] move two squadrons of patrol planes with tender support to GUAM or SAIPAN and inaugurate search operations therefrom.

—Excerpts from Commander Fifth Fleet Operation Plan 10-44, with guidance for Rear Adm. John H. Hoover, regarding utilization of patrol planes and their seaplane tenders.[1]

Operation FORAGER involved a giant step forward, 1,800 miles, by U.S. forces across the Central Pacific from Majuro Atoll, where the Fifth Fleet was based, to the Mariana Islands of Saipan, Guam, and Tinian, and to the southern Palau Islands in the Carolines. By spring 1944, Allied forces had established naval bases and airfields in the Marshalls, Admiralties, and north central New Guinea, which threatened enemy positions in the Caroline Islands, eastern Netherlands East Indies and southern Philippines. Enemy lines of communication had been cut eastward of Hollandia, New Guinea and to enemy bases in the Marshalls. Lines of communication to the Carolines had been weakened and enemy air strength there was deteriorated because of attacks by land-based and carrier aircraft. As a result, the Japanese were strengthening their positions in the Mariana Islands as a barrier against continued Allied advancement in the western Pacific.[2]

The Japanese still had, in the Carolines, three airfields at Truk and one field each at Satawan, Puluwat, Woleai, Palau and Yap. On 1 April 1944, two additional fields in Palau were under construction, and two fields at Ponape were operational but normally had no aircraft. In the Mariana Islands, there were three enemy airfields on Saipan and Tinian, two on Guam, and one each on Pagan and Rota. A major part of the Japanese Fleet was based in the southern Philippines-Singapore area. Palau served as a Japanese submarine base, Truk as an advanced base, and submarines occasionally stopped at Saipan. The enemy was using subs for reconnaissance and supply in the eastern Marshalls and for attacks on Allied surface forces throughout the Central Pacific.[3]

Map 23-1

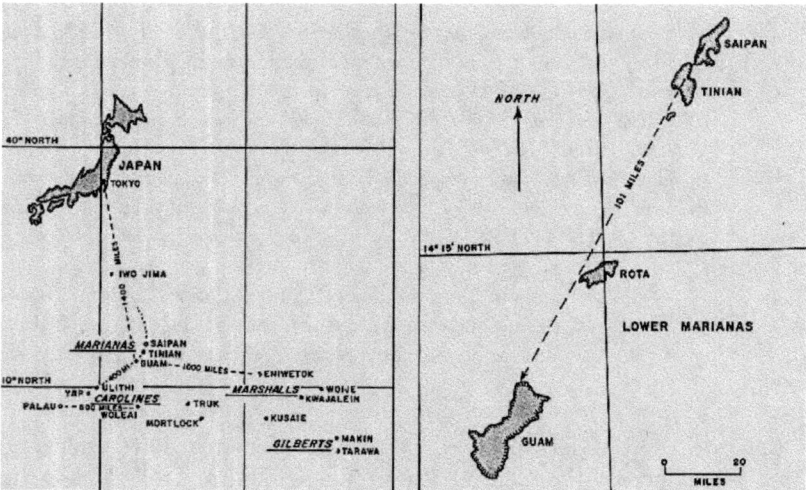

Side by side charts showing the relationships of Central Pacific Island chains to one another, and details of the Mariana Islands.
The Amphibians Came to Conquer: The Story of Admiral Richmond Kelley Turner

INVASION OF SAIPAN IN THE MARIANA ISLANDS

The purpose of Operation FORAGER was to neutralize Japanese bases in the Central Pacific, support the Allied drive to retake the Philippines, and provide bases for a strategic bombing campaign against Japan. It was launched on 15 June, when the 2nd and 4th Marine Divisions and the 27th Army Infantry Division began landing on Saipan. While these assault forces and the enemy ashore fought the Battle of Saipan between 15 June and 9 July 1944, the Japanese Combined Fleet sortied to engage the U.S. Navy Fleet supporting the landings. In the ensuing 19-21 June Battle of the Philippine Sea, the American battle force defeated the Japanese in what would be the greatest carrier battle of the war. Following the loss of two carriers, the *Shokaku* and *Taiho*, 346 planes, and an associated large numbers of pilots, Japanese naval air was unable for the duration of the war to engage Allied forces with parity. This reality resulted in Japanese leadership turning to the use of suicide planes.[4]

SEAPLANE TENDER SUPPORT

Eleven seaplane tenders supported the invasion of Saipan as part of the Northern Attack Force, Southern Attack Force, Task Group 57.1 (Aircraft Tenders), or other task groups as assignments changed. Seven of these ships earned a battle star at Saipan, and one of them, the *Williamson*, at Guam. The *Casco*, the flagship of Vice Adm. John H. Hoover, commander Forward Area, Central Pacific, arrived at Saipan on 11 August 1944. Hoover's command, previously titled Air Central Pacific, had been renamed in July.

Marinanas Operation: Capture and Occupation of Saipan

Northern Attack Force: Vice Adm. Richmond K. Turner (CTF-52)

Ship	Award Period	Commanding Officer
Ballard (AVD-10)	15 Jun-3 Jul 1944	Lt. Comdr. Gust C. Nichandros, USNR

Southern Attack Force: Rear Adm. Richard L. Conolly (CTF-53)

Williamson (AVD-2)	No battle star	Lt. Comdr. James A. Pridmore, USN

Forward Area, Central Pacific: Vice Adm. John H. Hoover (CTF-57)
Aircraft Tenders: Capt. Scott E. Peck, USN (CTG 57.1)

Casco (AVP-12)	No battle star	Comdr. Earl R. DeLong, USN
		Comdr. Reginald Rutherford, USN
Chandeleur (AV-10)	26 Jun-10 Aug 1944	Capt. Willard K. Goodney, USN
Curtiss (AV-4)	No battle star	Capt. Scott E. Peck, USN
Mackinac (AVP-13)	27 Jun-10 Aug 1944	Comdr. Gerald R. Dyson, USN
Onslow (AVP-48)	17 Jun-10 Aug 1944	Comdr. Alcen D. Schwarz, USN
Pocomoke (AV-9)	17 Jun-10 Aug 1944	Capt. Edward L. B. Weimer, USN
Yakutat (AVP-32)	27 Jul-10 Aug 1944	Comdr. George K. Fraser, USN

Arrived Later at Saipan

Kenneth Whiting (AV-14)	No battle star	Comdr. Raymond R. Lyons, USN
Shelikof (AVP-52)	4-10 Aug 1944	Comdr. Reuben E. Stanley, USN

Marianas Operation: Capture and Occupation of Guam

Williamson (AVD-2)	12 Jul-15 Aug 1944	Lt. Comdr. James A. Pridmore, USN

DUTIES OF THE DESTROYER SEAPLANE TENDERS

Two of the seaplane tenders were former destroyers. The *Ballard*, assigned to the Northern Force, arrived off Saipan with a task group that staged an amphibious demonstration (fake landing) off the northwest coast of the island while the main task group landed troops on southwest beaches. As bombardment groups covered the landings on 15 June with naval gunfire, the *Ballard* had occasion to fire at enemy aircraft. She took one plane under fire which was seen falling into a cloud, but it was undetermined whether or not it crashed into the water, or limped away in flight. *Ballard* served as part of a screen of ships around the transports, and that night retired with the task group out to sea. Upon returning to the island the following day, she anchored about four miles off shore and began setting up mooring buoys for PBM Mariner patrol planes. Six buoys were ready the next day, and six planes of VP-16 arrived in the mid-afternoon—the first Mariners to fly forward area patrols.[5]

While making preparations to get a patrol off that evening, 17 June, the *Ballard*'s crew was called to battle stations at 1845 when a Japanese plane made a run on the ship. While under fire, it dropped a bomb amidst the moored planes and one aft of *Ballard*. Neither the ship nor the seaplanes suffered any damage; the aircraft departed shot full of holes and missing a part of its wing but still aloft. On this occasion and in ensuing days, whenever the threat condition was Red, the *Ballard* slipped her anchor and got under way in order to have sea room to maneuver.[6]

WILLIAMSON REFUELS SCOUTING PLANES

The *Williamson* was assigned to the Southern Attack Force to carry out duties unique among the seaplane tenders. She had been fitted in May with a rig for the underway fueling of floatplanes from battleships and cruisers. Observation of the fall of gun rounds was critical to surface gunnery in World War II, particularly during the early years before radar was perfected, and battleships often had to fire on targets far beyond visual range. To assist them in directing gunfire, BBs carried up to four Vought OS2U Kingfisher floatplanes aboard. Cruisers, which had shorter range guns, used Curtis-Wright SOC Seagull floatplanes primarily to locate enemy surface ships and submarines, but the small biplanes could also "spot" the fall of rounds. The Seagulls had folding outer wings to enable their storage in aircraft hangars aboard the cruisers. Since battleships lacked hangars, Kingfishers had rigid non-folding wings. Accommodations were, however, not an issue. The aircraft were simply parked on launch rails when not used.[7]

Upon arriving at Saipan on 14 June the *Williamson* had reported for duty to commander Bombardment and Gunfire Support Force, Rear Adm. Walden L. Ainsworth, USN. Thereafter, she began refueling spotting planes from the battleships and cruisers of this force, positioned off the west side of Saipan. Her efforts enabled parent ships to continue pre-amphibious landing shore bombardment unencumbered by the necessity to retrieve and refuel the aircraft. The evening of 15 June, the *Williamson* departed Saipan at 1900 for Guam, arriving there the next day to service spotting planes of ships engaged in the bombardment of that island. At 1000 that morning the approach of the Japanese Fleet made consolidation of forces necessary to repel the threat. The result was the Battle of the Philippine Sea.[8]

Map 23-2

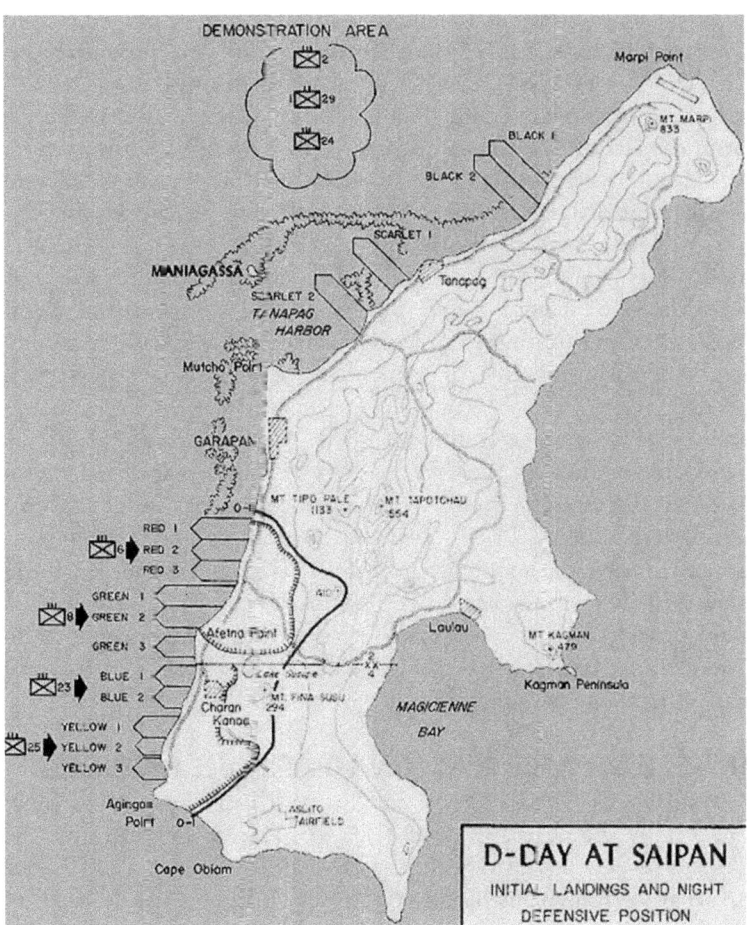

Landing beaches at Saipan Island
Breaching the Merianas: The Battle for Saipan,
Marines in World War II Commemorative Series Pamphlet

The *Williamson* returned to Saipan on 17 June and was assigned screening duties. She departed Saipan eight days later for Eniwetok. Here, the Bombardment and Gunfire Support Force was reassembled and prepared for the next operation, the invasion of Guam on 9 July. On arrival at Guam, the destroyer seaplane tender took up refueling planes of bombardment ships. After the landings were made, she functioned through 16 August as terminal vessel at Guam for mail and passenger seaplanes arriving from Eniwetok.[9]

ONSLOW AND *POCOMOKE* ARRIVE AT SAIPAN

The *Pocomoke* (AV-9) and the *Onslow* (AVP-48) were the next two seaplane tenders to arrive at Saipan. *Pokemoke*, escorted by *Onslow* and the destroyer *Downes* (DD-375) left Eniwetok a little past midnight on 16 June. The *Pocomoke* led the other ships out of the atoll using her 24-inch searchlights to pick up the channel buoys. Upon arrival in Saipan Harbor in the late afternoon on 18 June, the two tenders took up their duties, sharing the planes of VP-16 and furnishing sustenance and quarters for squadron personnel. In the following three months, the *Onslow* would also tend planes of VP-72, 202, and 216, and Rescue Squadron VH-1 in varying degrees and functions. The ship's regular duties consisted of gassing patrol planes, feeding and berthing flight personnel, guarding (monitoring) assigned radio frequencies, rearming planes, and furnishing boats for transportation of squadron personnel as needed.[10]

The *Pocomoke* took over the six PBM Mariner aircraft of VP-16 that had been tended by the *Ballard*, at which time the flight crews aboard her transferred as well. Once the balance of the squadron's aircraft, eight additional PBMs, flew in, 58 officers and 158 enlisted men spread among the tenders comprised VP-16 personnel. Among other bits of information offered the *Pocomoke* by the *Ballard* was that she could expect daily air raids at about sundown. This proved to be good advice and the evening meal aboard ship was moved forward one hour to facilitate eating without interruption.[11]

CHANDELEUR AND *MACKINAC* ARRIVE AS WELL

The *Chandeleur* (AV-10) arrived at Saipan from Eniwetok on 26 June, under escort by the destroyer *Steele* (DE-8). During her run into the island, it was necessary for her to make various courses and speed changes to avoid numerous patrol craft. Heavy firing was observed on Saipan and by various units of the U.S. Fleet offshore during the approach, but no enemy ships or planes were sighted. Upon reporting for duty, the *Chandeleur* received orders to anchor off Garapan town on Saipan's west coast and tend the fifteen PBM-3D Mariners of VP-216 engaged in long range searches. These aircraft were conducting daily search patrols covering 10-degree sectors to a distance of six hundred miles from Saipan. On 17 July, VP-202 arrived to augment the day search. Twelve of its PBM-3Ds operated from the *Chandeleur* and *Mackinac* and flew the same type sector searches. The remaining three planes were based on the *Pocomoke* as a separate detachment with VP-16, and flew one nightly anti-submarine patrol.[12]

Photo 23-1

A Martin PBM Mariner seaplane being lifted aboard the *Pocomoke* at Saipan
From History of U.S.S. *Pocomoke* (AV-9) From 28 April 1941 to 2 September 1945

The *Mackinac* (AVP-13) had arrived at Saipan a day after the *Chandeleur*. As she dropped anchor, the sight of Mt. Tapochau, 1,500 feet high, and the generally rugged terrain and neighboring island, *Tinian*, provided crewmembers a welcome change of scenery after viewing nothing but sea-level atolls for the past several months. The *Mackinac* joined the *Pocomoke, Chandeleur, Onslow,* and *Ballard* as part of Capt. Clarence O. Taff's Task Group 59.3 (Search, Reconnaissance, and Photographic). This force would further expand upon the arrival of the *Shelikop* and *Yakutat*, and again with the *Casco* and *Kenneth Whiting*, which were only present for a short time after delivering spares and personnel to the area.[13]

ENEMY ATTACKS AGAINST TENDERS/SEAPLANES

The occupation of Saipan was still in the assault phase during the latter part of June, with the front lines directly across the reef from the *Mackinac*'s anchorage in an area studded with PBMs. With binoculars it was possible from aboard ship to watch the land movements and naval bombardment. One morning the *Mackinac* came under fire from batteries in the Japanese lines. However, as offshore bombardment of the island progressed, the tenders and patrol planes were able to shift moorings closer to the reef and avail themselves of smoother water and better operating conditions. The limit on nearness was the range and location of such armament as the enemy retained. Assisted by the prevalent offshore winds, Japanese rounds and shrapnel occasionally reached the tender-seaplane area. Several patrol planes tended by the *Chandeleur* came under fire from anti-aircraft batteries during and immediately after take-off.[14]

Photo 23-2

Tenders and PBM Mariner seaplanes at Garapan Anchorage, Saipan Island
(History of U.S.S. *Pocomoke* (AV-9) From 28 April 1941 to 2 September 1945)

The shrapnel hitting the seaplane tender did no damage and that landing among the planes made small holes that were easily repaired. Shrapnel hit the *Ballard* on 21 June, while she was alongside the *Pocomoke* receiving aviation gasoline. A destroyer in the vicinity took the enemy battery under fire and silenced it. Three days later, the *Pocomoke* fired twelve rounds from her 3-inch/50s at machine gun nests on the western shore of Saipan Island. On two occasions when enemy shore batteries opened fire on the seaplane area, and she dearly wanted to respond in kind, the *Pocomoke* held her fire due to the fact that American troops were in the vicinity of the gun emplacements.[15]

The *Chandeleur*'s crew went to general quarters three times on 27 June, due to red alerts, but no planes were sighted. The following day brought more red alerts. This time enemy planes in the immediate vicinity were bombing U.S. military installations; shore battery fire brought one down. This scenario occurred again on 30 June, when shore battery fire once again brought down one fighter plane. During repeated night air raids in late June and early July (27, 28, and 30 June, and 1, 2, 5, 6, and 7 July), the *Chandeleur*'s gun did not open, because the attacking planes were not visible and, when they could be heard overhead, it was deemed advisable to hold fire and trust in chemical smoke for self-protection. The use of smoke generators to screen ships from view by aircraft was very effective in spite of bright moonlight.[16]

In addition to the threat that enemy aircraft and shore battery fire posed, the proximity of the seaplanes and their tenders to the shore made them particularly vulnerable to Japanese swimming out from the island for the purpose of damaging or destroying them. For this reason, all ships and aircraft were on strict watch against boarders.[17]

PATROL PLANE RECONNAISSANCE OPERATIONS

On 4 July, a VP-216 plane with the *Chandeleur*'s photographer aboard acquired photos of Pagan Island from an altitude of 3,500 feet. Located about two hundred miles north of Saipan, Pagan was the fourth largest island of the Northern Marianas and site of a Japanese airfield and garrison. However, no anti-aircraft fire was received and no unusual activity was observed on the island. A plane scouting Pagan later in the month received moderate damage from enemy fire on 23 July while observing the island's airstrip for unusual activity.[18]

There were several sightings in July 1944 by planes out on patrol of Japanese Betty and Emily aircraft, and of unknown submarines. On 8 July, a Mariner on regular patrol sighted and attacked an Emily. The planes flew a parallel course firing at each other for forty-five minutes.

Plane *216-6* suffered no damage, but her adversary was streaming large quantities of gasoline or oil from its port engines when it reversed course to the north. No attacks were made on submarines, because they were in a Class B area, and submerged immediately preventing identification. An area thus designated was normally reserved exclusively for submarine combat operations, but was one in which friendly aircraft could operate. Aircraft were not to attack a submarine under these circumstances unless identified as enemy beyond the possibility of doubt.[19]

TANAPAG SEAPLANE BASE PUT INTO SERVICE

> *All 4th MarDiv line Regiments reported infiltration and sniping during the night. The 24th Marines reported that at 0300 about 20 civilians approached the Regimental CP [command post] and when challenged they scattered and Jap soldiers behind them threw hand grenades. Some of the civilians, captured at daybreak, said they were forced by the soldiers to act in this way as shields. The Division continued mopping-up during the day.*
>
> —Excerpt from 4th Marine Division report on scattered enemy opposition encountered on Saipan Island on 13 July 1944; consisting mostly of sniper fire and grenade attacks.[20]

Garapan Town and Tanapag Harbor fell to American forces on 9 July, and the island was declared secure. Immediately thereafter, Comdr. Gerald R. Dyson, the *Mackinac*'s commanding officer, was assigned temporary additional duty as officer-in-charge of Seaplane Base, Tanapag, tasked with placing the ramp and apron in commission. The ship's officers and crew "turned to" on the job and the following day, VP-216 beached its first Mariner on the ramp of the captured Japanese seaplane base. This work was not without risk; each day individual or small groups of Japanese were engaged, killed or captured." VP-216 combat air crews assigned to guard the aircraft at the base encountered several snipers on 13 and 14 July and were instrumental in killing several and assisting in the capture of others. On the 18th, the crews encountered several enemy soldiers armed only with grenades. In the fight that followed, three soldiers were killed; none of the airmen were hurt. The previous day, four members of the Marine Corps Signal Battalion had killed two Japanese armed with grenades one-quarter mile south of the seaplane base.[21]

Enemy threats against the seaplane base persisted for some time. On the night of 29 July, a landing force comprised of four officers and thirty-seven men left the *Yakutat* to provide assistance to the base. This action followed receipt of a report from the base that the enemy had broken through U.S. Army lines and it was in immediate danger of attack. The landing force returned aboard ship a short time later, having determined that no action by its members was necessary, since the Army and Marines were able to handle the situation.[22]

The *Yakutat* had arrived at Saipan twelve days earlier on 17 July, with two officers and forty-eight men of Patrol Service Unit 2-6 embarked, and 5-inch star shell ammunition for the Southern Attack Force. During the ship's approach to the island, many dead Japanese were observed in the sea and the bombardment of Tinian was plainly visible. Upon arrival, Comdr. George K. Fraser reported for duty to Capt. Clarence O. Taff, commander Group 1, Fleet Air Wing Two. The *Yakutat* then immediately began servicing planes, assisting with setting up the seaplane base, and providing sustenance and quarters for the patrol service unit. Fraser relieved the commanding officer of the *Mackinac* as officer-in-charge Seaplane Base, Tanapag Harbor, two days later. Once the area around the base was judged sufficiently safe, an officers' club was established on the beach in the vicinity of the ramp. This "watering hole" was initially sponsored by the seaplane tenders and was well patronized.[23]

Shortly thereafter, two additional tenders arrived at Saipan. The *Shelikof* (AVP-52) entered Saipan Harbor on 4 August with 1,900 bags of U.S. mail, special ordnance material, a load of aviation gasoline, and passengers brought from Eniwetok. The following day, she shifted to Tanapag Harbor in preparation to commence squadron operations. On 6 August, VP-18 reported aboard. The *Curtiss* (AV-4) arrived on 12 August, and anchored in Tanapag Harbor to serve as the flagship of Vice Admiral Hoover—relieving the *Casco* of this duty.[24]

24

South Palau Islands

Peleliu is a horrible place. The heat is stifling and rain falls intermittently—the muggy rain that brings no relief, only greater misery. The coral rocks soak up the heat during the day and it is only slightly cooler at night. Marines are in the finest possible physical condition, but they wilted on Peleliu. By the fourth day there were as many casualties from heat prostration as from wounds. . . .

Peleliu is incomparably worse than Guam in its bloodiness, terror, climate and the incomprehensible tenacity of the Japs. For sheer brutality and fatigue, I think it surpasses anything yet seen in the Pacific, certainly from the standpoint of numbers of troops involved and the time taken to make the island secure.

—News correspondent Robert Martin describing Peleliu[1]

Before the Allies began the planned invasion of the Philippines, a few islands were considered necessary as advanced bases. The capture of Morotai was previously discussed. Two other important ones were Peleliu and Ulithi. Peleliu, the southernmost island in the Palau group, would serve as a staging point for aircraft and ships to Leyte; Ulithi Atoll was desired for its big deep lagoon, the perfect site for a fleet base. The 323rd regimental combat team of the U.S. 81st Infantry Division took Ulithi Atoll, midway between Peleliu and the Marianas, without opposition on 23 September.

Capturing Peleliu proved to be very costly. Bombardment of the island began on 12 September 1944. The 1st Marine Division landed three days later to find the Japanese defense force of approximately 11,000 under Col. Kunio Nakagawa had no intention of easily giving up the island. When the combat finally ended on 27 November, Marine casualties numbered 6,526 (including Navy corpsmen and doctors) of whom 1,252 were killed. The 81st Division suffered 3,089 casualties, 404 killed in action. Japanese casualties were estimated to be 10,900 with all but a tiny fraction of the defenders killed.[2]

Of the six seaplane tenders that would receive battle stars for the invasion of the Palau islands, only one, the *Ballard* (AVD-10), was directly involved with the D-day landings of Operation STALEMATE

II, code word for the Battle of Peleliu. The seaplane tender spent the first two days in September alongside the repair ship *Prometheus* (AR-3) at Gavutu Harbor, Florida Island, in the Solomons. The *Ballard* loaded bombs on 3 September after being fitted with streaming-cruiser-type recovery nets for use in refueling scout observation planes during the invasion of Peleliu. She conducted plane recovery exercises the following day, and on the 6th sailed with a bombardment group en route to Peleliu.[3]

Map 24-1

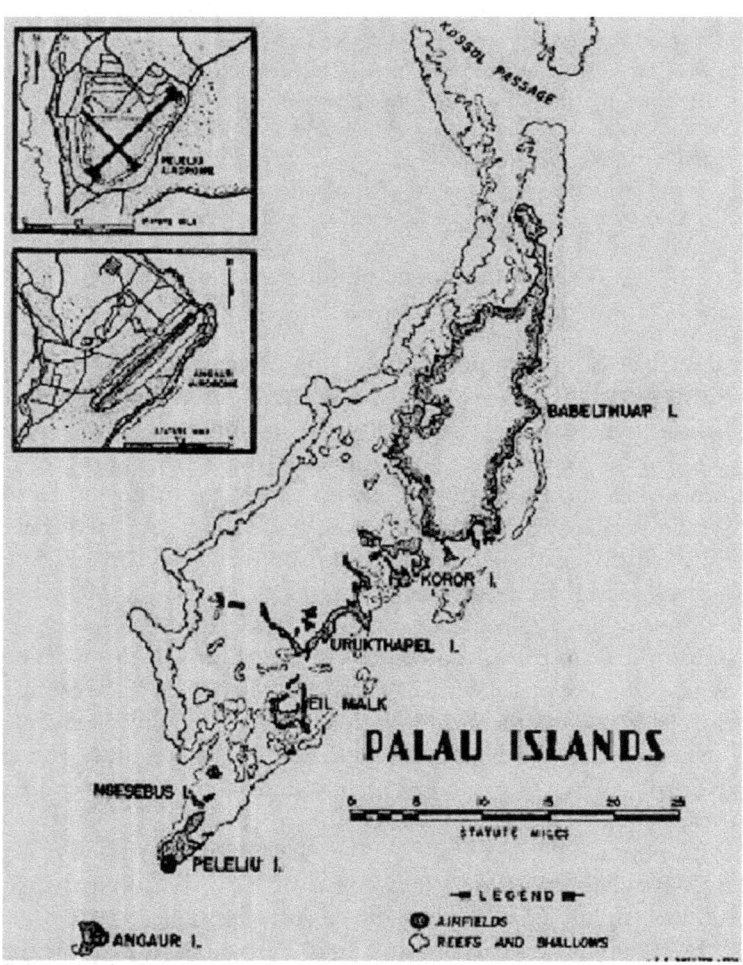

Palau Islands, Western Caroline Islands
The Army Air Forces in World War II, Vol. V, The Pacific: Matterhorn to Nagasaki June 1944 to August 1945

The *Ballard* arrived off Peleliu the morning of 12 September and witnessed "heavy" ships begin bombardment of the island at 0540, before she took up patrol and screening duties. Early the following afternoon, she streamed her "CAST" recovery net and refueled plane No. 2 from the cruiser *Honolulu* (CL-48). A day later she fueled plane No. 1 from the *Honolulu*, before making the *Pennsylvania*'s (BB-38) side to receive fuel while also discharging aviation gasoline to the battleship for her planes. During this period, the fleet would retire out to sea each night, and return off Peleliu the following morning. When not discharging aviation fuel to aircraft or ships, the *Ballard* screened ships or carried out anti-submarine patrols. During the afternoon of 19 September, she delivered AvGas to the cruiser *Denver* (CL-48).[4]

Following a sighting of floating mines along the beach on 24 September, the *Ballard* was sent to deal with them. Once in position, the word was passed for machine guns to open fire. So much racket was created the cease fire bell could not be heard. The ship's whistle was blown and one by one, the guns ceased fire. The two mines thus sunk off Angaur Island provided the crew some relief from the monotony of patrol operations. In September and October, the ship alternately performed anti-submarine screening duties and made short trips to Kossol Passage to fuel Navy ships or aircraft before returning south to support the capture of Peleliu and Angaur Islands.[5]

TENDERS AND SEAPLANES AT KOSSOL PASSAGE

The other five seaplane tenders operated from anchorage in Kossol Passage as part of Task Group 59.3 under Commodore Dixwell Ketcham, USN. Ketcham had relieved Capt. Clarence O. Taff as task group commander on 10 September. Two days later, the *Chandeleur* (AV-10) with Ketcham and staff of Fleet Air Wing One aboard had left Saipan in convoy with the *Pocomoke* (AV-9) screened by *Mackinac* (AVP-13), *Onslow* (AVP-48), and *Yakutat* (AVP-32) to take part in the invasion of Peleliu. Peleliu lay at the southern end of the Palau Group, the westernmost of the Caroline Islands. Located to the east within the Carolines was the powerful Japanese naval base at Truk. Similar to the Allied strategy employed to bypass Rabaul, the plan was to isolate and neutralize Truk by air and sea attack, in lieu of a direct assault. Likewise, rather than trying to seize the numerous enemy bases in the Carolines or bypass selected ones in the drive westward toward Truk, American forces would attack only the Palau Islands.[6]

The group of ships remained at sea until 16 September and then proceeded to the seaplane area in Kossol Passage, which lay north of Babelthuap, the largest island in the Palau group. Minesweepers of

Comdr. Wayne R. Loud's Task Group 32.9 were in the process of sweeping the anchorage. Moored mines were continually being cut and exploded by gunfire as they floated to the surface inside the large reef-enclosed area, and the tenders were happy to "drop anchor" without mishap with mines or the numerous uncharted coral heads or shoals present. The first few days were devoted primarily to marking navigation obstructions and making the seadrome as safe an operating area as possible for planes. The area was ringed by underwater reefs of which only a few were visible at low tide.[7]

A sharp lookout was also kept for any floating mines. After two were sighted in the vicinity of the *Mackinac*, a detail headed by the ship's gunnery officer disposed of them very neatly by securing a line to the mines and towing them to a safe area where they were exploded by automatic rifle fire. The minesweepers completed their dangerous work on 23 September, having swept 323 mines in Kossol Passage.[8]

On 17 September, forty-two PBM-3D Mariner aircraft of Patrol Bombing Squadrons VPB-16, 202, and 216, and a detachment of VH-1 arrived from Saipan. The *Pocomoke* tended VPB-16 planes, berthed its 61 officers and 165 men, and served as Fleet Post Office and Air Transportation Center for the area. Eight crews of VPB-202 based aboard the *Mackinac*, and continued to operate from her until relieved by VPB-21 in October. The officers and men of eight crews of VPB-216 went aboard the *Yakutat*, and VH-1 the *Onslow*. These squadrons conducted long-range searches, anti-submarine patrols and rescue flights, respectively. The crews of planes making daily searches were able to glimpse the Philippine coast.[9]

Air raids in the Kossol Passage area were rare, and no damage or casualties to tenders resulted from them. The *Mackinac*'s crew was called to battle stations on 26 September because of several raiders in the areas, but no bombs were dropped. On 3 October, the *Yakutat* was designated secondary fighter director unit, in the event she might be needed to vector (provide intercepts for) friendly fighters to engage enemy aircraft. Air alerts occurred on six occasions, and raiders remained in the area for varying lengths of time. Though they dropped bombs in the lagoon, none were observed by the *Yakutat*.[10]

TASK GROUP REORGANIZATION

Following the transfer on 28 September of the VH-1 detachment aboard *Onslow* to the *Chandeleur* and receipt from the *Mackinac*, the officers and crew of one aircraft of VPB-202, *Onslow* left for Ulithi to establish seaplane operations there. Upon her arrival on the 29th, the *Onslow* began tending transient planes of various squadrons. A few days later, Commodore Dixwell Ketcham's Task Group 59.3 was redesignated Task Group 30.5, to reflect its new assignment to Admiral Halsey's Third Fleet.

Task Group 30.5 (Search and Reconnaissance)

Task Unit	Title
30.5.1	Seaplane Squadrons and Tenders, Kossol Passage
30.5.2	Seaplane Squadrons and Tenders, Saipan
30.5.3	Land plane search group, Tinian
30.5.4	Seaplane and Tender Detachment, Ulithi[11]

Rescue Squadron VH-1 departed the *Chandeleur* on 6 October. Three of its planes and seven crews relocated to Saipan for basing aboard the *Kenneth Whiting*. The remaining two planes and two crews remained aboard the *Pocomoke* until 30 October when, with their duty completed, they left the ship. The activities of these two PBM planes in October had included five missions escorting B24 bombers to the Bonin Islands, four escorting B24s and P47s to the Kazen Islands, and two escorting B29s to Truk. The Bonin (Ogasawara) Islands, which included Iwo Jima, lay only 540 nautical miles south of Tokyo, and the Kazens were south of the Bonins.[12]

On 13 October, Capt. Willard K. Goodney in *Chandeleur* assumed duties of commander Task Unit 30.5.1 for seaplane operations in Kossol Passage. Commodore Ketchum was then making preparations to move Fleet Air Wing One administration and operations staff to Ulithi. Ketchum transferred to the *Hamlin* (AV-15) at Ulithi the next day, and on 15 October the personnel of Wing One departed the *Chandeleur*. The *Yakutat* stood out of Kossol Passage on 9 November to also proceed to Ulithi Atoll.[13]

SEAPLANES DAMAGED BY PASSING TYPHOON

The majority of the planes were not able to evacuate in time, and the night they rode out the height of the storm was a hectic one. Three planes were lost and one officer was lost as his plane was being abandoned.

—Excerpt from ship's history of the *Mackinac* (AVP-13), describing storm conditions at Kossol Passage, Palau, on 7 November 1944. Lt. Philip G. Unhock, USNR, was lost during a rescue attempt by a PT boat to save the crew of the sinking PBM-3D Mariner aircraft.[14]

Operations at Kossol Passage proved costly in numbers of planes lost to adverse operating conditions or storm damage. The anchorage was not ideal for seaplane operations; being exposed to wind and wave it picked up some really rough water at times. On 7 November, tenders and planes caught a good portion of a typhoon with winds over 75 knots at the peak. The ships had received warning the preceding day of a storm forming 200 miles to the northeast of the Palau Islands.[15]

The *Mackinac* managed to ride out the storm with 90 fathoms of chain out to her riding anchor and 15 fathoms to her second anchor under foot (beneath the ship). However, her 40-foot motor launch broke loose from its moor and disappeared in the first night of the storm. It was later recovered from a reef where it had been stranded. The worst of the storm had passed by midnight of the first day. The wind and seas abated from then on sufficiently for all remaining planes to ride out the storm at their buoys.[16]

The *Pocomoke* also lost her No. 4 motor whaleboat. In preparation for anticipated high winds and storm surge, her engineers had lit fires under No. 2 boiler at 0725 that morning to build up steam. Beginning in late afternoon, a number of additional steps were taken. At 1635, her whaleboat was returned by the crew of the infantry landing craft *LCI-397*. A few minutes later, gangways were "triced up" (hauled up and secured), all boats lifted out of the water, and booms swung in, in preparation for forecast winds of 50-60 knots. With the captain at the conn, engines were turned over at various revolutions to relieve strain on the anchor chains. At 2231, the main engines were stopped but remained in standby condition.[17]

SEAPLANE TENDER/SQUADRON BATTLE STARS

Western Caroline Islands:
Capture and Occupation of South Palau Islands

Ship	Award Period	Commanding Officer
Ballard (AVD-10)	6 Sep-14 Oct 1944	Lt. Comdr. Gust C. Nichandros, USNR
Chandeleur (AV-10)	6 Sep-14 Oct 1944	Capt. Willard K. Goodney, USN
Mackinac (AVP-13)	6 Sep-14 Oct 1944	Comdr. Gerald R. Dyson, USN
Onslow (AVP-48)	6 Sep-14 Oct 1944	Comdr. Alden D. Schwarz, USN
Pocomoke (AV-9)	6 Sep-14 Oct 1944	Capt. Edward L. B. Weimer, USN
Yakutat (AVP-32)	6 Sep-14 Oct 1944	Comdr. George K. Fraser, USN
VPB-216	17 Sep-14 Oct 1944	Comdr. Harry E. Cook Jr.

25

Liberation of the Philippines

Should we lose in the Philippines operations, even though the fleet should be left, the shipping lane to the south would be completely cut off so that the fleet, if it should come back to Japanese waters, could not obtain its fuel supply. If it should remain in southern waters, it could not receive supplies of ammunition and arms. There would be no sense in saving the fleet at the expense of the loss of the Philippines.

—Adm. Soemu Toyoda, Imperial Japanese Navy, discussing Vice Adm. Takeo Kurita's mission to destroy completely the transports in Leyte Bay following the American invasion of the Philippines, and why there were no restrictions as to the damage that his force might take.[1]

The U.S. Sixth Army went ashore at Leyte Island on 20 October, 1944, two months and two years after the first landings were conducted in the Guadalcanal area of the Solomon Islands. During the intervening period, Halsey's South Pacific Forces had occupied or neutralized the remainder of the Solomon Islands, and MacArthur's Southwest Pacific Forces had forged a route through the New Guinea/New Britain area. Nimitz's Central Pacific Forces had taken the Gilberts, the Marshalls, the Marianas, and the Southern Palau Islands. Amphibious landings in the Marianas (Saipan, Tinian, and Guam) in June and July breached Japan's strategic inner defense ring and gave the Americans a base from which B29 bombers could attack the Japanese home islands. Following the invasion of Saipan, the Japanese counterattacked in the Battle of the Philippine Sea, fought between the First Mobile Fleet and American Fifth Fleet from 19 to 21 June. In what one American aviator termed "The Great Marianas Turkey Shoot," the U.S. Navy destroyed three enemy aircraft carriers—the *Hijo*, *Shokaku*, and *Taiho*—some 480 planes, and nearly as many aviators. The devastating loss left the Japanese with virtually no carrier-based aircraft or experienced pilots for the forthcoming Battle of Leyte Gulf.[2]

The naval force (comprised of units of the American Third and Seventh Fleets) assembled for the invasion of Leyte was not quite as large as the one that had taken part in June in the invasion of Normandy, but it had more striking power. Embarked aboard the assault vessels were the Sixth Army's Tenth and Fourteenth Corps. The weather at the entrance to Leyte Gulf at daybreak on 20 October was cloudy with altostratus and partial swelling cumulus, a visibility to seaward of twelve miles, and light winds from the southeast. Planners had been concerned that a typhoon might pass through the area and cause retirement or diversion of the forces en route from New Guinea. However, the conditions on "A-Day" (Assault Day) were perfect as described by commander, Third Amphibious Force:

> The assault proceeded on schedule following the preliminary bombardment by ships' gunfire and aircraft, a slight onshore tendency of the almost imperceptible wind conveniently drifting the smoke and dust of the bombardment off the beaches and into the interior. The airborne beach observer had made his required report earlier, but the report was unnecessary in this case due to the almost complete absence of surf.[3]

The landings at Tacloban, located in northeast Leyte on an inlet of the Leyte Gulf, and at Dulag, twenty-five miles to the southward, were made against little opposition. Naval historian Samuel Eliot Morison noted about the operation: "The Leyte landings were easy, compared with most amphibious operations in World War II—perfect weather, no surf, no mines or underwater obstacles, slight enemy resistance, mostly mortar fire." With this beginning, the liberation of the Philippines was off to a good start.[4]

MACARTHUR'S RETURN TO THE PHILIPPINES

The light cruiser *Nashville* (CL-43)—MacArthur's flagship—arrived at 1050 that morning with the Supreme Commander Southwest Pacific Area embarked. Moments after he waded ashore that afternoon and thus fulfilled his pledge to return to the Philippines, the general spoke with great emotion as he delivered a rousing speech to the Filipino people—transmitted in a radio address from the beachhead—enjoining them to drive the Japanese invaders from the islands:

TO THE PEOPLE OF THE PHILIPPINES:

I have returned. By the grace of Almighty God our forces stand again on Philippine soil—soil consecrated in the blood of our two peoples. We have come, dedicated and committed, to the task of destroying every vestige of enemy control over your daily lives, and of restoring, upon a foundation of indestructible strength, the liberties of your people.

At my side is your President, Sergio Osmena, worthy successor of that great patriot, Manuel Quezon, with members of his cabinet. The seat of your government is now therefore firmly reestablished on Philippine soil. The hour of your redemption is here. Your patriots have demonstrated an unswerving and resolute devotion to the principles of freedom that challenges the best that is written on the pages of human history. I now call upon your supreme effort that the enemy may know from the temper of an aroused and outraged people within that he has a force there to contend with no less violent than is the force committed from without.

Rally to me. Let the indomitable spirit of Bataan and Corregidor lead on. As the lines of battle roll forward to bring you within the zone of operations, rise and strike. Strike at every favorable opportunity. For your homes and hearths, strike! For future generations of your sons and daughters, strike! In the name of your sacred dead, strike! Let no heart be faint. Let every arm be steeled. The guidance of divine God points the way. Follow in His Name to the Holy Grail of righteous victory![5]

The capture of Leyte was part of a strategy to isolate Japan from the countries it had occupied in Southeast Asia, and in particular, to deprive its forces and industries of vital oil supplies. Leyte Gulf was about forty miles wide east and west, and about fifty miles long, and the southern part of the gulf was, in effect, a part of the Surigao Strait which formed a wide waterway between the Pacific and the Sulu Sea. Allied control of the Leyte Gulf area and San Bernardino Strait only 100 miles to the north would deny the Japanese all water routes between the Pacific and the South China Sea except via the northern end of Luzon Island (the economic and political center of the Philippines, being home to the country's capital city, Manila) or the southern end of Mindoro Island.[6]

The lull following the lightly opposed Leyte landings was short-lived. After receiving word on 17 October of the presence of the advance American minesweeping and hydrographic group in the entrances to the Leyte Gulf, Adm. Soemu Toyoda, the commander-in-chief of the Combined Fleet issued the alert for SHO-1. This plan for a naval battle with the American Fleet off Leyte was a part of the larger Operation SHO-GO, a defense plan against American advances toward Japan. Thus, as amphibious ships were unloading on assault beaches and the Sixth Army was extending the beachhead, Japanese naval forces were en route to Leyte Gulf to give battle.[7]

BATTLE OF SURIGAO STRAIT

> *As the* Half Moon *proceeded very slowly up the coast of Leyte she had the privilege of being an eyewitness to a major Naval Battle, the Battle of Surigao Straits. Salvos from the big guns of both sides could be plainly seen. Through binoculars the burst of individual shells could be distinguished. Soon the fire power of the Japanese unit was observed to decrease and a very hasty retreat was made with the American forces in close pursuit.*
>
> —USS *Half Moon* (AVP-26) war diary entry for 24 October 1945, describing the seaplane tender's close proximity to Japanese and American naval surface forces engaged in combat.

The *Half Moon* (AVP-26) anchored in San Pedro Bay at noon on 21 October, having made an uneventful transit from Morotai in company with three motor torpedo boat tenders—the *Oyster Bay* (AGP-6), *Wachapreague* (AGP-8), and *Willoughby* (AGP-9)—forty-five PT boats, one Army QS boat and one Naval aviation rescue boat. Following receipt of orders, she proceeded down the eastern coast of Leyte Island the following morning to search for a seaplane mooring area. At Himunangen Bay, later nicknamed "Strafing Hollow," she found a spot which seemed to be ideal, anchored, and laid buoys to receive five planes of VPB-33.[8]

In early morning on 23 October, two Vals spotted the tender and immediately turned for an attack. Fortunately, four F6F Hellcat fighters arrived on the scene and drove the enemy off. The squadron's planes arrived that same day. The following afternoon, two Sallys came in to make a surprise low-altitude attack out of the sun. One made a run on the *Half Moon*, strafing on the approach and dropped two bombs, which failed to explode; one skipped over the fantail and the other fell thirty feet off the starboard side of the ship. The other plane made an attack on the moored seaplanes, dropping one bomb which did explode, but caused no damage. As both planes began a second run, heavy fire from the ship caused them to veer off. Hits were made on one, and then two U.S. fighters appeared and the planes retired. The only casualty suffered during the attack was one man slightly wounded from the strafing.[9]

Liberation of the Philippines   333

The *San Carlos* (AVP-51) was also present at Himunangen Bay, having arrived there the previous day to tend planes of VPB-34. At 0620, she opened fire on a "Jake" approaching from the southwest to prevent an attack on moored PBYs. The Jake turned and disappeared to the north over Leyte Island. At 0821 the *San Carlos* got underway bound for San Pedro Bay in Leyte Gulf. She anchored in the bay off the southwest coast of Samar Island that evening.[10]

Meanwhile that same evening at Himunangen Bay, 24 October, the commanding officer of the *Half Moon* received information of an impending surface battle which was to take place in Surigao Straits. Due to impending danger, Comdr. Jack I. Bandy decided to relocate the *Half Moon* to a spot between Cabugan Grande and Leyte Islands in an attempt to use land-masking to prevent detection. Following this movement, ship's surface radar detected approaching forces from both sides. Bandt requested to leave the area, permission was granted, and the *Half Moon* cautiously slipped from behind Cabugan Grande Island and proceeded up the coast of Leyte. She anchored for the night a mile south of Taytay Point, but at dawn returned to Hinunangan Bay. About 0800, three Vals appeared and came in strafing to attack the seaplane tender. All guns opened fire on the low flying aircraft. Two bombs were dropped, exploding about fifty yards away, but did no damage.[11]

After the three attacks against his ship, Bandy believed that the Japanese were using the area as a rendezvous point for their raids into Leyte Gulf, and upon spotting a U.S. Navy ship in the bay they would attack. Taking this into account, he decided to return to San Pedro Bay. En route there, the *Half Moon* came under attack four times on 26 October, and remained under way that night as a precautionary measure. She anchored in San Pedro Bay off the coast of Samar early the next morning. That evening, ten "Judys" appeared overhead. Three broke off and came in on the *Half Moon*. Her guns opened and after what seemed to be an interminable period of firing, one plane crashed fifty feet off the ship's port quarter and the others made a hurried retreat.[12]

The *San Carlos* had come under attack off Samar practically the entire day on the 26th. In order to avoid describing six relatively similar attacks, summary information is tabulated below. In each of the attacks, her gunners took the attacking aircraft under fire. Hits were made on planes in two of the attacks, gunfire twice forced the planes to abandon their attacks, and Navy F6F fighters chased off the enemy during the other two attacks. The Japanese designations of aircraft identified by their Allied names in this chapter and elsewhere in the book may be found in Appendix J. For example, the Allied code name Kate referred to a Nakajima B5N Type 97 Navy Carrier Attack Bomber.

Time	Enemy Aircraft	Fired upon by the Ship	Ship Strafed or Bombed	Disposition
0851	1 Oscar	yes	no	Chased off by F6Fs
1013	1 Kate	yes	no	Abandoned attack
1312	3 Jills	yes	bombed	Chased off by F6Fs
1823	1 Val	yes	no	Abandoned attack
1830	1 Hamp	yes	bombed	Hits made on plane
2015	1 Betty	yes	no	Hit made on plane[13]

The numbers and diversity of enemy aircraft attacking scores of Navy and merchants ships, including the *Half Moon* and *San Carlos*, indicated Japan's deep commitment to its defense of the Philippines. Moreover, among the many different variants of Navy carrier-based and Army and Navy land-based fighters and bombers carrying out such attacks, were Kamikazes—planes piloted by zealots willing to sacrifice their lives by crash diving into Allied ships.

Late that day, 26 October, while maneuvering as evasive action against a possible seventh attack, the *San Carlos* grounded on sand and mud. She remained thus until the following afternoon, when with the fleet tug *Chowanoc* (ATF-100) pulling astern and her engines back full, the tender came free of the shoal. No damage was sustained. That evening as the *San Carlos* proceeded with the *Half Moon* following her, she opened fire at a "Tony" that was diving at the latter ship. Hit, it crashed into the water.[14]

ARMY AND NAVY AIR-SEA RESCUE OPERATIONS

In addition to the *Half Moon* and *San Carlos*, four other tenders—*Currituck*, *Heron*, *Orca*, and *San Pablo*—supported operations in the Leyte Gulf that autumn. The *Orca* (AVP-49) arrived in San Pedro Bay the morning of 4 November and anchored off Jinamoc Island, before receiving aboard VPB-34 and two Army Air-Sea Rescue crews later that day. VPB-34 remained only three days before being transferred on 7 November to the *Tangier* at Morotai Island for temporary duty. A replacement squadron, VPB-11, reported aboard *Orca* two days later.[15]

The *Orca* moved to a new anchorage in San Juanico Strait on 12 November. That afternoon an Army rescue plane operating from her departed at 1230 on a mission. Escorted by P38 fighter cover, it arrived over Ponson Island, which lay to the east of Cebu and west of Leyte Island, an hour later. After making a water landing as a prelude to rescuing American servicemen sighted in the native village of Pilar, a native boat came alongside the plane to report that the men could not be brought out, as there were three boats with Japanese in them cruising around the bay. Undeterred, the pilot identified which boats contained the enemy and then taxied over to them and strafed them with .50-caliber machinegun fire. The fighter cover took over from there and eliminated the threat, and the plane was able to rescue five men. The Army plane then proceeded to Baybay on the west coast of Leyte, picked up four more men, and returned to the *Orca* in the early evening. As air-sea rescue operations from the seaplane tender continued, VPB-11 transferred to U.S. Seaplane Base, Mios Woendi on 22 November, and VPB-34 returned aboard the *Orca* for duty.[16]

COOPER SURVIVORS RESCUED BY PBY-5 PLANES

> *The actual rescue of the* COOPER*'s survivors was accomplished in two days. All but Lieutenant Orr and his party were picked up on the first day by five or six PBY trips. A world's record for weight carrying was established in the first two. One plane with Lieutenant Joe Ball had a total of 64 on board, which included 56 survivors. Another with Lieutenant (jg) Essary as pilot had 45 survivors. No one knows how they all got in the plane. However, the plane was approximately 3,000 pounds heavier than the designers said that it would fly.*
>
> —Commander Mell A. Peterson, commanding officer of the USS *Cooper* (DD-695), sunk by a Japanese torpedo in Ormoc Bay, Philippine Islands, the night of 3 December 1944.[17]

Around midnight on the 2nd, the destroyers *Cooper*, *Allen M. Sumner* (DD-692) and *Moale* (DD-693) were patrolling Ormoc Bay on the west side of Leyte Island, under orders to seek out and destroy Japanese transports attempting to reinforce Leyte through the port of Ormoc. Shortly before midnight a group of three enemy planes using land background to mask its approach attacked the three ships of Destroyer Division 120. Two of attackers were shot down.[18]

Two minutes into the new day on 3 December, the *Cooper* opened fire at a range of 12,000 yards on an enemy destroyer with troops aboard, located close to the beach in Ormoc Bay. Shelled by the *Sumner* as well, it caught fire and began to sink. The *Cooper*'s 5-inch battery then shifted to a second target, a ship the size of a destroyer escort, five miles distant in the same vicinity. The first salvo hit, and fire was continued until an immediate halt was necessary to avoid hitting the *Moale*, which had crossed her line of fire while taking a ship under fire northward of *Cooper*'s target. At least one of these targets was sunk. At 0017, a torpedo struck the *Cooper* on her starboard side and blew a large hole in her hull. The destroyer rolled 45-degrees to starboard, continued over onto her side, and broke in two and sank in less than thirty seconds.[19]

Photo 25-1

Destroyer USS *Cooper* (DD-695) under way in New York Harbor on 25 March 1944, two days before commissioning.
Courtesy of Destroyer History Foundation and NavSource

A majority of the survivors spent the bulk of the next fifteen hours in the water. Only one-quarter to one-third could be on a raft, in a floater net or in a rubber boat at a time. Some of the survivors made it to shore on northwest Leyte and on Ponson Island and were aided by Philippine guerillas. Comdr. Mell A. Peterson, the destroyer's commanding officer, expressed in an interview his gratitude for the assistance provided:

> The Philippine guerillas apparently have an organization to take individuals in the water or groups of survivors to the PBYs so that they do not have to taxi all over the area and pick up small groups.... On northwest Leyte, in the mountains, Lieutenant Orr of the *Cooper* and 22 men were kept the night of December 3rd.

These men were outfitted from a small store of Japanese clothing which somehow had been collected by the natives.... The performance of the Philippine guerillas was outstanding and they cared for my people in a very fine fashion.[20]

On 3 December, all the survivors except for Lt. (jg) John I. Orr Jr. and his party were picked up over the course of five or six PBY trips. The two seaplanes rescuing the first two groups set a record for weight taken aloft by Catalinas. An account by the *Orca*'s navigation officer, indicated one of the fifty-seven survivors picked up by the first PBY proved to be a Japanese sailor, presumably from one of the enemy ships sunk in battle—who seemingly adopted an "any port in a storm" philosophy about escaping from the sea. The account provided other details about the rescue effort as well:

> One plane had 57 survivors on board and the other had 45.... All these in addition to the regular 9 men in each plane's flight crew. About this time the Japs on shore, only a few hundred yards away, apparently woke up to what was going on, and they let go with quite a fusillade at the two Catalinas. The pilot of each was positive that the planes could not take off with such a load - but they had to "Get the Hell out of there - and quickly!! They poured on full throttle and away they went taxiing for dear life for the open sea. After about a three mile run, to the utter and complete astonishment of all hands, the old Cats gave a mighty grunt and heaved themselves into the air and flew![21]

Between 3 and 5 December 1944, PBY-5 Catalinas tended by the *Orca* were able by sheer daring to save 166 survivors of the *Cooper*, with 191 men lost. Lt. Joe Ball, the pilot of the plane that retrieved the first fifty-six *Cooper* survivors (and one Japanese), many of them severely injured, received the Navy Cross. The pilot of the plane that lifted the second group, Lt. (jg) Melvin S. Essary, USN, was awarded the Distinguished Flying Cross. Lt. Joe Ball's Navy Cross Medal citation reads:

> The President of the United States of America takes pleasure in presenting the Navy Cross to Lieutenant Joe Frederick Ball, United States Naval Reserve, for extraordinary heroism in operations against the enemy while serving as Commander of a Navy PBY-5 Patrol Plane in Patrol-Bombing Squadron THIRTY-FOUR (VPB-34). On 3 December 1944, Lieutenant Ball, as Patrol Plane Commander of a Navy Catalina aircraft landed his plane on the waters of Ormoc Bay, Leyte, and picked up a total of

56 survivors from the U.S.S. *COOPER* which had been sunk during the previous night. He carried out the entire rescue with consummate skill and with total and repeated disregard for his personal safety, remaining on the water for almost an hour with many enemy planes in the vicinity, and repeatedly taxiing his plane well within point-blank range of guns on the enemy-held coastline and of two enemy warships, in his effort to pick up survivors. When his plane could hold no more, he was forced to make a run of three miles in order to get off the water. Upon becoming airborne, he elected to fly his plane home unescorted in order to provide the quickest possible medical treatment for his passengers, many of whom were wounded, and succeeded in returning his plane and passengers safely to base. His courage and heroic conduct throughout were in keeping with the highest traditions of the United States Naval Service.[22]

"BLACK CAT" AND "NIGHTMARE" OPERATIONS

During the months of November and December in the Leyte area, the crews of seaplane tenders were kept busy working around the clock performing ship's work, operating and tending seaplanes, and manning battle stations. Aboard the flagship *Currituck* (AV-7) there was also additional work associated with being a supply and emergency base for non-aviation units. The *Currituck*, with commander Aircraft, Seventh Fleet aboard, had arrived in San Pedro Bay on 6 November and anchored off Dio Island. Being the only major ship in that area of the large bay, she served as a dispatch and communications ship in addition to tending patrol planes. In support of the Army, the *Currituck* fed both her crew and many guests—of which there were over 1,700 from other units in the Tacloban-Jinamoc area who came aboard seeking a dry place to sleep and a chance for a real meal.[23]

Of course, her primary mission was supporting the operation and repair of seaplanes. The *Currituck* tended PBY-5s of VPB-34 from 6 to 23 November, and PBM-3Ds of VPB-20 from 21 November 1944 to 4 January 1945. These squadrons were used mostly for "Black Cat" and "Nightmare" missions. Operating from the seaplane tender, VPB-20 conducted night search and attack missions, sector searches, barrier patrol, convoy coverage, tomcat (night gunfire spotting) and various other special missions throughout the Philippines, and as far south as the northern coast of Borneo. In December 1944, the patrol bombing squadron:

- Covered each of the destroyer attack force operations at night against enemy shipping and shore installations in the Ormoc Bay area on the west coast of Leyte

- Covered the amphibious forces participating in landings at Ormoc Bay
- Covered the convoys engaged in landings on the southwest coast of Mindoro
- Flew defensive patrols to protect the beachheads[24]

PBM MARINERS STRIKE JAPANESE TASK FORCE

In late afternoon on 26 December, the squadron received word of a Japanese task force, comprised of a heavy cruiser, a light cruiser, and six destroyers, approaching Mindoro. Five patrol bombers loaded with four 500-pound bombs each were ordered to intercept and attack the enemy force which, as feared, began shelling American beachheads following arrival in Mangarin Bay. Three of the PBM-3D Mariners had been preparing to take off on regular night searches; the remaining two had been standby aircraft. The three planes ready to go, piloted by lieutenants (junior grade) James A. Abele, Warren M. Cox, and John B. Muoio, took off shortly after 1700 to find the task force. Lt. James W. Fallon and Lt. (jg) William J. Ondrecka followed an hour later in the two other planes.[25]

Abele sighted the enemy force at 2043, but intense, accurate heavy and medium anti-aircraft fire prevented him from closing. Muoio dropped two bombs at a destroyer from 2,000 feet, but they fell short by about forty feet, and his remaining two bombs failed to release on a second run. Cox made a run at 0015; his bombs also failed to release. However, despite his aircraft having been hit by AA fire, he continued attempting attacks until 0430 when the starboard engine failed and he was forced to land in Mangarin Bay.[26]

As soon as the PBM Mariner hit the water, it was subjected to a bombing and strafing attack by an unidentified plane. The crew of the Mariner was able to get clear before it sank, and remained in the water with only their "May-Wests" (inflatable life preservers) and a bomb bay tank to keep them afloat until rescued after daylight. The plane captain, Donald A. Schnur, was fatally injured in the attack. Through the perseverance and heroism of Aviation Machinist's Mate Second Vernon K. Anderson, USN, Schnur was kept afloat and survived until after the crew was rescued. For his actions, Anderson received the Navy and Marine Corps Medal.[27]

In the face of heavy anti-aircraft fire, Fallon attacked a destroyer, dropping his bombs from 150 feet and scored two hits. Although his plane was riddled with holes and out of control, he successfully made a crash landing at sea a half mile from the enemy force. All of the crew were able to get out safely and into life rafts before the PBM sank. After drifting for two days and three nights, the rafts reached Canipo Island in the Calamian group. Guerrillas found them and took them to northern Palawan (a group of islands that stretch between Mindoro in the northeast and Borneo in the southwest) and the men were returned to the squadron three weeks later.[28]

Ondrejcka made an attack at 0100, dropping his bombs from 3,000 feet while trying for a hit on a destroyer. His plane was hit and damaged by enemy fire, but he continued to shadow the enemy force until, out of gas, he was forced to land near Biliran Island, north of Leyte. The plane returned to base at 1445 that afternoon after a crash boat came out and refueled it.[29]

HERON AND *SAN PABLO* ARRIVE IN LEYTE GULF

> *The first four days aboard were indeed impressive to a squadron that suddenly found itself in the "front line." Japanese bombers and fighters were very active in the Leyte Gulf and Tacloban area during this period. The group of AVP tenders of which we were a part, anchored in the western limits of San Pedro Bay, were responsible for the subtraction of several Japanese planes. A warm introduction it has been and an impressive one, of both our floating anti-aircraft efficiency and our very impressive fighter protection.*
>
> —Patrol Bombing Squadron VPB-25 war diary entry for November 1944, citing its reception in San Pedro Bay after arrival from Naval Air Station, Kaneohe, Oahu, Hawaii for war duty in the Philippines.

The *San Pablo* (AVP-30) and the *Heron* (AVP-2) were the last of the seaplane tenders supporting the invasion of the Philippine Islands to arrive in the Leyte Gulf. The two ships sailed from Morotai Island on 16 November for Leyte Island with the *San Pablo* serving as escort for Navy aviation rescue boats *C-24375* and *C-9485*, and the *Heron* with freight barge *YFN-613* in tow. Two Army crash boats, *P-716* and *P-717*, joined the convoy that afternoon. Enemy air attacks on ships in transit to Leyte were common, but the weather along their route was very poor, resulting in the temporary cessation of enemy air activity over the eastern approaches to the Philippine area.[30]

The *San Pablo* and *Heron* arrived at Leyte Island on 21 November and anchored in Anibong Bay in the vicinity of the *Half Moon* and *Orca* after which Comdr. Chauncey S. Willard reported to commander Task

Group 73.7 for duty. His ship, the *San Pablo*, was tasked with tending half of VPB-25, with responsibility for the squadron's 55 officers, 164 enlisted men, and fifteen PBM-3D Mariner aircraft shared with the *Half Moon*. Over the next several days there were air raids nearly every day. During evening twilight on the 24th, a flight of four or five twin-engine "Frances" bombers came in low over the nearby mountains for a surprise attack. All ships opened fire, and the planes were driven off. The following day, ten officers and thirty enlisted men—flight crews of land-based planes—reported aboard the *Heron* for messing and berthing due to inadequate shore facilities.[31]

Operations by the Mariner patrol bombers included flying 1,300-mile daylight patrols. Their search area between compass bearing 341 degrees and 041 degrees was made up of five adjacent 12-degree patrol sectors, with the westernmost sector extending to a point some fifty miles beyond the northern tip of Luzon. The primary mission of the planes was to detect and report any Japanese surface or submarine movements in opposition to U.S. ground combat operations on Leyte and the large numbers of cargo ships in Leyte Gulf. Their secondary function was to carry out attacks against enemy submarines that might be operating in the southern half of the patrol sectors. To this end, each PBM carried four 350-pound depth charges.[32]

The *Heron* closed out the month engaged in salvage operations. On 28 November, she got under way and proceeded to the vicinity of Manicani Island in Leyte Gulf to salvage PBM *#109*, with the work beginning immediately after she anchored off the island along the southern coast of Samar. Operations were interrupted by two enemy air attacks in the vicinity that day, four the next and three the day after that. However on the third day, 30 November, the Mariner was floated free of a reef and brought to the *Heron*. It remained moored to her stern overnight while the seaplane tender made preparations to tow the patrol bomber to the *Currituck* for repairs.[33]

LINGAYEN GULF LANDINGS

> *The enemy's large scale employment of suicide planes give rise to highly concentrated and desperate anti-aircraft fire....About forty-three planes reached their targets [Allied ships], many after flying through the heaviest concentration of gun fire. A plane diving at speed in excess of four hundred fifty knots becomes in effect a low velocity projectile; its momentum is so great that it may not be deflected by volume of hits alone. The loss of a tail or the total disintegration of a wing generally, but not always, causes the plane to swerve from its general course. Killing the pilot may or may not deflect the plane.*

—Vice Adm. Thomas C. Kinkaid, commander, Luzon Attack Force, highlighting the grave danger that kamikaze aircraft presented to Allied shipping during Lingayen Gulf Landings in January 1945.[34]

Less than 72 hours after I had taken command of the ship, we found ourselves underway with the very first convoy, headed for Lingayen; and we had been underway less than 12 hours, when the "Kamakaze boys" gave us our first working over. From then on, for the next six days, we caught it hot and heavy. Fortunately for us, our attackers appeared not to have been confirmed "Lodge Members – Kamakaze Local No. 269", for none of them made suicide dives, unless actually hit and out of control.

—Comdr. Everett O. Rigsbee Jr., USN, commanding officer USS *Orca* (AVP-49), describing enemy aircraft attacks made against the seaplane tender in January 1945.[35]

At 0930 on 9 January 1945, assault forces of the U.S. Sixth Army under Lt. Gen. Walter Krueger, commencing landing on Lingayen Gulf beachheads in the Lingayen-Dagupan-San Fabian-Rabon area of Luzon. The amphibious operation, code named MIKE ONE, was a part of MacArthur's Operation MUSKETEER, a four-phased plan to liberate the Philippine Islands. The objectives of the Lingayen Gulf landings were the prompt seizure of central Luzon, the reoccupation of the Manila-Central Plains area, the establishment of bases for the support of operations to the north of the Philippines, and the complete occupation of Luzon Island. The weather conditions that day were favorable; sea and surf conditions were slight, there was no precipitation, and visibility was limited only by bombardment smoke the morning carried offshore by land breezes. As the Lingayen Attack Force came ashore, the enemy offered little opposition to landing craft approaching the beach or soldiers disembarking, the only resistance coming on the northeastern flank. This reflected new tactics adopted by the Japanese to withdraw from established beach defenses and to instead fight inland in the jungle. The landing of the San Fabian Attack Force, a few miles to the east, was unopposed. Over the next two days, ship-to-shore movement of follow-on assault troops and equipment continued smoothly and on 11 January, Krueger assumed command of Sixth Army forces ashore. That afternoon MacArthur and his staff left the light cruiser *Boise* (CL-47), for his headquarters at Dagupan near the Lingayen Gulf.[36]

LUZON ATTACK FORCE

Vice Adm. Thomas C. Kinkaid commanded the Luzon Attack Force (Task Force 77) comprised of Task Force 78 (San Fabian Attack Force) under Vice Adm. Daniel E. Barbey and Task Force 79 (Lingayen Attack Force) under Vice Adm. Theodore S. Wilkinson Jr. In the final days leading up to the invasion of Luzon, there had been 138 ships in the Lingayen area engaged in minesweeping and bombarding the coastline. On the morning of the invasion, 9 January, 344 additional ships arrived to take part in the amphibious landings at Lingayen and nearby San Fabian.[37]

TASK GROUP 77.6—LEYTE TO LINGAYEN GULF

A week earlier, the seaplane tender *Orca* (AVP-49) had departed Leyte on 2 January to join the ships of Task Group 77.6 (hydrographic and minesweeping group), en route to the Mike ONE operation. The task group under Comdr. Wayne R. Loud was comprised of ten destroyer minesweepers (DMS), ten minesweepers (AM), forty-three yard minesweepers (YMS), two destroyer minelayers (DM), one high-speed transport (APD), the old minelayer *Monadnock* (CM-9), and the Australian frigate HMAS *Gascoyne* (K354) and sloop *Warrego* (U73). The minesweepers were to sweep Lingayen Gulf for moored and acoustic mines prior to landings by joint expeditionary forces. The *Orca* was designated Task Unit 77.2.9, the seaplane reservicing unit for Vice Adm. Jesse B. Oldendorf's Bombardment and Fire Support Group. Upon joining the convoy, she took position in the center column, 500 yards astern of the minelayer *Monadnock* and 500 yards ahead of the aviation gasoline tanker *Susquehenna* (AOG-5). A few warships were present to provide protection for the convoy, which also included merchant vessels, naval auxiliaries and amphibious craft headed for the Lingayen Gulf or destinations en route.

Task Force 77 Task Groups Supporting Both Task Force 78 and Task Force 79	Commander Task Group
TG 77.1 Fleet Flagship Group	Capt. A. M. Granum
TG 77.2 Bombardment and Fire Support Group	Vice Adm. Jesse B. Oldendorf
TG 77.3 Close Covering Group	Rear Adm. Russell S. Berkey
TG 77.4 Escort Carrier Group	Rear Adm. C. T. Durgin
TG 77.5 Hunter-Killer Group	Capt. J. C. Cronin
TG 77.6 Minesweeping and Hydrographic Group	Comdr. Wayne R. Loud
TG 77.7 Screening Group	Capt. John B. McLean
TG 77.8 Salvage and Rescue Group	Comdr. B. S. Huie
TG 77.9 Reinforcement Group	Rear Adm. Richard L. Conolly
TG 77.10 Service Group	Rear Adm. R. O Glover[38]

At 0724 the following morning, a report was received of six to eight enemy aircraft approaching the convoy. Four minutes later, a Val crashed into the oiler *Cowanesque* (AO-79). The plane's right wing struck the ship's rail on the port side, and its nose crashed into the top of a kingpost at a replenishment station. Its gasoline tank exploded, starting a small fire. The flames were quickly extinguished and a bomb, which had landed on the deck, but failed to explode, was thrown over the side. Two men were killed and two slightly wounded in the attack, but the ship suffered no significant damage. At 0732 the explosion of a near bomb miss off the port side of a second oiler, the *Pecos* (AO-65), momentarily caused her main engines to stop.[39]

One of the other Vals was hit by gunfire, and crashed into the sea to starboard of the formation while trying to reach Negros Island. A search of the wreckage found a Japanese map with the current position of the convoy and also its projected location at 1320 annotated on the diagram. Based on this information, another attack was anticipated but none materialized.[40]

The convoy continued its steady trek to Lingayen Gulf on 4 January, passing the Visayan Islands unhindered by enemy aircraft. The tankers left the formation that day and proceeded to Mindoro. In mid-afternoon the following day the destroyer *Bennion* (DD-662), frigate HMAS *Gascoyne*, and sloop HMAS *Warrego* were detached to intercept two Japanese destroyers overtaking the convoy about ten miles astern. The *Bennion* was able to close the evasive enemy but not sufficiently for effective gunfire. Apparently not wishing to fight, the DDs reversed course, made smoke, and headed south-southeast toward Manila at 28 knots.[41]

INCREASED AIR ATTACKS AGAINST THE CONVOY

In the early evening on 5 January, a sighting was made aboard *Orca* of a group of about nine planes, five to six miles off the starboard side of the ship, orbiting at 6,000-7,000 feet. The aircraft, which proved to be Japanese Zeros with bombs under their wings, staged a whirlwind attack on the convoy. Some of the planes successfully executed suicide dives and crashed into ships, others were hit by anti-aircraft fire and, aflame or encumbered, impacted the water. An entry from the *Orca*'s war diary describes the action near her and a group of 136-foot wooden-hulled minesweepers in the same area within the convoy:

> They immediately broke off in a diving turn, which brought them on the starboard quarter. The leading three planes, spaced at about 2,000 yards interval in column, then turned in toward this

ship in a 45° full-power dive.... When the leading plane was about 3,000 yards away, it had swung sufficiently astern for gun No. 42 to bear, and this gun began tracking.... Fire was commenced; supplemented by automatic-weapons fire from all of the YMS craft in the formation, toward the direction from which the attack was coming.[42]

Photo 25-2

Japanese Kamikaze Zeke-type ("Zero") aircraft diving on the cruiser *Columbia* (CL-56) during the Lingayen Gulf operation on 6 January 1945. Hit by the ship's guns and aflame, it crashed close aboard her.
Courtesy of John R. Henry, U.S. Naval History and Heritage Command Photograph #NH 79448

Anti-aircraft fire found the first Zero hurtling in at approximately 1,000 yards distant from the *Orca*, and it began to disintegrate and burst into flames. The pilot, apparently recognizing that he could not reach his primary target, the seaplane tender, executed a sharp wingover and crashed alongside a YMS, positioned 500 yards on the port quarter of the *Orca*. With this threat eliminated, the *Orca* prepared to engage the second of the three attackers—which got twice as close to her before being shot down:

Gun No. 43 on this ship, quickly shifted to the second enemy plane, which was closing at a terrific speed. Effective hits were not observed on this plane until it was within 1,000 yards, and it appeared to all observers on this ship that the plane would inevitably crash on deck. However ... when the plane was within 500 yards, numerous 20 and 40MM hits were observed on this second enemy plane, causing it to burst into flames. Apparently the pilot was killed instantly, because the nose of the plane began to rise very slightly, and the port wing dropped just sufficiently, to cause the plane to skim over the crane mast on the after end of the ship, about 50 feet away. The bomb it was carrying exploded on impact, and showered the ship with bomb fragments, parts of the airplane, and [of its occupants].[43]

All of *Orca*'s guns that could bear then shifted fire to the third plane coming in, which—hit by gunfire from one or more of the ships in the outer part of the formation—was trailing smoke. When about 3,000 yards from the *Orca*, it appeared to be hit again by fire from her and other ships, and it went out of control and crashed harmlessly in between columns of the formation.[44]

In other action within the convoy, a suicide plane crashed two hundred yards off the port bow of the minesweeper *Scrimmage* (AM-297) at 1734. Five minutes later, a suicide plane struck the fleet ocean tug *Apache* (ATF-67) and at 1740 one struck the *LCI(G)-70*, carrying away her mast and crashing on the foc's'le deck. Aboard the 158-foot infantry landing craft, four men were killed, nine were wounded, and eight knocked overboard, two of whom went missing. Later, while *LCI(G)-70* was transferring her wounded to the destroyer minesweeper *Hogan* (DMS-6), a Zero equipped with twin floats came in and dropped a bomb 100 yards off the craft's starboard bow. Hit by 40mm, 20mm, and .50-caliber fire, the attacker crashed into the water. A short time later, the three combatant ships—*Bennion*, *Gascoyne*, and *Warrego*—sent to intercept the enemy destroyers rejoined the formation at 1835.[45]

In early evening, night combat air patrol "splashed" a bogie at 1902. However, some of the enemy planes got by the friendly fighter aircraft and twenty minutes later bombs fell on the starboard quarter of the formation. The *Bennion* took a bogie six miles distant under fire at 1942 and a second one at the same range from her twelve minutes later. At 1955, an enemy plane dropped a bomb which failed to do any damage. The destroyer ceased firing a minute later, the action being over for the night.[46]

ARRIVAL IN LINGAYEN GULF

Just before daybreak on 6 January, the *Orca* and *Bennion* left the convoy as it neared the Lingayen Gulf to join the Bombardment and Fire Support Group. As the convoy broke up, groups of minesweepers proceeded to their assigned sweep areas inside the gulf. The destroyer minesweepers *Chandler* (DMS-9), *Dorsey* (DMS-1), *Hamilton* (DMS-18), *Hogan* (DMS-6), *Hopkins* (DMS-13), *Hovey* (DMS-11), *Howard* (DMS-7), *Long* (DMS-12), *Palmer* (DMS-5), and *Southard* (DMS-10) began working to clear a channel into the gulf for the battleships and cruisers of the bombardment group. However, Kamikaze aircraft proved more hazardous than sea mines, crashing the *Hovey*, *Long*, and *Palmer* and sinking the first two ships that day. The *Palmer*, also damaged on 6 January, succumbed and sank the following day.[47]

As the *Orca* entered Lingayen Gulf with the bombardment and fire control ships mid-afternoon on 6 January, her commanding officer wondered how plane reservicing could be carried out with swells of eight to twelve feet, and heavy air attacks imminent. And, as the seaplane tender shifted from one group of ships to another so too, it appeared, did the air attacks. At about 1725 the enemy came in to attack the cruisers and battleships in earnest, and again at 1800. Over the course of that one day, the *Orca* expended 44 rounds of 5-inch, 834 rounds of 40mm, and 696 rounds of 20mm ammunition.[48]

On 7 January, the "heavy ships" commenced pre-landing shore bombardment in late morning. Midafternoon, a SOC Seagull came in for refueling by the *Orca*, a few minutes later an OS2U Kingfisher, and the remainder of the afternoon was devoted to servicing SOCs and OS2Us. At about 1745, the *Orca* joined the Bombardment and Fire Support Group task group, which was forming for night retirement out to sea. While entering Lingayen Gulf the following morning with the group, the *Orca* took an enemy plane under fire at 0721. The bombardment ships then proceeded with shelling the shore, and the seaplane tender began servicing aircraft.[49]

The following morning, 9 January, the heavy ships continued to bombard shore installations and gun positions until about 1045, just before the first wave of troops landed. That afternoon, several crews of VPB-54 reported aboard the *Orca* for temporary duty in connection with air-sea rescue missions. The following day, she anchored near Cabalitian Island, and laid seaplane moorings in preparation to tend aircraft. Ensuing operations by VPB-54 aircraft operating from the tender would be planned by the U.S. Sixth Army General eadquarters, Fifth Army Air Force Air Sea Rescue Group 5276, and 308th Bombardment Wing. Missions assigned the squadron included air-sea rescue, parachute drops of supplies to guerrilla forces, postal service to beachheads at Subic Bay and in Batangas Providence, and the ferrying of Army and Navy officers between Leyte and Lingayen.[51]

Photo 25-3

Battleship *Mississippi* (BB-41) bombarding Luzon, during the Lingayen operation, on 8 January 1945. She is followed by the *West Virginia* (BB-48) and HMAS *Shropshire*. U.S. Navy photograph, now in the collections of the National Archives

ASSAULT FORCE ARRIVES IN LINGAYEN GULF

The *Orca* was a part of Rear Adm. Frank D. Wagner's Task Force 73. Wagner, commander Aircraft, Seventh Fleet, left San Pedro Bay on 6 January aboard the *Currituck* (AV-7), screened by the *Barataria* (AVP-33), for Lingayen Gulf. His tenders and squadrons identified in the below table were responsible for conducting VOS (observation and scouting), rescue, search, and anti-submarine missions in support of the Lingayen Gulf operation:

Task Force 73: Rear Adm. Frank D. Wagner, USN

Task Group	Ship/Squadron	Commander/ Commanding Officer	Type Aircraft
73.1	Flagship Group	Capt. William A. Evans Jr.	
	Currituck (AV-7)	Capt. William A. Evans Jr.	
	1 AVR (crash boat)		
73.2	Lingayen Group	Rear Adm. Frank D. Wagner	
73.2.1	Search & ASW Unit	Rear Adm. Frank D. Wagner	
	Currituck (AV-7)	Capt. William A. Evans Jr.	
	Barataria (AVP-33)	Comdr. Garrett S. Coleman	
	1 AVR (crash boat)		
	VPB-20	Lt. Comdr. Robert M. Harper	15 PBM-3D
	VPB-71	Comdr. Norman C. Gillette Jr.	12 PBY-5A
72.2.2	VOS & Rescue Unit	Comdr. Everett O. Rigsbee Jr.	
	Orca (AVP-49)	Comdr. Everett O. Rigsbee Jr.	
	1 AVR (crash boat)		
	½ VPB-54	Lt. Comdr. Kenneth J. Sanger	6 PBY-5A[52]

After crossing the Leyte Gulf, the tenders rendezvoused with the San Fabian Assault Force and sailed in company. Enemy aircraft attacked the force the first two days in transit and were shot down by the combat air patrol protecting the convoy. During an attack by several suicide planes the evening of 8 January, one came under fire from Assault Force ships including the *Barataria*, and was shot down.[53]

At daybreak on 9 January, a short time before U.S. Army assault forces began landing on Lingayen Gulf beachheads, the *Currituck* and *Barataria* departed the convoy and proceeded to an anchorage in the eastern Lingayen Gulf, five miles to the northwest of San Fabian, Luzon. After seaplane moorings, anchors, and buoys were broken out and laid south of Aringay Point, PBM-3D Mariner patrol bombers of VPB-20 began arriving in early afternoon and mooring. That evening, enemy planes attacked shipping in the harbor, dropping fragmentation bombs. A small bomb or unexploded 40mm projectile exploded on the *Currituck*'s boat deck, injuring five seamen.[54]

CATALINA AND MARINER AIRCRAFT OPERATIONS

> *With the arrival at Lingayen Gulf the most active phase of Patrol Bombing Squadron SEVENTY-ONE's combat duty began. It was to last through the month of February. Black Cat operations were resumed the night of January 12 when three planes flew offensive reconnaissance missions to Formosa and the Southeast China coast, and one plane flew a sector of the barrier patrol around the Lingayen Gulf area.*
>
> —Patrol Bombing Squadron VPB-71 War Diary entry, January 1945

The first night patrols at Lingayen Gulf began on 10 January, and two days later "Black Cat" and "Nightmare" anti-shipping flights from the gulf to the Formosa and China coasts. The term Nightmare referred to night anti-shipping missions carried out by PBM-3D Mariner patrol aircraft. Squadrons VPB-20 and VPB-71 flew all the patrols and anti-shipping in January. Additional barrier patrols were flown the last three days of the month to provide protection for troop landings at Nasugbu and San Antonio, Luzon, from attack by the sea.[55]

The Japanese were not expecting night attacks at Formosa, and on one occasion even turned on the landing lights at a seaplane base when a Mariner came in on a bombing run. During "Nightmare" missions, PBMs also frequently sighted unescorted merchant ships operating along the China coast near Formosa and made attacks on them. The enemy was soon alerted, however, and shore searchlights and anti-aircraft batteries became more prevalent. Merchant shipping, which had been poorly protected, was consolidated into convoys with naval escort. Nevertheless, VPB-71 aircraft continued to sink or damage enemy shipping in low-level night attacks. Additionally, thirteen night raids targeted barracks, harbor installations, radio stations, and industrial plants on Formosa and adjacent islands and in China.[56]

COMBAT ON LUZON CONTINUES FOR MONTHS

While the major combat contributions made by seaplane tenders and their patrol bombers to the Philippine Islands Campaign came to an end in January, the fighting ashore continued for months. The Battle of Luzon lasted from 9 January to 15 August 1945 during which, except for those forces surrendering at the end of the war, the Japanese lost virtually all of the 230,000 military personnel on Luzon. These losses were in addition to some 70,000 casualties from battle on

Leyte Island. By the summer of 1945, American forces had destroyed nine of Japan's best divisions and rendered another six combat-ineffective. American casualties were also high. Ground combat losses for the U.S. Sixth and Eighth Armies were almost 47,000, some 10,380 killed and 36,550 wounded.[57]

SEAPLANE TENDER/SQUADRON BATTLE STARS

Leyte Operation: Battle of Surigao Strait

Half Moon (AVP-26)	24-26 Oct 1944 No BS	Comdr. Jack I. Bandy
San Carlos (AVP-51)	24-26 Oct 1944 No BS	Lt. Comdr. De Long Mills
VPB-33	24-26 Oct 1944	Lt. Comdr. F. P. Anderson
VPB-34	24-26 Oct 1944	Lt. Comdr. Vadym V. Utgoff

Leyte Operation: Leyte Landings

Currituck (AV-7)	6-29 Nov 1944	Capt. William A. Evans Jr.
Half Moon (AVP-26)	20 Oct-29 Nov 1944	Comdr. Jack I. Bandy
Heron (AVP-2)	21-29 Nov 1944	Lt. John M. Norcott
Orca (AVP-49)	4-29 Nov 1944	Comdr. Morton K. Fleming Jr.
San Carlos (AVP-51)	10 Oct-29 Nov 1944	Lt. Comdr. De Long Mills
San Pablo (AVP-30)	21-29 Nov 1944	Comdr. Chauncey S. Willard
VPB-11	7-20 Nov 1944	Lt. Comdr. Thomas S. White
VPB-11	15-29 Nov 1944	Lt. Comdr. Thomas S. White
VPB-20	1-29 Nov 1944	Lt. Comdr. Robert M. Harper
VPB-25	16-29 Nov 1944	Lt. Comdr. James C. Skoroz
VPB-33	15-29 Nov 1944	Lt. Comdr. F. P. Anderson
VPB-34	15-29 Nov 1944	Lt. Comdr. Vadym V. Utgoff
VPB-101	10 Oct-29 Nov 1944	Lt. Comdr. Marvin T. Smith
VPB-104	5-29 Nov 1944	Lt. Comdr. Whitney Wright
VPB-130	9-29 Nov 1944	Lt. Comdr. Charles R. Dodds
VPB-146	17-26 Nov 1944	Lt. Comdr. Jesse P. Robinson Jr.
VPB-216	15 Oct-18 Nov 1944	Comdr. Harry E. Cook Jr.

Luzon Operation: Lingayen Gulf Landing

Currituck (AV-7)	9-18 Jan 1945	Capt. William A. Evans Jr.
Barataria (AVP-33)	9-18 Jan 1945	Comdr. Garrett S. Coleman
Orca (AVP-49)	4-18 Jan 1945	Comdr. Everett O. Rigsbee Jr.
VPB-20	10-18 Jan 1945	Lt. Comdr. Robert M. Harper
VPB-25	4-18 Jan 1945	Lt. Comdr. James C. Skoroz
VPB-33	4-18 Jan 1945	Lt. Comdr. F. P. Anderson
VPB-54	10-18 Jan 1945	Comdr. Kenneth J. Sanger
VPB-71	11-18 Jan 1945	Comdr. Norman C. Gillette Jr.
VPB-104	4-18 Jan 1945	Lt. Comdr. Whitney Wright
VPB-117	4-18 Jan 1945	Comdr. Harold W. McDonald
VPB-137	4-18 Jan 1945	Lt. Comdr. John A. Porter

26

Assault and Occupation of Iwo Jima

> *At great cost, you'd take a hill to find then the same enemy suddenly on your flank or rear. The Japanese were not on Iwo Jima. They were in it! I'd known combat in the Solomons with its sly ambushes and jungle firefights, but Iwo was another kind of war. On Iwo by the 8th day, only two officers of my second battalion (26th Marines, 5th Marine Division) were standing... We had one prisoner—unconscious, his clothes blown off.*

—Col. Thomas M. Fields, USMC (Ret.)

The Battles of Iwo Jima and Okinawa were fought by Allied forces between February and August 1945 to secure island bases for a final B29 bomber assault on Japan. The Iwo Jima operation was conducted first because it was expected to be easier than an assault on Okinawa. Because of the enemy's prolonged and bitter defense of Leyte and Luzon, the planned dates for both actions had slipped. Thus, the Pacific Fleet had to cover and support both invasions, while the Seventh Fleet and its amphibious forces were concurrently engaged in liberating the Southern Philippines.[1]

On 19 February as naval gunfire pounded the island, more than 450 ships massed off Iwo Jima. Marines of the 4th and 5th Divisions hit the four assault beaches shortly after 0900, initially finding little enemy resistance. Coarse volcanic sand hampered their movement as they struggled to move up the beach from the surf zone. As the protective naval gunfire subsided to allow for advancement, the Japanese emerged from fortified underground positions to begin a heavy barrage of fire against the invading force. The 4th Marines continued to push forward against heavy opposition to take the Quarry, a Japanese strong point, while the 5th Marine Division's 28th Marines isolated Mount Suribachi that same day. The 3rd Marine Division joined the fighting on the fifth day, charged with securing the center sector of the island. The fortified enemy defenses linked miles of interlocking caves, concrete blockhouses and pillboxes, which required frontal assaults to gain nearly every inch of ground. Maj. Gen. Harry Schmidt, commanding the Fifth Amphibious Corps—of which the 3rd, 4th, and 5th Marines were a part—declared Iwo Jima secured on 16 March. Ground fighting, however, continued between then and the official completion of the operation on 26 March 1945.[2]

Photo 26-1

Shells explode ashore during the bombardment of Iwo Jima on D-Day-minus-two, 17 February 1945. The view looks east toward Mount Suribachi's west side. The ship in the right foreground appears to be a YMS engaged in pre-invasion minesweeping. U.S. Navy Photograph #NH 104142

SEAPLANE TENDERS ARRIVE AT IWO JIMA

The *Hamlin* (AV-15) and *Chincoteague* (AVP-24) stood out of Guam on 17 February 1944 and rendezvoused at sea with Task Group 51.1 for transit to Iwo Jima. Three days later the seaplane tenders detached from the convoy at thirty-five minutes past midnight on 20 February (D-day + 1) and proceeded to Iwo Jima together. The *Hamlin* was a relatively new ship, having been commissioned on 26 June 1944, and her first experience of being in the front line was a thrilling one for many aboard. Night retirement groups of ships leaving the objective caused some ticklish moments during the approach to the island, and *Hamlin*'s radar proved its worth many times.[3]

Arriving at Iwo Jima at 0800 on 20 February, the two tenders received orders to lay off the southeast of the island in the transport area. Over the next several hours, air alerts were frequent although no visual sightings of the enemy were made. Later in the day, the *Hamlin* and *Chincoteague* proceeded to Area William to await orders to establish the seadrome. This did not occur due to bad sea conditions and heavy gunfire from the beach for four days. The morning of 24 February, the *Hamlin* anchored 600 yards from the shore, and began laying seaplane moorings, working in very close to the beach with a heavy sea still running. In preparation for receiving planes, her boats swept the area continuously removing as much floating debris as possible. Flotsam presented one of the major obstacles to seaplane operations at Iwo Jima. There was so much in fact that only the larger pieces could be removed, including rafts, timbers, ammunition cases, and other incidentals to the amphibious landing, which drifted continuously through the seadrome.[4]

During one of the frequent air raids, a 5-inch shell damaged the *Hamlin*'s port 24-inch searchlight and deflected through the port side of the stack, lodging in it within without exploding. It was jettisoned over the side. On another occasion, a 20mm shell struck her signal bridge slightly wounding four men.[5]

In addition to serving as a seaplane tender, the *Hamlin* was designated a rescue center to receive survivors. Such personnel were treated and berthed aboard her until arrangements could be made for further disposition. While at Iwo Jima, she provided care for nineteen aviators, survivors of the sea; four men that ship's force (crew) rescued from a sinking LCM landing craft; and twenty-three Marines.[6]

Photo 26-2

USS *Hamlin* (AV-15) at anchor in Tanapag Harbor, Saipan, on 13 February 1945.
U.S. National Archives Photograph #RG-80-G-306648

The large numbers of ships present at Iwo Jima and heavy swells caused by the prevailing easterly wind prevented the arrival of Patrol Bombing Squadron Nineteen until 27 February. Three of its PBM-3D Mariners arrived that day and the remaining twelve planes between 28 February and 3 March. During a week of operations at Iwo Jima, the squadron flew twenty-seven sector searches extending to within one hundred miles of Honshu Island, the largest and most populous island of Japan. The planes flew up to seven searches daily, despite having to land and take off under essentially open sea conditions. This precluded carrying any bombs in order to be sufficiently light to be able to take-off from the unprotected roadstead. Sightings and reports were made of nineteen enemy vessels, resulting in two actions. The squadron left Iwo Jima on 6 March for Parry Island in the Marshalls.[7]

During this period, the *Chincoteague* tended part of VPB-19 and two PB2B-2 Catalinas of Rescue Squadron VH-3 from her anchorage 500 yards off the beach under the shadow of Mount Suribachi. She and *Chincoteague* got under way for Saipan on 8 March. Upon arriving there, the *Hamlin* began loading provisions, ammunition and aviation spares. She was to next tend a squadron that flew PBM-5 planes, necessitating a change over from her PBM-3D allowance. The *Chincoteague* refueled and provisioned as well before proceeding to Ulithi Atoll in the Caroline Islands. For the next two-and-one-half months, she operated there as part of the Seaplane Base Group of Fleet Air Wing One and later Wing Eighteen.[8]

DEDICATED AIR-SEA RESCUE GROUPS FORMED

As the war in the Pacific expanded and Navy, Army, and Marine Corps combat and reconnaissance flights increased, so too did the requirement for rescue operations. Special rescue squadrons were organized and specially equipped, whose sole purpose was to locate and rescue fliers who failed to return from missions. These VH squadrons had no other duties but air-sea rescue. As a part of this effort, commander Air Force, Pacific Fleet created an air-sea rescue Group formed of the *Bering Strait* (AVP-34) and six PBM Mariners of Rescue Squadron VH-3. The purpose of this group was to furnish rescue service to the fast carrier task groups during their strikes and afterwards, in order to provide some assurance to downed aviators that they might expect eventual rescue.[9]

The six aircraft flew from Kaneohe to Eniwetok on 13 December 1944 and reported aboard the *Bering Strait*. One week was spent on her and the last week of the month aboard the *Cumberland Sound* (AV-17). The squadron moved to Saipan on 31 December, from which it flew thirty, 10-14 hour missions in January. These were largely either standby missions at Iwo Jima to cover airstrikes by B24s, or search missions for survivors reported down at sea. There also was one standby mission at Truk and a few along the B29 flight track to and from Japan.[10]

In February, the squadron conducted nine standby missions at Iwo Jima, guarding strikes on targets; eleven searches for survivors in the area north of Saipan; and two flights to carry press dispatches from Iwo Jima to Guam. From 1 to 12 March, the squadron flew thirteen missions: one open sea landing and rescue, participation in two other rescues, eight searches, an emergency flight delivering blood plasma to Iwo Jima, and one Dumbo standby mission.[11]

Photo 26-3

Boeing B29 bomber, which had crash landed at Motoyama Airfield on Iwo Jima. Army Signal Corps Photograph #SC 206875, now in the collection of the National Archives

The *Berang Strait* alternated in February and March between duty at sea as an air-sea rescue lifeguard station and short visits to Saipan. This duty involved her assisting bombers returning from Japan that had to ditch at sea, because damage or lack of fuel precluded them from making it to an airfield. Shortly before midnight on 10 February, she made contact with a homeward-bound B29 in duress, first by radar and then visually. To assist it in locating her, the tender switched on her standing lights and stood by for a landing, illuminating the sea and indicating wind direction with searchlights. After the bomber, named

"Deacon's Delight," ditched, the entire twelve-man crew was picked up by the *Bering Strait*'s motor whaleboat and brought to the ship. The seaplane tender then headed for the scene of "Homing Bird," another B29 that had ditched. Guided by a Dumbo to its location, the ship arrived on scene by late afternoon the following day and picked up the entire eleven-man crew.[12]

And so it went. The *Bering Strait* embarked seven survivors of a third B29 the morning of 12 February, and returned to Saipan three days later to disembark the airmen. On the night of her return to station, 19 February, a B29 ditched twelve miles north of Pagan Island, but broke up and sank upon landing. Five men, trapped in the wreckage, drowned. The remainder of the crew was unable to extract all of the life rafts, and lay at the mercy of the sea. Directed to the scene by a Dumbo, the *Bering Strait* picked up five survivors, one of whom had no life jacket and had been swimming for two hours. Fortunately, the airmen had been visible in the darkness because of tiny lights pinned to their life jackets, lights "obtained" from the Navy "on personal initiative." *Bering Strait* disembarked those survivors at Saipan on 21 February, and got under way later the same day to relieve the destroyer *Cummings* (DD-363) on station. Returning to Saipan on 3 March, she spent the next six days undergoing maintenance before resuming her lifeguard work at sea on 9 March.[13]

In the early afternoon on 10 March, the *Bering Strait* picked up the nine-man crew of a B29, nicknamed the "Hopeful Devil," that had ditched during its return from a bombing mission over the Japanese home islands. Almost immediately, she picked up a position report on another B29, which proved to be wrong. Fortunately, while en route to where the aircraft was thought to have come down at sea, she spotted a Dumbo orbiting southwest of Guguan Island in the Marianas and altered course to investigate. She found and retrieved the 11-man crew of the bomber there then returned to her lifeguard station. The *Bering Strait* remained at sea, twenty-eight miles from Pagan Island, from 11 to 14 March, and then relieved sistership *Cook Inlet* (AVP-36) at another air-sea rescue station.[14]

Returning to Saipan on 16 March, the *Bering Strait* put ashore the twenty airmen taken on board since the 10th, before sailing for Guam. Upon her detachment from lifeguard duties, the commanding general of the 313th Bombardment Wing sent the seaplane tender the below congratulatory message:

> Since you have been our guardian angel of the seas you have returned safely to us 50 combat crewmen. Many of them are

flying against the enemy again. We are grateful for the splendid work you have done and wish you all the best of luck.[15]

The *Cook Inlet* had been similarly employed on rescue station duty. Ten days into an earlier patrol, she had picked up nine survivors of the 21st Bomber Command on Farallon de Pajaros Island ("Birds Rock" in Spanish) the evening of 11 March. This uninhabited volcanic island was the northernmost member of the Northern Mariana Islands. The seaplane tender then returned to her rescue station. On the 15th, she entered Saipan Harbor for the night before returning to station the following day, expecting increased work following the departure of the *Bering Stait*.[16]

HEAVY CASUALTIES SUFFERED AT IWO JIMA

The acquisition of Iwo Jima—which would be strategically important as an air base for fighters escorting the B29s flying long-range bombing missions against mainland Japan, and as an emergency landing strip for crippled B29s unable to make it back to their base in the Mariana Islands—came at a high cost. The vital link in the chain of bases was gained through the individual and collective courage of Marines over a thirty-six day period. The brutal fighting resulted in 26,000 American casualties, including 6,800 dead. Only 1,083 of the 20,000 Japanese defenders of Iwo Jima survived.[17]

SEAPLANE TENDER/SQUADRON BATTLE STARS

Ship	Award Period	Commanding Officer
Bering Strait (AVP-34)	15 Feb-16 Mar 1945	Comdr. Walter D. Innis, USN
Chincoteague (AVP-24)	19 Feb-16 Mar 1945	Comdr. James A. Smith, USN
Cook Inlet (AVP-36)	2-16 Mar 1945	Comdr. William P. Woods, USN
Hamlin (AV-15)	19 Feb-8 Mar 1945	Capt. Gordon A. McLean, USN
VH-1	20 Feb-16 Mar 1945	Lt. Comdr. J. D. Adam
VH-2	20 Feb-16 Mar 1945	Lt. Comdr. H. A. Wells
VH-3	20 Feb-16 Mar 1945	Lt. Comdr. William D. Bonvillian
VPB-19	20 Feb-7 Mar 1945	Lt. Comdr. J. A. Masterson
VPB-23	3-16 Mar 1945	Lt. Comdr. William M. Stevens
VPB-102	15 Feb-16 Mar 1945	Lt. Comdr. Gerald R. Pearson
		Lt. Comdr. Louis P. Pressler
VPB-106	15 Feb-16 Mar 1945	Comdr. W. S. Sampson
VPB-116	15 Feb-16 Mar 1945	Lt. Comdr. A. R. Waggoner
VPB-118	15 Feb-16 Mar 1945	Comdr. C. K. Harper
VPB-151	15 Feb-16 Mar 1945	Comdr. Paul Masterton
VPB-208	15-22 Feb 1945	Lt. Comdr. Anton J. Sintic Jr.

27

Assault and Occupation of Okinawa

> *The arrival of this group in the battle area prior to the main assault and establishment within a few hours thereafter of an air base is, of course, a classic example of naval air force mobility. Outstanding ability was shown by the tender-patrol plane combination in maintaining an unprecedented schedule of operations per plane available, in spite of suicide attacks, smoked seadrome [smoke purposefully generated as a defensive measure] and 130 air raid alarms with 150 hours at General Quarters during the period.*
>
> —Capt. Gordon A. McLean, USN,
> Commander Seaplane Base Group
> during the invasion of Okinawa

The eighty-two-day-long Battle of Okinawa was fought on Okinawa in the Ryukyu Islands, and was the largest amphibious assault in the Pacific. The Ryukyus, a chain of Japanese islands stretching southwest from Kyushu to Formosa (now Taiwan), includes the Osumi, Tokara, Amami, Okinawa, and Sakishima Islands. The larger islands are mostly volcanic, the biggest being Okinawa, and the smaller ones are mostly coral. Four divisions of the U.S. Tenth Army (the 7th, 27th, 77th, and 96th) and two Marine divisions (the 1st and 6th) fought on Okinawa, supported by naval, amphibious, and air forces. The purpose of the operation, which lasted from 1 April through mid-June 1945, was to capture the island for use as a base for air operations during the planned invasion of Japan.[1]

Some Japanese accounts of the battle refer to it as *tetsu no ame* or *kou no kaze*, "iron rain" or "steel wind," respectively, due to the ferocity of the fighting, the intensity of kamikaze attacks from the Japanese defenders, and the sheer numbers of ships and armored vehicles that assaulted the island. The battle resulted in the highest number of casualties in the Pacific Theater during World War II. The Tenth Army suffered 7,613 killed or missing in action, and 31,800 wounded, while Marine Corps casualties overall—ground, air, and ships' detachments—exceeded 19,500. Navy losses were 34 vessels and craft sunk and 368 damaged, over 4,900 sailors killed or missing in action, and over 4,800 wounded. Japan lost over 100,000 soldiers, either killed, captured or committed suicide.[2]

Map 27-1

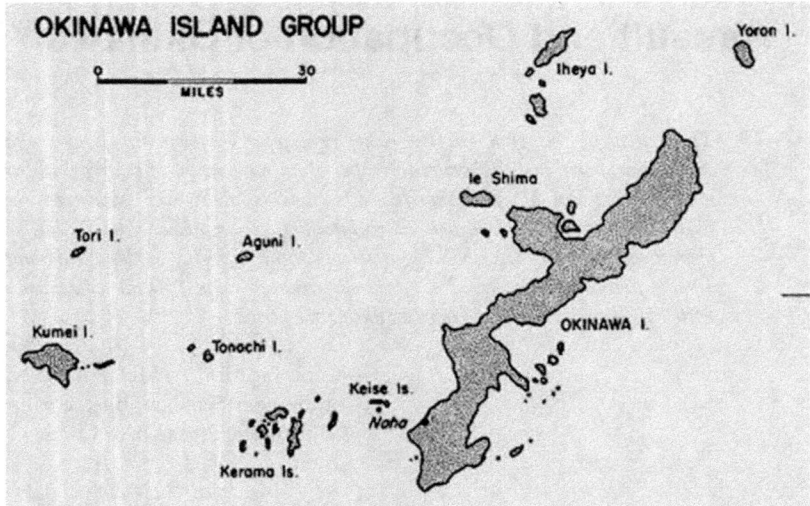

The U.S. 77th infantry division captured the Kerama Islands on 26 March 1945, for use as a seaplane anchorage and advanced base in support of the invasion of Okinawa.
United States Army in World War II, The War in the Pacific, Okinawa: The Last Battle

CAPTURE OF KERAMA RETTO, OKINAWA GUNTO

As a prelude to the invasion of Okinawa Gunto (meaning group of Okinawa Islands), Task Group 51.1 (Western Islands Attack Group) captured Kerama Retto, a small group of islands about fifteen miles southwest of Okinawa. The boldly conceived plan to invade these islands six days prior to the landings on Okinawa was designed to secure an advanced naval base for the logistics support of fleet units, and a sheltered anchorage for a seaplane base. The assault on Kerama Retto was carried out by the U.S. 77th Infantry Division under the command of Maj. Gen. Andrew D. Bruce, with a Marine Reconnaissance Battalion, less one company, attached from the Fleet Marine Force.[3]

In spite of narrow beaches, bad sea approaches, and rugged and difficult terrain, landings were quickly established against only light opposition, and all principal islands of the group except Kuba and Tokashiki were under American control by the afternoon of 26 March. Enemy reaction took the form of suicide plane attacks primarily, resulting in serious damage to one destroyer and two transports, and minor damage to two additional transports within the task group. The first seaplanes arrived at Kerama Retto and began operations from the seaplane base on 29 March.[4]

SEAPLANE BASE GROUP (TASK GROUP 51.20)

The ships of Task Group 51.20 (Seaplane Base Group)—*Bering Strait* (AVP-34), *Chandeleur* (AV-10), *Hamlin* (AV-15), *Onslow* (AVP-48), *Shelikof* (AVP-52), *St. George* (AV-16), and *Yakutat* (AVP-32)—had left Saipan on 23 March for Kerama Retto. En route to the invasion of Okinawa, code named ICEBERG, the task group was under the command of Commodore Ketchan embarked in *Hamlin*. Following arrival at Kerama Retto, Capt. Gordon A. McLean, commanding officer of the *Hamlin*, assumed duties of commander, Seaplane Base Group. Seven seaplane tenders initially comprised the seadrome, and others later joined the group.

It has been the convention in this book to cite seaplane tenders and patrol squadrons awarded battle stars for particular operations or events at the end of associated chapters. Such a summary is provided below to highlight early on, the large numbers of patrol aircraft and seaplane tenders assigned to Okinawa. The dates in the center column apply to periods of eligibility for battle stars earned, and in the case of VPB-18 and VH-3, to Navy Unit Commendations (NUC) awarded to these squadrons as well.

Initial Seaplane Base Group

Ship	Award Period	Commanding Officer
Hamlin (AV-15)	26 Mar-30 Jun 45	Capt. Gordon A. McLean, USN
St. George (AV-16)	26 Mar-30 Jun 45	Capt. Robert G. Armstrong, USN
Chandeleur (AV-10)	26 Mar-30 Jun 45	Capt. John S. Tracy, USN
Yakutat (AVP-32)	26 Mar-30 Jun 45	Comdr. George K. Fraser, USN
Onslow (AVP-48)	26 Mar-30 Jun 45	Comdr. Alden D. Schwarz, USN
Shelikof (AVP-52)	26 Mar-30 Jun 45	Comdr. Reuben E. Stanley, USN
Bering Strait (AVP-34)	26 Mar-30 Jun 45	Comdr. Walter D. Innis, USN
VPB-18	30 Mar-30 Jun 45	Lt. Comdr. R. R. Boettcher, USN
[NUC]	1 Apr-31 Jul 45	
VPB-21	29 Mar-30 Jun 45	Lt. Comdr. James D. Wright
VPB-27	29 Mar-30 Jun 45	Lt. Comdr. E. N. Chase II, USN
VPB-208	1 Apr-30 Jun 45	Lt. Comdr. Anton J. Sintic Jr., USN
VH-3	29 Mar-30 Jun 45	Lt. Comdr. Wm. D. Bonvillian, USN
[NUC]	29 Mar-30 Jun 45	

Ships and Squadrons which Reported Subsequently		
Williamson (AVD-2)	25 Mar-20 Apr 45	Lt. Comdr. William H. Ayer, USN
Gillis (AVD-12)	25 Mar-29 Jun 45	Lt. James C. Sullivan Jr., USNR
Thornton (AVD-11)	25 Mar-1 May 45	Lt. Laurence F. Geibel, USNR
Norton Sound (AV-11)	26 Apr-30 Jun 45	Capt. Benjamin S. Custer, USN
Kenneth Whiting (AV-14)	1-11 Apr 45	Comdr. Raymond R. Lyons, USN
Suisun (AVP-53)	26 Apr-30 Jun 45	Comdr. James J. Vaughan, USN
Casco (AVP-12)	25 Apr-30 Jun 45	Comdr. Reginald Rutherford, USN
Duxbury Bay (AVP-38)	26 Apr-30 Jun 45	Comdr. Frank N. Howe, USN
Mackinac (AVP-13)	11 May-30 Jun 45	Comdr. Paul L. Stahl, USN
Curtiss (AV-4)	22 May-25 Jun 45	Capt. Scott E. Peck, USN
		Capt. Henry C. Doan, USN
Gardiners Bay (AVP-39)	3-30 Jun 45	Comdr. Carlton C. Lucas, USN
VPB-13	26 Apr-30 Jun 45	Lt. Comdr. J. A. Ferguson, USN
VPB-26	26 Apr-20 Jun 45	Lt. Comdr. R. S. Null[5]

DUTIES OF THE DESTROYER SEAPLANE TENDERS

The three destroyer seaplane tenders that participated in ICEBERG had left Ulithi in the Caroline Islands two days earlier for Okinawa, to support the Gunfire and Covering Force conducting pre-landing shore bombardment of the island. In early morning on 21 March, the *Gillis* (AVD-12), *Thornton* (AVD-11), and *Williamson* (AVD-2) stood out and joined Task Force 54 for movement to Okinawa. While maneuvering to come alongside the port quarter of the *Thornton* to deliver mail, the *Gillis* suffered a steering casualty, and her bow struck the stern of the other ship. No damage was suffered by the *Gillis* except for the loss of her bullnose, but the *Thornton* was forced to return to port for the repair of her stern, buckled up to frame 174, and her steering engine, disabled by the collision.[6]

The crippled *Thornton* would be repaired but later, unfortunately, be involved in collisions with two other ships. On the night of 5 April 1945, while en route to Kerama Retto in company with the tank landing ship *LST-999*, she collided with the fleet oilers *Ashtabula* (AO-51) and *Escalante* (AO-71), part of a large convoy apparently steering a reciprocal course. With her starboard side severely damaged and open to the sea, the *Thornton* was towed on 14 April into Kerama Retto. Two weeks later, a board of inspection and survey recommended on the 29th that she be decommissioned, beached, stripped of all useful materiel as needed, and be abandoned. The *Thornton* was thereafter decommissioned on 2 May, and struck on 13 August 1945.[7]

Photo 27-1

The seaplane tender USS *Thornton* (AVD-11) being towed into Kerama Retto harbor by a fleet tug, after being heavily damaged in a collision on 5 April 1945 with the fleet oilers *Ashtabula* (AO-51) and USS *Escalante* (AO-70).
U.S. Navy Photograph #80-G-328478, now in the collections of the National Archives

During the initial assault and occupation of Okinawa and adjacent islands in the Ryukyu Islands, the *Gillis* and *Williamson* were assigned to Task Force 54, whose battleships and cruisers were charged with the systematic destruction of enemy coastal defense artillery positions and strongpoints, shore bombardment preparatory to the landing, and direct fire support of the troops after landing until victory was assured. During the period 21 March to 1 April, the *Gillis'* mission was to act as an escort and screening vessel and, when directed, to fuel observation planes attached to the battleships and cruisers. She was not called upon to fuel any planes. The *Williamson* operated as an anti-submarine screening vessel and spotting plane refueling unit with Fire Support Unit One. After the invasion forces were ashore on 1 April, the two destroyer seaplane tenders joined the Seaplane Base Unit. Their duties included refueling ship-based, patrol, and transport type seaplanes, supplying aviation gasoline to battleships and cruisers, and performing salvage and debris removal.[8]

PATROL BOMBING AND RESCUE SQUADRONS

> *The tenders had arrived with the occupational forces the preceding morning and our aircraft made their way to moorings in the shadow of rocky cliffs of the small islands of the group to the accompaniment of heavy gunfire and the rattle of small arms fire as our forces dynamited caves and cleared out snipers.*
>
> —Excerpt from the war history of VPB-21 describing the arrival of the squadron's planes at Kerama Retto on 29 March 1945.[9]

Following the establishment of the seadrome at Kerama Retto, Patrol Bombing Squadrons 18, 21, 27, and 208 were ordered forward from the Marianas and the Carolines. VPB-27 and 21 and Rescue Squadron VH-3 arrived on 29 March, and VPB-18 the following day. VPB-208, based at Ulithi, was unable to move forward until 1 April due to typhoon weather in that area of the Caroline Islands. The Mariners of VPB-27 had taken up anti-submarine patrols around Kerama and Okinawa on 29 March, which proved to be too much for a single squadron. Thus, despite the fact that neither VPB-18 nor VPB-21 were specially trained in anti-submarine warfare, nor had special ASW armament, they were assigned limited anti-submarine patrols until the arrival of VPB-208. Anti-submarine patrol was the primary mission during the first thirty days of the Okinawa operation, with long-range search of the waters between the Japanese Empire and Okinawa almost as important.[10]

Having just missed out on being involved in the invasion of Saipan, Palau and Ulithi, the personnel of VPB-21 were particularly excited about being a part of what would be the largest amphibious operation of the Pacific War. U.S. Navy carrier and battleship forces held down enemy air opposition, and battered shore installations prior to commencement on 1 April of the landings on Okinawa. Meanwhile, the distinction of being the first Navy flying boats in the heart of enemy-occupied territory went to VPB-21 and the other patrol bombing squadrons and rescue squadron VH-3. Their mission was to conduct:

- long range offensive search and reconnaissance
- offensive anti-shipping sweeps and block patrols
- anti-submarine and air-sea rescue services[11]

Assault and Occupation of Okinawa 367

The long range patrols flown by PBM Mariners differed widely from conventional sector searches. To prevent the enemy from anticipating their movements, the planes followed meandering tracks covering the entire Ryukyu chain and the vast area westward to the China coast, northward along Kyushu, northwestward to Korea and northeastward up along Kyushu, Shikoku and Honshu. No set schedule dictated operations, but the tracks were flown day and night.[12]

The patrols were broadly of two fundamental types: anti-shipping sweeps, and defensive blocks. The latter consisted of two "butterfly-type" patrols, flown back and forth to the eastward and westward of, and only thirty miles or so distant from, the south coast of Kyushu. The mission of the planes thus employed was to provide early warning of enemy surface units which might try to resupply the Japanese garrison on Okinawa or to attack the large concentrations of American shipping off the beachhead.[13]

Map 27-2

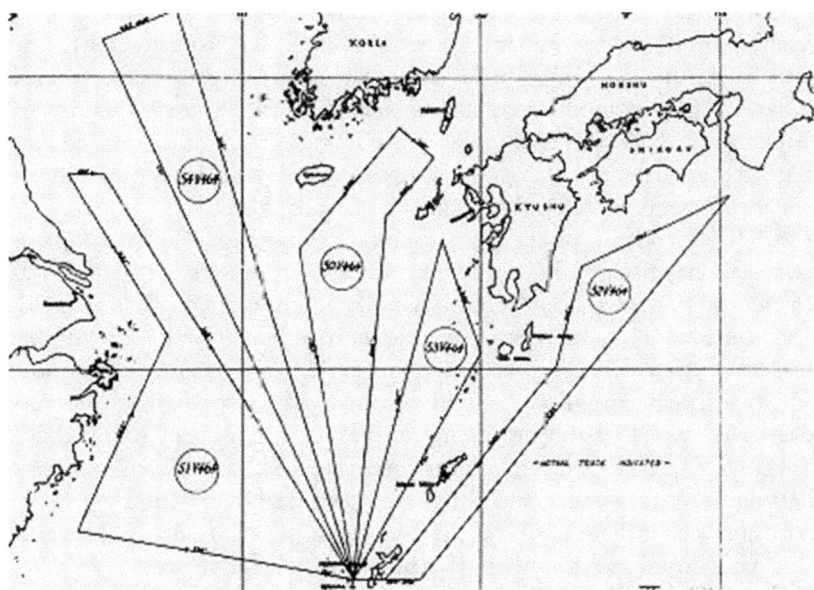

Mariner aircraft, based aboard seaplane tenders at Kerama Retto, flew long range searches and barrier patrols in Chinese, Korean, and the Japanese home islands waters. Commander Seaplane Base Group, General Action Report, Capture of Okinawa Gunto, Phases I and II, 25 March to 17 May 1945 – Submission of, 15 June 1945

The seadrome at Kerama Retto was reasonably satisfactory. However, at times aircraft taxiing or those under flight were confronted by one or more hazards, including approaching enemy aircraft, high winds and swells, small boats continuously crossing runways, and the necessity of getting flights in and out in minimal time. When winds blew from certain directions and were above 15 knots, a long, rolling swell hampered take-offs and landings of the heavy flying boats. There were also uncharted shoals and reefs in the immediate area that presented navigational hazards to taxiing aircraft.[14]

VPB-18/VH-3 EARN NAVY UNIT COMMENDATIONS

Based aboard the *St. George*, Patrol Bombing Squadron 18 flew aggressive armed reconnaissance patrols day and night and to the limit of pilot endurance and plane availability. During a hundred days in the area, the squadron participated in more offensive actions than it had previously encountered in its quiet though commendable career. In addition to routine reconnaissance patrols, which were the most numerous, its planes undertook special anti-shipping missions, night heckling and intruder flights in the confined waters of the Empire itself, night convoy tracking missions along the Korean coast, and attacks on enemy land installations. The latter targets were typically radio, radar, and lighthouse stations, and were usually well-defended by anti-aircraft batteries. Specific search and attack missions against reported enemy vessels or small convoys were also carried out, and the squadron frequently doubled as an air-sea rescue unit.[15]

The squadron policy was to attack any target a patrol plane commander thought he could get away with, and such action was carried out with vigor and enthusiasm by all concerned. During VPB-18's time at Kerama Retto, the squadron performed 422 combat missions, of which 236 were day patrols, 159 were night patrols, and 27 were special missions. In the course of these flights, Mariners destroyed twelve airborne enemy aircraft and damaged nine others. Seventy-six attacks were made on enemy vessels of 100 tons or more, netting forty-four sunk and thirty-two damaged. Varying degrees of damage was inflicted on twenty-four land installations, and twenty survivors could attest to VPB-18's proficiency in air-sea rescue.[16]

Six additional PBM-3Rs of Rescue Squadron VH-3 landed at Kerama Retto on 29 March and joined the detachment that had made the trip by sea aboard the *Bering Strait*. In April, the squadron made twenty-seven open-ocean landings and accomplished the rescue of thirty-nine survivors. Five of the landings were carried out in the face of hostile fire from shore batteries, and three others were made with enemy aircraft in the area, being discouraged by friendly fighter cover. The geographic area of these operations ranged from the Sakishima Gunto in the southern Ryukyus to the mouth of the Kagoshima bay in southern Kyushu.[17]

The month of May was much the same; squadron planes made fifteen open-ocean landings, rescuing another thirty-nine survivors. Three of the rescues were opposed by hostile fire from shore, and more than half of them took place within three miles of enemy islands. Operations extended the length of the Ryukyus chain from the mouth of Ariake Wan (Bay) in southern Kyushu to the Sakishima Gunto. Fourteen open-sea landings in June resulted in the rescue of forty-two survivors and assistance provided in saving thirteen others. Rescue Squadron Three "bagged" its first enemy plane when Lt. Edgar P. Palm, USN, returning from a search, shot down an attacking Val east of Okinawa on 3 June.[3]

Photo 27-2

A Martin SP-5B "Marlin" patrol plane uses JATO (jet assisted take-off) rockets to lift from the waters of Cam Rahn Bay, South Vietnam, in April 1967.
U.S. National Archives Photograph #USN 1122402

Palm had previously earned the Distinguished Flying Cross for extraordinary achievement as a patrol plane commander over the Ryukyus area on 30 April 1945. During a Dumbo search mission, Palm arrived on station midafternoon and found two fighters (likely F6F Hellcats from VF-9) orbiting a survivor and dye marker three miles west-southwest of the enemy island of Kikai Shima. Despite seemingly insurmountable conditions, and several failed attempts to land his plane on a foul sea, the intrepid pilot persisted and was successful in saving a fellow aviator. The squadron Air Intelligence Officer's report summarized Palm's actions:

> Landing in the face of 15 foot swells and a 20 knot wind, the plane bounced 70 feet in the air on first touching but was kept under control and after several lesser bounces was brought down undamaged. The port engine was out and the survivor brought aboard the bow hatch at 1520. A JATO [jet assisted] take-off was made and the accompanying VF warned the Dumbo he was being fired on by shore batteries. The plane returned to base at 1640.

The survivor was Lt. (jg) E. J. Warner of Fighting Squadron VF-9 based on the carrier *Yorktown* (CV-10). He had been making a strafing run on the airfield on Kiksi when an AA burst knocked out his engine which caught fire. He dropped his belly tank, ditched several miles out to sea, and had been in his raft for about an hour-and-a-half when rescued. (The acronym JATO refers to a jet-assisted take-off used to help overloaded planes get into the air by providing additional thrust in the form of small rockets—see photo previous page.)[19]

SEAPLANE TENDERS HIT BY KAMIKAZE AIRCRAFT

> *Seaplane operations at Kerama Retto were carried out under extraordinarily difficult conditions of maintenance. All the overhauling work was done by the tenders, and much of it was accomplished on planes in the water, without hoisting the aircraft on board the tenders.... Enemy air raids served to heighten the difficulties encountered by the seaplanes at Kerama. 70 Air raids and 88 hours at general quarters occurred in April.*
>
> —History of Fleet Air Wing One, 1 January - 2 September 1945.[20]

Due to the preponderance of enemy air attacks against Kerama Retto in April, the men aboard the *St. George* came to refer to the anchorage as "Kamikaze Cove." During the time she was at Kerama, her crew was called to their battle stations a total of 219 times. On 29 April, the *St. George*'s guns brought down a Val, which crashed about 900 yards from the ship. A week later, the *St. George* was hit by a suicide Tony aircraft. General Quarters was sounded aboard ship at 0832 on 6 May, and gunfire directed at an air target about 10,000 yards from the ship eight minutes later. Undeterred, the single Japanese plane coming in dove at the *St. George*, striking the starboard side of her seaplane deck, crashing into a PBM Mariner on deck and then into the base of the seaplane crane before penetrating the deck.[21]

The impact separated the plane's engine from the fuselage and propelled it through the skin of the ship into an officer's stateroom on the main deck, as the wreckage burst into flames. The ship's repair parties fought the fire and rescued the injured almost immediately. Due to their rapid actions the flames had no opportunity to get out of control. Sadly, three crewmen had died in the attack, two had received critical injuries and another twenty-five had suffered minor injuries. Following a funeral for the deceased men, their remains were buried in the U.S. Armed Forces Cemetery on Zamami Shima Island that afternoon. The *St. George* remained on station and continued to tend aircraft despite her seaplane crane being inoperative due to damage. A barge was brought alongside the tender and repairs to planes were accomplished aboard it versus lifting them up on her deck.[22]

Rear Adm. John D. Price, commander Fleet Air Wing One, came aboard the ship on 20 May, to award Purple Hearts to those wounded in the kamikaze attack. Carpenter Elwin R. Groseclose, USN, and Chief Carpenter's Mate Darrell C. Onstott, USNR, would later receive Silver Star Medals for conspicuous gallantry and intrepidity in action while serving on a damage control party. The men had unhesitatingly entered a stateroom containing burning gasoline, and in the face of imminent explosions and with complete disregard for their own safety, had remained until the fire was under control.[23]

The large seaplane tender *Curtiss* (AV-4), which had arrived at Okinawa on 22 May to serve as flagship for Rear Admiral Price, was damaged by a kamikaze on 21 June. The first hint of imminent danger came at 1843, when a sighting was made aboard the *Norton Sound* (AV-11) of two low-flying enemy planes—a "Frank" (Nakajima Ki-84 Hayate Army fighter) and a "Zeke—flying north through the south entrance of Kerama Retto at about 200 feet altitude. The Frank crashed into the forward, starboard side of the *Curtiss* just above the waterline. The detached engine pierced her hull and entered sick bay. The aircraft and bomb it carried plunged through the ship's hull, continued downward and exploded on the third deck, killing thirty-five and wounding another twenty-one crewmembers.[24]

Meanwhile the Zeke had flown about 1,500 yards farther north, before circling in a left hand turn. The *Norton Sound* and other ships in the vicinity—*Kenneth Whiting*, *Chandeleur*, and *Bering Strait*—opened fire with their ready gun crews. The Zero fighter was hit and crashed into the water forward of the *Kenneth Whiting*. That evening, Admiral Price shifted his flag from the *Curtiss* to the *Norton Sound*—the same day that Okinawa had been declared secured. Effective damage control kept the *Curtiss* afloat, and four days later she was able to get under way bound for the west coast of the United States and overhaul at Mare Island Navy Yard near San Francisco.[25]

Photo 27-3

Norton Sound (AV-11) hoisting aboard a Martin PBM Mariner patrol bomber while the seaplane tender lay anchored at Kerama Retto, Ryukyu Islands.
U.S. Naval Aviation Museum Photograph No# 2011.003.139.001

THE *GARDINERS BAY* ARRIVES AT OKINAWA

The *Gardiners Bay* (AVP-39) was the last of the seaplane tenders to arrive at Kerama Retto. She was the twenty-third vessel of her class built at the Lake Washington Shipyards, Houghton, Washington, and had been commissioned only a few months earlier on 11 February 1945. She reported for duty to commander Fleet Air Wing One on 7 June and over the next two weeks, refueled and tended planes for various patrol bombing squadrons. On 23-24 June, Rescue Squadron VH-4 reported aboard her and commenced air-sea rescue operations. Concurrently, Comdr. Carlton C. Lucas, USN, commanding officer of the *Gardiners Bay*, received orders from Wing One to form an Air-Sea

Rescue Unit (Task Unit 30.5.2), comprised of Rescue Squadrons VH-3 and 4, Motor Torpedo Boat Squadron 31, and the *Gardiners Bay* (flagship), *Bering Strait*, *Mackinac*, and *Suisun*.[26]

CONTRIBUTIONS OF FLEET AIR WING ONE

During the Ryukyus operation, the ship-tended Mariners and land-based Privateers of Fleet Air Wing One sank a total of 254 Japanese vessels and damaged 298 others. Wing aircraft shot down 46 enemy aircraft and damaged 29 others, and mined the southern Korean coastline, effectively closing it to enemy shipping. Patrol bombers bombed and strafed dozens of radar and weather stations, and destroyed Korean bridges, rolling stock and equipment, and sealed up railway tunnels. These actions in combination with those of U.S. Navy submarines, resulted in a complete blockade of the East China Sea and the Yellow Sea.[27]

28

Third Fleet Operations against Japan

> *After nearly three weeks of replenishment in Leyte Gulf, subsequent to their support of the Okinawa operation, the fast carrier forces of Admiral Halsey's Third Fleet, comprising the greatest mass of sea power ever assembled, proceeded northward on 1 July toward Japan. This huge armada was to complete the destruction of the Japanese fleet, conduct a pre-invasion campaign of destruction against every industry and resource contributing to Japan's ability to wage war, and maintain maximum pressure on the Japanese in order to lower their will to fight.*
>
> —Fleet Adm. Ernest J. King, from *United States Navy at War Final Official Report to the Secretary of the Navy covering the period March 1, 1945, to October 1, 1945.*

On 1 July 1945, after organized enemy resistance on Okinawa had ceased, Task Force 38 (the fast carrier task forces of the Third Fleet) proceeded northward from Leyte Gulf to operate close to Japan; and there it stayed during final phases of the War in the Pacific until Japan surrendered on 15 August. Task force aircraft struck at the city of Tokyo on 10 July and then attacked the islands of Honshu and Hokkaido on 14-15 July. Moving southward, the Third Fleet, joined by units of the British Pacific Fleet under Vice Adm. Sir Henry Bernard Hughes Rawlings, on July 17, made the first combined American-British bombardment of the Japanese homeland. Later that month the same force made extended air strikes in the Inland Sea area and on the Japanese naval base at Kure, returning to harass Tokyo for the third time in three weeks on 30 July.[1]

The Third Fleet had been formed on 15 March 1944 under the command of Adm. William F. Halsey, and had previously operated in and around the Solomon Islands, the Philippines, Formosa, Okinawa and the Ryukyu Islands. During this period of Third Fleet operations against Japan, Fleet Air Wing One units conducted long range search and reconnaissance in areas assigned. Other tasking included attacks on enemy shipping, anti-submarine patrols, and air-sea rescue operations. To best execute his responsibilities, Rear Adm. John D.

Price, USN, commander Fleet Air Wing One and Task Group 30.5 (embarked in the seaplane tender *Norton Sound*) allocated his forces among four task units. The identities of the tenders assigned to each task unit and the aircraft squadrons embarked aboard these ships are contained in tables in the text. The fourth task unit, aptly titled "Landplane Search Unit, Okinawa," operated from Yontan Airfield, Okinawa. PB4Y-2 Privateer aircraft of patrol bombing squadrons VPB-109, 118, 123, and 124, and Photo Group One aircraft, comprised this task unit. The patrol bombers carried out long-range search and attack missions against enemy shipping, as well as attacks on special land targets.[2]

Photo 28-1

PB4Y-2 Privateer patrol planes of VP-23 over Miami, Florida, in July 1949.
U.S. National Archives Photograph #80-G-440193

As a result of a shift in Japanese shipping routes due to submarine and aircraft attacks on its vessels in May and June, Fleet Air Wing One began attacks in July against the Korean railroad system, to which much of the cargo previously moved by water was believed to have been redirected. On 4 July, six Privateers of VPB-118, operating in pairs, made a series of attacks against the double-track railroad line between Keijo and Fusan (today Pusan) and single-track lines to other

South Korean ports. Ten days later, seven Privateers concentrated on the rail line between Keijo and Gunzan and on rail targets around Keijo. On the last day in July, six Privateers destroyed one span of the vital Seisen River Bridge, again severing the main north-south double-track railroad line in Korea.³

SEAPLANE TENDERS RELOCATE TO CHIMU WAN
The tenders were based at Kerama Retto during the first half of July. However, the increasing prevalence of southerly winds caused large swells in the seadrome much of the time and several planes were lost or damaged by choppy seas. A more suitable site for late summer operations became a necessity, and the seaplane base was shifted on 14 July from Kerama Retto, seventeen miles west of Naha, Okinawa, to Chimu Wan on the east coast of Okinawa. This body of water was known to servicemen as Buckner Bay in honor of Lt. Gen. Simon B. Buckner Jr., USA, who had been killed in action on Okinawa a month earlier on 18 June 1945.

The tenders moved there in two groups. The first one made the transit on 14 July, with the *Hamlin* leading the formation, *Kenneth Whiting* 800 yards directly astern of her, and the *Gardiners Bay*, *Mackinac*, and *Suisun* in a protective screen around the large tenders.⁴

Photo 28-2

Seaplane anchorage at Chimu Wan, Okinawa, which soldiers had named Buckner Bay in honor of Lt. Gen. Simon B. Buckner Jr., USA, who was killed on Okinawa. Photograph from "A History of the U.S.S. *Norton Sound* (AV-11), A Seaplane Tender," dated 5 September 1945

The following morning, the *Bering Strait*, *Chandeleur*, *Norton Sound*, *Onslow*, *Shelikof*, and *Yakutat* stood out of Kerama Retto in heavy rain, bound for Chimu Wan. Shortly after clearing the harbor, *Yakutat* was ordered to return to tend crippled aircraft. Upon reaching open water, the 311-foot seaplane tenders *Bering Strait, Onslow,* and *Shelikof* formed a screen around the 514-foot *Norton Sound*—the flagship of Admiral Price—and the 492-foot *Chandeleur* in column formation astern of her. The group proceeded around the southern end of Okinawa and up the eastern shore to Chimu Wan. As *Norton Sound* led the *Chandeleur* inside the bay, the screen patrolled outside and then followed the two larger seaplane tenders to the anchorage. The *Yakutat* joined the other ships the following day.[5]

Chimu Wan proved to be a much improved location for seaplane operations. The harbor was protected on all sides from the sea, except the east, and offered a larger landing and takeoff area, facilitating night operations. For a time, ship and squadron personnel were able to enjoy better recreational facilities than had been available at Kerama Retto. There, liberty parties had taken place on Zamami Island, and recreation had been very limited—about the only sport indulged in was beer drinking. However, liberty ashore at Chimu Wan proved to be short-lived. Within a few days after arrival of the seaplane tenders and patrol squadrons, Okinawa was placed out of bounds except for those going ashore on official business.[6]

AIRCRAFT ANTI-SUBMARINE PATROLS AND ANTI-SHIPPING OPERATIONS

The PBM-5 Mariners of the Anti-Submarine and Strike Unit (Task Unit 30.5.1), based on the *Hamlin, Norton Sound, Onslow, Shelikof,* and *Yakutat,* conducted anti-submarine patrols and strikes against enemy shipping. The purpose of the latter mission was reconnaissance and harassment of the already badly extended Japanese supply lines. Aircraft search sectors stretched out in all directions from Okinawa far into Japanese waters, to Kyushu, along the western coast of Korea, and almost to Tokyo along the eastern coast of Kyushu and Skikoku. Patrol bombers also scouted the Sakishima Islands, along the China coast between Foo Chow and Shanghai, and northwest to the Shantung Peninsula.[7]

The remaining tender assigned to the task unit, the *Duxbury Bay*, was responsible for supporting all Wing One tenders and embarked squadrons. Her diverse duties included laying seaplane mooring buoys at Chimu Wan, serving as a post office ship and movie exchange, and delivering aviation gasoline to an aircraft carrier.[8]

Anti-Submarine and Strike Unit (Task Unit 30.5.1)

Seaplane Tender	Commanding Officer	Embarked Squadron	Squadron Commander
Hamlin (until 11 July) (AV-15)	Capt. Gordon A. McLean, USN	VPB-208: 14 PBM-5	Comdr. Anton J. Sintic Jr., USN
Norton Sound (AV-11)	Capt. Benjamin S. Custer, USN	VPB-26: 12 PBM	Lt. Comdr. R. S. Null
Duxbury Bay (AVP-38)	Comdr. Frank N. Howe, USN		
Onslow (AVP-48)	Comdr. Alden D. Schwarz, USN	VPB-27: 4 PBM	Lt. Comdr. E. N. Chase II, USN
Shelikof (AVP-52)	Comdr. Reuben E. Stanley, USN	VPB-27: 4 PBM	Lt. Comdr. E. N. Chase II, USN
Yakutat (AVP-32)	Lt Comdr. William I. Darnell, USN	VPB-27: 4 PBM	Lt. Comdr. E. N. Chase II, USN

During July, VPB-26 aircraft primarily conducted anti-submarine patrols, and thus opportunities for the destruction of enemy shipping were rare. However, lieutenants Robert G. Turner and William L. Williams sank two "Sugar Dogs" and probably a third one (each about 300 tons displacement) on 23 July off the coast of China near the tip of the Shantung Peninsula. Sugar Dog was the Allied designation for a small coastal freighter. Four days later, Lt. Jacob O. Bach damaged three luggers (small sailing vessels), and set afire and burned two buildings on Miyako Island in Sakishima Gunto.[9]

VPB-208 inflicted damage on enemy shipping by sinking two Sugar Dogs, and damaging another small freighter, and "deep-sixing" a two-masted schooner and damaging three others. Squadron aircraft also severely battered a freighter transport, which possibly beached, and a small patrol craft. However, strike operations were usually not without risk for patrol bombers. One in particular demonstrated it was unwise for PBM-5 Mariners to press home attacks on vessels escorted by enemy warships unless the fire power of the latter had been reduced or eliminated.[10]

On 4 July, five Mariners loaded with two torpedoes each were sent to join three Privateers and eight Thunderbolts in a coordinated strike against an enemy convoy off the China coast. Rendezvous was made near the convoy, consisting of four merchant vessels under escort by three destroyers. The P47 Thunderbolts struck first; losing one of the fighter-bombers in the process, although a destroyer was set afire and one freighter was slightly damaged. The much lighter armed Privateers and Mariners broke off their runs without dropping due to heavy, intense, and accurate anti-aircraft fire. The VPB-208 Mariner patrol bombers eventually released their torpedoes well away from the convoy, at ranges of two-and-a-half to four miles distant and scored no hits on ships.[11]

While VPB-208 was engaged in strike missions, VPB-27 flew night anti-submarine patrol and search and reconnaissance missions. The squadron lost no planes during the course of fifty-eight of the former and fifty-three of the latter, but several aircraft suffered battle damage. The most serious resulted from an attack on two Mariners by enemy fighters near Shanghai, in which three Tojos (Nakajima Ki-44 Army Type 2 fighters) struck from out of the sun. Flying the lead plane of two PBMs on an anti-shipping search, Lt. R. S. Scott saw a Togo appear in the direction of the sun. He added power and nosed over to get down close to the water. However, the enemy quickly closed, and opened up with heavy caliber fire, severely damaging Scott's aircraft and wounding both pilots and two crewmen. One explosive round hit aft of the bow turret severely injuring the pilot about his legs, body, and face, and rendering him unconscious. The co-pilot received a facial wound and was blinded by the blood pouring from it.[12]

With both the pilot and co-pilot incapacitated, the navigator acted quickly to save the aircraft from crashing, as detailed by an entry in the squadron's war diary:

> Lieut. (jg) Guy Eby, the navigator, was near the flight engineer's panel when the shell hit. He ran forward and as the plane was still in a steep glide with full power and full RPMs, Lieut. (jg) Eby grabbed the yoke from the dazed co-pilot and attempted to pull the plane up. But the nose-up elevator control had been shot away and the plane failed to respond. Eby then immediately rolled nose-up tab and succeeded in pulling the plane up when it was less than 200 feet from the water and indicating better than 200 knots.
>
> With the plane heading upward Lieut. (jg) Eby helped Lieut. (jg) [W. H.] Dompier from the starboard seat and took over the controls, finally getting the plane squared away on level flight. After a few minutes when a fire in the bow had been extinguished, Lieut. (jg) Eby called the Plane Captain and others, who removed Lieut. Scott from the port seat and took him to a bunk where they provided emergency treatment.[13]

Even allowing for Eby's rapid and correct actions, it's remarkable that the patrol bomber was able to cripple back from the mission. A post-flight inspection of the aircraft revealed that damage wrought by the enemy fighter had almost completely demolished instrumentation and control surfaces, and caused the loss of much of the plane's fuel. One explosive shell exploded against the instrument panel destroying all instruments in the first pilot's seat and wounding both pilots. Another exploded in the starboard wing just inboard of the engine, punching several holes in the wing tank. Two other shells hit the tail assembly, one on the vertical stabilizer on the starboard side, and the other the port vertical stabilizer.[14]

AIR-SEA RESCUE OPERATIONS

While Patrol Bombing Squadrons VPB-26, 27, and 208 flew antisubmarine and strike missions, Rescue Squadrons VH-3 and 4, and four PT boats of Motor Torpedo Boat Squadron 31, conducted air-sea rescue in support of Third Fleet operations.

Air-Sea Rescue Unit (Task Unit 30.5.2)

Ship	Commanding Officer	Supported Squadron	Commander
Pine Island (AV-12) (reported 16 July)	Comdr. Henry T. Hodgkins Jr., USN	VH-3 embarked from *Bering Strait* and *Gardiners Bay* on 17 July	VH-4 embarked from *Suisun* and *Gardiners Bay* on 17 July
Gardiners Bay (AVP-39)	Comdr. Carlton C. Lucas, USN	VH-3 PBMs VH-4 PBMs	Total of 6 PBMs in each squadron
Bering Strait (AVP-34)	Comdr. Walter D. Innis USN	VH-3: 4 PBM Mariner aircraft	Lt. Comdr. William D. Bonvillian, USN
Casco (AVP-12) detached 5 July	Comdr. Reginald Rutherford, USN	MTB Squadron 31: 4 PT boats	Lt. John M. Searles, USNR
Mackinac (AVP-13)	Comdr. Paul L. Stahl, USN	MTB Squadron 31: 4 PT boats	Lt. John M. Searles, USNR
Suisun (AVP-53)	Comdr. James J. Vaughan, USN	VH-4: PBM Mariner aircraft	Lt. Forest H. Norvell Jr.

Six seaplane tenders served with the Air-Sea Rescue Unit in July. The *Bering Strait*, *Gardiners Bay*, *Pine Island*, and *Suisun* provided upkeep for the PBM-5 Mariner aircraft and personnel of Rescue Squadrons 3 and 4. The *Casco* and later the *Mackinac*, which replaced her, supported four PT boats of MTB Squadron 31, which carried out several successful air-sea rescue missions. The remaining boats of Lt. John M. Searles' squadron operated from Toguchi, Okinawa, maintaining "flycatcher patrols" between the northern coast of Okinawa and Yoron Island to prevent the enemy from reinforcing or evacuating Okinawa.

(The term "flycatcher" also applied to operations involving finding the locations of hidden Japanese suicide boats, and destroying the craft. This subject is discussed in ensuing pages.) In the course of these patrols, PT boats sank one 40-foot lugger and seven canoes, loaded with Japanese troops seeking to escape.[15]

Rescue Squadron VH-3 aircraft made twenty water landings in July, recovered sixty-two survivors, and assisted in the recovery of nine more survivors. Two of the rescues were made in the Inland Sea of Japan in support of Third Fleet strikes on the Japanese home islands. The others were made as far west as the China coast and south along the Ryukyus islands to Sakashima Gunto.[16]

PBM Mariners of Rescue Squadron VH-4 flew air-sea rescue missions covering strikes by the 21st Bomber Command, 2nd Marine Air Wing, Fifth Army Air Force, 308th Bombardment Wing, and Third Fleet on targets in Japan; the Miyako Islands southwest of Okinawa; Amami Oshima (a large island between Kyushu and Okinawa); and the China coast. During sixty-one such flights, eleven open-sea landings were made and thirteen survivors recovered. On three occasions, U.S. submarines picked up downed aviators located by seaplanes in waters too rough for them to land.[17]

SEAPLANE SEARCH UNIT

> *We had been tender-based before, off and on, but never all together and never for long enough to feel that the ship was ours, which is how we felt about the USS ST. GEORGE (AV-16). Capt. R. G. ARMSTRONG, USN, had made it clear to his officers and men that the sole purpose of the ship and crew was to keep VPB-18 flying. The friendly cooperation we received from the ship's company left little to be desired. Especially appreciated was the boat service; rarely did a VPB-18 plane make its buoy before a personnel boat was alongside to take off personnel. For this and the prompt bower-boat service we were the envy of our less fortunate brethren on the other tenders. Clean, comfortable quarters, fresh-water showers, ice-cold drinking water, daily gedunks [ice cream, candy, and other snack foods], excellent laundry service, and above all, chow that was varied, well prepared and attractively served - all those helped keep squadron morale at a high pitch.*

> —Lt. Comdr. R. R. Boettcher, USN, commander Patrol Bombing Squadron 18, praising the support and services provided VPB-18 by the large seaplane tender *St. George*.[18]

The remaining seaplane tenders—*Chandeleur*, *Kenneth Whiting*, and *St. George*, and later the *Hamlin*—were assigned to the Seaplane Search Unit. Commander Fleet Air Wing One's guidance to the aviation squadrons serviced by these ships was very brief and unambiguous, "Conduct aggressive reconnaissance in sectors assigned, observing enemy ship movements, and disrupting traffic in enemy sea lanes as opportunity permits."[19]

Seaplane Search Unit (Task Unit 30.5.6)

Ship	Commanding Officer	Supported Squadron	Commander
St. George (AV-16) detached 12 July	Capt. Robert G. Armstrong, USN	VPB-18: PBM-5 aircraft	Lt. Comdr. R. R. Boettcher, USN
Hamlin (AV-15) reported 11 July	Capt. Gordon A. McLean, USN	VPB-208: 14 PBM-5 aircraft	Lt. Comdr. Anton J. Sintic Jr., USN
Chandeleur (AV-10)	Capt. John S. Tracy, USN	VPB-21: PBM-5 aircraft	Lt. Comdr. James D. Wright, USN
Kenneth Whiting (AV-14)	Capt. Raymond R. Lyons, Capt. Alfred R. Truslow Jr.	VPB-13: 14 PB2Y-5 aircraft	Lt. Comdr. J. A. Ferguson, USN

The officers and men of VPB-18 aboard the *St. George* were informed by Lt. Comdr. R. R. Boettcher on 9 July that they were being recalled to Saipan for a period of rehabilitation and training. Boettcher described the pressing need for extensive maintenance and repairs to his remaining aircraft, and praised the efforts made to keep them operational for as long as possible:

> The rough water in the Kerama Retto area, coupled with enemy action and long grueling patrol hours day in and day out, had resulted in a good many engine and structural failures. The large ground swells already mentioned caused a great deal of prop trouble, as well as an oil or gas leak on practically every flight. The leaks were as much a result of the necessary high power settings as they were of heavy pounding and jolting during take-off and landing.
>
> During the quarter, six planes were lost. Two were shot down by enemy fighters; two were lost at sea to engine failures and lack of gas; one was lost in a taxiing accident; and the sixth was struck by a suicide plane while on the seaplane deck undergoing repairs. One plane was brought back a distance of 500 miles on single engine. In summary, though our availability was down to three planes at times, it was always possible to find enough to fly the

assigned missions. There was a lot of maintenance necessary and the facilities were definitely limited. But the PATSU (Aircraft Service Unit) attached to the tender did a very credible job and kept us in the air.[20]

Three of the squadron's planes flew to Tanapag, Saipan, on 10 July, followed by six more the next day. VPB-18 transferred its remaining planes to other squadrons in the area, and the excess flight and ground personnel left Guam aboard the *St. George* on 13 July. Following her arrival at Saipan four days later, the seaplane tender went into dry dock for general overhaul and replacement of a crane rendered useless by a Kamikaze attack in May.[21]

The *Hamlin* and VPB-208—which had been assigned to the Anti-Submarine and Strike Unit—replaced the *St. George* and VPB-18 in the Seaplane Search Unit on 11 July. While thus assigned, five of VPB-208's Mariners had joined three Privateers and eight Thunderbolts in the unsuccessful coordinated attack on an enemy ship convoy off the China coast described earlier.[22]

Photo 28-3

PB2Y Coronado patrol bomber.
U.S. National Archives Photograph #80-G-359435

"CORONADO" PATROL BOMBERS

All the squadrons tended by ships flew PBM Mariners except VPB-13 aboard the *Kenneth Whiting*, which had PB2Y-5 "Coronado" patrol bombers. This aircraft, like PBY Catalinas, was manufactured by the Consolidated Aircraft Company. However, it was bigger (79 feet in length with a 115-foot wingspan) than a PBY and had a correspondingly larger crew (normally ten men) and weapons payload. The Coronados were fitted with eight guns—six 12.7mm M2 Browning machine guns in twin nose, dorsal, and tail powered-turrets, and two Browning guns in manual waist mounts—and could either carry an ordnance load of two Mk. 13 torpedoes or up to 12,000 pounds of bombs. The robust planes could also carry three-times the weight in bombs of a Mariner.[23]

VPB-13 flew eighty-seven day armed reconnaissance and twenty-nine night armed reconnaissance flights in July, all long-range. The search sectors extended from Okinawa to the east coast of China and Shanghai area; over to the Yellow Sea (the northern part of the East China Sea between China and the Korean Peninsula); along the west coast of Korea; along the east coast of Kyushu and Shikoku; and in the areas southwest of Kyushu, and southeast of Kyushu and Shikoku. Although planes repeatedly covered this expansive area, contact with the enemy was moderate and targets difficult to find. Two PB2Ys did attack an enemy lugger near Chosin, Korea, on 8 July and set it aflame. Enemy lighthouses, radar locations, and installations along the China coast were strafed and bombed on the 30th and again on 31 July.[24]

The remaining Seaplane Search Unit patrol bombing squadron, VPB-21, was aboard the *Chandeleur*. The number of enemy sightings and attacks made by her aircraft in July were considerably less than previous monthly levels in April through June. The most important sighting was made by the pilots of a Mariner flying a Yellow Sea patrol on 13 July. They spotted four new Japanese destroyers and two escort vessels in the middle of the sea heading in the direction of Jeju, Korea's largest island, located approximately fifty miles south of the peninsula at the entrance to the Tsushima Strait. This island was then occupied by the Japanese; who referred to it as Saishu To.[25]

The Japanese destroyers sighted by the Mariner detected the patrol bomber when it was five miles away and immediately opened up with heavy anti-aircraft fire. From a safe distance, the aircraft tracked the ships for three hours before reaching its PLE (prudent limit of endurance). During this period, four reports were sent to base and twelve transmissions made to all submarines along the destroyers' course. At PLE, the pilots began their return leg to ensure adequate fuel to make it back to base. No attack was sent out against the enemy ships—presumably because available submarines and attack aircraft were otherwise occupied—and they got away during the night.²⁶

JAPANESE SUICIDE EXPLOSIVE MOTORBOATS

Photo 28-4

Japanese "Shinyo" (suicide) explosive motorboat discovered after the war in a cave at Sasagawa Chiba, Japan, on 22 September 1945.
U.S. National Archives Photograph #80-G-379177

Unbeknownst to the American military, large numbers of Shinyo ("Sea Quake") suicide explosive motorboats were based on Jeju Island. They were a part of KETSU-GO (Decisive Operation) the Japanese plan for defeating the expected Allied invasion of the home islands. Defensive in nature, the operation divided the Japanese home territory into seven zones from which the entire strengths of the Army, Navy and Air Force would fight the final decisive battles of the Japanese empire. "The sooner the Americans come, the better.... One hundred million die proudly" was a Japanese slogan in the summer of 1945. The U.S. Naval Technical Mission (an organization sent to Japan after the war) described the Shinyo program—which was a part of a larger

Special Attack Units program that included kamikaze aircraft, kaiten human-torpedoes, and other means of suicide attacks—in a report:

> On the surface of the water, it took the form of Shinyo, a small special attack boat which utilized the explosive charge in its bow by ramming the side of the intended victim. These motor boats were collected in special attack basins along the coast or carried on mother ships. Such suicide craft were manned by middle school boys of 15 and 16 years of age. It is reported that a supply of volunteer pilots was obtained because of special privileges, early responsibility, fast promotion, and the promise of a posthumous monetary award to the volunteer's parents.[27]

RESCUE OF A B24 BOMBER CREW FROM HAIMEN

Other minor attacks and harassing forays by VPB-21 patrol planes followed. These included an attack against a 50-foot vessel at Uotsuri Shima; attacks on a truck, bridge, and party of horseback riders in Sakashima Gunto; and on a lighthouse and installations on an island off the China coast. The most interesting mission took place on 27 July, when Lt. M. C. Stovall, accompanied by Lt. Floyd Harris, flew to Haimen, on the coast of China between Wenchow and Ningpo, to pick up an Army Air Force captain who had been shot down near Shanghai, and the crew of a B24 which had gone down over Shanghai on 17 July. Haimen was considered to be dangerous; Japanese troops in the area had retreated inland only days earlier.[28]

Stovall landed around noon at the mouth of the river at Haimen, an event of great interest to the local population. Hundreds of Chinese crowded onto waterfront streets and piers, while others sought the vantage point of a temple on a nearby hill to watch the Army evacuees ferried out to the plane. The passengers, still wearing the blue coolie attire that had facilitated their evasion of the Japanese, boarded the aircraft. Stovall then performed the formalities of departure, and took off to the wonderment of the native audience. The plane arrived back at Chima Wan in late afternoon, completing the five hundredth VPB-21 mission since the squadron's arrival in the Ryukyus on 29 March 1945. In Stovall's words, "there was nothing to it."[29]

SUMMATION OF FLEET AIR WING ONE'S EFFORTS

> *The month of July witnessed the almost entire elimination from the YELLOW SEA of enemy shipping of any size or importance. Sightings, particularly along the CHINA COAST, were limited to junks, motorboats and other small vessels. The heavy toll taken of JAPANESE shipping by submarines and Fleet Air Wing One planes in May and June apparently prompted the enemy to withdraw ships remaining in the YELLOW SEA to the SEA OF JAPAN and to rely on round about and already heavily overburdened rail routes to move vitally needed war materials from CHINA, MANCHURIA and NORTH KOREA to KOREAN railhead ports, for a relatively short haul by ship to the [Japanese] EMPIRE.*
>
> —Fleet Air Wing One War Diary, July 1945

Duty for the crews of seaplane tenders in July was characterized by the servicing of planes, interspersed with periodic battle stations for Flash Red air raid warnings. Aboard the *Kenneth Whiting*, General Quarters was set on twenty-four occasions due to enemy aircraft in the vicinity, with total time thus spent 17 hours 38 minutes. During dusk and night air raids, the ships laid smoke screen using fog generators or smoke pots. It was policy that ships screened by smoke did not fire at enemy aircraft overhead or in the vicinity, unless directly attacked, in order to not reveal their position.[30]

Photo 28-5

Seaplane tender *Onslow* (AVP-48) refueling a PBM Mariner.
U.S. Navy Photograph #NH 97673

Heavy squalls occurred at various times during the month, but did not materially affect flying conditions, with the exception of the threat posed by an approaching typhoon. This storm forced the evacuation of all flyable aircraft (seventy-three) to Saipan the evening of 18 July or the following morning, and suspension of aircraft operations until 21 July. The seaplane tenders put to sea on 19 July to ride out the storm, returning to their anchorages at Chimu Wan the following evening.[31]

LAURELS FOR SEAPLANE TENDERS AND VPB-18

Fourteen seaplane tenders and thirteen squadrons of Fleet Air Wing One received a battle star for the period 10-25 July 1945 for "Third Fleet Operations against Japan." Patrol Bombing Squadron VPB-18 also received the Navy Unit Commendation; a copy of the award citation may be found in Appendix K.

Ship	Commanding Officer	Ship	Commanding Officer
Chandeleur (AV-10)	Capt. John S. Tracy	*Floyds Bay* (AVP-40)	Comdr. James R. Ogden
Hamlin (AV-15)	Capt. Gordon A. McLean	*Gardiners Bay* (AVP-39)	Comdr. Carlton C. Lucas, USN
Kenneth Whiting (AV-14)	Comdr. Raymond R. Lyons, and Capt. Alfred R. Truslow Jr.	*Mackinac* (AVP-13)	Comdr. Paul L. Stahl
Norton Sound (AV-11)	Capt. Benjamin S. Custer	*Onslow* (AVP-48)	Comdr. Alden D. Schwarz
Pine Island (AV-12)	Comdr. Henry T. Hodgskin Jr.	*Shelikof* (AVP-52)	Comdr. Reuben E. Stanley
Bering Strait (AVP-34)	Comdr. Walter D. Innis	*Suisun* (AVP-53)	Comdr. James J. Vaughan
Duxbury Bay (AVP-38)	Comdr. Frank N. Howe	*Yakutat* (AVP-32)	Lt. Comdr. William I. Darnell
VH-1	Lt. Comdr. R. R. Barrett Jr. Lt. H. G. Crawford	VPB-27	Lt. Comdr. E. N. Chase II
VH-3	Lt. Comdr. William D. Bonvilian	VPB-109	Lt. Comdr. George L. Hicks
VH-4	Lt. Forest H. Norvell Jr.	VPB-118	Comdr. C. K. Harper
VH-6	Lt. Comdr. L. O. Ebey	VPB-123	Lt. Comdr. S. C. Shilling
VPB-13	Comdr. J. A. Ferguson	VPB-124	Lt. Comdr. John M. Miller
VPB-21	Lt. Comdr. James D. Wright	VPB-208	Lt. Comdr. Anton J. Sintic Jr.
VPB-26	Lt. Comdr. R. S. Null		

Navy Unit Commendation

Squadron	Award Period	Commanding Officer
VPB-18	1 Apr-31 Jul 1945	Lt. Comdr. R. R. Boettcher

29

War's End

> *The Americans had seen from April 1 to July 2 [1945] the damage that a cornered Japanese military—shorn of its navy, air force, and intermingled with civilians—could inflict on Americans. They clearly wanted no more Okinawas. Had the Americans not invaded Okinawa, it is more, not less, likely that they would have landed on the Japanese mainland in late summer and thereby suffered far greater casualties.*
>
> —Victor Davis Hanson postulating in *Ripples of Battle* that because the Japanese on Okinawa were so fierce in their defense, and because casualties were so appalling, many American strategists looked for an alternative means to end the war other than a direct invasion of mainland Japan. This means presented itself in the use of atomic bombs.

Following extensive Third Fleet Operations against the Japanese empire in July and early August 1945, Japan was finished as a war making nation, in spite of its four million men still under arms. But Japan's leaders were determined to fight on, because seemingly to not lose "face" was more important than the hundreds of thousands of lives that would be lost. To continue was no longer a question of military strategy, but an aspect of Japanese culture and psychology.

As American president Harry S. Truman was wrestling with the decision to drop an atomic bomb on the city of Hiroshima on Honshu Island, the Japanese government was mobilizing the entire population of Japan to impose massive casualties on any American invasion. Operation KETSU-GO called for the use of the Civilian Volunteer Corps—comprised of all boys and men ages fifteen to sixty and all girls and women seventeen to forty, except for those exempted as unfit. These men and women received weapons training in the use of hand grenades, swords, sickles, knives, fire hooks, and bamboo spears. Led by regular forces, they were to actively defend a few selected beach areas, and then to mass reserves for an all-out counterattack if the invasion forces succeeded in winning a beachhead. A Japanese slogan in 1945 was "The sooner the Americans come, the better.... One hundred million [Japanese will] die proudly."[1]

Diagram 29-1

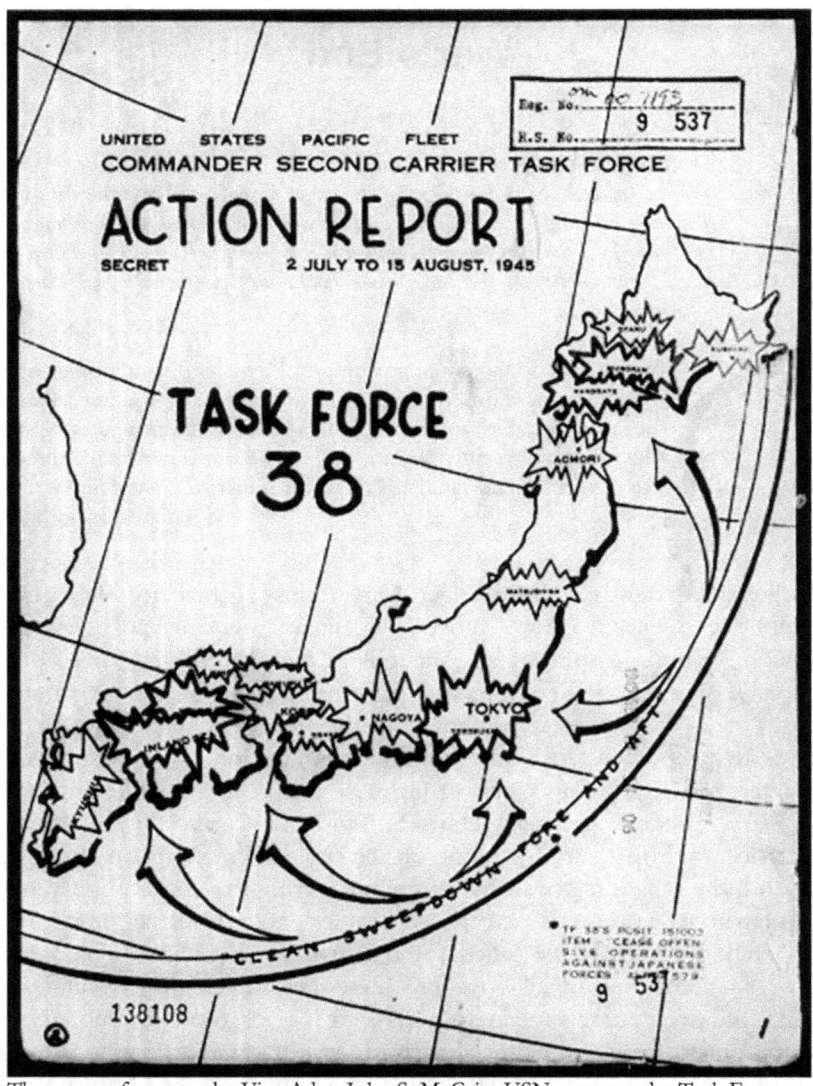

The cover of a report by Vice Adm. John S. McCain, USN, commander Task Force 38, on the operations from 2 July-15 August 1945 of his fast aircraft carriers against Japan, graphically depicts the last naval actions in the Pacific.

USE OF ATOMIC BOMBS ON JAPAN ENDS WAR

On 6 August 1945, the American B29 bomber "Enola Gay" dropped a five-ton bomb over Hiroshima, reducing four square miles of the city to ruins and immediately killing 80,000 people. Tens of thousands more died in the following weeks from wounds suffered and from radiation poisoning. Despite these horrific civilian casualties, the Japanese government refused to capitulate. As a result, a bomb was dropped three days later on the city of Nagasaki, on the northwest coast of the island of Kyushu, killing nearly 40,000 more people. Thereafter, Emperor Hirohito accepted the inevitable defeat of Japan. At noon on 15 August, a recording of his formal announcement of surrender was transmitted from the Imperial Palace in Tokyo all over the Japanese Empire. In the broadcast, Hirohito stated in part:

> Moreover, the enemy has begun to employ a new and most cruel bomb, the power of which to do damage is, indeed, incalculable, taking the toll of many innocent lives. Should we continue to fight, not only would it result in an ultimate collapse and obliteration of the Japanese nation, but also it would lead to the total extinction of human civilization.[2]

That same day, 15 August, Adm. William F. Halsey, commander Third Fleet, received orders from Fleet Adm. Chester W. Nimitz, commander-in-chief Pacific Fleet, to cease all operations against Japan. The cease fire order was received too late to stop the first of the day's air strikes against Tokyo, but the second strike which had been launched, was recalled in time. Two weeks later, Nimitz arrived in Tokyo Bay aboard a PB2Y Coronado seaplane, in preparation for Japan's formal surrender aboard the battleship *Missouri* (BB-63).[3]

SURRENDER CEREMONY IN TOKYO BAY

> *It is my earnest hope, and indeed the hope of all mankind, that from this solemn occasion a better world shall emerge out of the blood and carnage of the past—a world dedicated to the dignity of man and the fulfillment of his most cherished wish for freedom, tolerance and justice.*
>
> —Closing remark made by Gen. Douglas MacArthur during a speech at the Surrender Ceremony of Japan aboard the battleship USS *Missouri* (BB-63) on 2 September 1945.

Photo 29-1

Fleet Adm. Chester W. Nimitz, USN, arrives at Tokyo Bay in a seaplane on 29 August 1945. The battleship *Missouri* (BB-63) is in the background. U.S. Naval History and Heritage Command Photograph #NH 96809

Photo 29-2

Nimitz signs the formal instrument of Japanese surrender as representative of the United States.
Source: Fleet Adm. Ernest J. King, *United States at War Final Official Report to the Secretary of the Navy covering the period March 1, 1945, to October 1, 1945*

Present in Tokyo Bay on that day were 255 Allied naval ships and merchant vessels. Five were the seaplane tenders *Cumberland Sound* (AV-17), *Hamlin* (AV-15), *Gardiners Bay* (AVP-39), *Mackinac* (AVP-13), and *Suisun* (AVP-53).[5]

Ship Type	No.	Ship Type	No.	Ship Type	No.
battleships	10	motor minesweepers	12	repair ship	1
small aircraft carriers	2	auxiliary minelayer	1	landing craft repair ship	1
escort carriers	3	amphibious force flagships	3	fleet oilers	5
heavy cruisers	5	high-speed transports	13	civilian oilers	5
light cruisers	10	tank landing ships	8	gasoline tanker	1
destroyers	48	dock landing ships	2	destroyer tender	1
destroyer escorts	9	infantry landing craft	9	hospital ships	3
frigates	2	medium landing ships	13	large seaplane tenders	2
sloops	2	vehicle landing ships	2	small seaplane tenders	3
light minelayers	2	attack transports	21	submarine tender	1
high-speed minesweepers	7	transport	1	submarine rescue ship	1
submarines	12	attack cargo ships	9	fleet ocean tugs	2
submarine chasers	5	cargo ship	1	auxiliary ocean tug	1
motor gunboats	3	civilian cargo ships	2	old ocean tug	1
Minesweepers	9	stores issue ship	1		

Photo 29-3

Capt. Etheridge Grant, USN, (center), checks charts with a Japanese Navy pilot and Lieutenant Rogers, USN, as his ship, the seaplane tender *Cumberland Sound* (AV-17), prepares to enter Tokyo Bay on 28 August 1945.
U.S. Navy Photo #80-G-344500, now in the collections of the National Archives

Postscript

> *On 15 August [1945] President Truman was able to announce the unconditional surrender by the Japanese Imperial Government. Orders were sent out for the occupation of Japan and Korea.... Overnight [there was] a change in the attitude of the men in the combat zone from one of war to one of peace. Suddenly everybody wanted to go home. No one was interested in becoming a member of the occupational forces.*
>
> —Excerpts from a description by Vice Adm. Daniel E. Barbey, USN (Ret.) in *MacArthur's Navy* about the perspective of Sailors and Marines in the Pacific following the end of World War II, which could also describe the attitude of servicemen in Europe after the cessation of fighting there[1]

Following the war, the seaplane tenders in the Pacific did not all immediately return home to the United States. Some remained in Asian waters on occupational duty; others were sent there. In total, Navy men aboard twenty seaplane tenders earned Asia clasps to affix to their Occupation Service Medals. Two of these same ships, as well as one other tender, received Europe clasps for duty there in 1953. Eighteen of the tenders that performed Asia occupational service also received a China Service Medal. However, continued duty of most of the Navy's seaplane tenders would be short lived. As a result of a massive post-war demobilization, and ongoing disposal of its seaplane tenders, the Navy had in ensuing years, fewer and fewer of these type ships. A mere five took part in the Korean War, and only three in the Vietnam War.

The table on the following page provides a summary of the post-World War II service of the Navy's seaplane tenders, and the Vietnam duty of seven former seaplane tenders. Six of these ships—the *Half Moon* (WHEC-378), *Yakutat* (WHEC-380), *Barataria* (WHEC-381), *Bering Strait* (WHEC-382), *Castle Rock* (WHEC-383), and *Cook Inlet* (WHEC-384)—plied South Vietnam waters as Coast Guard high endurance cutters. The seventh one, *Rehoboth*, served the Navy as the survey ship AGS-50.

Included in the table are the number of periods of service of ships associated with occupational duty and China Service, and battle stars and service stars earned in Korea and Vietnam. Personnel assigned to seaplane tenders engaged in Occupation Duty and China Service were eligible to receive only a single award for each, no matter how many qualifying periods their ship participated in within the time frame authorized. The officers and men of ships that served in Korea and Vietnam could affix a star to their Korea and/or Vietnam Service Medals for each period of qualifying service in which they participated.

Post-World War II Service of Seaplane Tenders

Ship	Occupational Duty	China Service	Korean War	Vietnam War
Wright (AV-1)	1 Asia	1		
Curtiss (AV-4)	1 Asia	1		
Currituck (AV-7)	2 Asia	3		5
Tangier (AV-8)	2 Asia	1		
Pine Island (AV-12)	4 Asia	22		4
Salisbury Sound (AV-13)	5 Asia	6		4
Kenneth Whiting (AV-14)		4		
St George (AV-16)	2 Asia	1		
Cumberland Sound (AV-17)	1 Asia			
Chincoteague (AVP-24)	1 Asia	1		
Half Moon (WHEC-378)*				6
Yakutat (WHEC-380)*				8
Barataria (AVP-33)	1 Asia	1		
Barataria (WHEC-381)*				2
Bering Strait (WHEC-382)*				9
Castle Rock (WHEC-383)*				2
Cook Inlet (WHEC-384)*				5
Corson (AVP-37)	1 Asia	5	1	
Duxbury Bay (AVP-38)	3 Asia	2		
Gardiners Bay (AVP-39)	6 Asia	14	4	
Floyds Bay (AVP-40)	3 Asia	11	1	
Greenwich Bay (AVP-41)	1 Asia	2		
Onslow (AVP-48)	2 Asia	3	1	
Orca (AVP-49)	2 Asia	9		
Rehoboth (AVP-50)	3 Asia 1 Europe	2		
Rehoboth (AGS-50)**				4
Shelikof (AVP-52)	1 Asia 1 Europe			
Suisun (AVP-53)	3 Asia	9	1	
Timbalier (AVP-54)	1 Europe			

* Earned Vietnam Service Medals as U.S. Coast Guard cutters (WHEC)
** Earned Vietnam Service Medal as a U.S Navy survey ship (AGS-50)

POST-WAR DEMOBILIZATION

After World War II, following great loss of life and deprivation, Americans wanted a peace dividend and a return to the lives they had enjoyed before Japan's unprovoked attack on Pearl Harbor. Acceding to their wishes, legislators slashed funding and support for defense, resulting in the Navy's declaring scores of ships excess to the needs of the service and rapidly decommissioning and transferring them to the Maritime Commission or War Shipping Administration for disposal. Within five years, the fleet had decreased to only seven percent of its strength on 14 August 1945 (VJ Day), when there were 6,768 active ships in the U.S. Navy Following the first eleven months of post-war demobilization, the active ship force level stood at 1,248 ships and by 30 June 1950 had been reduced to 634 ships.[2]

One might well wonder what happened to the thousands of once proud U.S. Navy vessels. Many were transferred by sale or lease to allies and other foreign countries, including the Soviet Union. The remaining ships were scrapped, transferred to federal or state agencies, sold to private individuals, or laid-up in the "mothball" anchorages of the Atlantic and Pacific Reserve Fleets. These organizations, which had been established around 1912, were originally comprised of reserve ships operated on a greatly reduced schedule. However, because hundreds of ships were no longer needed following World War II, each fleet was reconstituted of naval vessels that although fully equipped for service were partially or fully decommissioned, held in reserve against a time when it might be necessary to call them back into service. In earlier times, these ships were said to be "laid up in ordinary." Now commonly referred to by sailors as the "ghost fleet," the eerily still, silent, and often fog-shrouded vessels were usually moored or anchored in backwaters near naval bases or shipyards for easier reactivation should the need arise.[3]

Such was the case with many of the seaplane tenders that survived the war. Three did not. The *Langley* (AV-3) had been lost as a result of a Japanese aircraft attack on 27 Feb 1942; the *Gannet* (AVP-8) torpedoed and sunk by the German submarine *U-653* on 7 June 1942; and the *Thornton* (AVD-11) decommissioned on 2 May 1945 and struck from the Naval Register on 13 Aug 1945, due to damage resulting from collisions at sea. The *Gannet* was one of nine World War I vintage minesweepers converted for duty as small seaplane tenders (AVP). Her eight sister ships were all decommissioned in 1945 and 1946. Similarly, the *Thornton* was one of fourteen "Flush Deck" destroyers of the same era pressed into duty as destroyer seaplane tenders (AVD). The remaining thirteen of these type ships were decommissioned, struck, and sold for scrap between 1944 and 1947.

The Navy hung on to its large seaplane tenders (AV) for quite some time. The Navy judged the *Wright* (AV-1) too old for continued service, and decommissioned and struck her in 1946. The Sea Service retained the other tenders into the 1960s and 1970s. The *Tangier*, *Pocomoke*, *Kenneth Whiting*, and *Cumberland Sound* were struck in 1961, the *Curtiss*, *Hamlin*, and *St. George* in 1963, and the *Currituck*, *Chandeleur*, and *Pine Island* in 1971.

At least two of these ships continued working as civilian vessels. The ex-*Tangier* was registered in 1963 by Beauregard Inc., Wilmington, Delaware, as the freighter *Detroit*—which was able to carry cars and sixty-two containers. A local change of ownership took place in 1969, and she remained in service, operated by Sea-Land Services, Inc. The freighter was scrapped in 1972. Ocean Ventures, Inc., of Portland, Oregon, registered the ex-*Cumberland Sound* in 1971 as the freight barge *Big Z*. She was scrapped in 1974.[4]

The two remaining AVs from World War II continued to serve the Navy, albeit not as seaplane tenders. The *Albemarle* was taken out of the National Defense Reserve Fleet on the James River (at Fort Eustis, Virginia) and placed in service in January 1966 as the USNS *Corpus Christi Bay* (T-ARVH-1). She served as a Helicopter Aircraft Repair Ship in Vietnam, operating out of Cam Ranh Bay during 1966. She was placed out of service on 31 December 1974, and was sold for scrapping the following year.

Photo Postscript-1

USS *Norton Sound* (AV-11) launches a V-1 "loon" missile on 12 October 1949. A "lark" missile can be seen on the fo'c'sle to its right.
U.S. National Archives Photograph #80-G-438269

The former seaplane tender with the longest Navy service was the *Norton Sound*. She was converted in 1948 at the Philadelphia Naval Shipyard for use as a mobile missile launching platform. After initially retaining her AV-11 hull number, the Navy re-designated her a guided missile ship (AVM-1) on 8 August 1951. During the next four decades, she supported a variety of Navy-conducted missile tests. *Norton Sound* was decommissioned on 11 December 1986, struck on 26 January 1987 and "laid up" in the Suisun Bay Reserve Fleet at Benicia, California. Following her sale to C. J. W. Shipping and Trading Company, San Francisco, she was towed to Taiwan for scrapping.[5]

BARNEGAT-CLASS SMALL SEAPLANE TENDERS

> *The workmanship on the vessel is generally quite superior to that observed on other vessels constructed during the war. The vessel has ample space for stores, living accommodations, ships, offices and recreational facilities. The main engine system is excellent . . . The performance of the vessel in moderate to heavy seas is definitely superior to that of any other cutter. This vessel can be operated at higher speed without storm damage than other Coast Guard vessels.*
>
> —Comdr. W. C. Hogan, commanding Officer, CGC *McCulloch* in a memorandum to the Commandant of the Coast Guard, titled: CGC McCulloch, Suitability for use as CG Cutter, 12 February 1947.[6]

Twenty-nine *Barnegat-class* small seaplane tenders served during World War II; two others, the *Timbalier* (AVP-54) and *Valcour* (AVP-55) were commissioned after the war on 24 May and 5 July 1946, respectively. The Navy having no requirement in peacetime for large numbers of these type ships wanted to dispose of the bulk of them. The Coast Guard, needing cutters, was happy to acquire sixteen of the relatively new and versatile vessels between 1946 and 1949. It designated fifteen as Seaplane Tenders (WAVP), and the *Rockaway* an Oceanographic Ship (WAGO). The classification of all of these ships was changed on 1 May 1966 to High Endurance Cutter (WHEC). Several years later, on 23 September 1971, that of *Rockaway* changed a third time to Offshore Law Enforcement Vessel (WOLE).

Photo Postscript-2

Coast Guard cutter *Dexter* (WAVP-385)—ex-*Biscayne* (AVP-11)—arriving at her new home port, San Francisco, California, on 11 August 1958.
U.S. Coast Guard Photograph No. 80458:12 CGD/ah

Six of the Coast Guard cutters—*Absecon, Bering Strait, Castle Rock, Chincoteague, Cook Inlet,* and *Yakutat*—were transferred to the Republic of Vietnam Navy (VNN) in 1971 and 1972. (The names of the ships in the below table, obtained from a VNN reference, differ slightly from American sources which cite the intended names of the ships upon their transfer to the Republic of Vietnam Navy.) These six ships continued their service to the Republic of Vietnam until the fall of Saigon to North Vietnam on 30 April 1975. Five were able to escape to the Philippines and became a part of that country's navy. The *Pham Ngu Lao* (HQ-15), was captured by North Vietnamese forces and served as *Pham Ngu Lao* (HQ-1) in the Vietnam Socialist Republic's Navy (PRVSN).[7]

Navy Seaplane Tenders Transferred to the Coast Guard

U.S. Navy	U.S. Coast Guard	South Vietnam Navy	Philippine Navy
Biscayne (AVP-11)	*Dexter* (WAVP-385)		
Casco (AVP-12)	*Casco* (WAVP-370)		
Mackinac (AVP-13)	*Mackinac* (WAVP-371)		
Humboldt (AVP-21)	*Humboldt* (WAVP 372)		

Matagorda (AVP-22)	Matagorda (WAVP-373)		
Absecon (AVP-23)	Absecon (WAVP-374)	Pham Ngu Lao (HQ-15)	Captured by North Vietnam; redesignated Pham Ngu Lao (HQ-1)
Chincoteague (AVP-24)	Chincoteague (WAVP-375)	Tran Binh Trong (HQ-5)	Andres Bonifacio (PF-7)
Coos Bay (AVP-25)	Coos Bay (WAVP-376)		
Half Moon (AVP-26)	Half Moon (WAVP-378)		
Rockaway (AVP-29)	Rockaway (WAGO-377)		
Unimak (AVP-31)	Unimak (WAVP-379)		
Yakutat (AVP-32)	Yakutat (WAVP-380)	Tran Nhat Duat (HQ-3)	Taken over by the Philippines, April 1975; used for parts
Barataria (AVP-33)	Barataria (WAVP-381)		
Bering Strait (AVP-34)	Bering Strait (WAVP-382)	Ly Thuong Kiet (HQ-16)	Diego Silang (PF-9)
Castle Rock (AVP-35)	Castle Rock (WAVP-383)	Ngo Quyen (HQ-17)	Francisco Dagohoy (PF-10)
Cook Inlet (AVP-36)	Cook Inlet (WAVP-384)	Tran Quang Khai (HQ-2)	Taken over by the Philippines, April 1975; used for parts

U.S. NAVY'S REMAINING *BARNEGAT*-CLASS SHIPS

Following the transfer of the sixteen *Barnegat*-class seaplane ships to the U.S. Coast Guard in 1946-1948, the Navy still had fifteen of these type small seaplane tenders. Five of the ships were disposed of by sale or lease in the late 1950s and early 1960s:

- *Gardiners Bay* (AVP-39) to Norway in 1958 as the Norwegian Navy training ship *Haakon VII* (A-537)
- *Shelikof* (AVP-52) and *Timbalier* (AVP-54) in 1960 as the Greek cruise ships MV *Kypros* and MV *Rodos*, respectively, and *Barnegat* (AVP-10) in 1962 as the cruise ship MV *Kentavros*
- *Orca* (AVP-49) to Ethiopia 1962 as *Ethiopia* (A-01)

Four of the remaining ten ships were employed by the Navy and Military Sealift Command for uses other than seaplane tender duty. *San Pablo* (AVP-30) and *Rehoboth* (AVP-50) were converted to Navy survey ships (with associated changes in hull numbers to AGS-30 and AGS-50), and *Valcour* (AVP-55) to Miscellaneous Command Flagship (AGF-1). The *San Carlos* was brought out of the Reserve Fleet and placed in service in 1958 as the oceanographic research ship USNS *Josiah Willard Gibbs* (T-AGOR-1). She functioned thereafter as the principal research vessel for the Hudson Laboratories of Columbia University. In 1971, she was deactivated and transferred to Greece as the torpedo boat tender HS *Hephaistas* (A413).

Of the six remaining seaplane tenders, the *Suisun* (AVP-53) and *Corson* (AVP-37) were decommissioned in 1955 and 1956 and were later sunk as targets. The *Floyds Bay* (AVP-40) and *Onslow* (AVP-48) were decommissioned in 1960, and the *Duxbury Bay* (AVP-38) and *Greenwich Bay* (AVP-41) in 1966. Readers desiring additional details about the disposition of the seaplane tenders may consult Appendix L.

Appendix A: Seaplane Tender and Patrol Squadron Battle Stars

Acronyms or abbreviations used in the table:

Det.: Detachment
FE: Fleet Echelon
No BS: No battle star was awarded to a particular ship because it had previously received one for another engagement during the same operation. A squadron earning more than one star for a single operation involved different groups of aircraft.
P-1: Plane 1. The letter P preceding a number or numbers denotes that a particular plane or planes earned the award.

American Theater

Escort/Anti-submarine Operations

Ship or Squadron	Award Period	Commanding Officer
VP-32	15 Jul 43	Lt. Comdr. B. C. McCaffree
VP-32	26 Jul 43	Lt. Comdr. B. C. McCaffree
VP-32	28 Jul 43	Lt. Comdr. B. C. McCaffree
VP-53 *P-1*	8 Mar 43	Lt. Comdr. Frank Nichols
VP-74 *P-1*	30 Jun 42	Lt. Comdr. Willis E. Cleaves
VP-74 *P-1*	20 Oct 42	Lt. Comdr. W. A. Thorn
VP-74 *P-2*	27 Sep 43	Lt. Comdr. G. C. Merrick
VP-74 *P-5*	19 Jul 43	Lt. Comdr. J. C. Toth
VP-74 *P-7*	31 Jul 43	Lt. Comdr. J. C. Toth
VP-74 *P-5, 6*	17 May 43	Lt. Comdr. J. C. Toth
VP-81 *P-7*	12 Jul 42	Lt. Comdr. T. B. Haley
VP-82 *P-8*	1 May 42	Lt. Comdr. W. L. Erimann
VP-82 *P-9*	15 Mar 42	Lt. Comdr. W. L. Erimann
VP-83 *P-10*	13 Jan 43	Lt. Comdr. Bertram J. Prueher
VP-83 *P-5, 12*	15 Apr 43	Lt. Comdr. Bertram J. Prueher
VP-92 *P-6*	26 Aug 42	Lt. Comdr. J. A. Moreno
VP-94 *P-1*	9 Jul 43	Lt. Comdr. Harold R. Swenson
VP-94 *P-4*	21 Jul 43	Lt. Comdr. Harold R. Swenson
VP-204	5 Aug 43	Lt. Comdr. William M. McCormick
VP-205 *P-6*	3 Aug 43	Lt. Comdr. Malcolm C. McGrath
VP-205 *P-4, 11*	5 Aug 43	Lt. Comdr. Malcolm C. McGrath

European Theater

Escort/Anti-submarine/Armed Guard: Russian Convoy Operations

VP-73 *P-9*	16 Dec 41-	Lt. Comdr. James E. Leeper
	31 Oct 42	Lt. Comdr. Alexander S. Heyward Jr.

North African Occupation: Algeria-Morocco Landings

Barnegat (AVP-10)	8-11 Nov 42	Comdr. Josephus A. Briggs, USN
VP-73	8-11 Nov 42	Lt. Comdr. Alexander S. Heyward Jr.
VP-92 *P-6*	8-11 Nov 42	Lt. Comdr. J. A. Moreno

Sicilian Occupation

Biscayne (AVP-11)	9-15 Jul 43	Comdr. Robert C. Young

Salerno Landings

Biscayne (AVP-11)	9-21 Sep 43	Comdr. Robert C. Young

West Coast of Italy Operations: Anzio-Nettuno Advanced Landings

Biscayne (AVP-11)	22 Jan-1 Mar 44	Comdr. Edward H. Eckelmeyer

Invasion of Normandy

Rockaway (AVP-29)	6-25 Jun 44	Comdr. James H. Mills Jr.
VPB-103	6-25 Jun 44	Lt. Comdr. William G. von Bracht
VPB-105	6-25 Jun 44	Lt. Comdr. Donald Gay Jr.
VPB-110	6-25 Jun 44	Lt. Comdr. Page Knight
VPB-114	6-25 Jun 44	Comdr. Lloyd H. McAlpine

Invasion of Southern France

Biscayne (AVP-11)	15 Aug-25 Sep 44	Comdr. Edward H. Eckelmeyer
		Lt. Comdr. R. H. Bates

Escort/Anti-submarine Operations

VP-63 *P-1, 12*	15 May 44	Lt. Comdr. Curtis H. Hutchings
VP-63 *P-1, 7, 8*	16 Mar 44	Lt. Comdr. Curtis H. Hutchings
VP-63 *P-14, 15*	24 Feb 44	Lt. Comdr. Curtis H. Hutchings
VP-73 *P-9*	16 Dec 41-	Lt. Comdr. James E. Leeper
	31 Oct 42	Lt. Comdr. Alexander S. Heyward Jr.
VP-73 *P-9*	20 Aug 43	Lt. Comdr. Alexander S. Heyward Jr.
VP-83 *P-2*	6 Jan 43	Lt. Comdr. Bertram J. Prueher
VP-84 *P-2*	25 May 43	Lt. Comdr. Poyntell C. Staley Jr.
VP-84 *P-3*	15 May 43	Lt. Comdr. Poyntell C. Staley Jr.
VP-84 *P-7*	24 Jun 43	Lt. Comdr. Poyntell C. Staley Jr.
VP-84 *P-8*	5 Nov 42	Lt. Comdr. Jesse J. Underhill
VP-84 *P-8*	10 Dec 42	Lt. Comdr. Jesse J. Underhill
VP-84 *P-9*	20 Jun 43	Lt. Comdr. Poyntell C. Staley Jr.
VP-92 *P-6*	15 Jul 43	Lt. Comdr. J. A. Moreno
VP-92 *P-4, 5*	13 Nov 42	Lt. Comdr. J. A. Moreno
VPB-63 *P-R*	30 Apr 45	Lt. Comdr. Carl W. Brown

VPB-103 *P-10*	25 Apr 45	Comdr. Warren J. Bettens
VPB-103 *P-14*	11 Mar 45	Comdr. Warren J. Bettens
VPB-112	27 Feb 45	Comdr. A. Y. Parunak

Pacific Theater

Pearl Harbor

Ship or Squadron	Award Period	Commanding Officer
Curtiss (AV-4)	7 Dec 41	Comdr. Samuel P. Ginder Sr.
Tangier (AV-8)	7 Dec 41	Comdr. Clifton A. F. Sprague
McFarland (AVD-14)	7 Dec 41	Lt. Comdr. Joseph L. Kane
Thornton (AVD-11)	7 Dec 41	Lt. Comdr. Wendell F. Kline
Avocet (AVP-4)	7 Dec 41	Lt. Comdr. William C. Jonson, Jr.
Swan (AVP-7)	7 Dec 41	Lt. Comdr. Finley E. Hall
VP-11	7 Dec 41	Lt. Comdr. Leon W. Johnson
VP-12	7 Dec 41	Lt. Comdr. John P. Fitzsimmons
VP-14	7 Dec 41	Lt. Comdr. William T. Rassieur
VP-21	7 Dec 41	Lt. Comdr. George T. Mundorff Jr.
VP-22	7 Dec 41	Lt. Comdr. Frank O'Beirne
VP-23	7 Dec 41	Lt. Comdr. Francis M. Hughes
VP-24	7 Dec 41	Lt. Comdr. T. U. Sisson

Philippine Islands Operation

Childs (AVD-1)	8 Dec 41-3 Mar 42	Comdr. John L. Pratt
William B. Preston (AVD-7)	8 Dec 41-3 Mar 42	Lt. Comdr. Etheridge Grant
Heron (AVP-2)	8 Dec 41-3 Mar 42	Lt. Comdr. William L. Kabler
VP-22	9 Jan-3 Mar 42	Lt. Comdr. Frank O'Beirne
VP-101	8 Dec 41-3 Mar 42	Lt. Comdr. John V. Peterson
VP-102	8 Dec 41-3 Mar 42	Lt. Comdr. Edgar T. Neale

Midway

VP-13 Det.	3-6 Jun 42	Lt. William M. Nation
VP-23	3-6 Jun 42	Lt. Comdr. Francis M. Hughes
VP-24	3-6 Jun 42	Lt. Comdr. John P. Fitzsimmons
VP-44	3-6 Jun 42	Lt. Comdr. Robert C. Brixner
VP-51	3-6 Jun 42	Lt. Comdr. D. T. Day Jr.

Guadalcanal-Tulagi Landings

Curtiss (AV-4)	7-9 Aug 42	Capt. Wilson P. Cogswell
Mackinac (AVP-13)	7-9 Aug 42	Comdr Norman R. Hitchcock
VP-11	7-9 Aug 42	Lt. Comdr. Clayton C. Marcy
VP-23	7-9 Aug 42	Lt. Comdr. Francis M. Hughes

Capture and Defense of Guadalcanal

Curtiss (AV-4)	10 Aug 42-8 Feb 43	Capt. Wilson P. Cogswell
McFarland (AVD-14)	16 Oct 42	Lt. Comdr. John C. Alderman
Thornton (AVD-11)	20 Nov 42-8 Feb 43	Lt. Comdr. James F. Walker
Long Island (AVG-1)	18-22 Aug 42	Comdr. James D. Barner

408   Appendix A

VP-11	10 Aug 42-8 Feb 43	Lt. W. P. Schroeder
		Lt. Comdr. Clayton C. Marcy
VP-12	15 Dec 42-8 Feb 43	Comdr. Clarence O. Taff
VP-14	10 Aug 42-8 Feb 43	Lt. Comdr. Clifford M. Campbell
VP-23	10 Aug 42-8 Feb 43	Lt. Comdr. Francis M. Hughes
		Lt. Comdr. James R. Ogden
VP-72	10 Aug 42-8 Feb 43	Comdr. Sidney J. Lawrence
VP-91 FE	10 Aug 42-8 Feb 43	Lt. Comdr. Joe B. Paschal
		Lt. Comdr. James O. Cobb

Santa Cruz Islands

Curtiss (AV-4)	26 Oct 42	Capt. Wilson P. Cogswell
VP-11	26 Oct 42	Lt. Comdr. Clayton C. Marcy
VP-23	26 Oct 42	Lt. Comdr. James R. Ogden
VP-24	26 Oct 42	Lt. Comdr. William L. Richards
VP-51	26 Oct 42	Lt. Comdr. William A. Moffett Jr.
VP-91 FE	26 Oct 42	Lt. Comdr. Joe B. Paschal

Pacific Raids: Tarawa Island Raid

VP-33	18 Sep 43	Lt. Comdr. R. C. Bengston

Treasury-Bougainville Operation: Supporting Air Actions

Chandeleur (AV-10)	27 Oct 43-1 May 44	Capt. Albert K. Morehouse
		Capt. Walter V. R. Vieweg
Pocomoke (AV-9)	27 Oct 43-1 May 44	Capt. Curtis S. Smiley
		Capt. Edward L. B. Weimer
Wright (AV-1)	27 Oct 43-1 May 44	Capt. Frank C. Sutton
		Capt. James E. Baker
Chincoteague (AVP-24)	27 Oct 43-1 May 44	Comdr. Robert A. Rosasco
Coos Bay (AVP-25)	27 Oct 43-1 May 44	Comdr. William Miller
		Comdr. Delbert L. Conley
VP-23 FE	27 Oct-15 Dec 43	Lt. Comdr. Frank A. Brandley
VP-54 FE	27 Oct-15 Dec 43	Lt. Comdr. Carl W. Schoenweiss
VP-71 FE	27 Oct-15 Dec 43	Lt. Comdr. C. K. Harper
VP-81 *P-7*	10 Dec 43-1 May 44	Lt. Comdr. E. P. Rankin
VP-91 FE	9 Nov-15 Dec 43	Comdr. E. L. Farrington

Consolidation of Southern Solomons

Curtiss (AV-4)	8 Feb-9 Jun 43	Capt. Wilson P. Cogswell, USN
VP-12	9 Feb-23 May 43	Comdr. Clarence O. Taff
VP-24	8 Feb-9 Jun 43	Lt. Comdr. William L. Richards
VP-44	8 Feb-9 Jun 43	Lt. Comdr. Robert A. Rosasco
VP-91 FE	8 Feb-9 Jun 43	Lt. Comdr. James O. Cobb
		Lt. Comdr. E. L. Farrington

Aleutians Operation: Attu Occupation

Gillis (AVD-12)	1-2 Jun 43	Lt. Comdr. William W. Fitts
Casco (AVP-12)	12 May-2 Jun 43	Comdr. Willis E. Cleaves
VP-43 *P-5*	11 May-2 Jun 43	Lt. Comdr. Gerald E. Pierson
VP-45	11 May-2 Jun 43	Lt. Comdr. Arthur S. Hill

VP-45	11 May-2 Jun 43	Lt. Comdr. Malcom C. McGrath
VP-61	11 May-2 Jun 43	Lt. Comdr. Frank Bruner
VP-62	11 May-2 Jun 43	Lt. Comdr. Francis R. Jones

Special Operations: Action off Vanikoro

Chincoteague (AVP-24)	17-21 Jul 43	Comdr. Ira E. Hobbs

New Georgia Group Operation:
New Georgia-Rendova-Vangunu Occupation

Chincoteague (AVP-24)	17 Jul 43	Comdr. Ira E. Hobbs
VP-1	20 Jun-5 Aug 43	Comdr. Lyle L. Koepke
VP-24	3 Jul-4 Aug 43	Lt. Comdr. William L. Richards
VP-44	20 Jun-6 Jul 43	Lt. Comdr. Robert A. Rosasco
VP-54	20 Jun-5 Aug 43	Lt. Comdr. Carl W. Schoenweiss

New Georgia Group Operation: Vella Lavella Occupation

VP-23	8 Sep-16 Oct 43	Lt. Comdr. George E. Garcia
VP-24	15 Aug-12 Sep 43	Lt. Comdr. William L. Richards
VP-54	15 Aug-16 Oct 43	Lt. Comdr. Carl W. Schoenweiss

Escort/Anti-submarine Operations

VP-23	15 Sep 43	Lt. Comdr. George E. Garcia
VP-43 *P-5*	31 Aug 42	Lt. Comdr. Carroll B. Jones
VP-52 *P-49*	16 Dec 43	Lt. Comdr. Harold A. Sommer
VPB-142 *P-37113*	27 Jun 45	Lt. Comdr. John H. Guthrie

Gilbert Islands Operation

Curtiss (AV-4)	13 Nov-8 Dec 43	Capt. Scott E. Peck
Mackinac (AVP-13)	2-8 Dec 43	Comdr. Paul D. Stroop
VP-13 Det.	13 Nov-8 Dec 43	Lt. Comdr. T. F. Connolly
VP-53 *P-1*	13 Nov-8 Dec 43	Lt. Comdr. David Perry
VP-72	13 Nov-8 Dec 43	Comdr. Sidney J. Lawrence

Marshall Islands Operation:
Air Attacks on Defended Marshall Islands Targets

VP-13 Det.	26 Nov 43-2 Mar 44	Lt. Comdr. T. F. Connolly
VP-53 *P-1*	26 Jan-2 Mar 44	Lt. Comdr. David Perry
VP-72	26 Jan-2 Mar 44	Comdr. Sidney J. Lawrence
VP-202	29 Jan-2 Mar 44	Comdr. Robert W. Leeman

Marshall Islands Operation:
Occupation of Kwajalein and Majuro Atolls

Casco (AVP-12)	4 Feb 44	Comdr. Earl R. DeLong

Marshall Islands Operation: Occupation of Eniwetok Atoll

Chincoteague (AVP-24)	26 Feb 44	Comdr. Robert A. Rosasco
VP-13 Det.	17 Feb-2 Mar 44	Lt. Comdr. T. F. Connolly

Bismarck Archipelago Operation: Supporting Air Actions

VP-12 FE	14 Feb-1 May 44	Lt. Comdr. Francis R. Drake
VP-14 FE	27 Dec 43-1 May 44	Lt. Comdr. Ernest L. Simpson Jr.
VP-23 FE	15 Dec 43-4 Jan 44	Lt. Comdr. George E. Garcia
VP-34 FE	4 Mar-1 May 44	Lt. Comdr. T. A. Christopher
		Lt. Comdr. Vadym V. Utgoff
VP-54 FE	15-20 Dec 43	Lt. Comdr. Carl W. Schoenweiss
VP-71 FE	15 Dec 43-7 Mar 44	Lt. Comdr. C. K. Harper
VP-81 FE	15 Dec 43-1 May 44	Lt. Comdr. E. P. Rankin
VP-91 FE	15 Dec 43-1 May 44	Comdr. E. L. Farrington
VPB-33	14 Feb-26 Mar 44	Lt. Comdr. R. C. Bengston
VP-34	31 Dec 43-30 Mar 44	Lt. Comdr. T. A. Christopher
VP-52	1 Dec 43-1 May 44	Lt. Comdr. Harold A. Sommer
VB-106 (later VPB)	27 Mar-10 Apr 44	Comdr. J. T. Hayward

Eastern New Guinea Operation: Finschhafen Occupation

San Pablo (AVP-30)	21 Jan-17 Feb 44	Comdr. Stanton B. Dunlap

Eastern New Guinea Operation: Seventh Fleet Supporting Operations

VPB-33	26 Mar-1 Jun 44	Lt. Comdr. R. C. Bengston
		Lt. Comdr. F. P. Anderson
VP-34	30 Mar-24 Jul 44	Lt. Comdr. T. A. Christopher
		Lt. Comdr. Vadym V. Utgoff
VB-106 (later VPB)	27 Mar-1 Jun 44	Comdr. J. T. Hayward

Bismarck Archipelago Operation: Admiralty Island Landings

Tangier (AV-8)	31 Mar-17 Apr 44	Comdr. Richard M. Oliver
Heron (AVP-2)	8-17 Apr 44	Lt. John M. Norcott
San Pablo (AVP-30)	24 Mar-17 Apr 44	Comdr. Stanton B. Dunlap

Hollandia Operation: Aitape-Humboldt Bay-Tanahmerah Bay

Orca (AVP-49)	23 May-1 Jun 44	Comdr. Morton K. Fleming Jr.

Consolidation of Northern Solomons

Chincoteague (AVP-24)	15 Apr-15 Jul 44	Comdr. Robert A. Rosasco
Coos Bay (AVP-25)	15 Dec 43-15 Aug 44	Comdr. Delbert L. Conley
Heron (AVP-2)	15 Aug-23 Sep 44	Lt. John M. Norcott
San Carlos (AVP-51)	23 Jun-23 Aug 44	Lt. Comdr. De Long Mills

Marianas Operation: Neutralize Japanese Bases in Bonins and Marianas

VP-13 Det.	10 Jun-27 Aug 44	Lt. Comdr. T. F. Connolly
VP-16	17 Jun 44	Lt. Comdr. William J. Scarpino
VP-18	4-27 Jul 44	Lt. Comdr. Charles M. Brower
VP-202	17 Jul 44	Comdr. Robert W. Leeman
VP-216	23 Jun 44	Comdr. Harry E. Cook Jr.
VPB-102	10 Jun-27 Aug 44	Lt. Comdr. Gerald R. Pearson
VPB-116	10 Jun-27 Aug 44	Comdr. Donald G. Gumz

Marianas Operation: Capture and Occupation of Saipan

Chandeleur (AV-10)	26 Jun-10 Aug 44	Capt. Willard K. Goodney
Pocomoke (AV-9)	17 Jun-10 Aug 44	Capt. Edward L. B. Weimer
Ballard (AVD-10)	15 Jun-3 Jul 44	Lt. Comdr. Gust C. Nichandros
Mackinac (AVP-13)	27 Jun-10 Aug 44	Comdr. Gerald R. Dyson
Onslow (AVP-48)	17 Jun-10 Aug 44	Comdr. Alden D. Schwarz
Shelikof (AVP-52)	4-10 Aug 44	Comdr. Reuben E. Stanley
Yakutat (AVP-32)	17 Jul-10 Aug 44	Comdr. George K. Fraser

Marianas Operation: Capture and Occupation of Guam

Williamson (AVD-2)	12 Jul-15 Aug 1944	Lt. Comdr. James A. Fridmore

Western New Guinea Operations

San Pablo (AVP-30)	13-26 May 44	Comdr. Stanton B. Dunlap

Western New Guinea Operations: Toem-Wakde-Sarmi Area Operation

Wright (AV-1)	22 Jun-16 Jul 44	Capt. James E. Baker
VP-115	1-21 Jun 44	Comdr. J. R. Compton

Western New Guinea Operations: Seventh Fleet Supporting Operations

Tangier (AV-8)	1 Aug-17 Sep 44	Capt. Richard M. Oliver
San Pablo (AVP-30)	12 Oct-7 Nov 44 No BS	Comdr. Chauncey S. Willard
VPB-11	7 Aug-6 Nov 44	Lt. Comdr. Thomas S. White
VP-52	26 Mar-19 Sep 44	Lt. Comdr. Harold A. Sommer
VPB-101	2 Jun-31 Aug 44	Lt. Comdr. Lauren E. Johnson
VP-115	26 May-31 Aug 44	Comdr. J. R. Compton

Western New Guinea Operations: Cape Sansapor Operation

Half Moon (AVP-26)	26-31 Aug 44	Comdr. Jack I. Bandy
Orca (AVP-49)	22-31 Aug 44	Comdr. Morton K. Fleming Jr.

Western New Guinea Operations: Morotai Landings

Tangier (AV-8)	15 Sep 44 No BS	Capt. Richard M. Oliver
Half Moon (AVP-26)	15 Sep 44 No BS	Comdr. Jack I. Bandy
San Carlos (AVP-51)	15 Sep 44	Lt. Comdr. De Long Mills
San Pablo (AVP-30)	15 Sep 44 No BS	Comdr. Chauncey S. Willard
VPB-71	15 Sep 44	Comdr. Norman C. Gillette Jr.
VPB-101	15 Sep 44	Lt. Comdr. Marvin T. Smith
VPB-104	15 Sep 44	Lt. Comdr. Whitney Wright
VPB-137	15 Sep 44	Lt. Comdr. John A. Porter
VPB-146	15 Sep 44	Lt. Comdr. Jesse P. Robinson Jr.

Western Caroline Islands: Capture and Occupation of South Palau Islands

Chandeleur (AV-10)	5 Sep-14 Oct 44	Capt. Willard K. Goodney
Pocomoke (AV-9)	5 Sep-14 Oct 44	Capt. Edward L. B. Weimer
Ballard (AVD-10)	6 Sep-14 Oct 44	Lt. Comdr. Gust C. Nichandros
Mackinac (AVP-13)	6 Sep-14 Oct 44	Comdr. Gerald R. Dyson
Onslow (AVP-48)	6 Sep-14 Oct 44	Comdr. Alden D. Schwarz

Yakutat (AVP-32)   6 Sep-14 Oct 44   Comdr. George K. Fraser
VPB-216   17 Sep-14 Oct 44   Comdr. Harry E. Cook Jr.

Leyte Operation: Battle of Surigao Strait

Half Moon (AVP-26)   24-26 Oct 44 No BS   Comdr. Jack I. Bandy
San Carlos (AVP-51) 24-26 Oct 44 No BS   Lt. Comdr. De Long Mills
VPB-33   24-26 Oct 44   Lt. Comdr. F. P. Anderson
VPB-34   24-26 Oct 44   Lt. Comdr. Vadym V. Utgoff

Leyte Operation: Leyte Landings

Currituck (AV-7)   6-29 Nov 44   Capt. William A. Evans Jr.
Half Moon (AVP-26)   20 Oct-29 Nov 44   Comdr. Jack I. Bandy
Heron (AVP-2)   21-29 Nov 44   Lt. John M. Norcott
Orca (AVP-49)   4-29 Nov 44   Comdr. Morton K. Fleming Jr.
San Carlos (AVP-51) 10 Oct-29 Nov 44   Lt. Comdr. De Long Mills
San Pablo (AVP-30)   21-29 Nov 44   Comdr. Chauncey S. Willard
VPB-11   7-20 Nov 44   Lt. Comdr. Thomas S. White
VPB-11   15-29 Nov 44   Lt. Comdr. Thomas S. White
VPB-20   1-29 Nov 44   Lt. Comdr. Robert M. Harper
VPB-25   16-29 Nov 44   Lt. Comdr. James C. Skoroz
VPB-33   15-29 Nov 44   Lt. Comdr. F. P. Anderson
VPB-34   15-29 Nov 44   Lt. Comdr. Vadym V. Utgoff
VPB-101   10 Oct-29 Nov 44   Lt. Comdr. Marvin T. Smith
VPB-104   3-29 Nov 44   Lt. Comdr. Whitney Wright
VPB-130   9-29 Nov 44   Lt. Comdr. Charles R. Dodds
VPB-146   17-26 Nov 44   Lt. Comdr. Jesse P. Robinson Jr.
VPB-216   15 Oct-18 Nov 44   Comdr. Harry E. Cook Jr.

Luzon Operation: Lingayen Gulf Landing

Currituck (AV-7)   9-18 Jan 45   Capt. William A. Evans Jr.
Barataria (AVP-33)   9-18 Jan 45   Comdr. Garrett S. Coleman
Orca (AVP-49)   4-18 Jan 45   Comdr. Everett O. Rigsbee Jr.
VPB-20   10-18 Jan 45   Lt. Comdr. Robert M. Harper
VPB-25   4-18 Jan 45   Lt. Comdr. James C. Skoroz
VPB-33   4-18 Jan 45   Lt. Comdr. F. P. Anderson
VPB-54   10-18 Jan 45   Comdr. Kenneth J. Sanger
VPB-71   11-18 Jan 45   Comdr. Norman C. Gillette Jr.
VPB-104   4-18 Jan 45   Lt. Comdr. Whitney Wright
VPB-117   4-18 Jan 45   Comdr. Harold W. McDonald
VPB-137   4-18 Jan 45   Lt. Comdr. John A. Porter

Iwo Jima: Assault and Occupation of Iwo Jima

Hamlin (AV-15)   19 Feb-8 May 45   Capt. Gordon A. McLean
Bering Strait (AVP-34) 15 Feb-16 Mar 45   Comdr. Walter D. Innis
Chincoteague (AVP-24) 19 Feb-16 Mar 45   Comdr. James A. Smith
Cook Inlet (AVP-36) 2-16 Mar 45   Comdr. William P. Woods
VH-1   20 Feb-16 Mar 45   Lt. Comdr. J. D. Adam
VH-2   20 Feb-16 Mar 45   Lt. Comdr. H. A. Wells
VH-3   20 Feb-16 Mar 45   Lt. Comdr. William D. Bonvillian
VPB-19   20 Feb-7 Mar 45   Lt. Comdr. J. A. Masterson

VPB-23	3-16 Mar 45	Lt. Comdr. William M. Stevens
VPB-102	15 Feb-16 Mar 45	Lt. Comdr. Gerald R. Pearson
		Lt. Comdr. Louis P. Pressler
VPB-106	15 Feb-16 Mar 45	Comdr. W. S. Sampson
VPB-116	15 Feb-16 Mar 45	Lt. Comdr. A. R. Waggoner
VPB-118	15 Feb-16 Mar 45	Comdr. C. K. Harper
VPB-151	15 Feb-16 Mar 45	Comdr. Paul Masterton
VPB-208	15-22 Feb 45	Lt. Comdr. Anton J. Sintic Jr.

Okinawa Operation: Assault and Occupation of Okinawa

Chandeleur (AV-10)	26 Mar-30 Jun 45	Capt. John S. Tracy
Curtiss (AV-4)	22 May-25 Jun 45	Capt. Scott E. Peck
		Capt. Henry C. Doan
Hamlin (AV-15)	26 Mar-30 Jun 45	Capt. Gordon A. McLean
Norton Sound (AV-11)	26 Apr-30 Jun 45	Capt. Benjamin S. Custer
St. George (AV-16)	26 Mar-30 Jun 45	Capt. Robert G. Armstrong
Kenneth Whiting (AV-14)	1-11 Apr 45	Comdr. Raymond R. Lyons
Gillis (AVD-12)	25 Mar-29 Jun 45	Lt. James C. Sullivan Jr.
Thornton (AVD-11)	25 Mar-1 May 45	Lt. Laurence F. Geibel
Bering Strait (AVP-34)	26 Mar-30 Jun 45	Comdr. Walter D. Innis
Casco (AVP-12)	25 Apr-30 Jun 45	Comdr. Reginald Rutherford
Duxbury Bay (AVP-38)	26 Apr-30 Jun 45	Comdr. Frank N. Howe
Gardiners Bay (AVP-39)	3-30 Jun 45	Comdr. Carlton C. Lucas
Mackinac (AVP-13)	11 May-30 Jun 45	Comdr. Paul L. Stahl
Onslow (AVP-48)	26 Mar-30 Jun 45	Comdr. Alden D. Schwarz
Shelikof (AVP-52)	26 Mar-30 Jun 45	Comdr. Reuben E. Stanley
Suisun (AVP-53)	26 Apr-30 Jun 45	Comdr. James J. Vaughan
Yakutat (AVP-32)	26 Mar-30 Jun 45	Comdr. George K. Fraser
Grumium (AVS-3)	2 Apr-30 Jun 45	Lt. Comdr. Byron J. Parylak
VH-3	29 Mar-30 Jun 45	Lt. Comdr. William D. Bonvillian
VPB-13	26 Apr-30 Jun 45	Lt. Comdr. J. A. Ferguson
VPB-18	30 Mar-30 Jun 45	Lt. Comdr. R. R. Boettcher
VPB-21	29 Mar-30 Jun 45	Lt. Comdr. James D. Wright
VPB-23	30 Apr-23 May 45	Lt. Comdr. William M. Stevens
VPB-26	26 Apr-20 Jun 45	Lt. Comdr. R. S. Null
VPB-27	29 Mar-30 Jun 45	Lt. Comdr. E. N. Chase II
VPB-106	1-22 Apr 45	Comdr. W. S. Sampson
VPB-116	17 Mar-5 Apr 45	Lt. Comdr. A. R. Waggoner
VPB-116	20 Apr-20 May 45	Lt. Comdr. A. R. Waggoner
VPB-116	20-30 Jun 45	Lt. Comdr. A. R. Waggoner
VPB-118	22 Apr-30 Jun 45	Comdr. C. K. Harper
VPB-123	28 May-30 Jun 45	Lt. Comdr. S. C. Shilling
VPB-124	16-30 Jun 45	Comdr. Charles E. Houston
		Lt. Comdr. John M. Miller
VPB-208	1 Apr-30 Jun 45	Lt. Comdr. Anton J. Sintic Jr.

Okinawa Operation: Raids in Support of Okinawa Gunto Operation

VPB-109	10-30 May 45	Lt. Comdr. George L. Hicks

Third Fleet Operations against Japan

Chandeleur (AV-10)	10-25 Jul 45	Capt. John S. Tracy
Hamlin (AV-15)	10-25 Jul 45	Capt. Gordon A. McLean
Norton Sound (AV-11)	10-25 Jul 45	Capt. Benjamin S. Custer
Pine Island (AV-12)	10-25 Jul 45	Comdr. Henry T. Hodgskin Jr.
Kenneth Whiting (AV-14)	10-25 Jul 45	Comdr. Raymond R. Lyons
		Capt. Alfred R. Truslow Jr.
Bering Strait (AVP-34)	10-25 Jul 45	Comdr. Walter D. Innis
Duxbury Bay (AVP-38)	10-25 Jul 45	Comdr. Frank N. Howe
Floyds Bay (AVP-40)	10-25 Jul 45	Comdr. James R. Ogden
Gardiners Bay (AVP-39)	10-25 Jul 45	Comdr. Carlton C. Lucas
Mackinac (AVP-13)	10-25 Jul 45	Comdr. Paul L. Stahl
Onslow (AVP-48)	10-25 Jul 45	Comdr. Alden D. Schwarz
Shelikof (AVP-52)	10-25 Jul 45	Comdr. Reuben E. Stanley
Suisun (AVP-53)	10-25 Jul 45	Comdr. James J. Vaughan
Yakutat (AVP-32)	10-25 Jul 45	Lt. Comdr. William I. Darnell
VH-1	10-25 Jul 45	Lt. Comdr. R. R. Barrett Jr.
		Lt. H. G. Crawford
VH-3	10-25 Jul 45	Lt. Comdr. William D. Bonvillian
VH-4	10-25 Jul 45	Lt. Forest H. Norvell Jr.
VH-6	10-25 Jul 45	Lt. Comdr. L. O. Ebey
VPB-13	10-25 Jul 45	Comdr. J. A. Ferguson
VPB-21	10-25 Jul 45	Lt. Comdr. James D. Wright
VPB-26	10-25 Jul 45	Lt. Comdr. R. S. Null
VPB-27	10-25 Jul 45	Lt. Comdr. E. N. Chase II
VPB-109	10-25 Jul 45	Lt. Comdr. George L. Hicks
VPB-118	10-25 Jul 45	Comdr. C. K. Harper
VPB-123	10-25 Jul 45	Lt. Comdr. S. C. Shilling
VPB-124	10-25 Jul 45	Lt. Comdr. John M. Miller
VPB-208	10-25 Jul 45	Lt. Comdr. Anton J. Sintic Jr.

Appendix B: Presidential Unit Citations/ Navy Unit Commendations

Presidential Unit Citations

Ship	Award Dates	Area(s)
McFarland (AVD-10)	20 Jun-16 Oct 42	Southwest Pacific

Squadron	Award Dates	Area(s)
VP-11	15 Sep 43-1 Feb 44	Bismarck Sea
VP-12	24 Nov 42-1 Jun 43	South Pacific
VP-22	15 Jan-3 Mar 42	Netherlands East Indies and Philippine Areas
VP-34	15 Sep 43-1 Feb 44	Bismarck Sea
VP-52	15 Sep 43-1 Feb 44	Bismarck Sea
VP-83	1 Jan-30 Apr 43	Atlantic waters of South America
	1 Jul 43-29 Feb 44	Atlantic waters of South America
	1-30 Sep 44	Atlantic waters of South America
VP-84	1 Nov 42-30 Jun 43	Atlantic area
VP-101	3 Dec 41-3 Mar 42	Netherlands East Indies and Philippine Areas
VP-102	3 Dec 41-3 Mar 42	Netherlands East Indies and Philippine Areas
VPB-33	1 Sep-4 Oct 44	Netherlands East Indies, southern Philippine Areas
VPB-104	15 Aug 43-19 Mar 44	Pacific
	6 Nov 44-7 Jun 45	Pacific
VPB-117	4 Oct 44-11 Aug 45	South China Sea
VPB-118	26 Apr-8 Aug 45	Sea of Japan and Korea

Navy Unit Commendations

Ship	Award Dates	Area(s)
Heron (AVP-2)	17 Dec 41-3 Mar 42	Netherlands East Indies

Squadron	Award Dates	Area(s)
VP-32	1-31 Jul 43	Waters off Cuba
VP-42	1 Jun-1 Aug 42	Northern Asiatic – Pacific Area
VP-43	1 Jun-1 Aug 42	Northern Asiatic – Pacific Area
VP-82	15 Jan-10 Jun 42	Newfoundland Waters
VP-91	15 Sep 42-1 Mar 43	Southern Asiatic – Pacific Area
VPB-18	1 Apr-31 Jul 45	North China Sea Area
VPB-20	1 Nov 44-1 Jun 45	Indo-China, Borneo, Netherlands East Indies
VPB-28	1 Mar-23 Apr 45	South China – Formosa Area
VPB-71	24 Nov 44-16 Mar 45	Central Pacific Area
VPB-74	7 Jun 42-31 Jul 43	Atlantic Waters
VPB-101	2 Jun-31 Dec 44	Central and Southwest Pacific Areas
VPB-111	2 Dec 44-31 Jul 45	Central Pacific Area

Appendix C: Medal Citations for Officers and Men of USS *Heron*

Lieutenant William Leverette Kabler, United States Navy:
The President of the United States of America takes pleasure in presenting the Navy Cross to Lieutenant William Leverette Kabler, United States Navy, for extraordinary heroism and distinguished service in the line of his profession as Commanding Officer of the Minesweeper U.S.S. *HERON* (AM-10), during operations in Dutch East Indies on 31 December 1941. When the U.S. warship he commanded was attacked by 15 hostile planes of various types, Lieutenant Kabler fought his ship with such skill that the crew was able to destroy one plane, damage others and frustrate the attack. The conduct of Lieutenant Kabler throughout this action reflects great credit upon himself, and was in keeping with the highest traditions of the United States Naval Service.

Lieutenant Franklin Duerr Buckley, United States Navy:
The President of the United States of America takes pleasure in presenting the Bronze Star Medal with Combat "V" to Lieutenant Franklin Duerr Buckley, United States Navy, for heroic service as Executive Officer of the Minesweeper U.S.S. *HERON* (AM-10), during operations in Dutch East Indies on 31 December 1941. When the U.S.S. *HERON* was attacked by hostile aircraft, Commander Buckley directed accurate and effective anti-aircraft fire to destroy one and damage at least one more of the hostile bomber planes, thereby disrupting the Japanese attack. By his skill, leadership and devotion to duty in the face of overwhelming odds, he upheld the highest traditions of the United States Naval Service. (Commander Buckley is authorized to wear the Combat "V".)

Chief Boatswain William Harold Johnson, United States Navy:
The President of the United States of America takes pleasure in presenting a Gold Star in lieu of a Second Award of the Navy Cross to Chief Boatswain William Harold Johnson, United States Navy, for exceptional courage, presence of mind, and devotion to duty and extreme disregard for his personal safety while serving on board the Minesweeper U.S.S. *HERON* (AM-10), during operations in Dutch East Indies on 31 December 1941, when his ship was attacked by 15 hostile planes of different types. During protracted air attacks delivered against the U.S.S. *HERON* on 31 December 1941, the ship being attacked by an overwhelming number of enemy aircraft of various types using bombs and torpedoes, he discharged his duties as After Machine Gun Battery Officer in a most efficient and commendable manner. He manned his machine gun after ordering the personnel of his battery to

take cover while bombs were falling, and carried on in his action duties while seriously wounded. Such action contributed not only to the survival of the ship but also to the fact that effective losses were sustained by the enemy aircraft. Chief Boatswain Johnson's conduct throughout was in keeping with the highest traditions of the Navy of the United States.

Machinist's Mate Second Class Robert Lee Brock, United States Navy:
The President of the United States of America takes pleasure in presenting the Navy Cross to Machinist's Mate Second Class Robert Lee Brock, United States Navy, for extraordinary heroism and devotion to duty while serving as a Machine Gunner on board the Minesweeper U.S.S. *HERON* (AM-10), in action against the enemy during operations in Dutch East Indies on 31 December 1941 when his ship was attacked by 15 hostile planes of different types. With extreme disregard of personal safety, Machinist's Mate Second Class Brock returned to his action station while bombs were falling near the ship and after the force of a bomb explosion had thrown him from the after machine gun platform to the main deck below. During protracted air attacks delivered against the U.S.S. *HERON* on 31 December 1941 in the Dutch East Indies, the ship being attacked by an overwhelming number of enemy aircraft of various types using bombs and torpedoes, Machinist's Mate Second Class Brock discharged his duties as After .50 Caliber Machine Gun Captain in a most efficient and commendable manner. Such action contributed not only to the survival of the ship but also to the fact that effective losses were sustained by the enemy aircraft. His conduct throughout was in keeping with the highest traditions of the Navy of the United States.

Appendix D: Patrol Wings/Fleet Air Wings

Acronyms used:
FAB: Fleet Air Base
NAF: Naval Airfield
NAS: Naval Air Station
NS: Naval Station

Wing	Date and Location Where Established	Relocated/Date and Area
One	1 Oct 1937: FAB San Diego, California	9 Oct 1941: NAS Kaneohe Bay, Oahu, Hawaii
12 Sep 1942: Noumea
Dec 1942: Espiritu Santo
Mar 1943: Guadalcanal
Feb 1944: Munda
Jul 1944: Espiritu Santo
11 Sep 1944: Schouten Islands aboard the *Hamlin* (AV-15)
15 Oct 1944: Ulithi
30 Dec 1944: Saipan
19 Feb 1945: Iwo Jima aboard the *Hamlin*
10 Mar 1945: NAF Agana, Guam
26 Mar 1945: Kerama Rhetto aboard the *Hamlin*
14 Jul 1945: NAF Chimu Wan, Okinawa
Two	1 Oct 1937: FAB Pearl Harbor, Hawaii	15 Sep 1942: NAS Kaneohe Bay, Oahu, Hawaii
Three	1 Oct 1937: FAB Coco Solo, Panama	10 Aug 1942: Albrook Army Airfield, Panama
Four	1 Oct 1937: FAB Seattle, Washington	27 May 1942: NAS Kodiak, Alaska
15 Mar 1943: NAS Adak, Alaska
26 Apr 1944: NAF Attu, Aleutian Islands
Five	1 Oct 1937: FAB Norfolk, Virginia	
Six	2 Nov 1942: NAS Seattle, Washington	29 Dec 1942: NAS Whidbey Island, Washington
Seven	1 Jul 1941: NAF Argentia, Newfoundland	15 Dec 1941: NAF Keflavik, Iceland
18 Feb 1942: NAS Quonset Point, Rhode Island
15 May 1942: NAF Argentia
21 Aug 1943: Plymouth, England
10 Jul 1945: NAS Dunkeswell,

		England
		15 Jul 1945: Aboard the *Albemarle* for return to Norfolk, Virginia
Eight	8 Jul 1941: NAF Breezy Point, Norfolk, Virginia	15 Dec 1941: NAS Alameda, California
Nine	1 Dec 1941 or April 1942 (exact date unknown): NAS Norfolk, Virginia	1 May 1942: NAS Quonset Point, Rhode Island
		24 Aug 1943: NAS New York
Ten	December 1940: NS Cavite, Philippines	18 Dec 1941: Ambon
		15 Jan 1942: Surabaya
		7 Mar 1942: Perth, Australia
		1 Sep 1944: Los Negros, Admiralty Islands
		17 Oct 1944: Leyte, Philippines aboard the *Currituck*
		30 Nov 1944: Jinamoc Island, Philippines
		15 Dec 1944: Tacoban, Philippines
		14 Apr 1945: Puerto Princessa, Palawan
Eleven	15 Aug 1942: NAS Norfolk, Virginia	20 Aug 1942: San Juan, Puerto Rico
Twelve	16 Sep 1942: NAS Key West, Florida	15 Sep 1943: NAS Miami, Florida
		1 Jun 1945: NAS Key West, Florida
Fourteen	15 Oct 1942: NAS San Diego, California	
Fifteen	1 Dec 1942: NAS Norfolk, Virginia	10 Jan 1943: NAF Port Lyautey, French Morocco
		10 Jun 1945: NAS Norfolk, Virginia
Sixteen	16 Feb 1943: NAS Norfolk, Virginia	14 Apr 1943: Natal, Brazil
		20 Jul 1943: NAF Recife, Brazil
Seventeen	15 Sep 1943: Brisbane, Australia	31 Dec 1943: Samari Island, Papua New Guinea
		27 Jul 1944: Manus, Admiralty Islands
		9 Sep 1944: Woendi, Schouten Islands
		19 Oct 1944: Morotai Island
		30 Dec 1944: Leyte Gulf, Philippines
		28 Jan 1945: Lingayen Gulf, Philippines aboard the *Tangier* in San Pedro Bay
		26 Feb 1945: Clark Field, Luzon, Philippines
Eighteen	5 May 1945: NS Agana, Guam, Marianas	25 May 1945: NAF Tinian, Marianas

Appendix E: Allied Vessels at Darwin, Australia

United States Navy and Merchant Vessels (6)

Destroyer USS *Peary* (sunk, 88 deaths), Seaplane Tender USS *William B. Preston* (14 deaths), Merchant Vessel S.S. *Admiral Halstead*, U.S Army Transport *Mauna Loa* (sunk), USAT *Meigs* (sunk, 1 death), Cargo Ship S.S. *Portmar* (beached, refloated 6 April, 1 death)

British Merchant Vessel (1)

Tanker M.V. *British Motorist* (sunk, 2 deaths)

Royal Australian Navy and Merchant Vessels (49)

Boom Defense Vessels	Hospital Ship	Auxiliary Minesweepers
HMAS *Kangaroo*	HMAHS *Manunda* (12 deaths)	HMAS *Gunbar* (1 death)
HMAS *Kara Kara* (ex-ferry, 2 deaths)	**Ketches**	HMAS *Terka* (ex-coastal steamer *Sir Dudley de Chair*)
HMAS *Karangi*	HMAS *Chinampa*	HMAS *Tolga* (ex-*Dorlonco*/*Sir T. Hugh Bell*)
HMAS *Koala*	HMAS *Sulituan*	**Patrol Boats**
HMAS *Kookaburra*	**Lighters**	HMAS *Coongoola* (ex-luxury yacht)
Cargo Ships	HMAS *Kalaroo*	HMAS *Kiara* (ex-*Penelope*)
S.S. *Barossa* (beached, refloated 17 April)	*Karalee* (sunk 5 March)	HMAS *Kuru*
M.V. *Tulagi* (beached, refloated 20 February)	Oil Lighter No. 1	HMAS *Larrakia*
M.V. *Neptuna*	*Yampi Lass* (ex-scow)	HMAS *Mako*
Coal Hulk	**Luggers**	HMAS *Mavie* (ex-lugger, sunk)
HMAS *Kelat* (ex-windjammer; sunk 24 February)	HMAS *Arthur Rose*	HMAS *Nereus*
	HMAS *Griffioen*	HMAS *Vigilant*
	HMAS *Ibis*	HMAS *Winbah*
Depot Ship	HMAS *Malanda*	**Sloops**
HMAS *Platypus*	*Mars*	HMAS *Swan* (3 deaths)
Examination Vessel	HMAS *Medic*	HMAS *Warrego*
	Plover	**Troop Ship**
HMAS *Southern Cross* (ex-yacht)	HMAS *Red Bill*	S.S. *Zealandia* (sunk, 2 deaths)
	HMAS *St. Francis*	**Tug**
Ferry	HMAS *Moruya*	HMAS *Wato* (W127)[6]
HMAS *Koompartoo*	**Minesweepers**	
	HMAS *Deloraine*	
	HMAS *Katoomba*	
	HMAS *Townsville*	
	HMAS *Warrnambool*	

Appendix F: Silver Star Citation for Lt. Comdr. Lester Wood

Lt. Comdr. Lester Wood, USN:

On 19 February 1942, the U.S.S. *WILLIAM B. PRESTON* (DD-344) was anchored at Port Darwin, Australia, acting as tender for several PBY airplanes. About 0900 the Commanding Officer went ashore to make arrangements for the delivery of fuel and gasoline, leaving Lieutenant Commander Wood in temporary command. About 1000 a large formation of enemy aircraft appeared over the harbor and commenced bombing the shipping and shore establishments. Lieutenant Commander Wood had the ship at general quarters and underway within 5 minutes and commenced zig-zagging down the harbor, dodging bomb salvos, and heading for the open sea. Several dive bombers attacking the ship were driven off by the ship's anti-aircraft fire before they released their bombs. About 1010, while making a full rudder turn at 25 knots, the ship was struck by a bomb just forward of the after deckhouse on the port side, rupturing fuel tanks and steam lines to the steering engine. Fire immediately broke out in the vicinity and steering control was lost. In spite of the damaged condition of the ship and the jammed rudder and in the face of continued attacks by the enemy, Lieutenant Commander Wood succeeded in maneuvering the ship to keep clear of shoals and other burning ships, in making his way out through the boom into the open sea. While proceeding down the coast in this damaged condition the ship was subjected to another bombing attack, but Lieutenant Commander Wood succeeded in dodging all bombs and bringing the ship safely through a narrow passage into a small bay where he awaited the arrival of the Commanding Officer. His actions were in keeping with the highest traditions of the United States Naval Service.

Appendix G: Japanese Midway Invasion Force

Commander, Midway Invasion Force: Vice Adm. Kondo Nobutake

Covering Group: Vice Adm. Kondo Nobutake

Battleship Division 3, Section 1: Rear Adm. Mikawa Gunichi	Hiei (BB-2), Kongo (BB-1)
Cruiser Division 4, Section 1: Rear Adm. Mikawa Gunichi	Atago (CA-9), Chokai (CA-11)
Cruiser Division 5: Vice Adm. Takeo Takagi	Haguro (CA-7), Myoko (CA-5)
Destroyer Squadron 4: Rear Adm. Shoji Nishimura	flagship: Yura (CL-11)
Destroyer Division 4	Harusame (DD-71), Murasame (DD-68), Samidare (DD-70), Yūdachi (DD-69)
Destroyer Division 9	Asagumo (DD-83), Minegumo (DD-82), Natsugumo (DD-80)
Carrier Group	Zuiho (CVL)
Supply Group	Akashi (RS), Kenyo Maru (AO), Genyo Maru (AO), Sata (AO), Tsurumi (AO)

Close Support Group: Rear Adm. Kurita Takeo

Cruiser Division 7	Kumano (CA-16), Mikuma (CA-14), Mogami (CA-13), Suzuya (CA-15)
Destroyer Division 8	Asashio (DD-76), Arashio (DD-79)
attached oiler	Nichiei Maru (AO)

Transport Group: Rear Adm. Tanaka Raizo

Destroyer Squadron 2:	flagship: Jintsu (CL-16)
Destroyer Division 15	Kuroshio (DD-19), Oyashio (DD-20)
Destroyer Division 16	Amatsukaze (DD-25), Hatsukaze (DD-23), Tokitsukaze (DD-26), Yukikaze (DD-24)
Destroyer Division 18	Arare (DD-84), Kagero (DD-17), Kasumi (DD-85), Shiranui (DD-18)
transports	Argentine Maru (AP), Azuma Maru (AP), Brazil Maru (AP), Goshu Maru (AP), Kano Maru (AP), Keiyo Maru (AP), Kinryu Maru (AP) Kirisima Maru (AP), Kyozumi Maru (AP), Nankai Maru (AP), Toa Maru (AP), Zenyo Maru (AP)
oiler	Akebono Maru (AO)

Seaplane Group: Rear Adm. Fujita Riutaro

11th Seaplane Tender Division — *Chitose* (AV), *Kamikawa Maru* (AV), *Hayashio* (DD-21), *Tsuta* (APD-35): Carrying embarked troops for Kure atoll occupation

Minesweeping Group: Capt. Miyamoto Sadatomo

Shonan Maru No. 7, Shonan Maru No. 8, Tama Maru No. 3, Tama Maru No. 5

Appendix H: Crews of PBY Seaplanes that made a Night Torpedo Attack against Japanese Ships at Battle of Midway

PBY *24-P-12*

Individual	Squadron	Award for Valor
Lt. William L. Richards, USN	VP-24	Silver Star
Lt. (jg) C. P. Hibberd, USNR	VP-24	
Ens. A. L. Mills, USNR	VP-24	
Ens. James C. Boyden, USNR	VP-24	DFC
ARM3c T. M. Roadruck	VP-24	
AMM3c J. S. Gordon	VP-24	
AMM3c G. M. Hughes	VP-24	
AMM2c D. L. Ellis	VP-24	
ARM1c C. G. Ream	VP-24	

PBY *24-P-7*

Individual	Squadron	Award for Valor
Lt. (jg) Douglas C. Davis, USNR	VP-24	Silver Star
Ens. R. J. Ney, USNR	VP-24	
AP1c J. E. Foster	VP-24	
ARM2c K. K. Anderson	VP-24	
AMM2c T. E. Kimmel	VP-24	
RM3c W. N. Thompson	VP-24	
AMM3c W. C. Henderson	VP-24	
AMM3c C. L. Hunt	VP-24	
AMM3c R. H. Neuman	VP-24	

PBY *24-P-11*

Individual	Squadron	Award for Valor
Ens. Gaylord D. Propst, USNR	VP-24	Silver Star
Ens. B. L. Amman, USNR	VP-24	
CAP H. C. Smathers	VP-24	
AMM3c D. M. Zech	VP-24	
AMM3c G. C. Harrison	VP-24	
AMM3c E. L. Kline	VP-24	
ARM3c V. Abate	VP-24	
ARM3c E. W. Hix	VP-24	
ARM3c J. F. Dwyer	VP-24	

PBY 51-P-5

Ens. Allan Rothenberg, USNR	VP-51	Silver Star
Lt. (jg) James Clair Nolan, USNR	VP-51	
Ens. John O. Adams, USNR	VP-51	DFC
AMM2c C. G. Lawler	VP-51	
AMM3c C. C. Roberts	VP-51	
ARM2c O. M. Spahr	VP-51	
Sea2c P. F. Arcidiacono	VP-51	
AOM3c M. R. Sugg	VP-51	

Appendix I: Restructuring of Pacific Fleet Aviation Forces

U.S. Naval Air Forces, Pacific Fleet absorbed Carriers Pacific Fleet (formerly Aircraft Battle Force, Pacific Fleet], and Patrol Wings, Pacific Fleet (formerly Aircraft Scouting Force, Pacific Fleet). When war broke out, Halsey and McCain were in command of Aircraft, Battle Force, and Aircraft, Scouting Force, respectively. A separate command, Aircraft, South Pacific Force, was established three-and-one-half months before U.S. Naval Air Forces, Pacific Fleet.[25]

Aircraft, Battle Force, Pacific Fleet
Vice Adm. William F. Halsey Jr., USN 7 Dec 1941-10 Apr 1942

Carriers, Pacific Fleet (Established 10 April 1942)
Vice Adm. William F. Halsey Jr., USN 10 Apr 1942-11 Jul 1942
Rear Adm. Aubrey W. Fitch, USN 11 Jul 1942-31 Aug 1942

Aircraft Scouting Force, Pacific Fleet
Rear Adm. John S. McCain, USN 7 Dec 1941-10 Apr 1942

Patrol Wings, Pacific Fleet (Established 10 April 1942)
Rear Adm. John S. McCain, USN 10 Apr 1942-1 May 1942
Rear Adm. Patrick N.L. Bellinger, USN 1 May 1942-9 Aug 1942
Rear Adm. Aubrey W. Fitch, USN 9 Aug 1942-31 Aug 1942

Air Force, Pacific Fleet (Established 1 September 1942)
Rear Adm. Aubrey W. Fitch, USN 1 Sep 1942-15 Sep 1942
Rear Adm. Leigh Noyes, USN 15 Sep 1942-15 Oct 1942
Vice Adm. John H. Towers, USN 15 Oct 1942-28 Feb 1944
Rear Adm. Charles A. Pownall, USN 28 Feb 1944-16 Aug 1944
Vice Adm. George D. Murray, USN 16 Aug 1944-20 Jul 1945
Vice Adm. Alfred E. Montgomery, USN 20 Jul 1945-2 Sep 1945

Aircraft, South Pacific Force (Established 20 May 1942)
Rear Adm. John S. McCain, USN 20 May 1942-20 Sep 1942
Vice Adm. Aubrey W. Fitch, USN 21 Sep 1942-21 Oct 1943
Maj. Gen. Ralph J. Mitchell, USMC 21 Oct 1943-15 Jun 1944
Rear Adm. Ernest L. Gunther, USN 15 Jun 1944-

Appendix J: Japanese Military Aircraft

Allied Name	Aircraft Designation	Type Aircraft
Betty	Mitsubishi G4M Navy Type 1	Land-based Attack Aircraft
Claude	Mitsubishi A5M Navy Type 96	Navy Carrier Fighter
Emily	Kawanishi H8K Type 2	Large Flying Boat (seaplane)
Frances	Yokosuka P1Y1 Ginga	Navy Land-Based Bomber
Frank	Nakajima Ki-84 Hayate Type 4	Army Fighter
Hamp	Mitsubishi A6M Type Zero	Navy Carrier Fighter
Jake	Aichi E13A Type 0	Navy Reconnaissance Seaplane
Jill	Nakajima B6N Tenzan	Navy Carrier Torpedo Bomber
Judy	Yokosuka D4Y Suisei	Navy Carrier Dive Bomber
Kate	Nakajima B5N Type 97	Navy Carrier Attack Bomber
Mavis	Kawanishi H6K Type 97	Large Flying Boat (seaplane)
Nell	Mitsubishi G3M Navy Type 96	Land-based Attack Aircraft
Oscar	Nakajima Ki-43 Hayabusa Type 1	Army Fighter
Sally	Mitsubishi Ki-21 Type 97	Army Heavy Bomber
Tojo	Nakajima Ki-44 Shoki Type 2	Army Single-Seat Fighter
Tony	Kawasaki Ki-61 Hien Type 3	Army Fighter
Val	Aichi D3A Type 99	Navy Carrier Bomber
Zeke	Mitsubishi A6M2-K & A6M5-K	Navy Carrier Fighter ("Zero")

Appendix K: VPB-18 Navy Unit Commendation

THE SECRETARY OF THE NAVY
WASHINGTON

The Secretary of the Navy takes pleasure in commending

PATROL BOMBING SQUADRON EIGHTEEN

for service as follows:

"For outstanding heroism in action against enemy Japanese forces in the North China Sea Area from 1 April to 31 July 1945. Flying unescorted in PBM seaplanes along hostile shores, into strongly fortified harbors and across Japanese sea lanes, Patrol Bombing Squadron EIGHTEEN carried out hazardous night and day offensive reconnaissance searches in the face of extremely inclement weather, enemy fighter opposition and intense antiaircraft fire from heavily armed convoys and shore batteries. Individually heroic and aggressive, this gallant squadron flew in from 50 to 300 feet over rough seas and coastal islands to launch perilous masthead attacks against hostile surface forces and to bomb heavily fortified land installations. Piloted, manned and serviced by skilled and fearless men who loyally coordinated their efforts for maximum effectiveness, and whose common purpose was to crush Japan's ability to make war, this intrepid group achieved an illustrious combat record in eleven hostile fighters destroyed in aerial combat and in many thousands of tons of warships and merchant vessels sunk or damaged. Tireless in their devotion to duty, unyielding in their sustained aggressiveness and highly efficient in their splendid teamwork, the airmen and crews of Patrol Bombing Squadron EIGHTEEN upheld the highest traditions of the United States Naval Service."

All personnel attached to and serving with Patrol Bombing Squadron EIGHTEEN from 1 April to 31 July 1945, are hereby authorized to wear the NAVY UNIT COMMENDATION Ribbon.

Secretary of the Navy

Appendix L: Post-WWII Disposition of Seaplane Tenders

The dates of commissioning listed in the tables for all the ships, reflect the dates of their original commissioning. The *Lapwing*-class AVPs were commissioned as minesweepers and the AVDs as destroyers. The *Langley* (AV-3) and *Wright* (AV-1) were originally commissioned as a Collier and a Lighter-than-Air Aircraft Tender in 1913 and 1921, respectively. The other AVs were commissioned in the 1940s as large seaplane tenders.

Small Seaplane Tenders (ex-WWI Minesweepers)

Ship	Builder's Yard	Commissioned	Year Struck
Lapwing AVP-1 (ex AM-1)	Todd Shipyard Co., Brooklyn, New York	12 Jun 1918	August 1946
Heron AVP-2 (ex AM-10)	Standard Shipbuilding Co., New York, New York	30 Oct 1918	1 May 1946
Thrush AVP-3 (ex AM-18)	Pusey and Jones Co., Wilmington, Delaware	25 Apr 1919	8 Jan 1946
Avocet AVP-4 (ex AM-19)	Baltimore Dry Dock and Shipbuilding Co., Baltimore, Maryland	17 Sep 1918	3 Jan 1946
Teal AVP-5 (ex AM-23)	Sun Shipbuilding and Dry Dock Co., Chester, Pennsylvania	20 Aug 1918	5 Dec 1946
Pelican AVP-6 (ex AM-27)	Gas Engine and Power Co., Morris Height, New York	10 Oct 1918	19 Dec 1945
Swan AVP-7 (ex AM-34)	Alabama Dry Dock and Shipbuilding Co., Mobile, Alabama	31 Jan 1919	8 Jan 1946
Gannet AVP-8 (ex AM-41)	Todd Shipyard Corp., Brooklyn, New York	10 Jul 1919	Torpedoed by *U-653* on 7 June 1942
Sandpiper AVP-9 (ex AM-51)	Philadelphia Navy Yard, Pennsylvania	9 Oct 1919	17 Apr 1946

Destroyer Seaplane Tenders (ex-WWI Destroyers)

Ship	Builder's Yard	Commissioned	Disposition
Childs AVD-1 (ex DD-241, ex AVP-14)	New York Shipbuilding Corp, Camden, New Jersey	22 Oct 20	Decom 10 Dec 1945, struck 3 Jan 1946, sold for scrapping 23 May 1946
Williamson AVD-2 (ex DD-244, ex AVP-15)	New York Shipbuilding Corp, Camden, New Jersey	29 Oct 20	Decom 8 Nov 1945, struck 30 Oct 1946, sold for scrapping 4 Nov 1948
George E. Badger AVD-3 (ex DD-196, ex AVP-16, later APD-33)	Newport News Shipbuilding and Dry Dock Co., Newport News, Virginia	28 Jul 20	APD-33 19 May 1944, decom 3 Oct 1945, struck 24 Oct 1945, sold for scrapping 3 Jun 1946
Clemson AVD-4 (ex DD-186, ex AVP-17, later APD-31)	Newport News Shipbuilding and Dry Dock Co., Newport News, Virginia	29 Dec 19	APD-31 17 Jul 1944, decom 12 Oct 1945, sold for scrapping, 21 Nov 1946
Goldsborough AVD-5 (ex DD-188, ex AVP-18, later APD-32)	Newport News Shipbuilding and Dry Dock Co., Newport News, Virginia	26 Jan 20	DD-188 1 Dec 1943, APD-32 7 Mar 1944, decom 11 Oct 1945, struck 24 Oct 1945, sold for scrapping, 21 Nov 1946
Hulbert AVD-6 (ex DD-342, ex AVP-19)	Norfolk Navy Yard, Portsmouth, Virginia	27 Oct 20	DD-342 1 Dec 1943, decom 2 Nov 1945, sold for scrapping in Oct 1946
William B. Preston AVD-7 (ex DD-344, ex AVP-20)	Norfolk Navy Yard, Portsmouth, Virginia	23 Aug 20	Decom 6 Dec 1945, struck 3 Jan 1946, sold for scrapping, 6 Nov 1946
Belknap AVD-8 (ex DD-251, later APD 34)	Bethlehem Shipbuilding Corp., Quincy, Massachusetts	28 Apr 19	APD-34 22 Jun 1944, decom 4 Aug 1945, sold for scrapping 30 Nov 1945
Osmond Ingram AVD-9 (ex DD-255, later APD-35)	Bethlehem Shipbuilding Corp., Quincy, Massachusetts	28 Jun 19	DD-255 4 Nov 1943, APD-35 22 Jun 1944, decom 8 Jan 1946, struck 21 Jan 1946, sold for scrapping 17 Jun 1946
Ballard AVD-10 (ex DD-267)	Bethlehem Steel Corp., Squantum, Massachusetts	5 Jun 19	Decom 5 Dec 1945, struck 3 Jan 1946, sold for scrapping, 23 May 1946
Thornton AVD-11 (ex DD-270)	Bethlehem Shipbuilding Corp., Quincy, Massachusetts	15 Jul 19	Damaged in collision at sea, decom 2 May 1945, struck 13 Aug 1945

Gillis AVD-12 (ex DD-260)	Bethlehem Steel Corp., Quincy, Massachusetts	3 Sep 19	Decom 15 Oct 1945, struck 1 Nov 1945, sold for scrapping, 29 Jan 1946

Large Seaplane Tenders

Ship	Builder's Yard	Commissioned	Disposition
Wright (AV-1) ex-cargo vessel	American International Shipbuilding Corp, Hog Island, Pennsylvania	16 Dec 21	AG-79 1 Oct 1944, decom 21 Jun 1946, struck 1 Jul 1946, sold for scrapping 20 Jul 1948
Langley (AV-3) ex-Collier #3	Mare Island Navy Yard, Vallejo, California	7 Apr 13	Lost to enemy aircraft attack 27 Feb 1942
Curtiss (AV-4)	New York Shipbuilding Corp., Camden, New Jersey	15 Nov 40	Decom 24 Sep 1957, struck 1 Jul 1963, sold for scrapping 1 Mar 1972
Albemarle (AV-5)	New York Shipbuilding Corp., Camden, New Jersey	20 Dec 40	Decom 14 Aug 1950, recom 21 Oct 1957, decom 21 Oct 1960, struck 1 Sep 1962, placed in service as *Corpus Christi Bay* (T-ARVH-1) in January 1966, placed out of-service in 1973, struck 31 Dec 1974, sold for scrapping 17 July 1975
Currituck (AV-7)	Philadelphia Navy Yard, Philadelphia, Pennsylvania	26 Jun 44	Decom 7 Aug 1947, recom 1 Aug 1951, decom 12 Feb 1958, recom 20 Aug 1960, decom 31 Oct 1967, struck 1 Apr 1971, sold for scrapping 10 Jan 1972
Tangier (AV-8) ex-merchant S.S. *Sea Arrow* MC hull 51	Moore Dry Dock Co., Oakland, California	8 Jul 40	Decom circa Jan 1947, struck 1 Jun 1961, sold 10 Jan 1962, scrapped in Dec 1974
Pocomoke (AV-9) ex merchant S.S. *Exchequer* MC hull 64	Ingalls Shipbuilding and Dry Dock Co., Pascagoula, MS	18 Jul 41	Decom 10 Jul 1946, struck 1 Jun 1961, sold for scrapping 12 Dec 1961
Chandeleur (AV-10) ex-merchant MC hull 173	Western Pipe and Steel Co., San Francisco, California	19 Nov 42	Decom 12 Feb 1947, struck 1 Apr 1971, scrapped in 1971
Norton Sound (AV-11)	Los Angeles Shipbuilding and Drydock Co., San Pedro, California	8 Jan 45	AVM-1 8 Aug 1951, decom 10 Aug 1959, recom 20 Jun 1960, decom 11 Dec 1986, struck 26 Jan 1987

Ship	Builder's Yard	Commissioned	Disposition
Pine Island (AV-12)	Todd Shipyard Corp., San Pedro, California	26 Apr 45	Decom 1 May 1950, recom 7 Oct 1950, decom 16 Jun 1967, struck 1 Feb 1971, sold for scrapping 7 Mar 1972
Salisbury Sound (AV-13)	Todd Shipyard, San Pedro, California	26 Nov 45	Decom 31 Mar 1967, sold for scrapping 7 Feb 1972
Kenneth Whiting (AV-14) ex-merchant C3 hull	Seattle-Tacoma Shipbuilding Co., Seattle, Washington	8 May 44	Decom 29 May 1947, recom 24 Oct 1951, decom 30 Sep 1958, stuck 1 Jul 1961, sold for scrapping, 21 Feb 1962
Hamlin (AV-15)	Todd Pacific Shipyards, Inc., Tacoma, Washington	26 Jun 44	Decom 18 Jan 1947, stuck 1 July 1963, sold for scrapping 8 Mar 1962
St. George (AV-16)	Seattle-Tacoma Shipbuilding Corp. Inc., Tacoma, Washington	24 Jul 44	Decom 1 Aug 1946, struck 1 Jul 1963, sold to Italy, *Andrea Bafile* (A5314)
Cumberland Sound (AV-17) ex-merchant C3-S-A1 hull	Todd Pacific Shipyards, Inc., Tacoma, Washington	21 Aug 44	Decom 27 May 1947, struck 1 Jul 1961, sold 23 Apr 1962

Small Seaplane Tenders (Purposeful-built)

Ship	Builder's Yard	Commissioned	Disposition
Barnegat (AVP-10)	Puget Sound Navy Yard, Bremerton, Washington	3 Jul 41	Decom 17 May 1946, struck 23 May 1958, sold 1962 as cruise ship *Kentavros*
Biscayne (AVP-11)	Puget Sound Navy Yard, Bremerton, Washington	3 Jul 41	AGC 18 1944, to USCG 1946 as *Dexter* (WAVP-385), sunk as target 1968
Casco (AVP-12)	Puget Sound Navy Yard, Bremerton, Washington	27 Dec 41	Decom 10 Apr 1947, to USCG 1949 as WAVP-370, sunk as target 1969
Mackinac (AVP-13)	Puget Sound Navy Yard, Bremerton, Washington	24 Jan 42	Decom in Jan 1947, to USCG 1949 as WAVP-371, sunk as target 1969
Humboldt (AVP-21)	Boston Navy Yard, Boston, Massachusetts	7 Oct 41	AG-121 1944, decom 17 Mar 1947, to USCG as WAVP 372 1949, scrapped 1970
Matagorda (AVP-22)	Boston Navy Yard, Boston, Massachusetts	16 Dec 41	AG 122 1944, decom 20 Feb 1946, to USCG as WAVP-373 1949, sunk as target 1969
Absecon (AVP-23)	Lake Washington Shipyard, Houghton, Washington	28 Jan 43	Decom 19 Mar 1947, to USCG as WAVP-374 1948, to South Vietnam 1972 as *Pham Ngu Lao* (HQ-15)

Post-WWII Disposition of Seaplane Tenders 439

Chincoteague (AVP-24)	Lake Washington Shipyard, Houghton, Washington	12 Apr 43	Decom 21 Dec 1946, to USCG as WAVP-375 1948, to South Vietnam as *Tran Binh Trong* (HQ-5), to the Philippines as *Andres Bonifacio* (PF-7) 1975, struck 1986
Coos Bay (AVP-25)	Lake Washington Shipyard, Houghton, Washington	16 May 43	Decom 30 Apr 1946, to USCG as WAVP-376 1948, sunk as target 1968
Half Moon (AVP-26)	Lake Washington Shipyard, Houghton, Washington	15 Jun 43	AGP 5 1944, decom 4 Sep 1946, to USCG as WAVP-378 1948, scrapped 1970
Rockaway (AVP-29)	Associated Ship Building Inc., Seattle, Washington	6 Jan 43	AG 123 1944, decom 21 Mar 1946, to USCG as WAVP-377 1948, scrapped 1973
San Pablo (AVP-30)	Associated Ship Building Inc., Seattle, Washington	15 Mar 43	AGS-30 1944, decom 13 Jan 1947, Recom AGS-30 17 Sep 1948, decom 29 May 1969
Unimak (AVP-31)	Associated Ship Building Inc., Seattle, Washington	31 Dec 43	Decom 25 Jan 1946, to USCG as WAVP-379 1948, scuttled as reef 1989
Yakutat (AVP-32)	Associated Ship Building Inc., Seattle, Washington	31 Mar 44	Decom 17 Apr 1946, to USCG as WAVP-380 1948, to South Vietnam 1971 as *Tran Nhat Duat* (HQ-3)
Barataria (AVP-33)	Lake Washington Shipyard, Houghton, Washington	13 Aug 44	Decom 24 Jul 1946, to USCG as WAVP-381 1948, scrapped 1971
Bering Strait (AVP-34)	Lake Washington Shipyard, Houghton, Washington	19 Jul 44	Decom 21 Jun 1946, to USCG as WAVP-382 1948, to South Vietnam as *Ly Thuong Kiet* (HQ-16) 1971, to the Philippines as *Diego Silang* (PF-9) 1975, struck 1986
Castle Rock (AVP-35)	Lake Washington Shipyard, Houghton, Washington	8 Oct 44	Decom 6 Aug 1946, to USCG as WAVP-383 1948, to South Vietnam as *Ngo Quyen* (HQ-17) 1971, to the Philippines as *Francisco Dagohoy* (PF 10) 1975, struck 1986
Cook Inlet (AVP-36)	Lake Washington Shipyard, Houghton, Washington	5 Nov 44	Decom 31 Mar 1946, to USCG as WAVP-384 1948, to South Vietnam as *Tran Quang Khai* (HQ-2) 1971, to the Philippines 1975
Corson (AVP-37)	Lake Washington Shipyard, Houghton, Washington	3 Dec 44	Decom 21 Jun 1946, recom 13 Feb 1951, decom 9 Mar 1956, sunk as a target 1966
Duxbury Bay (AVP-38)	Lake Washington Shipyard, Houghton, Washington	31 Dec 44	Decom 30 Apr 1966, scrapped 1967

Gardiners Bay (AVP-39)	Lake Washington Shipyard, Houghton, Washington	11 Feb 45	Decom 1 Feb 1958, to Norway 1958 as *Haakon VII* (A 537), scrapped 1974
Floyds Bay (AVP-40)	Lake Washington Shipyard, Houghton, Washington	26 Mar 45	Decom 26 Feb 1960, sold 20 Jul 1960
Greenwich Bay (AVP-41)	Lake Washington Shipyard, Houghton, Washington	20 May 45	Decom in June 1966, sold for scrapping 21 Jun 1967
Onslow (AVP-48)	Lake Washington Shipyard, Houghton, Washington	22 Dec 43	Decom in Jun 1947, recom in Jan 1951, decom 22 Apr 1960, scrapped 1961
Orca (AVP-49)	Lake Washington Shipyard, Houghton, Washington	23 Jan 44	Decom 31 Oct 1947, recom 15 Dec 1951, decom in Mar 1960, to Ethiopia 1962 as *Ethiopia* (A 01)
Rehoboth (AVP-50)	Lake Washington Shipyard, Houghton, Washington	23 Feb 44	Decom 30 Jun 1947, recom as AGS-50 2 Sep 1948, decom 15 Apr 1970, scrapped 1970
San Carlos (AVP-51)	Lake Washington Shipyard, Houghton, Washington	21 Mar 44	Decom 30 Jun 1947, in service as T-AGOR-1 on 15 Dec 1958, struck 7 Dec 1971, to Greece 1971 as *Hephaistos* (A 413)
Shelikof (AVP-52)	Lake Washington Shipyard, Houghton, Washington	17 Apr 44	Decom 30 Jun 1947, sold 1960 as cruise ship *Kypros*, sunk in January 1981
Suisun (AVP-53)	Lake Washington Shipyard, Houghton, Washington	13 Sep 44	Decom 5 Aug 1955, sunk as target in October 1966
Timbalier (AVP-54)	Lake Washington Shipyard, Houghton, Washington	24 May 46	Decom 15 Nov 1954, sold 1960 as cruise ship *Rodos*, scrapped 1989
Valcour (AVP-55)	Lake Washington Shipyard, Houghton, Washington	5 Jul 46	Reclassified AGF-1 15 Dec 1965, decom 17 Jun 1973, scrapped 1978

Bibliography

Barbey, Daniel E. *MacArthur's Amphibious Navy.* Annapolis: U.S. Naval Institute, 1969.

Bartsch, William H. *Every Day a Nightmare: American Pursuit Pilots in the Defense of Java, 1941-1942.* College Station, TX: Texas A&M University Press, 2010.

Bruhn, David D. *Battle Stars for the "Cactus Navy": America's Yachts and Fishing Vessels in World War II.* Berwyn Heights, MD: HeritageBooks, 2014.

—*MacArthur and Halsey's "Pacific Island Hoppers": The Forgotten Fleet of World War II.* Berwyn Heights, MD: Heritage Books, 2014

—*We are Sinking, Send Help!: The U.S. Navy's Tugs and Salvage Ships in the African, European, and Mediterranean Theaters in World War II.* Berwyn Heights, MD Heritage Books, 2015

—*Wooden Ships and Iron Men: The U.S. Navy's Coastal and Motor Minesweepers, 1941-1953.* Westminster, MD: Heritage Books, 2009

Building the Navy's Bases in World War II: History of the Bureau of Yards and Docks and the Civil Engineer Corps 1940-1946 Volume II. Washington, DC: U.S. Government Printing Office, 1947.

Bulkley Jr., Robert J. *At Close Quarters PT Boats in the United States Navy.* Washington DC: Naval History Division, 1962.

Charlton, Peter. *The Unnecessary War: Island Campaigns of the South-West Pacific 1944-45.* Crows Nest, New South Wales: Macmillan Australia, 1983.

Cox, Jeffrey. *Rising Sun, Falling Skies: The Disastrous Java Sea Campaign of World War II.* Oxford, UK Osprey, 2014.

Cressman, Robert C. *The Official Chronology of the U.S. Navy in World War II.* Annapolis: U.S. Naval Institute, 2000.

Day, David. *The Politics of War.* Sydney, Australia: Harper Collins, 2003.

Dorny, Louis B. *US Navy PBY Catalina Units of the Pacific War.* Oxford, UK: Osprey, 2007.

Evans, David C. *The Japanese Navy in World War II: In the Words of Former Japanese Naval Officers.* Annapolis: U.S. Naval Institute, 1986.

Friedman, Norman. *U.S. Destroyers: An Illustrated Design History.* Annapolis, MD: U.S. Naval Institute, 2004.

Garfield, Brian. *The Thousand-Mile War: World War II in Alaska and the Aleutians.* Garden City, NY: Doubleday, 1969.

Grey, Jeffrey. *A Military History of Australia.* Cambridge, England: Cambridge University Press, 1999.

Hammel, Eric. *Carrier Strike: The Battle of the Santa Cruz Islands, October 1942.* Lawrence, KS: Pacifica Press, 1999.

Hara, Tameichi. *Japanese Destroyer Captain.* New York, NY: Ballantine Books, 1961.

Howe, George F. *United States Army in World War II Mediterranean Theater of*

Operations Northwest Africa: Seizing the Initiative in the West. Washington DC: Dept. of the Army, 1957.

Lott, Arnold S. *Most Dangerous Sea*. Annapolis: U.S. Naval Institute, 1959.

Messimer, Dwight R. *In the Hands of Fate*. Annapolis: U.S. Naval Institute, 1985.

—*Pawns of War*. Annapolis: U.S. Naval Institute, 1983.

Morison, Samuel Eliot. *History of United States Naval Operation in World War II: Breaking the Bismarcks Barrier, 22 July 1942-1 May 1944*. Boston: Little, Brown, 1984.

—*History of United States Naval Operations in World War II, Coral Sea, Midway and Submarine Actions, May 1942-August 1942*. Boston: Little, Brown, 1984.

—*History of United States Naval Operations in World War II, The Liberation of the Philippines — Luzon, Mindanao, the Visayas, 1944-1945*. Edison, New Jersey: Castle Books, 2001.

—*The Rising Sun in the Pacific 1931-April 1942*. University of Illinois Press, 2001.

—*The Two-Ocean War*. Boston: Little, Brown, 1963.

Owen, Frank. *The Fall of Singapore*. Penguin Books, 2001.

Perkins, J. W. *Battle Stars and Naval Awards*. Seminole, Florida: 2004.

Roberts, Michael D. *Dictionary of American Naval Aviation Squadrons, Volume 2*. Washington, D.C.: Naval Historical Center, 2000.

Shaw Jr., Henry I., Bernard C. Nalty, and Edwin T. Turnbladh. *History of U.S. Marine Corps Operations in World War II Volume III: Central Pacific Drive*. Washington, DC: Headquarters, U.S. Marine Corps, 1966.

Williams, Greg H. *World War II U.S. Navy Vessels in Private Hands*. Jefferson, North Carolina: McFarland, 2013.

Winslow, Walter G. *The Fleet the Gods Forgot: The U.S. Asiatic Fleet in World War II*. Annapolis: U.S. Naval Institute, 1994.

Notes

ACRONYMS USED IN CHAPTER NOTES

CAW	Commander Air Wing
CGC	Coast Guard Cutter
CINC	Commander-in-Chief
CNO	Chief of Naval Operations
ComDesDiv	Commander Destroyer Division
ComFairWing	Commander Fleet Air Wing
ComFltAir	Commander Fleet Air
CoMinRon	Commander Mine Squadron
ComPatWing	Commander Patrol Wing
CTG	Commander Task Group
CTF	Commander Task Force
DANAS	Dictionary of American Aviation Squadrons
DANFS	Directory of American Naval Fighting Ships
HMAS	His/Her Majesty's Australian Ship
HMS	His/Her Majesty's Ship (Royal Navy)
ONI	Office of Naval Intelligence
USS	United States Ship
USCG	United States Coast Guard
VH	Rescue Squadron
VMBF	Marine Bomber Fighting Squadron
VMF	Marine Fighting Squadron
VNN	Republic of Vietnam
VP	Patrol Squadron
VPB	Patrol Bombing Squadron
VS	Scouting Squadron
VT	Torpedo Squadron

PREFACE NOTES
[1] VPB-216 History, 15 November 1943 to 8 November 1944.

CHAPTER 1 NOTES
[1] Narrative by Lt. Comdr. William L. Kabler, USN, Bombing of USS *Heron* in the Java Sea, Naval Records & Library, CNO Personal Interviews, 5 January 1942.

[2] Narrative by Capt. John V. Peterson, Patrol Wing 10, Naval Records & Library, CNO, Personal Interviews, 28 February 1944.
[3] Peterson, 28 February 1944; ComFltAir, West Coast, Information Concerning Naval Campaign in Orient, 1941-1942, 12 December 1944.
[4] Peterson, 28 February 1944.
[5] Ibid.
[6] Narrative by Capt. John L. Pratt, USN, USS *Childs* (AVD-1), Manila to Australia, December 1941 to February 1942, Naval Records & Library, CNO, Personal Interviews, 30 March 1945.
[7] David D. Bruhn, *Battle Stars for the "Cactus Navy": America's Yachts and Fishing Vessels in World War II* (Berwyn Heights, Maryland, Heritage, 2014), 111.
[8] Pratt, 30 March 1945; ComFltAir, West Coast, Information Concerning Naval Campaign in Orient, 1941-1942, 12 December 1944.
[9] Pratt, 30 March 1945.
[10] Pratt, 30 March 1945; *Langley*, *DANFS*.
[11] Kabler, 5 January 1942; Pratt, 30 March 1945; Dwight R. Messimer, *In the Hands of Fate* (Annapolis: U.S. Naval Institute, 1985), 87-88; ComFltAir, West Coast, Information Concerning Naval Campaign in Orient, 1941-1942, 12 December 1944.
[12] Kabler, 5 January 1942; Pratt, 30 March 1945.
[13] Kabler, 5 January 1942; Peterson, 28 February 1944; ComFltAir, West Coast, Information Concerning Naval Campaign in Orient, 1941-1942, 12 December 1944.
[14] ComFltAir, West Coast, Information Concerning Naval Campaign in Orient, 1941-1942,
12 December 1944.
[15] Kabler, 5 January 1942; "USS *Peary*," Destroyer History Foundation (http://destroyerhistory.org/flushdeck/usspeary/: accessed 3 November 2014).
[16] "USS *Peary*," Destroyer History Foundation; ComFltAir, West Coast, Information Concerning Naval Campaign in Orient, 1941-1942, 12 December 1944.
[17] Kabler, 5 January 1942; VP-10 War Diary, December 1941.
[18] Kabler ,5 January 1942.
[19] Ibid.; VP-10 War Diary, December 1941.
[20] "HMS *Prince of Wales* (53)," Uboat.net
(http://www.uboat.net/allies/warships/ship/4071.html: accessed 2 November 2014); Frank Owen, *The Fall of Singapore* (Penguin Books, 2001), 65; Messimer, *In the Hands of Fate*, 130.
[21] Kabler, 5 January 1942; Commanding Officer, USS *Heron*, War Damage Report, 12 June 1942; Combat Narrative The Java Sea Campaign (Washington, D.C.: ONI, 1943), 11
(http://www.ibiblio.org/hyperwar/USN/USN-CN-Java/index.html#page1: accessed 26 March 2015); VP-10 War Diary, December 1941.
[22] Kabler, 5 January 1942; VP-10 War Diary, December 1941.

[23] Kabler, 5 January 1942.
[24] Ibid.; ComFltAir, West Coast, Information Concerning Naval Campaign in Orient, 1941-1942, 12 December 1944.
[25] Pratt, 30 March 1945; Kabler, 5 January 1942; ComFltAir, West Coast, Information Concerning Naval Campaign in Orient, 1941-1942, 12 December 1944.
[26] ComFltAir, West Coast, Information Concerning Naval Campaign in Orient, 1941-1942, 12 December 1944; General Orders: Bureau of Naval Personnel Information Bulletin No. 304 (July 1942) and 328 (July 1944); General Orders: CINC, Asiatic Fleet: (January 23, 1942); General Orders: Board Serial 1429 (February 14, 1947).
[27] Kabler, 5 January 1942; Peterson, 28 February 1944; ComFltAir, West Coast, Information Concerning Naval Campaign in Orient, 1941-1942, 12 December 1944.
[28] Peterson, 28 February 1944; ComFltAir, West Coast, Information Concerning Naval Campaign in Orient, 1941-1942, 12 December 1944.
[29] Peterson, 28 February 1944.
[30] General Orders: Bureau of Naval Personnel Information Bulletin No. 304 (July 1942) & 317 (August 1943).
[31] Peterson, 28 February 1944.
[32] Ibid.

CHAPTER 2 NOTES
[1] "Seaplane Tenders," *Flying Magazine*, October 1944.
[2] "AVP -- Small Seaplane Tenders," Naval History and Heritage Command. (http://www.history.navy.mil/photos/shusn-no/avp-no.htm: accessed 1 November 2014); Andrew Toppan, "World Aircraft Carriers List: US Seaplane Tenders: Small Tenders."
(http://www.hazegray.org/navhist/carriers/us_sea3.htm: accessed 22 November 2014).
[3] "AVP -- Small Seaplane Tenders," Naval History and Heritage Command.
[4] Norman Friedman, *U.S. Destroyers: An Illustrated Design History* (Annapolis, Naval Institute, 2004), 49-50; Andrew Toppan, "World Aircraft Carriers List: US Seaplane Tenders: Small Tenders."
[5] "AVP -- Small Seaplane Tenders," Naval History and Heritage Command.
[6] Andrew Toppan, "World Aircraft Carriers List: US Seaplane Tenders: Small Tenders."
[7] Carl T. Musselman, "Tender Moments in United States Naval Aviation" (http://www.back-aft.com/: accessed 16 November 2014).
[8] Ibid.
[9] Ibid.
[10] Ibid.; "Seaplane Tenders," Uboat.net
(http://uboat.net/allies/warships/types.html?type=Seaplane+tender); "Ships of the U.S. Navy, 1940-1945 AV -- Seaplane Tenders," Hyperwar (http://www.ibiblio.org/hyperwar/USN/ships/ships-av.html: both accessed 22 November 2014).

[11] Andrew Toppan, "World Aircraft Carriers List: US Seaplane Tenders: Heavy Tenders" (http://www.hazegray.org/navhist/carriers/us_sea2.htm#curi-cl: accessed 22 November 2014).
[12] Ibid.
[13] Ibid.
[14] Ibid.
[15] Musselman, "Tender Moments in United States Naval Aviation."
[16] "Casualties: U.S. Navy and Coast Guard Vessels Sunk or Damaged Beyond Repair during World War II 7 December 1941-1 October 1945" (http://www.history.navy.mil/faqs/faq82-2.htm: accessed 23 November 2014).

CHAPTER 3 NOTES
[1] ComFairWing Three, History of Fleet Air Wing Three, 4 January 1945.
[2] Michael D. Roberts, *Dictionary of American Naval Aviation Squadrons, Volume 2* (Washington, D.C.: Naval Historical Center, 2000), 807-813.
[3] David D. Bruhn, *Wooden Ships and Iron Men: The U.S. Navy's Coastal and Motor Minesweepers, 1941-1953* (Westminster, Maryland: Heritage Books, 2009), 18.
[4] Roberts, *Dictionary of American Naval Aviation Squadrons, Volume 2*, 807-813.

CHAPTER 4 NOTES
[1] Samuel Eliot Morison, *The Two-Ocean War* (Boston: Little, Brown, 1963), 46-47; "Attack on U.S. Airfields at Pearl Harbor" (http://worldwar2headquarters.com/HTML/PearlHarbor/PearlHarborAirFields/airfields.html: accessed 7 September 2015); "Japanese Forces at Pearl Harbor" (http://www.history.navy.mil/our-collections/photography/wars-and-events/world-war-ii/pearl-harbor-raid/japanese-forces-in-the-pearl-harbor-attack.html: accessed 7 September 2015).
[2] "Attack on U.S. Airfields at Pearl Harbor."
[3] "PBY Catalinas at Pearl Harbor," Pacific Aviation Museum Pearl Harbor (http://www.pacificaviationmuseum.org/pearl-harbor-blog/pby-catalinas-at-pearl-harbor: accessed 7 September 2015).
[4] Bruhn, *Wooden Ships and Iron Men: The U.S. Navy's Coastal and Motor Minesweepers*, 1941-1953, 11-15.
[5] Ibid.
[6] Ibid.
[7] Louis B. Dorny, *US Navy PBY Catalina Units of the Pacific War* (Oxford, U.K.: Osprey, 2007), p. 16; CINC, United States Pacific Fleet, Report of Japanese Raid on Pearl Harbor, 7 December, 1941, 15 February 1942 "PBY Catalinas at Pearl Harbor," Pacific Aviation Museum Pearl Harbor (http://www.pacificaviationmuseum.org/pearl-harbor-blog/pby-catalinas-at-pearl-harbor: accessed 7 September 2015).

[8] CTF 9 (ComPatWing Two), Operations on December 7, 1941, 20 December 1941; Jack McKillop, "U.S. Navy Aviation Units" (http://homepage.ntlworld.com/Andrew.etherington/articles/level1/pearl_harbor_us_navy_aviation_units.htm: accessed 26 April 2015).
[9] CINC, U.S. Pacific Fleet, Report of Japanese Raid on Pearl Harbor, 7 December, 1941, 15 February 1942; Commander, VP-22, Summary of action and damage during Air Raid on December 7, 1941, 13 December 1941; Commanding Officer, VPB-23, History of VPB-23, 23 June 1945; Commander, VPB-24, VPB-24, History of, 31 December 1944; McKillop, "U.S. Navy Aviation Units."
[10] CINC, U.S. Pacific Fleet, Report of Japanese Raid on Pearl Harbor, 7 December, 1941, 15 February 1942.
[11] "Remembering Pearl Harbor" (http://www.nationalww2museum.org/assets/pdfs/pearl-harbor-fact-sheet-1.pdf: accessed 8 September 2015).
[12] CINC, U.S. Pacific Fleet, Report of Japanese Raid on Pearl Harbor, 7 December, 1941, 15 February 1942; ComPatWing One, Report of Japanese Air Attack on Kaneohe Bay, T.H., December 7, 1941, 1 January 1942.
[13] "Remembering Pearl Harbor;" "Japanese Forces at Pearl Harbor."
[14] CINC, U.S. Pacific Fleet, Report of Japanese Raid on Pearl Harbor, 7 December, 1941, 15 February 1942; ComPatWing One, Report of Japanese Air Attack on Kaneohe Bay, T.H., December 7, 1941, 1 January 1942.
[15] Commanding Officer, USS *Hulbert*, Report of Battle, Japanese Air Attack on Pearl Harbor, December 7, 1941, 8 December 1941.
[16] Morison, *The Two-Ocean War*, 46-47; "Ford Island History," Hawaii Aviation (http://hawaii.gov/hawaiiaviation/hawaii-airfields-airports/oahu-pre-world-war-ii/ford-island: accessed 8 September 2015).
[17] Commander, VP-22, Summary of action and damage during Air Raid on December 7, 1941, 13 December 1941.
[18] Commanding Officer, USS *Thornton* (AVD-11), Engagement, Report of, December 7, 1941, 17 December 1941.
[19] Ibid.; Commanding Officer, USS *Neosho* (AO-23), Raid on Pearl Harbor, T. H., December 7, 1941 – Report on, 11 December 1941.
[20] Commanding Officer, USS *Thornton* (AVD-11), Engagement, Report of, December 7, 1941, 17 December 1941; Commanding Officer, USS *Hulbert*, Report of Battle, Japanese Air Attack on Pearl Harbor, December 7, 1941, 8 December 1941.
[21] Commanding Officer, USS *Thornton* (AVD-11), Engagement, Report of, December 7, 1941, 17 December 1941.
[22] Commanding Officer, USS *Swan* (AVP-7), Action of December 7, 1941 – Report on, 11 December 1941.
[23] Commanding Officer, USS *Avocet* (AVP4), Offensive Measures Taken During December 7th Raid – Report of, 12 December 1941.
[24] Ibid.

[25] Commanding Officer, USS *Tangier* (AV-8), Raid, Air, December 7, 1941, U.S.S. *Tangier* (AV8) – Report on, 2 January 1942.
[26] *Monaghan* (DD-354) War Diary, 7 December 1941 – 31 January 1942.
[27] Commanding Officer, USS *Tangier* (AV-8), Raid, Air, December 7, 1941, U.S.S. *Tangier* (AV8) – Report on, 2 January 1942.
[28] Ibid.
[29] Commanding Officer, USS *Raleigh* (CL-7), Report of U.S.S. *Raleigh*'s participation in the battle of Pearl Harbor, December 7, 1941, 31 December 1941.
[30] Commanding Officer, USS *Tangier* (AV-8), Raid, Air, December 7, 1941, U.S.S. *Tangier* (AV8) – Report on, 2 January 1942.
[31] Ibid.
[32] "Type A-class Midget Submarine," World War II Database (http://ww2db.com/ship_spec.php?ship_id=486: accessed 17 April 2015); Commanding Officer, USS *Tangier* (AV-8), Raid, Air, December 7, 1941, U.S.S. *Tangier* (AV8) – Report on, 2 January 1942.
[33] "Type A-class Midget Submarine," World War II Database; Bruhn, *Wooden Ships and Iron Men: The U.S. Navy's Coastal and Motor Minesweepers*, 1941-1953, 15.
[34] Commanding Officer, USS *Tangier* (AV-8), Raid, Air, December 7, 1941, U.S.S. *Tangier* (AV8) – Report on, 2 January 1942.
[35] Ibid.
[36] Commanding Officer, USS *Curtiss* (AV-4), Raid on December 7, 1941, Report of, 16 December 1941.
[37] Ibid.
[38] Ibid.; USS *Curtiss* Bomb Damage, December 7, 1941 Pearl Harbor, Bureau of Ships, Navy Department, April 20, 1942.
[39] Commanding Officer, USS *Curtiss* (AV-4), Raid on December 7, 1941, Report of, 16 December 1941; USS *Curtiss* Bomb Damage, December 7, 1941 Pearl Harbor, Bureau of Ships, Navy Department, April 20, 1942.
[40] Commanding Officer, USS *Curtiss* (AV-4), Raid on December 7, 1941, Report of, 16 December 1941; Pearl Harbor Casualties (http://www.pearlharbor.org/history/casualties/pearl-harbor-casualties: accessed 22 April 2015).
[41] Coverage by the *Honolulu Advertiser*, date of article unknown.
[42] ComPatWing One, Report of Japanese Air Attack on Kaneohe Bay, T.H., December 7, 1941, 1 January 1942; CTF 9 (ComPatWing Two), Operations on December 7, 1941, 20 December 1941.
[43] ComPatWing One, Report of Japanese Air Attack on Kaneohe Bay, T.H., December 7, 1941, 1 January 1942.
[44] Ibid.
[45] Ibid.
[46] Ibid.
[47] Ibid.
[48] Ibid.

[49] "Remembering the Honor, Courage and Commitment of Lt. John W. Finn," Naval History Blog (http://www.navalhistory.org/2014/07/23/peoplematter-remembering-the-honor-courage-and-committment-of-lt-john-william-finn: accessed 26 April 2015).
[50] Ibid.
[51] Ibid.
[52] Commander, VPB-24, VPB-24, History of, 31 December 1944; Commanding Officer, VPB-23, History of VPB-23, 23 June 1945.
[53] Dorny, *US Navy PBY Catalina Units of the Pacific War*, 20; Commander Utility Wing, Service Force, Pacific Fleet, Unit History covering World War II, preparation and submission of, [month and day illegible] 1945.
[54] McKillop, "U.S. Navy Aviation Units."
[55] Ibid.
[56] Ibid.
[57] CINC, U.S. Pacific Fleet, Report of Japanese Raid on Pearl Harbor, 7 December, 1941, 15 February 1942.
[58] Barbara Maranzani, "5 Facts About Pearl Harbor and the USS *Arizona*" (http://www.history.com/news/5-facts-about-pearl-harbor-and-the-uss-arizona: accessed 7 May 2015).

CHAPTER 5 NOTES

[1] C. A. Keller, 8 March 1943.
[2] VP-10 War Diary, December 1941; C. A. Keller, 8 March 1943.
[3] VP-10 War Diary, December 1941; C. A. Keller, 8 March 1943; Peterson 28 February 1944.
[4] Peterson, 28 February 1944; ComFltAir, West Coast, Information Concerning Naval Campaign in Orient, 1941-1942.
[5] ONI Combat Narratives: The Java Sea Campaign; Robert C. Cressman, *The Official Chronology of the U.S. Navy in World War II* (Annapolis, MD: Naval Institute, 2000), 58-59.
[6] ONI Combat Narratives: The Java Sea Campaign; *Boise* War Diary, December 1941.
[7] *Boise* War Diary, December 1941.
[8] *Trinity* War Diary, December 1941.
[9] *William B. Preston, DANFS*; Robert Cressman, "Historic Fleets – The Saga of the Williebee," *Naval History Magazine*, December 2012.
[10] Commanding Officer, *William B. Preston* (AVD-7), History of the U.S.S. *William B. Preston* (AVD-7) – Forwarding of, 16 October 1945; Cressman, "Historic Fleets – The Saga of the Williebee."
[11] Cressman, "Historic Fleets – The Saga of the Williebee."
[12] History of the U.S.S. *William B. Preston* (AVD-7) – Forwarding of, 16 October 1945; Cressman, "Historic Fleets – The Saga of the Williebee"; VP-10 War Diary, December 1941.
[13] *William B. Preston, DANFS*; Cressman, "Historic Fleets – The Saga of the Williebee."

[14] History of the U.S.S. *William B. Preston* (AVD-7) – Forwarding of, 16 October 1945; Cressman, "Historic Fleets – The Saga of the Williebee."
[15] C. A. Keller, 8 March 1943.
[16] C. A. Keller, 8 March 1943; Samuel Eliot Morison, *The Rising Sun in the Pacific 1931-April 1942* (University of Illinois Press, 2001), 161.
[17] C. A. Keller, 8 March 1943.
[18] Ibid.
[19] Peterson, 28 February 1944.
[20] Ibid.
[21] ComFltAir, West Coast, Information Concerning Naval Campaign in Orient, 1941-1942; Messimer, *In the Hands of Fate*, 52.
[22] ComFltAir, West Coast, Information Concerning Naval Campaign in Orient, 1941-1942; Dorny, *US Navy PBY Catalina Units of the Pacific War*, 22.
[23] ComFltAir, West Coast, Information Concerning Naval Campaign in Orient, 1941-1942.
[24] ComFltAir, West Coast, Information Concerning Naval Campaign in Orient, 1941-1942; VP-10 War Diary, December 1941; Messimer, *In the Hands of Fate*, 59.
[25] ComFltAir, West Coast, Information Concerning Naval Campaign in Orient, 1941-1942.

CHAPTER 6 NOTES

[1] Pratt, 30 March 1945; C. Peter Chen, "Dutch East Indies Campaign, Celebes and Moluccas 11 Jan 1942 - 31 Jul 1942" (http://ww2db.com/battle_spec.php?battle_id=64: accessed 17 June 2015).
[2] Pratt, 30 March 1945; C. A. Keller, 8 March 1943,
[3] Pratt, 30 March 1945.
[4] Peterson, 28 February 1944; VP-10 War Diary, December 1941.
[5] Peterson, 28 February 1944; VP-10 War Diary, December 1941.
[6] Peterson, 28 February 1944; VP-10 War Diary, December 1941.
[7] Pratt, 30 March 1945; Interview of Lt. Cdr. Pratt, USN, Commanding Officer of the USS *Childs* (AVD), in the Bureau of Aeronautics, Navy Department, 28 April 1942; Interview of Lieutenant Commander Clarence Keller, USN, PatWing 10, in the Bureau of Aeronautics, 12 March 1943; VP-10 War Diary, December 1941.
[8] Pratt, 30 March 1945; C. A. Keller, 8 March 1943.
[9] Pratt, 30 March 1945; VP-10 War Diary, December 1941.
[10] Pratt, 30 March 1945; C. A. Keller, 8 March 1943; Hart, 11 June 1942; Morison, *The Two-Ocean War*, 87; Morison, *The Rising Sun in the Pacific 1931-April 1942*, 277.
[11] Hart, 11 June 1942.
[12] Ibid.
[13] Ibid.
[14] Peterson, 28 February 1944; ComFltAir, West Coast, Information Concerning Naval Campaign in Orient, 1941-1942, 12 December 1944.

[15] Peterson, 28 February 1944; ComFltAir, West Coast, Information Concerning Naval Campaign in Orient, 1941-1942, 12 December 1944.
[16] Peterson, 28 February 1944; Messimer, *In the Hands of Fate*, 114.
[17] Peterson, 28 February 1944; Messimer, *In the Hands of Fate*, 115, 121; General Orders: Bureau of Naval Personnel Information Bulletin No. 304 (July 1942).
[18] General Orders: Bureau of Naval Personnel Information Bulletin No. 304 (July 1942).
[19] Peterson, 28 February 1944; Messimer, *In the Hands of Fate*, 122; General Orders: Bureau of Naval Personnel Information Bulletin No. 304 (July 1942); Walter G. Winslow, *The Fleet the Gods Forgot: The U.S. Asiatic Fleet in World War II* (Annapolis, MD: Naval Institute, 1994).
[20] Messimer, *In the Hands of Fate*, 122; General Orders: Bureau of Naval Personnel Information Bulletin No. 304 (July 1942).
[21] Messimer, *In the Hands of Fate*, 122; General Orders: Bureau of Naval Personnel Information Bulletin No. 304 (July 1942).
[22] Messimer, *In the Hands of Fate*, 122; General Orders: Bureau of Naval Personnel Information Bulletin No. 304 (July 1942); VP-10 War Diary, December 1941.
[23] Peterson, 28 February 1944; Messimer, *In the Hands of Fate*, 115.
[24] General Orders: Bureau of Naval Personnel Information Bulletin No. 304 (July 1942).
[25] Hart, 11 June 1942.
[26] Pratt, 30 March 1945; C. A. Keller, 8 March 1943; Clarence Keller, 12 March 1943; Aircraft Asiatic Fleet and VP-10 War Diary, January 1942.
[27] Hart, 11 June 1942.
[28] C. A. Keller, 8 March 1943; Clarence Keller, 12 March 1943; Aircraft Asiatic Fleet and VP-10 War Diary, January 1942; Peterson, 28 February 1944.
[29] Peterson, 28 February 1944.
[30] Pratt, 30 March 1945; Aircraft Asiatic Fleet and VP-10 War Diary, January 1942.
[31] Pratt, 30 March 1945.
[32] Ibid.
[33] Pratt, 28 April 1942; Pratt, 30 March 1945; Aircraft Asiatic Fleet and VP-10 War Diary, January 1942.
[34] "Tarakan," The Pacific War Online Encyclopedia (http://pwencycl.kgbudge.com/T/a/Tarakan.htm: accessed 1 July 2015); Morison, *The Rising Sun in the Pacific 1931-April 1942*, p. 272-273.
[35] "The capture of Balikpapan, January 1942," (http://www.oocities.org/dutcheastindies/balikpapan.html: accessed 1 July 2015); *Parrot, DANFS*.
[36] "The capture of Balikpapan, January 1942," (http://www.oocities.org/dutcheastindies/balikpapan.html: accessed 1 July 2015); *Parrot, DANFS*

[37] Aircraft Asiatic Fleet and VP-10 War Diary, January 1942; Peterson, 28 February 1944.
[38] Peterson, 28 February 1944.
[39] Hart, 11 June 1942; "Fall of Ambon," Australia's War 1939-1945 (http://www.ww2australia.gov.au/japadvance/ambon.html: accessed 22 June 2015).
[40] Pratt, 30 March 1945.
[41] Pratt, 30 March 1945; Pratt, 28 April 1942; Hart, 11 June 1942.
[42] Pratt, 30 March 1945; Aircraft Asiatic Fleet and VP-10 War Diary, January 1942.
[43] Pratt, 30 March 1945.
[44] Ibid.
[45] Ibid.
[46] Ibid.
[47] Ibid.
[48] Hart, 11 June 1942.
[49] Ibid.
[50] Pratt, 30 March 1945.
[51] Ibid.
[52] Ibid.
[53] Pratt, 28 April 1942.
[54] Pratt, 30 March 1945; Hart, 11 June 1942.
[55] Morison, *The Rising Sun in the Pacific*, 298-300; Messimer, *In the Hands of Fate*, 234; Bob Hackett, Sander Kingsepp and Peter Cundall, Shokaitei! IJN Patrol Boat No. 106: Tabular Record of Movement (http://www.combinedfleet.com/PB-106_t.htm: accessed 23 July 2015).
[56] Hart, 11 June 1942; Morison, *The Rising Sun in the Pacific*, 301.
[57] Pratt, 30 March 1945; *Paul Jones, DANFS*.
[58] Hart, 11 June 1942.

CHAPTER 7 NOTES
[1] "A Darwin Eyewitness Account - Stoker 2nd Class Charlie Unmack" (http://www.pacificwar.org.au/battaust/CharlieUnmack.html: accessed 26 May 2015).
[2] Ibid.; Commanding Officer, USS *William B. Preston*, War Damage – Report of, 1 May 1944.
[3] The Japanese bombing of Darwin, Broome and northern Australia 26 June 2015 (http://www.australia.gov.au/about-australia/australian-story/japanese-bombing-of-darwin: accessed 6 June 2015); Commanding Officer, USS *William B. Preston*, War Damage – Report of, 1 May 1944.
[4] The Japanese bombing of Darwin, Broome and northern Australia 26 June 2015.
[5] Ibid.
[6] *William B. Preston, DANFS*; Commanding Officer, USS *William B. Preston*, History of the U.S.S. *William B. Preston* (AVD7) – Forwarding of, 16 October 1945.

[7] Commanding Officer, USS *William B. Preston*, History of the U.S.S. *William B. Preston* (AVD7) – Forwarding of, 16 October 1945; Commanding Officer, USS *William B. Preston*, War Damage – Report of, 1 May 1944.
[8] Commanding Officer, USS *William B. Preston*, War Damage – Report of, 1 May 1944; *Peary, DANFS*.
[9] Commanding Officer, USS *William B. Preston*, History of the U.S.S. *William B. Preston* (AVD7) – Forwarding of, 16 October 1945.
[10] Commanding Officer, USS *William B. Preston*, History of the U.S.S. *William B. Preston* (AVD7) – Forwarding of, 16 October 1945; Commanding Officer, USS *William B. Preston*, War Damage – Report of, 1 May 1944; General Orders: Bureau of Naval Personnel Information Bulletin No. 309 (December 1942).
[11] General Orders: Bureau of Naval Personnel Information Bulletin No. 309 (December 1942); *William B. Preston, DANFS*.
[12] Commanding Officer, USS *William B. Preston*, War Damage – Report of, 1 May 1944; General Orders: Board Serial 198 (February 25, 1943).
[13] Commanding Officer, USS *William B. Preston*, History of the U.S.S. *William B. Preston* (AVD7) – Forwarding of, 16 October 1945.
[14] Ibid.; *William B. Preston, DANFS*.
[15] Commanding Officer, USS *William B. Preston*, History of the U.S.S. *William B. Preston* (AVD7) – Forwarding of, 16 October 1945; *William B. Preston, DANFS*.
[16] Series no: AWM78 Control symbol 400/2 RAN Administrative Authority - Darwin Naval Base (HMAS MELVILLE): Reports of Proceedings [war diary]
[17] Royal Australian Navy Campaign and Battle Honours (http://www.navy.gov.au/history/battle-honours: accessed 26 June 2015).

CHAPTER 8 NOTES
[1] Peterson, 28 February 1944.
[2] Morison, *The Rising Sun in the Pacific*, 295.
[3] Morison, *The Rising Sun in the Pacific*, 335.
[4] Dwight R. Messimer, *Pawns of War* (Annapolis: U.S. Naval Institute, 1983), 3, 11-12; Messimer, *In the Hands of Fate*, 266.
[5] William H. Bartsch, *Every Day a Nightmare: American Pursuit Pilots in the Defense of Java, 1941-1942* (College Station, TX: Texas A&M University Press; 2010), 101-104.
[6] *Phoenix* War Diary, February 1942; Commanding Officer, USS *Langley* (AV-3), Operations, action and sinking of U.S.S. *Langley*, period from February 22 to March 5, 1942, 9 March 1942; Messimer, *Pawns of War*, 26, 28.
[7] Commanding Officer, USS *Langley* (AV-3), Operations, action and sinking of U.S.S. *Langley*, period from February 22 to March 5, 1942, 9 March 1942; *Edsall* War History; Messimer, *Pawns of War*, 28-29.
[8] Commanding Officer, USS *Langley* (AV-3), Operations, action and sinking of U.S.S. *Langley*, period from February 22 to March 5, 1942, 9 March 1942; ComDesDiv Fifty-seven, U.S.S. *Edsall*, Record of Known Activities Between

26 February, 1942, and 1 March, 1942, 21 May 1942; Messimer, *Pawns of War*, 42-43.

[9] Messimer, *Pawns of War*, 37, 41.

[10] Commanding Officer, USS *Langley* (AV-3), Operations, action and sinking of U.S.S. *Langley*, period from February 22 to March 5, 1942, 9 March 1942.

[11] Commanding Officer, USS *Langley* (AV-3), Operations, action and sinking of U.S.S. *Langley*, period from February 22 to March 5, 1942, 9 March 1942; ComDesDiv Fifty-seven, U.S.S. *Edsall*, Record of Known Activities, 21 May 1942.

[12] Commanding Officer, USS *Langley* (AV-3), Operations, action and sinking of U.S.S. *Langley*, period from February 22 to March 5, 1942, 9 March 1942; ComDesDiv Fifty-seven, U.S.S. *Edsall*, Record of Known Activities Between 26 February, 1942, and 1 March, 1942, 21 May 1942.

[13] ComDesDiv Fifty-seven, U.S.S. *Edsall*, Record of Known Activities, 21 May 1942.

[14] Commanding Officer, USS *Langley* (AV-3), Operations, action and sinking of U.S.S. *Langley*, period from February 22 to March 5, 1942, 9 March 1942.

[15] Ibid.

[16] Ibid.; Messimer, *Pawns of War*, 90; Jeffrey Cox, *Rising Sun, Falling Skies: The Disastrous Java Sea Campaign of World War II* (Oxford, UK: Osprey, 2014), 278.

[17] Commanding Officer, USS *Langley* (AV-3), Operations, action and sinking of U.S.S. *Langley*, period from February 22 to March 5, 1942, 9 March 1942; ComDesDiv Fifty-seven, U.S.S. *Edsall*, Record of Known Activities, 21 May 1942.

[18] Commanding Officer, USS *Langley* (AV-3), Operations, action and sinking of U.S.S. *Langley*, period from February 22 to March 5, 1942, 9 March 1942; Commanding Officer, ex. USS *Pecos*, Action and Sinking of U.S.S. *Pecos* 1 March, 1942, 7 March 1942; Messimer, *Pawns of War*, 90-91; Cox, *Rising Sun, Falling Skies: The Disastrous Java Sea Campaign of World War II*, 279.

[19] Commanding Officer, USS *Langley* (AV-3), Operations, action and sinking of U.S.S. *Langley*, period from February 22 to March 5, 1942, 9 March 1942; Commanding Officer, ex. USS *Pecos*, Action and Sinking of U.S.S. *Pecos* 1 March, 1942, 7 March 1942; ComDesDiv Fifty-seven, U.S.S. *Edsall*, Record of Known Activities, 21 May 1942.

[20] Commanding Officer, USS *Langley* (AV-3), Operations, action and sinking of U.S.S. *Langley*, period from February 22 to March 5, 1942, 9 March 1942; Commanding Officer, ex. USS *Pecos*, Action and Sinking of U.S.S. *Pecos* 1 March, 1942, 7 March 1942; Messimer, *Pawns of War*, 97-98, 152.

[21] Commanding Officer, USS *Langley* (AV-3), Operations, action and sinking of U.S.S. *Langley*, period from February 22 to March 5, 1942, 9 March 1942.

[22] Commanding Officer, USS *Langley* (AV-3), Operations, action and sinking of U.S.S. *Langley*, period from February 22 to March 5, 1942, 9 March

1942; Commanding Officer, ex. USS *Pecos*, Action and Sinking of U.S.S. *Pecos* 1 March, 1942, 7 March 1942.
[23] Commanding Officer, ex. USS *Pecos*, Action and Sinking of U.S.S. *Pecos* 1 March, 1942, 7 March 1942; Messimer, *Pawns of War*, 95.
[24] Commanding Officer, ex. USS *Pecos*, Action and Sinking of U.S.S. *Pecos* 1 March, 1942, 7 March 1942; Messimer, *Pawns of War*, 94, 96, 101.
[25] Ibid.
[26] Commanding Officer, ex. USS *Pecos*, Action and Sinking of U.S.S. *Pecos* 1 March, 1942, 7 March 1942.
[27] Commanding Officer, ex. USS *Pecos*, Action and Sinking of U.S.S. *Pecos* 1 March, 1942, 7 March 1942; Messimer, *Pawns of War*, 103-104.
[28] Commanding Officer, USS *Langley* (AV-3), Commanding Officer, ex. USS *Pecos*, Action and Sinking of U.S.S. *Pecos* 1 March, 1942, 7 March 1942; ComDesDiv Fifty-seven, U.S.S. *Edsall*, Record of Known Activities, 21 May 1942.
[29] Ibid.
[30] ComDesDiv Fifty-seven, U.S.S. *Edsall*, Record of Known Activities, 21 May 1942; Messimer, *Pawns of War*, 146, 157; *Mount Vernon, DANFS*.
[31] ComDesDiv Fifty-seven, U.S.S. *Edsall*, Record of Known Activities Between 26 February, 1942, and 1 March, 1942, 21 May 1942.

CHAPTER 9 NOTES
[1] ONI Combat Narratives: The Java Sea Campaign.
[2] Morison, *The Two-Ocean War*, 90; *Houston, DANFS*, Java Naval Battles (http://combinedfleet.com/battles/Java_Campaign#Java_Sea: accessed 25 July 2015).
[3] Morison, *The Rising Sun in the Pacific*, 332-334.
[4] Ibid., 342-347; *Houston, DANFS*; Java Naval Battles.
[5] Morison, *The Rising Sun in the Pacific*, 349-358; Java Naval Battles.
[6] Morison, *The Rising Sun in the Pacific*, 366-368; *Houston, DANFS*.
[7] Morison, *The Rising Sun in the Pacific*, 372-373.
[8] Ibid., p. 371; "Hr Ms *Evertsen* (EV)" (http://www.pacificwrecks.com/ships/HrMs/evertsen.html: accessed 27 July 2015); "Admiralen-class destroyers" (http://netherlandsnavy.nl/Admiralen.htm: accessed 27 July 2015).
[9] Morison, *The Rising Sun in the Pacific*, 355; Java Naval Battles.
[10] Morison, *The Rising Sun in the Pacific*, 375-379.
[11] Pratt, 30 March 1945; Messimer, *In the Hands of Fate*, 256.
[12] "Air Raids," Australia's War 1939-1945 (http://www.ww2australia.gov.au/underattack/broome.html: accessed 25 June 2015).
[13] Pratt, 30 March 1945; Messimer, *In the Hands of Fate*, 256-257, 262-265.
[14] Pratt, 30 March 1945; Messimer, *In the Hands of Fate*, 262-265.
[15] Pratt, 30 March 1945; "Air Raids," Australia's War 1939-1945.
[16] Pratt, 30 March 1945; "Air Raids," Australia's War 1939-1945.
[17] Pratt, 30 March 1945.

[18] Ibid.
[19] C. A. Keller, 8 March 1943.
[20] Pratt, 30 March 1945; Messimer, *In the Hands of Fate*, 270-271.
[21] Pratt, 30 March 1945; Messimer, *In the Hands of Fate*, 272-273.
[22] Commander, VPB-33, History of VPB-33, transmittal of, 1 January 1945.
[23] Pratt, 30 March 1945; Messimer, *In the Hands of Fate*, 275.
[24] Pratt, 30 March 1945; Pratt, 28 April 1942.
[25] Interview of Commander George T. Mundorff Jr.,USN, ComFairWing One, 20 Months in South Pacific VPB in Australia and New Guinea 23 August 1943, Office of the Chief of Naval Operations, Navy Department, Washington, D.C.; *DANAS* Vol. II (http://www.history.navy.mil/research/histories/naval-aviation-history/dictionary-of-american-naval-aviation-squadrons-volume-2.html: accessed 9 May 2015).
[26] Interview of Commander George T. Mundorff Jr., USN.
[27] Ibid.
[28] Commanding Officer, VPB-34, The History of VPB-34, 22 January 1945.
[29] Ibid.
[30] Interview of Commander George T. Mundorff Jr., USN.
[31] Ibid.
[32] Bureau of Naval Personnel Information Bulletin, July and September 1942.

CHAPTER 10 NOTES

[1] Brian Garfield, *The Thousand-Mile War: World War II in Alaska and the Aleutians* (Garden City, NY: Doubleday, 1969), 12.
[2] Ibid., 5.
[3] Garfield, *The Thousand-Mile War*, 6-7; Cressman, *The Official Chronology of the U.S. Navy in World War II - 1942*; "The Doolittle Tokyo Raiders" http://www.doolittleraider.com: accessed 14 October 2011)
[4] Garfield, *The Thousand-Mile War*, 6-7; Cressman, *The Official Chronology of the U.S. Navy in World War II - 1942*.
[5] CTF 8 War Diary May 22, 1942 to May 31, 1942; Garfield, The *Thousand-Mile War*, 11-14; U.S. Navy Joint Intelligence Center, *The Aleutians Campaign, June 1942-August 1943* (Washington, D.C.: Naval Historical Center, Department of the Navy, 1993) (http://www.ibiblio.org/hyperwar/USN/USN-CN-Aleutians.html: accessed 18 July 2011); "U.S. Pacific Fleet and Pacific Ocean Areas Order of Battle" (http://www.zipcon.com/~kestral/usn.html: accessed 15 July 2011); "Task Force 8" (http://pacific.valka.cz/forces/tf8.htm#midway: accessed 15 July 2011).
[6] Samuel Eliot Morison, *History of United States Naval Operations in World War II, Coral Sea, Midway and Submarine Actions, May 1942-August 1942*. (Boston: Little, Brown, 1984), 163-165; Garfield, *The Thousand-Mile War*, 45; USS *Charleston*, 1941 Cruise, diary entries, from the collection of N. G. Wade, CTC, USN (Ret.), crewmember November 1940-April 1941

(http://www.navsource.org/archives/12/120905118.pdf: accessed 2 August 2011).

[7] Morison, *Coral Sea, Midway and Submarine Actions*, 163-165; Garfield, *The Thousand-Mile War*, 45; USS *Charleston*, 1941 Cruise, diary entries.

[8] Morison, *Coral Sea, Midway and Submarine Actions*, 165; Garfield, *The Thousand-Mile War*, 56, 73; "Guide to the Olson & Winge Marine Works Photographs and Scrapbook 1914-1970" (http://nwda-db.orbiscascade.org/findaid/ark:/80444/xv50635: accessed 17 July 2011).

[9] ComNorWestSeaFron War Diary, May 1942.

[10] Ibid.

[11] CTF 8 War Diary, May 1942; ComPatWing 4 War Diary, 27 May to 30 June, 1942.

[12] ComPatWing 4 War Diary, 27 May to 30 June, 1942.

[13] CTF 8 War Diary, May 1942; ComNorWestSeaFron War Diary, May 1942; *Oriole*, *DANFS*.

[14] CTG 8.1 Operational Plan No. 1-42 of 28 May 1942; *Hulbert* War Diary, June 1942.

[15] CTF 8 Operational Plan 1-42 of 27 May 1942; USCGC *Onondaga*, *DANFS*; ComPatWing 4 War Diary, 27 May, 1942 to 30 June, 1942; Bulkley, *At Close Quarters*, 261.

[16] *Charleston* War Diary, May 1, 1942 to May 31, 1942.

[17] CTF 8 War Diary, June 1942; CTF 8 Letter of Instruction to Commander Destroyer Striking Force, A16-1/TF8 Serial T06 of May 31, 1942

[18] CTG 8 War Diary June 1942; *Louisville* War Diary June 1942; Morison, *Coral Sea, Midway and Submarine Actions*, 166-170.

[19] CTG 8 War Diary June 1942; *Louisville* War Diary June 1942; Morison, *Coral Sea, Midway and Submarine Actions*, 169, 175-176.

[20] CTF 8 War Diary June 1942; ComNorWestSeaFron War Diary, June 1942; Morison, *Coral Sea, Midway and Submarine Actions*, 176.

[21] ComPatWing 4 War Diary, 27 May to 30 June, 1942.

[22] CTG 8 War Diary June 1942; *Louisville* War Diary June 1942; Robert J. Bulkley Jr., *At Close Quarters PT Boats in the United States Navy* (Washington DC: Naval History Division, 1962), 261-262.

[23] CTF 8 War Diary for June 1942; *Gillis* War Diary, 23 May, 1942 to 30 June 1942; ComNorWestSeaFron War Diary, June 1942.

[24] *Gillis* War Diary, 23 May to 30 June 1942; ComNorWestSeaFron War Diary, June 1942.

[25] *Gillis* War Diary, 23 May to 30 June 1942; U.S. Navy Joint Intelligence Center, *The Aleutians Campaign*, 7.

[26] General Orders: CNC Pacific: Serial 20 (August 21, 1942).

[27] ComNorWestSeaFron War Diary, June 1942; U.S. Navy Joint Intelligence Center, *The Aleutians Campaign*, 9; Morison, *Coral Sea, Midway and Submarine Actions*, 176-178; "Marine Exchange of Alaska" (http://www.mxak.org/community/northwestern/northwestern.html:

accessed 2 September 2012); ComPatWing 4 War Diary, 27 May to 30 June, 1942.

[28] ComNorWestSeaFron War Diary, June 1942; U.S. Navy Joint Intelligence Center, *The Aleutians Campaign*, 9; Morison, *Coral Sea, Midway and Submarine Actions*, 176-178; "Marine Exchange of Alaska" (http://www.mxak.org/community/northwestern/northwestern.html: accessed 2 September 2012); ComPatWing 4 War Diary, 27 May to 30 June, 1942.

[29] CTF 8 War Diary, June 1942.

[30] Ibid.

[31] Ibid.

[32] Ibid.

[33] Ibid.

[34] ComPatWing 4 War Diary, 27 May to 30 June, 1942; CTF 8 War Diary, June 1942; Bulkley, *At Close Quarters PT Boats in the United States Navy*, 261-262.

[35] ComPatWing 4 War Diary, 27 May to 30 June, 1942; CTF 8 War Diary, June 1942

[36] ComPatWing 4 War Diary, 27 May to 30 June, 1942; *Gillis* War Diary, 23 May, 1942 to 30 June 1942.

[37] *Hulbert* War Diary, June 1942.

[38] ComPatWing 4 War Diary, 27 May to 30 June, 1942; *Gillis* War Diary, 23 May, 1942 to 30 June 1942.

[39] ComNorWestSeaFron War Diary May 1942; *Charleston* War Diary, June 1942; CTF 8 Operational Plan No. 4-42 dated 10 June 1942.

[40] ComPatWing 4 War Diary, 27 May to 30 June, 1942; *Gillis* War Diary, 23 May to 30 June, 1942.

[41] Ibid.

[42] ComPatWing 4 War Diary, 27 May to 30 June, 1942; ComNorWestSeaFron War Diary, June 1942.

[43] ComNorWestSeaFron War Diary, June 1942; CTF 8 War Diary, June 1942.

[44] Morison, *Coral Sea, Midway and Submarine Actions*, 162-163; Garfield, *The Thousand-Mile War*, 157.

[45] Morison, *Coral Sea, Midway and Submarine Actions*, 162-163; Garfield, *The Thousand-Mile War*, 157.

[46] ComNorWestSeaFron War Diary, June 1942; Magellan Ship Biographies (http://www.cimorelli.com/cgi-bin/magellanscripts/ship_bio1.asp?ShipName=Seine: accessed 17 July 2011).

(46) Commanding Officer, USS Williamson, Report of Operations of VP-43, 14 June 1942.

(47) ComPatWing Four, Report of Operations of VP-43, 6 July 1942.

(48) Bureau of Naval Personnel Information Bulletin No. 313 (April 1943)

CHAPTER 11 NOTES

[1] Bruhn, *Battle Stars for the "Cactus Navy": America's Fishing Vessels and Yachts in World War II*, 101.
[2] Ibid.
[3] Ibid.; Dorny, *US Navy PBY Catalina Units of the Pacific War*, 33.
[4] Bruhn, *Battle Stars for the "Cactus Navy,"* 101.
[5] Interrogation Nav 60, Captain Yasumi Toyama, 1 Nov 1945, World War II Database (http://ww2db.com/doc.php?q=188: accessed 21 March 2015).
[6] CINC, U.S. Pacific Fleet, Night Torpedo Attack, 3-4 June; report of, 2 July 1942,
[7] ONI Combat Narratives: Battle of Midway; Dorny, *US Navy PBY Catalina Units of the Pacific War*, 33; Interrogation Nav 60, Capt. Yasumi Toyama, 1 Nov 1945.
[8] ONI Combat Narratives: Battle of Midway.
[9] Lieutenant W. L. Richards, U.S. Navy, Night Torpedo Attack, 3-4 June; Report of, 18 June 1942.
[10] Richards, U.S. Navy, Night Torpedo Attack, 3-4 June; Report of.
[11] Ibid.
[12] Richards, U.S. Navy, Night Torpedo Attack, 3-4 June; Report of; ComPatWing Two, Action Reports 3, 4, and 5 to be added to CPW-2 War Diary, 13 July 1942.
[13] ComPatWing Two, Action Reports 3, 4, and 5 to be added to CPW-2 War Diary, 13 July 1942.
[14] Richards, U.S. Navy, Night Torpedo Attack, 3-4 June; Report of.
[15] Ibid.
[16] Bruhn, *Battle Stars for the "Cactus Navy": America's Fishing Vessels and Yachts in World War II*, 103-105.
[17] Ibid.
[18] Ibid.
[19] Richards, U.S. Navy, Night Torpedo Attack, 3-4 June; Report of.
[20] Bruhn, *Battle Stars for the "Cactus Navy,"* 103-105.
[21] Richards, U.S. Navy, Night Torpedo Attack, 3-4 June; Report of.
[22] Bruhn, *Battle Stars for the "Cactus Navy,"* 105-106.
[23] Ibid.
[24] Interrogation Nav 60, Captain Yasumi Toyama, 1 Nov 1945.
[25] Commanding Officer, USS *Ballard*, Ship's History –Forwarding of, 29 October 1945.
[26] Commanding Officer, USS *Ballard*, Ship's History –Forwarding of, 29 October 1945; John Ford Biography
(http://www.imdb.com/name/nm0000406/bio: accessed 5 April 2015)
[27] Commanding Officer, USS *Ballard*, Ship's History –Forwarding of, 29 October 1945.
[28] Ibid.
[29] Ibid.; Morison, *The Two-Ocean War*, 157.

[30] *Thornton* War Diary, May and June 1942; World War II Japanese Admiral Isoroku Yamamoto (http://armedforcesmuseum.com/world-war-ii-japanese-admiral-isoroku-yamamoto/: accessed 6 April 2015).
[31] *Thornton* War Diary, May and June 1942.

CHAPTER 12 NOTES
[1] North Atlantic Naval Coastal Frontier War Diary, January 1942.
[2] J. W. Perkins, *Battle Stars and Naval Awards* (Seminole, Florida: 2004), p. T4.
[3] Commanding Officer, USS *Gannet*, Report of Action, 22 June 1942; "Ships hit by U-boats," Uboat.net (http://uboat.net/allies/merchants/search.php: accessed 11 September 2015); NOB Bermuda War Diary, June 1942.
[4] "American Military Bases in Bermuda from 1941 to 1995" (http://www.bermuda-online.org/milquit.htm: accessed 11 September 2015); *Building the Navy's Bases in World War II: History of the Bureau of Yards and Docks and the Civil Engineer Corps 1940-1946 Volume II* (Washington, DC: U.S. Government Printing Office, 1947), 31.
[5] Commanding Officer, USS *Gannet*, Report of Action, 22 June 1942; Eric T. Wiberg, Esq., "USS *Gannet*, Attack & Survivor's Narrative" (http://uboatsbermuda.blogspot.com/2014/11/uss-gannet-sunk-by-u-653feiler-n-of.html: accessed 11 September 2015).
[6] Commanding Officer, USS *Gannet*, Report of Action, 22 June 1942.
[7] Commanding Officer, USS *Gannet*, Report of Action, 22 June 1942; "Ships hit by U-boats," Uboat.net.
[8] Commanding Officer, USS *Gannet*, Report of Action, 22 June 1942.
[9] Ibid.
[10] Ibid.
[11] Ibid.
[12] Ibid.
[13] Commanding Officer, USS *Gannet*, Report of Action, 22 June 1942; *Hamilton*, *DANFS*; VP-74 War Diary, June 1942.
[14] The Commandant U.S. Naval Operating Base Bermuda, Action Report, 6 July 1942.
[15] NOB Base Bermuda War Diary, June 1942.
[16] Wiberg, "USS *Gannet*, Attack & Survivor's Narrative."
[17] Ibid.
[18] Bruhn, *Battle Stars for the "Cactus Navy": America's Fishing Vessels and Yachts in World War II*, 146-148.
[19] Ibid., 132-133.

CHAPTER 13 NOTES
[1] ComFairWing One, Fleet Air Wing One – History of (1 January – 2 September 1945), undated document.

[2] Bruhn, *Battle Stars for the "Cactus Navy": America's Fishing Vessels and Yachts in World War II*, 4.; Dorny, *US Navy PBY Catalina Units of the Pacific War*, 39; Morison, *The Two-Ocean War*, p. 140-147; *Yorktown, DANFS*.
[3] Morison, *The Two-Ocean War*, 142.
[4] Morison, *The Two-Ocean War*, 142; CTF 17, The Battle of the Coral Sea, May 4-8, 1942, 27 May 1942.
[5] Bruhn, *Battle Stars for the "Cactus Navy,"*, 4.; Dorny, *US Navy PBY Catalina Units of the Pacific War*, 39; Morison, *The Two-Ocean War*, 140-147; *Yorktown, DANFS*.
[6] Bruhn, *Battle Stars for the "Cactus Navy,"* 4.
[7] Dorny, *US Navy PBY Catalina Units of the Pacific War*, 39.
[8] *Tangier* War Diary, May 1942; Commanding Officer, VPB-71, War History, Forwarding of, 11 July 1945.
[9] *Tangier, Curtiss*, VP-71 War Diary, June 1942; Robert J. Cressman, "The Official Chronology of the U.S. Navy in World War II" (http://www.ibiblio.org/hyperwar/USN/USN-Chron/USN-Chron-1942.html: accessed 4 February 2015); Commanding Officer USS Curtiss, Ship's History – Submission of, 1 March 1946
[10] Commander Air Center, Navy 140, History of Air Center Command, Navy 140 – Forwarding of, 13 June 1945.
[11] Bruhn, *Battle Stars for the "Cactus Navy": America's Fishing Vessels and Yachts in World War II*, 4.
[12] Commanding Officer USS *Mackinac*, Ship's History – Forwarding of, 3 April 1946; *Tracy* War Diary, August 1942; Dorny, *US Navy PBY Catalina Units of the Pacific War*, 39.
[13] Commanding Officer USS *Mackinac*, Ship's History – Forwarding of, 3 April 1946; *Tracy* War Diary, August 1942.
[14] Commander Air Center, Navy 140, History of Air Center Command, Navy 140 – Forwarding of, 13 June 1945.
[15] Bruhn, *Battle Stars for the "Cactus Navy,"* 4.
[16] *Mackinac* War Diary, September 1942.
[17] Dorny, *US Navy PBY Catalina Units of the Pacific War*, 42.
[18] *Ballard* War Diary, September 1942.
[19] VP-2 War Diary, September 1942.
[20] Commanding Officer USS *McFarland*, Action, Report of, 15 December 1942.
[21] Ibid.
[22] Ibid.
[23] Bruhn, *Battle Stars for the "Cactus Navy,"* 1-27.
[24] Commanding Officer USS *McFarland*, Action, Report of, 15 December 1942.
[25] Ibid.
[26] Ibid.
[27] Ibid.
[28] Ibid.
[29] Ibid.

[30] Bureau of Naval Personnel Information Bulletin No. 314 (May 1943).
[31] Commanding Officer USS *McFarland*, Action, Report of, 15 December 1942.
[32] Ibid.
[33] Ibid.
[34] General Orders: Commander Southern Pacific Area and Forces: Serial 1148p (December 31, 1942).
[35] Stephen Sherman, "Lt. Col. Harold W. Bauer Guadalcanal Hero, C.O. VMF-212, Medal of Honor Recipient" (http://acepilots.com/usmc_bauer.html: accessed 9 February 2015).
[36] Commanding Officer USS *Ballard*, Ship's History – Forwarding of, 29 October 1945; *McFarland, DANFS*.
[37] "Battle of the Santa Cruz Islands October 26, 1942," USS Enterprise CV-6 The Most Decorated Ship of the Second World War (http://www.cv6.org/1942/santacruz/santacruz.htm: accessed 17 February 2015).
[38] Morison, *The Two-Ocean War*, 193.
[39] Bob Fish, "Battle of Santa Cruz Islands (CV-8)" (http://www.usshornet.org/history/wwii/santa_cruz.shtml: accessed 17 February 2015).
[40] Ibid.
[41] Ibid.
[42] Eric Hammel, *Carrier Strike: The Battle of the Santa Cruz Islands, October 1942* (Lawrence, Kansas: Pacifica Press, 1999), p. 380; David C. Evans, *The Japanese Navy in World War II: In the Words of Former Japanese Naval Officers* (Annapolis, Maryland: Naval Institute, 1986), 520.
[43] Tameichi Hara, *Japanese Destroyer Captain* (New York, New York: Ballantine Books, 1961), 135.
[44] CINC, U.S. Pacific Fleet, Solomon Islands Campaign, Battle of Santa Cruz – 26 October 1942, 6 January 1943; Dorny, *US Navy PBY Catalina Units of the Pacific War*, 47.
[45] *Curtiss* War Diary, October 1942; Dorny, *US Navy PBY Catalina Units of the Pacific War*, 49.
[46] General Orders: Commander Southern Pacific Forces: Serial 020 (January 7, 1943).
[47] Bruhn, *Battle Stars for the "Cactus Navy": America's Fishing Vessels and Yachts in World War II*, 22-23.

CHAPTER 14 NOTES

[1] Bruhn, *Battle Stars for the "Cactus Navy": America's Fishing Vessels and Yachts in World War II*, 200.
[2] *Building the Navy's Bases in World War II: History of the Bureau of Yards and Docks and the Civil Engineer Corps 1940-1946 Volume II*, 195; Report of the Inspection of Noumea, New Caledonia, by a Board of Officers representing the Navy Department, Rear Admiral Richard E. Byrd, Senior Member, June 17-19, 1942.

[3] Bruhn, *Battle Stars for the "Cactus Navy": America's Fishing Vessels and Yachts in World War II*, 182.
[4] "Narrative History of Task Force 6814 Americal Division Jan. 23, 1942 to June 30, 1943" (http://www.ibiblio.org/hyperwar/USA/OOB/Americal-history.html: accessed 17 September 2015).
[5] Ibid.
[6] "Narrative History of Task Force 6814 Americal Division Jan. 23, 1942 to June 30, 1943"; Bruhn, *Battle Stars for the "Cactus Navy,"* 213.
[7] *Tangier* War Diary, April 1942; Report of the Inspection of Noumea, New Caledonia.
[8] Report of the Inspection of Noumea, New Caledonia.
[9] Ibid.
[10] *Tangier* War Diary, April and May 1942.
[11] CTF 17, The Battle of the Coral Sea, May 4-8, 1942, 27 May 1942.
[12] *Tangier* War Diary, May 1942; Michael W. Pocock, "Daily Event for May 5, 2014," MaritimeQuest.com (http://www.maritimequest.com/daily_event_archive/2014/05_may/05_ss_j ohn_adams.htm: accessed 18 September 2015).
[13] *Tangier* War Diary, May 1942; Pocock, "Daily Event for May 5, 2014."
[14] *Tangier* War Diary, May 1942; Pocock, "Daily Event for May 5, 2014."
[15] *Tangier* War Diary, May 1942.
[16] Pocock, "Daily Event for May 5, 2014"; Bob Hackett and Sander Kingsepp, "Sensuikan! IJN Submarine *I-21*: Tabular Record of Movement" (http://www.combinedfleet.com/I-21.htm: accessed 18 September 2015).
[17] Commander Destroyers, Pacific Fleet, Sinking of the U.S.S. *Sims* (DD409) by Japanese bombers in the Coral Sea on May 7, 1942, L11-1/A12 Serial 0724; *Sims, DANFS*.
[18] Commander Destroyers, Pacific Fleet, Sinking of the U.S.S. *Sims* (DD409) by Japanese bombers in the Coral Sea on May 7, 1942, L11-1/A12 Serial 0724; *Sims, DANFS*.
[19] Commanding Officer, USS *Neosho*, Engagement of U.S.S. *Neosho* with Japanese Aircraft on May 7, 1942; Subsequent Loss of U.S.S. *Neosho*; Search for Survivors, 25 May 1942; *Sims, DANFS*; *Henley* War Diary, May 1942.
[20] Staff History Officer, History of Commander Aircraft South Pacific, Forwarding of, 31 December 1945; "Principal Civilian Officials And Naval Officers In Command 7 December 1941 - 2 September 1945" (http://www.ibiblio.org/hyperwar/USN/USN-Chron/USN-Chron-I.html: accessed 13 September 2015); Mar Air Wing 1 War Diary, October 1943.
[21] *Building the Navy's Bases in World War II: History of the Bureau of Yards and Docks and the Civil Engineer Corps 1940-1946 Volume II*, 221-222.
[22] ComFairWing One, Fleet Air Wing One – History of (1 January – 2 September 1945), undated document.
[23] David H. Buss, "U.S. Naval Air Forces, Pacific Fleet, Marks 72nd Anniversary," 28 August 2014 (http://navylive.dodlive.mil/2014/08/28/u-s-naval-air-forces-pacific-fleet-marks-72nd-anniversary/: accessed 14 September 2015).

[24] Commander, U.S. Naval Air Forces, U.S. Pacific Fleet, Transfer of Patrol Wing One to South Pacific Area, 11 September 1942.
[25] Ibid.
[26] Ibid.

CHAPTER 15 NOTES
[1] Historical Officer, VT-3, Squadron History, Submission of, 21 March 1945.
[2] Bruhn, *Battle Stars for the "Cactus Navy": America's Fishing Vessels and Yachts in World War II*, 79.
[3] *Building the Navy's Bases in World War II, History of the Bureau of Yards and Docks and the Civil Engineer Corps, 1940-1946, Vol. II*, 191-192.
[4] Ibid., 193-194.
[5] *Swan, DANFS*.
[6] *Swan, DANFS*; Arnold S. Lott, *Most Dangerous Sea* (Annapolis: Naval Institute, 1959), 14-15.
[7] *Swan, DANFS*.
[8] Commanding Officer USS *Swan*, Action of December 7, 1941, Report on, 11 December 1941.
[9] *Swan, DANFS*.
[10] Commanding Officer, VS-66, VS-66 – History of, 5 July 1945.
[11] *Swan, DANFS*; "Pago Pago," *The Pacific War Encyclopedia* (http://pwencycl.kgbudge.com/P/a/Pago_Pago.htm: accessed November 11, 2014); Senior Member, South Pacific Advanced Base Inspection Board, Advanced Bases South Pacific, Inspection Report of, 15 August 1942.
[12] *Swan, DANFS*; "Pago Pago," *The Pacific War Encyclopedia*; Senior Member, South Pacific Advanced Base Inspection Board, Advanced Bases South Pacific, Inspection Report of, 15 August 1942.
[13] Senior Member, South Pacific Advanced Base Inspection Board, Advanced Bases South Pacific, Inspection Report of, 15 August 1942.
[14] "Pukapuka," Cook Islands Travel Guide (http://cookislands.southpacific.org/northern/pukapuka.html; "Pukapuka," *Wikipedia* (http://en.wikipedia.org/wiki/Pukapuka#World_War_II; Alvin Townley, "Stranded at Sea," April 25, 2011 (http://www.airspacemag.com/military-aviation/stranded-at-sea-2255498/?page=: all accessed 11 November 2014).
[15] *Swan* War Diary, May 1942; Senior Member, South Pacific Advanced Base Inspection Board, Advanced Bases South Pacific, Inspection Report of, 15 August 1942.
[16] Senior Member, South Pacific Advanced Base Inspection Board, Advanced Bases South Pacific, Inspection Report of, 15 August 1942.
[17] Ibid.
[18] *Swan* War Diary, May 1942; Senior Member, South Pacific Advanced Base Inspection Board, Advanced Bases South Pacific, Inspection Report of, 15 August 1942.

[19] *Swan, DANFS*; Senior Member, South Pacific Advanced Base Inspection Board, Advanced Bases South Pacific, Inspection Report of, 15 August 1942.
[20] Senior Member, South Pacific Advanced Base Inspection Board, Advanced Bases South Pacific, Inspection Report of, 15 August 1942.
[21] Ibid.
[22] *Swan* War Diary, July-October 1942.
[23] *Swan* War Diary, October 1942.
[24] Commanding Officer, VPB-34, The History of VPB-34, 22 January 1945.
[25] *Building the Navy's Bases in World War II, Vol. II*, 195.
[26] *Swan* War Diary, November 1942; *Building the Navy's Bases in World War II, Vol. II*, 232; Commanding Officer, VPB-34, The History of VPB-34, 22 January 1945.
[27] *Swan* War Diary, November and December 1942.

CHAPTER 16 NOTES
[1] Commanding Officer, USS *Barnegat* (AVP-10), Unit History – Submission of, 28 January 1946.
[2] *Barnegat* War Diary, October 1942; Fleet Air Wing Seven War Diary, 1 March 1941 to 31 December 1944.
[3] *Barnegat* War Diary, October and November 1942.
[4] ONI Combat Narratives: The Landings in North Africa; George F. Howe, *United States Army in World War II Mediterranean Theater of Operations Northwest Africa: Seizing the Initiative in the West* (Washington, DC: Dept. of the Army, 1957), 150.
[5] Interview of Admiral Henry K. Hewitt, USN Mediterranean Area Campaign – North Africa Landing to Southern France, Naval Records and Library CNO, Personal Interviews.
[6] ONI Combat Narratives: The Landings in North Africa; Commanding Officer USS *Kennebec*, Report of Action, 10 December 1942.
[7] ONI Combat Narratives: The Landings in North Africa.
[8] *Barnegat* (AVP-10), Unit History; ONI Combat Narratives: The Landings in North Africa.
[9] David D. Bruhn, *We are Sinking, Send Help!: The U.S. Navy's Tugs and Salvage Ships in the African, European, and Mediterranean Theaters in World War II* (Berwyn Heights, MD: Heritage Books, 2015), 9.
[10] *Barnegat* (AVP-10), Unit History; ONI Combat Narratives: The Landings in North Africa.
[11] *Barnegat* (AVP-10), Unit History; ONI Combat Narratives: The Landings in North Africa.
[12] Howe, *United States Army in World War II Mediterranean Theater of Operations Northwest Africa: Seizing the Initiative in the West*, 147.
[13] Bruhn, *We are Sinking, Send Help!*, 11, 13.
[14] ONI Combat Narratives: The Landings in North Africa.
[15] Howe, *United States Army in World War II Mediterranean Theater of Operations Northwest Africa: Seizing the Initiative in the West*, 169.
[16] Ibid.; *Barnegat* War Diary, November and December 1942.

CHAPTER 17 NOTES

[1] ONI Combat Narratives: The Landings in North Africa.
[2] Bruhn, *We Are Sinking, Send Help!*, 16-147.
[3] Stephen Williams, "Veterans keeping memories of D-day alive" (http://www.dailygazette.com/ accessed 29 September 2015).
[4] Bruhn, *We Are Sinking, Send Help!*, 149-150.
[5] Ibid, p. 150.
[6] Commanding Officer, USS *Rockaway* (AVP-29), U.S.S. *Rockaway* (AVP 29) – History of, 16 November 1945.
[7] "The Wartime Memories Project - USN Dunkeswell Station 173" (http://www.wartimememoriesproject.com/ww2/airfields/dunkeswell.php: accessed 30 September 2015); Gordon Peterson, "Lt. Joseph P. Kennedy VPB-110" (http://www.wartimememoriesproject.com/ww2/airfields/dunkeswell.php#jpkennedy: accessed 30 September 2015).
[8] "Operation Aphrodite," *Historic Wings*, August 2012.
[9] Elizabeth Schaper describing the duties of her father, Lt. Armin N. Schaper, at NAF Dunkeswell (http://www.wartimememoriesproject.com/ww2/airfields/dunkeswell.php#anschapper: accessed 30 September 2015).
[10] "A Bit of History: Appendix Submarines Sunk by Patrol Squadrons During World War II," Naval Historical Center, Washington, D.C., 4 May 2001.
[11] Peterson, "Lt. Joseph P. Kennedy VPB-110"; Ed Grabianowski, "The Secret Drone Mission that Killed Joseph Kennedy Jr." (http://io9.com/5985733/the-secret-drone-mission-that-killed-joseph-kennedy-jr: accessed 30 September 2015); "Operation Aphrodite," *Historic Wings*, August 2012.
[12] "Operation Aphrodite," *Historic Wings*, August 2012.
[13] Ibid.
[14] Ibid.; "Joseph P. Kennedy Jr." John F. Kennedy Presidential Library and Museum (http://www.jfklibrary.org/JFK/The-Kennedy-Family/Joseph-P-Kennedy-Jr.aspx: accessed 30 September 2015).
[15] "Operation Aphrodite," *Historic Wings*, August 2012.
[16] *Rockaway* War Diary, May 1944.
[17] Ibid.
[18] *Rockaway* War Diary, May and June 1944.
[19] *Rockaway, DANFS*.
[20] Bruhn, *We Are Sinking, Send Help!*, 162-163.
[21] Ibid, 158.
[22] *Rockaway* War Diary, June 1944.
[23] Ibid.; Bruhn, *We Are Sinking, Send Help!*, 100.
[24] Commander U.S. Bases France War Diary, June and July 1944; Bruhn, *We Are Sinking, Send Help!*, 151.
[25] *Rockaway* War Diary, June 1944.

CHAPTER 18 NOTES

[1] *Curtiss* and *Mackinac* War Diary, October and November 1943; ComAirCenPac War Diary, October 1943

[2] ComCenPacFor War Diary, August 1943; "World War II: Admiral Raymond Spruance" (http://militaryhistory.about.com/od/WorldWarIINavalLeaders/p/World-War-Ii-Admiral-Raymond-Spruance.htm: accessed 21 September 2015).

[3] David D. Bruhn, *MacArthur and Halsey's "Pacific Island Hoppers": The Forgotten Fleet of World War II* (Berwyn Heights, MD: Heritage Books, 2014), 131.

[4] Ibid.

[5] *Mackinac* War Diary, October 1943.

[6] *Curtiss* and *Mackinac* War Diary, November 1943.

[7] ComCenPacFor War Diary, November 1943; Bruhn, *MacArthur and Halsey's "Pacific Island Hoppers,"* 131.

[8] ComCenAirPac War Diary, November 1943.

[9] Ibid.

[10] Ibid.

[11] ComCenAirPac War Diary, *Curtiss* War Diary, November 1943; Bruhn, *Battle Stars for the "Cactus Navy,"* 243.

[12] Commanding Officer, USS *Independence*, Report of Events Surrounding the Torpedoing of this vessel, 25 November 1943.

[13] VP-72 War Diary, November 1943.

[14] VP-72 War Diary, November 1943; *Independence, DANFS*.

[15] Bruhn, *Battle Stars for the "Cactus Navy,"* 244.

[16] *Mackinac* War Diary, November 1943; Commanding Officer, VMBF-331, Squadron VMBF 331 History, 29 December 1944.

[17] *Mackinac* War Diary, November 1943.

[18] Ibid.

[19] Henry I. Shaw, Jr., Bernard C. Nalty, and Edwin T. Turnbladh, *History of U.S. Marine Corps Operations in World War II Volume III: Central Pacific Drive* (Washington, DC: Headquarters, U.S. Marine Corps, 1966), 117-118.

[20] Shaw Jr., Nalty, and Turnbladh, *History of U.S. Marine Corps Operations in World War II Volume III*, 125-127; Morison, The *Two-Ocean War*, 307.

[21] Shaw Jr., Nalty, and Turnbladh, *History of U.S. Marine Corps Operations in World War II Volume III*, 125-127; Burton Wright III, *Eastern Mandates*, U.S. Army Center of Military History brochure.

[22] Commanding General, Northern Landing Force, Final Report on Flintlock Operation, 17 March 1944; Wright III, *Eastern Mandates*.

[23] Ibid.

[24] Wright III, *Eastern Mandates*.

[25] Ibid.

[26] Ibid.

[27] Shaw Jr., Nalty, and Turnbladh, *History of U.S. Marine Corps Operations in World War II Volume III*, 125-127; CTG 51.2, Majuro Action Report – Submission of, 15 February 1944.

[28] CTG 51.2, Majuro Action Report – Submission of, 15 February 1944.
[29] CTG 51.2, Majuro Action Report – Submission of, 15 February 1944; *Casco*, and VP-202 War Diary, February 1944.
[30] *Casco* War Diary, January and February 1944.
[31] *Casco* War Diary, February 1944.
[32] Morison, *The Two-Ocean War*, 316.
[33] Ibid., 312.
[34] Ibid., 314.
[35] Ibid., 314-316.
[36] Ibid., 316.
[37] Ibid.
[38] *Casco*, *Chincoteague*, VP-72, VP-102, VP-202 War Diary, February 1944.
[39] *Chincoteague*, VP-13, VP-102 War Diary, February 1944.

CHAPTER 19 NOTES
[1] David D. Bruhn, *MacArthur and Halsey's "Pacific Island Hoppers,"* xxiv.
[2] Ibid., 49.
[3] Bruhn; *MacArthur and Halsey's "Pacific Island Hoppers,"* 138; Commanding Officer, USS *Mackinac* (AVP-13), Ship's History, Forwarding of, 3 April 1946.
[4] USS *Mackinac* (AVP-13), Ship's History, Forwarding of, 3 April 1946; Commanding Officer, VPB-71, War History, Forwarding of, 11 July 1945; *Curtiss* War Diary, July 1943.
[5] USS *Mackinac* (AVP-13), Ship's History, Forwarding of, 3 April 1946.
[6] Commanding Officer, USS *Chincoteague* (AVP-24), Narrative of Actions and Subsequent Events from 14 to 21 July, 25 July 1943; *Chincoteague* War Diary, July 1943.
[7] Commanding Officer, USS *Chincoteague* (AVP-24), Narrative of Actions and Subsequent Events from 14 to 21 July, 25 July 1943.
[8] Ibid.
[9] Ibid.
[10] Commanding Officer, USS *Chincoteague* (AVP-24), Narrative of Actions and Subsequent Events from 14 to 21 July, 25 July 1943; Commanding Officer, VPB-71, War History, Forwarding of, 11 July 1945.
[11] Yuki Tanaka, "Japanese Atrocities on Nauru during the Pacific War: The murder of Australians, the massacre of lepers and the ethnocide of Nauruans," *The Asia-Pacific Journal: Japan Focus* (http://japanfocus.org/-Yuki-TANAKA/3441/article.html: accessed 10 October 2015); Commanding Officer, USS *Chincoteague* (AVP-24), Narrative of Actions and Subsequent Events from 14 to 21 July, 25 July 1943.
[12] Commanding Officer, USS *Chincoteague* (AVP-24), Narrative of Actions and Subsequent Events from 14 to 21 July, 25 July 1943.
[13] Ibid.
[14] Ibid.
[15] Ibid.
[16] Ibid.
[17] Ibid.

[18] Ibid.
[19] Ibid.
[20] Ibid.
[21] Ibid.
[22] Ibid.; VMF-214 War Diary, July 1943; Stephen Sherman, "VMF-214 Marine Fighting Squadron in WW2" (http://acepilots.com/usmc_vmf214.html: accessed 10 October 2015).
[23] Commanding Officer, USS *Chincoteague* (AVP-24), Narrative of Actions and Subsequent Events from 14 to 21 July, 25 July 1943.
[24] Ibid.
[25] Ibid.
[26] Ibid.
[27] General Orders: Bureau of Naval Personnel Information Bulletin No. 337 (April 1945); General Orders: Commander South Pacific: Serial 01630 (September 13, 1943).
[28] ONI Combat Narratives: Solomon Islands Campaign: XII The Bougainville Landing and the Battle of Empress Bay.
[29] Ibid.
[30] Sherman, "VMF-214 Marine Fighting Squadron in WW2."
[31] ONI Combat Narratives: Solomon Islands Campaign: XII The Bougainville Landing and the Battle of Empress Bay; Bruhn, *MacArthur and Halsey's "Pacific Island Hoppers,"* 87.
[32] "Invasion of Treasury Islands – USS *Cony* hit" World War II Today Follow the war as it happened (http://ww2today.com/27th-october-1943-invasion-of-treasury-islands-uss-cony-hit: accessed 15 October 2015); John C. Chapin, *Top of the Ladder: Marine Operations in the Northern Solomons*, Marines in World War II Commemorative Series pamphlet (http://www.ibiblio.org/hyperwar/USMC/USMC-C-NSol/index.html: accessed 23 October 2015).
[33] ONI Combat Narratives: Solomon Islands Campaign: XII The Bougainville Landing and the Battle of Empress Bay; Morison, *The Two-Ocean War*, 291.
[34] Jeffrey Grey, *A Military History of Australia* (Cambridge, England: Cambridge University Press, 1999), 184–185; David Day, *The Politics of War* (Sydney, Australia: Harper Collins, 2003), 623–624; Peter Charlton, *The Unnecessary War: Island Campaigns of the South-West Pacific 1944 - 45* (Crows Nest, New South Wales: Macmillan Australia, 1983), 57.
[35] History of the USS *Coos Bay* (AVP-25), 15 May 1943-2 September 1945.
[36] Ibid.
[37] Ibid.
[38] Ibid.
[39] Ibid.
[40] Ibid.
[41] History of the USS *Coos Bay* (AVP-25), 15 May 1943-2 September 1945; "Wartime RNZAF Timeline," Wings Over Cambridge

(http://www.cambridgeairforce.org.nz/rnzaf%20timeline.htm: accessed 17 October 2016).
[42] History of the USS *Coos Bay* (AVP-25), 15 May 1943-2 September 1945.
[43] Ibid.
[44] Ibid.
[45] Ibid.; Chapin, *Top of the Ladder: Marine Operations in the Northern Solomons*, Marines in World War II, Commemorative Series pamphlet.
[46] VP-91 War Diary, April through June 1944.
[47] Chapin, *Top of the Ladder: Marine Operations in the Northern Solomons*, Marines in World War II, Commemorative Series pamphlet.
[48] "Richard Milhous Nixon 9 January 1913 - 22 April 1994," Naval History and Heritage Command
(http://www.history.navy.mil/research/histories/bios/nixon-richard.html: accessed 25 October 2015).
[49] Ibid.
[50] The Richard Nixon/Frank Gannon Interviews
(http://www.libs.uga.edu/media/collections/nixon/nixonday1.html: accessed 25 October 2015).
[51] Ibid; "Nixon WWII Service Revealed for the First Time," The Richard Nixon Foundation (http://nixonfoundation.org/news-details.php?id=706: accessed 25 October 2015).
[52] The Richard Nixon/Frank Gannon Interviews; Milton W. Bush, Jr., "Green Island in World War II 1944: Base No. 7 Black Cat PBY Catalinas and PT Boat Teams
(http://www.seabees93.net/GI%20Green%20Island%206th%20ED.htm: accessed 25 October 2015).
[53] "Richard Milhous Nixon 9 January 1913 - 22 April 1994."
[54] Ibid.
[55] CINC, U.S. Pacific Fleet, Ship's History, Forwarding of, 5 November 1945.
[56] Ibid.
[57] Ibid.
[58] History of USS *Pocomoke* (AV-9) (Large Seaplane Tender) From 28 April 1941 to 2 September 1945.
[59] Ibid.
[60] Ibid.
[61] *Wright, DANFS*; VP 14 War Diary, November and December 1943.
[62] *Chandeleur, DANFS*.

CHAPTER 20 NOTES

[1] Bruhn, *MacArthur and Halsey's "Pacific Island Hoppers,"* 82.
[2] Commanding Officer, USS *San Pablo* (AVP-30), U.S.S. *San Pablo* History, 20 October 1945.
[3] Commanding Officer, USS *San Pablo* (AVP-30), U.S.S. *San Pablo* History, 20 October 1945; *San Pablo, DANFS*.

[4] Commanding Officer, USS *San Pablo* (AVP-30), U.S.S. *San Pablo* History, 20 October 1945; *San Pablo, DANFS*.
[5] *San Pablo* War Diary, November 1943; Commanding Officer, VPB-34, The History of VPB-34, 22 January 1945.
[6] *San Pablo* War Diary, November 1943.
[7] *San Pablo* War Diary, November and December 1943; Commanding Officer, USS San Pablo (AVP-30), U.S.S. San Pablo History, 20 October 1945.
[8] Commander, VPB-52, Squadron History, Submission of, 31 December 1944.
[9] Ibid.
[10] Ibid.
[11] Ibid.
[12] Ibid.; Bruhn, *MacArthur and Halsey's "Pacific Island Hoppers,"* 95.
[13] *San Pablo* War Diary, January 1944; *San Pablo, DANFS*; Commanding Officer, VPB-34, The History of VPB-34, 22 January 1945.
[14] Commanding Officer, USS *San Pablo* (AVP-30), U.S.S. *San Pablo* History, 20 October 1945.
[15] Ibid.
[16] Bruhn, *MacArthur and Halsey's "Pacific Island Hoppers,"* 87.
[17] Commanding Officer, USS *San Pablo* (AVP-30), U.S.S. *San Pablo* History, 20 October 1945.
[18] *San Pablo* War Diary, January 1944; Commanding Officer, USS *San Pablo* (AVP-30), U.S.S. *San Pablo* History, 20 October 1945.
[19] Commander Naval Base 722, War Diary November, December 1943 and January 1944, 4 March 1944; *San Pablo* War Diary, January 1944.
[20] *San Pablo* War Diary, February 1944.

CHAPTER 21 NOTES

[1] Commander Attack Group, Admiralty Islands Operation, 29 February 1944 – Report on, dated 16 March 1944; Samuel Eliot Morison, *History of United States Naval Operation in World War II: Breaking the Bismarcks Barrier, 22 July 1942-1 May 1944* (Boston: Little, Brown, 1984), 435.
[2] Bruhn, *MacArthur and Halsey's "Pacific Island Hoppers"*, 145-146.
[3] Bruhn, *MacArthur and Halsey's "Pacific Island Hoppers*, 146-147; Morison, *The Two-Ocean War*, 294.
[4] Commanding Officer, USS *San Pablo* (AVP-30), U.S.S. *San Pablo* History, 20 October 1945.
[5] Ibid.; VP-52 War Diary, April 1944.
[6] Commanding Officer, USS *San Pablo* (AVP-30), U.S.S. *San Pablo* History, 20 October 1945; Aircraft Seventh Fleet War Diary, April 1944.
[7] Commanding Officer, VPB-34, The History of VPB-34, 22 January 1945.
[8] Commanding Officer, USS *San Pablo* (AVP-30), U.S.S. *San Pablo* History, 20 October 1945.
[9] Ibid.
[10] *Heron* War Diary, April 1944.

[11] Ibid.
[12] Aircraft Seventh Fleet, VP-34, and VB-106 War Diary, April 1944.
[13] Bruhn, *MacArthur and Halsey's "Pacific Island Hoppers,"* 149-150.
[14] Ibid, 150-151.
[15] Commanding Officer, USS *San Pablo* (AVP-30), U.S.S. *San Pablo* History, 20 October 1945; VP-52 War Diary, May 1944; Morison, *The Two-Ocean War*, 319-320.
[16] Commanding Officer, VPB-34, The History of VPB-34, 22 January 1945.
[17] Commanding Officer, USS *San Pablo* (AVP-30), U.S.S. *San Pablo* History, 20 October 1945.
[18] Ibid.
[19] CINC, U.S. Pacific Fleet, Ship's History – Forwarding of, 25 November 1945.
[20] *Orca* War Diary, May and June 1944; CINC, U.S. Pacific Fleet, Ship's History – Forwarding of, 25 November 1945.

CHAPTER 22 NOTES
[1] Aircraft, Seventh Fleet War Diary, June 1944.
[2] Seventh Fleet, and Aircraft, Seventh Fleet War Diary, June 1944.
[3] *Wright* War Diary, June 1944; Commander, VPB-33, History of VPB-33, Transmittal of, 1 January 1945.
[4] FAW-17 War Diary, July 1944; Commanding Officer, VPB-34, The History of VPB-34, 22 January 1945.
[5] "Battle of Biak Island, 27 May-29 July 1944" (http://www.historyofwar.org/articles/battles_biak.html: accessed 9 November 2015).
[6] FAW-17, *Half Moon*, and *Heron* War Diary, July 1944.
[7] *Wright* War Diary, June 1944.
[8] Morison, *The Two-Ocean War*, 424-435.
[9] *Wright* War Diary, June 1944.
[10] Daniel E. Barbey, *MacArthur's Amphibious Navy: Seventh Amphibious Force Operations 1943-1945* (Annapolis: U.S. Naval Institute, 1969), 211.
[11] Barbey, *MacArthur's Amphibious Navy*, 215-216.
[12] VP-11, Aircraft Seventh Fleet, *Orca* War Diary, August 1944; *The Jungle Air Force of WWII 1942-1945, Air Force The Official Service Journal of the U.S. Army Air Forces*, December 1944.
[13] Commanding Officer, USS *Half Moon* (AVP 26), History of the *Half Moon* (AVP-26) – Submission of, 21 September 1945.
[14] Commanding Officer, VPB-34, The History of VPB-34, 22 January 1945.
[15] Ibid.
[16] *Orca* War Diary, September 1944; Commander, VPB-33, History of VPB-33, Transmittal of, 1 January 1945.
[17] CTF 77 (Commander Seventh Amphibious Force), Morotai Operation – Report on, File No. FE25/A16-3, Serial No. 00875; Barbey, *MacArthur's Amphibious Navy*, 227.
[18] CTF 77 (Commander Seventh Amphibious Force), Morotai Operation.

[19] C. Peter Chen, "Battle of Morotai 15 Sep 1944 - 14 Jan 1945," World War II Database (http://ww2db.com/battle_spec.php?battle_id=203: accessed 9 November 2015); Barbey, *MacArthur's Amphibious Navy*, 225.
[20] *Half Moon, San Carlos, Tangier* War Diary, September 1944.
[21] *San Carlos* War Diary, September 1944.
[22] Ibid.
[23] *Half Moon, Tangier* War Diary, September 1944.
[24] Commander, VPB-33, History of VPB-33, Transmittal of, 1 January 1945.
[25] Ibid.
[26] Ibid.
[27] Ibid.
[28] General Orders: Commander 7th Fleet: Serial 0141 (January 7, 1945).

CHAPTER 23 NOTES
[1] Operation Plan ComFifthFleet No. Cen 10-44, 12 May 1944.
[2] Ibid.
[3] Ibid.
[4] Bruhn, *MacArthur and Halsey's "Pacific Island Hoppers,"* 155-156.
[5] Commanding Officer, USS *Ballard* (AVD-10), Ship's History - Forwarding of, 29 October 1945.
[6] Ibid.
[7] Bruhn, *MacArthur and Halsey's "Pacific Island Hoppers,"* 157-158.
[8] Commanding Officer, USS *Williamson* (DD-244C, History of the Ship, 30 September 1945.
[9] Ibid.
[10] History of U.S.S. *Pocomoke* (AV-9) (Large Seaplane Tender) From 28 April 1941 to 2 September 1945; Commanding Officer, USS *Onslow* (AVP-48), U.S.S. *Onslow* (AVP-48) – History of, 2 February 1946.
[11] History of U.S.S. *Pocomoke* (AV-9) (Large Seaplane Tender) From 28 April 1941 to 2 September 1945.
[12] Commanding Officer, USS *Chandeleur* (AV-10), U.S.S. *Chandeleur* (AV10) – Action Report, 14 August 1944; *Chandeleur*, VP-202, and VP-216 War Diary, July 1944.
[13] Commanding Officer, USS *Mackinac* (AVP-13), Ship's History, Forwarding of, 3 April 1946.
[14] Commanding Officer, USS *Chandeleur* (AV-10), U.S.S. *Chandeleur* (AV10) – Action Report, 14 August 1944; Commanding Officer, USS *Mackinac* (AVP-13), Ship's History, Forwarding of, 3 April 1946
[15] Commanding Officer, USS *Chandeleur* (AV-10), U.S.S. *Chandeleur* (AV10) – Action Report, 14 August 1944; Commanding Officer, USS *Mackinac* (AVP-13), Ship's History, Forwarding of, 3 April 1946; History of U.S.S. *Pocomoke* (AV-9) (Large Seaplane Tender) From 28 April 1941 to 2 September 1945.
[16] Commanding Officer, USS *Chandeleur* (AV-10), U.S.S. *Chandeleur* (AV10) – Action Report, 14 August 1944; *Chandeleur* War Diary, June 1944.

[17] History of U.S.S. *Pocomoke* (AV-9) (Large Seaplane Tender) From 28 April 1941 to 2 September 1945.
[18] *Chandeleur* and VP-216 War Diary, July 1944.
[19] Ibid.
[20] Commanding General, Northern Troops and Landing Force Operations Report [word redacted] Phase I (Saipan), 12 August 1944.
[21] VP-216 War Diary, July 1944; Commanding Officer, USS *Mackinac* (AVP-13), Ship's History, Forwarding of, 3 April 1946.
[22] Commanding Officer, USS *Yakutat* (AVP-32), Action report – Occupation of Saipan and Tinian, 16 August 1944; Commanding Officer, USS *Yakutat*, U.S.S. *Yakutat* – Supplemental Action Report, 18 November 1944.
[23] Commanding Officer, USS *Yakutat* (AVP-32), Action report – Occupation of Saipan and Tinian, 16 August 1944; Commanding Officer, USS *Yakutat*, U.S.S. *Yakutat* – Supplemental Action Report, 18 November 1944.
[24] *Curtiss* and *Shelikof* War Diary, August 1944.

CHAPTER 24 NOTES

[1] Gordon D. Gayle, *Bloody Beaches: The Marines at Peleliu*, Marines in World War II Commemorative Series Pamplet (Washington, DC: Marine Corps Historical Center, 1996)
[2] Ibid; Morison, *The Two-Ocean War*, 425-428.
[3] *Ballard* War Diary, September 1944.
[4] Ibid.
[5] Ibid.
[6] Commanding Officer, USS *Mackinac* (AVP-13), Ship's History, Forwarding of, 3 April 1946; History of U.S.S. *Pocomoke* (AV-9) (Large Seaplane Tender) From 28 April 1941 to 2 September 1945; *Chandeleur* War Diary, September 1944.
[7] Commanding Officer, USS *Mackinac* (AVP-13), Ship's History, Forwarding of, 3 April 1946; *Mackinac* and *Onslow* War Diary, September 1944; Commander, Task Group 32.9 (Commander Mine Squadron Two), Peleliu – Anguar and Kossol Passage Action Report – Submission of, 11 October 1944.
[8] *Mackinac* War Diary, September 1944; Commander, Task Group 32.9 (Commander Mine Squadron Two), Peleliu – Anguar and Kossol Passage Action Report – Submission of, 11 October 1944.
[9] *Mackinac*, *Pocomoke*, and *Yakutat* War Diary, September 1944.
[10] Ibid.
[11] *Mackinac* and *Pocomoke* War Diary, October 1944.
[12] *Chandeleur*, *Onslow*, and VH-1 War Diary, September and October 1944; Commanding Officer, USS *Mackinac* (AVP-13), Ship's History, Forwarding of, 3 April 1946.
[13] *Chandeleur*, *Pocomoke*, and VH-1 War Diary, September 1944.

[14] *Chandeleur, Mackinac, Pocomoke, Yakutat*, and VH-1 War Diary, September and October 1944.
[15] Commanding Officer, USS *Mackinac* (AVP-13), Ship's History, Forwarding of, 3 April 1946; *Mackinac* War Diary, November 1944.
[16] Commanding Officer, USS *Mackinac* (AVP-13), Ship's History, Forwarding of, 3 April 1946; *Mackinac* War Diary, November 1944.
[17] *Pocomoke* War Diary, November 1944

CHAPTER 25 NOTES

[1] United States Strategic Bombing Survey, Interrogation of Japanese Officials, OpNav P-03-100, Naval Analysis Division, 13-14 November 1945 (http://www.ibiblio.org/hyperwar/AAF/USSBS/IJO/IJO-75.html: accessed 9 November 2011).
[2] Morison, *The Two-Ocean War*, 330-345.
[3] Aerology and Amphibious Warfare The Assault Landings on Leyte Island NAVAER 50-30T-6, Chief of Naval Operations, Aerology Section, Washington, D.C. (www history.navy.mil/library/online/assault_leyte.htm: accessed 24 April 2013).
[4] Morison, *The Two-Ocean War*, 432-435; CTF 78, Leyte Operation – Report on, dated 10 November 1944.
[5] *PCE(R)-848* and *PCE(R)-849* War Diary, October 1944; Masterson, "U.S. Army Transportation in the Southwest Pacific Area 1941-1947," 422.
[6] Morison, *The Two-Ocean War*, 432-436; CTF 78, Leyte Operation – Report on, dated 10 November 1944.
[7] Morison, *The Two-Ocean War*, 432-436.
[8] Commanding Officer, USS *Half Moon* (AVP-26), History of the *Half Moon* (AVP 26) – Submission of, 21 September 1945.
[9] Ibid.
[10] *San Carlos* War Diary, October 1944.
[11] Commanding Officer, USS *Half Moon* (AVP-26), History of the *Half Moon* (AVP 26) – Submission of, 21 September 1945.
[12] Ibid.
[13] *San Carlos* War Diary, October 1944.
[14] Ibid.
[15] *Orca* War Diary, November 1944.
[16] Ibid.
[17] Commander Mell A. Peterson, USN, USS *Cooper* (DD 695), CNO Naval Records and Library, Personal Interviews.
[18] Commander Mell A. Peterson, USN, Personal Interviews; Commanding Officer, *USS Cooper* (DD 695), U.S.S. *Cooper* (DD695), Report of action the night of 2-3 December, 1944, 7 December 1944.
[19] Commander Mell A. Peterson, USN, Personal Interviews; Commanding Officer, *USS Cooper* (DD 695), U.S.S. *Cooper* (DD695), Report of action the night of 2-3 December, 1944, 7 December 1944.
[20] Commander Mell A. Peterson, USN, Personal Interviews.

[21] CINC, U.S. Pacific Fleet, Ship's History – Forwarding of, 25 November 1945.
[22] Ibid.; General Orders: Commander 7th Fleet: Serial 2350 (June 8, 1946); General Orders: Bureau of Naval Personnel Information Bulletin No. 368 (October 1947).
[23] CINC, U.S. Pacific Fleet, Ship's History – Forwarding of, 31 December 1945; *Currituck* War Diary, November 1944.
[24] *Currituck* War Diary, November 1944; VPB-20 War History, 15 February 1944 – 30 September 1945.
[25] VPB-20 War History, 15 February 1944 – 30 September 1945.
[26] Ibid.
[27] Ibid.
[28] Ibid.
[29] Ibid.
[30] *Heron* and *San Pablo* War Diary, November 1944.
[31] Ibid.
[32] VPB-25 War Diary, November 1944.
[33] *Heron* War Diary, November and December 1944.
[34] Commander Luzon Attack Force, Action Report – Luzon Attack Force, Lingayen Gulf – Musketeer Mike One Operation, dated 15 May 1945.
[35] CINC, U.S. Pacific Fleet, Ship's History – Forwarding of, 23 November 1945.
[36] Commander Luzon Attack Force, Action Report – Luzon Attack Force, Lingayen Gulf – Musketeer Mike One Operation, dated 15 May 1945; Samuel Eliot Morison, *History of United States Naval Operations in World War II, The Liberation of the Philippines — Luzon, Mindanao, the Visayas, 1944-1945* (Edison, New Jersey: Castle Books, 2001), 128-132.
[37] Commander Luzon Attack Force, Action Report – Luzon Attack Force, Lingayen Gulf – Musketeer Mike One Operation, dated 15 May 1945; Com7thFlt War Diary, January 1945.
[38] *Orca* and *Hopkins* War Diary, January 1945; Arnold S. Lott, *Most Dangerous Sea* (Annapolis: Naval Institute, 1959), 144.
[39] CTG 77.6 (CoMinRon 2), Action Report of Minesweeping Operations in Lingayen Gulf, 14 January 1945; *Cowanesque* and *Pecos* War Diary, January 1945.
[40] *Cowanesque* and *Pecos* War Diary, January 1945.
[41] *Apache*, *Orca*, and *Scrimmage* War Diary, January 1945; CTG 77.6 (CoMinRon 2), Action Report of Minesweeping Operations in Lingayen Gulf, 14 January 1945.
[42] CTG 77.6 (CoMinRon 2), Action Report of Minesweeping Operations in Lingayen Gulf, 14 January 1945; Lott, *Most Dangerous Sea*, 145; *Orca* War Diary, January 1945.
[43] *Orca* War Diary, January 1945.
[44] Ibid.
[45] CTG 77.6 (CoMinRon 2), Action Report of Minesweeping Operations in Lingayen Gulf, 14 January 1945; *Apache* and *Scrimmage* War Diary, January

1945; Commanding Officer, USS *LCI(G) #70*, Action Report - Anti-Aircraft Action, 17 January 1945.
[46] CTG 77.6 (CoMinRon 2), Action Report of Minesweeping Operations in Lingayen Gulf, 14 January 1945.
[47] Lott, *Most Dangerous Sea*, 145-146; CTG 77.6 (CoMinRon 2), Action Report of Minesweeping Operations in Lingayen Gulf, 14 January 1945.
[48] *Orca* War Diary, January 1945.
[49] Ibid.
[50] *Orca* and VPB-54 War Diary, January 1945.
[51] Aircraft, Seventh Fleet, *Barataria*, and *Currituck* War Diary, January 1945.
[52] *Barataria*, and *Currituck* War Diary, January 1945.
[53] Ibid.
[54] Aircraft, Seventh Fleet War Diary, January 1945; VPB-20 and VPB-71 War History.
[55] VPB-71 War History.
[56] *Currituck* War Diary, January 1945.
[57] Dale Andrade, *Luzon 1944-1945*, Brochure, CMH Pub 72-28 (Washington DC: U.S. Army Center of Military History).

CHAPTER 26 NOTES

[1] Morison, *The Two-Ocean War*, 513-514
[2] "Battle for Iwo Jima, 1945," Naval History and Heritage Command (http://www.history.navy.mil/library/online/battleiwojima.htm: accessed 22 October 2012).
[3] Commanding Officer, USS *Hamlin* (AV-15), Unit History – Submission of, 6 December 1945.
[4] Ibid.
[5] Ibid.
[6] Ibid.
[7] Commanding Officer, USS *Hamlin* (AV-15), Unit History – Submission of, 6 December 1945; VPB19 War Diary, 1 February-17 March 1945.
[8] Commanding Officer, USS *Hamlin* (AV-15), Unit History – Submission of, 6 December 1945; CINC, U.S. Pacific Fleet, Ship's History – Forwarding of, 5 November 1945; VH-2 War Diary, February and March 1945.
[9] Commanding Officer, VH-2, Historical Report as of 12 December 1944, Submission of, 12 December 1944.
[10] Historical Officer, VH-3, Historical Manual – Continuation of, 1 January 1945, 1 March 1945, and 1 June 1945.
[11] Historical Officer, VH-3, Historical Manual – Continuation of, 1 March 1945, and 1 June 1945.
[12] *Bering Strait*, *DANFS*.
[13] Ibid.
[14] Ibid.
[15] Ibid.
[16] *Cook Inlet* War Diary, February and March 1945.

[17] "Battle for Iwo Jima, 1945" Naval History and Heritage Command; Morison, *The Two-Ocean War*, p. 523.

CHAPTER 27 NOTES

[1] Bruhn, *Battle Stars for the "Cactus Navy": America's Fishing Vessels and Yachts in World War II*, 264.
[2] Bruhn, *Battle Stars for the "Cactus Navy"*, 265; Morison, *The Two-Ocean War*, 556; Joseph H. Alexander, *The Final Campaign: Marines in the Victory on Okinawa*, Marines in World War II Commemorative Series Pamphlet (Washington, DC: Marine Corps Historical Center, 1996).
[3] Commander Amphibious Group Seven (CTG 51.1), Action Report – Capture of Okinawa Gunto, Phases 1 and 2, 26 May 1945.
[4] Ibid.
[5] Commander Seaplane Base Group (CTG 51.20), General Action Report, Capture of Okinawa Gunto, Phases I and II, 23 March to 17 May 1945 – Submission of, 15 June 1945; Commanding Officer, USS *Hamlin* (AV-15), Unit History – Submission of, 6 December 1945; *Bering Strait, DANFS*.
[6] Commanding Officer, USS *Gillis* (AVD-12), Action Report 1-45 – Bombardment of Okinawa, 21 March to 1 April 1945, 4 May 1945; *Thornton* War Diary, March 1945.
[7] *Thornton* War Diary, April 1945; *Thornton, DANFS*.
[8] Commander Seaplane Base Group (CTG 51.20), General Action Report, Capture of Okinawa Gunto, Phases I and II, 23 March to 17 May 1945 – Submission of, 15 June 1945; CTF 54, Action Report – Bombardment and Occupation of Okinawa – Gunfire and Covering Force, 5 May 1945; Commanding Officer, USS *Williamson* (DD-244), History of Ship, 30 September 1945.
[9] Commanding Officer, VPB-21, History of VPB-21, Submission of, 1 June 1945.
[10] ComFairWing One, Fleet Air Wing One – History of (1 January – 2 September 1945).
[11] Commanding Officer, VPB-21, History of VPB-21, Submission of, 1 June 1945; Commander Seaplane Base Group (CTG 51.20), General Action Report, Capture of Okinawa Gunto, Phases I and II, 23 March to 17 May 1945 – Submission of, 15 June 1945; Commanding Officer, USS *Chandeleur* (AV-10), General Action Report – Addendum to, 21 June 1945.
[12] Commanding Officer, VPB-21, History of VPB-21, Submission of, 1 June 1945; ComFairWing One, Fleet Air Wing One – History of (1 January – 2 September 1945).
[13] Ibid.
[14] Commanding Officer, VPB-21, History of VPB-21, Submission of, 1 June 1945; Commanding Officer, USS *Chandeleur* (AV-10), General Action Report – Addendum to, 21 June 1945.
[15] Commanding Officer, VPB-18, Squadron History – Forwarding of, 6 November 1945.
[16] Ibid.

[17] VH-3 War Diary, March and April 1945.
[18] VH-3 War Diary, May and June 1945.
[19] VH-3 War Diary, April 1945.
[20] ComFairWing One, Fleet Air Wing One – History of (1 January – 2 September 1945).
[21] Commanding Officer, USS *St. George* (AV-16), History of the USS *St. George* (AV16) – Forwarding of, 31 January 1946.
[22] Ibid.
[23] Ibid.
[24] *Curtiss, DANFS*; *Curtiss* War Diary, June 1945; Commanding Officer, USS *Norton Sound* (AV-11), A History of the USS *Norton Sound* (AV-11), A Seaplane Tender, 5 September 1945; ComFairWing One, Fleet Air Wing One – History of (1 January – 2 September 1945).
[25] *Curtiss, DANFS*; *Curtiss* War Diary, June 1945; Commanding Officer, USS *Norton Sound* (AV-11), A History of the USS *Norton Sound* (AV-11), A Seaplane Tender, 5 September 1945; ComFairWing One, Fleet Air Wing One – History of (1 January – 2 September 1945).
[26] History of the *Gardiners Bay* (AVP-39), 1 December 1945.
[27] ComFairWing One, Fleet Air Wing One – History of (1 January – 2 September 1945).

CHAPTER 28 NOTES
[1] "William Frederick Halsey, Jr. 30 October 1882 - 16 August 1959," Naval History and Heritage Command
http://www.history.navy.mil/research/histories/bios/halsey-william-f.html: accessed 31 August 2015)
[2] FAW-1 War Diary, July 1945.
[3] Ibid.
[4] Commander, VPB-25, Historical Report – submission of, 2 October 1945; *Kenneth Whiting* War Diary, July 1945.
[5] FAW-1, VPB-13, *Norton Sound, Shelikof, Yakutat* War Diary, July 1945.
[6] VPB-208 Squadron History, 1 July-31 August 1945.
[7] FAW-1, VPB-27 War Diary, July 1945; VPB-208 Squadron History, 1 July-31 August 1945.
[8] *Duxbury Bay* War Diary, July 1945.
[9] VPB-26 War Diary, July 1945.
[10] VPB-208 Squadron History, 1 July-31 August 1945.
[11] Ibid.
[12] VPB-27 War Diary, July 1945.
[13] Ibid.
[14] Ibid.
[15] ComNavFor Okinawa War Diary, July 1945; MTB Ron 31 War Diary, July and August 1945; Bulkley, *At Close Quarters PT Boats in the United States Navy*, p. 439.
[16] VH-3 War Diary, July 1945.
[17] VH-4 War Diary, July 1945.

[18] Commanding Officer, VPB-18, Squadron history – Forwarding of, 6 November 1945.
[19] FAW-1 War Diary, July 1945.
[20] Commanding Officer, VPB-18, Squadron history – Forwarding of, 6 November 1945.
[21] Ibid.
[22] VPB-208 Squadron History, 1 July-31 August 1945.
[23] *Kenneth Whiting* War Diary, July 1945; *Kenneth Whiting, DANFS*; "PB2Y Coronado Flying Boats" (http://pb2y.org/: accessed 2 September 2015).
[24] VPB-13 War Diary, July 1945.
[25] VPB-21 Squadron History July 1945.
[26] Commanding Officer, VPB-21, History of VPB-21, Submission of, 31 August 1945.
[27] Bob Hackett and Sander Kingsepp, "SHINYO!," (http://www.combinedfleet.com/ShinyoEMB.htm: accessed 3 September 2015).
[28] Commanding Officer, VPB-21, History of VPB-21, Submission of, 31 August 1945.
[29] Ibid.
[30] *Kenneth Whiting* War Diary, July 1945.
[31] CAW-1 War Diary, July 1945.

CHAPTER 29 NOTES:

[1] Donald R. McClarey, "One Hundred Million Die Proudly," The American Catholic, August 3, 2015 (http://the-american-catholic.com/2015/08/03/one-hundred-million-die-proudly/: accessed 3 September 2015).
[2] "Emperor Hirohito, Accepting the Potsdam Declaration, Radio Broadcast" (https://www.mtholyoke.edu/acad/intrel/hirohito.htm: accessed 31 December 2015).
[3] Commander SECOND Carrier Task Force, Pacific, Action Report – Operations Against Japan – 2 July-25 August 1945, 31 August 1945; "William Frederick Halsey, Jr. 30 October 1882 - 16 August 1959," Naval History and Heritage Command (http://www.history.navy.mil/research/histories/bios/halsey-william-f.html: accessed 31 August 2015).
[4] "Tokyo Bay: The Formal Surrender of the Empire of Japan, USS Missouri, 2 September 1945," Naval History and Heritage Command (http://www.history.navy.mil/research/library/online-reading-room/title-list-alphabetically/t/ships-present-in-tokyo-bay.html: accessed 31 December 2015).
[5] "Allied Ships Present in Tokyo Bay During the Surrender Ceremony, 2 September 1945," Naval History and Heritage Command (http://www.history.navy.mil/research/library/online-reading-room/title-list-alphabetically/a/allied-ships-present-in-tokyo-bay.html: accessed 31 December 2015).

POSTSCRIPT NOTES

[1] Daniel E. Barbey, *MacArthur's Amphibious Navy* (Annapolis: U.S. Naval Institute, 1969), 323.

[2] Bruhn, *Wooden Ships and Iron Men: The U.S. Navy's Coastal and Motor Minesweepers, 1941-1953*, 119.

[3] Ibid, 119-120.

[4] Greg H. Williams, *World War II U.S. Navy Vessels in Private Hands* (Jefferson, North Carolina: McFarland, 2013), 115, 186.

[5] *Norton Sound*, DANFS.

[6] Memorandum, Cdr. W. C. Hogan, Commanding Officer, CGC *McCulloch* to Commandant "Subj: CGC *McCulloch* Suitability for use as CG Cutter," 12 February 1947.

[7] "The Inventory of VNN's Battle Ships" (http://vnafmamn.com/VNNavy_inventory.html: accessed 28 December 2015); "Cutters, Craft & U.S. Coast Guard Manned Army & Navy Vessels" (http://www.uscg.mil/history/webcutters/cutterlist.asp: accessed 28 December 2015).

INDEX

Abate, V., 427
ABDA (American-British-Dutch-Australian) Command, 8, 72-73, 78, 81, 89-90, 111-114
Abele, James A., 339
Abernethy, Paul E., 108
Adam, J. D., 359, 412
Adams, Kenneth G., 193
Adams, John O., 428
Ainsworth, Walden L., 314
Alderman, John Clement, 179, 181, 183, 191, 407
Aldrich, Gene, 209
Allmond, Dennis, 13
Amman, B. L., 427
Anderson, Charles E., 123, 125
Anderson, F. P., 351, 410, 412
Anderson, K. K., 427
Anderson, Vernon K., 340
Andrews, Adolphus, 169-170
Arcidiacono, P. F., 428
Armstrong, Robert G., 353, 382-383, 413
Atwell, Melvin K., 188-189
Australia(n),
   Army,
      "Gull Force" (2/21st Battalion, 23rd Brigade, 8th Division), 83
   Battle Honours DARWIN 1942-43, 98
   Brisbane, 194, 199, 201, 277-278, 292, 420
   Broome, 16, 96, 115-116
   Cockatoo Island near Sydney, 303
   Darwin, 6-7, 14, 73, 78, 83, 87, 91-92, 94, 96, 98, 101, 115, 119, 419
   Derby, 96, 115
   Exmouth Gulf, 114, 116-120
   Fremantle, 7, 87, 97, 101, 108, 110
   Melbourne, 194
   Newcastle, 200
   Nichol Bay, 119
   Palm Island, Challenger Bay, 120, 278-279
   Perth, 16, 106, 115-119, 121, 420
   Port Hedland, 119
   Royal Australian
      Air Force, 77-78, 92, 101, 120, 197, 288
         Lockheed Hudson light bomber, 8, 14, 78, 83
         Squadrons Eleven and Twenty, 288

484 Index

    Navy, 98, 419
  Shark Bay, 119
  Southport, 298
  Sydney, 97, 203, 278, 293, 299-300, 303
  Townsville, 121, 278
Ayer, William H., 364
Bach, Jacob O., 379
Baker, James E., 276, 309, 408, 411
Ball, Joe Frederick, 335, 337-338
Bandy, Jack I., 302, 309-310, 333, 351, 411-412
Bangust, Joseph, 75-76, 122
Barbey, Daniel E., 291, 301, 303-304, 343, 397
Barner, James D., 407
Barrett Jr., R. R., 389, 414
Bates, R. H., 224, 406
Battle of
  the Coral Sea, 124, 157, 171, 198-199
  Guadalcanal, 175, 189
  Iwo Jima, 354-359
  the Java Sea, 15, 111, 113
  Kwajalein and Majuro Atolls (Operation FLINTLOCK), 244-251
  Leyte Gulf, 329
  Luzon, 350
  Makassar Strait, 108
  Midway, 126, 131, 141, 145-161, 171-172, 427
  Normandy (Operation OVERLORD), 226-234
  Okinawa, 361-373
  Peleliu (Operation STALEMATE), 324
  the Philippine Sea, 312, 315, 329
  Saipan (Operation FORAGER), 311-321
  the Santa Cruz Islands, 185-191
  Sunda Strait, 15, 111-113, 332
  Surigao Strait, 332-333, 351, 412
  Tarawa Atoll (Operation GALVANIC), 239
Bauer, Harold, W., 184
Bellinger, Patrick N. L., 31-32, 34, 228, 429
Bengston, R. C., 408, 410
Berkey, Russell S., 343
Bettens, Warren J., 407
Binford, Thomas H., 114
Blair, Eugene, 95-96, 122
Boettcher, R. R., 363, 382-383, 390, 413
Bohannon, John M., 167
Bolser, Gordon E., 51
Bonvillian, William D., 359, 363, 381, 389, 412-414
Borodenko, Michael, 13

Bounds, Dave W., 76
Boyden, James C., 427
Boyington, Gregory, 263
Bozuwa, G. G., 73
Branyon, Howard H., 180
Brandley, Frank A., 276, 408
Brett, George H., 72-73
Briggs, Josephus A., 215, 218, 224, 406
Brixner, Robert C., 161, 407
Brock, Robert Lee, 14, 122, 406, 418
Brokenshire, D. R., 178
Brower, Charles M., 410
Brown, Carl W., 406
Brown Jr., Ira W., 76, 122
Brown, W. S., 49
Bruner, Frank, 409
Buckley, Franklin Duerr, 14, 122, 417
Buckley, J. D., 49
Buckner Jr., Simon B., 124-125, 128, 142, 377
Bull, Richard, 122
Butler, William O., 128
Butterfield, Horace B., 177
Byrd, Richard E., xx, 197, 210, 212
Campbell, Clifford M., 191, 279, 284, 408
Campbell, Duncan A., 77, 117, 122
Canada/Canadian,
    Naval Reserve Division HMCS Cataraqui, HMCS Chippawa, 169
Caro, Joseph I., 46
Carteret, Philip, 255
Castle Jr., Emra F., 262
Chambers, R. F., 76
Chase II, E. N., 363, 379, 389, 413-414
China,
    Foo Chow, 378
    Haimen, 387
    Hainan, 84
    Sakishima Islands, 361, 368-369, 378-379
    Shanghai, 57, 378, 380, 385, 387
Christman, Elwyn Lewis, 74-76, 122
Christopher, T. A., 401, 410
Churchill, Winston, 10, 226
Cleaves, Willis E., 405, 408
Cobb, James O., 191, 276, 408
Cogswell, Wilson P., 191, 276, 407-408
Coleman, Garrett S., 345, 351, 412
Combs, Thomas S., 144, 279, 287-288, 298

Compton, J. R., 309, 411
Conley, Delbert L., 276, 408, 410
Conolly, Richard L., 223, 313, 343
Connolly, T. F., 251, 409-410
Cook Jr., Harry E., 328, 351, 410, 412
Cox, Warren M., 339
Crace, John G., 172
Craig, E., 106
Craig Jr., J. G., 279, 284
Crawford, H. G., 389, 414
Cronin, J. C., 343
Crouch, Edwin M., 105, 109-110
Cumberland, John, 77
Custer, Benjamin S., 364, 379, 389, 414
Darnell, William I., 379, 389, 414
Davis, Douglas C., 150-155, 427
Davis, John F., 122
Dawley, Jack Baldwin, 74-76, 122
Day Jr., D. T., 144, 161, 407
DeBaun, George H., 198-199
Deede, LeRoy C., 77, 122
DeLong, Earl R., 251, 313, 409
Dicken, R. J., 200
Dixon, Harold, 209
Doan, Henry C., 364, 413
Dockery, Glen, 77
Dodds, Charles R., 351, 412
Doe, Jens A., 292
Dompier, W. H., 380
Doolittle, James H., 123, 157
Doorman, Karel, 15, 89, 111-114
Donovan, Thomas A., 106-107
Drake, Francis R., 410
Duke, Lee H., 46
Dunlap, Stanton B., 278-279, 284, 295, 309, 410-411
Durgin, C. T., 343
Dutch
   Aircraft,
      Brewster F2A Buffalo fighter, 83
      Dornier, 70
   Royal Netherlands Navy, 72-73, 77
   Royal Netherlands Naval Air Service, 73
Dwyer, J. F., 427
Dyson, Gerald R., 313, 320, 328, 411
Ebey, L. O., 389, 414
Eby, Guy, 380

Eckelmeyer, Edward H., 224, 406
Edmonds, Clifton E., 46, 232
Edwards, John Perry, 50-51
Eichelberger, Robert L., 257, 299
Eisenhower, Dwight D., 219
Ellis, D. L., 427
Erreca, Louie, R., 76
Essary, Melvin S., 337
Evans, Clyde H., 76
Evans Jr., William A., 349, 351, 412
Fechteler, William M., 291
Fallon, James W., 339-340
Farrington, E. L., 276, 408, 410
Ferguson, J. A., 364, 383, 339, 413-414
Fields, Thomas M., 353
Finn, John William, 46, 49-50,
Fitch, Aubrey W., 202, 429
Fitts, William W., 408
Fitzsimmons, John P., 53, 161, 407
Flanigan, Howard A., 232
Fleming Jr., Morton K., 295, 309, 351, 410-412
Fletcher, Frank J., 172, 198
Foley Jr., Paul, 129-130, 144
Fonseca, David, 195
Ford, John, 157-158
Formoe, C. M., 49
Foss, Joseph Jacob, 274-275
Foss, R. S., 49
Foster, J. E., 427
Fox Jr., L., 49
Fraser, George K., 313, 321, 328, 363, 411-413
Frazier, John W., 46
Freeman, Charles S., 127
French
   Algiers, Mers-el-Kebir, 223, 225
   Foreign Legion, 219-220
   Morocco,
      1st and 7th Regiments Moroccan Tirailleurs, 219
      Fedala, 217-225
      Mehedia (Mehdia), 215-220
      Port Lyautey, 217, 220-222, 420
      Rabat-Sale, 218, 220
      Safi, 217, 225
      Sebou River, 216, 222
   Mimoyeccques, 230
   New Caledonia (Noumea), 171, 173-174, 193-202, 271, 277, 419

488 Index

Vichy French, xx, 193, 211, 218-219, 225
Fuchida, Mitsuo, 33, 92
Gallery Jr., William O., 279-280
Ganas, Nickolas S., 46
Gannon, J. W., 168
Garcia, George E., 409-410
Garton, Norman Farquhar, 135, 144
Gates, Amon W., 76
Gay Jr., Donald, 406
Gehres, Leslie E., 128, 138-140, 144
Geibel, Laurence F., 364, 413
Geise, Emery C., 51
Ghormley, Robert L., 185
Gillette Jr., Norman C., 310, 349, 351, 411-412
Ginder Sr., Samuel P., 407
Glassford Jr., William A., 57, 72-73, 105, 109, 111, 114
Glover, R. O., 343
Gluba, E. F., 96
Goodney, Willard K., 313, 327-328, 411
Gordon, J. S., 427
Gordon, Nathan, 282
Gough Jr., William V., 75-76
Grant, Etheridge, 16, 57, 59-61, 92, 96, 396, 407
Granum, A. M., 343
Griffin, D. T., 49
Groseclose, Elwin R., 371
Gumz, Donald G., 410
Gunichi, Mikawa, 425
Gunther, Ernest L., 429
Guthrie, John H., 409
Guy, George H., 46
Hailey, Thomas E., 51
Haley, T. B., 405
Hall, Earle B., 76
Hall, Finley E., 53, 407
Hall Jr., John L., 234
Halsey Jr., William F., xxi, 17, 185-187, 189, 253-254, 262-263, 327, 329, 375, 393, 429
Harper, C. K., 276, 359, 389, 408, 410, 413-414
Harper, Robert M., 349, 351, 412
Harris, Floyd, 387
Harrison, G. C., 427
Hart, Thomas C., xix, 2, 4, 14, 57, 65, 73, 90, 99, 115
Hartley, Kenneth J., 46
Hastings, Burden Robert, 74, 76, 122
Haven Jr., Edward S., 46

Hawkins Jr., Anthony, 46
Hayward, J. T., 410
Hazelton, Edgar, 77
Hecking (Capt. Royal Netherlands Navy), 77
Helfrich, Conrad E. L., 72-73, 90, 99, 102, 113-115
Hembree, Thomas, 46
Henderson, W. C., 427
Heyward Jr., Alexander S., 224, 406
Hibberd, C. P., 427
Hicks, George L., 389, 414
Hill, Arthur S., 408
Hirohito, Michinomiya, 393
Hitchcock, Norman R., 191, 407
Hix, E. W., 427
Hobbs, Ira E., 256-260, 262, 276, 409
Hodgskin Jr., Henry T., 389, 414
Hoffman, Charles C., 122
Hogan, W. C., 401
Hoover, John H., 235, 239, 248, 311, 313, 321
Houston, Charles E., 413
Howe, Frank N., 364, 379, 389, 413-414
Huffman, Dale D., 262
Hughes, Francis M., 50, 53, 161, 191, 407-408
Hughes, G. M., 427
Huie, B. S., 343
Hunt, C. L., 427
Hutchings, Curtis H., 406
Hyakutake, Harukichi, 265
Hyland, John J., 77, 117
Hyman, Wilford M., 200
Iceland
    Keflavik, 419
    Skerjafjordr, 215
Ingram, G. W., 49
Innis, Walter D., 359, 363, 381, 389, 412-414
Jackson, Donald, 188
Jacobs, Randall, 69
James, Jules, 168-169
Japan
    Hiroshima, Nagasaki, xxii, 391, 393
    Kure, 147, 153, 375, 426
    Kyushu, 361, 367, 369, 378, 382, 385, 393
    Sasagawa, 386
    Skikoku, 378
    Tokyo, 25, 123, 145, 244, 327, 375, 378, 393-396
    Tsugen Jima, 24

490 Index

Tsushima Strait, 385
Japanese
  aircraft
    Betty, 10, 102-103, 241, 319, 334, 431
    Claude, 60, 431
    Emily, 160, 319, 431
    Frances, 341, 431
    Frank, 371, 431
    Hamp, Jake, Jill, Judy, Oscar, 333-334, 431
    Kate, 60, 172, 187, 334, 431
    Mavis, 9, 11-12, 96, 431
    Nell, 10, 89, 261, 431
    Sally, 240, 256-258, 284, 332, 431
    Tojo, 380, 431
    Tony, 334, 370, 431
    Val, 35, 181, 187, 334, 431
    Zeke (Zero fighter), 3, 63-65, 74-77, 86, 118, 156, 184, 345-346, 371, 431
  bases
    Kavieng (New Ireland Island), 269, 281-282
    Rabaul (New Britain Island), 174, 253-254, 263-265, 268-269, 277, 280-282, 285-286, 291, 325
    Truk Island (Caroline Islands), 185, 248, 286, 311-312, 325, 327, 357
  military forces/operations
    2 Base Force, 2 Kure Special Naval Landing Force, 21 Air Flotilla, 56 Independent Mixed Brigade, 80
    67 Naval Guard Force, 257
    Combined Fleet, 124, 155, 185, 187, 248, 312, 331
    First Mobile Fleet, 329
    Nauru Island, 357
      Expeditionary Force of the 3rd Special Naval Base Force, Special Construction Unit of the Fourth Fleet, 257
    Midway Invasion/Occupational Force, 148-149, 425-426
    Northern Force, 128-129
    Operation
      K (aerial reconnaissance of Pearl Harbor), 160
      KETSU-GO (defense of the home islands), 385, 391
      MO (Battle of the Coral Sea), 171
      SHO-GO (defense against American advances toward Japan), 331
    Pearl Harbor Striking Force, 29-30
    Sasebo Special Naval Landing Force, 67
    Second Destroyer Squadron, 148, 157
    Second Mobile Force, 132
    Special Attack Units
      Shinyo explosive motorboats, Kaiten human-torpedoes, 386
      Kamikaze aircraft, 334, 342, 345, 347, 361, 370-371, 384, 386

Johnson, Lauren E., 279, 309, 411
Johnson, Leon W., 53, 407
Johnson, R. A., 96
Johnson, Rudolph L., 241
Johnson Jr., William G., 39, 53
Johnson, William Harold, 14, 122, 405-406, 417-418
Jones, Carroll B., 144, 298, 409
Jones (Capt. USMC), 247-248
Jones, Francis R , 409
Jonson Jr., William C., 407
Kabler, William Laverette, 1, 9-16, 57, 122, 407, 417
Kajioka, Sadamichi, 171
Kakuta, Kakaji, 132
Kane, Joseph L., 53, 407
Keller Jr., Clarence Armstrong, 55, 61-62, 77, 117, 122
Kennedy, John F., xxi, 227
Kennedy Jr., Joseph P., xxi, 227-230
Kennedy-Purvis, Charles F., 169
Kerns, L. L., 96
Ketcham, Dixwell, 325, 327
Kimmel, Husband E., 30
Kimmel, T. E., 427
King, Andrew, 46
King, Ernest J., 187, 197, 202, 375, 394
Kinkaid, Thomas C., 185, 342-343
Kivette, Frederick N., 144
Kline, E. L., 427
Kline, Wendell F., 53, 407
Knight, Page, 406
Knight, William, 96
Knox, Frank, 69
Knudsen, Roy H., 262
Koepke, Lyle L., 409
Kondo, Nobutake, 111, 425
Korea
    Chosin, Saishu To (Jeju), 385
    Fusan (Pusan), Gunzan, Keijo, 376-377
Krueger, Walter, 297, 342
Kurita, Takeo, 329, 425
Kuzume, Naoyuki, 299
Lahodney, William J., 280
Landers, Paul H., 75
Lane, James Mills, 34, 53, 144
Larson, Nils R., 51
Lawler, C. G., 428
Lawrence, C., 49

Index

Lawrence, Sidney J., 191, 251, 408-409
Layton, Albert E., 60
Leeman, Robert W., 409-410
Leeper, James E., 406
LeFever, Robert, 117
Lloyd, Rundolph, 281
Loud, Wayne R., 326, 343
Lowe, Robert S., 46
Lucas, Carlton C., 364, 372, 381, 389, 413-414
Lucca, Anthony, 226
Lurvey, Donald D., 75-76, 122
Lyons, Raymond R., 313, 364, 383, 389, 413-414
Manning, M. A., 49
MacArthur, Douglas, xxi, 17, 172, 236, 253-254, 264, 277, 286, 291-292, 297, 299-301, 329-330, 342, 393, 397
Marcy, Clayton C., 191, 407-408
Mason, Charles P., 187
Massey, James E., 46
Masterson, J. A., 359, 412
Masterton, Paul, 359, 413
Mastrototaro, Maurice, 46
Mather (Lt.), 189
Matsumura, Kanji, 199
McAlpine, Lloyd H., 406
McCaffree, B. C., 405
McCain, John S., 173-174, 197-198, 201, 392, 429
McConnell, Robert, 64
McConnell, Robert P., 103-105, 110
McCormick, William M., 405
McDonald, Harold W., 351, 412
McGabe, Thomas E. L., 77
McGinnis, Knefler, 32, 46, 48
McGrath, Malcolm C., 405, 409
McKee (Mr. and Mrs.), 141
McLaughlin, Loren W., 167
McLawhorn, Evren C., 75-76, 122
McLean, Gordon A., 359, 361, 363, 379, 383, 389, 412-414
McLean, John B., 343
Merrick, G. C., 405
Meyer, Cord, 249
Milbourne, Jesse K., 46
Miller, John M., 389, 413-414
Miller, William, 266, 276, 408
Miller Jr., M. W., 76
Mills, A. L., 427
Mills, De Long, 310, 351, 410-412

Mills Jr., James H., 231-232, 234, 406
Mitchell, Ralph J., 429
Moffett Jr., William A., 191, 408
Montgomery, Alfred E., 429
Moon, Don Pardee, 234
Moran, Edmond J., 232
Morehouse, Albert K., 276, 408
Moreno, J. A., 224, 405-406
Moses, Paul R., 76
Mundorff Jr., George T., 53, 119-120, 407
Muoio, John B., 339
Murray, George D., 185, 429
Nagumo, Chuichi, 29, 35, 187
Nakagawa, Kunio, 323
Nation, William M., 161, 407
Neale, Edgar T., 16, 57, 83, 122, 407
Netherlands (Dutch) East Indies,
   Ambon Island, 7-9, 12, 14, 74, 77-80, 83-85, 301, 420
   Greater Sunda Islands, 88
      Borneo
         Balikpapan, 4-5, 7, 15, 58, 68-71, 74, 81-82, 99
         Bandjermasin, Samarinda, 99
         Makassar Strait, 15, 58, 73, 81, 89, 99, 101, 108, 303
         Tarakan, 75-76, 80-82, 99
      Celebes/Celebes Sea, 14, 56-59, 67-71, 78, 80, 83, 88, 99, 106, 301-302, 308-309
         Kendari, 14, 67, 80, 83-89
         Makassar/Makassar Strait, 15, 58, 71, 73, 81, 89, 99, 101, 106, 108, 303
      Java
         Batavia, 106
         Soerabaja (today Surabaya), 7-8, 14-15, 70-74, 78, 80, 83-89, 96, 99, 112-117, 420
         Tjilatjap, 15, 89, 96, 101-102, 104-106, 108, 114-115, 117
   Lesser Sunda Islands, 87-88
      Alor Islands, 85
      Bali/Bali Strait, 99, 102, 104, 114
      Flores Islands, 14, 83
      Soemba Islands, 14, 83, 87
      Sumbawa Island, 88
      Tanimbar Islands, Saumlaki, 14
      Timor/Timor Sea, 7, 14, 83, 85, 87, 91, 120
   Molucca Islands (Maitara, Ternate), 9
      Halmahera Islands, 8, 78, 300, 303-304
         Morotai Island, 300, 303-307, 310, 323, 332, 334, 340, 411, 420
   Molucca Sea/Molucca Passage, 1, 8-9, 73, 77-78

494   Index

Tukang Besi Islands, 86
Neuman, R. H., 427
Nevills, Roy W., 262
New Guinea (formerly Papua, New Guinea, and Dutch New Guinea)
  Babo, 298
  Dreger Harbor, 283-284
  Finschhafen/Finsch Harbor, 264, 283-284, 300, 410
  Geelvink Bay, 291, 294, 298-299
  Hollandia, Tanahmerah Bay, and Aitapi, 282, 285, 290-298, 311, 410
  Jefman Island, Sagan, 298
  Jenkins Bay, 121
  Langemak Bay, 281-284, 291
  Madang, 282
  Manokwari, 294, 298
  Milne Bay, 277, 286
    Sariba Island, 277
  Nadzab, 291
  Namoai Bay, 277, 279-281, 289
  Owen Stanley Mountains, 203
  Port Moresby, 171-172, 282, 286
  Samarai Island, 121, 281-282, 289, 298
  Sansapor/Cape Sansapor, 292, 301, 304, 309, 411
  Schouten Islands, 294, 299-300, 419-420
    Biak Island, 286, 292, 294, 297-301
    Noemfoor Island, 292, 294, 298, 301
    Woendi Island, 294, 299-301, 335, 420
  Sorong, 294
  St. George's Channel, 280
  Vitiaz and Dampier Straits, 253, 264, 280-281
  Vogelkop Peninsula, 292, 294, 301
  Wakde Island, 291-292, 297-298, 300-301, 309, 411
  Wewak, 266, 282, 291, 298
New Zealand, 203-204, 213, 272-273
  3rd Army Division, 264, 268
  Auckland, 201
  Royal New Zealand Airforce Maritime Squadron No. 6FB, 268
  Upolu Island, 204
Newman, L. G., 49
Ney, R. J., 427
Nichandros, Gust C., 313, 328, 411
Nichols, Frank, 405
Nimitz, Chester W., xxiii, 46, 119, 124, 128, 132, 138, 141, 145-146, 172, 185, 187, 202, 235, 244, 329, 393-394
Nishida, Yoshimi, 250
Nishimura, Shoji, 100, 425
Nixon, Richard M., xxi, 269-273

Index   495

Nobel, Albert G., 291
Nolan, James Clair, 152-155, 428
Norcott, John M., 279, 295, 351, 410, 412
Nordgram, Alagran H., 262
Norvell Jr., Forest H., 381, 389, 414
Noyes, Leigh, 429
Null, R. S., 364, 379, 389, 413-414
O'Beirne, Frank, 16, 53, 407
Ogden, James R., 191, 389, 408, 414
Okinawa/Okinawan Islands, 25-26, 223, 353, 361-378, 381-382, 385, 391, 413-414, 419
    Amami Oshima, 361, 382
    Chimu Wan, 377-378, 389, 419
    Kerama Retto, 362-283
    Sakashima Gunto (Miyako), 379, 382, 387
    Naha, 377
    Toguchi, Yoron Island, 381
    Zamami Island, 371, 378
Oldendorf, Jesse B., 343
Oliver, Richard M., 295, 309-310, 410-411
Ondrejcka, William J., 339-340
Onstott, Darrell C., 371
Operation
    APHRODITE, 228-230
    CARTWHEEL, 253
    CHERRY BLOSSOM, 265
    FLINTLOCK, 244-247
    FORAGER, 311-312
    GOODTIME, 264
    ICEBERG, 363-364
    MUSKETEER, MIKE ONE, 342
    OVERLORD, xx, 226-234
    SHINGLE, 226
    STALEMATE II, 323
    TOENAILS, 253
    TORCH, xx, 216, 225
    WATCHTOWER, 285
Orr Jr., John I., 337
Orwick, Dean B., 46
Osmena, Sergio, 331
Oswald, Harvey E., 95-96, 122
Otterstetter, C. W., 49
Owen, George Thomas, 53
Ozawa, Jisaburo, 100
Pace, Bill, 261
Pacific Islands/Island Groups (other than those elsewhere in the index),

Admiralty Islands, 282, 285-300, 410, 420
  Manus (Seeadler Harbor), 285, 288, 298-299, 420
  Los Negros, 285-289, 297, 300, 420
Anambas Islands, 199
Bismarck Archipelago, 253-254, 264, 269, 277, 285, 410
  Emirau Island, 269
  New Britain
    Arawe, Gasmate, 281
    Rabaul, 174, 253-254, 263-269, 277, 280-282, 285-286, 291, 325
  New Ireland Island (Kavieng), 269, 277, 281-282
Bismarck Sea, 277, 280-282, 284, 405
Bonin (Ogasawara) Islands, 327, 410
  Iwo Jima, 25, 223, 327, 353-360, 412, 419
Bora Bora, 203
Canton Island, 212-214, 239, 274
Caroline Islands (Truk), 185, 236, 248, 286, 297, 311-312, 324-325, 327-328, 356-357, 364, 366, 411
  Palau Islands, 286, 297, 311-312, 323-329, 366, 411
    Angaur Island, Babelthuap, 325
    Kossol Passage, 325-328
    Peleliu Island, 323-325
  Puluwat, Satawan, 311
  Ulithi Atoll, 323, 326-327, 356, 364-366
  Woleai Island, 288, 311
  Yap Island, 297
Christmas Island, 89, 106-108, 115
Cocos Island, 89, 108, 115
Cook Islands, 203, 209
Ellice Islands, 202, 213, 235, 237-242, 273
  Funafuti, 213-214, 235, 237, 239-243, 273-274
Fijian Islands, 202, 212-213
Gilbert Islands, 213, 235-236, 241-244, 251, 409
  Apamama, 235-236
  Makin, 235-236, 239-242
  Tarawa, 235-244, 248, 251, 274
Hawaiian Islands/Hawaii, 29-54, 78, 121, 123, 146-147, 171, 173, 184, 195, 198, 201-203, 206, 212-213, 237, 239, 248, 251, 273, 279, 340, 419
Kazen Islands, 327
Marcus Island, 157
Mariana Islands, 237, 250, 273, 297, 299, 311-329, 358-359, 366, 410-411, 420
  Guam, 203, 311-316, 323, 329, 354, 357-358, 384, 411, 419-420
  Pagan, 312, 319, 358
  Rota, 312
  Saipan, 25, 299, 311-329, 355-359, 363, 366, 383-384, 389, 411, 419
  Tinian, 311-312, 317, 321, 327, 329, 420

Marshall Islands, 25, 145, 160, 213, 235-237, 244-251, 273, 275, 311-312, 329, 356, 409
Nauru Island, 357
New Caledonia, 173, 193-204, 271, 277
New Hebrides, 174, 201, 204, 255, 273, 275
    Espiritu Santo, 174-189, 202, 255, 258, 260-261, 266, 274-277, 419
Palmyra Island, 214, 274
Phoenix Islands, 212-214, 273
Samoan islands, 123, 173, 196, 203-210, 239, 274
    Fita Fita Guard, 208
    Tutuila Island (Pago Pago), 173, 204-212, 274
Santa Cruz Islands, 17, 25, 177, 179, 185-191, 254-255, 408
    Utupua Island, Swallow or Reef Islands, Duff Islands, 255
    Vanikoro, 179, 188, 202, 254-261, 266, 276, 409
Solomon Islands
  Bougainville, 262-276, 285, 408
  Green Islands, 268-273
  Guadalcanal, 171-195, 201, 237, 253-254, 266, 269, 271-275, 285, 329, 407, 419
  Guadalcanal area
    Florida Island, 172, 173, 266, 274-275, 324
    Gavutu Island, 174, 183, 275, 324
    Lunga Point Airfield/Henderson Field, 172-181, 185, 189
    Malaita Island, Maramasike Island, 174-175
    New Georgia Sound ("The Slot"), 171-173, 176, 266, 269
    Russell Islands, 184, 263
    Tulagi Island, 171-174, 179-184, 190-191, 267, 269, 407
  New Georgia Islands, 263
    Rendova Island, 267, 275-276, 409
  Shortland Island, 263
  Tanambogo Island, 174
  Treasury Islands, 262-276, 408
  Wallis Island, 204, 207-212, 239, 242
  Wake Island, 145-146, 157, 203
Palliser, Arthur, 114
Palm, Edgar P., 369-370
Parker, Ralph C., 124-128, 142
Parks, Clyde G., 76
Parks, Floyd D., 95-96, 122
Parunak, A. Y., 407
Paschal, Joe B., 191, 408
Pastula, Tony, 209
Patch, Alexander M., 194
Payne, Earl D., 64
Pearson, Gerald R., 359, 410, 413
Peck, Edward R., 278-279

498 Index

Peck, Scott E., 251, 313, 364, 409, 413
Peirse, Richard E. C., 73
Perkins, Charles E., 129-130
Perry, David, 251, 409
Perry, John (Rear Adm.), 171, 202
Perry, John (Ens.), 51
Peterson, Conrad, 199
Peterson, John V., 14-16, 55, 57, 62-63, 69, 74, 78, 83, 99, 117, 122, 407
Peterson, Mell A., 335-336
Pettingill, W. L., 168
Petit, Jack, 261
Pettit, Robert L., 75-76, 122
Peyton, T. J., 196
Phares, E. L., 74
Philippine Islands,
    Canipo Island, Palawan, 340
    Cebu Island, 4, 68, 334
    Leyte Island, 25, 292, 323, 329-353, 412
        Cabugan Grande Island, 333
        Dulag, 330
        Himunangen Bay, 332-333
        Jinamoc Island, 334, 338, 420
        Leyte Gulf, 329-334, 340-341, 349, 375, 420
        Ormoc Bay, 335-339
        Tacloban, 330, 338, 340
        San Pedro Bay, 332-334, 338, 340, 348, 420
    Luzon Island, 2-3, 6, 25, 61-65, 331, 341-343, 348-353, 420
        Corregidor Island, 68, 203, 331
        Lingayen Gulf, 65, 341-351, 412, 420
        Laguna de Bay/Los Banos, 3, 55, 62, 64-65
        Manila/Manila Bay, 2, 5-8, 28, 55, 57, 61-68, 73, 203, 331, 342, 344
        Nasugbu, San Antonio, 350
        Olongapo, 3, 55, 65
        San Fabian, 342-343, 349
    Mindanao, 6, 61, 68, 236
        Davao/Davao Gulf, 3, 55, 60, 68, 73, 80, 84, 100, 301
        Jolo, 61, 73-77, 100
        Lake Lanao (Malanao), 68-70
        Malalag Bay, 55, 60
        Mangarin Bay, 339
        Polloc Harbor, 61
    Palawan Island, 56, 340, 420
    Ponson Island, 334, 336
    Samar Island, 333, 341
    San Bernardino Strait, 331
    San Juanico Strait, 334

Index   499

Surigao Strait, 68, 331-333, 351, 412
Sulu Sea/Sulu Archipelago, 3, 6, 73-75, 100, 303, 331
Pidinkowski, A. F., 96
Pierson, Gerald E. 408
Poorten, Hein ter, 73
Porter, John A., 310, 351, 411-412
Porterfield, R. K., 49
Powell, William T., 46
Pownall, Charles A., 429
Pratt, John L., 4, 16, 57, 67-68, 71, 77, 79-80, 85-87, 115-118, 407
Pressler, Louis P, 359, 413
Price, John D., 371-372, 376, 378
Pridmore, James A., 313, 411
Propst, Gaylord D., 150, 152, 154, 427
Prueher, Bertram J., 405-406
Purnell, William R., 115
Quezon, Manuel, 331
Quinlan, Walter A., 294-295
Rankin, E. P., 276, 408, 410
Rassieur, William T., 53, 407
Rawlings, Henry Bernard Hughes, 375
Ray, H. L., 144
Ream, C. G., 427
Reeves Jr., John W., 142
Reid, Jack, 148
Renard, Jack C., 57, 74
Reynolds, William, 145
Rheindt, Robert Lee, 182
Rice, Wilson A., 46
Richards, William L., 149-151, 155, 160, 191, 276, 408-409, 427
Rider, Eugene C., 95, 122
Rigsbee Jr., Everett O., 342, 349, 351, 412
Roadruck, T. M., 427
Robb Jr., James W., 51
Roberts, C. C., 428
Roberts, J. H., 96
Robertson, John Mott., 122
Robinson, J. H., 49
Robinson Jr., Jesse P., 310, 351, 411-412
Robinson, William S., 122
Roosevelt, Elliott, 230
Roosevelt, Franklin D., 2, 225, 230
Rosasco, Robert A., 251, 273, 276, 408-410
Rosenau, Howard A. 46
Rothenberg, Allan, 150, 152, 155, 428
Russell, James S., 129-130, 144

Ruth, Wesley H., 51
Rutherford, Reginald, 313, 364, 381, 413
Sakaguchi, Shizuo, 81
Sampson, W. S., 359, 413
Sanger, Kenneth J., 349, 351, 412
Scarpino, William J., 410
Sceek, George, 65
Schlect, Benjamin, 46
Schmidt, Harry, 354
Schnur, Donald A., 339
Schoenweiss, Carl W., 276, 408-410
Schroeder, W. P., 191, 408
Schwarz, Alden D., 313, 328, 363, 379, 389, 411, 413-414
Scull, Herbert, M., 239
Scott (wing commander, Royal Australian Air Force), 77
Scott, R. S., 389
Scribner, James M., 76
Searles, John M., 381
Sedor, William B., 263
Sellers Jr., Frank E., 262
Sheldon (Army Lt. Col.), 247
Shilling, S. C., 389, 413-414
Shima, Kiyohide, 171
Ships and Craft
Australian
Arthur Rose, Barossa, Griffioen, Kalaroo, Mako, Malanda, Mars, Medic, Nereus, Plover, St. Francis, Sulituan, Tulagi, Winbah, Yampi Lass, 421
Australia, 172
Chinampa, Coongoola, Deloraine, Ibis, Kangaroo, Kara Kara, Karalee, Karangi, Kelat, Kiara, Koala, Kookaburra, Koompartoo, Kuru, Larrakia, Mavie, Moruya, Platypus, Red Bill, Southern Cross, Swan, Terka, Tolga, Townsville, Vigilant, Warrnambool, Wato, Zealandia, 98, 421
Duntroon, 101
Gascoyne, 343-344, 346
Gunbar, 91-92, 98, 421
Hobart, 172
Katoomba, 98, 101, 421
Manunda, 92, 421
Neptuna, 91, 98, 421
Perth, 112-114
Shropshire, 348
Warrego, 98, 343-344, 346, 421
Wilcannia, 200
British
British Motorist, 98, 421
Cyclops, 170

Electra, Encounter, Exeter, Jupiter, 112-114
Oceanway, Warspite, 233-234
Prince of Wales, Repulse, 10
Sumar, 164-159
Swallow, 255
Westmoreland, 164-167
Canadian,
Cathcart, 167
Dutch
Banckert, Piet Hein, Van Ghent, 89
Evertsen, Java, Kortenaer, Witte de With, 112-114
De Ruyter, 89, 111-113
Ethiopian, *Ethiopia*, 403, 440
German
E-boat, 233-234
U-123, U-701, 170
U-566, 164
U-653, xix, 26, 164, 395, 435
Greek
Chloe, 198-200
Kentavros, Kypros, Rodos, 403, 438, 440
Japanese
Akagi, Kaga, Soryu, 29, 108, 112, 155
Akashi, Amatsukaze, Arare, Arashio, Argentine Maru, Asagumo, Asashio, Azuma Maru, Brazil Maru, Chokai, Genyo Maru, Goshu Maru, Hayashio, Kagero, Kamikawa Maru, Kano Maru, Kasumi, Keiyo Maru, Kenyo Maru, Kinryu Maru, Kirisima Maru, Kuroshio, Kyozumi Maru, Nankai Maru, Natsugumo, Nichiei Maru, Oyashio, Sata, Shiranui, Shonan Maru 7 and 8, Toa Maru, Tsurumi, Zenyo Maru, Tsuta, 425-426
Akebono, Hagikaze, Ikazuchi, Kawakaze, Maikaze, Nachi, Natori, Nowaki, PC-4, 5, 6, 16, 17, 18, Sazanami, Takao, Ushio, Wakataka, Yamakaze, Yudachi, 112-113
Akebono Maru, 148, 151, 425
Akigumo, Makigumo, 187
Arashi, Atago, Haguro, Harusame, Hatsukaze, Kumano, Mikuma, Minegumo, Mogami, Murasame, Myoko, 112-113, 425
Asakaze, Matsukaze, Kuma, 61
Ashigara, 61, 112
Chikuma, 108, 136
Chitose, 157, 426
Hiei, 108, 425
Hijo, 329
Hiryu, 29, 108, 112, 155, 158-159
Hyuga, Ise, 157
Jintsu, 112-113, 148, 425
Junyo, 132, 188

Kongo, 63, 425
Krishima, Tone, 108
Minesweepers *15, 16*, 112
Naka, 100, 112
Ryujo, 60, 112, 132
Samidare, 112, 425
Sendai, 112, 180
Shoho, 172
Shokaku, 29, 112, 172, 186, 312, 329
Suzuya, Tokitsukaze, Yukikaze, Yura, 112, 425
Taiho, 312, 329
Tama Maru *3* and *5*, 426
Type-*A* midget submarine, 30, 42
I-16, I-18, I-20, I-22, I-24, 42-43
I-21, 199
Type-*I* mother-submarine, 31, 42-43
Zuikaku, 29, 112, 172, 188
Zuiho, 186, 425
Philippino
Andres Bonifacio, 402, 438
Diego Silang, 439
Francisco Dagohoy, 403, 439
South Vietnamese
Ly Thuong Kiet, Ngo Quyen, Pham Ngu Lao, Tran Binh Trong, Tran Nhat Duat, Tran Quang Khai, 402-403, 438-439
North Vietnamese, *Pham Ngu Lao*, 402
Norwegian, *Haakon VII*, 403, 439
United States
Army/Army Air Force
P-716 and *P-717*, 340
Coast Guard
Aurora, Bonham, Cyane, Haida, 129
McCulloch, 401
Nemaha, 134
Onondaga, 129, 133
Merchant Marine/Army and Marine Corps Transports
Admiral Halsted, Portmar, 421
Argentina, Barry, Cristobal, Erickson, Island Mail, McAndrew, Santa Elena, Santa Rosa, 194
Contessa, 218, 222
Henry R. Mallory, 167
Irvin McDowell, 179
John Adams, 199
John Muir, 284
Lurline, Matsonia, 207
Mauna Loa, Meigs, 98, 421

Index 503

  Monroe, 271
  Morlen, 134
  Northwestern, 135-137
  President Fillmore, 130, 134-135
  Sea Witch, William A. Holbrook, 101
Navy
  amphibious ships/craft/aviation rescue boats
    C-9485 and *C-24375*, 340
    LCI-397, 328
    LCI(G)-70, 346
    LST-999, 364
  auxiliaries/hospital ships/supply ships/transport ships
    Algorab, Henry T. Allen, 218
    American Legion, 265
    Antares, 30
    Apache, 346
    Ashtabula, Escalante, 26, 364-365
    Black Hawk, 114
    Brant, Cherokee, 220
    Cascade, Catalpa, Phaon, 239
    Chowanoc, 334
    Corpus Christi Bay, 400, 437
    Cowanesque, 343
    Electra, Florence Nightingale, John Penn, 218
    George Clymer, 218, 220
    Josiah Willard Gibbs, 404
    Jupiter, Kaskaskia, Lassen, 207
    Kaloli, Vireo, 147
    Kennebec, 218
    Kingfisher, Turkey, 210
    Medusa, 41, 43
    Mount Vernon, 110
    Neosho, 37, 199-201
    Owl, 168
    Pecos, 5, 57-58, 87, 106-110, 343
    Pigeon, 57
    Prometheus, 324
    Sabine, 131-132
    Seminole, 180
    Solace, 45
    Sonoma, 261
    Sumner, 37
    Susquehanna, 343
    Trinity, 5, 57-58
    Vestal, 53, 239
    Wharton, 290

YP (ex-*Bendora*), YP (ex-*Hiram*), YP (ex-*Point Reyes*), YP (*Northern Light*), YP (*Washington*), 127
YP-72, YP-74, YP-92, YP-151, YP-155, 127, 133
YP-73, YP-83, YP-84, YP-85, YP-86, YP-88, YP-93, YP-94, YP-95, YP-96, YP-148, YP-149, YP-152, YP-153, YP-154, YP-197, YP-250, YP-251, YP-333, YP-338, YP-396, YP-397, YP-401, 127
YP-236, 279
YP-239, 179-181, 183
YP-284, 147, 154, 180
YP-290, 147, 154-155
YP-345, YP-350, 147
YP-346, 179-180
YP-347, 193
YP-389, 170

combatants
  battleships
    Arizona, 40, 43, 53
    California, 38, 53
    Maryland, 52-53
    Mississippi, 348
    Nevada, 38, 43, 53
    Oklahoma, 37, 42, 51-53
    Pennsylvania, 35, 37, 53, 325
    South Dakota, 185
    Tennessee, 53
    Texas, 216, 218-221
    Utah, 35, 40-42, 53
    West Virginia, 43, 53, 348
  carriers
    Chenango, 217, 220
    Enterprise, 124, 155-156, 158, 185-186, 209
    Hornet, 123-124, 155, 185-187
    Independence, 241
    Lexington, 124, 172, 238
    Long Island, 407
    Ranger, 228
    Saratoga, 175
    Yorktown, 124, 155-156, 158, 172, 370
  cruisers
    Boise, 57, 343
    Chicago, 172
    Denver, 325
    Helena, 53
    Honolulu, 53, 124, 132, 325
    Houston, 57, 89, 108, 110, 112-114
    Indianapolis, 124, 132, 136, 141

Index   505

    Louisville, 124
    Marblehead, 53, 89, 108, 110, 114
    Nashville, 124, 131-132, 136-137, 330
    Northampton, 187
    Phoenix, 101
    Raleigh, 40-41, 53
    Savannah, 218, 220
    St. Louis, 124, 132
destroyers
    Alden, 112, 114
    Allen M. Sumner, Cooper, Moale, 335-338
    Anderson, Mustin, 187
    Barker, 5, 57, 89
    Bennion, 344, 346-347
    Brooks, Case, Dent, Gilmer, Kane, Sands, Talbot, 131-133
    Bulmer, 89
    Cassin, Shaw, 38, 53
    Clark, 147
    Cummings, 358
    Dallas, 218, 220-221
    Downes, 38, 53, 316
    Eberle, Livermore, Parker, Roe, 218
    Edsall, 102-103, 105, 108
    Ericson, 217-218
    Gridley, 124, 132, 137
    Hammann, 156
    Helm, Henley, Sims, 199-201
    Humphreys, McCall, 124, 131-132
    Jenkins, 261
    John D. Edwards, John D. Ford, Parrot, Pope, 81, 89, 112, 114
    Monaghan, 31, 39-40, 42
    Landsdowne, 266
    Paul Jones, 5, 57-58, 81, 112, 114
    Peary, 8-9, 78, 92-94, 98, 421
    Reid, 124-125
    Steele, 316
    Stewart, 89, 108, 110
    Trippe, 168
    Ward, 30-31
    Whipple, 26, 102-114
gunboats,
    Charleston, 125-126, 128-130, 140
    Luzon, Oahu, 57
    Tulsa, 105, 114
motor torpedo (PT) boats,
    tenders

506 Index

  Oyster Bay, 22, 293, 332
  Wachapreague, Willoughby, 22, 332
 PT boats
  PT-20, PT-21, PT-22, PT-24, PT-25, PT-26, PT-27, PT-28, PT-29, PT-30, 147
 patrol yacht
  Crystal, 147
  Isabel, 3, 114
 screw sloop-of-war, *Lackawanna*, 145
 seaplane tenders
  Absecon, 22, 402, 438
  Albemarle, 23, 400, 420, 437
  Avocet, 18, 32, 35, 38-39, 53, 178, 407, 435
  Ballard, 20, 147, 157-160, 177-179, 184, 188, 313-319, 323-328, 411, 436
  Barataria, 22, 348, 349, 351, 397-398, 403, 412, 439
  Barnegat, xx, 20-22, 215-216, 218-219, 222, 224, 255, 277, 293, 401, 403, 406, 438
  Belknap, Clemson, George E. Badger, Goldsborough, Osmond Ingram, 20, 436
  Bering Strait, 22, 356-359, 363, 368, 371-378, 381, 389, 397-398, 402-403, 412-414, 439
  Biscayne, xxiii, 22, 223-224, 402, 406, 438
  Casco, 22, 128-130, 139, 144, 248-249, 251, 313, 318, 321, 364, 381, 402, 408-409, 413, 438
  Castle Rock, 22, 397-398, 402-403, 439
  Chandeleur, 23-24, 255, 266, 275-276, 313, 316-319, 325-328, 363, 371, 377-378, 382-383, 385, 389, 400, 408, 411-414, 437
  Childs, 1, 3-4, 7-8, 13-16, 19-20, 55, 57, 65, 67-68, 70-71, 74, 77, 79-80, 83-89, 96, 114-118, 120-121, 407, 435
  Chincoteague, 17, 22, 251, 253-263, 266-269, 273, 275-276, 354-356, 359, 398, 402, 408-410, 412, 438
  Cook Inlet, 22, 358-359, 397-398, 402-403, 412, 439
  Coos Bay, 22, 266-269, 273, 275-276, 402, 408, 410, 439
  Corson, 22, 398, 404, 439
  Cumberland Sound, 23-25, 356, 395-396, 398, 400, 438
  Currituck, 23, 45, 306, 334, 338, 341, 348-349, 351, 398, 400, 412, 420, 437
  Curtiss, 23, 32, 35, 39-46, 53, 173-175, 178-179, 188, 190-191, 235, 237-243, 251, 255, 275-276, 313, 321, 364, 371-372, 398, 400, 407-409, 413, 437
  Duxbury Bay, 22, 364, 378-379, 389, 398, 404, 413-414, 439
  Floyds Bay, 22, 389, 398, 404, 414, 440
  Gannet, xix, 18, 26, 164-170, 399, 435
  Gardiners Bay, 22, 25, 364, 372-373, 377, 381, 389, 395, 398, 403, 413-414, 439

Gillis, 20, 128-130, 133-135, 138-141, 144, 364-365, 408, 413, 436

Greene, 20

Greenwich Bay, 22, 398, 404, 440

Half Moon, 22, 277-280, 291, 293, 299-302, 305-310, 332-334, 340-341, 351, 397-398, 403, 411-412, 439

Hamlin, 23-25, 327, 354-356, 359, 363, 377-379, 382-384, 389, 395, 400, 412-414, 419, 438

Heron, xv, xviii-xix, 1-16, 18, 56-58, 61, 68, 70-78, 83, 96, 114-115, 119-122, 204-205, 279, 289-300, 334, 340-341, 351, 407, 410, 412, 415, 417-418, 435

Hulbert, 20, 32, 34-39, 53, 129-130, 139, 141, 144, 436

Humboldt, 22, 291-300, 402, 438

Kenneth Whiting, 23-24, 313, 318, 327, 364, 371-372, 377, 382-384, 388-389, 398, 400, 413-414, 438

Langley, 1-8, 22-26, 55-58, 68, 71, 74, 87, 101-110, 399, 435, 437

Lapwing, xvi, 17-18, 205, 210, 435

Mackinac, 25, 174-178, 190-191, 235-243, 251-255, 313-328, 364, 373, 377, 381, 389, 395, 402, 407, 409, 411, 413-414, 438

Matagorda, 22, 403, 438

McFarland, xvii, 20, 32-33, 53, 173, 178-185, 190-191, 407, 415

Norton Sound, 23, 364, 371-389, 400-401, 413-414, 437

Onslow, 22, 313-317, 325-328, 363, 377-379, 388-389, 398, 404, 411, 413-414, 440

Orca, 22, 293-303, 309, 334-351, 398, 403, 410-412, 440

Pelican, Sandpiper, Teal, 18, 435

Pine Island, 23, 381, 389, 398, 400, 414, 437

Pocomoke, 23, 256, 273-276, 313-319, 325-328, 400, 408, 411, 437

Rehoboth, 22, 397-398, 403, 440

Rockaway, xx, 22, 226-234, 401, 403, 406, 439

Salisbury Sound, 23-24, 298, 437

San Carlos, 22, 303-310, 333-334, 351, 403, 410-412, 440

San Pablo, 22, 277-300, 309-310, 334, 340-341, 351, 403, 410-412, 439

Shelikof, 22, 313, 321, 363, 377-379, 389, 403, 411, 413-414, 440

St. George, 23-24, 280, 363, 368, 370-371, 382-384, 400, 413, 438

Suisun, 22, 25, 364, 373, 377, 381, 389, 395, 398, 401, 404, 413-414, 440

Swan, 18, 32, 35, 37, 39, 53, 178, 203-214, 407, 435

Tangier, xx, 23-24, 32, 35, 39-44, 53, 173, 178, 197-201, 288-289, 295, 299-300, 305-310, 334, 398, 400, 407, 410-411, 420, 437

Thornton, 20, 26, 32, 35-39, 53, 147, 157, 160, 178, 190-191, 255, 260-262, 364-365, 399, 407, 413, 436

Thrush, 18, 435

Timbalier, 22, 398, 401, 403, 440

Unimak, 22, 403, 439

Valcour, 22, 401, 403, 440
William B. Preston, 1, 3, 5, 7-8, 14, 16, 20, 55, 57-61, 68, 70-71, 77, 80, 83, 85, 92-98, 114-115, 120-122, 407, 421, 436
Williamson, 19-20, 128-130, 139, 144, 313-316, 364-365, 411, 436
Wright, 22-23, 32-33, 178, 266-267, 275-276, 298-300, 309, 398, 400, 408, 411, 435, 437
Yakutat, 22, 125, 313, 318, 321, 325-328, 363, 377-379, 389, 397-398, 402-403, 411-414, 439

mine warfare
    coastal minesweeper, *Condor* (ex-fishing boat *New Example*), 30
    destroyer minesweeper
        Chandler, Dorsey, Hopkins, Hovey, Howard, Long, Palmer, Southard, 347
        Hamilton, 168, 347
        Hogan, 346-347
        Tracy, 174
        Trever, 261
    minelayer
        Monadnock, 343
        Oglala, 53
    minesweeper
        Finch, 57
        Lark, 115
        Oriole, 128-129
        Osprey, Raven, 218
        Scrimmage, 346
        Whippoorwill, 105, 115
    Submarines
        S-27, 132
        S-34, S-35, 128
        Shark, 73

Sigel, Dick, 261
Simpler, Leroy C., 181
Simpson Jr., Ernest L., 410
Simpson, F. J., 96
Singapore, 2, 8, 73, 203, 312
Sintic Jr., Anton J., 359, 363, 379, 383, 389, 413-414
Sisson, T. U., 53, 407
Skoroz, James C., 351, 412
Smartt, J. G., 49
Smathers, H. C., 427
Smiley, Curtis S., 276, 408
Smith, James A., 359, 412
Smith, Marvin T., 310, 351, 411-412
Smith, W. W., 141
Sommer, Harold A., 279, 284, 309, 409-411

Spahr, O. M., 428
Sperling, Joseph, 46
Spradley, William H., 241
Sprague, Clifton A. F., 39-40, 43, 53, 407
Spruance, Raymond A., xxi, 17, 148, 235, 244, 297
Sri Lanka (formerly Ceylon), 89, 113
Stahl, Paul L., 364, 381, 389, 413-414
Staley Jr., Poyntell C., 406
Stanley, Reuben E., 313, 363, 379, 389, 411, 413-414
Stevens, William M., 359, 413
Stovall, M. C., 387
Stroop, Paul D., 251, 409
Stump, Felix B., 57
Sueto, Hirose, 80
Sugg, M. R., 428
Sullivan Jr., James C., 364, 413
Summers, J. H., 288
Sumpter, William B., 307-309
Sutton, Frank C., 276, 408
Swenson, Harold R., 405
Taff, Clarence O., 191, 276, 317, 321, 325, 408
Takagi, Takeo, 101, 112, 171, 425
Takahashi, Ibo, 61
Tanabata, Yoshinobu, 102
Thompson, Harold A., 303
Thompson, W. N., 427
Thorn, W. A., 405
Tills, Robert G., 60
Toguri, Iva ("Tokyo Rose"), 268
Toone, J. D., 110
Toth, J. C., 405
Towers, John H., 429
Toyama, Yasumi, 148-149, 157
Toyoda, Soemu, 329, 331
Tracy, John S., 363, 383, 389, 413-414
Truman, Harry S., xxii, 391, 397
Truslow Jr., Alfred R., 383, 389, 414
Turner, Richmond K., 312-313
Turner, Robert G., 379
Uhlmann, R. W., 49
Unmack, Charlie, 91
United Kingdom
    England/British
        Blyth Estuary, 230
        Bristol, 230-231
        Devon, 228

510   Index

    Devonport, 232
    Lee-on-the-Solent, 231-234
    Lyneham, 222
    Plymouth, 232, 234, 419
    Territory, Bermuda, 164
    The Seaman's Aid, 118
  Royal Air Force, 165, 228
    205 Squadron, 73
    Coastal Command, 215
    De Havilland Mosquito aircraft, 230
    Fersfield, 228-229
  Royal Navy
    American and West Indies Command, 169
    Destroyers for Bases Agreement, 164
    HM Dockyard, Bermuda, 164
    Mulberry Artificial Harbors, 332-333
    Pacific Fleet, 114, 375
  Ireland
    Lisahally, Londonderry Port, Lough Foyle Inlet, 215-216
  Scotland, 205
    Orkney Islands, 205, 228
    Rhynns Point, 216
United States
  Army
    1st Cavalry Division, 285-286, 300
    7th Infantry Division, 244, 246, 361
    26th Signal Company, 195
    27th Infantry Division, 242, 312, 361
    31st Infantry Division, 304
    34th Infantry Division, 297, 299
    41st Infantry Division, 297, 299-300
    77th Infantry Division, 361
    81st Infantry Division, 323
    96th Infantry Division, 361
    106th Infantry Division, 247
    106th Infantry Regiment, 250
    Alamo Task Force, 297
    Americal Division (former Task Force 6814), xx, 195
    Fort Mears, 133-135
    Sixth Army, 297, 329-330, 332, 342, 347
    Tenth Army, 361
  Army, Army Air Force
    5th Air Force, 282, 300
    11th Air Force, 128
    11th and 30th Bombardment Groups, 239
    19th Bombardment Group, 99

Index   511

21st Bomber Command, 259, 382
35th Pursuit Group, 102
308th Bombardment Wing, 347, 382
313th Bombardment Wing, 358
Airfield,
    Albrock (Panama), 419
    Clark (Luzon), 61, 420
    Hickam (Pearl Harbor), 29, 33-34, 37
    Iba (Luzon), 61
    Nichols (Luzon), 55, 61
    Wheeler (Pearl Harbor), 29
Bombardment Squadron 36, 129
Heavy Bombardment Groups 11 and 30, 239
Coast Guard, 125, 128, 132, 163, 170, 397-398, 401-403, 443
Marine Corps
    2nd Brigade, 207
    5th Amphibious Corps Reconnaissance Company, 247
    7th Defense Battalion, 208
    Marine Division,
        1st, xx, 174, 195, 323, 361
        2nd, 242-243, 312
        3rd, 265, 353
        4th, 244, 247, 269, 312, 320
        5th, 353
        6th, 361
    Aviation
        2nd Marine Air Wing, 282
        Air Group 13, 208
        Air Station Ewa, 29, 40
        Fighting Squadron
            VMF-111, 209
            VMF-121, 274
            VMF-212, 184
            VMF-214, 261, 263
            VMF-222, 275
            VMF-532, 274
        Observation Squadron VMO-151, 209
        Scout Bomber Squadron VMSB-331, 242
military aircraft
    Boeing
        B17 Flying Fortress heavy bomber, 30, 33, 85, 129, 138, 148-149, 187-188, 229-230
        B29 Superfortress heavy bomber, 299, 327, 329, 353, 357-359, 393
    Curtiss
        P40E Warhawk fighter aircraft, 101-102, 217, 220, 222
        SBC-4 Helldiver scout bomber, 209

SOC Seagull scout observation biplane, 1, 18-19, 55, 57, 118, 314, 347

Consolidated
- B24 Liberator bomber, 141, 228, 239-240, 304, 327, 357, 387
- PB2B-2 Catalina patrol aircraft, 356
- PB2Y Coronado patrol aircraft, 161, 249, 251, 383-385, 393
- PB4Y-1 Liberator patrol bomber, xxi, 227-230, 239, 290
- PB4Y-2 Privateer patrol bomber, 228, 376
- PBY3 Catalina patrol aircraft, 33, 35
- PBY4 Catalina patrol aircraft, 1-2, 8, 33, 55, 57, 59, 61-63, 74-77
- PBY5 Catalina patrol aircraft, 2, 33, 119, 126, 146-150, 160, 174, 177-178, 195-198, 202, 239, 251, 255, 257, 266-267, 277-281, 290, 292, 298-302, 307, 335, 337-338, 349

Douglas
- C47 Skytrain cargo aircraft, 240, 271
- SBD Dauntless scout plane and dive bomber, 158, 242
- TBD Devastator torpedo bomber, 209

Grumman
- F4F Wildcat fighter aircraft, 181, 209, 274-275
- F6F Hellcat fighter aircraft, 332-334, 369
- J2F Duck amphibious biplane, 1, 4, 8, 48, 57, 70-71, 74, 118, 209-210, 212, 242

Lockheed
- P38 Lightning fighter aircraft, 230, 275, 334
- PV-1 Ventura patrol bomber, 243, 287

Martin
- P5M-2/SP-5B Marlin patrol plane, xiii, 24, 369
- PBM-1/PBM-3D/PBM-3R/PBM-5 Mariner patrol bomber, 168, 231, 248-251, 314-318, 326-327, 338-341, 349-350, 356, 367-368, 371-372, 378-383, 385, 388

North American
- B25 Mitchell bomber, 123
- SNJ-3 Texan training aircraft, 209

Republic P47 Thunderbolt fighter aircraft, 327, 379

Sikorsky JRS-1 "flying boat" amphibian aircraft, 51-52

Vought F4U Corsair fighter aircraft, 261, 263, 274
- OS2U Kingfisher observation floatplane, 1, 3-4, 7-8, 19, 21, 47-48, 56-57, 61, 70, 74, 197, 204, 206-207, 210-212, 306, 314, 347

Navy/Naval
- Aviation
  - Air Facility/Air Field/Air Station
    - Adak (Alaska), Agana (Guam), Argentia (Newfoundland), Attu (Alaska), Breezy Point (Norfolk, Virginia), Keflavik (Iceland), Miami (Florida), New York (New York), Recife (Brazil), Seattle (Washington), Tinian (Marianas), 419-420
    - Alameda (California), 144, 420

Cavite (Philippines), 55, 64, 420
Coco Solo (Panama), 27, 419
Dunkeswell (England), 228, 419
Dutch Harbor (Alaska), 133
Kaneohe (Hawaii), 32, 34, 46, 50, 202, 212, 340, 419
Key West (Florida), 420
Kodiak (Alaska), 137, 141-142, 419
Norfolk (Virginia), San Diego (California), 27, 419-420
Pearl Harbor (Hawaii), 27, 205, 419
Port Lyautey (French Morocco), 220-222
Quonset Point (Rhode Island), 270
Air Transport Service, 213
Bureau of Aeronautics, 211, 272
Commander
    Air Central Pacific, 235, 241, 244, 313
    Aircraft, Battle Force, Pacific Fleet, 429
    Aircraft, Scouting Force, Pacific Fleet, 157, 429
    Aircraft Seventh Fleet, 279-280
    Aircraft, South Pacific Force, 173, 201, 429
    Carriers, Pacific Fleet, 202, 429
    Naval Air Forces, Pacific Fleet, 202, 429
    Patrol Wings, Pacific Fleet, 202, 429
Fleet Air Wing (Formerly Patrol Wing), 27-28
    One, 27, 31-32, 46, 49-50, 171, 201-202, 266, 325, 327, 356, 370-373, 375-375, 383, 388-389, 419
    Two (former Hawaiian Patrol Wing), 27, 31-32, 50, 160, 178, 198, 202, 205, 321, 419
    Three, Five, 27, 419
    Four, xxiii, 27, 125-144, 178, 419
    Six, 419
    Seven, xxi, 215, 228, 231, 234, 419
    Eight, 272, 420
    Nine, Eleven, Twelve, Fourteen, Fifteen, Sixteen, Eighteen, 420
    Ten, 1-16, 55-90, 99, 101, 117, 119-120, 122, 420
    Seventeen, 278-279, 298-299, 420
Naval Reserve Aviation Base, Ottumwa, Iowa, 270
South Pacific Combat Air Transport Command (SCAT), 269, 271
Squadron (aviation)
    Air Transport Squadron VMJ-353, 239
    Bombing Squadron
        VB-106, 290-291, 410
        VB-108, VB-137, VB-143, 239
    Fighting Squadron VF-9,
    Patrol Squadron/Patrol Bombing Squadron,
        VP-1, 409
        VP-11/VPB-11, 32-33, 53, 175, 178, 188, 190-191, 202, 277,

279-280, 284, 301, 305, 309, 334-335, 351, 407-408, 411-412, 415
VP-12, 32-33, 53, 191, 202, 276, 407-408, 410, 415
VP-13/VPB-13, 161, 251, 364, 383, 385, 389, 407, 409-410, 413-414
VP-14, 31-32, 53, 173, 191, 275, 407-408, 410
VP-16/VPB-16, 314, 316-317, 326, 410
VP-18/VPB-18, 321, 363, 366, 368, 382-384, 389-390, 410, 413, 415, 433
VPB-19, 356, 359, 412
VPB-20, 338, 349-351, 412, 415
VP-21/VPB-21, 31-33, 53, 118-119, 326, 363, 366, 383, 385, 387, 389, 407, 413-414
VP-22, 16, 32-33, 44, 53, 78, 407, 415
VP-23/VPB-23, 32-33, 50, 53, 147, 161, 175, 191, 255, 276, 359, 376, 407-410, 413
VP-24, 32-33, 50, 53, 146, 161, 175, 191, 276, 407-409, 427
VPB-25, 340-341, 351, 412
VPB-26, 364, 379, 381, 389, 413-414
VPB-27, 363, 366, 379-380, 389, 413-414
VPB-28, VP-32, 405, 415
VP-33/VPB-33, 118, 288, 298, 300, 303, 305, 307, 332, 351, 408, 410, 412, 415
VP-34/VPB-34, xvii, 120, 213, 279, 281-282, 284, 288, 291, 293, 300-302, 333-338, 351, 410, 412, 415
VP-41, 130, 139, 144,
VP-42, 144, 405, 415
VP-43, 139, 144, 408-409, 415
VP-44, 146, 160-161, 213, 269, 276, 407-408, 427
VP-45, 408
VP-51, 144, 147, 161, 189, 191, 407-408, 428
VP-52, 279-282, 284, 288, 292-294, 300, 309, 409-411, 415
VP-53, 239, 251, 405, 409
VPB-54, 276, 347, 349, 351, 408-410, 412
VP-61, VP-62, 409
VP-63/VPB-63, 406
VP-71/VPB-71, 173-174, 198, 257-258, 275-276, 310, 349-351, 408, 410-412, 415
VP-72, 191, 198-199, 239, 242, 251, 316, 408-409
VP-73, 216, 222, 224, 406
VPB-74, 405-406, 415
VP-81, 276, 405, 408, 410
VP-82, 405, 415
VP-83, 405-406, 415
VP-84, 406, 415
VP-91, 147, 189, 191, 269, 276, 408, 410, 415

VP-92, 224, 405-406
VP-94, 405
VP-101/VPB-101, 1, 16, 55, 64, 68, 74, 78, 277, 279-280, 300, 407, 411, 415
VP-102/VPB-102, 16, 249, 251, 407, 410, 413, 415
VPB-103, 228, 406-407
VPB-104, 310, 351, 411-412, 415
VPB-105, 228, 406
VPB-106, 359, 413
VPB-109, 376, 389, 414
VPB-110, xxi, 228-229, 406
VPB-111, 415
VPB-112, 407
VPB-114, 406
VP-115, 359, 411
VPB-116, 359, 410, 413
VPB-117, 351, 412, 415
VPB-118, 359, 376, 389, 413-415
VPB-123, VPB-124, 389, 413-414
VPB-130, 351, 412
VPB-137, 310, 351, 411-412
VPB-142, 409
VPB-146, 310, 351, 411-412
VPB-151, 359, 413
VP-202/VPB-202, 248-249, 317, 326, 409-410
VP-204, VP-205, 405
VPB-208, 359, 363, 366, 379-380, 383-384, 389, 413-414
VP-216/VPB-216, xvii, 317, 319-320, 326, 328, 351, 410, 412
Photo Group One, 376
Photographic Squadron VD-3, 239
Rescue Squadron
VH-1, 316, 327, 412, 414
VH-2, 412
VH-3, 356, 366, 368, 369, 373, 381-382, 412-414
VH-4, 372-373, 381-382, 389, 414
VH-6, 389, 414
Scouting Squadron
VS-1D-11, VS-1D-13, 206
VS-1D-14, 204, 211
Torpedo Squadron VT-3, 203
Utility Squadrons, 1, 4 50-51, 74
Base
Operating Base/Section Base
Bermuda, 164, 168
Cordova, Ketchikan, Kodiak, Sitika, 127

516   Index

        Dutch Harbor, 127, 135
      U.S. Naval Bases, France, 234
    Destroyer
      Division 2, 40
      Division 7, 201
      Division 11, 124
      Division 57, 105, 109
      Division 58, 114
      Division 59, 81
      Division 120, 335
    District
      Thirteenth, 125, 127
      Fourteenth, 31, 53
      Fifteenth, 205
    Fleet, United States
      Asiatic, 1-16, 26-28, 55, 57-59, 61, 71-73, 78, 81, 89, 111, 114, 116, 118, 273
      Atlantic, 27-28, 216, 228
      Pacific, 27, 31, 33, 36, 50, 124, 142, 148, 157, 171, 353, 356, 425
        Third, 327, 375-391, 393, 414
          Fifth (former Central Pacific Force), 235
          Seventh (former Southwest Pacific Force), 253, 279, 329
        Twelfth (former Naval Forces, Europe), 231
    Force,
      Landing Craft, Eleventh Amphibious Force, 234
      Seventh Amphibious Force, 325
      South Pacific, 185-186, 189, 253, 255, 263, 298, 329, 425
    Frontier
      Eastern Sea (former North Atlantic Naval Coastal Frontier), 163, 169-170
      Northwest Sea (Alaskan and Northwestern Sectors), 127, 142
    Mine Division 2, 205.
    Mining Squadron, Yankee, 205
    Motor Torpedo Boat Squadron
      MTB Ron 1, 147
      MTB Ron 31, 373, 381
    Naval Construction Battalion ("Seabees") 17, 210-213, 272
    NOAA, Hawaii Undersea Research Laboratory, 42
    Service Squadron 4, 239
    Submarine
      Base, Pearl Harbor, 34-42
      Division 41, 128
    Yangtze River Patrol, 57
    Yard, Cavite, 4, 55, 62-65
Underhill, Jesse J., 406
Unhock, Philip G., 327

Utgoff, Vadym V., 351, 410, 412
Utter, Harmon T., 64, 122
Vaughan, James J., 364, 351, 389, 413-414
Vibert, O. N., 96
Vieweg, Walter V. R., 276, 408
von Bracht, William G., 406
Waggoner, A. R., 356, 413
Wagner, Frank Dechant, 55, 57, 68-74, 77-78, 117, 122, 298, 348-349
Walcott, Fredman J., 204
Walker, James P., 191, 407
Warner, E. J., 370
Waterman, Andrew K., 75-76, 122
Watson, J. C., 65
Watson, R. A., 49
Wavell, Archibald, 73
Weaver, L. D., 49
Weimer, Edward L. B., 276, 313, 328, 408, 411
Wells, H. A., 359, 412
White, Thomas S., 309, 351, 411-412
Whitehead, Ennis C., 300
Whitford, N. T., 76
Wilkes, John E., xxi, 232, 264
Wilkinson Jr., Theodore S., 343
Willard, Chauncey S., 309-310, 340, 351, 411-412
Williams, William L., 379
Willy, Wilford J., xxi, 228-230
Wilson, LeRay, 95-96, 122
Wood, Lester Orin, 93-93, 122, 423
Woods, Russel W., xvii
Woods, William P., 359, 412
Wright, Harold, 127
Wright, James D., 263, 383, 389, 413-414
Wright, Orville, 275
Wright, Whitney, 310, 351, 411-412
Yamamoto, Isoroku, 124, 142, 155, 160
Young, Robert C., 224, 406
Zech, D. M., 427

About the Author

Commander David D. Bruhn, U.S. Navy (Retired) served twenty-two years on active duty and two in the Naval Reserve, as both an enlisted man and as an officer, between 1977 and 2001.

Following completion of basic training, he served as a sonar technician aboard USS *Miller* (FF 1091) and USS *Leftwich* (DD 984). He was commissioned in 1983 following graduation from California State University at Chico. His initial assignment was to USS *Excel* (MSO 439), serving as supply officer, damage control assistant, and chief engineer. He then served in USS *Thach* (FFG 43) as chief engineer and Destroyer Squadron Thirteen as material officer.

After graduation from the Naval Postgraduate School, Commander Bruhn was assigned to Secretary of the Navy and Chief of Naval Operation staffs as a budget analyst and resources planner before attending the Naval War College in 1996, following which he commanded the mine countermeasures ships USS *Gladiator* (MCM 11) and USS *Dextrous* (MCM 13) in the Persian Gulf.

Commander Bruhn's final assignment was executive assistant to a senior (SES 4) government service executive at the Ballistic Missile Defense Organization in Washington, D.C.

Following military service, he was a high school teacher and track coach for ten years, and is now a USA Track & Field official. He lives in northern California with his wife Nancy and has two sons, David and Michael.

www.ingramcontent.com/pod-product-compliance
Lightning Source LLC
Chambersburg PA
CBHW071431300426
44114CB00013B/1385

Eyes of the Fleet

The U.S. Navy's Seaplane Tenders and Patrol Aircraft in World War II

Cdr. David D. Bruhn, USN (Retired)

Cloaked by jungle foliage, the unheralded seaplane tenders operated ahead of the Fleet, like the Navy's famed PT boats. As Halsey's South Pacific, MacArthur's Southwest Pacific, and Spruance's Central Pacific forces advanced toward Japan, these ships served as afloat-bases for patrol planes referred to as the "eyes of the fleet." The large fabric-clad PBY "Catalinas" and later PBM "Mariners" combed the seaways for Japanese forces and carried out bombing, depth charge, and torpedo attacks on enemy ships and submarines. Nighttime anti-shipping operations—"Black Cat" or "Nightmare" missions—were dangerous and daytime combat operations even more so, when encounters with more maneuverable and heavily-armed fighters necessitated hiding in clouds to survive. The Japanese were keen to destroy the scouts and their floating bases, and seaplane tenders often lived a furtive existence, particularly early in the war. Pilots, plane crews and shipboard personnel received scores of awards for valor, including the Medal of Honor, Navy Cross, Distinguished Flying Cross, and Silver and Bronze Star Medals.

U.S.A. $40.00
B5707

ISBN 978-0-7884-5707-4

www.HeritageBooks.com